PSYCHOLOGY IN FOCUS

AS Level

Edited by David Rice
and Mike Haralambos

Written by
David Rice, Mike Haralambos,
Steve Jones, Nigel Foreman, Wendy Askam,
with Tracey Holland

CPL

Causeway Press

Dedication

To Jane, Kate and Kathleen

Acknowledgements

Cover and page design	Caroline Waring-Collins (Waring-Collins Design Consultancy)
Graphic origination	John A. Collins (Waring-Collins Design Consultancy)
Graphics	Elaine M. Sumner, Chris Collins (Waring-Collins Design Consultancy)
Author index and typing	Ingrid Hamer
Reader	Mary Walton
Advisers	David Alcorn, Olwyn Hamer, Martyn Wigfield, Merseyside Police

Picture credits

Advertising Archives 127; Alexandra Milgram (from the film *Obedience* by Stanley Milgram © 1965, distributed by Pennsylvania State University, Audio Visual Services) 206, 224 (l and r); Allen Lane, Penguin Books Ltd 83 (t and b); Brick 163, 170, 221, 266 (b); Bruce Coleman 242 (l and r), Camera Press 20 (tl), 49, 73, 93 (tl and r), 112, 115 (l), 192, 236, 238; David Hoffman 143, 172; Harlow Primate Laboratory, University of Wisconsin 65 (l and r), 66 (l and r); Hulton Deutsch 53, 133 (t); Imperial War Museum 78 (t); John Collins 7, 26 (l), 272; Mary Evans Picture Library 151 (r), 159; Mike Haralambos 273; Network 26 (r), 58, 67, 99, 110 (b), 158; Peter Newark's Military Pictures 111; Peter Newark's Western Americana 146 (l); P.G. Zimbardo, Inc., Stanford, CA. 194 (l and r), 228, 229: Popperfoto 29, 78 (b), 187, 204, 212 (t); Rex Features 20 (tr and bl), 37 (r), 44 (l and r), 86 (l), 93 (bl), 115 (r), 139, 147, 179 (tr and br), 182, 193, 211, 212 (bl), 244; Royal Geographical Society 184, 185 (l, tr and br); Science Photo Library 103, 128; Topham Picturepoint 30 (br), 52, 86 (r), 110 (t), 114 (l and r), 133 (b), 146 (r), 151 (l), 200, 205, 216, 249.

Cover picture

DALI, Salvador.
The Persistence of Memory (Persistance de la mémoire). 1931.
Oil on canvas, 9½ x 13" (24.1 x 33 cm).
The Museum of Modern Art, New York, Given anonymously.
Photograph © 2000 The Museum of Modern Art, New York.

British Library Cataloguing in Publication Data
A catalogue record for this book is available from the British Library.

ISBN 1 902796 04 7

Causeway Press Limited
PO Box 13, Ormskirk, Lancs L39 5HP

First impression 2000, reprinted 2001
Printed and bound by Scotprint, Haddington, East Lothian.

1 Short-term and long-term memory

Introduction

Memory is essential to all our lives. Without a memory of the past, we cannot operate in the present or think about the future. We would not be able to remember what we did yesterday, what we have to do today or have planned to do tomorrow. Without memory we could not learn anything. We would not even know who we are without a memory of ourselves.

Memory is involved in processing vast amounts of information. This information takes many different forms. It may be images – for example, the faces of people we know; it may be sounds – for example, the sound of spoken words in a conversation; it may be meanings – for example, the meanings of words printed on a page. Memory involves not only taking in this vast range of information, but also storing it, and retrieving it when it is needed.

Chapter summary

- **Unit 1 examines the two main types of memory store – short-term memory and long-term memory.**
- **Unit 2 outlines and assesses some of the main models of memory – the multistore model, the levels of processing model, the working memory model, and models of long-term memory.**
- **Unit 3 looks at the methods used in memory research.**

Unit 1 Types of memory

KEY ISSUES

1. **What are the three stages of the memory process?**
2. **What are the two main types of memory store?**

1.1 The three stages of the memory process

Psychologists believe that the process of memory involves three stages: *encoding*, *storage* and *retrieval*. For anything to be remembered, it must go through all of these stages. First, it must be encoded or put into some form that can be stored. Information may be encoded visually (as images), acoustically (as sounds), or semantically (as meanings). Second, the encoded information must be stored or held in memory until it is needed. Third, the stored information must be available to be retrieved or recovered from memory when required. Figure 1 provides a diagram of the three stages of the memory process.

Figure 1 The three stages of memory

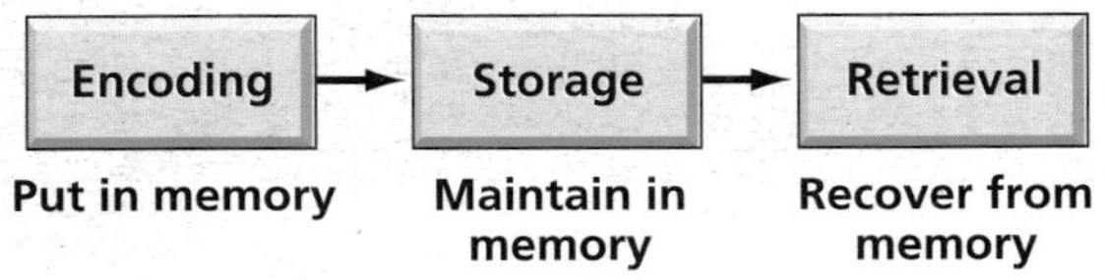

For remembering to take place, information must be successfully encoded, stored and retrieved. If failure occurs at any of these stages, the information will not be retrieved – it will be forgotten. Some forgotten material was never encoded properly in the first place and, as a result, was lost. Some was encoded, but for some reason not stored. Some was encoded and stored, but, for various reasons, cannot be retrieved. Forgetting is examined in the following chapter.

Key terms

Encoding *Transforming incoming information into a form that can be stored in memory.*

Storage *Holding information in memory until it is needed.*

Retrieval *Locating information in memory and 'getting it out' so it can be used.*

1.2 Short-term memory

Over a century ago, the American philosopher and psychologist William James (1890) suggested that there are two main types of memory store. The first holds information for a few seconds until you have used it – for example, remembering a phone number you have looked up just long enough to dial it. The second holds information for longer periods – from a few minutes to the rest of your life. James called these memory stores primary and secondary memory. Nowadays, psychologists usually call them short-term memory (STM) and long-term memory (LTM).

Short-term memory and long-term memory differ from each other in three main ways.

- Capacity: the amount of information the memory store holds.
- Duration: the length of time the memory store holds information.
- Coding: the way information is encoded in the memory store.

The capacity of STM

The digit span technique This is a simple but effective way of measuring the capacity of STM. The experimenter reads out lists of digits (numbers) and asks people to repeat them in the same order as they were presented. By making the lists longer and longer, you can find the point at which STM is 'full' and no longer able to take in any more information. You can test your own short-term memory storage capacity by using the lists in Table 1. Read each horizontal line of numbers out loud to yourself, then cover up the numbers immediately. Repeat the numbers and check your answer. What is the longest sequence of digits you can remember?

Table 1 Digit span technique

1	9	2	6							
3	6	7	1	4						
9	7	3	4	5	8					
7	2	4	0	8	6	1				
9	0	6	7	4	3	2	5			
9	7	3	4	1	5	2	0	6		
5	6	7	4	8	5	8	7	8	1	
3	6	4	1	9	8	7	2	3	2	4

Most people can remember about 7 numbers. George Miller (1956) described the capacity of STM as 'the magical number seven, plus or minus two'. In a series of experiments, Miller found that the short-term memory store could hold, on average, between 5 and 9 items of information. How does that compare with your score on the digit span test?

Chunking Miller found, however, that the actual amount of information STM can hold can be greatly increased by a process known as *chunking*. This refers to the grouping of items into larger units or chunks. So instead of struggling to remember a string of letters like H P T P M P S U I O A O, we find it easy to remember the same letters rearranged into a word – HIPPOPOTAMUS. The string of letters is made up of 12 items of information, which overloads STM; the word is one chunk, which takes up only one space in STM leaving room to spare.

Miller suggested that no matter how large a chunk is, it takes up only one space in STM, so we can store up to 'seven plus or minus two' chunks, regardless of their size. However, later research does not confirm this. Simon (1974) found that STM was quite capable of holding 7 or so chunks of information if each chunk was a single word, but if the chunks were larger, then capacity drops. For example, capacity drops to 4 for two-word phrases and 3 for eight-word phrases. In the world of chunks, size does matter.

Chunking works if a list is simply divided into segments. So, for example, a list of 12 digits:

1 4 9 1 6 2 5 3 6 4 9 6

is easier to store in STM as 4 chunks:

1 4 9 - 1 6 2 - 5 3 6 - 4 9 6.

Chunking is even more effective if the chunks have meaning. For example, try and remember these pairs of letters: BB-CA-BC-IT-VC-DR-OM. As these letters are presented in pairs, they are already chunked, and should fit within short-term memory. However, you might still find it difficult to remember the letters. If they are chunked differently, then they become much easier to remember: BBC-ABC-ITV-CDROM. These are the same letters presented in the same order, yet they suddenly become much easier to remember. This illustrates an important point: simply breaking a sequence up into fewer segments is not as helpful to memory as breaking the sequence up into fewer *meaningful* segments.

Companies often provide freephone numbers which can be easily chunked to aid memory, eg 0900 45 46 47.

Key terms

Digit span technique *A method of measuring the capacity of short-term memory by asking people to remember and repeat ever-longer lists of digits.*

The 'magical number seven plus or minus two' *Miller proposed that short-term memory could hold between five and nine items.*

Chunking *Organising items of information into groups (or chunks) to make the most efficient use of short-term memory's limited capacity.*

The duration of STM

Short-term memory is so called for a good reason – information is held there for a short time. This time can be extended by *rehearsal* – the repeating of information. For example, if you keep repeating a phone number to yourself, it will stay longer in STM.

Brown (1958) and Peterson and Peterson (1959) claimed that information held in STM disappears within about 20 seconds if it is not rehearsed. In one experiment, participants were asked to learn sets of three consonants, for example VGT and FCN. Before being asked to recall the letters, they were asked to count backwards in threes from a three-digit number (eg, 997, 994, 991 and so on). The point of doing this was to prevent rehearsal of the letters. After 6 seconds of counting backwards, 50% of the letters were correctly recalled. After 18 seconds of counting, recall dropped to under 10%. This suggests that information held in STM is quickly lost if rehearsal is prevented. The results of this experiment are shown in Figure 2.

Figure 2 The duration of STM

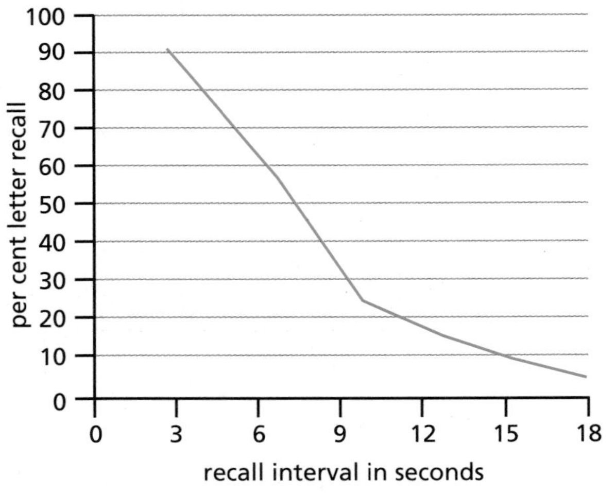

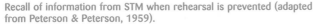

Recall of information from STM when rehearsal is prevented (adapted from Peterson & Peterson, 1959).

However, the graph in Figure 2 is misleading. Recall of the first set of letters is nearly 100%. Recall of the second set of letters drops slightly, and there is a steady drop in recall for each subsequent set of letters. It appears that participants were confusing later sets of letters with earlier ones. Figure 2 shows what happens when participants are tested repeatedly with different sets of letters. This suggests that measuring the duration of STM is more complicated than Peterson and Peterson's experiment suggests (see Chapter 2, Activity 1, p 24). However, despite this, researchers generally agree that STM has a limited duration – that information rapidly disappears from STM if it is not rehearsed.

The method of measuring the duration of STM by preventing rehearsal is known as the *Brown-Peterson technique* after the researchers who first used it. The rapid loss of information in STM when rehearsal is prevented is known as the *Brown-Peterson effect.*

Key terms

Rehearsal *Repeating information in order to retain it in STM.*

Brown-Peterson technique *A method of measuring the duration of STM by preventing rehearsal of information.*

Brown-Peterson effect *The rapid loss of information from STM when rehearsal is prevented.*

Encoding in STM

There is evidence that information can be coded in STM semantically (in terms of meaning), acoustically (in terms of sound) or visually (in terms of images). However, the main coding system used in STM appears to be acoustic.

Semantic coding Evidence from chunking suggests that information can be coded in STM semantically – that is, on the basis of meaning. If we can give meaning to numbers, letters and groups of words, we can chunk them, and so increase the amount of information we can hold in STM. Thus, a meaningful set of numbers – such as 2 4 6 8 10; a meaningful set of letters – such as A B C D E; and a meaningful set of words – such as 'I picked up the pen' are coded to some extent in terms of their meaning.

Acoustic coding Evidence suggests that the principal coding system used in STM is acoustic – that is, information is stored largely as sound. When a person is presented with a list of numbers or letters, they will try to hold them in STM by rehearsing them. Rehearsal involves saying the items over and over to themselves. Rehearsal is a verbal process, regardless of whether the list of items is presented acoustically (someone reads them out), or visually (on a sheet of paper).

Conrad (1964) demonstrated this. He showed lists of

printed letters to participants and asked them to write down as many as they could remember. He found that the mistakes they made tended to be a result of mixing up the *sounds* of the letters rather than their appearance. For example, participants typically mixed up B and V, because they sound similar. They didn't confuse F and E, even though they look similar. Conrad suggested that this happened because people *said* the letters to themselves rather than just looked at them. When the letters were sounded out in this way, similar sounding letters were confused.

You may have experienced this yourself. When you are rehearsing a phone number as you pick up the receiver to dial for a pizza, you will not be put off by the sight of other numbers written on a pad by the phone. But, if anyone starts to say numbers to you, your rehearsal is interrupted and you forget the number you were trying to dial.

Hinztmann (1967) suggested that information is usually coded in STM in an articulatory way. Articulatory means 'in the form of speech' or 'in words'. This implies that we have an 'inner voice' rehearsing items in STM.

Key terms

Semantic coding *The coding of information in terms of meaning.*

Acoustic coding *The coding of information in terms of sound.*

Articulatory coding *The coding of information in the form of speech.*

1.3 Long-term memory

Name three different vegetables. What was the date of the Battle of Hastings? Think of an event from your childhood. What did you have for breakfast yesterday? Assuming you know the answers, all this information has been retrieved from long-term memory (LTM). Stored in LTM is each person's knowledge of the world, their past life and their plans for the future. And much of this information can be recalled in an instant.

Activity 1 Coding in STM

Item A Remembering words

Read List A once. Cover the list. After a short interval (about 15 seconds) write the list down in the same order as it is printed. Now do the same with List B.

List A	List B
MAD	PEN
CAP	COW
CAT	BAR
MAP	DAY
CAD	SUP
The words in List A are similar in sound.	The words in List B have distinct sounds.

Item B Experimental results

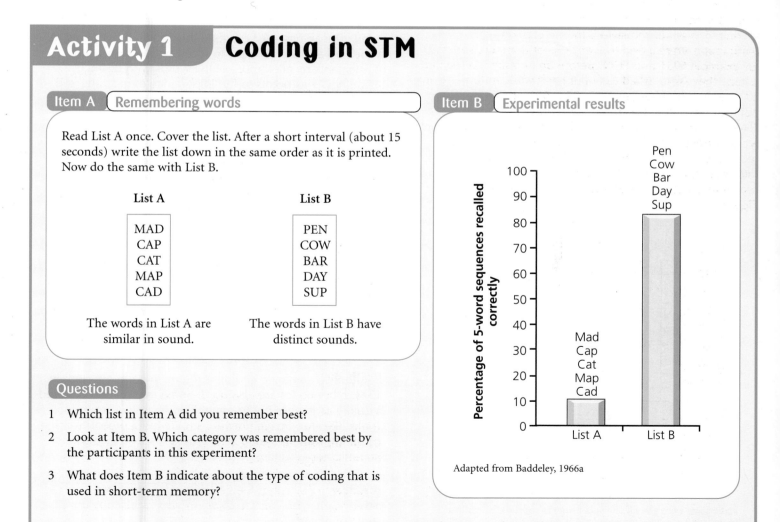

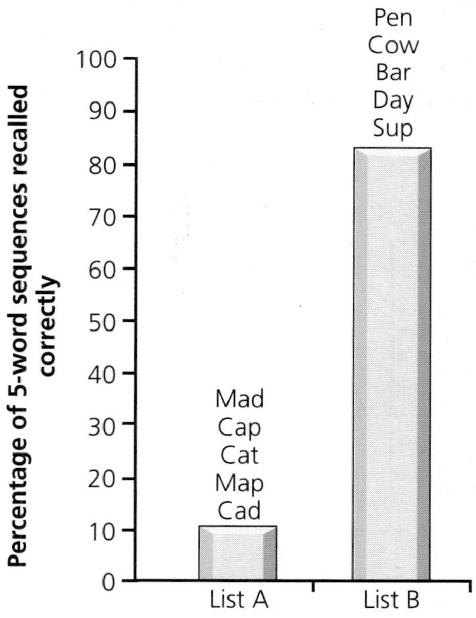

Adapted from Baddeley, 1966a

Questions

1. Which list in Item A did you remember best?
2. Look at Item B. Which category was remembered best by the participants in this experiment?
3. What does Item B indicate about the type of coding that is used in short-term memory?

The capacity of LTM

As noted earlier, for most people the capacity of short-term memory is limited to between 5 and 9 items of information – 'the magical number seven, plus or minus two'. There is no magical number for long-term memory. Its capacity appears to be unlimited. LTM holds vast amounts of information – so vast it is not possible to measure its extent.

The duration of LTM

Compared with the 20 seconds or so duration of STM, the duration of LTM seems limited only by the length of human life. Many people in their old age can readily recall events from their childhood. In STM, information that is not rehearsed disappears quickly. The same is not true of LTM – which is probably just as well. If LTM was dependent on rehearsal, we would spend our entire lives repeating our names so as not to forget them.

Figure 3 Sound and meaning in LTM

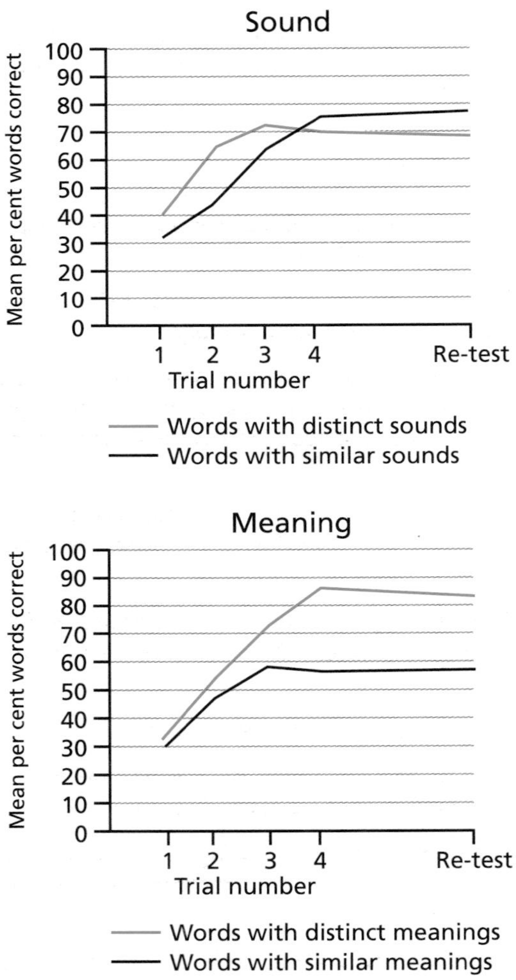

Participants were given 4 attempts (trials) to recall the words then re-tested after a delay (adapted from Baddeley, 1966b).

Encoding in LTM

As noted earlier, the coding of information in short-term memory appears to be mainly acoustic. Support for this view is provided by the experiment in Activity 1. It indicates that words with distinct sounds are easier to recall from STM than words with similar sounds. It is easier to discriminate words with distinct sounds – they stand out from each other. The results of this experiment point to the importance of sound and suggest that information in STM is mainly coded acoustically (Baddeley, 1966a).

Researchers generally agree that coding in long-term memory is largely semantic – information is coded in terms of meaning. If this is the case, then words with distinct meanings should be easier to learn and recall than words with similar meanings. Words with distinct meanings will be easier to discriminate because they will stand out from each other. This was demonstrated in an experiment. Participants were asked to learn 10 words with distinct meanings – for example, old, late, thin, wet, hot – and 10 words with similar meanings – for example, big, huge, broad, long, tall. When asked, after a delay, to recall both sets of words, participants recalled more of the words with distinct meanings. This points to the importance of meaning and suggests that information in LTM is coded semantically. When groups of words with distinct and similar *sounds* were learned, recall from LTM was more or less the same for both groups. Sound apparently makes little difference, meaning does. Again, this points to the importance of semantic coding in LTM (Baddeley, 1966b). The results of these experiments are shown in Figure 3.

In everyday life, people rarely learn things 'word for word'. However, studies of retrieval from LTM in everyday situations indicate that coding is mainly semantic. Try and remember a conversation you had in the last two days. You won't remember it word for word, but you will probably remember the gist of the conversation, in other words, its overall meaning. This explains why simply 'memorising' word for word for an exam is so ineffective. The key to successful revision is meaning, which allows you to understand and remember what you are learning.

Although semantic coding is the main coding system in LTM, other codes are also used. Some information is stored visually as images (try to remember what your front door looks like – an image drawn from LTM will probably come to mind); some is stored acoustically (especially music); some is stored as tastes and smells.

1.4 Evidence for two memory stores

There is considerable evidence to support the idea that STM and LTM really are two distinct memory stores. As this unit has shown, they differ in terms of capacity, duration and the main coding system used by each. The following evidence provides further support for the idea of two memory stores.

Awareness We are conscious or aware of information in STM at any given moment. Often this is because we are busy rehearsing the information so as not to lose it before we have a chance to use it. LTM, by contrast, is a vast memory bank of material which is available to consciousness when needed, but which otherwise lies quietly outside our conscious awareness.

Serial position effect Experiments show that when participants are presented with a list of words, they tend to remember the first few and the last few words and are more likely to forget those in the middle of the list. This is known as the *serial position effect* – it is illustrated in Figure 4. The tendency to recall the earlier words is called the *primacy effect*; the tendency to recall the later words is called the *recency effect*. The usual explanation is that the first few words have been transferred to LTM while the last few – the most recent – are still in STM. This explanation is supported by experiments using the Brown-Peterson technique – preventing rehearsal in STM by asking participants to count backwards. This cuts out the recency effect – words in STM are lost, but not the primacy effect – the first few words have been transferred to LTM. This supports the idea that STM and LTM are separate memory stores (Glanzer & Cunitz, 1966).

Brain damage Studies of patients with brain damage also indicate the existence of two separate memory stores. For example, chronic alcoholics sometimes develop Korsakoff's syndrome which causes damage to parts of the brain. This has little effect on STM but severely impairs LTM (Butters & Cermak, 1980). Some patients experience the opposite effect. For example, a patient known as KF suffered brain

Figure 4 The serial position effect

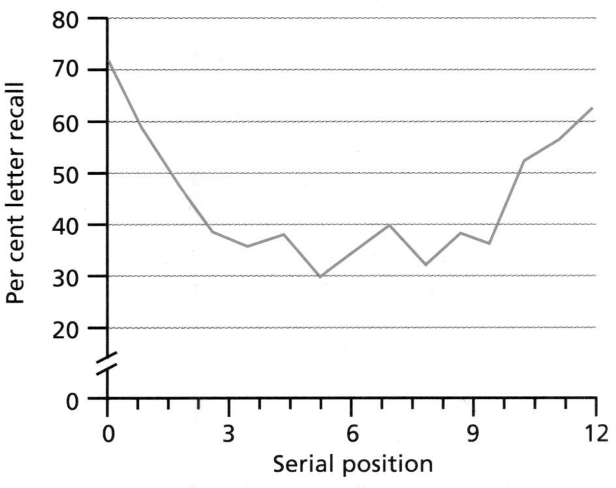

Adapted from Glanzer & Cunitz, 1966

Key terms

Serial position effect *The tendency to recall the first and last few items on a list and to forget those in the middle.*

Primacy effect *The tendency to recall the first items on a list.*

Recency effect *The tendency to recall the last (most recent) items on a list.*

damage as a result of a motorcycle accident. This had no effect on LTM but led to poor performance on many STM tasks (Shallice & Warrington, 1970). It is difficult to explain the evidence from brain-damaged patients without assuming there are two distinct memory systems (Eysenck & Keane, 1995).

Brain activity Various techniques, such as brain scans, have been developed for investigating activity in the brain. These techniques indicate different kinds of brain activity when STM is in use and when LTM is in use (Baddeley, 1997).

Forgetting The process of forgetting appears to be different in STM and LTM. This is examined in the following chapter.

Summary

1. Memory consists of three processes – encoding, storage and retrieval.
2. There are two main memory stores – short-term memory and long-term memory.
3. STM has a limited capacity – Miller measured it as between 5 and 9 items of information. The actual amount of information in STM can be expanded by chunking.
4. The duration of STM is around 20 seconds if information is not rehearsed. Rehearsal can increase duration.
5. The main method of encoding information in STM is acoustic – by sound. Other forms of encoding are also used.
6. LTM appears to have unlimited capacity.
7. The duration of LTM can be a lifetime. Rehearsal is not needed to retain information in LTM.
8. The main method of encoding information in LTM is semantic – by meaning. Other forms of encoding are also used.
9. There is considerable evidence to support the view that STM and LTM are two distinct memory stores. This includes differences in capacity, duration, encoding and awareness; the serial position effect, evidence from brain damaged patients, and differences in brain activity.

Unit 2 Models of memory

KEY ISSUES

1. **What are the main models of memory?**
2. **What are their strengths and weaknesses?**

2.1 Multistore models of memory

Models of memory seek to provide a picture of how the whole memory system works. They attempt to identify the various parts which make up the system, indicate what each part does, and to show how the parts work together.

A number of multistore models of memory have been developed, so called because they suggest that memory consists of several stores. The most influential multistore model was developed by Richard Atkinson and Richard Shiffrin (1968). It consists of three main stores – the sensory memory store, the short-term memory store and the long-term memory store. This section outlines Atkinson and Shiffrin's model.

Sensory store

The sensory store transfers information to short-term memory. It is made up of five stores, one for each of the senses – sight, hearing, touch, taste and smell. Research has focused on the visual or *iconic* store and the auditory or *echoic* store.

The iconic store Iconic memory was investigated in a series of experiments conducted by George Sperling (1960). He presented participants with 3 rows of 4 letters on a card for 50 milliseconds. They recalled only 4 or 5 of the 12 letters, though they claimed to have seen more. To test this claim, Sperling devised a procedure to 'jog their memory'. He sounded a tone immediately after the presentation to signal which row of letters participants were to recall – each row was signalled by a different tone. Participants now recalled 3 items from whichever row they were asked to remember. This indicated that, for a split second, most of the information (9 out of 12 letters) was being held in iconic memory. When the tone was sounded 0.3 seconds after the letters were presented, recall dropped from 9 to 6 letters. It dropped to an average of 4.5 letters when the tone was sounded 1 second after the presentation. This indicates that information disappears rapidly from iconic memory.

Iconic memory does not appear to use a coding system – it simply holds a brief image of what was in front of us. This brief image held in iconic memory is the cause of 'after-images' – as, for example, when a child 'writes' her name in the air with a sparkler on bonfire night.

The echoic store This store holds sounds for up to 4 seconds. This enables a sentence to be held in echoic memory. As a result, when we are listening to someone talking, we hear them saying whole sentences rather than separate words (Baddeley, 1997).

Transferring sensory information We are flooded with sensory information and pay no attention to most of it. As you are reading this book, you are probably paying no attention to the sounds and smells around you, or to other images within your range of vision. Information which is attended to passes into STM. Information which is not attended to is rapidly lost as new information enters the sensory memory store and pushes the old information out.

STM and LTM

Atkinson and Shiffrin's multistore model sees STM as a crucial part of the memory system. Without it, information cannot get into or out of LTM. Information can only be retrieved from LTM by entering STM. Information can only be stored in LTM by passing through STM.

In terms of the multistore model, rehearsal has an important part to play. It increases the time information can be held in STM and it is vital for transferring information to LTM. Atkinson and Shiffrin suggest that the longer information is held in STM, the more likely it is to be transferred into LTM. There is some experimental evidence to support this view. Participants were asked to rehearse a list of items out loud. In general, the more frequently an item was rehearsed, the more likely it was to be recalled from LTM (Rundus, 1971).

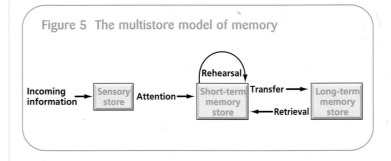

Figure 5 The multistore model of memory

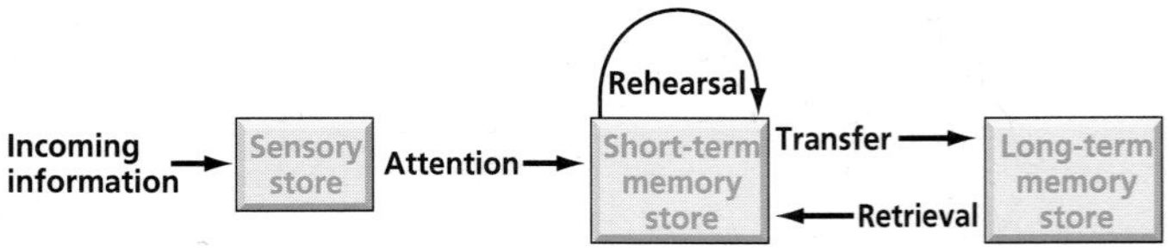

Evaluation of the multistore model

The three stores The multistore model is based on evidence from a wide range of sources – from the findings of experiments, to studies of brain-damaged patients. As outlined in Section 1.4, there is considerable evidence for the existence of STM and LTM as separate memory stores. And, as this section has indicated, there is evidence for the existence of a sensory store. Most researchers still accept the idea of three different memory stores (Eysenck & Keane, 1995).

Are the three stores unitary? Atkinson and Shiffrin do not see the sensory store as a single, unitary (one part) store. Instead, they suggest there are five sensory stores – one for each sense. But they see no such divisions within STM and LTM – they see them as unitary stores. However, both STM and LTM may well have different memory systems operating within them.

Take the case of KF discussed earlier. He suffered brain damage from a motorcycle accident which severely impaired his STM but left his LTM intact. In terms of the multistore model, this cannot happen since all information in LTM passes through STM. However, further investigation revealed that KF's STM impairment was mainly for verbal material such as spoken letters, words and numbers. His short-term memory for visual material and meaningful sounds, such as telephones ringing and cats mewing, was largely unaffected (Shallice & Warrington, 1974). This suggests the possibility of more than one short-term memory store.

A similar point can be made about LTM. LTM contains an enormous range of diverse material. It contains knowledge about the world, personal experiences, and skills such as how to play a guitar and how to ride a bicycle. Most researchers now reject the view that this vast range of diverse information is contained in a simple, unitary long-term memory store. Instead, they suggest there are different types of LTM, different subsystems within LTM. Again, the multistore model presents an oversimplified picture.

A linear model For the most part, the multistore model is a linear model. Information travels in a straight line from the sensory store to STM to LTM. It is then retrieved from LTM when required. The model leaves little room for the possibility that LTM influences, or even directs, other parts of the memory system. Yet there is evidence that LTM does just this. For example, expert chess players have a much better short-term memory for the arrangement of pieces on a chessboard. They can remember the positions of around 24 pieces compared to about 10 pieces for novice players. However, this only applies if the pieces are arranged according to the rules of chess. If they are arranged randomly, then the experts do no better than anyone else (de Groot, 1966). This suggests that the STM of expert chess players is informed by their knowledge of the game – which is held in LTM. In this case, LTM is directly influencing STM.

Similarly, chunking into meaningful units is only possible if STM 'knows' what a meaningful unit is – and that requires STM to be able to draw on LTM in order to chunk information in the first place.

This kind of evidence questions whether STM and LTM are as separate and distinct as the multistore model suggests. It also questions the idea that information just sits in LTM until it is retrieved by STM. It suggests that LTM plays an active role in memory, influencing, and maybe even directing, STM.

How important is rehearsal? The multistore model suggests that the longer information is in STM and the more it is rehearsed, the more likely it is to be transferred to LTM. A number of studies have questioned this view. For example, in one experiment, participants were asked to read a list of words over and over again. These words were then included in a longer list which they were asked to recall. The 'old' words, which had been well rehearsed, were not recalled any more frequently than the 'new' words included in the longer list (Tulving, 1967). Judging from this experiment, rehearsing words does not increase the probability of their recall.

Evidence from everyday situations suggests that rehearsal is a lot less important than the multistore model suggests. People rarely rehearse information in their everyday lives yet information is constantly entering LTM (Eysenck & Keane, 1995).

A passive and mechanical model. The multistore model has been criticised as a rather passive model of memory. For example, it tends to picture LTM as a passive storage dump. Information just sits there until it is needed. However, there is evidence to suggest that LTM is actively involved in the memory system as a whole. The multistore model has also been criticised for providing a rather mechanical model of memory. For example, it tends to picture information being mechanically shunted from one store to another.

Key terms

Multistore model *A model that pictures memory as a series of memory stores.*

Sensory memory store *A number of memory stores which hold incoming sensory information for very short periods of time.*

Iconic store *A sensory memory store for visual information.*

Echoic store *A sensory memory store for auditory information.*

2.2 Levels of processing model

The levels of processing model was introduced by Fergus Craik and Robert Lockhart in 1972. It provided an alternative to the multistore model. Craik and Lockhart did not reject the idea of memory stores – for example they accepted the existence of STM and LTM. However, rather than focusing on stores and how information is transferred from one store to another, they focused on how information is encoded and processed.

Levels of processing

According to Craik and Lockhart (1972), information can be encoded and processed at different *levels*. They argued that the level at which information is processed accounts for the likelihood of it being learned and remembered. They identified various levels of processing from the shallowest to the deepest. The following examples, based on processing words, are taken from one of their experiments in which participants were presented with questions on printed cards.

- At the shallowest level, words are processed visually in terms of their physical appearance. For example, is the following word in capital or lower case letters? FISH.
- At a deeper level, words are processed acoustically, in terms of their sound. For example, does the following word rhyme with 'pin'? STYLE. This is a deeper level of processing since it involves an analysis of both the appearance of the word and its sound.
- At the deepest level, words are processed semantically, in terms of their meaning. For example, is a PANCAKE a form of transport? To answer this, participants must focus on the meaning of the words.

Craik and Lockhart claimed that the deeper the level of processing, the stronger, more durable and longer lasting the memory.

The results of one of Craik and Lockhart's experiments are shown in Figure 6. Participants were asked a series of questions similar to those in the above paragraph. Later, they were asked to recall the words they had been questioned about. Figure 6 suggests that 'deep' processing in terms of meaning is a more effective way of remembering information than visual or acoustic processing.

Figure 6 Processing by appearance, sound and meaning

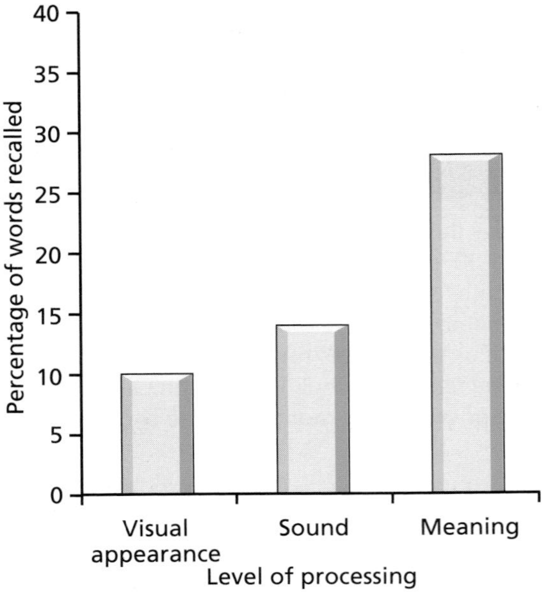

Adapted from Craik and Lockhart, 1972

Rehearsal

According to Atkinson and Shiffrin (1968), the more times information is rehearsed, the more likely it is to be remembered. According to Craik and Lockhart, it is the level of processing rather than the frequency of rehearsal that affects the durability of the memory. They distinguished between two types of rehearsal.

- **Simple maintenance rehearsal** This simply holds information. It prevents information from being forgotten during the holding process but does not lead to long-term memories.
- **Elaborative rehearsal** This increases the depth at which information is processed. It involves some kind of analysis or evaluation of the information. Only elaborative rehearsal leads to long-term memories.

Elaboration

Craik and Tulving (1975) developed the levels of processing model with the idea of *elaboration*. They suggested that how well information is remembered depends not only on the level of processing, but also on how complex or elaborate the processing is within each level. Thus, semantic processing produces better memory, but more complex semantic processing produces even better memory.

The following experiment illustrates the kind of evidence on which the idea of elaboration is based. Participants were presented with sentences containing a blank space followed by a word. They were asked whether the word fitted the space. Some of the sentences were very simple and others were more complex. Craik and Tulving assumed that the more complex the sentence, the more elaborate the processing would be. Here is an example of a simple sentence and a more complex sentence.

Simple sentence	**Word**
She read the ----------------------	newspaper
Complex sentence	
The great bird swooped down and carried off the struggling ------------	chicken

Later, the participants were shown the sentences without the additional words. This time they were asked to remember the word that had accompanied each sentence. Recall was twice as high for words accompanying complex sentences, suggesting that elaboration improves long-term memory. Craik and Tulving argued that the words had to be more thoroughly processed to fit into a complex sentence and, as a result, they became easier to remember. It was not just whether semantic encoding took place that was important, but also the amount of elaboration of that semantic encoding.

Evaluation

Change of direction The levels of processing model changed the direction of memory research. It showed that encoding was not a simple, straightforward process. This widened the focus from seeing long-term memory as a simple storage unit to seeing it as a complex processing system.

Supporting evidence Craik and Lockhart's ideas led to hundreds of experiments, most of which confirmed the superiority of 'deep' semantic processing for remembering information.

Measurement The ideas of 'depth' and 'elaboration' are vague and ill-defined. As a result, they are difficult to measure. This can lead to a circular argument – it is predicted that deeply processed information will be remembered better, but the measure of depth of processing is how well the information is remembered.

Distinctiveness Later research indicated that processing is more complex and varied than the levels of processing model suggests. In other words, there is more to processing than depth and elaboration. For example, research by Bransford et al. (1979) indicated that a sentence such as, 'A mosquito is like a doctor because both draw blood' is more likely to be recalled than the more elaborated sentence, ' A mosquito is like a racoon because they both have head, legs and jaws'. It appears that it is the distinctiveness of the first sentence which makes it easier to remember – it's unusual to compare a doctor to a mosquito. As a result, the sentence stands out and is more easily recalled.

2.3 Working memory model

The working memory model was introduced by Alan Baddeley and Graham Hitch in 1974. It is a model of short-term memory. Baddeley and Hitch argue that the picture of STM provided by the multistore model is far too simple. According to the multistore model, STM holds limited amounts of information for short periods of time with relatively little processing. It is a unitary system. This means it is a single system without any subsystems. It does not have various components or parts which specialise in different tasks.

Baddeley and Hitch's working memory presents a more complex picture of STM. Working memory is not a unitary system. It has a number of components or subsystems, each of which specialise in particular tasks – learning, reasoning, comprehension and problem solving. The traditional view saw information being held and rehearsed in STM and little more. From the point of view of working memory, information is analysed, evaluated and 'worked on'.

Key terms

Levels of processing *The idea that the way information is encoded affects how well it is remembered. The deeper the level of processing, the easier the information is to recall.*

Simple maintenance rehearsal *Holding information to prevent it from being forgotten in the short term.*

Elaborative rehearsal *Increases the depth at which information is processed. This leads to long-term memories.*

Elaboration *The idea that within a 'level', information can be processed to different extents. The more complex or elaborate the processing, the more likely the information is to be remembered.*

Distinctiveness *The more distinctive – different or unusual – the information, the more likely it is to be remembered.*

Evidence for working memory

What evidence is there that working memory exists, that it is made up of a number of parts, that it performs a number of different tasks? Baddeley (1986) conducted an experiment in which participants were asked to perform two tasks at the same time – a digit span task which required them to remember a list of numbers (see p 7) and a reasoning task which required them to answer true or false to the type of questions shown in Table 2.

Table 2 Reasoning tasks

BA	A follows B (true or false)
AB	B is not preceded by A (true or false)

Adapted from Baddeley, 1986

According to the traditional view of STM, once participants reach around 7 digits in their digit span task, there would be no room left to do anything else. STM has a limited capacity – it would be full. As a result, there would be no room left in STM to perform the reasoning task. This did not happen in Baddeley's experiment. As the number of digits increased in the digit span tasks, participants took longer to answer the reasoning questions, but not much longer – only fractions of a second. And, they didn't make any more errors in the reasoning tasks as the number of digits increased. The results of this experiment are shown in Figure 7.

Baddeley and Hitch (1974) conducted similar 'two-task' experiments on digit span and learning tasks, and digit span and comprehension tasks. The results were similar to those shown in Figure 7.

These results cannot be explained in terms of the traditional unitary model of STM. A new model – working

Figure 7 Reasoning and digit span tasks

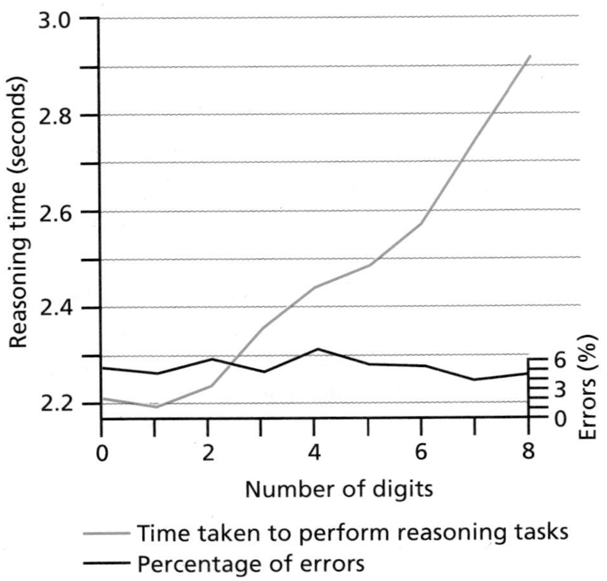

Adapted from Baddeley, 1986

memory – was needed to provide an explanation. A multicomponent or multipart system makes sense of these results. One component of working memory can be working on the digit span task while another component can be working on the reasoning task. Just because the component working on the digit span task reaches the limit of its capacity (with around 7 digits) does not mean that other components cannot operate successfully on other tasks.

The parts of working memory

Baddeley and Hitch's model sees working memory as having a controlling system, called the *central executive,* which supervises and coordinates a number of subsidiary systems or 'slave systems'. They studied two of these systems – the *articulatory* or *phonological loop* which deals with information in the form of speech, and the *sketchpad* or *visuo-spatial sketchpad* which deals with visual images. A simplified diagram of working memory is shown in Figure 8.

Figure 8 Working memory

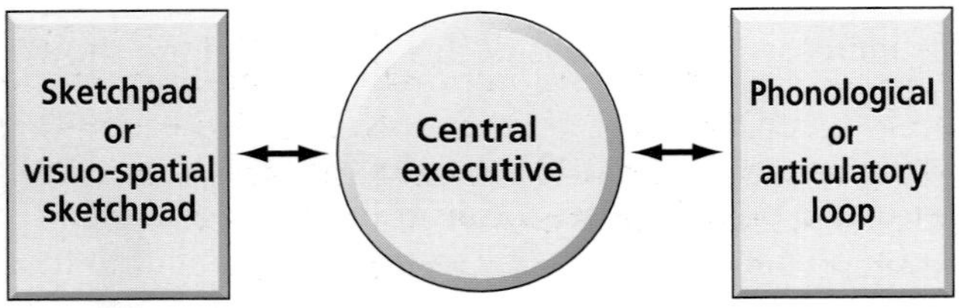

Adapted from Baddeley, 1986

It does not show other possible subsidiary systems which may be contained in working memory.

The phonological loop

The phonological or articulatory loop consists of two parts (see Figure 9).

The phonological store This store holds spoken words for 1½-2 seconds. Spoken words enter the store directly. Written words must first be converted into an articulatory (spoken) code before they can enter the phonological store.

The articulatory control process This process acts like an inner voice rehearsing information from the phonological store. It circulates information round and round like a tape loop. This is how we remember a telephone number we have just heard. As long as we keep repeating it, we can retain the information in working memory.

The articulatory control process also converts written material into an articulatory code and transfers it to the phonological store (Baddeley, 1997).

Figure 9 The phonological loop

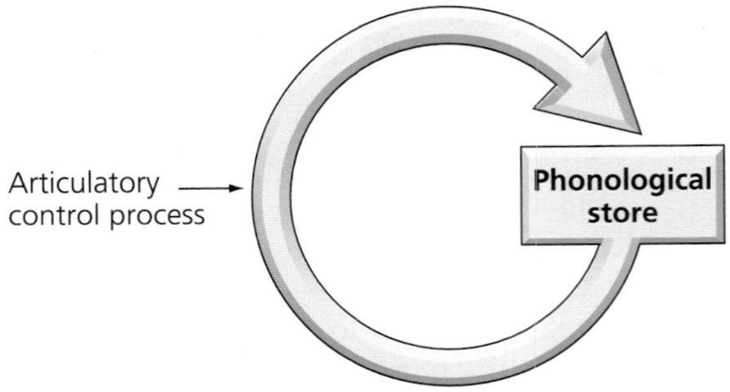

Adapted from Baddeley, 1986

The capacity of the phonological loop was demonstrated by the following experiment (Baddeley et al., 1975). Participants were given lists of short words and long words to recall. They recalled more of the short words than the long words. The researchers found that the phonological loop can hold the number of items that can be said in about 2 seconds. Since short words can be said in a shorter time than long words, more short words were recalled. This is known as the *word-length effect.* Try it yourself in Activity 2.

The sketchpad

The sketchpad or visuo-spatial sketchpad deals with visual and spatial information. Visual information refers to what things look like – there is a circle and a square in Figure 10. Spatial information refers to the layout of items relative to each other – the circle is above the square in Figure 10.

Activity 2 The word-length effect

Item A Short words

Some
Harm
Bear
Love
Snack

Item B Long words

Interrogation
Satisfactory
Simultaneous
Configuration
Opportunity

Questions

1 Read the list of words in Item A once. Close your eyes and try and repeat the words in order 4 times.

2 Do the same with the words in Item B.

3 Assuming you had difficulty with Item B, what does this suggest about the capacity of the phonological loop?

The sketchpad does not simply store visual and spatial information, it also analyses and manipulates this information. There is evidence that images are constructed and displayed on the sketchpad and 'looked at'. In one experiment, participants were asked to memorise a drawing of a boat like the one in Figure 11 (Kosslyn & Shwartz, 1981). They were then asked questions about different aspects of the boat. They appeared to answer the questions by 'looking' at an image in their head. Participants who had just answered a question about the motor at the back of the boat took longer to answer a question about the front of the boat than those who had been asked a question about the porthole in the middle of the boat. It was as if they were taking time to move their eyes along the image of the boat in their memory, and the further they had to move their eyes, the longer it took.

The sketchpad also displays and manipulates visual and spatial information held in long-term memory. For example, the spatial layout of your house is held in LTM. Try answering this question: How many windows are there in the front of your house? You probably find yourself picturing the front of your house and counting the windows. An image has been retrieved from LTM and pictured on the sketchpad.

Figure 10 Visual and spatial information

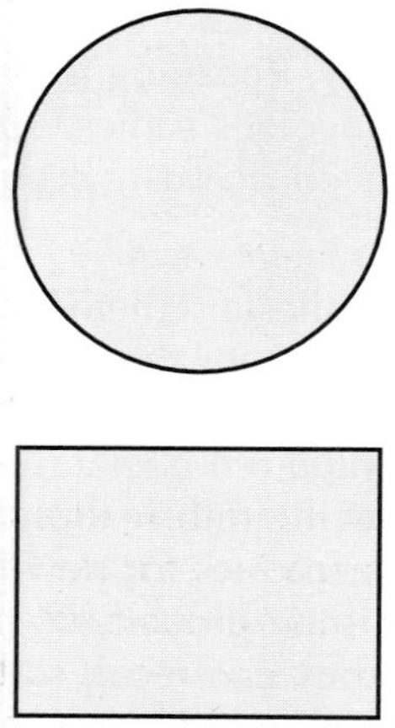

Figure 11 Drawing of a boat

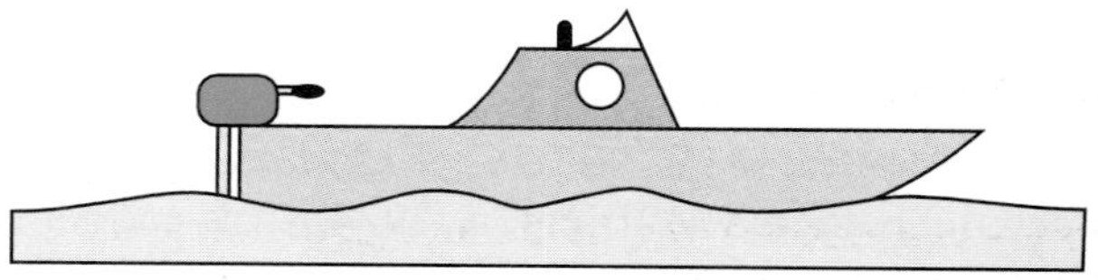

Evidence suggests that working memory uses two different systems for dealing with visual and verbal information. A visual processing task and a verbal processing task can be performed at the same time. It is more difficult to perform two visual tasks at the same time because they interfere with each other and performance is reduced. The same applies to performing two verbal tasks at the same time. This supports the view that the phonological loop and the sketchpad are separate systems within working memory.

The central executive

The central executive controls the phonological loop and the sketchpad. It decides which system is required and coordinates the retrieval of information from LTM. In the example given earlier, the central executive decided that the sketchpad was the best way of working out the number of windows in the front of your house, and retrieved an image of your house from LTM.

The central executive decides what working memory pays attention to. For example, two activities sometimes come into conflict such as driving a car and talking.

Rather than hitting a cyclist who is wobbling all over the road, it is preferable to stop talking and concentrate on driving. The central executive directs attention and gives priority to particular activities (Baddeley, 1997).

Evaluation of working memory

Multipart system Researchers today generally agree that short-term memory is made up of a number of components or subsystems. The working memory model has replaced the idea of a unitary (one part) STM as suggested by the multistore model.

Explanations The working memory model explains a lot more than the multistore model. It makes sense of a range of tasks – verbal reasoning, comprehension, reading, problem solving and visual and spatial processing. And the model is supported by considerable experimental evidence.

Brain damage As noted earlier (see p13), the multistore model could not explain memory impairment in certain brain-damaged people. For example, KF suffered brain damage from a motorcycle accident which impaired his short-term memory. KF's impairment was mainly for verbal information – his memory for visual information was largely unaffected (Shallice & Warrington, 1974). This cannot be explained in terms of a unitary STM. However, it can be explained in terms of the multicomponent working memory model – only one component of STM was damaged.

Rehearsal This plays a central part in the multistore model of memory – it is the only way information can pass from STM into LTM. However, evidence from everyday situations suggests that people rarely rehearse information. Rehearsal plays a relatively small part in the working memory model. It takes place in only one component – the phonological loop. In this respect, the working memory model reflects the operation of memory in everyday life.

The central executive There is little direct evidence for how the central executive works and what it does. However, the idea of a central executive 'makes sense' in terms of the working memory model. In any system made up of different parts, something must activate, coordinate and control the parts. More research is needed in order to discover how the central executive does this (Eysenck & Keane, 1995).

Key terms

Working memory *A model which sees short-term memory as made up of a number of parts, each specialising in particular tasks.*

Phonological or articulatory loop *The part of working memory that deals with spoken and written material.*

Phonological store *A short-term store which forms part of the phonological loop.*

Articulatory control process *Rehearses information from the phonological store. Also converts written material into an articulatory code and transfers it to the phonological store.*

Word-length effect *The retention of information in STM depends not so much on the number of words, but on how long it takes to articulate those words. STM appears to hold as many words as a person can speak in about 2 seconds.*

Sketchpad or visual-spatial sketchpad *The part of working memory that deals with visual and spatial information.*

Central executive *Activates, coordinates and controls the various parts of working memory.*

2.4 Models of long-term memory

Atkinson and Shiffrin's multistore model presented a unitary model of long-term memory. Most researchers now reject this view. They see LTM as a multipart system made up of two or more components or subsystems.

Procedural and declarative memory

A number of researchers make a distinction between *procedural* and *declarative* long-term memory (Cohen & Squire, 1980; Tulving, 1983).

Procedural memory This is a memory for skills – knowing how to do things. It includes memories for brushing your teeth, playing a guitar, riding a bicycle, tying your shoelaces and using a computer keyboard. These memories are only consciously recalled during the early stages of learning. For example, once the procedure has been learned, you brush your teeth with little or no awareness of the skills involved.

Declarative memory This is a memory for specific information. It includes, for example, knowledge that London is the capital of the United Kingdom, zebras are animals with striped coats and the Mississippi is a river in the USA. It also includes personal information such as the date of your birthday, the make of your car and what you had for lunch yesterday. Recalling information from declarative memory involves some degree of conscious effort – information is consciously brought to mind and 'declared'.

Evidence Studies of amnesia – memory loss due to brain damage – provide support for the distinction between procedural memory and declarative memory. Amnesiacs often have severely impaired declarative memory – they cannot remember specific information they have learned in the past, or form memories for new information they encounter. However, their procedural memory remains largely unaffected – they can recall skills they have already learned and are able to learn and retain new skills (Cohen, 1984).

Further support for the view that procedural and declarative memory are separate parts of LTM, is provided by people with Huntington's disease. There is evidence that their declarative memory is largely unaffected – they can learn and recall new information – but their procedural memory is impaired – they have difficulty learning new skills (Heindel et al., 1988).

Episodic and semantic memory

Endel Tulving (1972) suggested that declarative memory is made up of two components – *episodic memory* and *semantic memory*.

Episodic memory This part of LTM stores personal experiences which are often associated with a particular time and place – your first date, your driving test and what you did and where you were on the eve of the millennium.

Semantic memory Whereas episodic memory is like an autobiography, semantic memory is more like an encyclopaedia. It contains information about the world. Tulving (1972) described semantic memory as a 'mental thesaurus' since it contains knowledge of words and their meanings.

Evidence To what extent are episodic and semantic memories different memory systems? Clearly, they work together. Knowing what you had for breakfast yesterday – an episodic memory – requires a knowledge of cereals, toast and coffee drawn from semantic memory. However, there is evidence for a distinction between these types of memory.

There is an increase in blood flow to parts of the brain which are active. Participants in an experiment were asked to think about personal events – episodic memories. This resulted in increased blood flow to the frontal region of the brain, suggesting a high level of activity there. They were then asked to think about general knowledge, such as the capital cities of various countries – semantic memories. This resulted in increased blood flow to areas at the back of the brain (Tulving, 1989). This suggests that episodic and semantic memory are located in different parts of the brain and may, to some extent, be different memory systems.

Figure 12 Models of LTM

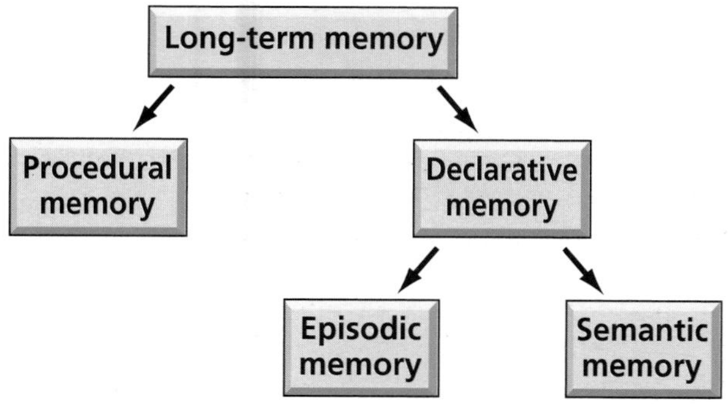

Key terms

Procedural memory *Memory for skills – knowing how to do things.*

Declarative memory *Memory for specific information.*

Episodic memory *Memory for personal experiences, often linked to particular times and places.*

Semantic memory *Memory for information about the world, including knowledge of words and their meanings.*

Summary

1. The multistore model of memory consists of three memory stores – the sensory store, STM and LTM.
2. Rehearsal increases the time information can be held in STM. It also transfers information from STM to LTM.
3. The multistore model has been criticised for presenting an oversimplified picture of memory.
4. The levels of processing model states that the level at which information is processed affects the likelihood of it being learned and remembered.
5. The deeper the level, the more thorough the processing and the greater the likelihood of retrieval. Information encoded semantically appears to be more deeply processed than information encoded visually or acoustically.
6. Elaboration of processing states that the likelihood of retrieval is affected not only by the level of processing but also by further processing – elaboration – within a level.
7. Although there are problems with measuring depth and elaboration, the levels of processing model has provided important insights into the working of memory.
8. Working memory is a model of short-term memory. It sees STM as a multipart system. The various parts specialise in different tasks.
9. The parts or components of working memory include the phonological loop which deals with spoken and written material, the sketchpad which deals with visual and spatial material, and the central executive which coordinates and controls the various parts.
10. There is considerable evidence to support the working memory model. However, there is little direct evidence for the functions of the central executive.
11. Most researchers now see LTM as a multipart system made up of two or more parts or subsystems.

Unit 3 Experiments

KEY ISSUES

1. **How true-to-life are memory experiments?**
2. **Can the findings of experiments be applied to everyday life?**
3. **What are the advantages of laboratory experiments?**

A large part of the research on memory is based on experiments conducted in laboratories. Those who take part in the experiments – the participants – are asked to perform tasks such as recalling lists of words and numbers. Both the setting – the laboratory – and the tasks are a long way from everyday life. In many cases, the setting is artificial and the tasks fairly meaningless. Does this matter?

3.1 Ecological validity

Psychologists use the term *ecological validity* to refer to the extent to which the findings of research studies can be generalised to other settings. An experiment has high ecological validity if its findings can be generalised, that is applied or extended, to settings outside the laboratory.

It is often assumed that if an experiment is realistic or true-to-life, then there is a greater likelihood that its findings can be generalised. If it is not realistic – if the laboratory setting and the tasks are artificial – then there is less likelihood that the findings can be generalised. In this case, the experiment will have low ecological validity.

Many experiments designed to investigate memory have been criticised for having low ecological validity. First, the laboratory is an artificial situation. People are removed from their normal social settings and asked to take part in a psychological experiment. They are directed by an 'experimenter' and may be placed in the company of complete strangers. For many people, this is a brand new experience, far removed from their everyday lives. Will this setting affect their actions, will they behave normally?

Often, the tasks participants are asked to perform can appear artificial and meaningless. Few, if any, people would attempt to memorise and recall a list of unconnected words in their daily lives. And it is not clear how tasks such as this relate to the use of memory in everyday life. The artificiality of many experiments has led some researchers to question whether their findings can be generalised to real life. As a result, many memory experiments have been criticised for having low ecological validity.

3.2 The case for experiments

Consider the following example. A researcher wishes to find out the importance of light on the growth of plants. She conducts the following experiment. Every factor or variable, except one, which is known to affect the growth of plants is held constant – kept the same. Plants of the same species and size are kept at the same temperature and humidity, grown in the same type and amount of soil and given the same volume of water at the same time. Only the light changes – one group of plants is exposed to more of the same light than the other group. A single variable – light – has been isolated from all other variables in order to discover the effect it has on plant growth. Experiments allow researchers to *control* variables and to discover the effect of one variable (eg light) on another variable (eg plant growth).

Researchers who study human memory in the laboratory adopt a similar approach. They claim that only by controlling variables can reliable findings about memory be produced. They argue that the world outside the laboratory contains a vast number of variables that cannot be controlled by the researcher. As a result, it is not possible to say what affects what.

Take the following example. How do people remember faces in the 'real world'? The researcher has no control over the range of factors that affect people's memory for faces in everyday life. For example, the researcher cannot control the amount of attention people give to the face in the first place, the length or number of times they see the face, their relationship to the person concerned, the similarity of other faces they have seen, and so on (Cohen, 1996).

In the laboratory, participants can be shown the same faces, for the same length of time, in the same setting. In this way, at least some of the variables which may affect memory for faces can be controlled.

Conclusion Many researchers believe that an understanding of human memory requires both experimental and naturalistic studies, that is research in the laboratory and studies of people in their 'natural' everyday settings. Alan Baddeley (1997) states, 'We need to blend the control of the laboratory with the richness of the everyday world if we are to understand the whole of human memory'. The value of combining experimental and naturalistic research is examined in Chapter 3 which looks at eyewitness testimony.

Key terms

Ecological validity *The extent to which the findings of research studies can be generalised to other settings.*

Control of variables *Control by the researcher over the factors which are assumed to affect behaviour.*

Naturalistic studies *Studies of people in their natural, everyday settings.*

Summary

1. Many laboratory experiments on memory have been criticised for being artificial and unrealistic.
2. Researchers have questioned whether the findings from experiments can be applied to the use of memory in everyday life. As a result, memory experiments have been criticised for having low ecological validity.
3. Laboratory experiments allow researchers to control many of the variables which may affect memory.
4. Many researchers argue that the findings of both experimental and naturalistic research must be combined for a full understanding of human memory.

References

Atkinson, R.C. & Shiffrin, R.M. (1968). Human memory: A proposed system and its control processes. In K.W. Spence (Ed.), *The psychology of learning and motivation: Advances in research and theory*, Vol.2. New York: Academic Press.

Baddeley, A.D. (1966a). Short-term memory for word sequences as a function of acoustic, semantic and formal similarity. *Quarterly Journal of Experimental Psychology, 18*, 362-365.

Baddeley, A.D. (1966b). The influence of acoustic and semantic similarity on long-term memory for word sequences. *Quarterly Journal of Experimental Psychology, 18*, 302-309.

Baddeley, A.D. (1976). *The psychology of memory.* London: Harper & Row.

Baddeley, A.D. (1986). *Working memory.* Oxford: OUP.

Baddeley, A.D. (1997). *Human memory: Theory and practice* (2nd ed.). Hove: Psychology Press.

Baddeley, A.D. & Hitch, G. (1974). Working memory. In G.A. Bower (Ed.), *Recent advances in learning and motivation, Vol. 8.* New York: Academic Press.

Baddeley, A.D., Thomson, M. & Buchanan, M. (1975). Word length and the structure of short-term memory. *Journal of Verbal Learning and Verbal Behavior, 14*, 575-589.

Bransford, J.D., Franks, J.J., Morris, C.D. & Stein, B.S. (1979). Some general constraints on learning and memory research. In L.S. Cermak & F.I.M. Craik (Eds.), *Levels of processing in human memory.* Hillsdale, NJ: Lawrence Erlbaum Associates.

Brown, J. (1958). Some tests of the decay theory of immediate memory. *Quarterly Journal of Experimental Psychology, 10*, 12-21.

Butters, N. & Cermak, L.S. (1980). *Alcoholic Korsakoff's syndrome: An information-processing approach.* London: Academic Press.

Cohen, G. (1996). *Memory in the real world* (2nd ed.). Hove: Psychology Press.

Cohen, N.J. (1984). Preserved learning capacity in amnesia: Evidence for multiple memory systems. In L.R. Squire & N. Butters (Eds.), *The neuro-psychology of memory.* New York: Guilford.

Cohen, N.J. & Squire, L.R. (1980). Preserved learning and retention of pattern analysing skill in amnesia: Dissociation of knowing how and knowing that. *Science, 210*, 207-210.

Conrad, R. (1964). Acoustic confusions in immediate memory. *British Journal of Psychology, 55*, 429-432.

Craik, F.I.M. & Lockhart, R.S. (1972). Levels of processing: A framework for memory research. *Journal of Verbal Learning and Verbal Behaviour, 11*, 671-684.

Craik, F.I.M. & Tulving, E. (1975). Depth of processing and the retention of words in episodic memory. *Journal of Experimental Psychology: General, 1*, 268-294.

de Groot, A.D. (1965). *Thought and choice in chess.* The Hague: Mouton.

Eysenck, M.W. & Keane, M.T. (1995). *Cognitive psychology: A student's handbook* (3rd ed.). Hove: Lawrence Erlbaum Associates.

Glanzer, M. & Cunitz, A.R. (1966). Two storage mechanisms in free recall. *Journal of Verbal Learning and Verbal Behavior, 5*, 351-360.

Heindel, W.C., Butters, N. & Salmon, D.P. (1988). Impaired learning of a motor skill in patients with Huntingdon's disease. *Behavioural Neuroscience, 102*, 141-147.

Hintzmann, D.L. (1967). Articulatory coding in short-term memory. *Psychonomic Science, 3*, 161-162.

James, W. (1890). *Principles of psychology, Vol. 1.* New York: Holt.

Kosslyn, S.M. & Shwartz, S.P. (1981). Empirical constraints of theories of visual mental imagery. In J. Long & A.D. Baddeley (Eds.), *Attention and Performance IX.* Hillsdale, NJ: Lawrence Erlbaum Associates.

Miller, G.A. (1956). The magical number seven plus or minus two: Some limits on our capacity for processing information. *Psychological Review, 63*, 81-97.

Peterson, L.R. & Peterson, M.J. (1959). Short-term retention of individual verbal items. *Journal of Experimental Psychology, 58*, 193-198.

Rundus, D. (1971). Analysis of rehearsal processes in free recall. *Journal of Experimental Psychology, 89*, 63-77.

Shallice, T. & Warrington, E.K. (1970). Independent functioning of verbal memory stores: A neuropsychological study. *Quarterly Journal of Experimental Psychology, 22*, 261-273.

Shallice, T. & Warrington, E.K. (1974). The dissociation between long-term retention of meaningful sounds and verbal material. *Neuropsychologia, 12*, 553-555.

Sperling, G. (1960). The information available in brief visual presentations. *Psychological Monographs: General and Applied, 74*, 1-29.

Tulving, E. (1967). The effects of presentation and recall of material in free-recall learning. *Journal of Verbal Learning and Verbal Behaviour, 6*, 175-184.

Tulving, E. (1972). Episodic and semantic memory. In E. Tulving & W. Donaldson (Eds.), *Organisation of memory.* London: Academic Press.

Tulving, E. (1983). *Elements of episodic memory.* Oxford: OUP.

Tulving, E. (1985). How many memory systems are there? *American Psychologist, 40*, 385-398.

Tulving, E. (1989). Memory: Performance, knowledge and experience. *European Journal of Cognitive Psychology, 1*, 3-26.

2 Forgetting

Introduction

Why do we forget? There are two simple answers to this question. First, the memory has disappeared – it is no longer there. Second, the memory is still stored in the memory system but, for some reason, it cannot be retrieved. These two answers summarise the main theories of forgetting developed by psychologists. The first answer is more likely to be applied to forgetting in short-term memory, the second to forgetting in long-term memory.

Chapter summary

- **Unit 1 outlines theories of forgetting in short-term memory.**
- **Unit 2 examines theories of forgetting in long-term memory.**
- **Unit 3 looks at the relationship between forgetting and emotion.**

Unit 1 Forgetting in short-term memory

KEY ISSUES

1. **What are the main theories of forgetting in STM?**
2. **What are their strengths and weaknesses?**

As outlined in the previous chapter, STM has a limited duration and a limited capacity. It can only hold information for a short period of time. It can only hold small amounts of information. These observations form the basis for the first two theories of forgetting discussed below. Both theories assume that forgetting occurs because information is lost from STM.

1.1 Trace decay

This explanation of forgetting in short-term memory assumes that memories leave a *trace* in the brain. A trace is some form of physical and/or chemical change in the nervous system. *Trace decay theory* states that forgetting occurs as a result of the automatic decay or fading of the memory trace.

Trace decay appears to occur rapidly. As the previous chapter indicated, STM has a limited duration – information is held there for only a short period of time. The Brown-Peterson effect states that information disappears from STM within about 20 seconds if it is not rehearsed (see p 8). Peterson and Peterson (1959) explained this rapid loss in terms of trace decay. The memory trace fades over time until it disappears completely. At this point, information is forgotten.

Evaluation Evidence from experiments questions the idea of trace decay. In one experiment (Waugh & Norman, 1965), participants were presented with a series of 16 numbers, for example 4, 9, 7, 3, 6 etc. They were then given a number from the series – this number was known as the probe – and asked which number followed it. For example, if the probe is 7, the correct answer is 3. This procedure is known as the *serial probe technique*.

The numbers were presented at different speeds. If information fades away due to the passage of time, then numbers presented at a faster rate have less time in which to decay than numbers presented at a slower rate. If trace decay is occurring, then memory should be better – more correct answers should be given – when the numbers are presented quickly. Presentation rate appeared to make little difference. There was no significant relationship between the speed of presentation and recall of the correct numbers. This finding throws doubt on the trace decay theory of forgetting.

Key term

Trace decay theory *Forgetting in STM occurs as a result of the automatic decay of the memory trace.*

1.2 Displacement

Trace decay theory focuses on time – the limited duration of STM. *Displacement theory* focuses on capacity – the limited amount of space in STM. In George Miller's famous phrase, the capacity of STM is 'the magical number seven, plus or minus two'. In other words, STM can hold between 5 and 9 items – numbers, words or chunks.

Displacement theory provides a very simple explanation of forgetting. Because of its limited capacity, STM can only hold small amounts of information. When STM is 'full', new information displaces or 'pushes out' old information. The old information which is displaced is forgotten in STM.

Evaluation There is some evidence to support the idea of displacement. In one experiment, participants were presented with a list of numbers. The more numbers that followed a particular probe number, the less likely that probe number was to be remembered (Shallice, 1967). It can be argued that the later numbers tended to displace the earlier numbers. As a result, the earlier numbers became more difficult to remember. However, it can also be argued that because the earlier numbers were presented earlier in time, they were forgotten as a result of trace decay. Shallice investigated this possibility and claimed that although time appeared to have some effect on recall, the number of items following a probe number seemed to have a greater effect. This experiment suggests that displacement provides a better explanation of forgetting in STM than trace decay.

Key term

Displacement theory *Forgetting occurs when information is displaced or 'pushed out' of STM when its capacity is exceeded.*

1.3 Interference

Interference theory states that forgetting occurs because memories interfere with and disrupt one another. Old memories can disrupt new memories – this is known as *proactive interference*, meaning forward interference. Alternatively, new memories can disrupt old memories – this is known as *retroactive interference*, meaning backward interference.

Interference is more likely when memories are similar. For example, if you change your telephone number, the old number can interfere with the new number. This may result in you forgetting the new number. This is an example of proactive interference – the old memory disrupts the new one. And, the similarity of the memories – two telephone numbers – makes interference more likely.

The following experiment on forgetting in STM supports the idea of interference (Loess, 1968). Participants were presented with lists of three words from a particular category, for example animals. They were asked to count backwards for 15 seconds to prevent rehearsal, then asked to recall the three animals. This was done six times with six different lists of animals. The first list of words was well recalled, the second list less well recalled and by the third or fourth list, recall was reduced to an even lower level. In terms of interference theory, this is an example of proactive interference – the earlier lists of words interfered with the later lists resulting in an increase in forgetting. Since all the words belong to the same semantic or meaning category – animals – they are similar. As a result, interference is likely.

The category was then changed, for example to vegetables, and the same procedure was followed. Recall improved immediately. In terms of interference theory, the old category did not interfere with the new category because the categories were different. Proactive interference ceased because vegetables are distinct from animals. This is known as *release from proactive interference*. However, after the first list of vegetables, proactive interference began again because the following lists of vegetables belonged to the same category.

Evaluation Support for interference theory is based mainly on the findings of laboratory experiments. However, these experiments may have little relationship to what happens in everyday life. As a result, it may not be possible to generalise from the findings. In other words, these experiments may have low ecological validity. The following experiment provides a more realistic test of interference theory (Slamecka, 1966).

Participants were given a word, for example, 'animal' and asked for a word they associated with it, for example 'dog'. They gave the first word which came to mind which probably reflects what would happen in an everyday situation. They were then asked to learn a new set of words which were linked to 'animal' such as 'cow', 'bear', 'cat', and so on. They were then asked to recall these words including the first word they associated with 'animal' – in this example 'dog'. In terms of interference theory, this should result in retroactive interference because the words belonged to the same semantic category. New learning should disrupt older memories and participants would probably forget the first word – 'dog' – they associated with 'animal'. They didn't. There was no evidence of interference. They remembered the word they were most likely to associate with the category 'animal'. This experiment suggests that when participants behave 'normally' and select their usual associations, interference may not occur.

Key terms

Interference theory *Forgetting occurs as a result of similar memories interfering with and disrupting each other.*

Proactive interference *Older memories interfering with newer memories.*

Retroactive interference *Newer memories interfering with older memories.*

Release from proactive interference *Proactive interference ceases to affect recall.*

Conclusion

This unit has looked at three theories of forgetting in short-term memory. There is experimental evidence both to support and question each theory. It is possible that, at various times, forgetting in STM may be a combination of two or all of these processes – trace decay, displacement and interference. The answer is far from clear. One of the foremost experts on memory, Alan Baddeley (1997), concludes that, 'The explanation of forgetting … remains an open question'.

Many ingenious experiments have been devised to examine forgetting in STM. However, as noted earlier, they may have low ecological validity. As a result, the findings of laboratory research may not be applicable to forgetting in everyday situations.

Summary

1. Trace decay theory explains forgetting in terms of the limited duration of STM. It states that forgetting occurs as a result of the progressive decay of the memory trace over time.
2. Displacement theory explains forgetting in terms of the limited capacity of STM. It states that forgetting occurs when information is displaced from STM when its capacity is exceeded.
3. Interference theory states that forgetting occurs as a result of similar memories interfering with and disrupting each other.
4. The findings on forgetting in STM are inconclusive – no firm conclusions can be reached.

Activity 1 Forgetting in STM

Item A The Brown-Peterson effect

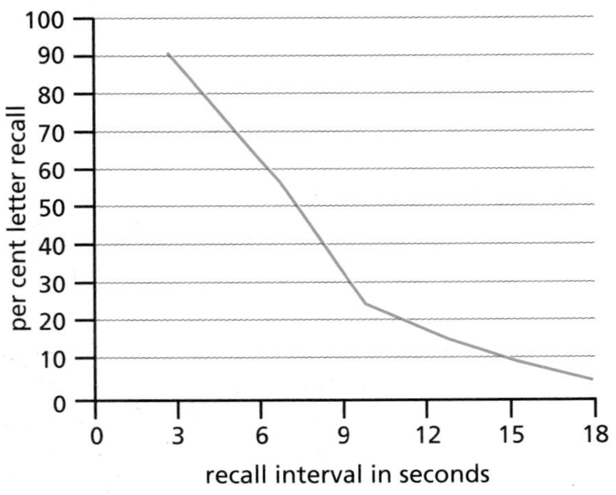

This graph shows the recall of information from STM when rehearsal is prevented (see p 8 for a fuller description of this experiment).

Adapted from Peterson & Peterson, 1959

Item B Experimental results

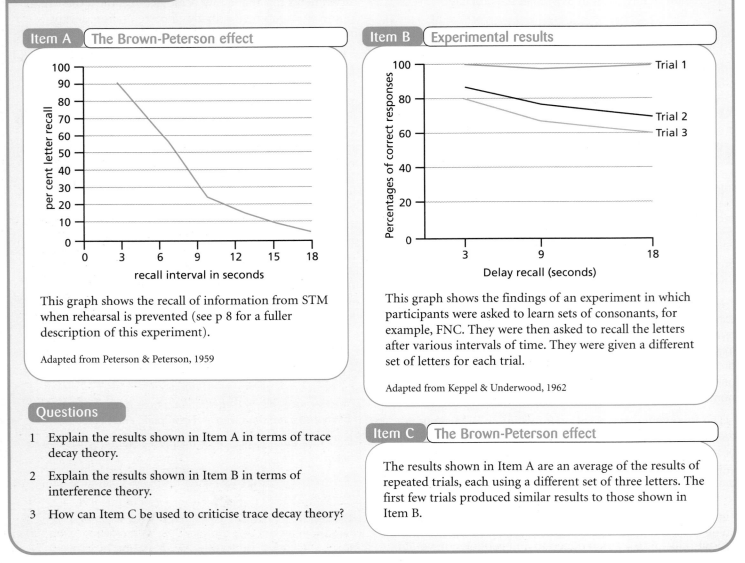

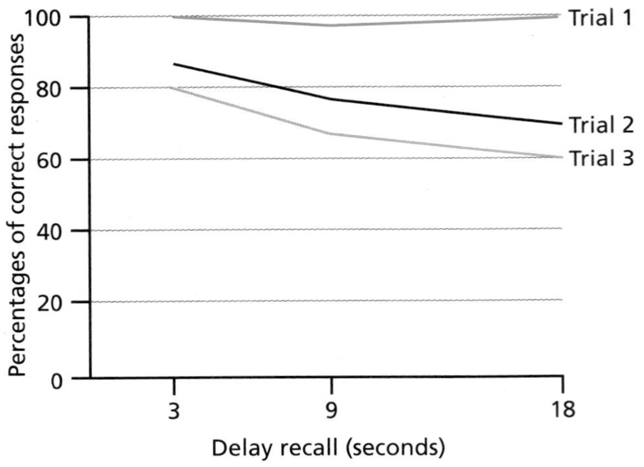

This graph shows the findings of an experiment in which participants were asked to learn sets of consonants, for example, FNC. They were then asked to recall the letters after various intervals of time. They were given a different set of letters for each trial.

Adapted from Keppel & Underwood, 1962

Item C The Brown-Peterson effect

The results shown in Item A are an average of the results of repeated trials, each using a different set of three letters. The first few trials produced similar results to those shown in Item B.

Questions

1 Explain the results shown in Item A in terms of trace decay theory.

2 Explain the results shown in Item B in terms of interference theory.

3 How can Item C be used to criticise trace decay theory?

Unit 2 Forgetting in long-term memory

KEY ISSUES

1. **What are the main theories of forgetting in LTM?**
2. **What are their strengths and weaknesses?**

Most psychologists assume that long-term memory has an unlimited capacity. If this is correct, then forgetting from LTM cannot be due to displacement. LTM cannot 'fill up' and 'overflow' as new information pushes out old information.

Many psychologists believe that once information enters LTM, it stays there permanently. If this is the case, then forgetting is not due to a loss of information from LTM, but a failure to access and retrieve information. However, not all researchers accept this point of view as the following section indicates.

2.1 Trace decay

Trace decay theory has also been used to explain forgetting in long-term memory. It states that memories automatically decay over time. There is little evidence to support this explanation. If the memory trace decays steadily over time, then older memories will always be forgotten before more recent ones. If you remember your first day at school or work but cannot remember your second day, this suggests that memories do not necessarily fade with time. Older people often recall events and friends from their youth more readily than recent events and friends. Again, this suggests that memories do not automatically decay over time.

The importance of time is questioned by the following experiment (Jenkins & Dallenbach, 1924). Participants were asked to learn lists of nonsense syllables. Their recall was better if they slept after learning the lists rather than stayed awake for the same period of time. This suggests it is not the passage of time itself that causes information to be forgotten – memories do not appear to progressively fade over time. Instead, it seems to be what happens during that time that is important.

2.2 Interference

Hundreds of experiments have indicated that interference plays a part in forgetting in long-term memory. As noted in Unit 1, interference can be proactive – earlier memories disrupt later memories, or retroactive – later memories disrupt earlier memories. Experimental evidence indicates that the more similar the information, the more likely that interference will occur. The following example illustrates the type of experiment designed to examine the role of interference in forgetting (McGeoch & McDonald, 1931).

Participants learned a list of adjectives until they could recall them perfectly. Some of the participants then spent 10 minutes resting while others learned new material. The new material varied in similarity to the original list – from very different (3-digit numbers such as 268), to very similar (synonyms – adjectives with the same meaning to those in the first list). The more similar the new material to the original, the more the recall of the original list declined. Participants who spent 10 minutes resting without any new material to learn had the highest recall, those who had to learn the synonyms had the lowest recall. This suggests that retroactive interference affected recall. It indicates that the more similar the later material, the greater the interference and the higher the level of forgetting. The results of this experiment are shown in Table 1.

Table 1 Retroactive interference

Activity	Average (mean) recall of ten adjectives
Rest	4.50
Learn 3-digit numbers	3.68
Learn nonsense syllables	2.58
Learn unrelated adjectives	2.17
Learn antonyms (adjectives with opposite meanings)	1.83
Learn synonyms (adjectives with the same meanings)	1.25

Adapted from McGeoch & McDonald, 1931

Evaluation Laboratory experiments are carefully designed to produce interference. The above study indicates this. Participants were asked to learn a list of adjectives with the same meanings as those on the original list. Situations like this are unlikely to occur in everyday life. As a result, generalisations from the laboratory to the wider world must be treated with caution. Such experiments might have low ecological validity.

Many researchers believe that interference is unlikely to be a major factor in forgetting in everyday life (Eysenck & Keane, 1995). However, it can occur as an oft-quoted example from Loftus (1980) indicates. A young woman in moments of passion with her present boyfriend tended to cry out the name of her previous boyfriend. This is a rather unfortunate example of proactive interference.

Experiments on interference are compressed into a relatively short period of time and information is encoded in the same setting – the laboratory. Again this indicates low ecological validity. In everyday life, the encoding of information which might interfere with existing information, is usually spread out over a longer period of time and often takes place in different settings. This may well reduce the effects of interference. For example, the new information may be associated with a particular time, place or person which will make it different from existing information. The importance of such factors can be seen from the following section.

Activity 2 Interference in LTM

Item A Finding your car

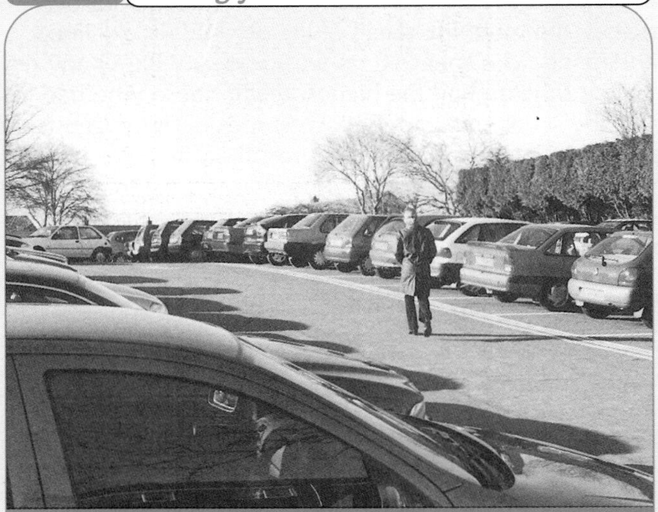

You park your car in a different place every day. You often have problems finding it.

Item B Remembering names

Teachers sometimes have difficulty remembering the names of their students, especially when they teach different groups every day.

Questions

1 Use the idea of interference to explain why you often have problems finding your car.

2 How does the idea of interference explain why teachers sometimes have difficulty remembering their students' names?

2.3 Retrieval failure

If information is stored in long-term memory, then it is available. However, it may or may not be accessible. If it is accessible, then it is retrieved when required. If it is not accessible, it is not retrieved when required and, at that point in time, it is forgotten. This is known as *retrieval failure.*

Tip-of-the-tongue effect The distinction between availability and accessibility is illustrated by the tip-of-the-tongue (TOT) effect. This occurs when people know they know something but are unable to recall it. Brown and McNeill (1966) devised an experiment to create TOT effects. Participants were presented with definitions of uncommon words and asked to identify the words that fitted the definitions. Often they produced words that were similar in sound or meaning to the correct words. For example, when the correct word was 'sampan' (a small Chinese boat), participants' answers included 'sarong', 'Cheyenne', 'barge' and 'junk'. The first two words sound like the correct answer, the last two words have similar meanings.

The TOT effect illustrates the distinction between availability and accessibility. The words are available in LTM – participants recognised them immediately they were told. However, they were not accessible and so could not be retrieved.

Key terms

Retrieval failure *The failure to retrieve information from memory.*

Availability *Whether or not information is stored in memory.*

Accessibility *Whether or not information which is available can be retrieved.*

Tip-of-the-tongue effect *Knowing that information is available in memory but being unable to retrieve it.*

Retrieval cues

There is considerable evidence that information is more likely to be retrieved from long-term memory if appropriate *retrieval cues* are present. This evidence comes from both laboratory experiments and everyday experience. A retrieval cue is a hint or clue that can help retrieval. Tulving (1974) argued that information will be more readily retrieved if the cues present when the information was encoded are also present when its retrieval is required. For example, if you proposed to your partner when a certain song was playing on the radio, you will be more likely to remember the details of the proposal when you hear the same song again. The song is a retrieval cue – it was present when the information was encoded and retrieved.

Context Retrieval cues may be based on *context* – the setting or situation in which information is encoded and retrieved. Examples include a particular room, driving along a motorway, a certain group of people, a rainy day and so on. Context also refers to the way information is presented. For example, words may be printed, spoken or sung, they may be presented in meaningful groups – in categories such as lists of animals or furniture – or as a random collection without any link between them. Evidence indicates that retrieval is more likely when the context at encoding matches the context at retrieval.

State Retrieval clues may also be based on *state* – the physical or psychological state of the person when information is encoded and retrieved. For example, a person may be alert, tired, happy, sad, drunk or sober when the information was encoded. They will be more likely to retrieve the information when they are in a similar state.

Cue-dependent forgetting This occurs when information in LTM cannot be retrieved because appropriate retrieval cues are absent. The information is available but not accessible because of a lack of retrieval cues.

Context-dependent retrieval

A number of experiments have indicated the importance of context-based cues for retrieval. An experiment conducted by Tulving and Pearlstone (1966) asked participants to learn lists of words belonging to different categories, for example names of animals, clothing and sports. Participants were then asked to recall the words. Those who were given the category names recalled substantially more words than those who were not. The categories provided a context, and naming the categories provided retrieval cues. Tulving and Pearlstone argued that cue-dependent forgetting explains the difference between the two groups of participants. Those who recalled fewer words lacked appropriate retrieval cues. (See Activity 3 for further details of this experiment).

An interesting experiment conducted by Godden and Baddeley (1975) indicates the importance of setting for retrieval. Participants learned lists of words either on land or 15 feet underwater. They were then asked to recall the words either in the same setting (for example, learning on land and recalling on land), or in the opposite setting (for example, learning on land and recalling underwater). The results, shown in Figure 1, indicate that when the settings for learning and recall are the same, participants retrieved significantly more words. The similarity of the contexts provided retrieval cues. Forgetting was due, in part, to an absence of context-dependent retrieval cues.

Figure 1 Context-dependent retrieval

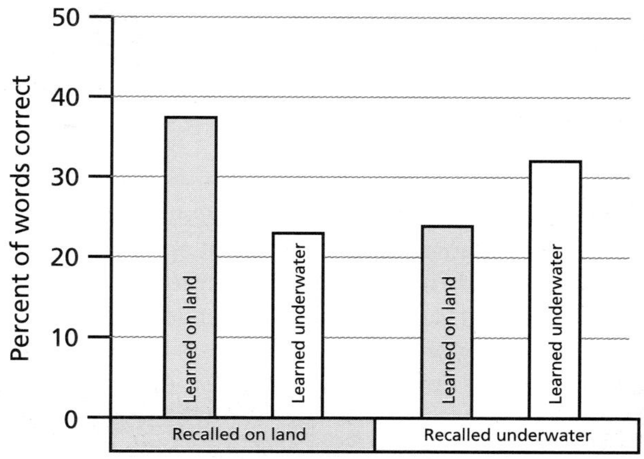

Adapted from Godden & Baddeley, 1975

State-dependent retrieval

The basic idea behind state-dependent retrieval is that memory will be best when a person's physical or psychological state is similar at encoding and retrieval. For example, if someone tells you a joke on Saturday night after a few drinks, you'll be more likely to remember it when you're in a similar state – at a later date after a few more drinks. Stone cold sober on Monday morning, you'll be more likely to forget the joke.

A study by Goodwin et al. (1969) investigated the effect of alcohol on state-dependent retrieval. They found that when people encoded information when drunk, they were more likely to recall it in the same state. For example, when they hid money and alcohol when drunk, they were unlikely to find them when sober. However, when they were drunk again, they often discovered the hiding place. Other studies found similar state-dependent effects when participants were given drugs such as marijuana or barbiturates.

Evidence for state-dependent retrieval in terms of mood is less convincing. From this point of view, recall should be better when a person's mood state, for example, happy or sad, at encoding is the same as their mood at retrieval (Bower, 1981). A review of 40 studies indicates a tendency, but not a particularly strong one, for people to recall information when their mood at encoding matches their mood at retrieval (Ucros, 1989). However, mood effects are usually greater when participants are asked to recall personal experiences rather than the lists of words often used in experiments. This suggests that mood effects may be stronger in real life than in laboratory settings. This calls into question the ecological validity of laboratory experiments.

Forgetting and retrieval-failure theory – evaluation

According to retrieval-failure theory, forgetting occurs when information is available in LTM but is not accessible. Accessibility depends in large part on retrieval cues. Forgetting is greatest when context and state are very different at encoding and retrieval. In this situation, retrieval cues are absent and the likely result is cue-dependent forgetting.

There is considerable evidence to support this theory of forgetting from laboratory experiments. The ecological validity of these experiments can be questioned, but their findings are supported by evidence from outside the laboratory. For example, many people say they can't remember much about their childhood or their schooldays. But returning to the house in which they spent their childhood or attending a school reunion often provides retrieval cues which trigger a flood of memories.

How does cue-dependent forgetting compare to the other theories of forgetting in LTM? According to Michael Eysenck (1998), a leading researcher, 'It has proved easy to demonstrate powerful effects of cue-dependent forgetting inside and outside the laboratory. It seems probable that this is the main reason for forgetting in long-term memory.'

Key terms

Retrieval cue *A clue or hint which helps retrieval.*

Context *The setting or situation in which information is encoded and retrieved.*

State *The physical or psychological state of a person when information is encoded and retrieved.*

Cue-dependent forgetting *Forgetting due to the absence of appropriate retrieval cues.*

Summary

1. There is little evidence for trace decay in LTM.
2. There is considerable evidence from laboratory experiments for interference in LTM. However, interference does not appear to be a major factor in forgetting in everyday life.
3. Evidence from both laboratory experiments and everyday experience supports the idea of cue-dependent forgetting. Forgetting appears to be greatest when context and state are very different at encoding and retrieval.

Activity 3 Retrieval cues – part 1

Word list

dog	grenade	knife	doctor
cat	gun	spoon	lawyer
horse	rifle	fork	teacher
cow	bomb	pan	dentist
apple	cotton	hammer	football
orange	silk	saw	cricket
pear	wool	spanner	basketball
banana	rayon	screwdriver	tennis
chair	blue	oil	shirt
table	red	gas	socks
bed	green	coal	skirt
sofa	yellow	wood	shoes

Adapted from Tulving & Pearlstone, 1966

Questions

1. Read the list three times.
2. Cover the list and write down as many of the words as you can remember.
3. Ask a friend to do the same. Show them the retrieval cues on page 32 before and during the time when they write the words down.
4. Have they recalled more words than you? If so, suggest why.

Unit 3 Emotional factors in forgetting

KEY ISSUES

1. **What are flashbulb memories and repressed memories?**
2. **How is emotion related to the recall of these memories?**

This unit examines the part played by emotion in the retrieval of information from long-term memory. It looks at two types of emotionally-charged memories. The first, flashbulb memories, are readily recalled, often in vivid detail. The second, repressed memories, are extremely difficult to recall. Emotion appears to have a significant, but very different, effect on the retrieval of these two types of memories.

3.1 Flashbulb memories

People sometimes have very vivid and detailed memories of where they were and what they were doing when a major event occurred. These memories are known as *flashbulb memories*. They are shaped by events which are experienced as emotionally charged, dramatic, surprising and important.

Brown and Kulik (1977) asked people a series of questions about ten major events, for example the assassination of President John F. Kennedy in 1963. They found that memories for such events were particularly vivid, detailed and long lasting. People usually remembered where they were when they heard the news, how they heard the news, what they and others were doing at the time, and the emotional impact of the news on themselves and those around them.

The Challenger explosion

According to Brown and Kulik (1982), flashbulb memories are special – they are quite different from other memories. They suggest that there is a special mechanism in the brain which is activated by events which produce high levels of emotion and surprise, and which are seen as particularly significant. As a result, the entire scene is 'printed' in memory in a 'flash'. This is why flashbulb memories are so accurate and long lasting.

Other researchers have questioned this view. First, they argue that flashbulb memories are no different from ordinary memories which are long lasting and important to the person concerned. A study by Rubin and Kozin (1984) found that significant and distinctive personal events such as graduating from high school and a first romance were recalled in much the same way as flashbulb memories.

Second, researchers have questioned the accuracy of flashbulb memories. In 1986, the American space shuttle *Challenger* exploded shortly after lift-off, killing all the astronauts on board. One study tested participants' memories for the *Challenger* disaster a few days after it happened and again nine months later. There was evidence of forgetting during the nine-month interval and some participants gave different, and sometimes inaccurate, details on the two occasions. Despite this, 92% of the participants retained complete and accurate memories of the event over the nine-month period (McCloskey et al., 1988). Somewhat different results were obtained from a similar study which tested memory for the *Challenger* explosion at two weeks and again at eight months after the event. Accuracy fell from 77% to 55% over the eight months, suggesting that so-called flashbulb memories are prone to forgetting just like ordinary memories. Memory for the event was best when it produced a strong emotional reaction (Bohannon, 1988). This suggests that participants who tended to forget did not find the *Challenger* explosion emotionally and personally significant. If this is the case, then a flashbulb memory would not have been formed (Conway, 1995).

A study of the resignation of the British prime minister Margaret Thatcher in 1990 helps to distinguish flashbulb memories from ordinary memories (Conway et al., 1994). Participants from a number of countries were tested a few days after the news of her resignation, and again after eleven months. Eighty-six per cent of the British participants had flashbulb memories of the event 11 months later, compared to only 29% of non-British participants. For most of the British participants, the event produced a strong emotional response and it was seen as very important. Most of the non-British participants were not emotionally involved, not particularly interested and, as a result, did not form flashbulb memories. They forgot many aspects of the event – it was just an 'ordinary memory'.

Evaluation Researchers disagree about the existence of flashbulb memories. Some argue they are a distinctive type of memory characterised by the emotional response an event produces and the importance attached to the event (Conway, 1995). Others see nothing special about so-called flashbulb memories. They see them as subject to the normal processes of forgetting just like any other memories. There is some evidence to support both points of view.

Key term

Flashbulb memory *A long-lasting, and vivid memory of a person's circumstances and feelings when they heard the news of a major event which affected them emotionally and which they saw as important. The memory also includes specific details of the event.*

Activity 4 Flashbulb memories

Item A Death of Princess Diana

People often remember what they felt and where they were when they of heard the news of Diana's death in 1997.

Item B Turkish earthquake, 1999

People who survive earthquakes often have flashbulb memories of the event.

Item C Assassinations

Malcolm X

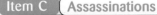

Martin Luther King (centre) on the balcony of the Memphis motel where he was shot the next day.

African Americans had more flashbulb memories than white Americans for the assassinations of Malcolm X in 1965 and Martin Luther King in 1968 (Brown & Kulik, 1982).

Questions

1 Suggest why the events pictured in Items A and B might produce flashbulb memories.

2 Why are African Americans more likely than white Americans to have flashbulb memories of the events in Item C?

3.2 Motivated forgetting

Sometimes we do not want to remember something. Forgetting information because we do not want to remember it is known as *motivated forgetting*. We may or may not be aware of this process.

Suppression

Deliberate and conscious motivated forgetting is known as *suppression*. Suppression has been demonstrated in laboratory experiments. For example, Weiner and Reed (1969) showed that participants are able to forget information they have just been given when instructed to do so. People can 'forget on demand'. This may work in real-life situations, too. As a motor-racing driver begins a race, he might deliberately try to forget the start of the last race when he stalled the car, or the race before that when he crashed at the start.

Repression

Repression is motivated forgetting without conscious awareness. It makes memories very difficult to retrieve. The idea of repression was introduced by Sigmund Freud in the nineteenth century. According to Freud, most forgetting is simply the discarding of information that is no longer needed (Freud & Breuer, 1895). However, certain memories are repressed – pushed out of consciousness and into the unconscious. These are traumatic memories – extremely distressing memories – which threaten an individual's wellbeing. Consider the following case.

Irene, a young 20-year-old woman, lived with her mother in an attic. Her mother had reached the final stages of tuberculosis. Irene watched her slowly dying for 60 days and nights. When her mother finally died, Irene was highly distraught. She tried repeatedly to revive the corpse. Soon after, Irene apparently had no memory of the events surrounding her mother's death. She would ask: 'When did she die? What did she die from? Was I not there to take care of her?'

Some time later, Irene began to have fits during which she would act out events from her life in great detail, including the period leading up to her mother's death and the death itself. She remembered none of this and still had no conscious memory that her mother had died. Clearly the event had not disappeared from memory – Irene's behaviour during her fits would not have been possible if she had no memory for her mother's death. The event remained in long-term memory but had been repressed (Hunter, 1957).

Repressed childhood memories

There is increasing evidence of repressed memories from cases of sexual abuse in childhood. One study examined hospital records of young girls who had been treated for sexual abuse (Williams, 1994). Seventeen years later, the women were tracked down. Thirty-eight per cent had no conscious memory of the events for which they were treated, though many reported later incidents of sexual abuse.

Repressed memories are difficult but not impossible to retrieve. Take the following case. In 1969, Eileen's eight-year-old friend Susan disappeared. Twenty years later Eileen suddenly remembered what had happened to her friend. Eileen's daughter reminded her of Susan. One day she was looking into her daughter's eyes and the long-repressed memory returned. Eileen had seen her own father sexually abuse Susan and then beat her to death with a rock. He threatened to kill Eileen if she told anyone. Twenty years after the event, her father was found guilty of murder and sentenced to life imprisonment (Zimbardo et al., 1995).

Evaluation of repression

It is difficult to evaluate the evidence on repressed memories for the following reasons.

- They are not easy to retrieve.
- Creating the kind of traumatic experiences described above would be extremely difficult in the laboratory.
- Even if this could be done, it would be unethical. The British Psychological Society's ethical guidelines for research state that participants should be protected from physical and psychological harm (BPS, 1998).
- Researchers have tried to create repressed memories in the laboratory by making participants feel anxious. But the mild anxiety that results is hardly the basis for repression. These experiments have provided little or no evidence for repressed memories (Holmes, 1990).

Most of the evidence for repressed memories comes from clinical studies in which psychiatrists ask their clients detailed and probing questions about past events. This approach has its own problems as the next section indicates.

False memory syndrome

To the person retrieving repressed memories, the events they recall are real. Often, however, there is no independent evidence to support or refute their stories. This has led to the idea of *false memory syndrome* – the possibility that so-called repressed memories are false, that they refer to events that never happened.

There is evidence that memories for traumatic events can be false. For example, Pynoos and Nader (1989) studied children's memories of a sniper attack in a school playground. One of the children recalled hearing shots and seeing someone lying on the ground. This seemed a plausible memory, until Pynoos and Nader discovered that the child had been on holiday at the time and so could not possibly have witnessed the event. Where did the memory come from?

The possibility that false information can be 'planted' in

people's memories was investigated by Loftus (1993). She asked the older brother of a 14-year-old boy to tell him that he had been lost in a shopping centre when he was five years old. The younger brother was convinced that the memory was true and, within two weeks, began to 'remember' details of this non-existent event, including the names of shops, details of the person who found him, and how he felt at the time. When he was told that the memory was false, the boy found this very difficult to believe and said he definitely remembered being lost and looking for his family.

False memories do exist. However, this does not necessarily mean that repressed memories are false. What it does mean is that when repressed memories are retrieved, they should be treated with caution. Wherever possible, independent evidence of their accuracy should be obtained. (For further discussion of false memory syndrome, see p 42).

3.3 Emotion and everyday forgetting

Clearly, most everyday events are very different from the traumatic experiences that lead to repressed memories or the emotionally-charged events that produce flashbulb memories. Does emotion affect the recall of everyday events?

Diary studies Marigold Linton (1975), a psychologist, kept a diary of events in her life over a six-year period. She rated the events in terms of their importance and her emotional response to them. She found little relationship between importance, emotional involvement and recall. However, she found she was more likely to forget unpleasant events and to remember pleasant ones.

A similar study was conducted by Willem Wagenaar (1968), a Dutch psychologist. He recorded 2400 events in his daily life over a six-year period. He found, unlike Linton, that he was more likely to remember events in which he was emotionally involved. Like Linton, he was more likely to forget unpleasant events. However, this applied only to recall over shorter intervals of time.

These two studies fail to show a clear-cut relationship between everyday forgetting and emotion. However, they are studies of particular individuals. Because of this, it is not possible to make generalisations from them.

Depression Studies of people with depression indicate a *response bias* in recall – a tendency to remember certain things and to forget others. Laboratory experiments indicate that depressed people are more likely to recall negative items (for example, negative adjectives) and to forget positive items (Zuroff et al., 1983). Similarly, when people with depression look back over their lives, they are more likely to forget happy events and to remember unhappy events. In this respect, their response bias colours their recall (Eysenck & Keane, 1995).

In terms of state-dependent retrieval, events are more likely to be recalled if a person's psychological state at encoding, matches their state at retrieval. This may explain why people with depression are more likely to forget happy events from their past life.

Key terms

Motivated forgetting *Forgetting information because of a desire not to remember it.*

Suppression *Deliberate and conscious motivated forgetting.*

Repression *Motivated forgetting without conscious awareness.*

False memory syndrome *A memory of an event that never happened.*

Response bias *A tendency to respond in a particular way.*

Summary

1. Emotion plays an important part in the formation of flashbulb memories. Usually, they are easily retrieved and remarkably accurate.
2. Some researchers argue that flashbulb memories are little different from many other significant and emotionally-charged memories.
3. Emotion also plays an important part in the formation of repressed memories. They are extremely difficult to retrieve.
4. It is difficult to distinguish repressed memories from false memories.
5. The relationship between emotion and the recall of everyday events is not clear-cut.

Activity 3 Retrieval cues - pt 2

Retrieval cues

animals fruit furniture	weapons cloth colours	cutlery tools fuels	professions sports clothing

Adapted from Tulving & Pearlstone, 1966

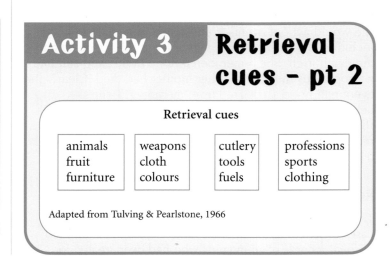

References

Baddeley, A.D. (1997). *Human memory: Theory and practice* (2nd ed.). Hove: Psychology Press.

Bohannon, J.N. (1988). Flashbulb memories for the Space Shuttle disaster: A tale of two theories. *Cognition, 29*, 179-196.

Bower, G.H. (1981). Mood and memory. *American Psychologist*, 32, 129-148.

BPS (British Psychological Society). (1998). *Code of conduct, ethical principles and guidelines.* Leicester: BPS.

Brown, R. & Kulik, J. (1977). Flashbulb memories. *Cognition, 5*, 73-99.

Brown, R. & Kulik, J. (1982). Flashbulb memory. In U. Neisser (Ed.), *Memory observed: Remembering in natural contexts.* San Francisco: W.H. Freeman.

Brown, R. & McNeill, D. (1966). The 'tip of the tongue' phenomenon. *Journal of Verbal Learning and Verbal Behavior, 5*, 325-337.

Cohen, G. (1996). *Memory in the real world* (2nd ed.). Hove: Psychology Press.

Conway, M.A. (1995). *Flashbulb memories.* Hove: Lawrence Erlbaum Associates.

Conway, M.A., Anderson, S.J., Larsen, S.F., Donnelly, C.M., McDaniel, M.A., McClelland, A.G.R. & Rawles, R.E. (1994). The formation of flashbulb memories. *Memory and Cognition, 22*, 326-343.

Eysenck, M. (1998). Memory. In M. Eysenck (Ed.), *Psychology: An integrated approach.* Harlow: Longman.

Eysenck, M.W. & Keane, M.T. (1995). *Cognitive psychology: A student's handbook* (3rd ed.). Hove: Lawrence Erlbaum Associates.

Freud S. & Breuer, J. (1895). *Studies on hysteria.* Penguin Freud Library Vol. 3 (published 1991). London: Penguin.

Godden, D. & Baddeley, A.D. (1975). Context-dependent memory in two natural environments: On land and under water. *British Journal of Psychology, 66*, 325-331.

Goodwin, D.W., Powell, B., Bremer, D., Hoine, H. & Stern, J. (1969). Alcohol and recall: State dependent effects in man. *Science, 163*, 1358.

Holmes, D.S. (1990). The evidence for repression: An examination of sixty years of research. In J. Singer (Ed.), *Repression and dissociation: Implications for personality theory, psychopathology, and health.* Chicago: University of Chicago Press.

Hunter, I.M.L. (1957). *Memory: Facts and fallacies.* Baltimore: Penguin.

Jenkins, J.G. & Dallenbach, K.M. (1924). Obliviscence during sleep and waking. *American Journal of Psychology, 35*, 605-612.

Keppel, G. & Underwood, B.J. (1962). Proactive inhibition in short-term retention of single items. *Journal of Verbal Learning and Verbal Behavior, 1*, 153-161.

Linton, M. (1975). Memory for real-world events. In D.A. Norman & D.E. Rumelhart (Eds.), *Explorations in cognition.* San Francisco: Freeman.

Loftus, E.F. (1980). *Memory.* Reading MA: Addison-Wesley.

Loftus, E.F. (1993). The reality of repressed memories. *American Psychologist, 48*, 518-537.

Loess, H. (1968). Short-term memory and item similarity. *Journal of Verbal Learning and Verbal Behavior, 7*, 87-92.

McCloskey, M., Wilbe, C.G. & Cohen, N.J. (1988). Is there a special flashbulb-memory mechanism? *Journal of Experimental Psychology: General, 117*, 171-181.

McGeoch, J.A. & McDonald, W.T. (1931). Meaningful relation and retroactive inhibition. *American Journal of Psychology, 43*, 579-588.

Peterson, L.R. & Peterson, M.J. (1959). Short-term retention of individual verbal items. *Journal of Experimental Psychology, 58*, 193-198.

Pynoos, R.S. & Nader, K. (1989). Children's memory and proximity to violence. *Journal of the American Academy of Child and Adolescent Psychiatry, 28*, 236-241.

Rubin, D.C. & Kozin, M. (1984). Vivid memories. *Cognition, 16*, 81-95.

Shallice, T. (1967). Paper presented at NATO symposium on short-term memory. Cambridge, England. Cited in A.D. Baddeley (1976). *The psychology of memory.* New York: Harper & Row.

Slamecka, N.J. (1966). Differentiation versus unlearning of verbal associations. *Journal of Experimental Psychology, 71*, 822-828.

Tulving, E. (1974). Cue-dependent forgetting. *American Scientist, 62*, 74-82.

Tulving, E. & Pearlstone, Z. (1966). Availability versus accessibility of information in memory for words. *Journal of Verbal Learning and Verbal Behavior, 5*, 381-391.

Ucros, C.G. (1989). Mood state-dependent memory. A meta-analysis. *Cognition and Emotion, 3*, 139-167.

Wagenaar, W.A. (1986). My memory: A study of autobiographical memory over six years. *Cognitive Psychology, 18*, 225-252.

Waugh, N.C. & Norman, D.A. (1965). Primary memory. *Psychological Review, 72*, 89-104.

Weiner, B. & Reed, H. (1969). Effects of the instructional sets to remember and to forget on short-term retention: Studies of rehearsal control and retrieval inhibition (repression). *Journal of Experimental Psychology, 79*, 226-232.

Williams, L.M. (1994). Recall of childhood trauma: A prospective study of women's memories of child sexual abuse. *Journal of Consulting and Clinical Psychology, 62*, 1167-1176.

Zimbardo, P.G., McDermott, M., Jansz, J. & Metaal, M. (1995). *Psychology: A European text.* London: Harper Collins.

Zuroff, D.C., Colussy, S.A. & Wielgus, M.S. (1983). Selective memory and depression: A cautionary note concerning response bias. *Cognitive Therapy and Research, 7*, 223-232.

3 Eyewitness testimony

Introduction

Eyewitness testimony is a legal term. It refers to an account given by people of an event they have witnessed. For example, they may be required to give a description at a trial of a robbery or a road accident they have seen.

Clearly, memory is very important for eyewitness testimony. An accurate memory for an event can lead to the conviction of a guilty person or the release of an innocent person. Alternatively, an inaccurate memory can lead to the conviction of an innocent person or a failure to convict a guilty person.

This chapter looks at the various factors which affect eyewitness testimony.

Chapter summary

- **Unit 1 outlines different perspectives on the study of memory.**
- **Unit 2 looks at eyewitness memory for faces and people.**
- **Unit 3 examines eyewitness memory for events.**
- **Unit 4 looks at ways of improving eyewitness memory.**

Unit 1 Perspectives on memory

KEY ISSUES

1. **How does the study of everyday memory differ from traditional laboratory research?**
2. **What is constructive memory?**

1.1 Introduction

Eyewitness testimony is an example of everyday memory – the use of memory in the world outside the laboratory. The study of everyday memory differs in important respects from the more traditional laboratory-based research described in the previous two chapters. They represent two different research traditions. Each has tended to use different methods and adopt different perspectives. Before looking at eyewitness testimony, it will be useful to look at these two traditions.

1.2 Two research traditions

Chapter 1 closed with a brief look at some of the methods used in memory research. This section returns to the question of methods.

Traditional laboratory research Over the last 100 years, memory research has been dominated by traditional laboratory experiments. These experiments have attempted to isolate some of the variables which are believed to affect memory. This means separating them from the vast range of factors which may influence memory. Once they have been isolated in the laboratory, these variables can be controlled and their effects measured. For example, a variable such as word length can be controlled – the length of words can be systematically varied by the experimenter. In this way, the effect of word length, for example on the capacity of short-term memory, can be measured.

However, as noted in previous chapters, laboratory experiments have been criticised for a lack of ecological validity. They have been seen as unrealistic and artificial. The tasks performed in experiments often bear little relationship to everyday life. For example, learning nonsense syllables, then counting backwards in threes, then attempting to recall these syllables, is hardly an everyday activity. Nor is it a particularly meaningful activity. As a result, critics have argued it is not possible to generalise from the findings of laboratory experiments – to apply the results of experiments to the wider world outside the laboratory (Neisser, 1978).

Naturalistic research Naturalistic research focuses on behaviour in terms of 'natural', normal, everyday situations. In this respect, its methods generally have higher ecological validity than traditional laboratory experiments. Experiments are still used, but the focus is on recreating or simulating events and experiences from outside the laboratory, and on the performance of tasks which are meaningful and relevant to the participants.

This can be seen from research on eyewitness testimony. Participants have been asked to recall events from films, pictures or reports of a robbery or a car crash. Researchers do their best to make such material realistic and to ensure it reflects the 'real thing' – real events in the real world.

1.3 Two perspectives

The traditional perspective The first two chapters have been mainly concerned with what can be called traditional questions on memory. Examples of such questions are: 'What is the capacity and duration of STM?' and 'Is STM a single or multipart memory system?' Researchers have tended to assume that the best way to answer these questions is the controlled laboratory experiment. According to their critics, both the questions and the methods are inappropriate. The questions and the experiments designed to answer them ignore many of the factors which affect memory in everyday life.

The everyday memory perspective From this point of view, what matters is how memory operates in everyday settings. This results in different methods and different questions. Consider the following quotations from Gillian Cohen, one of the leading researchers on everyday memory. Memory is 'influenced by a lifetime of past experiences, by history and culture, by current motives and emotions, by intelligence and personality traits, by future goals and plans'. In addition, 'remembering usually occurs in a social context and one of its main functions is to serve interpersonal communication. Memory is not just a private data bank: it is shared, exchanged, constructed, revised and elaborated in all our social interactions' (Cohen, 1996).

In many respects, this is a very different view of memory from that presented in the previous chapters. And, it results in different questions, for example: How is recall affected by the social context? As we shall see, eyewitness testimony occurs in social contexts such as police stations and courtrooms. And, the questions asked by police and lawyers can substantially affect the information 'remembered' by eyewitnesses.

1.4 Constructive memory

Previous chapters have presented a fairly simple picture of the basic memory process. It involves putting information in, storing it, and then getting that same information out again. Problems can arise – such as forgetting – but the overall process is not that complicated.

A rather different picture is presented by studies of everyday memory. They indicate that people's beliefs about the world influence how they see the world and how they remember events. And they indicate that memories are partly shaped by the social situations in which they are formed and retrieved. The following experiment illustrates these points. It was conducted in the USA in the 1940s.

All the participants were white Americans. They were divided into groups of seven. One participant from each group was shown the picture in Figure 1, described it to a second participant, who described it to a third, and so on. Over half the participants who received the final description reported that the black man, not the white man was holding the razor. Some even had him waving the razor in a threatening manner.

Figure 1 Argument on a subway train

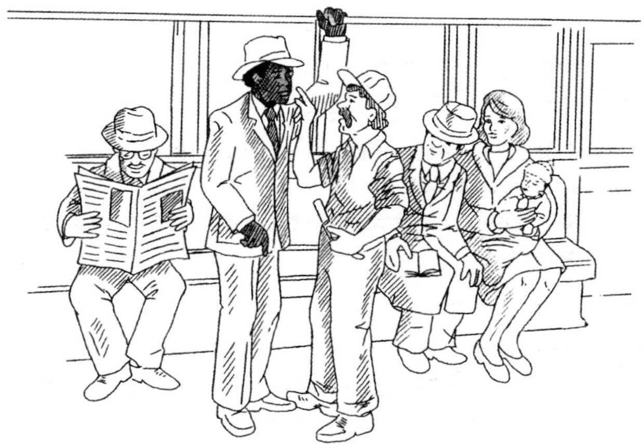

Adapted from Allport & Postman, 1947

Some of the questions raised by this experiment and probable answers to them are outlined below.

- Does it matter that the participants were white? Yes.
- Did they hold stereotypes that pictured blacks as hot-tempered and violent? Yes.
- Did these factors colour what they saw and what they heard? Yes.
- Does this mean that both the original memories and the memories as they were recalled were influenced by these factors? Yes.

The authors of this research concluded, 'When an actual perceptual fact is in conflict with expectations, expectation may prove a stronger determinant of perception and memory than the situation itself' (Allport & Postman, 1947). In other words, we see what we expect to see and this forms the basis of memory for an event.

People are constantly trying to make sense of the world around them, and in doing so, they strive to make everything meaningful. They apply existing knowledge, beliefs and expectations about the world – which they draw from long-term memory – in order to understand what's going on.

The terms *constructive memory* and *reconstructive memory* are used to describe this process of shaping, interpreting and making sense of information. These terms are used because they emphasise the view that people do not just passively absorb information and regurgitate it at a later date. Instead they actively shape information and build their own memories. As a result, they are constantly constructing and reconstructing their memories.

Reconstruction The view of memory outlined above was first put forward by Sir Frederick Bartlett (1932) in his book *Remembering*. He argued that people are constantly searching for meaning. As a result, they 'reconstruct' memories in ways which make sense to them. In a famous experiment, Bartlett asked British participants to read a story entitled *The war of the ghosts* – a folktale told by Native Americans from British Columbia in western Canada (see Activity 1). They were then asked to recall the story. Bartlett found that his participants reconstructed *The war of the ghosts* in terms of their experience, knowledge, expectations and beliefs, which at times were very different from those of the Native Americans. Their memory of the story was shaped by British *culture* – the learned, shared beliefs, attitudes and values of members of British society. For example, references to ghosts were played down by the participants since ghosts are not a major aspect of British culture. And the more often the participants recounted the story, the more 'British' it became.

Schemas Bartlett used the idea of *schemas* to explain the process of reconstructing memories. Schemas are mental representations of situations, events, people and objects. For instance, the stereotype of African Americans which participants used to interpret the picture of an argument on the subway train is an example of a schema. Stereotypes represent classes of people – nationalities, women, gays, ethnic minorities, the elderly and so on.

The importance of schemas to everyday life and to the construction of memory can be seen from the following example. If you hear the words, 'Mike ate in a restaurant', you would probably assume that Mike was eating food he had purchased in that restaurant. Why do you assume that? It doesn't say that at all. Your assumption is based on a 'restaurant schema' which contains information about what a restaurant is and what normally happens in one. By using a 'restaurant schema' you could probably give a fairly accurate description of Mike's behaviour from entering to leaving the restaurant. And if you recalled an actual meal you had eaten in a restaurant, you would probably add details from your 'restaurant schema' rather than recalling exactly what happened during your meal.

Schemas make sense of situations. They make life predictable, they provide people with guides for action. Think of the following events – a wedding, a birthday party, a funeral, bonfire night, Christmas Day. Each has a schema which gives meaning to the event, and which tells people how to behave and what to expect.

Bartlett's view of reconstructive memory focuses on the retrieval of memories. The process of recalling a memory involves a reconstruction of that memory in terms of schemas. The idea of constructive memory focuses more on the formation of the original memory. It suggests that this memory is constructed in terms of schemas (Eysenck, 1993).

Key terms

Constructive and reconstructive memory *The idea that memories are constructed and reconstructed in terms of existing knowledge, beliefs and expectations.*

Schemas *Mental representation of classes or categories of people, objects, events and situations.*

Culture *The learned, shared behaviour of members of a particular society. It includes shared beliefs, attitudes and values.*

Summary

1. Traditional laboratory research has been criticised as unrealistic and artificial.
2. Naturalistic research focuses on the use of memory in everyday situations. When experiments are used, they are often fairly realistic.
3. The idea of constructive and reconstructive memory assumes that people's beliefs and social contexts shape memories, both when they are encoded and retrieved.
4. Schemas are a major factor in the construction of memories.

Activity 1 Constructing memories

Item A The war of the ghosts

One night two young men from Egulac went down to the river to hunt seals, and while they were there it became foggy and calm. Then they heard war-cries, and they thought: 'Maybe this is a war-party'. They escaped to the shore, and hid behind a log. Now canoes came up, and they heard the noise of paddles, and saw one canoe coming up to them. There were five men in the canoe, and they said:

'What do you think? We wish to take you along. We are going up the river to make war on the people.'

One of the young men said, 'I have no arrows'.

'Arrows are in the canoe,' they said.

'I will not go along. I might be killed. My relatives do not know where I have gone. But you,' he said turning to the other, 'may go with them'.

So one of the young men went, but the other returned home.

And the warriors went on up the river to a town on the other side of Kalama. The people came down to the water, and they began to fight, and many were killed. But presently the young man heard one of the warriors say: 'Quick, let us go home: that Indian has been hit'. Now he thought: 'Oh, they are ghosts'. He did not feel sick, but they said he had been shot.

So the canoes went back to Egulac, and the young man went ashore to his house, and made a fire. And he told everybody and said: 'Behold I accompanied the ghosts, and we went to fight. Many of our fellows were killed, and many of those who attacked us were killed. They said I was hit, and I did not feel sick.'

He told it all, and then he became quiet. When the sun rose he fell down. Something black came out of his mouth. His face became contorted. The people jumped up and cried.
He was dead.

From Bartlett, 1932

Item B A bullfight

Costa Del Sol, Spain

Questions

1 a) Read *The war of the ghosts.*

b) After a 15 minute interval, rewrite the story staying as closely as possible to the original.

c) How does your version differ from the original?

d) Suggest reasons for the difference.

2 Imagine you have made your first visit to a bullfight.

a) How might your memory of the bullfight differ from the memory of a regular fan?

b) Why might the memories differ?

Unit 2 Eyewitness memory for faces and people

KEY ISSUES

1. **How reliable is eyewitness memory for faces and people?**
2. **What factors affect the selection of suspects from identity parades?**

2.1 The importance of eyewitness testimony

In 1976, a committee headed by Lord Devlin issued a report on eyewitness testimony and identity parades. All the identity parades in England and Wales in 1973 – over 2000 – were examined. Forty-five per cent resulted in a suspect being identified, and 82% of these suspects were later convicted. In over 300 cases, eyewitness identification was the only evidence of the suspect's guilt. Seventy-four per cent of these suspects were later convicted (Baddeley, 1997). This gives some indication of the importance given to eyewitness testimony, particularly by jurors. The following experiment illustrates this.

Participants acted as jurors in a case of armed robbery and murder. When they were presented with circumstantial evidence, such as the defendant being seen entering the building where the victim lived, only 18% thought he was guilty. Then eyewitness testimony was added to the evidence. An eyewitness claimed to have seen the defendant committing the crime. Now, 72% of the participants thought he was guilty. Even when the participants were told that the eyewitness had very bad eyesight and was not wearing his glasses at the time, 68% still thought the defendant was guilty (Loftus, 1974). This indicates the power of eyewitness testimony.

Mistaken identity

Eyewitnesses can be mistaken – from time to time, innocent people are fined or imprisoned purely on the basis of eyewitness testimony. It has been estimated that even a fairly low rate of mistaken identity might result in hundreds, or even thousands of people being wrongly convicted (Fruzetti et al., 1992).

The unreliability of eyewitness identification is indicated by the following study. A 13-second film of a mugging was shown on prime-time television. Following this, an identity parade of six suspects was shown, and viewers were asked to telephone and pick the mugger out of the parade. More than 2000 viewers responded, but only 14% chose the right person. As there were six suspects, it would be expected that 17% of viewers would choose correctly if they were choosing at random. In all probability, people who had *not* witnessed the crime would be more likely to choose the correct suspect than the actual eyewitnesses (Buckhout, 1980).

2.2 Face recognition

In an identification parade, eyewitnesses are asked to recognise people they have usually seen only once before. In other words, they are asked to recognise strangers. The television experiment described above suggests they are not very good at this.

Laboratory studies Face recognition studies conducted in laboratories typically involve showing participants a set of photographs to be remembered. They are then shown a second set, which includes some of the first set and asked to identify the faces from the first set. Face recognition from this type of experiment is usually better than face recognition from eyewitness experiments. These experiments usually simulate an incident, such as a robbery, then ask participants to identify the suspect in an identity parade.

In the experiments using photographs, participants are given exactly the same picture to recognise – usually a full-face head and shoulders. In the eyewitness experiments, participants see the person to be recognised in very different contexts (in the incident and in the line-up) and often from different angles (for example, a side view in the incident and a full face in the line-up). These differences make recognition more difficult. However, such experiments provide greater insights into the problems of eyewitness identification in real life since they reflect the 'real thing'. As a result, they probably have greater ecological validity.

Everyday face recognition In everyday life, faces are not often seen in isolation from other aspects of a person. We usually recognise people rather than faces – by their clothes, voices, build and context, as well as by their faces. Context is an important factor. In Gillian Cohen's words, 'It is hard to recognise your bank manager at the disco or your dentist in evening dress' (Cohen, 1996). It is even harder when you may only have seen a person for a few seconds and then try to recognise them in a different context. In terms of identity parades, this suggests it is difficult to recognise someone seen robbing a bank when they are placed in a line-up. The contexts are very different so one of the main cues which can aid memory is missing.

In everyday life, the less familiar people are – the less well we know them – the more likely we are to wrongly identify them. In one study, 22 people recorded the errors they made in recognising people during an eight-week period. There were 314 cases of mistaking an unfamiliar person for a person they knew, often because of similarities in clothing, build and hair (Young et al., 1985). In such cases, the cues which often aid memory gave the wrong impression and resulted in mistaken identity. Again, this indicates the kind of error that can occur in eyewitness identification. Usually the suspect is unfamiliar to the eyewitness.

Cross-race identification bias Research indicates that people find it easier to recognise and identify people from their own race then people from a different race (see Item C in Activity 2). This is known as *cross-race identification bias*. It is reflected in the phrase 'they all look the same to me' which is sometimes used by people to describe members of a different race than themselves. In terms of eyewitness testimony, this suggests that if an eyewitness and a suspect belong to a different racial group, then the identification must be treated with considerable caution.

2.3 Identity parades

In view of the points outlined so far, selecting the correct suspect from an identity parade is problematic. The composition of identity parades and the way they are conducted can magnify the problem.

Functional size The number of people in the line-up who are similar to the eyewitness's description of the suspect can affect the chances of a correct identification. The more people who match the eyewitness's description, the greater the *functional size* of the parade. Doob and Kirshenbaum (1973) report the unfortunate case of Ron Shatford. Following the robbery of a shop, an eyewitness described the robber as 'very neatly dressed and rather good-looking'. Shatford was arrested as a suspect. He was good-looking and was placed in an identity parade alongside eleven unattractive men. The witness immediately identified Shatford as the robber. In this case, the functional size of the parade was one, because the witness described the robber as being attractive, and only one attractive man was present. After Shatford had served 15 months of a prison sentence, another man confessed to the robbery. Shatford had been wrongly imprisoned because the identity parade had a small functional size.

Assuming the suspect is present It is also important for the witness to be told that the suspect might not actually be in the parade. Wells (1993) points out that if the police fail to do this, then it is natural for the witness to assume that the suspect is present. Why else would the police have gone to the trouble of setting up the identity parade? This leads to the witness feeling that they must make a positive identification. Based on the assumption that the suspect is present, eyewitnesses may compare the people in the parade and choose the person who is closest to their memory of the suspect.

Type of parade Lindsay et al. (1991) found that the problems of functional size and witnesses mistakenly choosing the person most like the suspect could be reduced by presenting the people in the parade one at a time. This reduces the opportunity for the witness to compare people and so reduces the likelihood of mistakenly identifying one of them as the suspect. Witnesses are also more likely to say that the suspect is not there than when a traditional identity parade is used.

Key terms

Cross-race identification bias *The likelihood that people will correctly recognise and identify members of their own race rather than members of other races.*

Functional size of an identity parade *The number of people in the parade who are similar to they eyewitness's description of the suspect.*

Summary

1. Eyewitness identification of a suspect can strongly influence the decisions of juries.
2. Eyewitness identification is often unreliable.
3. Face recognition is affected by a range of factors. These include context and familiarity with the person concerned.
4. A number of factors influence eyewitness identification from an identity parade. They include:
    - The functional size of the parade
    - Whether the eyewitness is informed that the suspect may not be present in the parade
    - Whether members of the parade are presented singly or together.

Activity 2 Identifying people

Item A That daft hat!

BRICK
That's him! He's the culprit!
I'd recognise that daft hat anywhere....

Item B Instructing witnesses

After witnessing a crime, participants were told either that the suspect was in the identity parade (biased instructions) or that he might or might not be present (unbiased instructions). Participants then viewed a parade in which the suspect was either present or absent.

	Percentage of false identifications	
	Unbiased instructions	Biased instructions
Suspect present	0	25
Suspect absent	33	78

Adapted from Malpass & Devine, 1981

Item C Cross-race identification bias

Eighty-six shopworkers in Texas were asked to identify three customers – one white, one African American and one Mexican American – who had purchased something from the shop earlier that day. One third of the shop-workers were white, one third African American, and one third Mexican American.

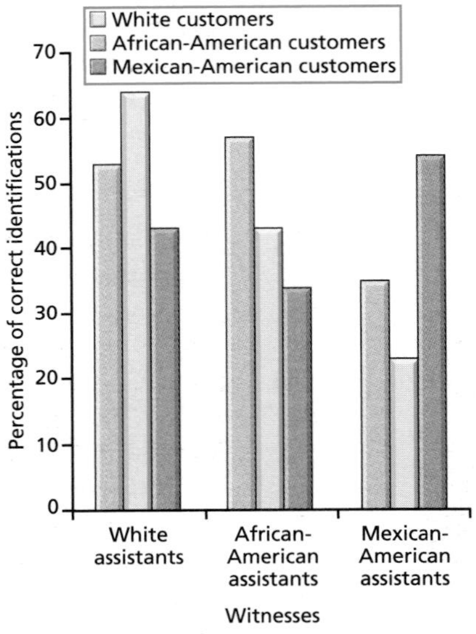

Adapted from Platz & Hosch, 1988

Questions

1 What problem with identity parades does Item A illustrate?

2 Summarise and explain the results of the experiment shown in Item B.

3 Explain the results shown in Item C in terms of cross-race identification bias.

Unit 3 Eyewitness memory for events

KEY ISSUES

1. **What factors affect the accuracy of eyewitness memory for events?**
2. **What are the limitations of experimental research in this area?**

Research has indicated that eyewitness memory for events can be changed by various factors. These include the addition of new information after the event has occurred and the way eyewitnesses are questioned about the event. This has been shown by a series of experiments conducted by Elizabeth Loftus and her colleagues.

3.1 The effects of leading questions

If a case reaches court, an eyewitness might be asked to give evidence and will be questioned by lawyers for the prosecution and the defence. Their memory of an event can be changed by this questioning. For example, they may be asked *leading questions* which direct them to give a particular interpretation of the event. This interpretation may be incorrect. The following experiment shows how this can happen.

Loftus and Palmer (1974) showed participants a film of a road accident involving a number of cars. After seeing the film, participants described what had happened, as if they were eyewitnesses giving evidence. Following this, they were asked a series of specific questions about the incident. Some of the participants were asked, 'About how fast were the cars going when they *smashed* into each other?' Others were asked, 'About how fast were the cars going when the *bumped* into each other?' Those who were asked the 'smashed' question thought the cars were going faster than those who were asked the 'bumped' question. The information presented in the question systematically affected the way in which the participants remembered the accident.

One week later, the same participants were asked if they had seen any broken glass at the scene of the accident. Thirty-two per cent of the participants who had previously been asked the 'smashed' question said that they had seen broken glass, compared with just 14% of the participants asked the 'bumped' question. In fact, there had been no broken glass in the accident. The addition of false detail to the memory of an event is called *confabulation*.

Figure 2 Two memories

Original memory

Memory after the 'smashed' question

Key terms

Leading question *A question which leads a person to give a particular answer.*

Confabulation *The addition of inaccurate information which changes a memory.*

3.2 What happens to original memory?

What happened to the participants' original memory of the car crash? There are a number of possibilities.

- The original memory has been lost and replaced by a new one.
- The original memory remains intact but participants give the answer they believe the researcher wants to hear.
- The original memory has been reconstructed.

The original memory has been lost

The road accident experiment indicated that memory can be changed by asking leading questions and supplying misleading information. Does this mean that the original memory has been lost and replaced with a false one? Loftus argues that this is the case. In one experiment she offered participants $25 if they recalled an event accurately (Loftus, 1979). She found that this incentive did not prevent their testimony from being affected by leading questions. Loftus claims that if their original memory had been intact, then the offer of money would prevent the influence of leading questions. She believes the original memory has been permanently changed.

Some support for this view is provided by the following experiment (Lindsay, 1990). Participants were shown a series of slides in which a man stole money and a calculator from an office. Following this, they were presented with an account of the crime that included misleading information. They were then questioned about the crime and told *not* to rely on this account or they would get the answers wrong. This instruction should have ensured that participants relied on their original memory rather than the inaccurate information presented after the event. However, they were affected by the misleading information – they added false details to the series of slides they had been shown. One interpretation of this is that the original memory has been lost and replaced by a new memory.

The original memory is intact

Other researchers disagree with Loftus. They argue that the original memory remains intact (McCloskey & Zaragoza, 1985). The apparent change in memory occurs because participants are responding to *demand characteristics*. These are characteristics of an experiment which direct and encourage participants to behave in a particular way. For example, the 'bumped' and 'smashed' questions in the Loftus experiment encouraged participants to give different answers. Participants may respond to demand characteristics by giving answers they feel are desired or expected by the experimenter. As a result, they are responding to the situation rather than changing their original memory.

Evidence from the Lindsay experiment described above, questions this view. Participants were explicitly told to ignore the misleading account which followed the slide presentation. This should have more effect on their recall than the less obvious and more subtle demand characteristics of the original Loftus experiment. Yet despite the instructions to ignore the misleading account, participants added some of the false information it contained. This suggests that demand characteristics alone cannot explain changes in the original memory.

The original memory is reconstructed

Unit 1 outlined the idea of constructive and reconstructive memory. From this point of view, memories are constructed and reconstructed in terms of existing knowledge, beliefs and expectations. People are constantly trying to make sense of available information. If new information is introduced which appears relevant to an existing memory, then it can form the basis for a reconstruction of that memory. Thus, additional information suggested by a leading question can be built into a reconstructed memory. In this way, incorrect details may be 'remembered' or confabulated.

This may have happened in the car crash experiment described earlier when participants were asked if they'd seen broken glass. A number of the participants built this new and inaccurate information into their reconstruction. It may be that many of the distortions of memory that occur are brought about by the reconstructive processes described in Unit 1.

3.3 Resisting misleading information

So far, this unit has given the impression that eyewitnesses are easily misled. It has presented evidence of errors and distortions of memory resulting from leading questions and false information. However, eyewitnesses are unlikely to be misled when false information is obviously and 'blatantly' incorrect. Also, they are less likely to be misled when false information refers to a central rather than a peripheral aspect of an event they have witnessed. False information is most likely to change a memory if it is plausible – if it seems probable and reasonable. The following experiment conducted by Elizabeth Loftus (1979) illustrates these points.

Participants were shown a series of slides which pictured a man stealing a large red wallet from a woman's bag. When questioned later, 98% of participants correctly identified the colour of the wallet. They were then read an account of the crime in which the colour of the stolen wallet was given as brown and the colours of other items, which were peripheral to the scene, were changed. The participants were given a further test. All but two maintained that the wallet was red. Many more were misled by the inaccurate description of the colour of unimportant items. It appears that memory for important items is not easily distorted by misleading information.

An experiment conducted by Loftus and Greene (1980) indicated that to be effective, misleading information must be plausible and not too obvious. Participants were more likely to be misled into 'remembering' a man's moustache, when he did not have one, if the misleading information was stated in passing ('Did the intruder, who was tall and had a moustache, say anything to the professor?') rather than being the main focus of a sentence ('Was the moustache worn by the intruder light or dark brown?').

3.4 False memory syndrome

One of the most controversial areas of eyewitness testimony is *false memory syndrome*. This was introduced in Chapter 2 – see pp31-32. If parts of memory for an event can be altered through the use of leading questions and inaccurate information, there is also the possibility that entirely false memories can be constructed. Can a completely new 'fictional memory', which has nothing to do with what a person actually witnessed, be constructed?

In the real world, it is extremely difficult to provide firm evidence to prove that false memories exist. However, experimental evidence indicates that completely false memories can be created, especially in young children. The following experiment illustrates this.

Children in a nursery school were told about a man called Sam Stone who was very clumsy and broke things. A month later, a man visited the school and spent some time in the classroom. Next day, the children were shown a ripped book and a grubby teddy bear. None of the children made connections between Sam Stone, the man who visited the school, and the damaged book and grubby toy. For the next ten weeks they were asked leading questions which suggested these connections – for example, 'I wonder if Sam Stone was wearing long pants or short pants when he ripped the book?' At the end of ten weeks, 72% of the children blamed Sam Stone for the damage and 45% said they actually saw him do it. One child 'saw' Sam Stone paint melted chocolate on the bear, another 'saw' him rip the book in a temper, and another 'saw' him soak the book in warm water until it fell apart (Leichtman & Ceci, 1995). These 'eyewitness accounts' were, of course, based on completely false memories.

This type of evidence raises the possibility of false accusations, particularly in cases of alleged child abuse. The child's memory may be affected by repeated and suggestive questioning. False memories – which seem completely real to the child – may be created (Ceci & Bruck, 1993).

3.5 Effects of expectation

Sometimes memories of an event reflect the observer's expectations rather than what actually happened. This is known as *confirmation bias*. It is illustrated by the following experiment. Students from two universities in the United States were shown a film of a violent football game between their two teams. They reported afterwards that their opponents had committed many more fouls than their own team. This confirmed each group's bias in favour of their own team. Their memories were influenced by seeing their own team as the 'good guys' and the opposition as the 'bad guys'. The opposition were also seen as an inferior team who needed to commit fouls in order to have any chance of winning (Hastorf & Cantrill, 1954). Similar confirmation bias is seen regularly in Britain when people discuss a football match – the number of fouls committed by the opposition is often exaggerated and those committed by their own team minimised.

3.6 Violence and weapon focus

Another factor influencing memory for events is the degree of violence contained in the event. Loftus and Burns (1982) showed participants two filmed versions of a crime. In one version, the robbers made a clean getaway without any violence. In the other version, a small boy was shot in the face as the robbers escaped. Loftus and Burns found that the inclusion of violence in the film impaired participants' memory for other details occurring up to two minutes before the shooting happened. If violent events lead to poorer memory, this has major implications for the use of eyewitness testimony in cases of violent crime.

A related factor influencing eyewitness memory is *weapon focus*. This refers to an eyewitness's concentration on a weapon to the exclusion of other details of a crime. In crimes where a weapon is involved, it is not unusual for witnesses to be able to describe the weapon much more clearly than the person holding it! Loftus et al. (1987) showed participants a series of slides of a customer in a restaurant. There were two versions. In one version the customer was holding a gun, in the other version the same customer held a chequebook. Participants who saw the gun version tended to focus on the gun. As a result, they were less likely to identify the customer in an identity parade than those who had seen the chequebook version.

Key terms

Confirmation bias *The idea that people tend to seek out evidence that confirms their own beliefs and expectations. This can result in a biased and distorted memory of an event.*

Weapon focus *The tendency of an eyewitness to focus on a weapon to the exclusion of other aspects of an event.*

3.7 Limitations of experimental evidence

The experiments conducted on eyewitness testimony are usually more realistic than the more traditional laboratory experiments described in the first two chapters. They attempt to recreate and simulate actual events, they aim to be true-to-life. But, despite these efforts, they are not 'real'. Participants know they are experiments and this knowledge will, to some extent, affect their behaviour. And, because of this, generalisations from laboratory experiments must be treated with caution. This can be seen from comparing the findings of experiments with real-life eyewitness testimony.

Summary

1. Eyewitness memory for an event can be distorted by leading questions and misleading information.
2. Some researchers argue that this means the original memory has been lost and replaced by a false one.
3. Others disagree. They argue that the original memory remains intact. The apparent change in memory is due to demand characteristics.
4. Memory involves a process of reconstruction. The addition of new information can form the basis for a reconstructed memory. This may result in confabulation.
5. Eyewitnesses are less likely to be misled if false information is obviously incorrect and refers to a central rather than peripheral aspect of the event.
6. There is evidence for the construction of completely false memories – memories of events that never happened.
7. The way in which an event is perceived and remembered is affected by the eyewitness's expectations.
8. Violent events can be more difficult to recall accurately, especially if a weapon is involved. Eyewitnesses tend to focus on the weapon to the exclusion of other aspects of the event.
9. Evidence from real-life eyewitness testimony appears to contradict some of the findings of laboratory experiments.

A number of experiments have indicated that high levels of stress impair eyewitness memory. This is suggested by the Loftus experiments on violent crime and the weapon focus. However, the following evidence from an actual crime contradicts this view. A robber stole guns and money from a gunshop. There was a shootout on the street which resulted in the death of the robber and serious injury to the owner. Eyewitnesses who reported most stress provided the most accurate accounts of this event. Despite suffering nightmares as a result of their experience, these witnesses produced remarkably accurate and detailed accounts.

The eyewitnesses were interviewed by researchers 4-5 months after the incident. The researchers asked misleading questions in an attempt to distort their memories of the event. These questions had no effect – none of the eyewitnesses were misled. Again, this finding appears to contradict the results of a number of laboratory studies (Yuille & Cutshall, 1986).

This study does not necessarily undermine the findings of laboratory experiments. What it does do is suggest that these findings be treated with caution. And, it indicates the need for naturalistic observations – observation of behaviour in 'natural', real-life settings (Stephenson, 1996).

Activity 3 Memory for events

Item A Crowd trouble

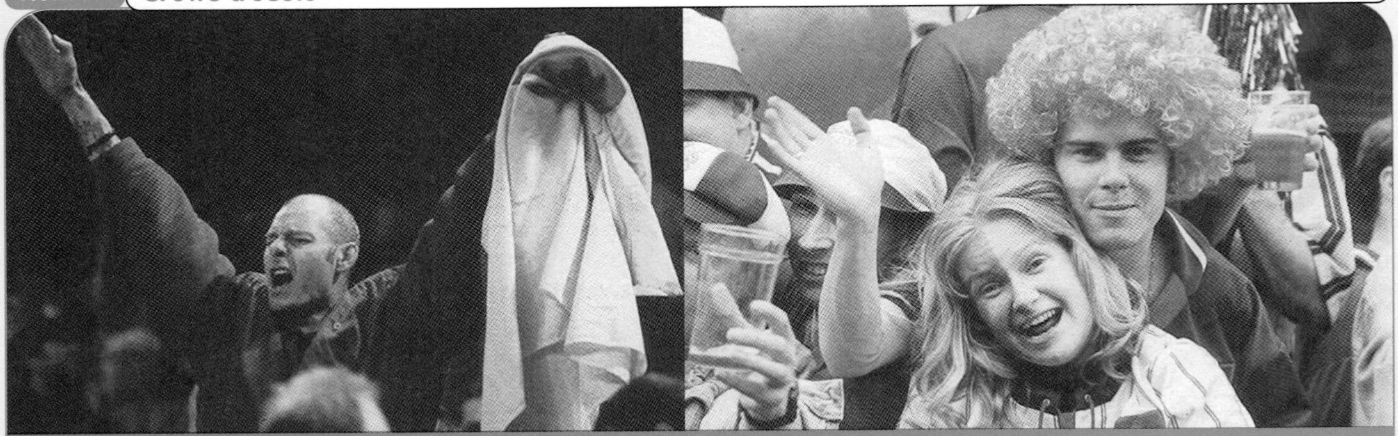

There has been trouble at a football match. Eyewitnesses have been asked to identify the troublemaker from a series of photographs. Most chose the man on the left.

Item B Sexual abuse

In 1988, Margaret Michaels, a 26-year-old nursery school teacher from New Jersey was sentenced to 47 years in prison for sexually abusing children in her care. Apart from the children, there were no other witnesses and no physical evidence of abuse. However, the testimonies of 19 child witnesses were remarkably consistent. For example, they all stated that Ms Michaels danced naked round the classroom and forced them to strip. The social workers who conducted the interviews often asked leading and suggestive questions. They told the children that Ms Michaels was a bad person, urged them to describe acts which they had previously said didn't happen, and offered them bribes for information. After 5 years, the appeals court overturned the verdict on the grounds that the children's testimony could not be trusted.

Adapted from Brehm et al., 1999

Item C Bank robbery

One hundred and ten eyewitnesses to bank robberies were interviewed. Some had been bystanders, others were bank workers who had been directly threatened by the robbers. The bankworkers recalled more than the bystanders. Even after 15 months, they still recalled a wide range of detail from the event, including not only the weapons of the bank robbers but their clothing and their behaviour.

Adapted from Christianson & Hubinette, 1993

Questions

1 Use the idea of confirmation bias to explain why most people chose the man on the left in Item A.

2 What light can studies of false memory syndrome throw on the case in Item B?

3 Why does the study in Item C suggest that experimental evidence should be treated with caution?

Unit 4 Improving eyewitness memory

KEY ISSUES

1. **Can hypnosis improve eyewitness memory?**
2. **Do police reconstructions improve eyewitness testimony?**
3. **Are there ways of questioning witnesses which increase the accuracy of their testimony?**

So far, this chapter has focused on the factors that contribute to the low reliability of eyewitness testimony. This unit looks at ways in which eyewitness testimony might be improved.

4.1 Hypnosis

Occasionally there are newspaper reports of an eyewitness being helped to remember the details of an event through the use of hypnosis. Hypnosis helps witnesses to relax, and, in theory, allows the hypnotist to reconstruct the known details of the event in the mind of the witness. The use of hypnosis has met with mixed results. In 1977, a bus driver, whose bus containing 26 children had been hijacked, was successfully hypnotised to recall all but one of the letters and numbers on the registration plate of the hijackers' van. The three suspects were tracked down.

However, an analysis of the results of the large number of studies on hypnosis and eyewitness testimony found that there was no evidence that hypnosis reliably aided recall (Orne et al., 1984). If anything, hypnosis results in more confabulation as the suggestible witness 'remembers' false details. Hypnosis makes people less cautious. This can lead to 'memories' of events that never happened.

Putnam (1979) showed how suggestible hypnotised witnesses could be. Participants were shown a videotape of an accident involving a car and a bicycle. After a delay, they answered a series of questions about the accident. Some of the participants were later hypnotised. They were told that under hypnosis it would be possible for them to see the entire accident again, only this time they would be able to slow it down and zoom in on details if they chose to. Putnam found that more errors were made by the participants who had been hypnotised, especially when leading questions were asked. Participants who were hypnotised were more open to suggestion than those who were not hypnotised.

Given these considerations, it is not surprising that British courts are very unlikely to accept testimony based on hypnosis.

4.2 Police reconstructions

Police reconstructions are used for crimes such as murder and robbery, and in cases of missing persons. In cases of robbery, reconstructions are filmed for television programmes such as *Crimewatch*. In murder cases, a person dressed in similar clothes to the victim retraces the victim's last known movements. This usually takes place a week later, in the same place and at the same time.

The aim of reconstructions is twofold. First, to obtain eyewitnesses who have not yet come forward. Second, to 'jog the memory' of eyewitnesses who have come forward – they are invited to attend the reconstruction. The hope is that they will remember further details of the victim's movements, and, in particular, any other persons who were in the vicinity. The person representing the victim is accompanied by police officers who question people along the route.

Reconstructions are based on the idea of cue-dependent recall. In the above example, the cues are similar clothes, time and place. As the previous chapter indicated, recall is more likely when the context at encoding matches the context at retrieval (see p 27).

Reconstructions sometime produce useful information. However, a word of warning is necessary. As this chapter has shown, testimony is often inaccurate when eyewitnesses are reporting on actual events. A reconstruction, which does not exactly mirror the real thing, may lead to further inaccuracies. In particular, it may lead to confabulation – the adding of false detail to the memory of an event.

4.3 Cognitive interviewing

The *cognitive interview* aims to help eyewitnesses recall events accurately. It is based on four general principles.

- It aims to reinstate the environmental and personal context of the crime in the mind of the witness. This includes sights, sounds, smells, feelings and emotions.
- It asks witnesses to report every detail, even if they think that the detail is trivial.
- It encourages witnesses to recount the details of the event in different orders.
- It asks witnesses to report the incident from a range of perspectives, including those of other bystanders, or even those of the criminals themselves (Geiselman et al., 1985).

A laboratory experiment compared the cognitive interview with a standard police interview and hypnosis. A standard police interview asks witnesses to recall the event and then answer detailed questions about the aspects of the event that the police think are important. Participants watched a short film of a violent crime. Two days later, they were divided into three groups and interviewed by a police officer. Participants interviewed using the standard police interview made an average of 29.4 correct statements. Participants interviewed using the cognitive interview made an average of 41.1 correct statements. Those interviewed using hypnosis produced an average of 38.0 correct statements (Geiselman et al., 1985).

Leading questions A further experiment investigated whether the cognitive interview could reduce the influence of leading questions. Participants watched a film of an incident in which an intruder carrying a blue backpack entered a classroom. They were asked the leading question, 'Was the guy with the green backpack nervous?' Later on, they were questioned about the event using either the cognitive interview or the standard police interview. Those questioned using the cognitive interview were less likely to be influenced by the leading question. They were more likely to correctly recall that the intruder was carrying a blue backpack (Geiselman et al., 1985).

The enhanced cognitive interview

A revised version of the cognitive interview – the *enhanced cognitive interview* – was developed by Fisher et al., (1987). It encouraged interviewers to use open-ended questions (eg, 'What did the suspect do next?') rather than fixed-choice questions which often result in very short answers (eg, 'Did the suspect walk or run?' Answer – 'He ran.'). Interviewers were also encouraged to follow the witness's train of thought. For example, if a witness remembered a detail 'out of sequence', they should be questioned about that detail there and then rather than waiting for its 'proper place' in the sequence of events to come round.

The enhanced cognitive interview was tested in a laboratory experiment. Participants were questioned about a violent crime. Those interviewed with the enhanced cognitive interview correctly recalled 45% more details than those interviewed with the basic cognitive interview. However, this improvement was accompanied by a 28% increase in the number of incorrect statements (Fisher et al., 1987).

Evidence from outside the laboratory indicates the benefits of the enhanced cognitive interview. Police in Miami were trained in this technique. It resulted in a 46% increase in the number of details reported by eyewitnesses. Where additional evidence was available to assess their statements, it appeared that 90% of the reported details were correct (Fisher et al., 1990).

These studies make an obvious but important point – the way eyewitnesses are questioned can make a significant difference to what they remember and report.

Key terms

Cognitive interview *An interviewing technique which aims to improve the detail and accuracy of eyewitness testimony.*

Enhanced cognitive interview *A revised version of the cognitive interview.*

Summary

1. The use of hypnosis to improve eyewitness memory has produced mixed results.
2. Police reconstructions may improve eyewitness testimony, but they may lead to confabulation.
3. Techniques such as the cognitive interview can improve the detail and accuracy of eyewitness testimony.

References

Allport, G.W. & Postman, L.J. (1947). *The psychology of rumour.* New York: Holt.

Baddeley, A.D. (1997). *Human memory: Theory and practice* (2nd ed.). Hove: Psychology Press.

Bartlett, F.C. (1932). *Remembering: A study in experimental and social psychology.* New York: Macmillan.

Brehm, S.S., Kassin, S.M. & Fein, S. (1999). *Social psychology* (4th ed.). Boston MA: Houghton Mifflin.

Buckhout, R. (1980). Nearly 2,000 witnesses can be wrong. *Bulletin of the Psychonomic Society, 16,* 307-310.

Ceci, S.J. & Bruck, M. (1993). Suggestibility of the child witness: A historical review and synthesis. *Psychological Bulletin, 113,* 403-439.

Christianson, S.A. & Hubinette, B. (1993). Hands up! A study of witnesses' emotional reactions and memories associated with bank robberies. *Applied Cognitive Psychology, 7,* 365-379.

Cohen, G. (1996). *Memory in the real world* (2nd ed.). Hove: Psychology Press.

Doob, A.N. & Kirshenbaum, H.M. (1973). Bias in police lineups – partial remembering. *Journal of Police Science and Administration, 1,* 287-293.

Eysenck, M.W. (1993). *Principles of cognitive psychology.* Hove: Erlbaum.

Fisher, R.P., Geiselman, R.E. & Amador, M. (1990). A field test of the cognitive interview: Enhancing the recollections of actual victims and witnesses of crime. *Journal of Applied Psychology, 74,* 722-727.

Fisher, R.P., Geiselman, R.E., Raymond, D.S., Jurkevich, L.M. & Warhaftig, M.L. (1987). Enhancing enhanced eyewitness memory: Refining the cognitive interview. *Journal of Police Science and Administration, 15,* 291-297.

Fruzetti, A.E., Toland, K., Teller, S.A. & Loftus, E.F. (1992). Memory and eyewitness testimony. In M. Gruneberg & P. Morris (Eds.), *Aspects of memory: The practical aspects.* London: Routledge.

Geiselman, R.E., Fisher, R.P., MacKinnon, D.P. & Holland, H.L. (1985). Eyewitness memory enhancement in police interview: Cognitive retrieval mnemonics versus hypnosis. *Journal of Applied Psychology, 70,* 401-412.

Hastorf, A.H. & Cantrill, H. (1954). They saw a game: A case study. *Journal of Abnormal and Social Psychology, 97,* 399-401.

Leichtman, M.D. & Ceci, S.J. (1995). The effects of stereotypes and suggestions on preschoolers' reports. *Developmental Psychology, 31,* 568-578.

Lindsay, D.S. (1990). Misleading suggestions can impair eyewitnesses' ability to remember event details. *Journal of Experimental Psychology: Learning, Memory and Cognition, 16,* 1077-1083.

Lindsay, R.C.L., Lea, J.A., Nosworthy, G.J., Fulford, J.A., Hector, J., Le Van, V. & Seabrook, C. (1991). Biased lineups: Sequential presentation reduces the problem. *Journal of Applied Psychology, 76*, 741-745.

Loftus, E.F. (1974). Reconstructing memory: The incredible eyewitness. *Psychology Today, 8*, 116-119.

Loftus, E.F. & Burns, T.E. (1982). Mental shock can produce retrograde amnesia. *Memory and Cognition, 10*, 318-323.

Loftus, E.F. & Greene, E. (1980). Warning: Even memory for faces may be contagious. *Law and Human Behaviour, 4*, 323-334.

Loftus, E.F., Loftus, G.R. & Messo, J. (1987). Some facts about 'weapon focus'. *Law and Human Behaviour, 11*, 55-62.

Loftus, E.F. & Palmer, J.C. (1974). Reconstruction of automobile destruction: An example of the interaction between language and memory. *Journal of Verbal Learning and Verbal Behavior, 13*, 585-589.

Malpass, R.S. & Devine, P.G. (1981). Eyewitness identification: Lineup instructions and the absence of the offender. *Journal of Applied Psychology, 66*, 482-489.

McCloskey, M. & Zaragoza, M.S. (1985). Misleading postevent information and memory for events: Arguments and evidence against memory impairment hypotheses. *Journal of Experimental Psychology: General, 114*, 1-16.

Neisser, U. (1978). Memory: What are the important questions? In M.M. Gruneberg, P.E. Morris & R.N. Sykes (Eds.), *Practical aspects of memory*. London: Academic Press.

Orne, M.T., Soskis, D.A., Dinges, D.F. & Orne, E.C. (1984). Hypnotically-induced testimony. In G.L. Wells & E.F. Loftus (eds.), *Eyewitness testimony: Psychological perspectives*. New York: Cambridge University Press.

Platz, S.J. & Hosch, H.M. (1988). Cross-racial/ethnic eyewitness identification: A field study. *Journal of Applied Social Psychology, 18*, 972-984.

Putnam, B. (1979). Hypnosis and distortions in eyewitness memory. *International Journal of Clinical and Experimental Hypnosis, 27*, 437-448.

Stephenson, G.M. (1996). Applied social psychology. In M. Hewstone, W. Stroebe & G.M. Stephenson (Eds.), *Introduction to social psychology* (2nd ed.). Oxford: Blackwell.

Wells, G.L. (1993). What do we know about eyewitness identification? *American Psychologist, 48*, 553-571.

Young, A.W., Hay, D.C. & Ellis, A.W. (1985). The faces that launched a thousand slips: Everyday difficulties and errors in recognising people. *British Journal of Psychology, 76*, 495-523.

Yuille, J.C. & Cutshall, J.L. (1986). A case study of eyewitness memory of a crime. *Journal of Applied Psychology, 71*, 291-301.

4 The development and variety of attachments

Introduction

Think of a mother duck swimming along with her ducklings following her in single file. It is as if there is some kind of tie between them.

Think of a mother sitting on a park bench on a warm spring day. Her two-year-old son toddles around on the grass. Every now and again he returns to his mother just to touch her knee or smile at her. He never wanders far. Again, it is as if there is a tie between them.

This invisible tie joins the young to their caregivers. Psychologists believe that it is important for the young of many species, both human and non-human, to form a close relationship with their caregivers – their survival may depend on it. For example, young animals who have a tendency to wander off may be unable to find food, they may injure themselves, they may be killed. Clearly, a strong tie to a caregiver is a valuable asset – it promotes survival.

For the relationship to be effective it needs to work both ways – the young must be tied to caregivers *and* caregivers need to be tied to the young. For example, if parents don't establish a close relationship with their children, they may neglect them – they may not feed them properly or they may not protect them.

In humans, the tie between infant and caregiver is known as attachment. This chapter looks at attachment.

Chapter summary

- **Unit 1 looks at the development of attachments.**
- **Unit 2 outlines the main types of attachment.**
- **Unit 3 looks at explanations for different types of attachment.**
- **Unit 4 examines the relationship between culture and attachment types.**
- **Unit 5 looks at the relationship between attachment types and later life.**
- **Unit 6 outlines and assesses various theories of attachment.**

Unit 1 The development of attachments

KEY ISSUES

1 What are the stages of development of attachments?

2 How is attachment related to other aspects of the infant's development?

1.1 Attachment

Attachment is a strong, long-lasting emotional tie or bond to a particular individual. Psychologists believe that it is both normal and healthy for infants to form an attachment to one or more of their caregivers, and that this attachment is important for later development.

One of the most influential child psychologists, John Bowlby, suggested that a single, primary attachment relationship is essential for the healthy psychological development of the child. In his view, this first and most important attachment is ideally with the mother or a 'mother figure'. He believed that, 'mother love in infancy and childhood is as important for mental health as are vitamins and proteins for physical health' (Bowlby, 1951).

Attachments in infancy usually have the following characteristics.

- They are selective – they are formed with specific individuals.
- They involve proximity seeking – efforts are made to be physically close or near to the attachment figure.
- They provide comfort and security.
- They lead to distress on separation from the attachment figure (Schaffer, 1996).

Key terms

Attachment *A strong, long-lasting emotional tie to a particular individual.*

Proximity seeking *Seeking to remain physically close to an attachment figure.*

This unit looks at the development of attachment between infants and caregivers. Most psychologists see it as a gradual process. Attachments are not created in an instant – they develop over a period of months.

1.2 Stages of attachment

Most researchers believe that attachment develops through a series of stages. Two of the most influential accounts of the development of attachment are by Rudolph Schaffer and Peggy Emerson (1964) and John Bowlby (1969). Both accounts suggest three main stages to the attachment process.

Table 1 Stages of attachment

Stage 1	Birth to around 6 weeks – asocial or pre-attachment stage
Stage 2	6 weeks to 7 months – indiscriminate attachments or attachment-in-the-making
Stage 3	From 7 months – specific attachments or clear-cut attachment

Stage 1 Birth to 6 weeks

Schaffer and Emerson called this the *asocial stage*. Asocial means non-social. According to Schaffer and Emerson, babies during this period do not act in a social manner. They respond to people in much the same way as they do to balloons, puppets and anything else that comes their way. Nor do they show any recognition of individual people. Everyone is much the same as everyone else, and everything else, at this stage.

Bowlby did not entirely agree. Whilst he accepted that infants at this stage make little or no distinction between different people, he did believe that they are equipped with a range of behaviours (including crying, babbling, smiling, clinging and reaching) that form the basis for *sociability* – for behaving in social ways towards people. These behaviours are designed to create and maintain proximity (physical closeness) with the primary caregiver – ordinarily the mother. For example, crying brings the mother to the infant, clinging keeps her close. Bowlby's version of this stage is usually called the *pre-attachment phase* (Schaffer, 1966).

Later research suggests that human infants are not as asocial as Schaffer and Emerson claim. Infants appear more settled when held by their caregiver, and smile more broadly when they hear her (or his) voice. There is evidence that one-week-old babies are able to recognise their mother's face (Bushnell et al., 1989), and that two-week-old babies who have been breast-fed can identify their mother's smell (Cernoch & Porter, 1985). Stern (1977) claims that infants are innately prepared – they have an inborn *predisposition* – to look into their caregiver's eyes, look away and look back again in a kind of rhythmic social dance.

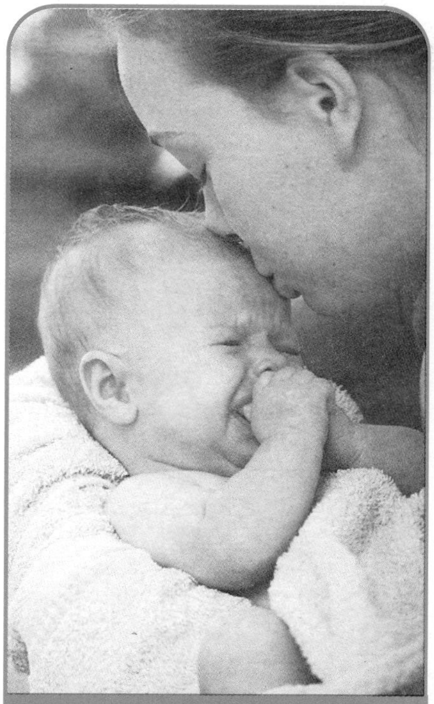

Mother and baby

Meltzoff and Moore (1977) showed that infants can imitate facial expressions, and Wolff (1969) sees crying as a sophisticated form of communication, with different types of cry meaning different things.

This evidence suggests that very young babies do respond in a special way to human beings, and that they are able to recognise specific individuals, in particular their main caregiver. However, researchers generally agree that actual attachment has not yet occurred.

Stage 2 From 6 weeks to 7 months

Schaffer and Emerson called this the *indiscriminate attachment* stage. Indiscriminate means making no distinctions, seeing no difference. According to Schaffer and Emerson, infants can now distinguish between people and things, and show a general sociability towards people. This claim is supported by Ahrens (1954) who suggested that young children begin to smile 'socially' at around 6 weeks. Infants can now distinguish between familiar and unfamiliar people, but pay little attention to differences between individuals. They show no fear of strangers, will cry for attention from anyone and can be comforted by anyone.

Again, Bowlby did not entirely agree. He accepted that infants at this stage are not yet fully attached to a specific person. However, he suggested that they are beginning to distinguish between people, and are already showing a preference for one particular person – usually the mother. The infant is more likely to smile at the mother and be comforted by her when distressed. Bowlby's version of this stage is usually called the *attachment-in-the-making phase*.

Sociability is more developed and more clearly expressed at this stage. Infants show a clear preference for, and pleasure from, the company of other human beings. This can be seen from infants responding to and seeking responses from others, and from the pleasure they derive from this. Some researchers see sociability as an inborn tendency or predisposition (Buss & Plomin, 1984). They see it as the basis for the development of attachment.

Schaffer later divided Stage 2 into two parts: a) 6 weeks to 3 months when the infant shows a preference for human company and develops a general sociability towards people, and b) 3 to 7 months when the infant begins to distinguish between people and recognises familiar and unfamiliar people (Schaffer, 1977).

Stage 3 From 7 months

At around 7 months, Schaffer and Emerson suggest the infant enters the *specific attachment stage*, and forms a strong emotional bond with a particular individual. This individual is usually the mother, but not necessarily. Specific attachment is indicated by the infant showing distress when they are separated from the attachment figure or preferred adult. This is known as *separation protest* and is taken as evidence for *separation anxiety*. From around 7 months infants protest if separated from their attachment figure, and show special joy when they are reunited with them. The attachment figure can comfort them more effectively than anyone else. Schaffer and Emerson used separation protest as an indicator that attachment has occurred, as a way of identifying the main attachment figure, and as a way of measuring the strength of the attachment.

Around the same time that infants develop specific attachments and separation anxiety, they are also likely to develop *stranger anxiety* – a fear of strangers. It is no longer possible to leave an infant with just anyone without them showing distress. Infants are likely to withdraw from strangers, turn to the caregiver for support when a stranger is near, or whimper, cry or bawl in the presence of strangers.

Bowlby also sees this third stage as the time when the infant forms a strong emotional bond with an attachment figure. Like Schaffer and Emerson, he sees separation anxiety and stranger anxiety appearing at this stage. Bowlby notes how infants often become visibly upset and make strenuous efforts to maintain proximity when separated from their attachment figure. For example, they crawl after her or cry for her attention. Bowlby's version of this stage is usually called the *clear-cut attachment phase*.

Who is the primary attachment figure? For Bowlby, the first and most important attachment figure is nearly always the mother. In most cases, she is also the main caregiver – the main provider of emotional and physical care for the infant.

Schaffer and Emerson's (1964) research questions this view. They studied 60 infants in Scotland, observing them once a month from birth to 12 months, then again at 18 months. 60% of the infants formed their *primary attachment*, their first and most important attachment, with their mother. However, 40% formed their primary attachment with someone other than their mother – with their father, older sister or brother, or grandparent. Schaffer and Emerson found that caregiving, as such, was not the main basis for attachment. Infants did not necessarily form their primary attachment with the person who provided them with physical care – the person who fed, washed and dressed them and changed their nappies. Nor does the amount of time spent with the infant appear to be the basis for the primary attachment. Instead, infants were likely to form a primary attachment with the most responsive and stimulating person around them.

One or more attachments? Bowlby believed that infants form their main attachment with their mother. He accepted that they form other attachments but saw these as secondary – less important and less strong – compared to the primary attachment relationship. Schaffer and Emerson's research questions this 'special relationship'. Although most infants have only one attachment at 7 months, most have *multiple attachments* by 18 months – 29% had more than one attachment at 7 months; 60% more than one at 10 months; 87% more than one at 18 months.

Many of the infants who formed multiple attachments did not appear to have a primary attachment. In other words, their attachments with various people were equally strong – there was no special relationship with one particular attachment figure.

Evaluation

This section has focused on the development of attachment and the *stages* this development goes through. Many researchers believe that most children in all societies go through these stages in much the same way. If this is so, then the idea of stages is a useful model for the first part of a child's development.

However, there are a number of problems with this view.

- First, the idea of stages suggests that early development is 'fixed' – that children automatically go through particular stages at particular ages. In fact, development is more fluid than this. Although most children do appear to follow this general path of development, the age at which they do so varies more than the model suggests.
- Second, there are important differences between infants in terms of their attachment behaviour. Some may become more securely attached than others. This point will be examined in the following unit.
- Third, before reaching any firm conclusions about stages of development, the idea needs to be examined in different societies with different patterns of

childrearing. The stage model was first developed from observations of children raised in Western societies. It may not apply to other societies. This point will be examined in Unit 4.

Key terms

Asocial *Non-social. Responding in similar ways to inanimate objects and people.*

Sociability *A preference for, and pleasure from, the company of other human beings. Behaviour which fosters the development of attachment and social relationships in general.*

Indiscriminate attachments *Having equal preference for various people.*

Specific attachment *Forming an attachment to a particular person who is preferred to others.*

Multiple attachments *Forming attachments with two or more people.*

Primary attachment *The first and most important attachment relationship.*

Separation protest *Protest at separation from an attachment figure.*

Separation anxiety *The anxiety felt when separated from an attachment figure.*

Stranger anxiety *The anxiety felt in the presence of a stranger.*

1.3 Attachment and development

Social development As noted earlier, psychologists see the formation of attachments as a normal and healthy part of the child's development. In particular, it is a major part of the child's *social development* – the development of social skills and the ability to form relationships with others. This aspect of the child's development is linked to other aspects of development such as cognitive and physical development.

Cognitive development This refers to the development of thinking, reasoning and problem-solving skills. An important aspect of cognitive development is the ability to form *schemas* (see p 36). A schema is an organised framework of information which represents things in the world. In order to form specific attachments, the infant will need to develop basic schemas of their attachment figures which will include what they look like, what they do, and the infant's relationship with them.

In order to form these schemas, infants need to develop the concept of *object permanence* – an awareness that when an object is no longer visible, it still exists (Piaget, 1957). Very young infants lose interest in an object which moves out of sight. If you shake a rattle in front of them and then hide it, they turn their attention elsewhere. Some researchers believe that object permanence develops around the age of 7 months, when specific attachments and separation anxiety appear. Object permanence means that the infant realises that when their attachment figure is out of sight, they are still somewhere but not with them. This awareness is important for the formation of attachments and for the development of separation anxiety. As Schaffer and Emerson (1964) noted, separation anxiety and separation protest appear around 7 months, the time at which object permanence develops.

Visual perception Research indicates that the newborn infant's vision is more fuzzy and blurred than an adult's (Atkinson & Braddick, 1981). As infants' visual perception develops, they are increasingly capable of making fine distinctions which are necessary to recognise things, particularly individual faces. This development is important – it allows the infant to distinguish between people and helps them to recognise their attachment figures.

As infants grow older, their interest in human faces increases as does their ability to distinguish between different faces and respond to different facial expressions. In one experiment infants were shown a picture of a human face and two other pictures in which the facial features were scrambled (see Item A, Activity 1). At one month, infants showed no preference between the three 'faces', at two months they showed a marked preference for the realistic face (Maurer & Berrera, 1981). By the age of four months, it appears that infants not only distinguish between different facial expressions, but respond appropriately to them, for example by smiling at a picture of a happy face (Serrano et al., 1995). These developments, indicated by evidence from experiments, mirror the development of sociability at Stage 2.

Physical development This also plays a role in attachment. Separation anxiety begins around the time the child starts to crawl. This is when proximity seeking – the attempt to stay close to the attachment figure – becomes especially important. In Bowlby's view, from around 7 months infants use their attachment figure as a *secure base*. The infant is

Key terms

Social development *The development of social skills and the ability to form relationships with others.*

Cognitive development *The development of thinking, reasoning and problem-solving skills.*

Object permanence *An awareness that when an object is no longer visible it still exists.*

Schema *An organised framework of information which represents things in the world.*

Secure base *The base provided by an attachment figure from which the infant can explore, and return to for security.*

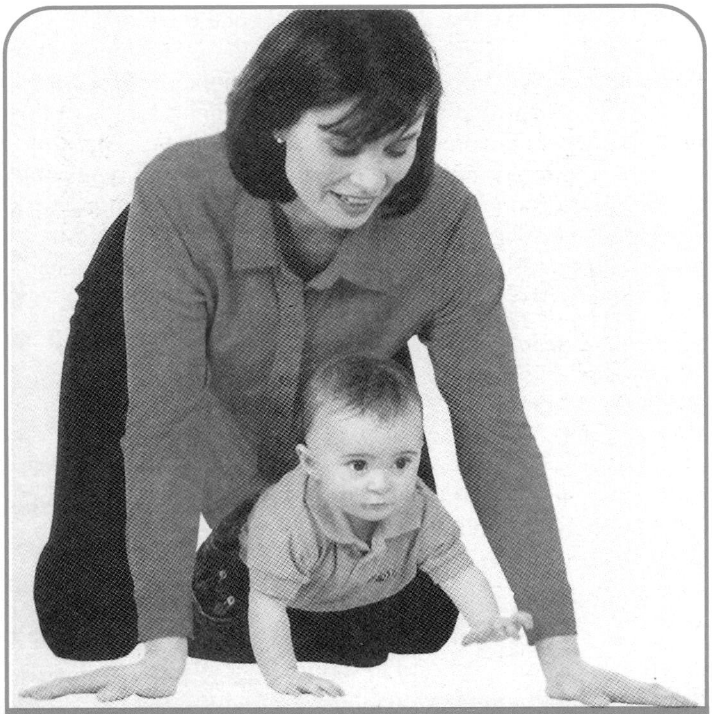

A secure base

starting to crawl and is becoming increasingly mobile. They use their attachment figure as a base from which to explore the world around them. Every so often they come back and 'touch base' before returning to their explorations. In this way, the attachment figure provides a safe and secure base from which infants investigate the world. This can be seen as the beginnings of independence.

Summary

1. Some researchers believe that attachment develops through a number of stages.
2. Three main stages have been identified.
   - The asocial or pre-attachment stage
   - Indiscriminate attachments or attachment-in-the-making
   - Specific attachments or clear-cut attachment.
3. Separation anxiety and stranger anxiety appear when infants have formed one or more specific attachments.
4. Bowlby believed that infants form a strong emotional bond with a primary attachment figure – usually the mother. All other attachments are secondary – less important and less strong.
5. Research evidence indicates that infants are likely to form primary attachments with the most responsive and stimulating person around them who may or may not be the mother and/or main caregiver.
6. Evidence suggests that most infants have formed multiple attachments by the age of 18 months.
7. The idea of stages for the development of attachment has been criticised. In particular, the process appears more fluid than fixed stages suggest.
8. The development of attachment is related to other aspects of the infant's development – for example, their cognitive and physical development.

Activity 1 Attachment

Item A Looking at 'faces'

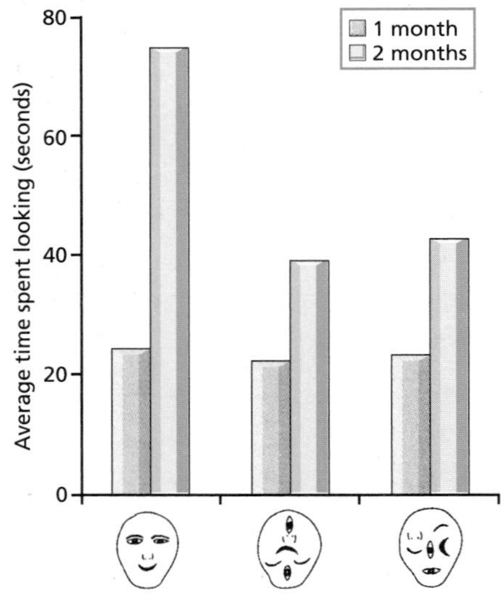

This bar graph shows the average length of time babies aged 1 month and 2 months spent looking at the 3 'faces'.

Adapted from Maurer & Barrera, 1981

Item B Object permanence

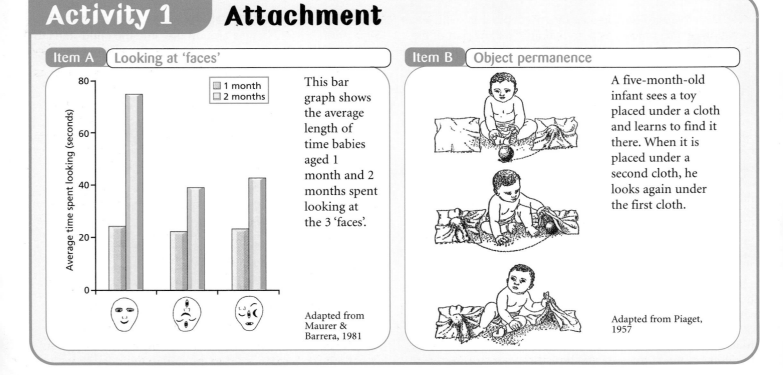

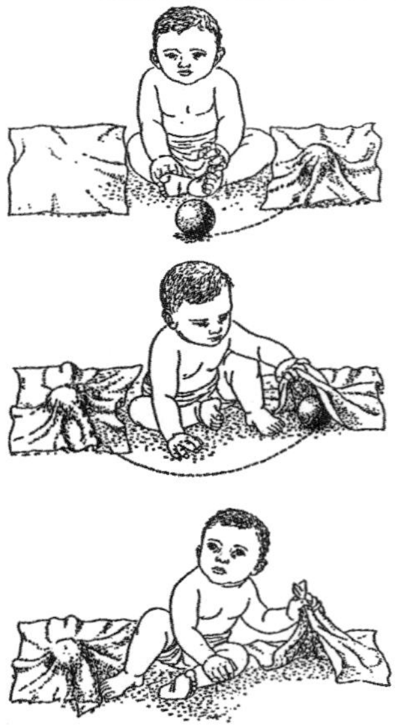

A five-month-old infant sees a toy placed under a cloth and learns to find it there. When it is placed under a second cloth, he looks again under the first cloth.

Adapted from Piaget, 1957

Item C Collective childrearing

Children and metapelets on a kibbutz

In Israel about 3% of the population live in about 270 kibbutzim. These settlements vary in size from 100 – 2,000 members. Most are based on agriculture with some light industry.

Many kibbutzim had a system of collective childrearing, though today it has all but disappeared. Married couples shared a single bedroom/living room. Children spent most of the day and all of the night away from their parents in children's houses. They were cared for by metapelets – caregivers and educators.

Mothers visited their infants in the communal nursery four or five times a day. These visits continued for six months until breastfeeding stopped. Then parents spent about two hours a day, after work, with their children. This was seen as 'fun time'. It was the only time when parents and brothers and sisters came together as a group. As they grew up, children moved through a series of children's houses, the same age group staying together until adulthood. The peer group was an important source of security and companionship. Children of the same age group tended to see each other as brothers and sisters.

A study by Fox (1977) found that one and two-year-old children were equally attached to their mother and the metapelet who cared for them. Both provided a secure base for exploration and both could reassure the infant when they felt insecure. In some cases, although the children protested equally when left by either their mother or their metapelet, they appeared to be more comforted by their mother at reunion and more likely to seek her out. This may have been due to the fact that some metapelets came and went as often as every four months. Attachment appeared stronger when the metapelet was a more permanent figure.

Adapted from Bettelheim, 1969; Fox, 1977

Questions

1 a) What does the bar chart in Item A show?
  b) How might the findings of this research relate to the development of attachment?

2 What does the experiment in Item B suggest about the infant's ability to form specific attachments?

3 What support does Item C provide for the idea of multiple attachments?

Unit 2 Types of attachment

KEY ISSUES

1 How is attachment measured and classified?

2 What are the main types of attachment?

Like all relationships, attachment relationships vary – they are not all the same. This unit is concerned with differences between types of attachments. It looks at ways of assessing and classifying attachment relationships. In particular, it compares secure and insecure attachments between infants and caregivers.

2.1 Classifying attachment types: the Strange Situation

Mary Ainsworth and her colleagues designed an experiment to describe and assess the attachment relationship between caregiver and infant (Ainsworth et al., 1978). It is known as the Strange Situation because it takes place in an environment which is strange to the participants – a room with toys scattered around which can be observed by the researchers. The experiment contains a number of episodes which provide various measures of the attachment relationship. The procedure is outlined in Table 2.

The experiment is designed to become increasingly stressful for the infant. For example, in later episodes the infant is left alone, and in the company of a stranger. There are three main sources of possible distress.

- A strange or unfamiliar environment
- Separation from the caregiver
- The presence of a stranger.

The experiment provides various measures of the attachment relationship. They include the following.

- The infant's reaction to separation from their caregiver.
- The infant's reaction to reunion with their caregiver.

Table 2 The Strange Situation

No. of episode	Persons	Time present	Activity
1	Caregiver, infant and and observer	30 secs	Observer shows caregiver and infant the experimental room then leaves.
2	Caregiver and infant	3 mins	Caregiver sits and watches, infant explores and plays with toys.
3	Stranger, caregiver and infant	3 mins	Stranger enters, silent at first, then talks to caregiver, then interacts with infant. Caregiver leaves room quietly.
4	Stranger and infant	3 mins	First separation from caregiver. Stranger interacts (talks and plays) with infant.
5	Caregiver and infant	3 mins	First reunion. Caregiver returns, stranger leaves. Caregiver greets, comforts and tries to settle infant. Caregiver leaves and says goodbye.
6	Infant alone	3 mins	Second separation. Infant left alone in room.
7	Stranger and infant	3 mins	Continuation of second separation. Stranger enters and interacts with infant.
8	Caregiver and infant	3 mins	Second reunion. Caregiver enters, greets infant and picks infant up. Stranger leaves quietly.

Adapted from Ainsworth et al., 1978

- The infant's reaction to the presence of a stranger.
- The infant's willingness to explore a strange environment with their caregiver, with a stranger, or alone.

The experiment lasts around 21 minutes and is normally used with infants from 12 to 18 months old. If the infant becomes very upset, or the caregiver wants to return, then episodes 4, 6 or 7 are cut short (ie, when the infant is left either alone, or with the stranger). The caregiver in most experiments is the mother.

2.2 Types of attachment

Ainsworth identified three types of attachments from observations of a large sample of infants in the Strange Situation (Ainsworth et al., 1978).

Securely attached When the caregiver is present, the infant explores the strange environment, plays happily with the toys, and uses the caregiver as a secure base. The infant shows moderate distress when separated from the caregiver, goes to her for comfort when she returns, and is easily soothed. The infant clearly prefers the caregiver to the stranger.

Insecurely attached – avoidant The infant pays little attention to the caregiver and shows little concern when she leaves. For her part, the caregiver tends to ignore the infant. The infant shows little stranger anxiety and, if distressed, is as likely to be comforted and calmed down by the stranger as by the caregiver. On reunion with the caregiver, the infant makes little effort to renew contact and sometimes actively avoids contact by looking or turning away. Shows no real preference for caregiver or stranger.

Insecurely attached – resistant The infant is very distressed when separated from the caregiver and is difficult to comfort on reunion. The infant rushes to her but may show anger, and struggle to be put down. The caregiver's behaviour is similarly inconsistent – sometimes rejecting and angry toward the infant, sometimes overly sensitive and responsive. The infant tends to ignore the stranger and resists the stranger's attempts to interact and provide comfort. Exploration of the environment is limited as the infant has difficulty moving away from the caregiver.

A fourth attachment type, insecure attachment – disorganised, was later suggested by Main and Solomon (1986)

Insecure attachment – disorganised The infant shows no set pattern of behaviour at separation or reunion, hence the term 'disorganised'. They may appear wary of the caregiver rather than the stranger, and may move towards the caregiver yet not look at her. This kind of behaviour is associated with abused infants or those whose mothers are severely depressed.

The above classification was based on studies of infants in the USA, where most of the experiments using the Strange Situation have been conducted. Most researchers use the first three classifications. A survey of 18 studies from the USA reveals the following percentages of infants in each of these three classifications – secure 65%; avoidant 21%; resistant 14% (van IJzendoorn & Kroonenberg, 1988).

Most researchers see a secure attachment as 'normal' and 'best'. This is based on the view that a secure attachment is the most beneficial for the child's later development. Some research indicates that children with secure attachments in infancy are more likely to be popular with their peers, friendly and cooperative; independent and confident with strangers; curious, ready to investigate and eager to learn; positive in their outlook and emotionally mature (Carlson & Stroufe, 1995). Other research suggests that insecurely attached children are more likely to be hostile and socially inadequate (Bretherton, 1985). The relationship between attachment types and later development is examined in Unit 5.

Key term

Strange Situation *An experimental procedure designed to measure and classify attachment relationships between infants and caregivers.*

2.3 Stability of attachment

Various questions arise concerning attachment. How stable is the attachment relationship over time? For example, if an infant has a secure attachment at 12 months, is it likely to remain secure at 18 months? How stable is the attachment relationship with different attachment figures at the same time period? For example, if an infant has a secure relationship with their mother at 12 months, is a secure relationship with their father at 12 months also likely?

Research indicates that if family circumstances do not change and are fairly stress-free, then the type of attachment relationship is likely to remain the same from 12 to 18 months. In other words, a stable family environment leads to a stable attachment, both with the same attachment figure over time, and with different attachment figures at the same time. For example, one study using the Strange Situation found that only 2 out of 50 infants (4%) changed their type of attachment between 12 and 18 months (Waters, 1978).

The type of attachment is more likely to be unstable, ie to change, when the infant's family situation is unstable. The change is usually from a secure to an insecure attachment. This tends to occur when there is conflict between the parents, unemployment, or illness in the family. Unstable attachments are also linked to poverty. All these situations place pressure on the family.

2.4 The Strange Situation – evaluation

The Strange Situation has been described as 'the most powerful and useful procedure' for the study of infant development (Lamb et al., 1985). It is widely used and has generated a massive amount of research. The following reasons have been given for this positive evaluation.

- The Strange Situation is easily replicated – its systematic procedures allow the experiment to be repeated under the same conditions. This means that all the infants are responding to a similar situation. As a result, differences in their behaviour are not due to differences in the experiment.
- The Strange Situation provides a variety of measures for assessing the attachment relationship. This is important as a single measure can give a false impression. For example, the attachment may appear secure if an infant is moderately distressed when *separated* from their caregiver. However, when *reunited* with their caregiver, the infant might do their best to escape from her arms. Only when this further measure – reunion – is used, does it become possible to classify the attachment as insecure-avoidant.
- Research evidence indicates the possibility that different types of attachment, as measured by the Strange Situation, may have different effects on the child's development. If this is so, then it gives a real point to studying and classifying attachment patterns from 12 to 18 months. The relationship between attachment types and later development is examined in Unit 5.

Not all evaluations of the Strange Situation have been so positive. There are three main criticisms of the procedure.

- First, it has been criticised for being unrealistic. This means the setting for the experiment is not true to life, it does not reflect everyday situations. As a result, it may not be possible to generalise the findings to real-life settings. If this is so, the Strange Situation lacks ecological validity. As its name suggests, the Strange Situation provides a strange and unfamiliar environment for the caregiver and infant. Does their attachment classification reflect the Strange Situation rather than their actual attachment? Research indicates that attachment appears much stronger in the Strange Situation than when caregiver and infant are observed at home (Bronfenbrenner, 1979). Clearly, in this setting, the situation is less strange.
- Second, the Strange Situation was created in the USA and the classification of attachment types was based on studies of American infants. Can the same procedures and the same classifications be applied to other societies with different cultures? If the answer is no, as some researchers argue, then the use of the Strange Situation is limited to the USA or, at best, to Western societies. Again, this questions the ecological validity of the Strange Situation. This point will be examined in Unit 4.
- Third, the ethics of the Strange Situation have been questioned. Is it acceptable to place infants and caregivers in situations which can produce mild and, in some cases, extreme anxiety? As noted earlier, certain episodes in the experiment are cut short if the infant appears extremely distressed. And, the caregiver can return if she feels the infant really needs her. Even so, should these situations be allowed to arise in the first place? Many researchers would argue that any distress has only short-term effects and that these are outweighed by the benefits of the research.

Summary

1. The Strange Situation is normally used with infants from age 12 to 18 months. It measures and classifies the attachment relationship between the infant and their main caregiver – usually the mother.

2. Four main types of attachment relationship have been identified. Most researchers use the first three. The four types are:
   - Secure
   - Insecure-avoidant
   - Insecure-resistant
   - Insecure-disorganised.

3. Attachment relationships are usually stable from 12 to 18 months if family circumstances remain the same during that time. They are more likely to change if family circumstances change.

4. The Strange Situation is easily replicated. It provides a variety of measures for assessing the attachment relationship.

5. The Strange Situation has been criticised
   - for lacking ecological validity – it may not be possible to generalise its findings to other settings;
   - as ethically unsound – it may result in stress for infants and caregivers.

Unit 3 Explaining attachment types

KEY ISSUES

1 What effect does the caregiver's behaviour have on the attachment relationship?

2 What effect does the infant's temperament have on the attachment relationship?

3 What effect do the circumstances of the family have on the attachment relationship?

3.1 Attachment and the caregiver

A number of researchers believe that the behaviour of the primary caregiver, usually the mother, shapes the attachment relationship. Different types of behaviour from the mother will therefore lead to different types of attachment. For example, the *sensitivity hypothesis* states that the more responsive mothers are to infants during their early months, the more secure the attachment will be at 12 months (Ainsworth & Bell, 1969).

Mary Ainsworth and her colleagues studied infants throughout their first 12 months (Ainsworth et al., 1978). They found the following relationships between attachment type and the mother's behaviour.

Secure attachment Mothers are sensitive to the infant's needs. They respond appropriately and readily to the infant's signals and communicate positively. They provide warmth and close physical contact, especially when the infant is distressed. They are accepting, cooperative and accessible to the child. This is likely to result in a secure attachment at 12 months.

Insecure-avoidant Mothers are not sensitive and responsive to the infant's signals. They tend to be impatient and neglect the infant.

Insecure-resistant The mother's behaviour is inconsistent. She sometimes responds positively and sensitively, at other times she ignores the infant's attempts to gain her attention.

Evaluation These suggested links between the mother's behaviour and the type of attachment are neat and tidy and appear to make sense. For example, the behaviour of the infant in an insecure-resistant attachment is inconsistent and this reflects their mother's inconsistent behaviour.

A survey of research from the USA provides support for the view that sensitive and responsive mothering leads to secure attachment (Lamb et al., 1985). However, the link between the mother's behaviour and other types of attachment is not as clear-cut as Ainsworth's research indicates. Research from outside the USA raises further questions. For example, research in Germany found no difference in sensitivity between mothers with securely attached children and mothers with insecure-avoidant children (Grossmann et al., 1985). This research will be examined in more detail in Unit 4.

The sensitivity hypothesis places the major responsibility for the type of attachment on the mother's shoulders. And, if different types of attachment have different effects on the child's development, then the mother can be praised or blamed. However, as the following section suggests, this may be uncalled for.

3.2 Attachment and infant temperament

There are two sides to a relationship. In terms of the attachment relationship, the two sides are caregiver and infant. The previous section looked at the mother's contribution to the attachment relationship. This section looks at the infant's contribution. It examines the argument that differences in infants' *temperament* can result in different types of attachment. This is known as the *temperament hypothesis* (Kagan, 1984). It states that infants rather than caregivers shape the attachment relationship.

Temperament refers to personality, to an individual's

characteristics. For example, infants can be even-tempered or irritable, responsive or withdrawn, active or inactive, soothed easily or with difficulty. A longitudinal study – a study of the same group over time – of 138 infants in New York by Thomas and Chess (1977) classified 40% of the infants as having 'easy' temperaments, 10% 'difficult' temperaments, 15% as 'slow to warm up' and 35% as 'mixed'. Since many aspects of temperament are evident during the first weeks of life and continue into adulthood, some researchers, including Thomas and Chess, assume they are largely inborn or innate.

What effect does infant temperament have on the attachment relationship? There is some evidence to support the temperament hypothesis. For example, one study found that newborn babies who became upset when their feeding was interrupted were more likely to be classified as insecurely attached at 12 months (Miyake et al., 1985). However, other studies have found no relationship between temperament and type of attachment (Vaughn et al., 1989).

Evaluation The evidence relating to the temperament hypothesis is inconclusive – no firm conclusion can be reached. Some researchers argue that the attachment relationship is probably shaped by a combination of the infant's temperament and the mother's behaviour (Belsky & Rovine, 1987).

One study indicated that the mother's responsiveness was influenced by her perception of the infant's temperament. Mothers who saw their children as 'difficult' became less responsive to them by 24 months (Spangler, 1990). Research such as this suggests that a combination of the sensitivity hypothesis and the temperament hypothesis explains attachment type.

Some researchers argue that many aspects of the infant's temperament are inborn. They imply that these characteristics are fixed at birth and largely unchangeable. However, temperament is also shaped by a child's experiences. For example, a child who cries easily but is effectively comforted by their mother may learn to cry less. Again, this suggests that what matters is a combination of infant temperament and caregiver response.

3.3 Attachment and family circumstances

As Section 2.3 indicated, changes in family circumstances can lead to changes in the type of attachment relationship. This suggests that factors other than the sensitivity of the main caregiver and the temperament of the child will affect attachment relationships.

In general, research indicates that attachment types in middle-class families are stable between 12 and 18 months. However, major changes in family life, such as the mother taking a job outside the home, can lead to a change in attachment. In one study of middle-class families, 47% of infants and mothers changed their type of attachment relationship from 12 to 19 months in response to a change in family circumstances (Thompson et al., 1982).

Such changes are more common in low-income families. For example, unemployment, illness and marital breakup are more common in families living in poverty (Haralambos & Holborn, 2000). A study of low-income families indicated that a third of mothers and infants changed their type of attachment – usually from secure to insecure – from 12 to 18 months (Vaughn et al., 1979).

Conclusion The evidence presented in this unit suggests that no one factor can explain attachment types. A multitude of factors can affect family life, which in turn can affect the attachment relationship.

Key terms

Sensitivity hypothesis *The idea that the more responsive and sensitive mothers are to infants during their early months, the more secure the attachment relationship will be at 12 months.*

Temperament *An individual's personality, their characteristics.*

Temperament hypothesis *The idea that differences in infants' temperament can result in different types of attachment.*

Summary

1. Research from the USA provides support for the sensitivity hypothesis in terms of secure attachment. However, the link between sensitivity and other types of attachment is not particularly strong.
2. Evidence relating to the temperament hypothesis is inconclusive – no firm conclusion can be reached.
3. Some researchers argue that a combination of the mother's sensitivity and the infant's temperament shape the attachment relationship.
4. Family circumstances and social class can affect attachment relationships.

Activity 2 Explaining attachment types

Item A Responsiveness training

100 low-income mothers in Holland, whose children were assessed as extremely irritable shortly after birth, were selected to take part in an experiment. Half the mothers were chosen at random to take part in three short training sessions to improve their sensitivity and responsiveness to their child. The other mothers received no training. At 12 months all the mothers and babies were observed at home and in the Strange Situation. Those who had participated in the training sessions were more likely to be responsive to their children who, in turn, were more likely to be securely attached to the mother.

Attachment and responsiveness training

	Attachment classification	
	Number secure	Number insecure
Training	31	19
No training	11	39

Adapted from van den Boom, 1994

Item B Irritable infants

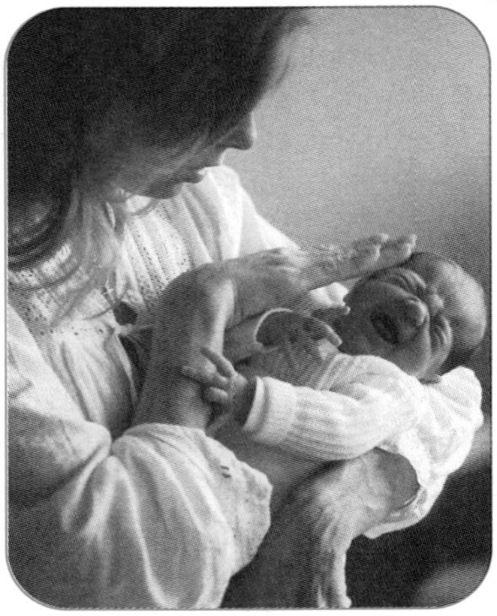

A study of mothers with highly irritable infants found no link between the infant's temperament and the type of attachment formed. However, when the researcher looked at the mother's social situation, a link was found. Irritable infants were likely to form secure attachments if their mother had social support from relatives and friends. Irritable infants whose mothers had little social support were more likely to form insecure attachments.

Adapted from Crockenberg (1981)

Questions

1 What support, if any, does Item A provide for
   a) the sensitivity hypothesis
   b) the temperament hypothesis?

2 No one factor alone can explain attachment types. What evidence does Item B provide for this statement?

Unit 4 Culture and attachment types

KEY ISSUES

1. **What is the relationship between culture and attachment?**
2. **Is the Strange Situation an appropriate method for studying attachment in different cultures?**

Culture is the learned shared behaviour of members of society. It includes norms – accepted and expected ways of behaving, and values – beliefs about what is good and worthwhile. To some extent, different cultures have different norms about childrearing and different values about the way children and parents ought to behave. What effect does culture have on attachment?

Table 3 is a survey of various studies which have used the Strange Situation to investigate attachment in different countries. It indicates that, in all countries, secure attachment is the most common type of attachment. However, there are significant differences between countries. For example, Germany has a relatively high proportion of insecure-avoidant attachments. What accounts for these differences?

Table 3 Culture and attachment

		Percentage of each attachment type		
Country	Number of studies	Secure	Insecure-avoidant	Insecure-resistant
Germany	3	56.6	35.3	8.1
Great Britain	1	75.0	22.2	2.8
Netherlands	4	67.3	26.3	6.4
Sweden	1	74.5	21.6	3.9
Israel	2	64.4	6.8	28.8
Japan	2	67.7	5.2	25.0
China	1	50.0	25.0	25.0
United States	18	64.8	21.1	14.1
Overall average		65.0	21.3	13.7

Adapted from van IJzendoorn & Kroonenberg, 1988

Japan Studies of Japanese infants and mothers using the Strange Situation show a relatively high proportion of insecure-resistant attachments. One of the main characteristics of this type of attachment is extreme distress on separation from the caregiver. Researchers have explained this in terms of traditional Japanese childrearing norms. Under normal circumstances, children are never left alone at 12 months, and their mothers rarely leave them in the care of anyone else. As a result, they are more likely to be distressed when left with a stranger or left alone in the Strange Situation.

Researchers argue that the relatively high proportion of attachments classified as insecure-resistant is due to traditional Japanese childrearing practices. Some of the procedures used in the Strange Situation place considerable stress on Japanese children (Takahashi, 1990).

Israel Studies of infants raised in Israeli kibbutzim show a similarly high proportion of insecure-resistant attachments. The traditional system of communal childrearing in kibbutzim is described in Activity 1 on page 53. One study using the Strange Situation classified over half the attachments as insecure-resistant and only 37% as secure (Sagi et al., 1985). This has been explained as follows. Infants have little contact with strangers. The kibbutz is a largely self-contained community, which, in some respects, is like a large extended family – children are seen as 'children of the kibbutz'. As a result, being left alone or with a stranger in the Strange Situation can be particularly distressing and lead to a high proportion of attachments being classified as insecure-resistant (Lamb et al., 1985).

Germany A study of German infants and mothers using the Strange Situation classified 49% of attachments as insecure-avoidant and only 33% as secure (Grossmann et al., 1985). Insecure-avoidant relationships are characterised by the infant paying little attention to the caregiver and showing little concern when she leaves. For her part, the caregiver tends to ignore the infant. The researchers observed the German mothers at home and found no evidence that they were insensitive, unresponsive or indifferent to their children. The parents valued independence – they wanted their children to be self-reliant, to 'stand on their own two feet' and not make demands on them. Some of the behaviour in the Strange Situation which is supposed to indicate secure attachment was seen by German parents as evidence of 'clinging' and 'spoilt' children. As a result of the norms and values which directed childrearing, a high proportion of attachments were classified as insecure-avoidant.

Conclusion

What does the research evidence from different cultures mean? How can it be interpreted? There are no simple answers to these questions.

Culture and the Strange Situation A number of researchers have questioned the use of the Strange Situation across cultures. It may not be suitable for measuring and classifying attachment in different cultures. The Strange Situation was developed in the USA; the classifications were based on observations of American infants and mothers. Certain types of behaviour were seen as indicating a secure attachment. And a secure attachment was seen as the best form of attachment, as the type most likely to benefit the child's development.

Does the Strange Situation, the way it is designed, and the way its findings are interpreted reflect, at least to some extent, the norms and values of one particular culture? Evidence from the studies outlined above suggests the answer may be yes. Behaviour seen as normal and beneficial in the USA may be seen differently in other societies. As noted earlier, infant behaviour seen as indicating a secure attachment in the USA was seen by many German parents as reflecting a 'spoilt' and 'clinging' child. And, in terms of an American designed experiment, a large proportion of German infants were labelled as insecure-avoidant. But was their attachment *really* insecure? Just because the German infants were encouraged to be independent doesn't necessarily mean their attachment was insecure. If this is the case, then the Strange Situation may be flawed – it was unable to measure the true nature of their attachment. The Strange Situation assumes that the behaviour of all children in all cultures means the same thing. This is a highly questionable assumption.

Culture and childrearing Whatever the strengths and weaknesses of the Strange Situation, the evidence indicates that childrearing practices vary from culture to culture and, as a result, so do attachment relationships. Thus in some cultures the attachment relationship emphasises independence (eg Germany), and in other cultures dependence (eg Japan).

But, to go on to say that one type of attachment is better than another is highly questionable. Who is to say that American infants are better prepared for later life than German or Japanese infants? Making this kind of judgement can be seen as *ethnocentrism* – seeing the world and judging other cultures in terms of the norms and values of your own culture. Bearing this in mind, Gavin Bremner (1994) concludes that 'at least when considering attachment across cultures we should probably abandon the notion that there is a single correct style of parenting or even that an insecure attachment is inevitably poorer than a secure attachment'.

Key term

Ethnocentrism *Seeing and evaluating other cultures in terms of the norms and values of your own culture.*

Summary

1. To some extent childrearing practices vary from culture to culture.
2. Most studies suggest that secure attachment is the most common form of attachment in all societies.
3. There are marked differences between societies in terms of the proportion of attachment types.
4. These differences may be due to differences in culture – in particular, differences in the norms and values associated with childrearing.
5. The Strange Situation may not produce valid (true) measures and classifications of attachment across cultures.
6. The view that one type of attachment is better than another may be unjustified. It may simply be a reflection of ethnocentrism.
7. Evidence from different cultures can be used to support the view that there is a universal tendency to form a secure attachment. It can also be used to argue that there is not such a tendency.

Unit 5 The effects of attachment types

KEY ISSUES

1 What effects might attachment relationships have on a child's early development?

2 What effects might they have on later life?

The significance of attachment Do attachment relationships matter? One answer is yes they do if they affect children's development. Bowlby (1973) argued that a secure attachment between an infant and mother figure is essential for later life. He believed that the primary attachment relationship provides a child with a model or template for all their future relationships. He called this model the *internal working model*. For example, if an infant experiences a warm and close relationship with a mother figure, this will form the basis for their future relationships. They will tend to expect and develop similar relationships in later life. Mary Ainsworth (1978) took a similar position arguing that different attachment types will have different effects on the child's later development and behaviour.

5.1 Effects on early development

Most of the research has looked at possible relationships between attachment types measured between 12 and 18 months and the child's development up to age 6 or 7 years. Researchers typically begin with the hypothesis that secure attachments are more beneficial for development than insecure attachments. In general, their findings appear to support this view. In terms of cognitive, social and emotional development, a secure attachment seems to be advantageous. Research indicates that children with secure attachments in infancy are more likely to be popular with their peers, friendly and cooperative; independent and confident with strangers; curious, ready to investigate and eager to learn; positive in their outlook and emotionally mature (Carlson & Sroufe, 1995). Children with insecure attachments in infancy tend to be hostile and to have problems with social relationships (Bretherton, 1985).

Evaluation

At first sight, the above evidence is very impressive. The links between early attachment and later development seem strong. And the links appear to make sense. For example, a securely attached child will develop an internal working model which leads to positive relationships. This explains why they are more likely to make friends and be popular with their peers. In addition, a securely attached child uses their main caregiver as a secure base from which to explore and investigate. This will encourage cognitive development and therefore explains their readiness to investigate and eagerness to learn in later years.

Family stability The relationship between early attachment and later development is not as neat and tidy as it appears. Some studies find little evidence to support a direct link. The strongest evidence for a link comes from families in which child care and family circumstances remain stable over the period when the child is assessed. It may well be this stability, rather than the attachment relationship itself, which accounts for the child's development. For example, the child might be receiving the same quality of parenting at 6 years as they did at 12 months. Maybe it is the quality of parenting at 6 years which affects the child's behaviour rather than their attachment relationship at 12 months. If this is the case, then the apparent link between attachment and development simply reflects a third factor – stability. In other words, it is the stability of child care and the circumstances of the family which shapes both the attachment relationship and the child's development (Lamb et al., 1985). This is an important point. It suggests that the child's development is not fixed by attachment relationships formed between 12 and 18 months. It suggests that these relationships are not as crucial and formative as many researchers believe.

Family instability Research indicates that the link between attachment and development is weakest when major changes occur in family life. As noted earlier, such changes include divorce, remarriage, unemployment and serious illness. They tend to produce instability and can result in changes to the type and quality of parenting. When a child's development is assessed at 6 or 7 years, the assessment may reflect these factors rather than attachment at 12 months.

Conclusion Early attachments may be significant, they may have important influences on development. But we can't be sure – the link is not definitely established. Parents may not be as crucial to the child's development as attachment theorists claim. Researchers such as Judith Harris (1999) argue that the peer group has a greater influence than parents on the child's social development. In other words, the child's friends may have more effect on their social development than their attachment relationship. As Schaffer (1996) concludes, the relationship between attachment and later development is 'nowhere near as straightforward as has been suggested by many attachment theorists'.

Key terms

Internal working model *A model or template for relationships. It develops from the primary attachment relationship and forms the basis for all future relationships.*

Peer group *A group made up of people with similar social characteristics, for example age and status.*

5.2 Effects on later life

Does the type of attachment in infancy affect behaviour in adulthood? Research by Hazen and Shaver (1987) indicated that romantic relationships in adult life often reflect the three attachment types identified by Ainsworth. People who had secure attachments as infants tended to form similar relationships in adult life. They were likely to have close and trusting relationships with their partner. Those who experienced insecure-avoidant attachments during infancy tended to feel uncomfortable about becoming close to their partner and fearful about making a commitment. And those who had insecure-resistant attachments as infants tended to feel they weren't receiving enough love from their partner and to worry that their partner might leave them. Research also indicates a similar link between the type of friendships people develop as adults and their attachment type in infancy (Bartholomew & Horowitz, 1991).

Evaluation

Although there is evidence to support a link between types of infant attachment and relationships in adult life, there are problems with the research.

Identifying attachment types The identification of the type of attachment in infancy is based on participants' descriptions of their relationships with their parents. There are three main problems with this approach.

- First, it relies on participants' memories which may be unreliable.
- Second, participants may try to present themselves in the best possible light to researchers. They may claim to have had secure attachments when, in fact, their attachments were less desirable.
- Third, participants' present romantic relationship may colour their views of their early attachments. For example, in one study, 80% of the participants in secure, long-term romantic relationships rated their infant attachments as secure. However, when their interviews were analysed, only 50% were judged to have had secure attachments (Bartholomew, 1993).

The intervening years A lot of things happen between infancy and adult life. These include a variety of relationships, some romantic, some not, all of which will have some effect on present relationships.

Some researchers argue that the suggested link between attachment types in infancy and adult relationships tends to ignore experiences during the intervening years (Levitt, 1991). While early attachment may have some influence on adult life, it is far from being the only influence.

Summary

1. Many researchers start from the assumption that secure attachments are more beneficial for development than insecure attachments. There is considerable evidence to support this view.
2. However, both the type of attachment and the child's development may be shaped by the stability of parenting and family circumstances. This suggests that attachment relationships may not be as formative and significant for development as many researchers believe.
3. Research indicates that relationships in adult life reflect attachment types in infancy. However, the evidence is not conclusive.

Unit 6 Theories of attachment

KEY ISSUES

1 What are the main theories of attachment?

2 What contribution has animal research made to understanding attachment in humans?

6.1 Early theories of attachment

Up until the 1950s, there was broad agreement in psychology that the human infant forms an attachment to the mother because she provides the baby with milk and comfort.

Psychoanalysis

Sigmund Freud (1856-1939), the founder of psychoanalysis, believed that both infants and adults possess a *libido*, an inborn drive or appetite for physical pleasure. This libido provides our main motivation or driving force from the moment of birth. Many of our physical pleasures are supplied by other people, and Freud believed we form emotional attachments to those people who gratify our libidinal desires.

In new-born infants, the libido expresses itself primarily as a desire to be fed and kept warm and secure, and the child forms an attachment to the person who satisfies these desires. In most cases, this person is the mother. Freud claimed 'by her care of the child's body' the mother establishes a relationship to the child which is 'unique, without parallel, established unalterably for a whole lifetime as the first and strongest love-object and as the prototype of all later love relations' (Freud 1940, cited in Young-Breuhl, 1990).

In psychoanalytic theory then, the child forms an attachment to the mother because she satisfies the child's need for feeding and comfort. Forming a secure attachment to a caring mother is crucial to the future wellbeing of the child, as the success of later relationships is determined by the security of this first attachment. Infants who fail to form a secure attachment to the mother are unlikely to form successful relations with anyone else in childhood or adulthood.

Psychoanalytic theory also provides an explanation for the mother's attachment to the child. It states that physical contact with the child, especially breastfeeding, provides satisfaction for the mother's own libidinal desires for physical stimulation.

Evaluation Psychoanalytic theory has always been open to the criticism that it uses abstract ideas (like libido) that are not open to direct observation or measurement, and are therefore difficult to study scientifically. However, while some condemn psychoanalysis as unscientific (eg Eysenck, 1985), others praise it as rich and insightful (eg Mitchell, 1975).

Learning theory

The main alternative to psychoanalysis in explaining the social development of the child is *learning theory*. There are two main strands to learning theory: the first, *behaviourism*, was launched in the USA by John Watson in 1913, and was enormously influential in psychology up until the 1960s; the second, *social learning theory*, grew out of behaviourism in the 1940s and largely replaced it in influence from the 1960s. It is still very significant in child psychology today.

Behaviourism explained all animal and human behaviour in terms of learning by *conditioning*. One important feature of conditioning is that rewards have a major effect on learning. Behaviours or responses that are rewarded are more likely to be learned than those that are ignored or punished. The behaviourists call rewards *positive reinforcers*.

B.F. Skinner (1904-1990), one of the most important behaviourists, showed that a rat could be conditioned to press a lever by rewarding (or *reinforcing*) it for approaching, touching and pressing the lever. The rat was rewarded with food pellets automatically released from a food dispenser when the lever was pressed. Every time a food pellet was released, the food dispenser clicked. Interestingly, Skinner found that a rat would continue to press the lever even when the food dispenser was empty, provided it could hear the food dispenser click. Skinner explained that the rat had learned an association between the food pellets and the clicking of the food dispenser, until in the end the click became a kind of reward in itself. In Skinner's terminology, the food pellets were the *primary reinforcer*, while the clicking of the food dispenser had become a *secondary reinforcer*.

Social learning theory In the 1950s, social learning theorists like Dollard and Miller (1950) tried to link behaviourist ideas with those of psychoanalysis. They suggested that the human infant, when hungry, feels uncomfortable, and enters a *drive state* – that is, the baby is motivated to find some way to alleviate or lessen the discomfort of being hungry. Of course, in early infancy the baby can do little more than howl, and it is up to other people, usually the mother, to feed it. Being fed satisfies the infant's hunger and makes it feel comfortable again. In social learning theory terminology, *drive reduction* (that is, alleviating the infant's hunger and releasing it from the drive state of being hungry) is rewarding, and the child learns that food is a reward or primary reinforcer. The person who supplies the food, the mother, is associated with the food and becomes a secondary reinforcer (just as the click of the food dispenser became a secondary reinforcer to Skinner's rat). After a while, the mere presence of the mother is a source of comfort and security to the child, and the child develops an attachment to her. Social learning theory suggests that hunger is a *primary drive* – an innate or inborn drive state that emerges naturally when the infant needs to be fed. Attachment is a *secondary drive* that the child learns through the mother being so strongly associated with feeding.

Social learning theory also provides an explanation for the mother's attachment to the child. It suggests that the infant's behaviour like smiling and cooing (or at the very least stopping crying!) provides reinforcement to the mother to repeat her feeding behaviour.

Later versions of social learning theory placed less emphasis on reinforcement and drives. Albert Bandura (1965), for example, argued that learning can occur without any reward or positive reinforcement. People can learn simply by observing the behaviour of others. This is known as *imitation* or *modelling*. People simply watch, listen to and learn from others, and model their own behaviour accordingly.

Caregivers can provide models for infants to copy. If they are loving, attentive and responsive, then infants may imitate this behaviour. This can contribute to the formation of attachments to their caregivers (Hay & Vespo, 1988).

Evaluation of early theories

Behaviourism has been widely criticised for being *reductionist*. This means it 'reduces' the complexities of human behaviour to over-simple ideas such as learned responses and reinforcement. It then uses these ideas as building blocks to explain complex human behaviours such as attachment. Much of the time, behaviourism seemed to be trying to explain human psychology in terms of the behaviour of rats pressing levers.

Social learning theory goes beyond behaviourism, recognising that human behaviour is complex, as is the social environment in which infants are raised. As a result, behaviour cannot be reduced to a few basic processes. For example, social learning theory recognises there is more than one way of learning with its addition of the idea of imitation or modelling.

Psychoanalysis and learning theory have both been referred to by John Bowlby as 'cupboard theories' of love and attachment. Both see infants as forming an attachment with the person who feeds them (much as a cat loves you when you go to the cupboard to get its food). However, research into attachments does not bear out the claim that infants necessarily form attachments with those who feed them. Schaffer and Emerson (1964) conducted a study of 60 infants in Glasgow, observing them every four weeks from birth until 12 months and then again at 18 months (see p 50). For many of the children, their primary attachment figure – the individual they were most strongly attached to – was the person who usually fed, bathed and changed them. However, for a large minority (40%), their primary attachment figure was not responsible for any of these caregiving activities. In general, infants formed primary attachments with people who were responsive to their behaviour and provided them with stimulation, for example, by talking, singing, laughing, touching and playing. Infants tend to attach to the most stimulating adult, not necessarily the most nurturing one. Feeding, as such, did not appear to be a major factor in the formation of attachments. These findings provide some support for later social learning theories which suggest that responsive behaviour by caregivers may be imitated by infants and this contributes to the formation of attachments.

Key terms

Libido *An important drive in motivating people to seek physical, sensual and sexual pleasure.*

Drive *An appetite or desire that motivates people. Examples include hunger, thirst and sexual desire.*

Conditioning *A form of learning in which a person or animal is trained to give a response to a stimulus.*

Positive reinforcer *A reward. Rewarding behaviour leads to that behaviour being learned and repeated.*

Association *A connection or link made between two things that are often presented together, for example, milk and mother.*

Primary reinforcer *A positive reinforcer that is rewarding in itself, for example, food.*

Secondary reinforcer *A neutral stimulus that is associated with a primary reinforcer often enough that it becomes a reward itself.*

Drive state *A state of motivation arising from being in a state of need. For example, hunger is a drive state arising from lack of food.*

Drive reduction *The reduction of a drive state. For example, food reduces the drive state of hunger.*

Primary drive *An innate drive arising from a biological need such as hunger or thirst.*

Secondary drive *An acquired or learned drive. For example, a desire for mother's company because her presence has become associated with the satisfaction of the primary drive for food.*

Imitation or modelling *Leaning by observing and copying the behaviour of others. Can occur without positive reinforcement.*

Reductionist *An approach which attempts to explain something in terms of its basic components.*

6.2 Evidence from animal research

Psychoanalytic theory and some social learning theories argue that infants become attached to their caregivers because the caregivers provide them with food. They see the desire for food as a primary drive and attachment as a secondary drive. Attachment is therefore seen as a by-product of feeding. This view was challenged by evidence from animal research.

Ethology and imprinting

Ethology is the study of animals in their natural environment. It assumes that animal behaviour is in part innate or genetically based. Innate behaviours are seen to have evolved because they are adaptive – they increase the likelihood that the individual will survive and reproduce.

Although ethology is primarily concerned with animal behaviour, ideas from ethology have provided insights into human behaviour. In particular, they influenced John Bowlby's theory of attachment which is examined in Section 6.3.

One of the most famous experiments in ethology was conducted by Konrad Lorenz (1935). He divided a large clutch of greylag goose eggs into two groups. One group was hatched by the mother goose and the goslings followed her around. The second group was placed in an incubator. On hatching, the first thing the goslings saw was Lorenz – they promptly followed him around as if he were their mother. Lorenz then marked each group to distinguish it from the other and placed all the goslings under an upturned box. They were then released in the presence of the mother goose and Lorenz. Each group went straight to their 'mother figures'. Lorenz's goslings followed him everywhere and became distressed if they lost sight of him.

Lorenz called this form of tie *imprinting*. In the case of the goslings, imprinting directs them to attach themselves to the first moving object they see after hatching. In a very short space of time they learn what the object looks like and how it differs from other objects. Lorenz believed that imprinting only occurs during a *critical period* – a short period of time when the individual is particularly sensitive and impressionable. In the case of the goslings, the critical period was the first few hours after hatching.

Lorenz and his goslings

Lorenz saw imprinting as *adaptive behaviour*. It protected the young by keeping them close to their mother so promoting their chances of survival and reproduction.

In summary, Lorenz argued that imprinting is:

- An innate predisposition to establish a bond
- A rapid process which occurs during a fairly short critical period
- An adaptive behaviour which has evolved over millions of years as a means of protecting the young.

Evaluation Lorenz applied his idea of imprinting to certain species of birds. Since then, ethologists have modified his views and applied them to a wider range of species. Imprinting is now seen to occur in many *precocial* animals – animals that can feed themselves and move around freely shortly after birth.

The idea of a critical period has been replaced with the idea of a *sensitive period*. A critical period suggests that if imprinting does not occur during this period, it won't occur at all. Later research indicates that this is not so – imprinting can occur outside the so-called critical period. Because of this, the term sensitive period is now used. Imprinting is more likely to occur and occurs more easily during sensitive periods. For example, a duck imprints more readily during the first 24 hours after hatching but it can imprint outside this period (Hess, 1958).

Lorenz's research had an important influence on theories of attachment in humans. Imprinting occurs without any food being involved. For example, goslings and ducklings feed themselves – they are *not* fed by their mothers. This suggests that imprinting is itself a primary drive, that it is not a by-product of feeding by the mother. This raises the possibility

Key terms

Adaptive behaviour *Behaviour which helps organisms adapt to their environment. In terms of ethology, adaptation often refers to genetically based behaviour patterns which have evolved because they increase the likelihood that the individual will survive and reproduce.*

Imprinting *A partly innate, partly learned process during which an infant rapidly forms a strong tie with a mother figure.*

Innate *Inborn, genetically based, inherited through the genes.*

Critical period *A period of time when imprinting must take place if it is to occur at all.*

Sensitive period *A period of time when infants are particularly sensitive to imprinting.*

Precocial animals *Animals that are born late in their development, and can feed themselves and move around freely shortly after birth.*

The two 'mothers'

Contact comfort

that attachment in humans might be a primary drive. If this is the case, then it calls into question the 'cupboard love' theories of psychoanalysis and early social learning theory which see attachment as a by-product of feeding.

Harlow's research with rhesus monkeys

The significance of feeding in forming attachments was also challenged by Harry Harlow's research with rhesus monkeys (Harlow, 1959). He believed that comfort and security rather than food were the crucial factors involved in attachment. To test this hypothesis, he designed the following experiment.

Eight newborn monkeys were separated from their mothers and isolated in individual cages. Each was provided with two *surrogate mothers* made of wire cylinders (surrogate means substitute). One of the 'mothers' was wrapped in soft towelling cloth which, in Harlow's words, provided 'contact comfort'. Four of the monkeys received milk from a bottle attached to the wire 'mother', four from a bottle attached to the cloth 'mother'. The two groups drank the same amount of milk and gained weight at the same rate. However, those who were fed by the wire 'mother' visited her *only* to feed. Babies in both groups spent most of their time nestled close to the cloth 'mother'. When they were frightened they always ran to the cloth 'mother' – regardless of whether or not 'she' was the one who provided food.

Harlow concluded that comfort and security rather than food formed the basis for attachment. The babies who were fed by a wire 'mother' failed to form an attachment to her. Instead, they spent much of the time clinging to the soft, cuddly 'mother' who provided them with contact comfort.

However, this attachment was not sufficient for healthy social development. In later life the monkeys were either indifferent or abusive to other monkeys and had difficulty with mating and parenting. For example, the first monkey to have a baby ignored the infant and pushed it away when it tried to make contact.

Key term

Contact comfort *Direct physical contact which provides comfort and security.*

Evaluation Harlow's research was very influential. His single most important claim was that comfort and security rather than feeding formed the basis for attachment. As with ethology, this challenged the view of psychoanalysis and early social learning theory that attachment was a by-product of feeding.

Harlow saw the cloth 'mother' as ideal for contact comfort. In his words, 'She is available 24 hours a day to satisfy her infant's overwhelming compulsion to seek bodily contact' (1959). In the short term, the cloth 'mother' may have provided for the baby's needs. However, in the long term she failed to do so – the babies had problems with social relationships in later years. In another experiment, babies with cloth 'mothers' were allowed to play with three other young monkeys for an hour a day. When they grew up they were no different from monkeys who had been raised with their natural mothers. This suggests that for healthy psychological development, social contact may be more important than contact comfort or even 'mothering' (Harlow & Suomi, 1970).

Harlow's research was based on rhesus monkeys. It may not be appropriate to generalise from non-human animals to humans. Findings which apply to non-human animals may not apply to humans. One reason for this is that non-human animal behaviour is based less on learning and more on innate, genetically-based behaviour patterns. Despite these cautions, findings from animal behaviour can provide insights into human behaviour.

Harlow's research has been criticised on ethical grounds. In terms of today's morality, it is wrong to manipulate animals in this way. In addition, the consequences were

Activity 3 Comfort and security

Item A Fear

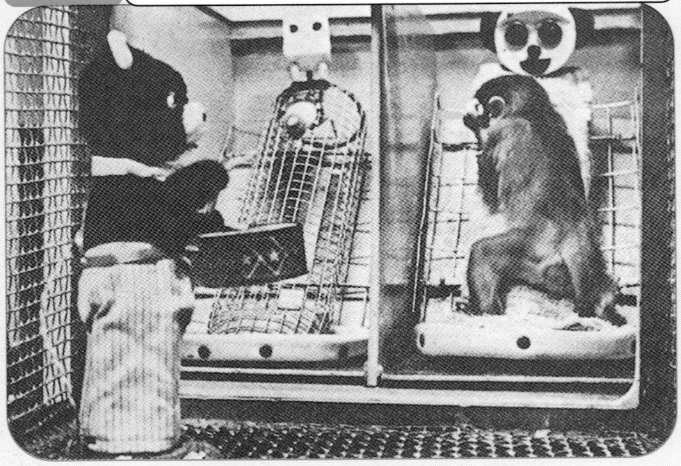

A mechanical teddy bear beating a drum is brought into the cage. The terrified baby clings to its cloth 'mother'.

Item B Curiosity

After a while, the baby 'would turn to look at the previously terrifying bear without the slightest sign of alarm. Indeed, the infant would sometimes even leave the protection of the "mother" and approach the object that a few minutes before had reduced it to abject terror' (Harlow, 1959).

Question

Look at Items A and B. What support does this experiment provide for Harlow's view that attachment is based on comfort and security rather than feeding?

very damaging – both for the monkeys involved in the experiment and their young. This breaks the British Psychological Society's code of ethics for the use of animals in research (BPS, 1998).

6.3 Bowlby's theory of attachment

In a series of publications from the 1940s to the 1980s, John Bowlby developed what many consider the most comprehensive and influential theory of attachment.

Proximity Bowlby was strongly influenced by ethology. He saw attachment behaviour in all species as innate. He believed it had evolved as a means of protecting the young. As such it was adaptive behaviour – it promoted their survival. Bowlby saw the key to attachment as *proximity* – it served to keep the infant and caregiver near to each other. This provided protection from predators who might injure or kill the infant.

Bowlby saw attachment as a two-way process. Both infant and caregiver are genetically 'programmed' to maintain proximity – each has developed behaviours which keep them physically close. For example, human infants coo and smile and their caregivers respond with warmth and affection; infants cry and their caregivers respond with attention and concern. Separation leads to feelings of anxiety in both infant and caregiver, which also serves to maintain proximity. In many species infants are wary of strangers. Bowlby suggests that this is an innate survival mechanism. It may alert the infant to danger. And a cry at the sight of someone strange or unfamiliar usually brings a caregiver running.

From proximity – a *physical* attachment – grows a strong *emotional* bond between infant and caregiver. Proximity, and the behaviours which have developed to maintain it, lead to emotional closeness. In humans, we use the word 'love' to describe this closeness between infant and caregiver. Bowlby argues that this emotional bond is essential for the child's development.

Monotropy Bowlby believed that human infants have an innate tendency to become attached to one particular person. He called this idea of one special relationship *monotropy*. Bowlby recognised that infants eventually form many attachments – to parents, siblings (brothers and sisters), grandparents, aunts and uncles and family friends. However, he believed that a single primary attachment relationship was essential for the healthy psychological development of the child. Ideally, this attachment is with the mother. In his words the child needs, 'a warm, intimate, and continuous relationship with his mother (or permanent mother-substitute – one person who steadily "mothers" him) in which both find satisfaction and enjoyment' (Bowlby, 1953). Bowlby believed there was a sensitive period for the establishment of this special relationship. For most children it must take place during their first 12 months.

Internal working model Bowlby believed that a child's relationship with their mother figure provides a model or template for all their future relationships. He called this model the *internal working model*. It develops from the primary attachment relationship. For example, if a child experiences a warm, close relationship with their mother, they will tend to expect and develop similar relationships in later life. The primary attachment relationship also provides a model for the child's self-image. For example, if the mother is cold and rejecting, the child will tend to develop a negative self-image and experience low self-esteem and a lack of worth. This may well lead to unsatisfactory relationships in later life.

Cognitive development Bowlby believed that a strong attachment with a mother figure was essential for the child's cognitive development – the development of thinking, reasoning and problem-solving skills. Exploration of the environment is critical for cognitive development. Bowlby argued that attachment provides a base from which the infant can explore new environments, secure in the knowledge that the mother figure provides a safe haven to which it can return.

Evaluation

Is attachment innate? Bowlby's theory of attachment suffers from the same problems as all theories which claim that behaviour is directed or influenced by genes – it is difficult, if not impossible to verify. Despite rapid advances in genetics, there is no direct evidence of a gene or genes for attachment. They may exist but they have yet to be discovered. In view of this, Bowlby's claim that attachment is innate is, at best, a possibility.

Is attachment adaptive? How can we be sure that attachment is adaptive, that it serves to promote the chances of infants surviving and reproducing? Bowlby argued that it evolved to protect the young from predators. This may apply to the early stages of human evolution, but predators – in the sense of wild animals – are hardly a problem in modern human societies. If we accept Bowlby's argument, attachment appears little more than a 'hangover' from a previous era.

And why did Bowlby single out protection from predators as basis for attachment? As Rudolph Schaffer notes, 'attachment serves so many useful functions that to single this one out as the biological basis seems somewhat far-fetched' (1989).

Multiple attachments To what extent does monotropy exist in practice? In other words, to what extent do infants have a single primary attachment figure? Schaffer and Emerson's (1964) study of 60 infants from Glasgow showed that most formed their first attachment with one particular person. But nearly one third formed multiple attachments – to two or more persons – in which there appeared to be no preferred attachment figure. This became increasingly common as the infants grew older – by 18 months most had developed multiple attachments with no preferred attachment figure. Schaffer (1971) claims that Bowlby's idea of monotropy is 'not borne out by the facts'. And Thomas (1995) suggests that multiple attachments may be more desirable than a single primary attachment. The child's social, emotional and cognitive development may well benefit more from a network of attachments.

The role of the father For Bowlby the mother-infant relationship was central to the attachment process. The mother was the primary caregiver and the primary attachment figure. Bowlby saw the main role of the father as supporting the mother. He supports her financially, allowing her to devote herself to caring for the child. He supports her emotionally, providing her with love and companionship. This helps the mother to 'maintain that harmonious and contented mood' which creates an atmosphere in which the infant thrives (Bowlby, 1953).

However, a number of studies have shown that fathers are often a lot more than supporting actors. Research evidence indicates that infants usually show no preference for mothers or fathers in unstressful situations. However, in stressful situations, they tend to favour the mother (Lamb, 1976). As the infant grows older, this preference for the mother tends to disappear. One study indicated that boys between the ages of 15 and 24 months showed a preference for their fathers (Lamb, 1977). This type of evidence suggests that fathers are not the marginal figures pictured by Bowlby. Instead, it suggests they play an important part in the attachment process.

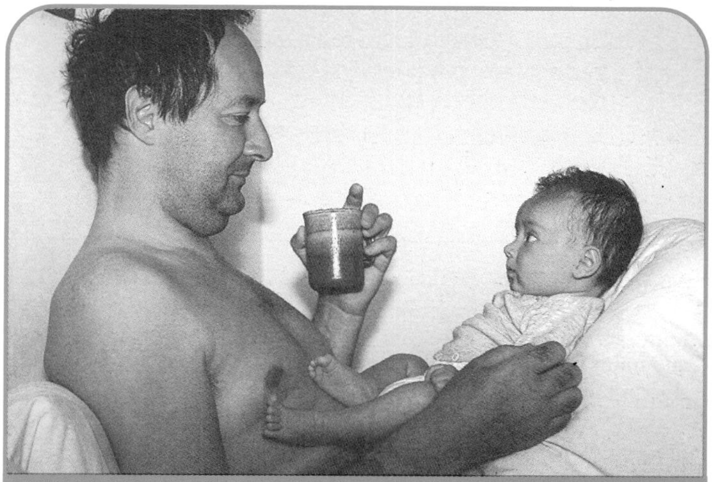

Father and child

A sensitive period Bowlby was clearly influenced by the ideas of imprinting and sensitive periods derived from ethology. He suggested that powerful and lasting attachments are made to a mother figure during a sensitive period. And, if they are not made during this period, they are unlikely to be made later. However, as Durkin (1995) points out, attachments in humans are not all-or-nothing relationships with one person 'getting stuck' to another. Relationships develop and change over time. Infants do not 'blindly' and mechanically imprint on a mother figure during a sensitive period. They have some degree of choice when making their attachments. In this respect, attachment relationships in infancy are similar to social relationships in later life.

Cognitive development There is evidence to support Bowlby's claim that secure attachment is important for cognitive development. For example, Hazen and Durrett (1982) found that securely attached young children were more independent explorers of their environment and were also more innovative in their approach to problem solving.

Conclusion It is generally recognised that forming attachments to a few people is part of the normal process of child development. The evidence suggests that Bowlby overestimated the importance of a single attachment to a mother figure. And, as this evaluation has noted, there are other aspects of Bowlby's theory which are questionable. However, in some respects, it was an advance on earlier theories which saw attachment as a by-product of feeding and pictured the infant as a passive individual who was fed and, as a result, became attached. Bowlby saw both caregivers and infants actively involved in attachment behaviour and the formation of attachments.

Key term

Monotropy *The idea of one special relationship. In terms of attachment, the view that infants have an innate tendency to form a single primary attachment to their mother or a mother figure.*

Summary

1. Psychoanalytic theory states that the infant forms an attachment to the mother because she satisfies their need for feeding and comfort.
2. Early versions of social learning theory state that the infant becomes attached to the person who feeds it.
3. Animal research suggests that infants do not necessarily form attachments to the person who feeds them.
4. Lorenz saw imprinting as a largely instinctive process which occurs during a fairly short critical period. It keeps infants in close proximity to their mothers and evolved as a means of protecting the young.
5. From his research with rhesus monkeys, Harlow claimed that contact comfort – direct physical contact which provides comfort and security – was the basis for attachment.
6. Bowlby saw attachment behaviour as innate. It had evolved as a means of protecting infants by maintaining proximity with their mothers. From this physical closeness develops a strong emotional bond.
7. Bowlby believed that a single primary attachment to a mother figure was essential for the child's healthy psychological development.
8. The following criticisms have been made of Bowlby's theory.
   - It is not possible to prove that attachment is innate and adaptive.
   - Research evidence indicates that he overestimated the significance of a primary attachment to a mother figure.
   - His idea of a sensitive period for attachment is questionable.

References

Ahrens, S.R. (1954). Beitrage zur entwicklung des physiognomie und mimiker-kennes (Contributions on the development of physiognomy and mimicry recognition). *Zeitschrift fur Experimentelle und Angewandte Psychologie, 2*, 412-454.

Ainsworth, M.D.S. & Bell, S.M. (1969). Some contemporary patterns of mother-infant interaction in the feeding situation. In A. Ambrose (Ed.), *Stimulation in early infancy*. New York: Academic Press.

Ainsworth, M.D.S., Blehar, M.C., Waters, E. & Wall, S. (1978). *Patterns of attachment: A psychological study of the strange situation*. Hillsdale, NJ: Erlbaum.

Atkinson, J. & Braddick, O.J. (1981). Acuity, contrast sensitivity and accommodation in infancy. In R.N. Aslin, J.R. Roberts & M.R. Petersen (Eds.), *The development of perception: Psychobiological perspectives, vol. 2: the visual system*. New York: Academic Press.

Bandura, A. (1965). Influence of model's reinforcement contingencies on the acquisition of imitative responses. *Journal of Personality and Social Psychology, 1*, 589-595.

Bartholomew, K. (1993). From childhood to adult relationships: Attachment theory and research. In S. Duck (Ed.), *Learning about relationships*. Newbury Park, CA: Sage.

Bartholomew, K. & Horowitz, L.M. (1991). Attachment styles among young adults: A test of a four-category model. *Journal of Personality and Social Psychology, 61*, 226-244.

Belsky, J. & Rovine, M. (1987). Temperament and attachment security in the Strange Situation: a rapprochement. *Child Development, 58*, 787-795.

Bettelheim, B. (1969). *The children of the dream*. London: Thames & Hudson.

Bowlby, J. (1953). *Childcare and the growth of love*. Harmondsworth: Penguin.

Bowlby, J. (1969). *Attachment and loss, vol. 1: Attachment*. London: Hogarth.

Bowlby, J. (1973). *Attachment and loss, vol. 2: Separation.* London: Hogarth.

BPS (British Psychological Society). (1998). *Code of conduct, ethical principles and guidelines.* Leicester: BPS.

Bremner, J.G. (1994). *Infancy* (2nd ed.). Oxford: Blackwell.

Bretherton, I. (1985). Attachment theory: Retrospect and prospect. In I. Bretherton & E. Walters (Eds.), Growing points of attachment theory and research. *Child Development Monographs, 50,* nos. 1-2.

Bronfenbrenner, U. (1979). *The ecology of human development: Experiments by nature and design.* Cambridge, Mass: Harvard University Press.

Bushnell, I.W.R., Sai, F. & Mullin, J.T. (1989). Neonatal recognition of the mother's face. *British Journal of Developmental Psychology, 7,* 3-15.

Buss A.H. & Plomin, R. (1984). *Temperament: Early developing personality traits.* Hillsdale, NJ: Erlbaum.

Carlson, E.A. & Sroufe, L.A. (1995). Contribution of attachment theory to developmental psychopathology. In D. Cicchetti & D.J. Conen (Eds.), *Developmental psychopathology: Vol 1. Theory and methods.* New York: Wiley.

Cernoch, J.M. & Porter, R.H. (1985). Recognition of maternal axillary odours by infants. *Child Development, 56,* 1593-1598.

Crockenberg, S.B. (1981). Infant irritability, mother responsiveness, and social support influences on the security of infant-mother attachment. *Child Development, 52,* 857-865.

Dollard, J. & Miller, N.E. (1950). *Personality and psychotherapy.* New York: McGraw-Hill.

Durkin, K. (1995). *Developmental social psychology.* Oxford: Blackwell.

Eysenck, H. (1985). *The decline and fall of the Freudian Empire.* Harmondsworth: Penguin.

Fox, N. (1977). Attachment of Kibbutz infants to mother and metapelet. *Child Development, 48,* 1228-1239.

Grossmann, K., Grossmann, K.E., Spangler, S., Suess, G. & Unzner, L. (1985). Maternal sensitivity and newborn orientation responses as related to quality of attachment in Northern Germany. *Monographs of the Society for Research in Child Development, 50,* (1-2 Serial No. 209).

Haralambos, M. & Holborn, M. (2000). *Sociology: Themes and perspectives* (5th ed.). London: Collins Educational.

Harlow, H.F. (1959). Love in infant monkeys. *Scientific American, 200,* 68-74.

Harlow, H.F. & Suomi, S.J. (1970). The nature of love – simplified. *American Psychologist, 25,* 161-168.

Harris, J.R. (1999). *The nurture assumption.* London: Bloomsbury.

Hay, D.F. & Vespo, J.E. (1988). Social learning perspectives on the development of the mother-child relationship. In B. Birns & D.F. Hay (Eds.), *The different faces of motherhood.* New York: Plenum Press.

Hazen, N.L. & Durrett, M.E. (1982). Relationship of security of attachment to exploration and cognitive mapping abilities in 2-year olds. *Developmental Psychology, 18,* 751-759.

Hazen, C. & Shaver, P.R. (1987). Conceptualizing romantic love as an attachment process. *Journal of Personality and Social Psychology, 52,* 511-524.

Hess, E.H. (1958). Imprinting in animals. *Scientific American,* March, 71-80.

Kagan, J. (1984). *The nature of the child.* New York: Basic Books.

Lamb, M.E. (1976). Effects of stress and cohort on mother- and father-infant interaction. *Developmental Psychology, 12,* 435-443.

Lamb, M.E. (1977). The development of mother-infant and father-infant attachments in the second year of life. *Developmental Psychology, 13,* 637-648.

Lamb, M.E., Thompson, R.A., Gardner, W. and Charnov, E.L. (1985). *Infant-mother attachment: The origins and significance of individual differences in Strange Situation behaviour.* Hillsdale, NJ: Erlbaum.

Levitt, M.J. (1991). Attachment and close relationships: A life-span perspective. In J. L. Gewirtz & W.M. Kurtines (Eds.), *Intersections with attachment.* Hillsdale, NJ: Erlbaum.

Lorenz, K.Z. (1935). The companion in the bird's world. *Auk, 54,* 245-273.

Main, M. & Soloman, J. (1986). Discovery of a disorganised disoriented attachment pattern. In T.B. Brazelton & M.W. Yogman (Eds.), *Affective development in infancy.* Norwood, NJ: Ablex.

Maurer, D. & Barrera, M. (1981). Infants perception of natural and distorted arrangements of a schematic face. *Child Development, 52,* 196-202.

Meltzoff, A.N. & Moore, M.K. (1977). Imitation of facial and manual gestures by human neonates. *Science, 198,* 75-78.

Mitchell, J. (1975). *Psychoanalysis and feminism.* Harmondsworth: Penguin.

Miyake, K., Chen, S.J. & Campos, J.J. (1985). Infant temperament, mother's mode of interaction and attachment in Japan: An interim report. In I. Bretherton & E. Waters (Eds.), Growing points of attachment theory and research. *Monographs of the Society for Research in Child Development, 50,* 276-297.

Piaget, J. (1957). The child's view of reality. *Scientific American,* March.

Sagi, A., Lamb, M.E., Lewkowicz, K.S., Shoham, R., Dvir, R. & Estes, D. (1985). Security of infant-mother, -father, and -metapelet attachments among kibbutz reared Israeli children. *Monographs of the Society for Research in Child Development, 50,* (1-2 Serial No. 209).

Schaffer, H.R. (1977). *Mothering.* London: Fontana.

Schaffer, H.R. (1989). Early social development. In A. Slater & G. Bremner (Eds.), *Infant development.* Hove: Lawrence Erlbaum Associates.

Schaffer, H.R. (1996). *Social development.* Oxford: Blackwell.

Schaffer, H.R. & Emerson, P.E. (1964). The development of social attachments in infancy. *Monographs of the Society for Research on Child Development, 29.*

Serrano, J.M., Iglesias, J. & Loeches, A. (1995). Infants' responses to adult static facial expressions. *Infant Behaviour and Development, 18,* 477-482.

Spangler, G. (1990). Mother, child, and situational correlates of toddlers' social competence. *Infant Behaviour and Development, 13,* 405-419.

Stern, D. (1977). *The first relationship: Infant and mother.* Cambridge, MA: Harvard University Press.

Takahashi, K. (1990). Are the key assumptions of the 'strange situation' procedure universal? *Human Development, 33,* 23-30.

Thomas, A. & Chess, S. (1977). *Temperament and development.* New York: Brunner/Mazel.

Thomas, L.K. (1998). Multicultural aspects of attachment. http://bereavement.demon.co.uk/lbn/attachment/lennox/htlm.

Thompson, R.A., Lamb, M.E. & Estes, D. (1982). Stability of infant-mother attachment and its relationship to changing life circumstances in an unselected middle-class sample. *Child Development, 53,* 144-148.

van den Boom, D.C. (1994). The influence of temperament and mothering on attachment and exploration: An experimental manipulation of sensitive responsiveness among lower-class mothers with irritable infants. *Child Development, 65,* 1457-1477.

van IJzendoorn, M.H. & Kroonenberg, P.M. (1988). Cross-cultural patterns of attachment: A meta-analysis of the Strange Situation. *Child Development, 59,* 147-156.

Vaughn, B.E., Lefever, G.B., Seifer, R. & Barglow, P. (1989). Attachment behaviour, attachment security, and temperament during infancy. *Child Development, 60,* 728-737.

Waters, E. (1978). The reliability and stability of individual differences in infant-mother attachment. *Child Development, 49,* 483-494.

Wolff, P.H. (1969). The natural history of crying and other vocalisations in early infancy. In B. Foss (Ed.), *Determinants of infant behaviour, vol. 4.* London: Methuen.

Young-Breuhl, E. (1990). *Freud on women.* London: Hogarth.

5 Deprivation and privation

Introduction

Chapter 4 looked at attachment between the child and its caregiver – usually the mother or a 'mother figure' – during the child's early years. A number of researchers have argued that this attachment is essential for the child's wellbeing during infancy and in later life. In particular, it is seen as important for the child's emotional development, social development, cognitive development, and physical development.

If the child fails to form an attachment during infancy, or if an attachment is formed but is then disrupted or broken, this may have harmful effects throughout life. First, it may result in psychological problems. Second, it may affect social development – the ability to form close and lasting relationships with others and to follow social norms (the accepted and expected ways of behaving in society). Third, it may impair cognitive development – for example, it may retard intelligence. Fourth, it may affect physical development leading to ill-health and stunted growth.

This chapter looks at research which investigates the possible effects of a failure to form an attachment and the disruption or loss of an existing attachment.

Chapter summary

- **Unit 1 examines early research into the possible effects of a lack of attachment or a disruption or loss of attachment.**
- **Unit 2 looks at the possible effects of a disruption or loss of attachment.**
- **Unit 3 looks at the possible effects of a failure to form an attachment.**

Unit 1 Early research

KEY ISSUES

1. **What is maternal deprivation?**
2. **How might it harm children's development?**
3. **What other factors might harm children's development?**

1.1 Bowlby's maternal deprivation hypothesis

John Bowlby (1951) claimed that a strong attachment to a mother figure was essential for a child's psychological health, both in infancy and in later life. Bowlby used the term *maternal deprivation* to refer to either 1) a failure to form this attachment during the early months or 2) a disruption or loss of an existing attachment. In both cases the child is deprived of the love of a mother figure. In Bowlby's words, 'The young child's hunger for his mother's love and presence is as great as his hunger for food'. This love and presence are as essential for healthy psychological development as 'vitamins and minerals are for physical development' (Bowlby, 1973).

In short, if attachment to a mother figure is absent or broken, then the effects on the child could be serious. However, Bowlby believed that these effects could be reduced by the return of an absent mother or the provision of a mother substitute.

According to Bowlby, fostering or adoption may provide adequate care since they involve a single mother figure with whom a primary attachment can be made. Institutional care, for example local authority care homes and orphanages, is unlikely to provide a replacement mother figure.

Internal working model Bowlby believed that the importance of the mother figure lies in the model she provides for all future relationships. This model or template develops out of the primary attachment relationship. Bowlby called it the internal working model. He argued that there is a link between early and later relationships. In particular, if the child has experienced maternal deprivation, then this may well lead to unsatisfactory relationships in later life – for example, the inability to form close and long-lasting relationships.

Key term

Maternal deprivation *According to Bowlby, the absence of the love and care of a mother or mother figure due to either a failure to form an attachment or the loss of an existing attachment.*

1.2 Deprivation and psychopathy

Bowlby's maternal deprivation hypothesis was based in part on his own research. Bowlby worked as a psychiatrist at the London Child Guidance Clinic during the 1930s. He recorded case histories of some of the boys he saw which formed the basis for his research, published in 1946 and titled *Forty-four juvenile thieves: Their characters and their home lives*. Bowlby selected a sample of 44 'thieves' and compared them to 44 boys with no criminal record who had attended the clinic. He classed 14 of the thieves as *affectionless psychopaths*.

According to Bowlby, affectionless psychopaths act impulsively with little regard for the consequences of their actions. They show no shame or remorse and have little or no concern for others. They are unable to form close, meaningful and long-lasting relationships. Bowlby believed that affectionless psychopathy often results from maternal deprivation. 12 out of the 14 'affectionless thieves' had 'early and prolonged separations from their mothers'. They had spent most of their early years in residential homes or hospitals. Of the remaining 74 children in the sample, only 7 had experienced early separations. This evidence appears to support Bowlby's claim that maternal deprivation in early life results in psychological and behavioural problems in later life.

However, there are problems with Bowlby's research. First, his sample was not representative. The vast majority of juvenile thieves are not referred to children's clinics for treatment. Second, much of the data was retrospective – based on looking back and recalling past events. It relied on the memories of the juveniles and their mothers. As a result, it may be inaccurate. Third, the diagnosis of affectionless psychopathy was made by Bowlby himself. He may have been biased, looking hard for what he hoped and expected to find. Fourth, a correlation between two things doesn't necessarily mean that one causes the other. We cannot be sure that the separations themselves caused the maladjustment. For example, both the separations and the maladjustment may have been caused by discord and conflict within the family. This possibility is examined in the next section.

Key term

Affectionless psychopathy *A lack of affection and concern for others. An inability to form close and lasting relationships. A lack of guilt or remorse for antisocial behaviour.*

1.3 Deprivation or discord?

Michael Rutter (1981) questioned Bowlby's view that separation, in and of itself, produced harmful effects for the child. He argued that the events and experiences that preceded the separation may be more important than the separation itself. Consider the following.

First, a child is separated from its mother because of the mother's longstanding illness or death. Second, a child is separated from its mother because of the mother's divorce, psychological disorder, or addiction to alcohol or heroin. Rutter suggests that the second examples are more likely to produce harmful effects. And, in his words, these effects are '*not* because of the separation involved but rather because of the discord and disharmony which led to the break'.

Evidence to support this view was provided by Rutter's study of over 2000 boys between the ages of 9 and 12 living on the Isle of Wight and in London (Rutter et al., 1976). He looked at the relationship between separation and delinquency. If the separation was due to the physical illness or death of the mother, there was no correlation with delinquency. However, if the separation was due to the psychological disorder of one or both parents, or to discord within the family, then the boys were four times more likely to become delinquent. Rutter concluded that it is the conflict and stress which precedes separation rather than the separation itself which is likely to be the underlying cause of antisocial behaviour.

However, two critical points should be made about Rutter et al's study. Like Bowlby's *Forty-four juvenile thieves*, the data was collected retrospectively (after the event) and may, therefore, be unreliable; and the evidence is correlational, therefore no cause and effect can be established.

1.4 The effects of institutions

Apart from his own research, Bowlby based his maternal deprivation hypothesis on a number of other studies. During the 1930s and 40s, there was a growing body of research which seemed to indicate that psychological health, cognitive development and social development were linked to early attachment experience. For example, Goldfarb (1943) looked at the effects on children of being raised in an institution. He compared two groups of 15 children. The first group went directly from their 'natural' mothers to foster parents before the age of one. The second group were raised in a residential nursery then fostered between the ages of 6 months and $3^1/2$ years.

The two groups were assessed between the ages of 10 and 14. The institutional group lagged behind on every measure of development. They had lower IQs, poorer language skills, they were less able to form relationships and less likely to follow rules and social norms.

What accounts for these differences? The physical care – food, clothing, hygiene – in the residential and foster homes was similar. The quality of care provided by the two groups of foster parents was similar. The main difference seemed to be the presence or absence of attachment during the early months. This, Goldfarb suggested, explains the differences between the two groups. In his words, 'strong anchors to specific adults were not established' in the case of the children who spent their early years in the institution.

Evaluation Although it appeared to provide strong support for Bowlby's maternal deprivation hypothesis, there are problems with Goldfarb's research. His sample was not random. Infants in the first group had been selected for immediate fostering. Those in the second group had been kept in the nursery before being fostered. This might mean there were differences between the two groups. Maybe members of the institutional group were more prone to illness, more socially withdrawn, less attractive, and therefore less likely to appeal to foster parents. Differences such as these, rather than attachment, may account for the differences between the two groups in later life.

Goldfarb argued that the problems of the children raised in the nursery were due to a failure to form attachments during infancy. But, these problems may be due, at least in part, to the conditions within the nursery. Babies under 9 months were kept in single cubicles and their only human contact was when they were fed and changed. In view of this, it is not surprising that they had poor language and social skills. Later research has shown that babies raised in a stimulating environment in institutions have far fewer problems than those in Goldfarb's study (Smith et al., 1998). Thus the lack of stimulation resulting from social isolation, rather than a failure to form attachments, may have caused the developmental problems experienced by the children in Goldfarb's research.

1.5 Deprivation and privation

In *Maternal deprivation reassessed* (1981), Michael Rutter argues that Bowlby's use of the term deprivation was vague and imprecise. Rutter felt there was an important distinction to be made between *privation* and *deprivation*. He defined privation as a lack or absence of attachment due to a failure to form an attachment between infant and caregiver. A newborn baby who is placed in an orphanage and fails to make an attachment is an example of privation. Deprivation refers to the loss of an attachment that has already been made, in other words, the loss of something that was previously there. The separation of mother and child due to the mother's illness or death is an example of deprivation.

Key terms

Social norms *The accepted and expected ways of behaving in society.*

Stimulation *Something outside the individual to which they respond. In the case of infants and children, stimulation includes attention and affection from others and physical contact and social interaction with others.*

Privation *A lack of attachment due to the failure to form an attachment.*

Deprivation *A loss of an existing attachment due to the separation of an infant and its attachment figure.*

Rutter argues that the distinction between privation and deprivation is important because each may have different effects. He believes that harmful, long-term effects are due more to privation than deprivation. For example, an inability to form lasting relationships in later life is more likely to result from a *lack* of attachment (privation) than a *loss* of attachment (deprivation).

Despite this criticism, Rutter accepted Bowlby's main argument, that attachment is important for healthy psychological development.

Summary

1. Bowlby believed that a single primary attachment to a mother figure was essential for the child's healthy psychological development.

2. Early research often failed to consider factors other than privation and deprivation which may contribute to developmental problems. These include:
   - Lack of stimulation during infancy
   - The conflict and stress which may precede separation.

3. According to Rutter, Bowlby failed to distinguish between privation and deprivation. This distinction is important because each may have different effects.

Activity 1 Deprivation and privation

Item A Separation and antisocial behaviour

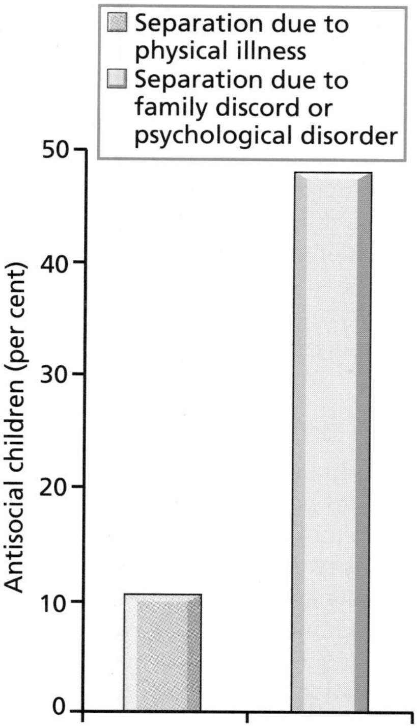

This bar chart shows the reasons for parent-child separation in relation to antisocial behaviour.

Adapted from Rutter et al., 1976

Item B The 'non-recoverables'

After the overthrow of the dictator Nicolae Ceaucescu in 1990, the appalling conditions in Romanian orphanages were revealed to the world. Many of the 40,000 infants and children in these institutions were referred to as 'non-recoverables'. They were found tied to their beds, starving and filthy. Often, they had never been held. No one had talked to them. They rock back and forth, staring blankly.

Adapted from Sachs, 1990, quoted in Zimbardo et al., 1995

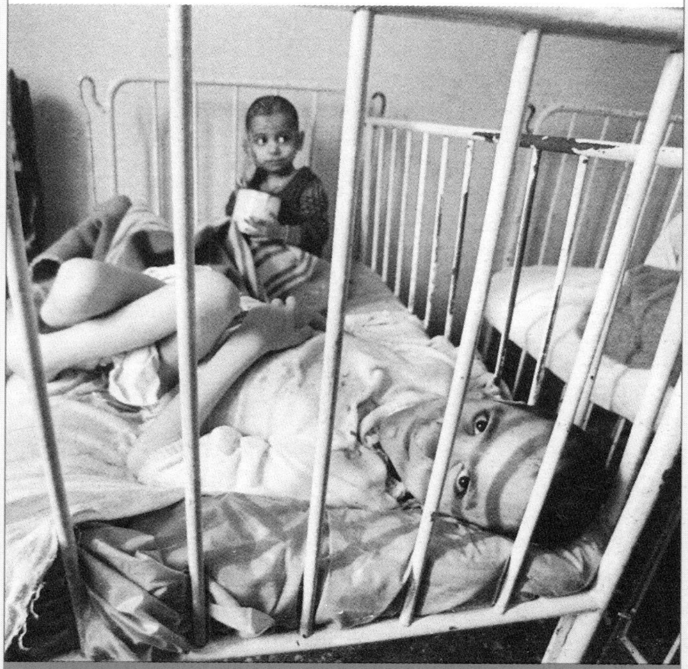

Children in a Romanian orphanage

Questions

1 Use Item A to argue that Bowlby overestimated the importance of maternal deprivation.

2 Suggest reasons for the behaviour of the children in Item B.

Unit 2 The effects of deprivation/separation

KEY ISSUES

1. **What are the short-term effects of separation?**
2. **What are the long-term effects of separation?**

Separation is an alternative term for deprivation. It is a more neutral term and sounds less problematic. The word separation does not necessarily imply that the experience is harmful.

Children may be separated from their caregivers in a number of ways. They may experience separation for a few hours every day if their caregiver goes out to work. They may be placed in day care – with a childminder or in a nursery school. They may experience temporary separations for days or weeks due to hospitalisation – when they or their caregiver stays in hospital. Or they may experience long-term separation due to the death or divorce of their parents.

This unit looks at the possible short-term and long-term effects of separation on the child's development. The possible effects of day care are examined in the following chapter.

2.1 Short-term effects

In an early study, Spitz and Wolf (1946) looked at 123 babies whose mothers were in prison. While in prison, the women cared for their babies from birth to around nine months. Then, for a three month period, the babies were taken away from their mothers and placed in a nursery. Although the standard of physical care provided was high, the babies showed signs of distress – frequent crying, a loss of appetite and a failure to gain weight. Spitz and Wolf believed that this distress was due to the absence of the mothers and the loss of the love they provided. The babies resumed their normal behaviour and gained weight when they were returned to their mothers.

Bowlby used this research to support his maternal deprivation hypothesis. However, as with Goldfarb's (1943) research on infants raised in institutions (see p 71-72), it is not clear whether the effects were due to an absence of maternal love or to a lack of stimulation in the institution.

Hospitalisation Evidence of the significance of short-term separation was provided by James and Joyce Robertson who worked closely with Bowlby and were involved in developing the maternal deprivation hypothesis. The Robertsons and Bowlby made a series of films about short-term separation, for example *A two-year-old goes to hospital* (1952). At the time, many psychologists believed that children experience anxiety when deprived of the care of their primary caregiver, but most felt that this anxiety could be easily overcome by good physical care. The Robertsons and Bowlby disagreed. They suggested that this anxiety might lead to an extreme and pathological reaction. (Pathological means diseased. They used this term to suggest that the consequences were similar to a physical illness.)

One of their films was about a two-year-old boy going into hospital. Another film showed a boy, also two years old, being admitted to a residential nursery. Despite good *physical* care, the emotional support wasn't there. Both boys displayed acute distress. This was the central point of the films. The boys experienced *bond disruption* – a temporary break in the attachment to their primary caregiver. The boy in residential care was only there for nine days. But he changed rapidly from a cheerful and affectionate to a withdrawn and despairing child. On his return home, he was sullen, rejecting towards his mother, and there were severe behaviour problems throughout his childhood including repeatedly running away from home.

This was in contrast to two young girls, also filmed by the Robertsons. Aged around two, the girls stayed with the Robertsons while their mother was in hospital. They had visited the Robertsons beforehand, and when they came to stay they brought personal items, such as toys, and maintained contact with their father. They also followed their normal daily routine and the Robertsons made a point of being mother substitutes. The girls showed some signs of distress but generally adapted well. The Robertsons claimed that the key was continued maternal care during separation – the stress of bond disruption was reduced because there was substitute emotional care.

Evaluation The films were based on very small samples so it is not possible to make generalisations. However, the separation distress they reveal reflected what staff in hospitals and residential nurseries had regularly observed. The films were extremely influential. In particular, they changed hospital visiting policies and raised awareness about the importance of emotional as well as physical care.

The protest-despair-detachment model

When a child is separated from its main caregiver, the first response is likely to be crying. Some children stop crying quite quickly and turn their attention elsewhere. If separation continues then the child is likely to respond in a recognisable sequence of stages. Bowlby and the Robertsons were the first to outline this *protest-despair-detachment model* which may occur over a period of days or weeks. In response to separation, a child may go through the following stages.

1. **Protest** The child cries but can be comforted. The child is agitated, fearful and angry and tries to regain the attention of their attachment figure.
2. **Despair** The child becomes outwardly calmer and appears apathetic – showing little emotion or interest in their surroundings. Inwardly, the fear and anger remain. The child no longer looks for the attachment figure, shows little interest in comfort offered by others, and may seek self-comfort through thumb-sucking or rocking.
3. **Detachment** This stage may occur after prolonged separation. The child appears to be coping well and responds to other people. However, the child seems emotionally detached – not really involved in relationships with others. Little interest is shown when the attachment figure eventually reappears.

It is important to note that a) this is only one possible response to separation and b) if a child goes through the first stage, they do not necessarily go on to the second and third.

Factors affecting the separation response

Infants and young children respond to temporary separation in a variety of ways. Some find it extremely distressing, other do not. Some go through the three stages of protest, despair and detachment, others do not. This section looks at

Key terms

Bond disruption *A temporary break in the attachment relationship due to separation.*

The protest-despair-detachment model *The stages a child may go through in response to separation from their main caregiver.*

some of the factors which may affect the way young children experience and respond to separation.

Age Distress from temporary separation seems less evident in infants below the age of 6 months or so, as firm attachments have yet to be formed. It appears most frequently between the ages of 7 months and three years, particularly during the period 12-18 months (Maccoby, 1980). Older children cope better, probably because they have learned that separation is followed by reunion. Also their language skills have developed, so parents can explain that the separation will be short – a few hours or a few days – and so children can look forward to the reunion. Younger children may feel abandoned and may even blame themselves for the separation.

Strange environment Distress appears greater when separation takes place in a strange environment rather than a familiar one (Ross et al., 1975). However, young children admitted to hospital with their mother show less distress than those admitted alone (Fagin, 1966). This suggests that both separation and the strangeness of the environment affect the level of distress.

Multiple attachments As noted in Chapter 4, most children form multiple attachments – with their mother, father, siblings (brothers and sisters) and grandparents. Distress resulting from separation from their primary caregiver can be reduced by the presence of other attachment figures. For example, distress on entry to a residential nursery can be reduced if the child is accompanied by a sibling (Heinicke & Westheimer, 1965).

Multiple attachments mean that the child is not dependent on a single caregiver. When both parents are regularly involved with caregiving, children show less distress when left alone with strangers (Kotelchuk, 1976).

Continuity In general, the more the child's everyday routines can be maintained, the less serious the distress. The Robertsons' film about the young girls whose mother was in hospital illustrated this point. Although living with the Robertsons, the girls continued their daily routines. This provided some continuity with their lives before the separation.

Experience of separations If children have regular experience of short-term separations (and reunions), they are less likely to experience distress. A study of four-year-old children who spent four days in hospital having their tonsils removed showed that those who had experienced regular separations were less likely to find their stay distressing. They were used to being away from home having stayed overnight, without their parents, at grandparents and friends (Stacey et al., 1970).

Individual differences No two people are the same. Children differ in terms of their characteristics and personalities. For example, some are confident and outgoing, others are shy and lacking in confidence. Such differences will affect their experience of and response to separation.

Family circumstances Research indicates that children from low-income, so-called 'disadvantaged' families, may experience separation as more stressful than children from higher-income families. It has been suggested that conflict and insecurity are more likely in low-income families due to the pressures of poverty. This magnifies the negative effects of separation (Quinton & Rutter, 1976).

Conclusion There is general agreement that the effects of temporary separation can be distressing for many young children. However, in most cases, the effects are likely to be short-term – most children soon resume their normal behaviour when reunited with their caregiver. As a result, temporary separation is unlikely to have long-term effects on the child's development.

This section has shown that the separation experience is affected by a range of factors. These factors must be taken into account in any explanation of children's response to separation. However, researchers generally agree that in times of distress children are in greatest need of their caregivers. Therefore, even if distress is caused by something other than separation, then separation will probably make it worse.

Working mothers

So far, this unit has looked at irregular and infrequent separations, such as stays in hospital. What about regular and frequent separations, for example when both parents go out to work?

Bowlby (1953) issued the following warning to mothers – 'If you don't do your five years' hard labour when the child is young, you do it later'. This implied that the mother should stay at home and look after her children, at least until they start full-time education. This reflected the general view of the role of mothers during the 1950s. From the 1950s, there has been a steady growth in the employment of mothers with young children. How might the resulting separations affect the child?

Most researchers now agree that early fears about the effects of working mothers on their children were greatly exaggerated. In fact some research indicates that the effects can be beneficial – children of working mothers tend to be more independent and self-sufficient then children who receive full-time mothering. However, the main finding from research is that there is no simple answer to the question of how working mothers affect children's development. There are a wide range of factors which need to be taken into account. These include:

- The child's age – some researchers believe that full-time mothering is essential during the first year though others disagree
- The child's sex – there is some evidence that boys tend to experience more ill effects than girls
- The child's temperament
- The number of hours the mother works
- The quality of childcare when she is at work
- The amount of support provided by the father.

These are some of the many factors which contribute to the atmosphere in which the child is raised and the relationship between children and their mothers. As a result, there is no simple, straightforward cause and effect relationship between working mothers and child development (Schaffer, 1996).

2.2 Long-term effects

So far, this unit has focused on the short-term effects of separation, effects that tend to last for days and weeks rather than years. Are there longer-term effects?

Separation and disadvantage A longitudinal study (a study of the same group over time) looked at 5000 children born in 1946 (Douglas, 1975). The study indicated a link between prolonged or repeated hospital admissions, especially under the age of four, and behaviour disturbance and antisocial behaviour in adolescence.

However, this correlation does not necessarily mean that separation caused antisocial behaviour in adolescence. Both the separation and the behaviour may have been caused by other factors. Clarke and Clarke (1976) re-analysed the data and concluded that, in many cases, both the hospital admissions, which led to the separations, and the antisocial behaviour were due to poverty and disadvantage. Children raised in poverty are more likely to suffer from ill-health as a result of inadequate housing and poor nutrition. They are also more likely to be arrested for alleged crimes and to behave in ways seen as disruptive and antisocial, particularly by teachers. This behaviour may result, in part, from discord and conflict within the family which stems from the stress of living in poverty. It may result from failure at school which again might be due, in part, to poverty. Or it can be seen, more generally, as a reaction to their disadvantaged situation. Behaviour in adolescence may therefore be a response to disadvantage rather than a response to separation at an early age.

Reasons for separation There are all sorts of reasons for temporary separations. Some may be joyful, such as the child going on holiday with a friend's family. Others may be distressing, such as a serious illness which results in the mother's admission to hospital. Do the reasons for separation make a significant difference to the long-term effects?

Rutter's study of over 2000 boys between the ages of 9 and 12 suggests a possible answer to this question. As outlined in Unit 1, Rutter looked at the relationship between separation and delinquency. If the separation was due to the physical illness or death of the mother, or to holidays or housing difficulties, there was no correlation between delinquency and separation. However, if the separation was due to the psychological disorder of one or both parents, or to discord and conflict within the family, then the boys were four times more likely to become delinquent. Rutter suggests it is the reasons for the separation, not simply the separation itself, which produce long-term effects.

Conclusion As with short-term effects, there is no simple, straightforward relationship between separation and long-term effects. A child experiences a whole range of significant events between their early years and later life. Any of these can affect future behaviour. It is extremely difficult to separate the effects of these events from the effects of separation during the early years.

Parental death

The death of a parent results in a permanent separation from an attachment figure. Bifulco et al. (1992) studied a group of 249 women who were separated from their mothers before they were 17, either through separation for more than a year, or through the mother's death. The group as a whole had twice the normal rate of depression and anxiety disorders in adulthood. However, the women who were under the age of 6 when their mothers had *died* had a particularly high rate of depression. This was not true where *separation* occurred before the age of 6. This suggests two things. First, there is a sensitive period before the age of 6 when children are particularly attached to their main caregiver. Second, there is a difference between permanent separation (even where there is substitute maternal care from a father, grandparent or step-parent) and temporary separation.

There are some similarities between the response to death and the response to other forms of separation. Bowlby (1953) notes the similarity between adult mourning and the despair stage of response to separation in a young child.

A number of factors will modify the effect of parental death. They include the amount and quality of substitute care which is subsequently provided and the effect the death has on the rest of the family, particularly the remaining parent. Recovery may depend to some extent on how well children are helped to cope with their mourning. For example, Bowlby (1953) believes that adults should encourage children to grieve 'naturally' rather than trying to divert their attention from the bereavement.

Divorce

The divorce rate rose rapidly in all Western societies during the 20th century. It is estimated that if present trends continue, around 40% of marriages in the UK will end in divorce. During the 1990s, about 65% of divorces involved couples with children under the age of 16. In 1997, around 30% of the children affected were under 5, and over 70% under 10 (*Social Trends*, 1999).

It is difficult to separate the long-term effects of divorce from the many other factors which affect children's development. Findings from a range of studies suggest the following long-term effects of divorce.

- A lower level of self control. Children of divorced parents tend to be more disruptive and disobedient both at home and at school. This applies particularly to boys who tend to be aggressive, while girls are more likely to withdraw into themselves.
- A lower level of academic attainment – progress at school suffers.
- A tendency to leave school early and to take low-paid, low-skill jobs. Children of divorced parents are more likely to start a family before the age of 20 and more likely to get divorced themselves. The combination of low qualifications, low pay and dependent children often leads to financial difficulties.
- A high level of emotional and psychological problems – young men in particular are more likely to suffer from depression.
(Richards, 1994; Schaffer, 1996).

These findings are generalisations. They do not apply to all children of divorced couples. As with all types of separation, the effects of divorce are influenced by a wide range of factors. These include the age of the child when the parents divorce, the financial circumstances of the family unit after the parents divorce, the relationship of the divorced couple, their relationship with the children, whether the parents re-marry and the relationship between step-parent and children.

The pre-divorce family A number of researchers have suggested that relationships within the family before the divorce may be as important, if not more important, than the divorce itself. Using data from two large-scale longitudinal studies – the British National Child Development Study and the US National Survey of Children – Cherlin et al., (1991) found that the apparent effects of divorce were often present well before the divorce took place. For example, if children's progress at school was poor and their conduct disruptive, this often occurred before as well as after the divorce.

According to Schaffer (1996), many of the effects attributed to divorce may be due to parental conflict which was present before, during and after the divorce. Research indicates that children from divorced families in which there is little conflict are better adjusted than children from two-parent families where there is regular conflict between the parents (Amato & Keith, 1991).

How might parental conflict harm children's development? Young children are often frightened by parental conflict. Most, if not all, children are unsettled, distressed and hurt. Children don't get used to parental conflict and learn to live with it. Things get worse rather than better. Parents are short-tempered and often take out their frustration on the children. They tend to be preoccupied with their own conflict and neglect the child's emotional development. Faced with this daily conflict, children have difficulty controlling their own emotions. Like their parents, who provide a model for their behaviour, children often have difficulty regulating emotions such as aggression. This suggests that the actual separation produced by divorce is only part of a wider pattern of behaviour which affects the child's development (Cummings, 1994; Schaffer, 1996).

Conclusion

This unit has examined the short-term and long-term effects of separation on children's development. The evidence suggests there is no simple, straightforward relationship between separation and development. Separation affects children in all sorts of ways for all sorts of reasons. A multitude of factors modify the effects of separation. Many

Summary

1. Studies of hospitalisation indicate that infants and young children may find separation distressing. However, the effects are usually short-term.
2. A number of factors may affect the separation response. These include:
   - The age of the child
   - The familiarity of the environment
   - The presence of other attachment figures
   - Whether or not daily routines are maintained
   - Previous experience of separations
   - Individual differences
   - Family circumstances
   - The reasons for the separation
3. There is no simple cause and effect relationship between working mothers and children's development.
4. Research indicates that divorce may have long-term, harmful effects on children's development.
5. Some researchers argue that these effects are due to a history of parental conflict rather than divorce itself.
6. The separation experience is influenced by a range of factors. As a result, generalisations about the effects of separation must be treated with caution.

of the supposed effects of separation are, at least in part, due to factors which precede the separation. In view of this, generalisations about the effects of separation must be treated with caution.

Activity 2 Evacuation

Item A The evacuation

Children waiting to be evacuated.

Returning home

In September 1939, 1.5 million children were evacuated from major British cities that were likely to be bombed by the Germans. Most of them returned home within a year. They were sent to live with families in the countryside. Children under 5 were accompanied by their mothers. Many of the children were distressed as they left home – they didn't know where they were going or how long they were going to be there. Others were apprehensive but excited at the prospect of life in the countryside.

Many were lucky. Often from low-income, inner-city slums, this was their first experience of the countryside, of fresh air, good food and a decent home. With kind foster parents they flourished. Others were not so lucky. They felt unloved and uncared for. Some missed their mums and could think of little else. There were sometimes problems when the behaviour of working-class children clashed with the expectations of their middle-class foster parents. A minority of evacuees had dreadful experiences. They were overworked and, in some cases, physically and sexually abused.

Adapted from Lynn, 1989; Lancaster & Lancaster, 1993

Item B Contrasting reactions

After nearly 50 years, two women look back on their lives as evacuees. Margaret wouldn't have missed it 'for anything'. Freda, despite being cared for by a kind woman, wished it had never happened.

Margaret I learned to appreciate so many things in life and even today I much prefer the country to the town.

For years and years after I came home I kept in touch with my foster parents and I still visit Ulverston, my second home. I am sorry to say that my foster parents are now no longer with us, but they will always have a special place in my heart.

The first family I stayed with, and mostly my second, they did a wonderful job of looking after me and it must have been from love, it certainly can't have been for the 37$^{1}/2$p the government gave them.

Freda The whole experience marked me for life. Until fairly recent years I suffered bad bouts of homesickness if I was away from home for any time; I find it exceptionally difficult to trust anyone other than my husband; for a large part of my young adult life I suffered badly from depression and feelings of rejection. I am angry that the whole scheme was so ill thought out and put into operation – they were messing about with children's lives, for God's sake, how dare they give it so little thought.

Adapted from Wicks, 1988

Question

Generalisations about the experience and effects of separation should be treated with caution. Discuss, with some reference to the evacuation during World War II.

Unit 3 The effects of privation

KEY ISSUES

1. **What effect does privation during the early years have on later life?**
2. **To what extent can these effects be reversed?**

Privation refers to a failure to form an attachment to a main caregiver. Early researchers, such as Bowlby and Goldfarb, believed that privation in infancy resulted in harmful effects in later life. These effects were seen as largely irreversible and permanent. The child was therefore pictured as a prisoner of their early experience.

Privation has generally been seen as more harmful than separation. For example, Rutter (1981) argued that long-term, harmful effects were more likely to be due to privation.

This unit looks at two types of privation – children raised in institutions during their early years, and 'isolated' children who have been locked away by their parents and isolated from the wider society.

3.1 Institutional childcare

This section looks at children who have spent their early years in institutions – orphanages or residential nurseries. The first part looks at institutions in which the quality of care is low, the second part at institutions where the quality of care is high. This comparison provides some indication of the importance of different types of care.

Low quality care

A longitudinal study of children brought up in a Lebanese orphanage was conducted by Wayne Dennis (1973). The children were placed in the orphanage shortly after birth. They were looked after by caregivers who had themselves been raised in the orphanage until the age of 6. The caregivers provided the children with basic physical care – they bathed, dressed, changed and fed them. However, they rarely spoke to or played with them – babies were left to lie in their cribs all day. Once they could walk they were left in playpens with only a ball to play with.

Dennis assessed the infants at 2 months and they appeared normal for their age. However, at the end of a year their cognitive development had slumped to only half the normal level. At age 6, the boys and girls were sent to separate institutions. The girls continued to receive little attention and stimulation. At 16, they had an average IQ of 50 (100 is the average for the general population). They could hardly read, they could not tell the time or dial a telephone number.

The boys were luckier. They were trained for jobs outside the institution by workers who came from the surrounding area. They were also taken on trips. Compared to the girls, their experiences were more varied and their environment was more stimulating. By age 15, the boys' average IQ was 80, a substantial improvement on their early years and within the range that would allow them to function normally in the wider society.

Some of the children from the orphanage were adopted. Those who were adopted before they were 2 (when their IQ averaged 50) had normal IQs (around 100) when they were tested 2-3 years later. Those who were adopted between the ages of 2 and 6 were only slightly below normal in terms of IQ when tested later.

This study indicates that, at least to some extent, the effects of privation depend on the environment. The more stimulating the environment, the more normal the child's intellectual development. It also suggests that to some degree children can catch up when their development has fallen behind. However, it appears that the amount of catching up depends partly on the age of the child. There may be a critical period of intellectual development between the ages of 2 and 6. Children adopted before the age of 2 developed normally, those adopted between 2 and 6 improved considerably but their IQ remained below normal. However, there is another possibility – children selected for early adoption may have been more intelligent than those adopted later.

High quality care

Barbara Tizard and her colleagues studied 65 English working-class children who had been raised in a residential nursery from just after birth until 2 or more years of age (Hodges & Tizard, 1989). The children were assessed at age $4^1/_2$, 8 and 16 and compared with a similar group of working-class children who had been raised at home.

The nursery had well-trained staff who provided high standards of care. The children were given plenty of attention and there was no shortage of books and toys. This was reflected in the children's cognitive development. By age $4^1/_2$, they had an average IQ score of 105 and their language development was normal for children of their age.

The children had little opportunity to form close attachments to their caregivers. There was a high turnover of staff and by age 2, an average of 24 caregivers had looked after each child for at least a week; by age 4 the average was 50. In addition, the nursery discouraged strong attachments between staff and children.

Most of the children in the nursery were adopted or restored to their biological families between the ages of 2 and 7. Tizard assessed their development at age 4½, 8 and 16. By age 8, most of the adopted and some of the restored children had formed close attachments to their parents. The adoptive parents really wanted a child and put considerable effort into building a relationship. The biological parents were less sure about their child's return – often they had financial problems and other children to care for. As a result, fewer of the restored children formed close attachments. According to their teachers, some of the children from both groups (adopted and restored) showed problems. They described them as attention-seeking, particularly from adults, restless, disobedient, quarrelsome and unpopular with their peers.

At 16, this picture was largely repeated. Adopted children in general had close and affectionate relationships with their parents. Restored children were more likely to have poor family relationships. But some members of *both* groups were still rated by teachers as attention seeking, unpopular with their peers and quarrelsome. They were less likely to have a 'special friend' but more likely to be friendly to any of their classmates. However, this assessment applied to only *half* the children raised in the nursery. And the researchers point out that their behaviour characteristics are *differences* and not necessarily *difficulties.*

Conclusion

What does this study show?

- First, 'early institutional care and the lack of close attachments had not had the drastically damaging effects predicted by Bowlby' (Hodges & Tizard, 1989).
- Second, the quality of care and the stimulation received by children raised in an institution can have real effects on their cognitive development. This is indicated by a comparison of the studies of Lebanese and English children.
- Third, attachments to parents can be made *after* the age of 2, though the strength of the attachment depends, to some extent, on the amount of love and care provided by the parents.
- Fourth, despite these attachments, there do appear to be lasting effects of privation in the case of some children which continue at least to the age of 16
- Fifth, these lasting effects applied to only half the institutionalised children. This suggests the effects of privation are *not* inevitable.
- Sixth, these effects are *differences* and not necessarily difficulties or problems.

Reversing the effects of privation

The studies examined so far in this unit indicate that the effects of privation are not inevitable, that they are not necessarily permanent, that they can be reversed. This section looks at two studies which suggest that the effects of privation are reversible.

A longitudinal study examined 13 children classified as 'mentally retarded' (Skodak & Skeels, 1945). Their average IQ was 64. They had been raised in an understaffed, overcrowded orphanage where they received little attention. Aged between 11 and 21 months, they were moved to a woman's ward in an institution for the mentally retarded. There, both staff and inmates lavished them with love and attention, played with them and took them on outings.

The transformation was dramatic. Within 19 months they changed from apathetic, withdrawn infants to lively, alert young children. Their average IQ rose from 64 to 92. Over the same period, the average IQ of a control group of 12 children who remained in the orphanage dropped from 87 to 61. By the age of 3 or 4, most of the children in the experimental group (those who had been moved to the woman's ward) had been adopted by families and went on to standard schools.

Over 20 years later, a follow-up study showed that the gains made by these children were lasting. Their grades at school were significantly higher than those of the control group, four went to college and one achieved a PhD. They had a wide range of jobs including teacher, sales manager and airline stewardess. Only one member of the control group had a skilled job. The rest either had unskilled jobs, were unemployed, or still lived in the orphanage (Skeels, 1966).

This study suggests that the effects of early privation can be reversed given the right environment. It indicates that the effects of early childhood experience need not be permanent.

The following investigation is not a study of privation as such, but again it suggests that the effects of early childhood experience can be reversed. Kagan (1976) studied Native American children in an isolated village in Guatemala in Central America. During their first year, the children spent most of their time in dark, windowless huts – it was assumed that sunlight and fresh air were harmful to babies. They slept a lot, they had no toys, and their parents rarely played with or talked to them. They appeared passive, withdrawn and unresponsive. In terms of their development at age one, they were 3 to 4 months behind infants of the same age in the United States.

Once they could walk, at around 13-16 months, the infants were allowed out and soon learned to play and interact like 'normal' infants. In a follow-up study in late childhood, they achieved normal scores for their age on a range of cognitive and social tests (Kagan, 1976).

This was not a study of privation – the children had formed relationships with their mothers from an early age. However, it does indicate that being deprived of stimulation during the first year of life does not necessarily have permanent effects on children's development. They can catch up – the effects are reversible.

Methodological problems

There have been a number of criticisms of the methods used in studies of institutional privation. They include the following.

Samples This unit has looked at three studies of children raised in institutions. Unit 1 looked at a further study conducted by Goldfarb (1943). In each case, the sample size was different and, in terms of their social background and nationality, the members of each sample were different. In addition, the numbers in each sample were small – for example, 13 in Skeels' study, 15 in Goldfarb's, and 65 in Tizard's. Because of the differences between the samples it is difficult to compare the studies. Because of the small samples it is difficult to generalise from the results.

Dropout All four studies were longitudinal – they studied members of the same group over time. All longitudinal studies face the problem of 'dropout' – some of the children or their parents may refuse to take part or cannot be contacted at later stages of the research. Tizard's original sample of 65 was reduced to 51 at age 8 and to 42 at age 16 – a 35% reduction. This can affect the results, especially if those who drop out are different in important respects from those who remain.

Validity of data Tizard's study was based largely on questionnaires and interviews with nursery staff, parents and teachers. They were asked to make assessments of the children. How valid (true) were these assessments? For example, the assessments made by teachers were probably influenced by the fact that they knew which of their pupils had been raised in the nursery. This knowledge may well have led them to see these children differently.

Time scale Longitudinal studies of children raised in institutions usually stop when the children are teenagers. To fully gauge the effects of privation, the children should be studied throughout their lives. This raises at least two problems. First, the original researchers will be dead before the study ends. Second, in view of the dropout rate in Tizard's study (35% between ages 4½ and 16), how many will be left in the sample when they approach old age?

3.2 Isolated children

Isolated children provide examples of extreme privation. During their early years they have usually been locked away by their parents and isolated from the wider society.

The Czech twins Identical twin boys were born in Czechoslovakia in 1960. Their mother died shortly after their birth. They spent their first 18 months in an institution then went to live with their father and his new wife. She took an instant dislike to them. The twins were shut away in a small, unheated room and kept apart from the rest of the family. The only time they left the room was when they were locked in the cellar as a punishment. They were deprived of proper food, exercise, sunshine and, apart from each other, human companionship.

When they were rescued at the age of 7, they looked like 3-year-olds. They were abnormally small, they could hardly walk because of rickets, they relied mainly on gestures to communicate and could barely talk. At first, they were terrified of the new sights and sounds around them – traffic, television, mechanical toys.

The twins were placed in a residential nursery for preschool children. At age 8, they were placed in the care of two sisters who provided a loving and secure family environment. The twins soon put on weight and learned to walk and talk. At first, they were sent to a school for retarded children. They then went on to primary and secondary schools. By age 14, they were in a class of children who were only 18 months younger than themselves. Their language development was now normal for their age and their IQ, estimated to be 40 when they were discovered, was now around 100. The twins later married and had children and are reported to be enjoying warm and stable relationships (Koluchová, 1972, 1991).

Isabelle Apart from her mother, who was a deaf mute, Isabelle hardly saw anybody until she was 6½. She spent her early years in a darkened room. When she was discovered, she was thought to be deaf and mentally retarded. After considerable loving care and expert help, she developed in leaps and bounds. She learned more quickly than children of her own age and went through several stages of development at an accelerated rate. By the time she finished high school at 16, Isabelle had caught up with her classmates (Davis, 1949).

Genie Some time before she was 2, Genie was locked in a darkened room by her father who thought she was retarded. During the day she was tied to a chair, at night she was tied up in a sleeping bag. Other members of the family were forbidden to speak to her and she was beaten by her father if she made a sound. When she was 13, her mother escaped with her – at which point her father committed suicide. On admission to hospital, Genie weighed 59 lbs, she was unable to walk and the only sounds she made were a few whimpers.

Despite being placed with a family and receiving expert help, Genie's development was limited. She remained in schools for mentally retarded students and though her IQ increased, it was well below normal at age 20. Her use of language was restricted to short phrases such as, 'Father hit arm. Big wood. Genie cry'. Her social behaviour never developed to the point where she could function in the wider society (Curtiss, 1977).

Conclusion It is difficult to draw any firm conclusions from studies of isolated children for the following reasons.

- The cases are few in number, and even fewer are well-documented and researched.

- The experiences of the children, both during their early and later years, vary considerably. For example, the Czech children had each other, Isabelle had her mother – albeit a deaf mute, and Genie had nobody.
- There is no way of knowing whether they were retarded at birth. For example, Genie's backwardness may have been innate (inborn).

However, researchers have drawn the following tentative conclusions from studies of isolated children.

- Extreme isolation, a lack of caregiving and normal social relationships during the early years can severely limit a child's development.
- However, this setback is not always irreversible. Children are not necessarily prisoners of their early childhood experience. In developmental terms, they can catch up as the cases of the Czech twins and Isabelle suggest.
- This indicates that some researchers may have placed too much emphasis on the early years with ideas such as critical and sensitive periods. Studies of isolated children suggest that these periods are not as crucial as was once thought. Effective learning and normal development can occur even if they have not occurred during the early years.

3.3 The outcomes of privation

As with separation, there is no simple, straightforward relationship between privation during the early years and behaviour in later life. Even when children have similar experiences of privation, as in the Tizard study, some are apparently affected by this experience as teenagers, others are not.

Summary

1. Studies of children raised in institutions indicate that privation does not necessarily have harmful effects.
2. The quality of care provided by the institutions has important effects on the child's development.
3. Strong attachment to foster parents can be made after the child leaves the institution. These attachments can be formed after the age of 2.
4. For *some* children raised in institutions, privation does appear to have lasting effects, at least until the age of 16.
5. Extreme isolation can severely restrict a child's development. However, some children can recover from this experience and develop normally.
6. It is difficult to reach firm conclusions from studies of isolated children.
7. The effects of privation can be reversed, modified and changed by a child's experience after the early years.

Clarke & Clarke (1998) point out that early experience represents 'no more than an initial step on the ongoing path of life'. This means that privation is only a first step. Its effects may be modified or changed by later 'steps' in the path of life. This point is illustrated by the studies examined in this unit. They have shown that early experience matters but is not irreversible. Many of the children raised in institutions and even some of those who experienced extreme isolation develop normally, despite their early years of privation.

Activity 3 Isolated children

Item A Changes in IQ scores

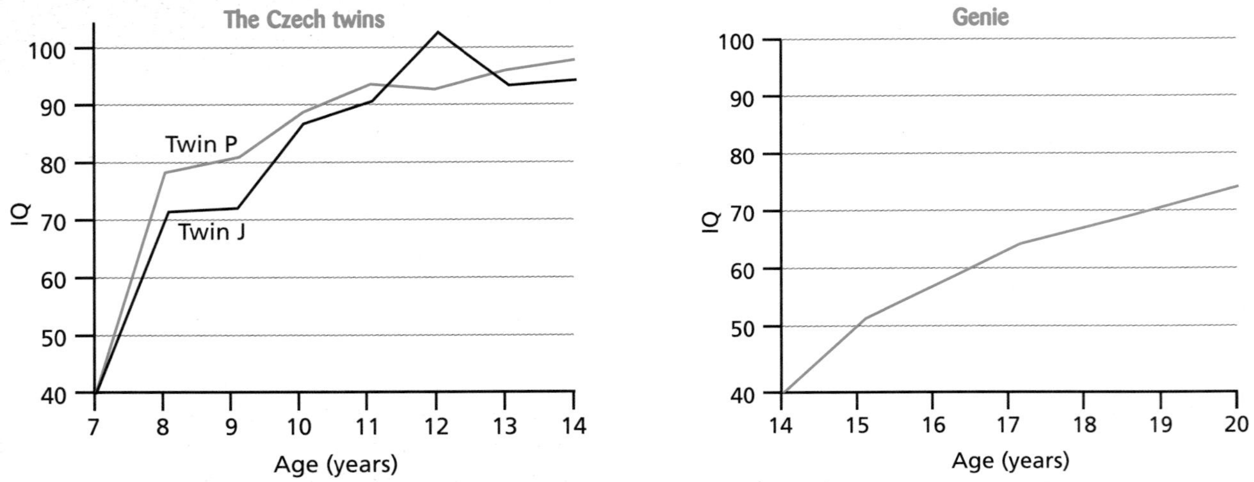

Adapted from Smith et al., 1998

Item B Kamala and Amala

In 1920 two girls were reportedly discovered in a wolf den in Bengal, India. Aged about two and eight years, they were taken to an orphanage where they were looked after by the Reverend J.A.L. Singh and his wife. The young child, Amala, died soon after she arrived at the orphanage, the elder girl, Kamala, remained in the orphanage until 1929 when she too died. Despite the fact that Amala and Kamala were called 'wolf-children' and found in a wolf's den, there is no evidence that they were actually raised by wolves. The Reverend Singh wrote the following description of their behaviour in 1926.

'At the present time Kamala can utter about forty words. She is able to form a few sentences, each sentence containing two, or at the most, three words. She never talks unless spoken to, and when spoken to she may or may not reply. She is obedient to Mrs Singh and myself only. Kamala is possessed of very acute hearing and evidences an exceedingly acute animal-like sense of smell. She can smell meat at a great distance. Never weeps or smiles but has a 'smiling appearance'. Shed a single tear when Amala died and would not leave the place where she lay dead. She is learning very slowly to imitate. Does not now play at all and does not mingle with other children. Once both Amala and Kamala somewhat liked the company of an infant by the name of Benjamin while he was crawling and learning to talk. But one day they gave him such a biting and scratching that the infant was frightened and would never approach the wolf-children again. Amala and Kamala liked the company of Mrs Singh, and Kamala, the surviving one of the pair, is much attached to her. The eyes of the children possessed a peculiar glare, such as that observed in the eyes of dogs or cats in the dark. Up to the present time Kamala sees better at night than during the daytime and seldom sleeps after midnight. The children used to cry or howl in a peculiar voice neither animal nor human. Kamala still makes these noises at times. She is averse to all cleanliness, and serves the calls of nature anywhere, wherever she may happen to be at the time. Used to tear her clothes off. Hence a loin cloth was stitched to her in such a fashion that she could not open or tear it. Kamala used to eat and drink like a dog, lowering her mouth down to the plate, and never used her hands for the purpose of eating or drinking. She would gnaw a big bone on the ground and would rub it at times in order to separate the meat from the bone. At the present time she uses her hands for eating and walks straight on two legs but cannot run at all.'

Kamala and Amala soon after they were brought to the orphanage.

Kamala receiving a biscuit from Mrs Singh

Adapted from Hurd, 1973

Questions

1 a) Briefly summarise the changes in IQ scores shown on the graphs in Item A.

b) Suggest reasons for the differences between the scores of the Czech twins and Genie.

2 Read Item B. Assuming Kamala had not died, do you think she would ever have been ready to enter the wider society? Give reasons for your answer.

References

Amato, P.R. & Keith, B. (1991). Parental divorce and the well-being of children: A meta-analysis. *Psychological Bulletin, 110*, 26-46.

Bilfulco, A., Harris, T. & Brown, G.W. (1992). Mourning or early inadequate care? Re-examining the relationship of maternal loss in childhood with adult depression and anxiety. *Development and Psychopathology, 4*, 433-449.

Bowlby, J. (1946). *Forty-four juvenile thieves.* London: Balliere, Tindall and Cox.

Bowlby, J. (1951). *Maternal care and mental health.* Geneva, Switzerland: World Health Organisation.

Bowlby, J. (1965). *Child care and the growth of love* (2nd ed.). Harmondsworth: Penguin.

Bowlby, J. (1973). *Attachment and loss, vol. 2: Separation.* London: Hogarth.

Cherlin, A.J., Furstenberg, F.F. Jr., Chase-Lonsdale, P.L., Kiernan, K.E., Robins, P.K., Morrison, D.R. & Teitler, J.O. (1991). Longitudinal studies of effects of divorce on children in Great Britain and the United States. *Science, 252*, 1386-1389.

Clarke, A.M. & Clarke, A.D.B. (1976). *Early experience: Myth and evidence.* London: Open Books.

Clarke, A.M. & Clarke, A.D.B. (1998). Early experience and the life path. *The Psychologist, 11*, 433-436.

Cummings, E.M. (1994). Marital conflict and children's functioning. *Social Development, 3*, 16-36.

Curtiss, S. (1977). *Genie: A psycholinguistic study of modern-day 'wild child'.* New York: Academic Press.

Davis, K. (1949). *Human society.* New York: Macmillan.

Dennis, W. (1973). *Children of the crèche.* New York: Appleton-Century-Crofts.

Douglas, J.W.B. (1975). Early hospital admissions and later disturbances of behaviour and learning. *Developmental Medicine and Child Neurology, 17*, 456-480.

Fagin, C.M.R.N. (1966). *The effects of maternal attendance during hospitalisation on the post-hospital behaviour of young children: A comparative study.* Philadelphia: Davis.

Goldfarb, W. (1943). The effects of early institutional care on adolescent personality. *Journal of Experimental Education, 12*, 106-129.

Heinicke, C.M. & Westheimer, I.J. (1965). *Brief separations.* London: Longman.

Hodges, J & Tizard, B. (1989). Social and family relationships of ex-institutional adolescents. *Journal of Child Psychology and Psychiatry, 30*, 77-97.

Hurd, G. (Ed.). (1973). *Human societies: An introduction to sociology.* London: Routledge & Kegan Paul.

Kagan, J. (1976). Resilience and continuity in psychological development. In A.M. Clarke and A.D.B. Clarke (Eds.), *Early experience: Myth and evidence.* New York: Free Press.

Koluchová, J. (1972). Severe deprivation in twins: A case study. *Journal of Child Psychology and Psychiatry, 13*, 107-114.

Koluchová, J. (1991). Severely deprived twins after twenty-two years' observation. *Studia Psychologica, 33*, 23-28.

Kotelchuk, M. (1976). The infant's relationship to the father: Experimental evidence. In M.E. Lamb (Ed.), *The role of the father in child development.* New York: Wiley.

Lancaster, T. & Lancaster, S. (1993). *The era of the Second World War.* Ormskirk: Causeway.

Lynn, V. (1989). *We'll meet again.* London: Sidgwick & Jackson.

Maccoby, E.E. (1980). *Social development : Psychological growth and the parent child relationship.* New York: Harcourt Brace Jovanovich.

Quinton, D. & Rutter, M. (1976). Early hospital admissions and later disturbances of behaviour. *Developmental Medicine and Child Neurology, 18*, 447-459.

Richards, M.P.M. (1994). The international year of the family: Family research. *The Psychologist, 8*, 17-24.

Ross, G., Kagan, J., Zelazo, P. & Kotelchuk, M. (1975). Separation protest in infants in home and laboratory. *Developmental Psychology, 11*, 256-7.

Rutter, M. (1981). *Maternal deprivation reassessed.* (2nd ed.). Harmondsworth: Penguin.

Rutter, M., Graham, P., Chadwick, D.F.D. & Yule, W. (1976). Adolescent turmoil: Fact or fiction. *Journal of Child Psychology and Psychiatry, 17*, 35-56.

Schaffer, H.R. (1996). *Social development.* Oxford: Blackwell.

Skeels, H.M. (1966). Adult status of children with contrasting early life experiences: A follow-up study. *Monographs of the Society for Research in Child Development, 31*, no. 3.

Skodak, M. & Skeels, H.M. (1945). A follow-up study of children in adoptive homes. *Journal of Genetic Psychology, 66*, 21-58.

Smith, P.K., Cowie, H. & Blades, M. (1998). *Understanding children's development* (3rd ed.). Oxford: Blackwell.

Spitz, R.A. & Wolf, K.M. (1946). Anaclitic depression. *Psychoanalytic Study of the Child, 2*, 313-342.

Stacey, M., Dearden, R., Pill, R. & Robinson, D. (1970). *Hospitals, children and their families: The report of a pilot study.* London: Routledge & Kegan Paul.

Wicks, B. *No time to wave goodbye.* London: Bloomsbury.

Zimbardo, P.G., McDermott, M., Jansz, J. & Metaal, N. (1995). *Psychology: A European text.* London: Harper Collins.

6 Day care

Introduction

The demand for day care – nurseries, play groups and childminders – is growing rapidly in Western societies. This is due mainly to changing attitudes – in particular views of the role of mothers – and the increasing numbers of women entering the labour force. In the United Kingdom in 1971, just over 50% of women in the 25 to 44 age group were economically active – either in work or seeking work. By 1997, this figure had risen to over 75%. In 1998, 60% of married or cohabiting women (living with a partner but not married) with preschool children were economically active compared to 36% of lone mothers with preschool children. A survey by the Department of Education revealed that 4 out of 5 non-working mothers would take up paid employment if they could find and afford adequate day care (*Social Trends*, 1999).

Day care is now at the forefront of British government policy. The Labour government's National Childcare Strategy aims to provide good quality, affordable day care for children up to 14 years of age.

This chapter looks at the possible effects of day care on children.

Chapter summary

- **Unit 1 looks at the variation in children's day care experience.**
- **Unit 2 examines research into the possible effects of day care on attachment, cognitive development and social development.**

Unit 1 Variation in day care

KEY ISSUES

1. **How might variations in day care affect children?**
2. **Why does this make it difficult to generalise about the effects of day care?**

Varieties of day care The type of day care available for children varies considerably. It ranges from playgroups, usually organised by parents, to childminders, to day nurseries. There is also variation within each type. Playgroups may, as their name suggests, focus on play. However, they may also involve an educational component. Stories may be read to the children, educational toys provided, and children may be taught the alphabet and how to write the letters.

Similar variation exists in nurseries. Some are organised along the lines of reception classes in primary schools with an emphasis on preparation for full-time education. Others may be little different from playschools.

Similarly, childminders vary in terms of what they do with the children in their care and how many children they look after.

Quality of day care The quality of day varies enormously. For example, in day nurseries the number of staff to children varies as does their commitment to and involvement with the children. The quality of the buildings, equipment and toys also varies.

Researchers suggest that the following factors are found in high quality day care.

- A rich, varied and stimulating environment
- Small groups, particularly for infants
- A variety of activities, some structured, some unstructured
- Qualified staff who are responsive to children.

Many day nurseries fall short of these standards. For example, one survey in the USA described 86% of day nurseries as 'poor or mediocre', with only 14% described as 'good' (Cost, Quality and Outcomes Study Team, 1995).

Studies of childminding indicate similar variations in quality. A study of 66 childminders in London found that many were highly competent, but some provided little love, attention or stimulation for the children in their care (Mayall & Petrie, 1983).

Age and time in day care Children's experience of day care is affected by the age at which they enter day care – for example, before the age of one or later – and how long they spend in day care – how many hours a day, how many days a week, how many months or years. Their experience may also be affected by how often their day care is changed – for example from childminder to nursery, or from one childminder to another.

Numbers in childcare As Table 1 shows, the number of children in day care has grown rapidly. In England and Wales, the number of day care places for children under 8 rose from 648,000 in 1987 to 998,000 in 1997. This does not include unregistered childminders – those who are not registered with (and regularly inspected by) the local authority (*Social Trends*, 1999).

Problems with the evidence

As the previous section indicates, there are wide variations in the type of day care, the quality of day care, the age at which children enter day care, the length of time they spend there and the number of times their day care provision changes. All these factors will have an effect on the child's day care experience. Because of these variations, any conclusions about the effects of day care on children must be regarded with caution. Researchers must take great care about generalising from particular studies.

In addition, a number of other factors must be taken into account. They include:

- **The social background of the children** – for example, their social class and ethnicity. Parents from low-income families may be able to afford only the least expensive day care which may be the lowest quality care. As a result, the effects of day care on children may vary from rich to poor.
- **Relationships within the family** – children's response to day care may reflect relationships within the family rather than day care itself. For example, if relationships between their parents are strained, then this may result in a negative experience of day care.

Table 1 Day care places for children

England & Wales	*Thousands* 1987	1997
Day nurseries		
Local authority provided	29	20
Registered	32	180
Non-registered	1	2
All day nursery places	62	202
Childminders		
Local authority provided	2	4
Other registered	152	379
All childminder places	154	383
Playgroups		
Local authority provided	3	2
Registered	423	408
Non-registered	7	3
All playgroup places	433	413

Adapted from Social Trends, 1999

- **Individual differences** – children are different, their personalities vary. Some may benefit more from day care than others. For example, children who are shy and unsociable may find day nurseries threatening.

Most of the research on day care has been conducted in the USA. And much of this research has been conducted in day care centres attached to universities. These centres are not typical. They are usually of high quality and those who use them – the university staff – have high status, well-paid jobs. As a result, their children are hardly representative of the day care population as a whole. Again, these findings and, in particular, any generalisations from them, must be treated with caution (Howes & Olenick, 1986).

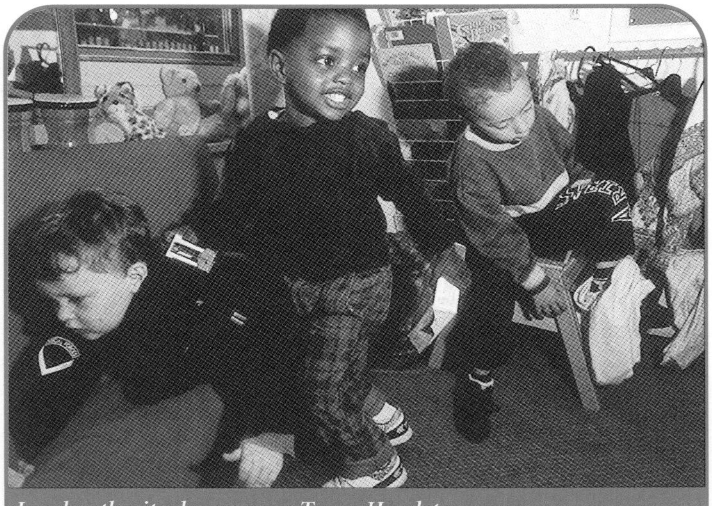

Local authority day nursery, Tower Hamlets

Playgroup for under 4s

Key terms

Day care *The care of children during the day outside the family unit.*

Day nurseries *Organisations set up to care for preschool children during the day. They usually employ qualified staff.*

Childminders *Individuals who take care of one or more preschool children.*

Playgroups *Voluntary groups organised and run by parents to take care of children.*

Individual differences *Differences in personality and characteristics between people.*

Summary

1. There are wide variations in the type and quality of day care, the age at which children enter day care, the length of time they spend there, and the number of times their day care provision changes.
2. In addition to these factors, the children's social background, relationships within the family, and individual differences will affect their experience of day care.
3. In view of the above factors, it is difficult to generalise about the effect of day care on children. Any conclusions must be treated with caution.

Unit 2 The effects of day care

KEY ISSUES

1. **What effect might day care have on attachment?**
2. **What effect might day care have on cognitive development?**
3. **What effect might day care have on social development?**

2.1 Day care and attachment

What effect does day care have on the children's attachment to their parents?

As outlined in Chapter 4, there was concern, particularly during the 1950s and 1960s, that temporary separations from the main caregiver during infancy could lead to insecure attachments. And this insecurity may lead to long-term psychological harm. However, by the 1980s most researchers believed that good quality day care had no negative effects on attachment.

In the late 1980's, some researchers had a change of mind. In the USA, Belsky and Rovine (1988) analysed the results of five studies which had measured attachment security using the Strange Situation (see pp 53-55). They claimed that for children under the age of one, day care for over 20 hours a week increased the risk of insecure attachments. Data from the five studies indicated there was a 43% chance of insecure attachment when infants were in day care for over 20 hours a week compared with 26% for those with no day care or less than 20 hours. After the age of one, day care appeared to have no negative effects on the security of the child's attachment.

Other researchers have questioned these findings. Clarke-Stewart (1989) makes the following points.

- First, the higher levels of insecure attachment may have more to do with the mothers than day care as such. Mothers who place their children in day care as infants may find child care particularly difficult and frustrating. This, rather than the day care experience, may result in less secure attachment.
- Second, it is questionable whether insecure attachments lead to more general emotional insecurity in the child as Belsky and Rovine (1988) suggested.
- Third, is the Strange Situation a valid measure of attachment security? The method was developed mainly using infants who had been raised without regular separation from their mothers. It may not be a true measure of attachment for children with working mothers since those children experience regular, everyday separations.

Some researchers argue that day care does not pose a serious threat to attachment. Others argue that there are so many factors involved, there is insufficient evidence to blame day care. In their view, further research is needed before reaching any firm conclusions.

2.2 Day care and cognitive development

Cognitive development refers to intellectual growth from infancy to adulthood. It refers to thinking, reasoning, problem solving, language skills and mathematical skills.

The traditional view is that good quality day care, particularly if it has an educational component, benefits the cognitive development of working-class children, but has little effect on middle-class children. According to this view, middle-class parents are more likely to read to their children, provide them with educational toys, play with them, talk to them at greater length, and teach them to perform a wider variety of tasks. As a result, day care has little to add.

However, a number of studies suggest that the cognitive

development of children from all social classes may benefit from day care. For example, a study of 146 Swedish children compared children in day nurseries with those looked after by a childminder and those who remained at home. When these children were assessed at the age of 8, those who had been in day nurseries were consistently better than the other groups on tests of verbal and mathematical ability. Moreover, the longer the children had been in day care, the higher their scores. Childminding came out worst (Broberg et al., 1997).

Similar findings come from an American study based on 150 children, aged 2-4 years. Those who attended day nurseries had better intellectual development then those placed with childminders or those remaining at home (Clarke-Stewart, 1991).

The results of other studies are not so straightforward. An American study, based on a sample of 1000 3-4 year olds, found that white (but *not* black) children who began day care before the age of one had the lowest vocabulary scores whatever their social class. Starting day care after the age of one appeared to have no effect (Baydar & Brooks-Gunn, 1991). Rather different results came from another American study. Children from low-income families who started day care before the age of one had higher reading and maths scores when they started school than similar children who stayed with their mothers. However, middle-class children who started day care before the age of one had lower scores than middle-class children who spent their preschool years at home (Caughy et al., 1994).

Interpreting the results The above findings are not straightforward. At times they appear contradictory. This may result from a number of factors.

- The type of day care provision varies both between countries and within countries.
- Children enter day care at different ages.
- They are assessed at different ages, using different tests.
- Samples vary in size and composition – for example in the social background of the children in each sample.
- The quality of day care can vary considerably.

Helen Bee (1997) suggests that this last point may explain many of the differences between research findings. In her words, 'When the day-care setting for a child provides *more* enrichment that the child would normally receive at home, we see some beneficial cognitive effects. When day care is less stimulating that the child's home care would have been, it has negative effects.' However, Bee admits that there is insufficient evidence to support this explanation – it therefore remains a suggestion.

Head Start

This section looks briefly at preschool day centres specifically designed to improve cognitive development. It focuses on the Head Start programmes in the USA where much of the research on preschool education has been conducted.

Operation Head Start was launched in the USA in the 1960s. It was a massive programme of preschool education designed for children from low-income families. These children were failing in droves in the school system. Their failure was seen to result from a lack of stimulation and 'richness' in their family lives. They were labelled as 'culturally deprived' – deprived of many of the things middle-class children received in their preschool years such as a wide vocabulary. Preschool education was seen as a way of compensating for this so-called 'deficiency' in their home background. It would provide additional stimulation, it would enrich their lives, boost their cognitive development and give them a 'head start' when they began elementary (primary) school. Similar thinking lay behind British programmes of preschool compensatory education which began in the late 1960s in low-income areas.

Children usually entered the Head Start programme at the age of 3 or 4. A large amount of research was conducted to examine the effectiveness of Head Start. A summary of the research findings indicates the following (Zigler & Styfco, 1993).

Children typically gain around 10 IQ points after a year of Head Start. This gain usually disappears within a few years of starting elementary school. But there are some advantages. Children who went through the programme were less likely to be placed in special education classes, they appeared to adjust better to the school environment and were more likely to obtain a high school certificate. As adults, they were less likely to be unemployed, to have a criminal record and to depend on welfare (Barnett, 1993).

In terms of cognitive development, as measured by IQ tests, reading and maths tests, it appears that unless preschool programmes are followed on by further special programmes throughout the child's educational career, then the initial gains provided by Head Start largely disappear (Cole & Cole, 1996).

2.3 Day care and social development

Social development refers to the development of the child's relationships with other people. It is concerned with the process by which the child becomes a part of the wider society while, at the same time, becomes a separate and distinct individual. This involves learning and acting in terms of the norms – the accepted ways of behaving – which operate in the wider society, and also learning to become a relatively independent person. Psychologists tend to have the following picture of the socially well-adjusted child. This child gets on with other people and stands on their own two feet. In other words, they have developed relationship skills and a certain level of independence.

A large body of research, mainly from the USA, has been concerned with how day care affects children's social development. To some extent the findings are contradictory. Some studies indicate that day care has positive effects on social development. Children who attend day centres appear to be more independent and self-sufficient, they cope better with new situations, they are more popular with their peers (children of the same age), they are more cooperative and helpful both with other children and their parents. In general, their social skills and their knowledge of the wider social world are more developed than children who do not attend day care centres.

Other studies point to the negative effects of day care on social development. These studies suggest that children who attend day care centres are more aggressive and less likely to comply with the requests and follow the instructions of their parents and teachers. It is important not to overstate this level of aggression – it is well within the range found in children in general (Cole & Cole, 1996).

Interpreting the results Why are the findings apparently contradictory? A number of reasons have been suggested.

- The effect of day care on social development may depend on the quality of day care. A number of researchers have argued that if day care is well organised, with stimulating and clearly structured tasks, then this will contribute to the child's social development. Children will tend to be aggressive in an unstimulating and unstructured environment (Clarke-Stewart et al., 1994).
- Assessing children's aggression involves a difficult judgement. Behaviour seen as aggressive by one person may be seen as indicating independence by another. Children who want to do things their way may be seen as either aggressive or independent (Clarke-Stewart, 1989).
- Even if some children in day care are more aggressive, this may have nothing to do with day care as such. Children who are aggressive may be more likely to be placed in day care because their parents find them difficult to handle. Alternatively, their aggression may stem from their family relationships. If both parents are in full-time employment, they may well be under stress, especially with one or more preschool children. In some cases, it may be stress within the family unit, rather than day care, that results in aggressive children (Clarke-Stewart, 1989).

Conclusion Most researchers believe that high quality day care is beneficial for children's social development. The child is exposed to a wider social world and most children learn to get along with larger groups of people. In doing so, they develop a wider range of social skills and greater independence from the family unit.

Culture and day care

The material on day care presented in this chapter is based on research conducted in Western Europe and, particularly, in the USA. To what extent do these findings apply to all cultures?

Culture refers to the learned, shared behaviour of members of a society. It is the 'way of life' of people in society. It includes the norms (accepted and expected ways of behaving), the values (what people consider important and worthwhile), the attitudes (the opinions and ways of thinking), and the beliefs (what people hold to be true), which are generally shared by members of society.

Culture varies from society to society. To what extent will this affect day care?

The USA and Japan A comparison of nursery schools in the USA and Japan indicates the importance of culture (Tobin et al., 1989). The American teachers were shown a video of a Japanese school and the Japanese teachers a video of an American school. In the Japanese classrooms there were 30 children and one teacher, in the American classrooms 18 children with two teachers. Both the Americans and the Japanese were surprised by the size of the other's classes. The Japanese felt that the small class sizes would be harmful to the children's social development. In the words of one teacher, children 'need to have the experience of being in a large group in order to learn to relate to lots of children in lots of kinds of situations'.

The American teachers emphasised the importance of independence, self-reliance and self-sufficiency. This reflected the importance placed on individualism in American culture. The Japanese teachers disapproved of this emphasis. In the words of one Japanese teacher, 'a child's humanity is realised most fully not so much on his ability to be independent from the group as his ability to cooperate and feel part of the group'.

When children misbehaved and when there were arguments and fights, American teachers tended to intervene, taking the children on one side and discussing the problem. To the Japanese, 'that is a bit too heavy, too

Key terms

Cognitive development *Intellectual growth from infancy to adulthood. The development of reasoning and problem-solving skills.*

Operation Head Start *A programme of preschool education for children from low-income families, begun in the 1960s in the USA.*

Compensatory education *Education designed to make up or compensate for what is seen as lacking in low-income children's social background.*

Social development *The development of the child's relationship with other people. The growth of social skills and, in Western Europe and particularly in the USA, independence and self-reliance.*

Culture *The learned, shared behaviour of members of society. It includes shared norms, values, attitudes and beliefs.*

adult-like, too severe and controlled for young children'. They preferred to let the children settle disputes and solve problems amongst themselves without what they saw as adult interference.

This is an important study. It shows that the way day care is organised reflects, to some extent, the culture of society. It shows that social development means different things in different cultures. The Japanese and American teachers encouraged behaviour which was valued in their particular cultures. It is important to realise that many aspects of day care in our society reflect the norms and values of our culture. It follows that what we consider high quality day care cannot automatically be applied across the board to all cultures.

Summary

1. In the 1950s and 1960s, there was concern that temporary separations from the main caregiver during infancy could lead to insecure attachments.

2. By the 1980s, most researchers believed that high quality day care had no negative effects on attachment.

3. In the late 1980s, some researchers argued that day care for over 20 hours a week before the age of one could lead to insecure attachments. Other researchers questioned this view.

4. Research findings on the effect of day care on cognitive development vary.
   - Some research indicates that high quality day care benefits cognitive development in all children.
   - Other research suggests that only certain children benefit from day care. For some, day care may hold back their cognitive development.

   A number of factors may account for the different findings. They include the quality of day care, the age at which children enter day care, and the social background of the children.

5. Research suggests that day care can have positive effects – for example, the development of social skills – and negative effects – for example, aggressiveness – on children's social development.

6. The organisation of day care and the behaviour encouraged by the staff reflects the culture of society.

References

Barnett, W.S. (1993). Benefit-cost analysis of preschool education: Findings from a 25-year follow-up. *American Journal of Orthopsychiatry, 63*, 500-508.

Baydar, N. & Brooks-Gunn, J. (1991). Effects of maternal employment and child-care arrangements on preschoolers' cognitive and behavioural outcomes: Evidence from the children of the National Longitudinal Survey of Youth. *Developmental Psychology, 27*, 932-945.

Bee, H. (1997). *The developing child* (8th ed.). New York: Longman.

Belsky, J. & Rovine, M. (1988). Nonmaternal care in the first year of life and the security of infant-parent attachment. *Child Development, 59*, 157-167.

Caughy, M.O., DiPietro, J.A. & Strobino, D.M. (1994). Day-care participation as a protective factor in the cognitive development of low-income children. *Child Development, 65*, 457-471.

Clarke-Stewart, K.A. (1989). Infant day care: Maligned or malignant? *American Psychologist, 44*, 266-273.

Clarke-Stewart, K.A. (1991). A home is not a school. *Journal of Social Issues, 47*, 105-123.

Clarke-Stewart, K.A., Gruber, C.P. & Fitzgerald, L.M. (1994). *Children at home and in day care.* Hillsdale, NJ: Erlbaum.

Cole, M. & Cole, S.R. (1996). *The development of children* (3rd ed.). New York: W.H. Freeman.

Cost, Quality, & Child Outcomes Study Team (1995). *Cost, quality, and child outcomes in child care centres, executive summary* (2nd ed.). Denver: Economics Department, University of Colorado at Denver.

Howes, C. & Olenick, M. (1986). Family and childcare influences on toddlers' compliance. *Child Development, 57*, 202-216.

Mayall B. & Petrie, P. (1983). *Childminding and day nurseries: What kind of care?* London: Heinemann Educational Books.

Social Trends (1999). London: The Stationery Office.

Tobin, J.J., Wu, D.Y.H. & Davison, D.H. (1989). *Preschool in three cultures: Japan, China, and the United States.* New Haven: Yale University Press.

Zigler, E. & Styfco, S.J. (1993). Using research and theory to justify and inform Head Start expansion. *Social Policy Report, Society for Research in Child Development, 7*, 1-21.

7 Stress as a bodily response

Introduction

A headteacher sits at her desk. The day had started badly. Her new car had broken down and she was forced to walk the last two miles of her journey to work, arriving hot and flustered. She is working through the school accounts – they don't balance. Constant interruptions make matters worse. The Head of Psychology walks in demanding money for textbooks which the school can't afford. A parent phones worried about his son's progress in mathematics. Just as she returns to the school accounts, her secretary walks in with a pile of urgent papers to sign. By this time, the headteacher is under stress. Her pulse is racing, she is sweating and her stomach feels as though it is in a tight knot.

This example illustrates several aspects of stress. First, stress is often caused by external events, largely outside a person's control. Second, stress affects a person's internal state, for example it can lead to an increase in heart rate. Third, stress is usually seen as a negative experience.

This chapter is mainly concerned with the physiological aspects of stress, with stress as a bodily response.

Chapter summary

- **Unit 1 outlines different views of stress.**
- **Unit 2 looks at the relationship between the brain and the nervous system and stress.**
- **Unit 3 looks at the effects of short-term and long-term stress on the body.**
- **Unit 4 discusses the relationship between stress and the immune system.**
- **Unit 5 examines the relationship between stress and coronary heart disease.**

Unit 1 Defining stress

KEY ISSUES

1. **What are the different views of stress?**
2. **Can stress have both negative and positive effects?**
3. **What is the relationship between arousal and stress?**

1.1 Views of stress

Stress as an external stimulus

The term stress was first used in physics. In this sense, it refers to the application of an outside or external force which places strain on an object. For example, a large weight is hung on a metal rod. The rod is placed under stress by the weight, bends, and may eventually break. The weight acted as a *stressor*.

Similar definitions of stress are used in psychology. For example, stress can be seen as an external stimulus which places a strain on the individual (a stimulus is anything that affects an individual's behaviour). Examples of stressful external stimuli or stressors include taking an exam, moving house, divorce and a new job. In each case, these examples can be seen as external forces which place strain on the individual and which might, like the force on the metal rod, cause them to 'snap'.

Stress as an internal response

Other approaches see stress as an internal response to external stressors. In this sense, stress is something happening *inside* the person rather than an *outside* force acting on the person. It is the psychological and physiological changes produced by a stressor. These changes are known as the *stress response*.

Psychological aspects of the stress response may include a state of tension involving emotions such as fear, anxiety and anger. Examples of physiological aspects of the stress response include an increase in heart rate and the release of sugar into the bloodstream. These changes increase alertness and energy. If the stressor is prolonged, as in the case of long-term unemployment, or if there are repeated stressors, one after the other, then the stress response can be long lasting and harmful. It may lead to illness or even death.

Stress as a transaction

The first approach to stress focuses on the stressor, the external stimulus which places a strain on the individual. The second approach focuses on the stress response, the individual's internal reaction to a stressor. A third view sees stress as a *transaction* between the individual and their environment. From this point of view, stress is seen in terms of the meanings people give to both their environment and their ability to cope with it. In this respect, an event only becomes a stressor when a person perceives or interprets it as such. For example, one person may see a divorce as a calamity, another person may see it as a welcome release and an opportunity for a fresh start. In the first case divorce will probably be experienced as a stressor, in the second case, as a relief.

As well as giving meanings to events, people also assess their ability to cope with those events. Faced with redundancy, one person may feel they cannot cope and this may lead to a stress response. Another person may feel they can cope quite adequately and, as a result, take things in their stride.

Stress as a transaction sees stressors and the stress response resulting from the meanings and interpretations people give both to events and their ability to cope with those events. If they feel they cannot cope, then they experience the psychological and physiological aspects of the stress response (Cox, 1978).

1.2 Negative and positive aspects of stress

Approaches which focus on the stress response tend to see stress as a negative and harmful state. Stress can threaten psychological and physical wellbeing, it can result in illness and even death. For example, Lazurus and Folkman (1984) define stress as 'the negative emotional and physiological process that occurs as individuals try to adjust to or deal with environmental circumstances that disrupt, or threaten to disrupt, their daily functioning'.

This view of stress as harmful is particularly appropriate for severe and prolonged stress. However, in the short term, moderate levels of stress 'can be stimulating, motivating and desirable' (Bernstein et al., 1997). Without stress life would have no challenges – there would be no progress, no striving to achieve higher standards. Overcoming challenges is essential for a species' adaptation and survival and this involves the positive use of stress.

1.3 Arousal and the fight-or-fight response

Arousal The idea of arousal is central to many definitions of stress. Stress is seen to involve mental and physical arousal. This means the brain and the body are in a state of heightened alertness. There is a readiness for action, a readiness to respond mentally and physically to a stressor. High levels of arousal usually accompany highly emotional states – fear, anger, excitement, apprehension. They also involve physiological changes such as a rise in the heart rate which increases energy and alertness.

The fight-or-flight response Walter Cannon's (1932) idea of the fight-or-flight response provides an understanding of the relationship between arousal and stress. Cannon saw the fight-or-flight response as a reaction to stressors. He argued that it is a biologically-based survival mechanism which evolved in humans and other animals. The basis of his idea is summed up in the following example. Faced with a predator which threatened their life, human beings had two main options – fight or flight. They could either stand their ground, defend themselves and kill or ward off the predator or they could escape by flight – running away or climbing to safety. Their chances of survival would be improved if

Key terms

Stress *There are three main ways of looking at stress. As:*

1. *An external stimulus which places a strain on the individual.*
2. *An internal state of psychological and physiological change in response to a stressor.*
3. *A transaction between the individual and their environment. This transaction results in a stress response if the individual believes they cannot cope with the demands they see placed upon them.*

Stressor *Something which causes stress.*

Stress response *The psychological and/or physiological response to a stressor.*

Arousal *A heightened state of mental and physical alertness. A readiness to respond.*

Fight-or-flight response *A response to a situation seen as a threat or an emergency. It involves physiological changes which prepare the body for rapid activity.*

Summary

1. Approaches to stress tend to focus on a) the stressor and the strain it places on the individual, b) the response to that stressor, in other words the stress response, c) the way the individual perceives both a possible stressor and their ability to cope with it.
2. The effects of stress can be positive or negative. Stress can be used positively to overcome a challenge. It can also have negative effects leading to illness and even death.
3. Arousal is a major part of the stress response.
4. The fight-or-flight response sees stress as a biologically-based survival mechanism which evolved to prepare the body for rapid activity.

their minds and bodies changed in ways which increased their ability to fight or flee. The short-term physiological aspects of the stress response do just this.

In response to a stressor, chemicals are released in the brain and the body producing the following physiological changes. The heart rate accelerates increasing the blood pumped round the body and brain. Sugar is released from the liver for extra energy and muscle strength. Saliva and mucus dry up increasing the size of air passages to the lungs. Breathing deepens which increases the oxygen in the blood. These and other physiological changes increase energy and alertness in preparation for a rapid response to a threat.

Activity 1 Stress and stressors

Item A Stressors

Moving house

Taking an examination

Item B Positive stress

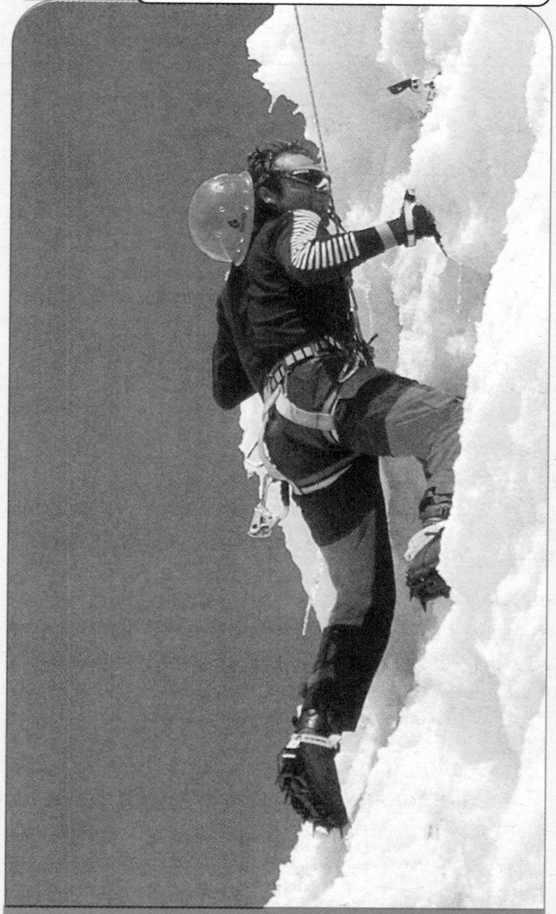

Mountain climbing

Item C Homo erectus

Homo erectus, an ancestor of homo sapiens, appeared around 1.3 million years ago and, judging from the fossil remains, evolved in Africa and spread across Europe and Asia. Homo erectus was a hunter. At one site in southwestern Kenya archaeologists found the bones of over 50 adult baboons, apparently ambushed and clubbed or stoned to death by homo erectus hunters. Baboons are big-boned, formidable creatures with long, sharp canine teeth. The males are about the size of a man. At a site 100 miles northeast of Madrid in Spain, archaeologists have managed to reconstruct an elephant hunt which took place about 400,000 years ago. The hunters set fire to dry summer grass and stampeded the herd into a bog. They rushed in jabbing the elephants with spears and beating them with rocks while attempting to avoid flailing trunks and sharp tusks. At times the hunters could become the hunted. The bones of predators, such as sabre-toothed big cats, have been found at a number of homo erectus sites.

Adapted from E. White and D. Brown, 1973

Questions

1 Re-read the description of the headteacher in the introduction. Which parts illustrate a) the idea of stress as an external stimulus; b) the idea of stress as an internal response?

2 Use the pictures in Item A to illustrate the view of stress as a transaction.

3 With reference to Item B, suggest how the stress response can have a positive effect.

4 Hunting has been a major source of food for humans for 99% of their existence. Using information from Item C, suggest how and why the fight-or-flight response may have evolved.

Unit 2 The nervous system

KEY ISSUES

1. **What is the nervous system?**
2. **How does the nervous system respond to stressors?**
3. **What effects does this response have on bodily functions?**

This unit introduces the idea of the *nervous system* as the biological control system that organises behaviour. The way people see, hear, dream, remember, plan, think and act is controlled by the nervous system, especially by the brain.

2.1 Stress and the nervous system

Brain processes are involved in every aspect of stress behaviour from interpreting an event as a stressor to organising and directing stress responses. The following summarises some of the brain processes that are involved.

- The brain receives information from the outside world through the senses – sight, hearing, smell, touch and taste.
- This information is processed – organised, interpreted and given meaning.
- Processing draws on memory – past experience and knowledge.
- Decisions are made about how to respond to incoming information.
- On the basis of these decisions, the brain sends output signals to muscles and organs to bring about responses.
- Responses include bodily movements such as running, reaching, gesturing and speaking, and physiological changes within the body, such as speeding or slowing the heart rate.

The following examples indicate the importance of the brain in stress behaviour. On a visit to the zoo, you see a lion pacing up and down its cage. On a safari holiday in Africa, a lion comes charging towards you. All the above brain processes are involved in interpreting and directing responses to these events. In the first example, you would be unlikely to see the situation as dangerous and simply walk on by. In the second example, you would, in all likelihood, interpret the event as a stressor and make an appropriate stress response which would involve physiological changes and activity – in all probability, flight.

Both the interpretation of an event as a stressor and the activation of the stress response are directed by the nervous system. An understanding of stress therefore requires an understanding of how the nervous system works.

2.2 Neurons

The nervous system is composed of a huge number of nerve cells, known as *neurons*. Neurons are the basic building blocks of the nervous system. They operate together, processing information and transferring information from one neuron to another, thereby organising our behaviour. Neurons carry information from the eyes, ears, skin and other senses to the brain. They form the connections within the brain that transfer information to memory, access information from memory, and produce output signals to control responses.

There are 10,000,000,000 neurons in the brain – more than the number of stars in our universe. In one region of the brain, a group of neurons may process visual information from the eyes, in another, auditory information from the ears. In other regions, groups of neurons are involved in such things as memory, planning behaviour, organising movements and gestures, and speaking.

Neurons are extremely small, but they can be seen under a microscope. They vary in appearance. A typical neuron is shown in Figure 1. It consists of:

- a *cell body* or *soma*, which has *dendrites* extending from it – this is the receiving and information processing part of the neuron
- an *axon* which carries information in the form of small electrical signals
- *synaptic terminals* which are the points at which these electrical signals can be transferred to other neurons.

Figure 1 A Neuron

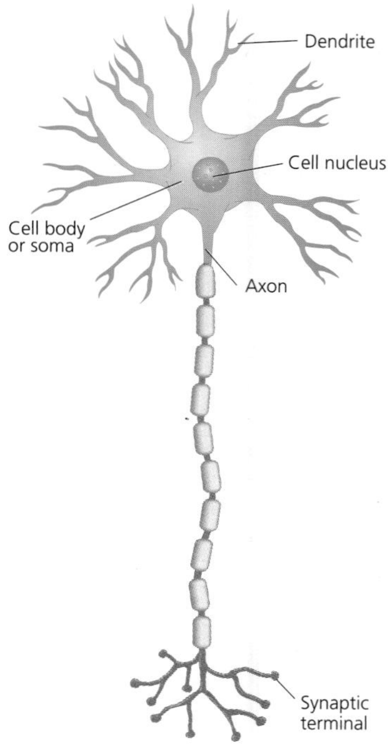

Figure 2 The transmission process

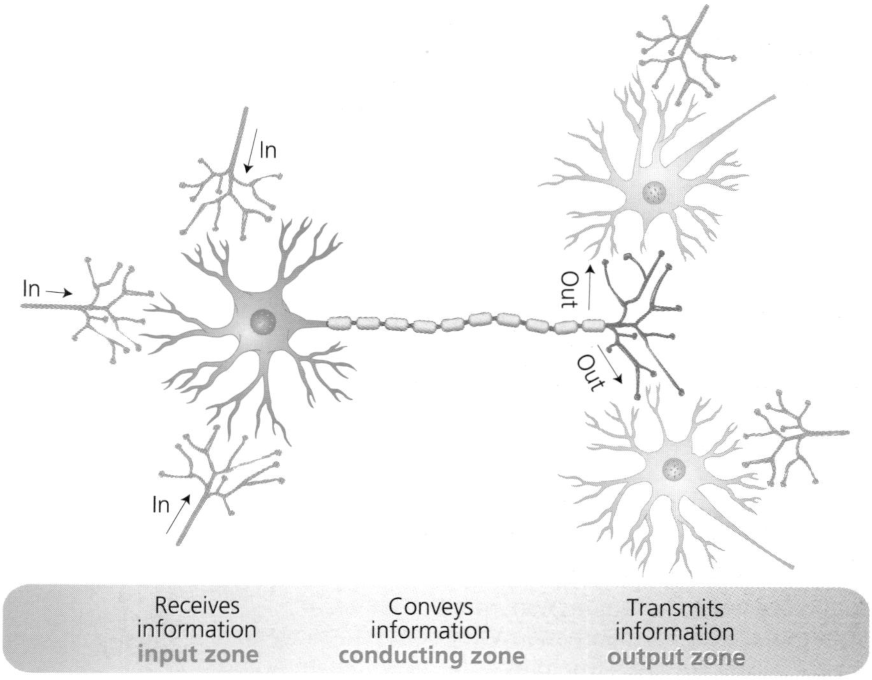

Neurotransmitters

Communication between neurons is achieved by the release of chemicals known as *neurotransmitters*. Neurotransmitters are released from the synaptic terminals of the sending neuron and picked up by the surface of the receiving neuron (see Figure 2). The receiving neuron has special receptors on the dendrites and the cell body to which the neurotransmitter molecules attach. The neurotransmitter molecules, by locking on to the receptors, influence the electrical activity of the receiving neuron, making it more (or sometimes, less) likely to send signals itself. As we shall see, certain neurotransmitters are directly involved in the stress response.

Key terms

Nervous system *The biological control system that organises behaviour.*

Neuron *The main processing unit within the nervous system. It passes information from one place to another, communicating with other neurons via chemical transmission.*

Neurotransmitter *A chemical used to communicate between neurons.*

Cerebral cortex *The cortex is the surface of the brain where higher processing – thinking and problem solving – takes place.*

2.3 The brain

The brain is the centre of all intelligent processing in the nervous system. It is a large, complex organ in which pathways of neurons transport information from one region to another. The surface of the human brain is called the *cerebral cortex* (see Figure 3). This is where a lot of higher processing takes place – where we think and process information. It is within the cortex that information from the senses is interpreted as stressors.

Figure 3 The surface of the human brain

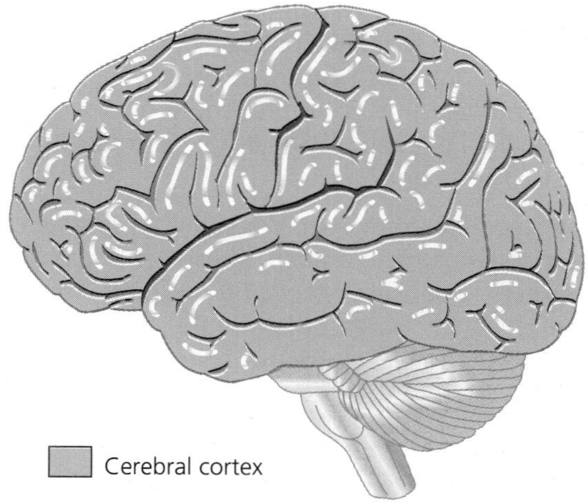

Figure 4 The hypothalamus and pituitary gland

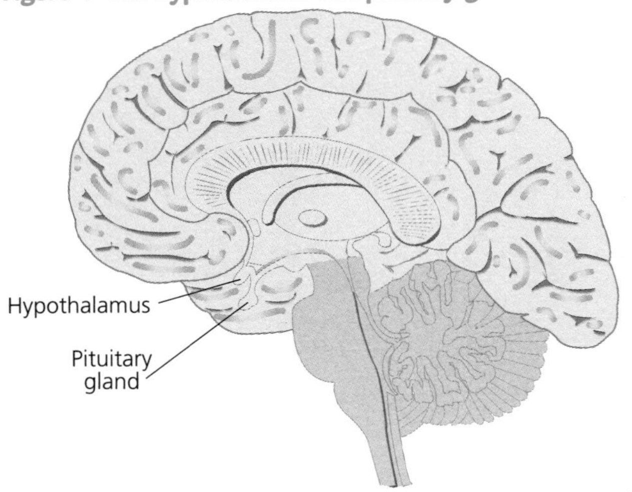

Beneath the cortex, there are many hidden structures which can only be seen directly by opening the brain. These are referred to as *subcortical*, meaning under the cortex. Many perform vital tasks, in conjunction with the cortex, in relation to memory, emotion and motor control – movement of muscles. Two of these structures – the *hypothalamus* and the *pituitary gland* – play an important part in the stress response (see Figure 4). Their role will be examined shortly.

2.4 The central and peripheral nervous systems

Together the brain and spinal cord form the *central nervous system* (CNS), where information processing takes place. The other main division of the nervous system is the *peripheral nervous system* (PNS). It is divided into two parts, the *somatic nervous system* and the *autonomic nervous system*. The somatic nervous system (soma means body), connects the CNS with the rest of the body, by means of pathways which conduct information to and from the brain and the muscles and glands (see Figure 5).

Figure 5 The human nervous system

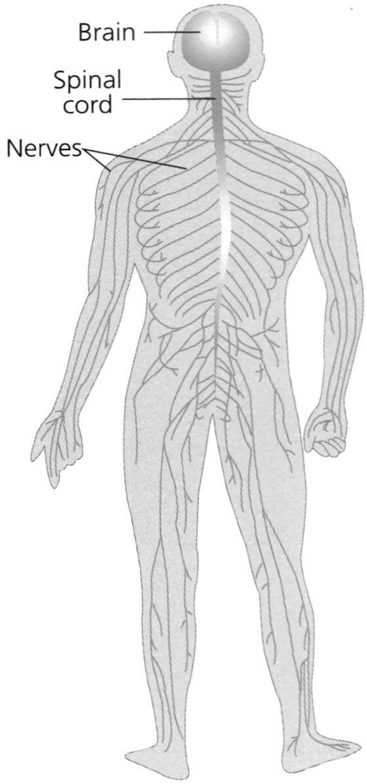

The brain and spinal cord (central nervous system) and spinal nerves.

The autonomic nervous system

The autonomic nervous system (ANS) is responsible for a variety of functions that keep the body in a stable state. These include control of heart rate, perspiration, eye sensitivity and digestion. These functions are involved in the stress response. For example, heart rate increases in response to a stressor.

The ANS is divided into two parts, the *sympathetic branch* and the *parasympathetic branch*. These act in parallel, but they often have opposing effects. For example, the sympathetic branch increases heart rate and the parasympathetic branch decreases heart rate (see Figure 6).

The autonomic nervous system is so called because it is relatively 'autonomous'. Many of its functions are 'automatic' – they require little or no conscious thought. The ANS is somewhat independent of the central nervous system, though the two work together, since the hypothalamus has an important controlling influence on activity within the ANS.

The sympathetic branch This branch comes into play and dominates the ANS when we are alerted or aroused. In response to a stressor, the hypothalamus releases the neurotransmitter chemical noradrenaline which is the main neurotransmitter activating the sympathetic branch. This directs the sympathetic branch to produce many of the changes associated with the stress response. These include releasing sugar from the liver (for use by the muscles in fighting or in rapid escape), increasing heart rate and the strength of heart contractions (so that the body has plenty of blood pumped to it, again for sudden action), increasing lung function to oxygenate the blood, and diverting blood supply from the stomach and skin to the muscles of the limbs for vigorous action. The pupils of the eye dilate (widen) to increase the sensitivity of the eye by allowing more light to enter. The sympathetic branch comes into action swiftly to release and use energy when we need to be active. It produces many of the changes which Cannon described as the fight-or-flight response.

Many of the functions associated with activity in the sympathetic branch are arousing or activating. Arousal is not easily defined and measured, but it is taken to mean the general level of activation within the nervous system. High levels of arousal are associated with stressful states.

The parasympathetic branch In many ways, the parasympathetic branch of the ANS has opposite effects to the sympathetic branch. The parasympathetic branch works alongside the sympathetic branch to ensure a balance in the ANS. Whether the heart is beating quickly (speeded by the sympathetic branch) or slowly (slowed by the parasympathetic branch) is determined by the balance of activity in these two systems.

Activity in the parasympathetic branch results in the storage of energy and the building up of energy for future use. For example, when an emergency is over, it is necessary to conserve energy and build up resources again. Here the parasympathetic branch takes over and slows the heart, stores sugars and stimulates stomach secretions and digestion. This builds up energy in preparation for future emergencies.

So far, this unit has provided a brief description of the various parts which make up the nervous system. Although each part has separate functions, they are all interconnected. This can be seen from Figure 7 which provides a diagrammatic representation of the nervous system.

Figure 6 Branches of the autonomic nervous system

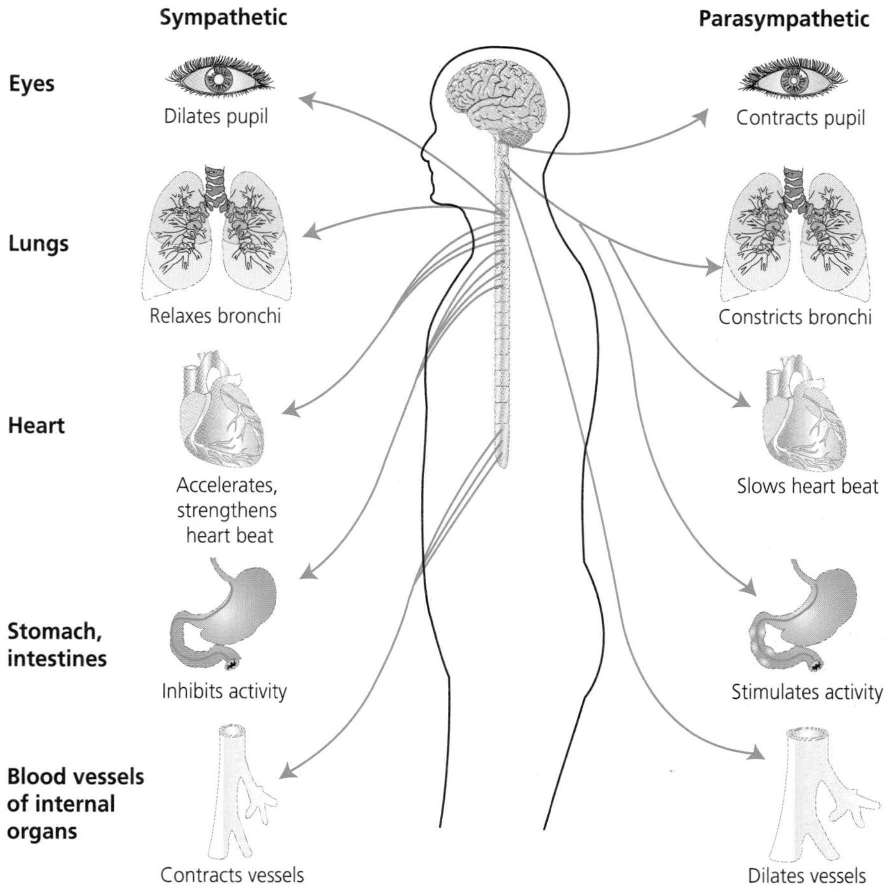

Figure 7 The nervous system

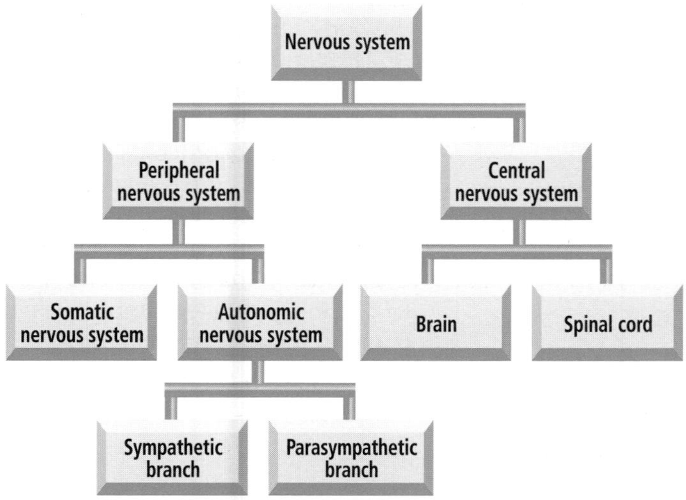

Key terms

Central nervous system (CNS) *Consists of the brain and the spinal cord. The part of the nervous system where information processing takes place.*

Peripheral nervous system (PNS) *Consists of two parts – the somatic nervous system and the autonomic nervous system.*

Somatic nervous system *Connects the CNS with the organs and muscles of the body.*

Autonomic nervous system (ANS) *Keeps the body in a stable state by controlling basic functions such as heart rate. The ANS is divided into two branches.*

Sympathetic branch *The part of the ANS which is concerned with the release and use of energy when activity is required.*

Parasympathetic branch *The part of the ANS which is concerned with the storage of energy.*

2.5 The endocrine system

The *endocrine system* consists of glands – collections of cells that secrete (release) hormones into the bloodstream. Hormones are chemicals that circulate in the blood and act as messengers, affecting particular target cells or organs. In some ways, hormones are similar to neurotransmitters. Both are chemicals, both transmit messages, and in some cases, both involve the same chemicals. The messages sent from neuron to neuron by neurotransmitters are almost instantaneous – they take a few thousandths of a second. Hormones are slower-acting, taking seconds, or even minutes, to travel through the bloodstream and produce an effect. The initial physiological response to a stressful situation would die down rapidly without hormones – they are responsible for prolonging the stress response.

The stress response in the endocrine system operates in the following way. The adrenal gland, (see Figure 9), is stimulated by the sympathetic branch of the ANS. Directed by the hypothalamus, the sympathetic branch sends messages, via neurotransmitters, to the inner core of the adrenal gland – the adrenal medulla. This results in the secretion of adrenaline, which constricts the blood vessels and increases the heart rate, and noradrenaline which stimulates the secretion of a hormone which directs the liver to increase the blood sugar level. The stress response described in this paragraph is sometimes called the *sympathetic-adrenal-medullary system* (SAM).

Figure 8 The physiological stress response (1)

```
                    STRESSOR
                       │
                       ▼
                  Hypothalamus
                  ┌────┴────┐
                  ▼         ▼
             Pituitary   Sympathetic
              gland       branch
                │           │
                ▼           ▼
             Adrenal     Adrenal
             cortex      medulla
                │           │
                ▼           ▼
           Glucocorticoids  Adrenaline
                            and
                            noradrenaline
```

Hypothalamic-pituitary-adrenal axis (HPA) | Sympathetic-adrenal-medullary system (SAM)

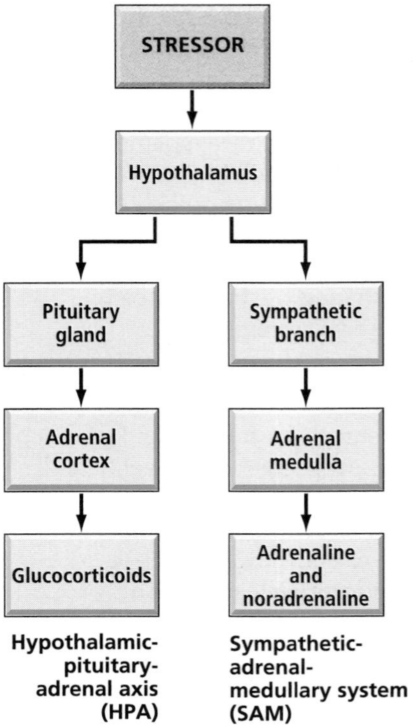

The two main systems in the stress response

Figure 9 The physiological stress response (2)

Hypothalamus
Pituitary gland

Respiration rate increases

Heart rate increases

Blood flow to skeletal muscle increases, blood pressure increases, blood sugar increases

Adrenal glands

Kidneys

Hypothalamus

Pituitary gland

ACTH

Adrenal cortex
Adrenal medulla

Blood vessel

⌐ Nerve impulses from sympathetic branch ■ Adrenaline

→ Hormones from endocrine system ● Noradrenaline

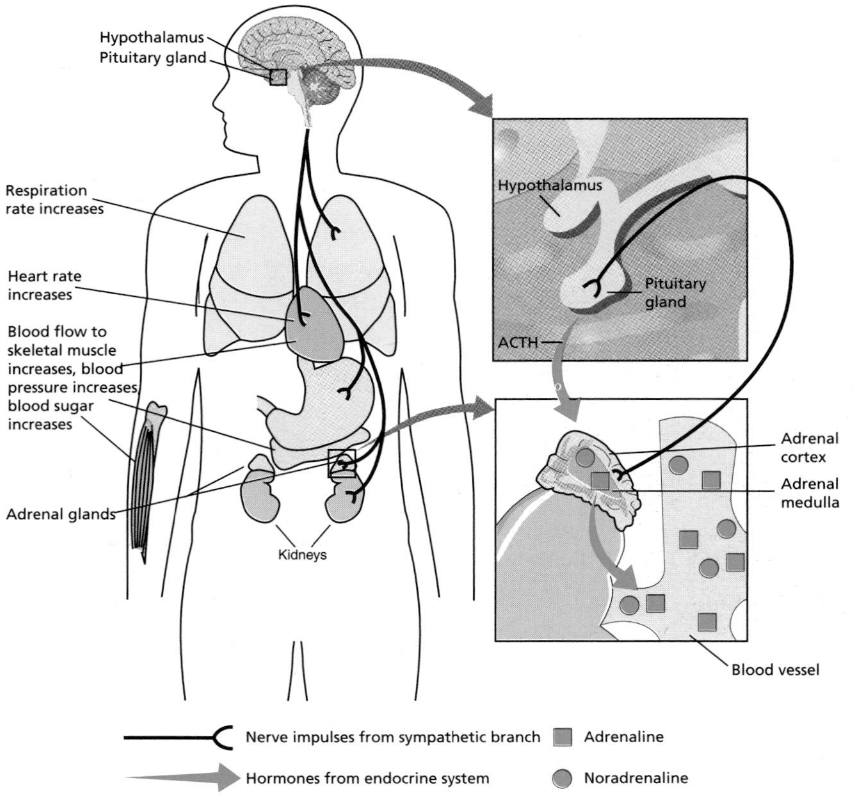

The adrenal gland is also stimulated by the pituitary gland. The pituitary gland is situated just below the hypothalamus and is sometimes known as the 'master gland' as it controls the other glands in the endocrine system. In response to a stressor, the pituitary gland is directed by the hypothalamus to release adrenocorticotropic hormone (ACTH), the body's major 'stress hormone'. ACTH stimulates the outer layer of the adrenal gland – the adrenal cortex – to secrete a group of hormones known as glucocorticoids which help to increase the body's energy level. The system described in this paragraph is sometimes known as the *hypothalamic-pituitary-adrenal axis* (HPA). It is illustrated simply in Figure 8 and in more detail in Figure 9.

Key terms

Hypothalamus *A small structure at the base of the brain which is involved in controlling the autonomic nervous system and the endocrine system.*

Endocrine system *The system of glands which secretes hormones into the bloodstream.*

Hormones *Chemicals released by glands which circulate in the bloodstream and act as messengers affecting particular cells and organs.*

Pituitary gland *The main endocrine gland. Sometimes known as the 'master gland' because it regulates the other glands in the endocrine system.*

Adrenal glands *The main 'stress glands', so called because they play a major role in the stress response.*

Sympathetic-adrenal-medullary system (SAM) *The route through which the brain directs the sympathetic branch of the autonomic nervous system to activate the stress response.*

Hypothalamic-pituitary-adrenal axis (HPA) *The route through which the brain directs the endocrine system to activate the stress response.*

Summary

1. To some extent, all parts of the nervous system, the endocrine system, and the body, are involved in the stress response.
2. The brain is involved in perceiving and interpreting an event as a stressor and organising and initiating the stress response. It directs the autonomic nervous system and the endocrine system to respond to a stressor. It also directs motor responses such as running.
3. The hypothalamus activates the sympathetic branch of the autonomic nervous system. The sympathetic branch produces many of the physiological changes involved in the stress response, for example, accelerating the heart rate and dilating the pupils.
4. In response to a stressor, the hypothalamus stimulates the pituitary gland to secrete ACTH, the body's major 'stress hormone'.
5. The adrenal gland is stimulated by both the sympathetic branch of the ANS and the pituitary gland to secrete hormones which activate the stress response.

Activity 2 The stress response

Item A Train journeys

A crowded London commuter train

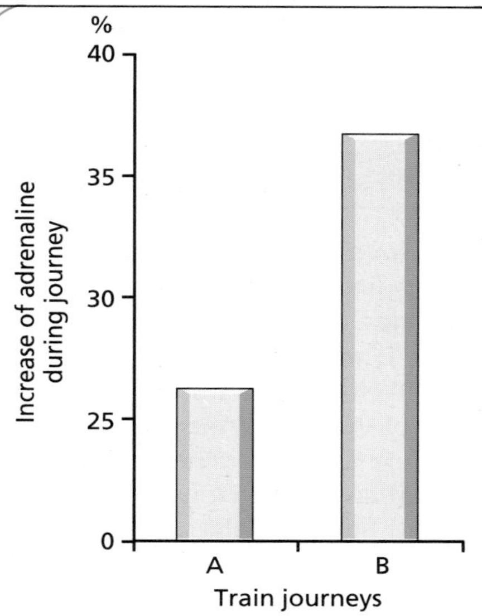

Adapted from Frankenhaeuser, 1978

The bar chart shows the percentage increase in adrenaline secretion during two commuter train journeys. Journey A is a normal commuter trip, journey B has a 10% increase in passengers.

Item B Taking exams

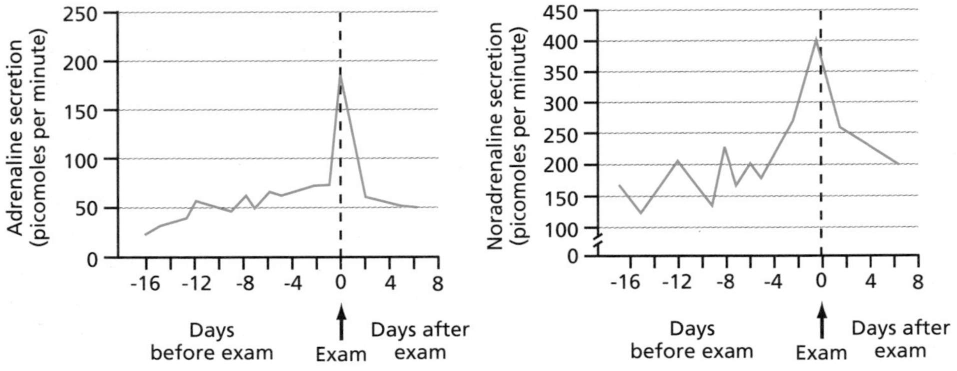

These graphs show the levels of adrenaline and noradrenaline in a student before, during and after an exam.

Adapted from Frankenhaeuser, 1978

Questions

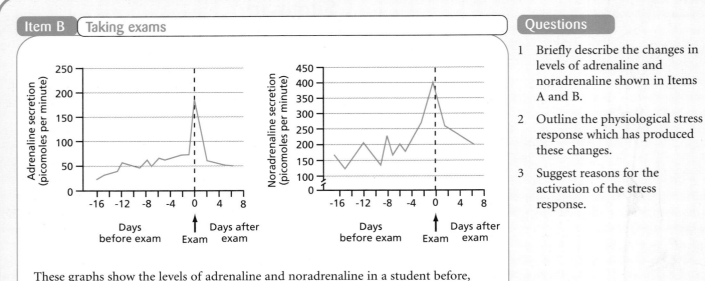

1 Briefly describe the changes in levels of adrenaline and noradrenaline shown in Items A and B.

2 Outline the physiological stress response which has produced these changes.

3 Suggest reasons for the activation of the stress response.

Unit 3 The effects of stress

KEY ISSUES

1. **What are short-term and long-term stress?**
2. **What are the main stages in the physiological response to short-term and long-term stress?**
3. **What is the relationship between long-term stress and physical illness?**

3.1 Short-term and long-term stress

Short-term stress refers to a sudden burst of energy and emotional feelings in response to situations which are seen as emergencies. Short-term stress is sometimes known as acute stress. It may result in a spurt of activity in order to deal with the emergency. Usually people describe their experience of short-term stress in terms of their feelings – fear, anger, excitement – rather than in terms of their physiological responses. However, they may say their heart was racing or they were dripping with sweat. Short-term stress is quite different from, and generally considered far less dangerous than, long-term stress. However, the sudden shock produced by severe short-term stress can result in physical harm, for example a heart attack.

Long-term stress can occur either when a stressor is prolonged, for example long-term exposure to cold, or because several stressful events occur one after the other. Long-term stress is sometimes known as chronic stress.

People sometimes describe their experience of long-term stress with phrases like, 'I always feel tense', 'I'm constantly under pressure', 'I feel like I'm going to pieces'. Long-term stress might involve months or years of coping with bullying, a serious illness, the gradual collapse of a business, or long-term unemployment. It may result in poor concentration, poor memory and a lack of clear thinking.

3.2 The General Adaptation Syndrome (GAS)

The term stress was introduced into psychology in the 1950s by Hans Selye (pronounced 'selyay'). He was the first researcher to make detailed studies of the physiological changes that take place under conditions of short-term and long-term stress. Much of his research was based on experiments with laboratory animals. He exposed them to a variety of stressors including bacterial infections, toxins (poisons), physical restraint and extreme heat and cold. Based on the results of his experiments, Selye argued that all stressors, no matter how different they are, produce much the same reaction, the same *general* bodily response. He therefore defined stress as 'the nonspecific response of the body to any demand made upon it' (Selye, 1956). This means that the body does not have a specific response to a particular stressor, it has the same response to all stressors.

Selye's model of the stress response is known as the *General Adaptation Syndrome (GAS)*. 'General' refers to his belief that there is the same general bodily response to all stressors. 'Adaptation' refers to his view that the stress response enables organisms to adapt to stressors. 'Syndrome' means a typical or characteristic combination of factors – in this case the typical combination of factors that make up the stress response.

Selye identified three main stages in the stress response – alarm, resistance and exhaustion (see Figure 10).

Alarm reaction The first stage, the alarm reaction, mobilises the body for swift action such as Cannon's fight-or-flight response. It occurs over seconds or minutes in the face of a sudden stressor. An abrupt increase in arousal of the autonomic nervous system is produced by a release of adrenaline and noradrenaline. The rate and strength of heart beat increase, raising blood pressure, and stored red blood cells are released from the spleen, increasing oxygen carriage in the blood. Stored sugar is released from the liver, for extra energy (particularly for the muscles), and blood supply is shifted away from the skin and viscera (stomach and intestines) toward the muscles and brain. There is increased tone (tension) in the muscles, respiration deepens, and the pupils dilate (widen) to allow more light into the eye for improved visual function. The blood increases its ability to coagulate (to clot in order to form scar tissue) and there is enhancement of the body's systems for repairing damaged tissue. All of these changes improve survival chances in a fight-or-flight situation – they increase the body's level of resistance to a stressor. A very severe stress response, however, can be life threatening – the shock produced by sudden physiological changes can lead to a heart attack. But, if the stressor disappears or subsides, the body can return to its resting level. This is the typical response to short-term stress. The body has successfully adapted to a stressor and the stress response ends.

Resistance stage The resistance stage occurs when a stressor persists. The release of hormones from the pituitary gland and the adrenal cortex increases, but the alarm symptoms of the first stage disappear, giving an appearance of a return to normal physiological functioning. However, at this stage, arousal is still high as the body's resistance to the stressor is raised. But resistance is lowered if new stressors appear.

Figure 10 The General Adaptation Syndrome

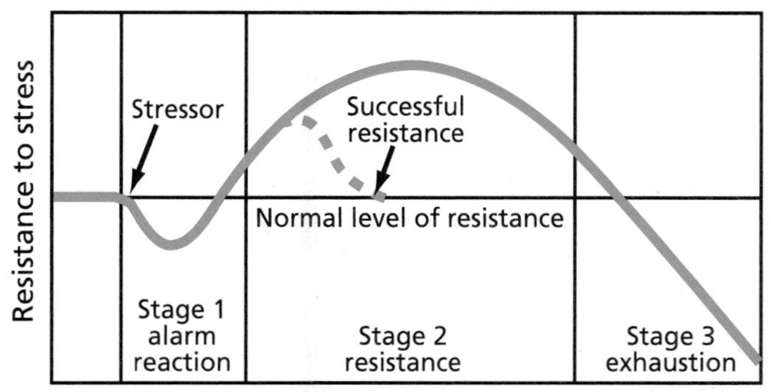

The resistance stage can harm health. For example, it can reduce the effectiveness of the immune system, so lowering the body's resistance to disease.

Exhaustion stage The exhaustion stage is reached when a stressor persists still longer, and the body's defences can no longer cope. The adrenal glands cease to function normally. There is a drastic fall in blood sugar levels. At this stage the individual has few if any reserve resources – even a mild additional stressor has an exaggerated effect. The symptoms associated with the alarm stage such as raised blood pressure can reappear irreversibly – that is, blood pressure remains permanently high and does not return to normal even when the stressor has passed. At this stage, although there is a massive decline in resistance to all forms of stress, there is still a readiness for immediate activity and energy expenditure.

The exhaustion stage is associated with the development of *psychosomatic illness* – disorders of the body which are caused in part by psychological (mental and emotional) factors. These include stomach ulcers and other digestive problems, heart disease and hypertension (permanently raised blood pressure). Selye called these the *diseases of adaptation*. They occur when the energy needed for the body's defence mechanisms in the adaptation stage has been exhausted. Illness is the cost of an unsuccessful defence against long-term stress. In extreme cases, it can result in death.

Evaluation of the GAS

Strengths The General Adaptation Syndrome has been extremely influential. It is based on a great deal of careful observation and has led to a large amount of research. In particular, it has identified a link between psychological factors and physical illness. Many common stressors such as unemployment, marital conflict, preparing for an examination and the death of a close relative are associated with the stress response outlined by the General Adaptation Syndrome. These stressors are often accompanied by the physiological changes described by Selye and sometimes result in the psychosomatic illnesses he identified. (The relationship between stress and illness is examined in the following unit.)

Weaknesses As the transaction approach states, people do not always respond in the same way to stressors and the experience of stress. Selye largely ignored the importance of individual differences. People differ in their interpretation of a possible stressor. They may see it as having little or no effect on them, as mildly stressful or extremely stressful. They also differ in their assessment of their ability to cope with a stressor. Some feel they can cope quite adequately, others feel they are unable to cope. All these interpretations and assessments will affect every stage of the General Adaptation Syndrome. In this respect, Selye ignored the psychological aspects of stressors and stress response.

Selye claimed that all stressors produce the same physiological response. In other words, the response is general and non-specific. However, there is evidence to suggest that there are specific physiological responses to specific stressors. For example, stressors which lead to anxiety appear to result in the release of more adrenaline than noradrenaline, and stressors which lead to aggression appear to result in the release of more noradrenaline (Cox, 1978). This suggests that Selye overstated his case. Although stressors may often produce the same physiological response, they may not always do so.

Summary

1. The General Adaptation Syndrome states that
   - All stressors produce the same physiological response
   - This response can continue through three stages
   - It can result in physical illness.
2. The General Adaptation Syndrome has been criticised
   - For failing to recognise individual differences in the stress response
   - On the basis of evidence which suggests that there may be specific physiological responses to specific stressors.

Key terms

Short-term stress *A sudden burst of energy in response to a stressor. It dies down rapidly once the stressor has passed.*

Long-term stress *Longer-lasting stress in response to a prolonged stressor or a number of stressors.*

General Adaptation Syndrome *A model which identifies the main physiological changes in the stress response. These are the alarm stage, the resistance stage and the exhaustion stage.*

Diseases of adaptation *Physical illnesses caused by stress when the body's energy levels are considerably reduced.*

Psychosomatic illness *A physical illness caused in part by psychological factors ('psycho' means psychological, 'soma' means body).*

Unit 4 Stress and the immune system

KEY ISSUES

1. What is the immune system?

2. How might stress affect the immune system?

3. How might this increase the risk of illness?

Traditionally, the medical profession assumed that physical illness had little or nothing to do with the mind. Thoughts, perceptions and emotions were seen to have little or no effect on physical health. This view has been increasingly challenged over the past fifty years, partly as a result of the large body of research which indicates a link between stress and illness.

Today, health psychologists recognise that many factors may contribute to the onset and development of illness. These include genetic factors, diet, exercise, age, gender and ethnicity. Because of this it makes little sense to ask: Does stress cause illness? Given the many factors involved, the question becomes: Does stress increase the likelihood of illness? Health psychologists are therefore concerned with the *contribution* stress makes to the onset and development of illness.

4.1 Stress and the common cold

Many studies of the link between stress and illness are vague and imprecise. They point to stressors in the individual's environment and link them to past, present or future illness. Often there is little indication of the strength of the stressor, people's perception of the stressor, or the level of stress they are experiencing. Other factors which may contribute to the onset of illness are often left out of the equation. In other words, they are not controlled for. The following study makes good many of these shortcomings. It looks at the relationship between stress and the common cold (Cohen et al., 1991).

Three hundred and ninety-four healthy participants completed a questionnaire designed to measure their stress level. They listed the stressful events they had experienced over the last year, assessed their ability to cope with these events and noted how often they felt negative emotions such as hostility, anger and depression. On the basis of this information, each participant was given a 'psychological stress index' from 3 (lowest stress) to 12 (highest stress).

The participants were then given nasal drops which exposed them to one of five common cold viruses. Most showed signs of infection, but only around a third were judged by a doctor to have an actual cold. Comparing these results with participants' stress index indicated a direct relationship between stress and illness. The higher the stress index, the more likely participants were to catch a cold. This is shown graphically in Figure 11. Figure 12 shows the percentage of participants who developed a cold from each of the five viruses. In each case there is a direct relationship between stress levels and catching a cold.

Figure 11

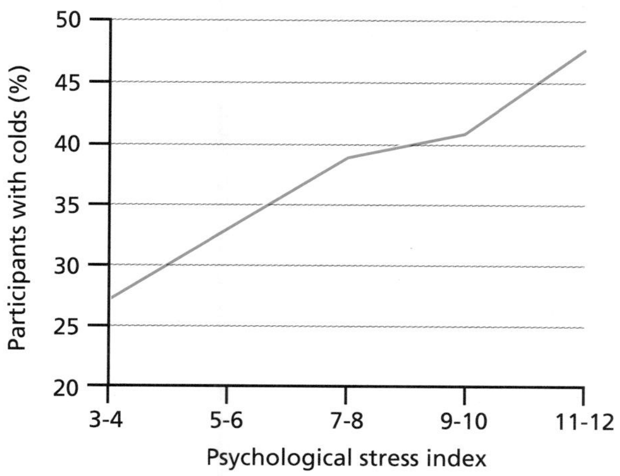

Adapted from Cohen et al., 1991

The researchers attempted to control for other variables which may have affected these results. In other words, they tried to control for factors other than stress which may have contributed to the onset of a cold. They controlled for age, gender, education, allergies, weight, smoking, alcohol consumption, diet, sleep, exercise, and a range of personality factors. None of these variables appeared to make a difference. In addition, the participants were carefully monitored in special housing for a few days before and after their exposure to the viruses. In view of all these checks and controls, the researchers concluded that there was a direct relationship between stress and illness.

But how exactly did stress contribute to the onset of colds? What was the actual mechanism involved? It appeared that in some way stress lowered the body's resistance to cold viruses. In other words, stress may have affected the body's *immune system*.

4.2 The immune system

The immune system protects the body from harmful viruses and bacteria. To take a simple case: a virus attacks the body. It gets into the bloodstream and circulates around the body. The immune system is designed to identify the virus as a harmful 'foreign' agent, to seek it out, and to destroy it.

The immune system contains cells known as *lymphocytes* which recognise and destroy harmful viruses and bacteria which invade the body. They lock on to the invaders, multiply rapidly, and destroy them. There are two types of lymphocytes – B cells and T cells. B cells produce *antibodies* which are released into the fluid surrounding the body's cells to destroy the invading viruses and bacteria. If the invader gets inside a cell, T cells lock on to the infected cell, multiply, and destroy it.

If there is a link between stress and illness, then one possibility is that stress reduces the efficiency of the immune

Figure 12

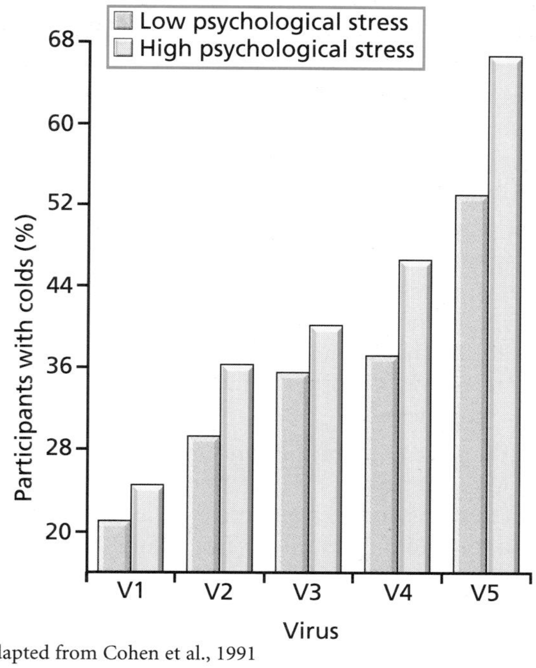

Adapted from Cohen et al., 1991

system. This will lower the body's resistance to disease-causing viruses and bacteria. If there is a link between stress and the immune system, then this suggests there is also a link between the immune system and the brain. As noted earlier, the brain is directly involved in the perception of stressors and the stress response.

The immune system and the brain Numerous direct neural connections appear to exist between the brain and the immune system. For example, many nerve fibres connect the brain to the sympathetic branch of the autonomic

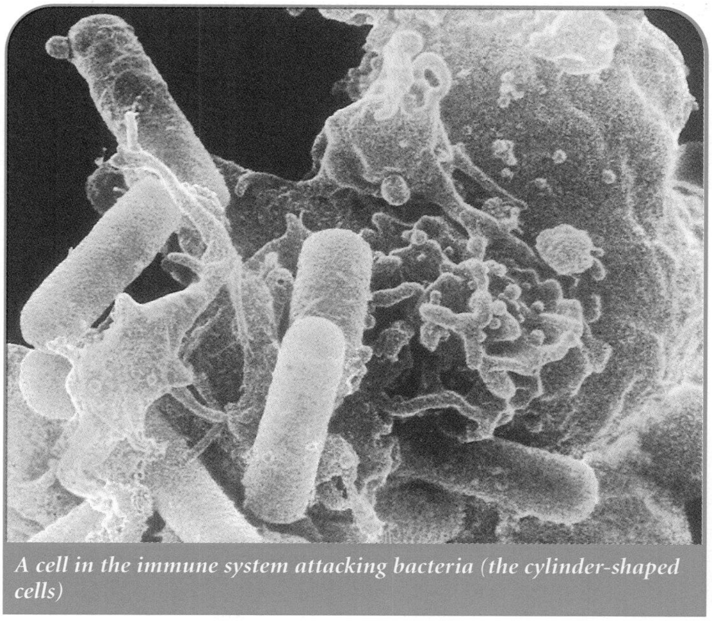

A cell in the immune system attacking bacteria (the cylinder-shaped cells)

nervous system. And, many of the nerve fibres from the sympathetic branch end among lymphocytes in the thymus gland – a gland in the neck which produces lymphocytes. Lymphocytes have receptors – specially designed receivers – for a number of different neurotransmitters. In view of these connections, it is possible that the brain can communicate directly with the immune system and affect its functioning. For example, messages from the brain may affect the production and the effectiveness of B cells and T cells.

The brain may also influence the immune system via the endocrine system. As outlined earlier, in response to a stressor the hypothalamus directs the pituitary gland to release ACTH hormone which travels to the adrenal cortex and causes further hormones to be released. Some of these hormones are known to suppress the immune system, so reducing its effectiveness.

Measuring the efficiency of the immune system Does stress reduce the effectiveness of the immune system? Before this question can be answered, some measure of the efficiency of the immune system is required. Two main measures have been used. First, counting the number of T cells and B cells and assessing the antibody levels in the blood. Second, assessing how well the immune cells are functioning. For example, are they able to reproduce effectively? This can be done by artificially stimulating them with a chemical.

4.3 Stress, illness and the immune system

A large number of studies have indicated a link between stress, the immune system and illness. They suggest that stress reduces the efficiency of the immune system which lowers the body's resistance to disease. First, a look at some of the evidence.

A number of studies have looked at the relationship between taking examinations – a well-known stressor – and the functioning of the immune system. Various measurements indicating the efficiency of the immune system have been taken. In general, these studies indicate that the stress of examinations reduces the effectiveness of the immune system. For example, one study examined 40 medical students six weeks before their exams and again during their exams. The students revealed higher levels of stress during their exams and the percentage of T cells showed significant reductions at exam time (Glaser et al., 1986).

Key terms

Immune system *Protects the body from disease-causing viruses and bacteria.*

Lymphocytes *Specialised cells – B cells and T cells – which recognise and destroy harmful viruses and bacteria.*

Antibodies *Proteins released by B cells which destroy harmful viruses and bacteria.*

Studies of men and women who have recently divorced or separated – often an extremely stressful experience – indicate poorer functioning of the immune system compared with married couples of similar age and social position. For example, immune cells from divorced and separated people did not reproduce as effectively as those from their married counterparts (Kiecolt-Glaser et al., 1987).

A whole range of stressors appear to reduce the effectiveness of the immune system. They include events such as the death of a husband or wife, everyday events which people find annoying and frustrating, and living in an environment which is perceived as threatening – for example in the vicinity of a nuclear accident (Taylor, 1995).

Evaluation The description of the immune system outlined above is far from complete. The system is extremely complex and includes many components. Far more research is needed to unravel its complexities, to discover how its parts work together to defend the body, and to pinpoint its relationship to the nervous system and the endocrine system.

A number of studies have indicated that while a stressor may suppress one or more parts of the immune system, it appears to leave other parts unaffected. Again, more research is needed to discover why this is so.

In addition, the immune system may be affected by a whole range of factors in people's lives. These include drugs such as alcohol, caffeine and nicotine, a person's general health, their diet, physical activity, sleep patterns, age and medication. Although many studies attempt to control for such factors in order to isolate the effect of stress, complete control is unlikely (Kiecolt-Glaser & Glaser, 1988)

Despite this, the weight of evidence suggests that apart from short-term acute stress, the experience of stress does suppress the immune system. This provides an important explanation for the relationship between stress and illness. Suppression of the immune system makes the body more vulnerable to illness.

Summary

1. A reduction in the efficiency of the immune system will reduce the body's resistance to disease.
2. There is evidence which indicates that stress can reduce the efficiency of the immune system.
3. The brain directs the perception of stressors and the stress response.
4. There are connections between the brain and the immune system. This raises the possibility that the brain may affect the immune system as part of the stress response.
5. In view of the complexity of the immune system, these findings are suggestive rather than conclusive. In other words, we cannot be certain that stress suppresses the immune system.

Activity 3 Control, stress and the immune system

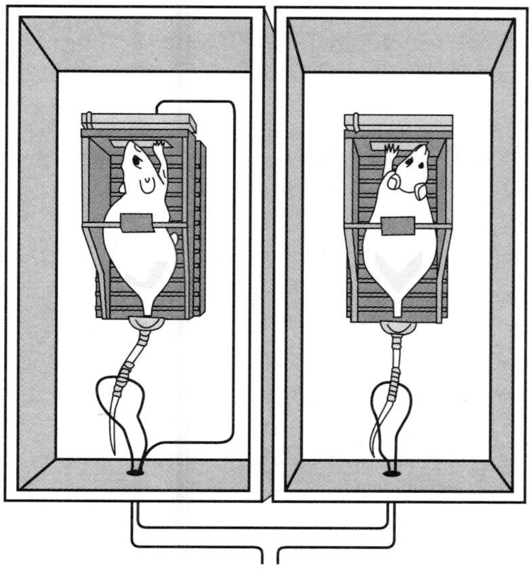

In this experiment, two rats experience the same stressors – a series of electric shocks. Each rat has a lever which it can press. The rat on the left can end each shock by pressing its lever. The rat on the right has no control over the shocks – its lever does nothing. However, it receives exactly the same series of shocks as the first rat.

The researchers then investigated the effect of this procedure on one aspect of the rats' immune system – the reproduction of T cells. T cells from the rat that could end the shock multiplied in the same way as those of rats who were not exposed to the shocks. However, the reproduction of T cells from the rat who received uncontrollable shocks was significantly reduced. Similar experiments have supported these findings.

Adapted from Laudenslager et al., 1983

Question

Using the above data, provide an explanation for the relationship between control, stress and the immune system.

Unit 5 Stress and coronary heart disease (CHD)

KEY ISSUES

1. **What is coronary heart disease?**
2. **How might stress contribute to coronary heart disease?**

Coronary heart disease (CHD) refers to illnesses caused by the narrowing of the arteries which supply the heart with blood. This process is known as *atherosclerosis*. It is caused by fatty material being deposited on the walls of the arteries. A narrowing of the arteries reduces the flow of oxygen carried in the blood to the heart.

There are two main types of CHD – *angina pectoris,* commonly known as angina and *myocardial infarction,* commonly known as a heart attack. Angina is less serious. It results in chest pains, usually after physical exertion, because the blood flow to the heart muscle is insufficient to provide the additional oxygen required. A heart attack results from a blockage of an artery supplying the heart with blood. A narrowed artery is more easily blocked by a deposit or a blood clot. This can reduce oxygen supply to the point where part of the heart dies. The result is a heart attack which can prove fatal. CHD is one of the main causes of death in Western industrial societies.

5.1 Risk factors and CHD

Before looking at possible relationships between CHD and stress, other factors, which have been linked to CHD, will be briefly outlined. The following risk factors have been identified:

- Gender – men are more likely than women to suffer from CHD
- Age – the elderly are most at risk
- High levels of cholesterol in the blood
- High blood pressure
- Cigarette smoking
- Diabetes
- Low levels of physical activity
- Obesity – being seriously overweight
- Diet – particularly diets high in saturated fat
- Family history of CHD which suggests genetic factors may be involved.

None of these risk factors is particularly good at predicting who will get CHD. And, there is some evidence which does not appear to support them. For example, people living in the midwestern states of the USA have high smoking rates and their diets are extremely high in saturated fats. Despite this, their level of CHD is significantly below the more industrialised parts of the USA (Davison & Neale, 1998).

On their own, each of the risk factors listed above explains only a tiny proportion of CHD. Even taken together, or in various combinations, they leave most of CHD unexplained (Evans, 1998). Because of this, some researchers have turned to psychological factors. In particular, they have looked at stress as a possible risk factor for CHD.

5.2 Stress and CHD

This section outlines a number of studies which indicate a relationship between stress and CHD.

Life events A number of studies indicate that the physiological stress response to life events may increase the risk of CHD. Life events are significant events in people's lives which they usually experience as stressful. One study looked at negative life events over a period of one year – events such as divorce and the death of a close friend or relative. These events were accompanied by rises in blood pressure and in the production of fatty acids which leads to an increase in blood cholesterol. This can lead to atherosclerosis – a narrowing of the arteries by deposits of fatty material (Theorell & Emlund, 1993).

Stress at work A number of studies have looked at stress at work in relation to CHD. The following factors appear to increase the level of stress and the risk of CHD: lack of control over work, few opportunities to make decisions, low job satisfaction, monotonous and repetitive tasks, and a lack of job security, all of which are associated with low status occupations. A number of these factors have been linked to high blood pressure and high blood cholesterol, both of which increase the risk of CHD (Evans, 1998).

Type A behaviour pattern

A large amount of research has indicated that individuals with particular behaviour patterns are more likely to experience stress and to suffer from CHD. Two heart specialists, Friedman and Rosenman (1974), identified the *Type A behaviour pattern* which they claimed made people more vulnerable to CHD. The Type A individual is driven to achieve, highly competitive, aggressive, hostile, impatient, fast talking and fast thinking, and often involved in two or more activities at the same time. The first major study to examine the relationship between Type A behaviour and CHD was based on a sample of 3524 Californian men between the ages of 39 and 59. All were free from CHD at the start of the research. They were studied over an 8½ year period. At the end of that time, 7% of the sample had developed at least some signs of CHD. Of this 7%, two-thirds were Type A individuals. The research showed that Type A individuals generally had higher blood cholesterol levels and higher levels of adrenaline and noradrenaline than Type Bs. The secretion of adrenaline and noradrenaline is part of the physiological stress response. They increase the level of fatty acids in the blood which may lead to atherosclerosis.

More recent studies have not supported the link between Type A behaviour and CHD. This may be because different methods were used to identify the Type A behaviour pattern. It may also be due to the possibility that the behaviours included in Type A are too broad.

A number of researchers have focused on particular aspects of the Type A pattern. One study divided the Type A behaviour into 12 distinct parts. Only two parts predicted atherosclerosis – 'potential for hostility' and 'anger-in' (feeling uncomfortable about expressing anger openly). Atherosclerosis was marked in individuals who scored highly on measurements of hostility and suppressed anger (Dembroski et al., 1985).

Cynical hostility Some researchers claim that *cynical hostility* is a better predictor of CHD than the broader Type A pattern. Cynical means having little faith in human sincerity or goodness. Those with a cynically hostile attitude assume that people are basically selfish and will use unfair means for their own gain. This attitude encourages a hostile and oppositional approach to others marked by suspicion, distrust, resentment, aggression and anger.

There is evidence that individuals who score highly on measures of cynical hostility react more readily to stressors and their stress response lasts longer. In particular, their heart rate and blood pressure are particularly high, as are their secretions of adrenaline and noradrenaline. A number of studies have indicated a link between cynical hostility and CHD (Taylor, 1995). However, not all studies support these findings. Again, one of the problems is measurement. It is not easy to measure vague and imprecise things like cynicism and hostility. Different measuring scales often produce different results.

The stress response and CHD

What are the mechanisms which link the stress response to CHD? First, stress activates the sympathetic branch of the autonomic nervous system. This leads to a constriction of the blood vessels and a rise in blood pressure and the heart rate. As a result, more and more blood is pushed through shrinking arteries. Long-term stress may lead to wear and tear on, and damage to, the arteries. Activation of the sympathetic branch also leads to an increase in the release of fatty acids into the bloodstream which can increase the chance of atherosclerosis.

Second, stress also activates parts of the endocrine system via the hypothalamic-pituitary-adrenal axis (see p 98). This leads to the secretion of 'stress hormones' including adrenaline and noradrenaline which again leads to an increase in the release of fatty acids into the bloodstream. This increases blood cholesterol levels which, in turn, increase the risk of atherosclerosis and CHD.

Evaluation

The evidence for a link between stress and CHD is not simple and clear-cut. Some of the results of research are contradictory. This may be partly due to the difficulty of measuring vague concepts such as stress, hostility and cynicism. In addition, the physiological stress response is extremely complex and only partially understood. Despite these problems, the weight of evidence does suggest a link between stress and CHD. This is not to say that stress causes CHD, only that in many cases, it might be one of the causes. In other words, stress is probably a contributory factor to CHD.

Summary

1. Apart from stress, a number of risk factors for CHD have been identified. On their own, or in various combinations, these risk factors leave most of CHD unexplained. Partly because of this, some researchers have looked at stress as a possible risk factor for CHD.
2. Research has indicated that a range of stressors are accompanied by rises in blood pressure and blood cholesterol levels. An increase in fatty acids in the bloodstream can lead to atherosclerosis.
3. Some research has indicated that people with Type A behaviour patterns are more vulnerable to CHD. Not all research supports this finding.
4. More recent research points to cynical hostility as a risk factor for CHD.
5. The stress response produces physiological changes which may contribute to CHD.

Key terms

Coronary heart disease *Illnesses caused by the narrowing of the arteries which supply the heart with blood.*

Atherosclerosis *A narrowing of the arteries caused by a build up of fatty material on the artery walls.*

Angina pectoris *Commonly known as angina. An illness caused by insufficient blood flow to the heart. Results in chest pains, usually after physical exertion.*

Myocardial infarction *Commonly known as a heart attack. Results from a blockage of an artery supplying the heart with blood. Can reduce oxygen supply to the point where part of the heart dies.*

Type A behaviour pattern *A pattern of behaviour characterised by competitiveness, impatience, hostility and aggression.*

Cynical hostility *A behaviour pattern characterised by cynicism and hostility. It assumes that others are basically selfish and insincere and regards them with distrust and hostility.*

References

Bernstein, D.A., Clarke-Stewart, A., Roy, E.J. & Wickens, C.D. (1997). *Psychology* (4th ed.). Boston: Houghton Mifflin.

Cannon, W.B. (1932). *The wisdom of the body*. New York: Norton.

Cohen, S., Tyrrell, D.A.J. & Smith, A.P. (1991). Psychological stress and susceptibility to the common cold. *New England Journal of Medicine, 325,* 606-612.

Cox, T. (1978). *Stress*. London: Macmillan.

Davison, G.C. & Neale, J.M. (1998). *Abnormal psychology* (7th ed.). New York: John Wiley.

Dembroski, T.M., MacDougall, J.M., Williams, R.B., Haney, T.L. & Blumenthal, J.A. (1985). Components of type A, hostility, and anger-in: Relationships to angiographic findings. *Psychosomatic Medicine, 47,* 219-233.

Evans, P. (1998). Stress and coping. In M. Pitts & K. Phillips, (Eds.), *The psychology of health: An introduction*. London: Routledge.

Frankenhaeuser, M. (1978). Psychoneuroendocrine approaches to the study of emotion as related to stress and coping. *Nebraska Symposium on Motivation, 26,* 123-162.

Friedman, M. & Rosenman, R.H. (1974). *Type A behaviour and your heart*. New York: Knopf.

Glaser, R., Rice, J., Speicher, C.E., Stout, J.C. & Keicolt-Glaser, J.K. (1986). Stress depresses interferon production by leukocytes concomitant with a decrease in natural killer cell activity. *Behavioural Neuroscience, 100,* 675-678.

Kiecolt-Glaser, J.K., Fisher, L., Ogrocki, P., Stout, J.C., Speicher, C.E. & Glaser, R. (1987). Marital quality, marital disruption and immune function. *Psychosomatic Medicine, 49,* 13-34.

Kiecolt-Glaser, J.K. & Glaser, R. (1988). Methodological issues in behavioural immunology research with humans. *Brain, Behaviour, and Immunity, 2,* 67-78.

Laudenslager, M.L., Ryan, S.M., Drugan, R.C., Hyson, R.L. & Maier, S.F. (1983). Coping and immunosuppression: Inescapable but not escapable shock suppresses lymphocyte proliferation. *Science, 211,* 68-570.

Lazarus, R.S. & Folkman, S. (1984). *Stress, appraisal, and coping*. New York: Springer.

Selye, H. (1956). *The stress of life*. New York: McGraw-Hill.

Taylor, S.E. (1995). *Health psychology* (3rd ed.). New York: McGraw-Hill.

Theorell, T. & Emlund, N. (1993). On physiological effects of positive and negative life changes: A longitudinal study. *Journal of Psychosomatic Research, 37,* 653-659.

White, E. & Brown, D. (1973). *The first men*. New York: Time-Life.

8 Sources of stress

Introduction

A list of the events, situations and experiences that people perceive as stressors is practically endless. Psychologists have therefore looked at this multitude of stressors and tried to discover whether they have anything in common. It appears they have. For example, events which are perceived as unpredictable and uncontrollable are often experienced as stressful. The first part of this chapter classifies stressors in terms of the characteristics they share.

Different people perceive different events as stressors and respond to them in different ways. Why? The short answer is individual differences – people differ in terms of their personality, behaviour patterns, gender, social class, ethnicity and culture. The second part of this chapter looks at the relationship between individual differences and the experience of stress.

Chapter summary

- **Unit 1 identifies and classifies sources of stress.**
- **Unit 2 examines the effect of individual differences on the perception of stressors and the experience of stress.**
- **Unit 3 considers the question of measurement in stress research. It assesses the strengths and weaknesses of various methods of measuring the stress response.**

Unit 1 Sources of stress

KEY ISSUES

1 What is a transactional model of stress?

2 What are the main sources of stress?

1.1 The transactional model of stress

The previous chapter provided a brief outline of the transactional model of stress. This model states that stress results from a transaction between the individual and their environment. Environment includes all the events and relationships the individual experiences. Events may include marriage and divorce, moving house, changing jobs and going on holiday. Relationships include relationships with friends, family, and colleagues at work.

Whether or not the individual experiences stress depends on the way they perceive both their environment and their ability to cope with it. This is where the idea of transaction come in – the individual interacts with their environment, perceives it in a certain way and gives meaning to it. Stress arises from an individual's perception that the demands of the environment place a strain on, or are greater than, their resources. Resources include their time, energy, money, strength of will, and level of support from family and friends.

Stress occurs when a person feels they will have difficulty coping or cannot cope. This is an important point. It means that a stressor is not simply out there in the environment – it only becomes a stressor when people define it as such and feel it will strain or overcome their resources for dealing with it.

Take the following examples of redundancy. A teacher in his mid-50s is made redundant. He welcomes this event as it includes a generous package – a large lump sum and an enhanced pension. It's the opportunity he's been waiting for to take early retirement, to travel and to improve his golf. A second teacher in his mid-40s is made redundant. He has a family to support and is worried about his prospects of finding another job. To him, redundancy is a disaster and he is concerned about his ability to cope with the situation. Redundancy is perceived very differently by these two teachers. And, because of this difference in perception, it will probably be experienced as far more stressful by the second teacher than by the first.

Cognitive appraisal

Richard Lazarus (1976) developed one of the first transactional models of stress. He argued that *cognitive appraisal* is the key to understanding stress. Cognitive means thinking; appraisal means making a judgement or evaluating.

Figure 1 Cognitive appraisal

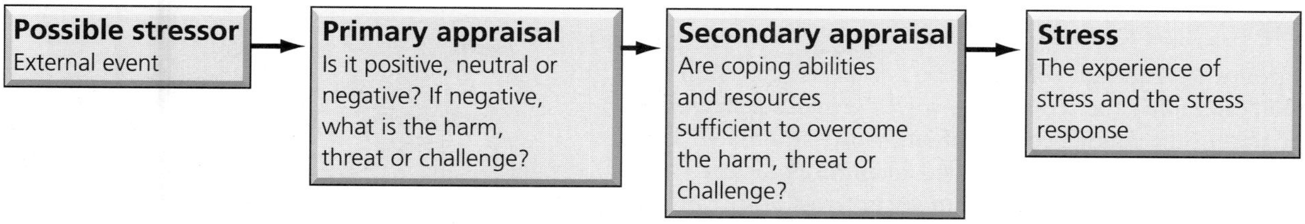
Possible stressor
External event
Primary appraisal
Is it positive, neutral or negative? If negative, what is the harm, threat or challenge?
Secondary appraisal
Are coping abilities and resources sufficient to overcome the harm, threat or challenge?
Stress
The experience of stress and the stress response

Adapted from Billings & Moos (1981)

Primary appraisal is the first appraisal people make. They decide whether an event is positive, neutral or negative. If they decide the event is negative, they then make a further appraisal in terms of its possible *harm, threat*, or *challenge*. If a person has been fired from their job they may see present harm as shame and embarrassment, threat as possible future damage such as problems due to lack of income, or they may see the situation as a positive challenge – an opportunity to train for the job they always wanted.

Secondary appraisal involves an evaluation of coping abilities and resources for dealing with the situation. The experience of stress will depend on both the primary and secondary appraisal. If harm and threat are seen as high and coping abilities and resources perceived as low, then a high level of stress is probable. If coping abilities and resources are seen as high, then the experience of stress may well be minimal.

The transactional model has the advantage of accounting for *individual differences* in the stress response – the differences between people, which lead them to respond in different ways to a possible stressor. Individual differences are examined in Unit 2.

Many recent views of stress adopt a transactional model. In terms of this model, the source of stress is the cognitive appraisal of events. Only when an event is perceived as stressful does it become a stressor. However, research has indicated that some events are more likely than others to be perceived as stressors. The rest of this unit looks at these events and asks what it is about them which makes them likely to be appraised as stressful.

Key terms

Transactional model *Stress is the result of a transaction between the individual and their environment.*

Cognitive appraisal *An evaluation or judgement of an event (primary appraisal) and of the resources available to cope with it (secondary appraisal).*

Individual differences *The difference between individuals, for example differences in personality, age, gender and social class.*

1.2 Lack of control

Research evidence indicates that people often experience stress when they believe they have little or no control over a situation.

Lack of control at work A study of Swedish sawmill workers indicated a relationship between lack of control and high levels of stress (Frankenhaeuser, 1975). The workers did little more than feed timber into cutting and planing machines. The work was repetitive and monotonous and the workers felt there was nothing they could do about it. Machines controlled the speed of their work and their work operations. Since the machines had to be constantly 'fed' and tended, workers were prevented from moving round the factory floor, so having little opportunity for social contact. Their control over their work was minimal.

Compared to other workers in the mill, these workers had high blood pressure, a high rate of stomach and intestinal disorders, including ulcers, and they were more likely to suffer from headaches. Urine analysis showed they had high levels of adrenaline and noradrenaline. These findings suggest they were experiencing stress. The study concludes that this was primarily due to a lack of control over their work environment.

Experimental evidence Two groups were shown colour transparencies of victims of violent deaths. Participants in the first group were told they could stop the 'slide show' by pressing a button. Those in the second group were not given this option. As it happened, both groups saw the same pictures for the same length of time. However, the results indicated that the second group – those *without* the stop button – found the viewing more stressful. Stress was measured by the electrical resistance of the skin which indicates the level of arousal in the autonomic nervous system. This experiment suggests that the perception of having control over the situation will affect the level of stress experienced (Geer & Maisel, 1973).

Activity 1 Primary appraisal

Item A A study of primary appraisal

Four groups of American college students were shown a film of an initiation ceremony. The ceremony involved genital surgery which formed part of the young people's initiation into adulthood. The soundtrack for the first group provided an anthropological description which discussed the ceremony in terms of the young people's culture and described it as a normal part of growing up. The soundtrack for the second group focused on the young people's excitement in participating in the initiation rite and their pride in the transition from adolescence to adulthood. The soundtrack for the third group emphasised the apprehension and fear felt by the initiates and the pain they suffered. The fourth group watched the film without any soundtrack.

The stress levels of the four groups of students were measured. The highest level of stress was experienced by the group who listened to the soundtrack which emphasised the pain the initiates were going through. The lowest levels of stress were experienced by the first two groups.

Stress was measured by self-reports – reports by group members of the stress levels they thought they experienced. It was also measured by their heart rate and the electrical resistance of their skin, both of which indicate the level of arousal of the autonomic nervous system.

Adapted from Speisman et al., 1964

Azande boys from Sudan in Africa during their initiation ceremony. They are pictured here in the circumcision camp.

Question

How does this study indicate the importance of primary appraisal?

Activity 2 Lack of control

Item A Choosing seats

A study of male passengers on a commuter train indicated that, in general, stress levels increased the more crowded the train became, even though all the passengers managed to get a seat. Stress was measured by the amount of adrenaline in urine samples. Interestingly, those who joined the train at the first stop, and had a longer journey to the city, had lower levels of adrenaline than those who joined the train later. Apparently, what made the difference was the wider choice of seats available to the first passengers. Though they still found a seat, choice was limited for the passengers who joined the train later in the journey.

Adapted from Lundberg, 1976

Item B Stuck in traffic

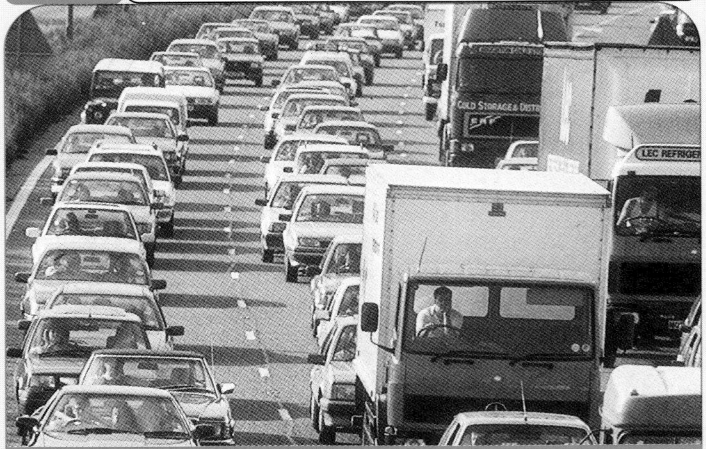

Traffic jam on M1 near London

Questions

1 How can lack of control help to explain the different levels of stress experienced by the passengers in Item A?

2 Look at Item B. People often experience stress when they are stuck in a traffic jam. Use the idea of lack of control to explain this.

1.3 Unpredictability

Events which are unpredictable often produce higher levels of stress than events which are predictable. If an event is predictable, people expect it and can prepare for it. As a result, it comes as less of a shock than something unexpected which comes 'out of the blue'. In addition, they have time to develop coping strategies which may reduce the stress. For example, research indicates that the sudden and unexpected death of a child is often more stressful for the parents than the death of a child after a long-term illness (Hazzard et al., 1992).

Unpredictability is linked with high levels of stress in many areas of life. The stress associated with life-threatening illnesses is magnified by unpredictability. A study of people with AIDS reveals many areas of uncertainty. Was the diagnosis correct – have I really got AIDS? Will I be able to function normally tomorrow? Symptoms of AIDS often flare up and die down rapidly which means people can't make even short-term plans. Is there a cure around the corner? How long have I got to live? (Weitz, 1989)

Unpredictability is a feature of many jobs associated with high stress levels. These include firefighters, ambulance drivers and paramedics, and doctors and nurses in accident and emergency departments. Workers in these occupations are often unable to predict what they will be doing, what demands will be placed on them, and where they will be from one hour to the next.

Experimental evidence Laboratory experiments with both humans and animals indicate that unpredictable stressors produce more stress than predictable stressors. In one experiment, rats were given a series of shocks. They were unable to predict when the shocks would occur. They were then given the opportunity to press a bar at the start of a series of shocks. This provided a warning tone before each shock. The rats soon learned to press the bar indicating they preferred predictable to unpredictable shocks (Abbott et al., 1984). Experiments with humans produced similar results. Participants show less arousal and report lower levels of stress when shocks are predictable, even when the shocks were of exactly the same intensity (Katz & Wykes, 1982).

These results have been explained in the following ways. First, if a stressor is predictable, people can prepare for it. Second, if there are a number of predictable stressors, this gives people the opportunity to relax until the next warning signal.

Disasters are often unpredictable. They include natural disasters such as earthquakes, volcanic eruptions, floods, avalanches and mud slides, and human-made disasters such as terrorist bombs in peacetime and missile attacks and bombing raids in wartime. Even when a warning is available or given, people are usually unable to predict the scale of the disaster and exactly when it will occur. Consider the following example.

At 5.04 pm on Saturday, October 17, 1989, an earthquake hit San Francisco. Within minutes, 63 people were dead, nearly 3,800 injured and more than 28,000 homes and businesses damaged or destroyed. The city was blacked out apart from fires fed by broken gas mains, roads were fractured, and bridges collapsed (Canby, 1990). After the earthquake a team of psychologists interviewed nearly 800 people from the area. They found the stress response tended to follow a typical pattern. The *emergency phase* lasted 3-4 weeks during which people were extremely anxious and distressed, preoccupied with the quake, and keen to talk about it. The *inhibition phase* (3-8 weeks) followed. There was a sudden decline in talking about the quake, but an increase in stress-related behaviour such as arguments and irritability. By the *adaptation phase*, from 8 weeks onwards, most people seemed to have got back to normal. However, one year later, around 20% still felt distressed about the earthquake (Pennebaker & Harber, 1991).

Activity 3 Unpredictability

Item A Missing in action

The USA became involved in the Vietnam War during the early 1960s. By the end of the war in 1975, over 57,000 American servicemen had died. Many others had been in prison camps or were 'missing in action'. A study showed that the wives of those missing in action suffered more emotional stress and physical illness than wives whose husbands were in prison camps or killed in action.

Adapted from Hunter, 1979

US troops in Vietnam move forward in a rice field under helicopter gunship cover.

Item B Mt St Helens

On May 18, 1980, Mount St Helens in northwestern USA erupted. It was the most powerful volcanic eruption the world had known for 60 years. Although there were warnings, and most people were evacuated from the area, the exact time of the eruption could not be predicted, nor was the scale and power of the blast anticipated. Sixty people were killed and the blast of hot gas, ash and rock destroyed an area of 150 square miles.

Psychologists studied the behaviour of people in the small agricultural town of Othello near the disaster area. After the eruption they found a 198% increase in stress-related illness, a 235% increase in the diagnosis of mental health problems, and an 18.6% increase in the death rate. Crisis calls to the emergency services increased dramatically, as did appointments at the local mental health clinic.

Adapted from Adams & Adams, 1984

Mt St Helens erupting in 1980

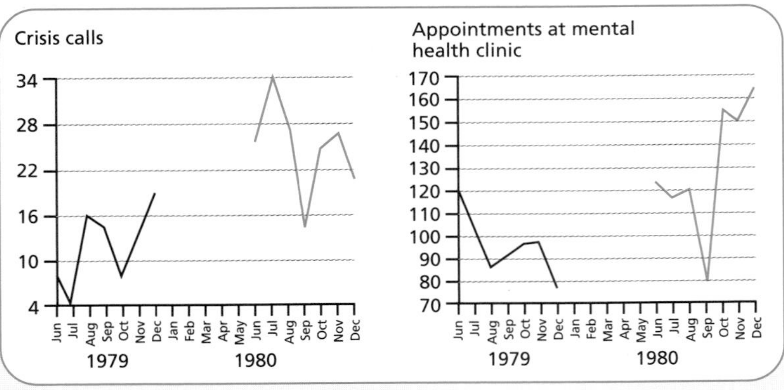

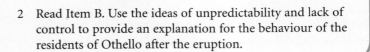

Questions

1 Look at Item A. Suggest an explanation for the high levels of stress experienced by the wives of servicemen missing in action.

2 Read Item B. Use the ideas of unpredictability and lack of control to provide an explanation for the behaviour of the residents of Othello after the eruption.

1.4 Conflict and frustration

Conflict is used here to refer to internal conflict. People often experience conflict when they have two incompatible goals or courses of action. They can only attain one goal or follow one course of action at the expense of the other. For example, a couple are forced to choose between the following – 1) a family holiday which they really need because they haven't been away for four years; 2) a new car because the old one is only fit for the scrap heap. However, they can only afford one of these options. Internal conflict can result from this incompatibility, especially if there is little to choose between the goals.

Conflict can produce frustration. In fact, frustration is often defined as a negative feeling that results from delaying or preventing the attainment of a goal or a course of action. Examples of situations which typically produce frustration are: missing an important appointment because the train was late; being overlooked for promotion which you feel is long overdue.

Internal conflict and frustration can be sources of stress.

Role conflict This occurs when a person feels that, to some extent, their roles are incompatible – the performance of one social role is impaired by other, equally important, roles. For example, women often find difficulty combining their roles as wife, mother, employee and housewife. Each role is demanding in terms of time, emotion and energy and the effective performance of one role can impair the performance of others. The result can be stressful, especially in emergency situations – for example, if a child is ill and requires nursing and taking time off work is out of the question.

Key terms

Incompatible goals *The presence of two or more goals where the attainment of one goal prevents the attainment of another goal.*

Frustration *A negative feeling that results from the delay or prevention of a course of action or the attainment of a goal.*

Role conflict *A situation in which the requirements for the successful performance of two or more social roles conflict.*

Increasing numbers of women are entering the labour force in Western societies. However, they still have the main responsibility for domestic tasks – housework and childcare (Haralambos, 1996). This suggests that, for many women, role conflict and the stress it produces may be increasing.

1.5 Life events

Life events are significant changes in a person's life which disrupt their normal routines. They include marriage and divorce, a new job or the loss of an existing job, moving house, the death of a close relative or the birth of a new member of the family. They include both positive and negative events, events which are seen as desirable and undesirable. A number of researchers argue that life events are a major source of stress.

The most famous application of this idea is the Social Readjustment Rating Scale (SRRS) devised by Holmes and Rahe (1967). They argued that whenever an individual had to make 'a substantial adjustment to the environment, the likelihood of stress is high'. Holmes and Rahe began their research by examining the medical records of around 5000 people. They found that, in many cases, significant life changes occurred in the months preceding the onset of illness. They selected 43 of these life events and asked a sample of 394 people to rate the degree of 'social readjustment' required for each event. Based on the results, they constructed the SRRS – see Table 1. Each life event was ranked and assigned a number of *life change units* (LCUs) from 100 (death of spouse – husband or wife) to 11 (minor violations of the law such as a speeding ticket). A person's *stress score* is the sum of all the life change units for events they have experienced within a period of 12 months.

Table 1 Social Readjustment Rating Scale

Rank	Life event	Value
1	Death of spouse	100
2	Divorce	73
3	Marital separation	65
4	Jail term	63
5	Death of close family member	63
6	Personal injury or illness	53
7	Marriage	50
8	Fired at work	47
9	Marital reconciliation	45
10	Retirement	45
11	Change in health of family member	44
12	Pregnancy	40
13	Sex difficulties	39
14	Gain of new family member	39
15	Business readjustment	39
16	Change in financial state	38
17	Death of a close friend	37
18	Change to different line of work	36
19	Change in number of arguments with spouse	35
20	Mortgage or loan over $10,000	31
21	Foreclosure of mortgage or loan	30
22	Change in responsibilities at work	29
23	Son or daughter leaving home	29
24	Trouble with in-laws	29
25	Outstanding personal achievement	28
26	Wife begins or stops work	26
27	Begin or end school	26
28	Change in living conditions	25
29	Revision of personal habits	24
30	Trouble with boss	23
31	Change in work hours or conditions	20
32	Change in residence	20
33	Change in schools	20
34	Change in recreation	19
35	Change in church activities	19
36	Change in social activities	18
37	Mortgage or loan less than $10,000	17
38	Change in sleeping habits	16
39	Change in number of family get-togethers	15
40	Change in eating habits	15
41	Vacation	13
42	Christmas	12
43	Minor violations of the law	11

Holmes and Rahe (1967)

Evaluation of the SRRS

Advantages

Ease of measurement and use The SRRS offers a simple, straightforward measure of stress. It is quick and easy to administer – people just tick off the events that have happened to them over a period of 12 months. It is easy to score – the researcher simply adds up the total of life change units. Partly as a result of this, the SRRS was used in thousands of studies.

Stress and illness (1) If the SRRS is an effective instrument for measuring stress, then the higher the individual's stress score, the greater their risk of subsequent illness. Many studies have claimed to have found this relationship. For example, people with heart disease have been shown to have higher life change unit scores than healthy people. However, as we shall see, the relationship between high LCU scores and the onset of illness is not particularly strong.

Disadvantages

Stress and illness (2) Although there is a correlation between high LCU scores and later illness, it is not a particularly strong one. A survey of studies using the SRRS indicates a correlation of around 0.3 (Sarafino, 1994). If a high LCU score is always associated with illness, the correlation would be 1.0. If it is never associated with illness, the correlation would be 0. A correlation of 0.3 indicates a fairly weak relationship.

Correlation vs causation Just because two things are correlated does not necessarily mean that one causes the other. Some illnesses can develop undetected over long periods of time. Some of the life events included in the SRRS may result from the early stages of an illness rather than causing that illness. Possible examples are changes in eating and sleeping habits, trouble with in-laws and the boss, and sex difficulties, all of which may be a response to a developing illness (Brown, 1986).

Cognitive appraisal and individual differences Those who complete the SRRS questionnaire simply tick off the life events they have experienced. This says nothing about the meaning they give to these events, nothing about their cognitive appraisal of these life changes. In terms of the transactional model, the only valid (true) measurement of stress is of perceived stress. The 43 life events on the SRRS may be perceived very differently by different people. For example, a son or daughter leaving home may be experienced as a loss by one set of parents, as a blessed relief by another set. The SRRS does not take individual differences in response to possible stressors into account.

More recent measuring instruments have tried to correct these shortcomings. For example, the Life Experiences Survey takes cognitive appraisal into account by asking participants for their assessments of the life events they have experienced (Sarason et al., 1978).

Retrospective data Information about life events is usually collected at least 6 months and often up to 18 months after the events have happened. Asking people to recall events may produce invalid data. They may simply forget. And, there is evidence to suggest that people who are ill when they are filling in the questionnaire are more likely to remember negative events.

To overcome the problems of retrospective data, researchers have used a prospective approach which follows healthy individuals over a number of years, noting their life events and illnesses. This method has produced stronger correlations (Brown & Harris, 1989).

Do change and readjustment lead to stress? The basic idea behind the SRRS is that the change and readjustment produced by life events leads to stress. A number of researchers have questioned this view, arguing that factors other than change and readjustment may account for many of the SRRS life events being perceived as stressful. There is evidence that changes seen as negative, eg divorce, produce more stress than changes seen as positive, eg marriage. The top 6 events in the SRRS would probably be perceived as negative. This, rather than the readjustment they require, may result in stress. In the same way, many of the events on the SRRS may be perceived as uncontrollable and/or unpredictable. Again this perception, rather than change and readjustment, may lead to stress (Brown, 1986).

Conclusion Because of the above criticisms, the SRRS is rarely used today. Despite this, it was a landmark in the measurement of stress. Without it, the more recent scales, which represent refinements of and improvements on the SRRS, would not have been developed.

Key term

Life events *Significant changes in a person's life which require a substantial readjustment in their normal routines.*

Activity 4 Life events and stress

Marriage, number 7 on the SRRS

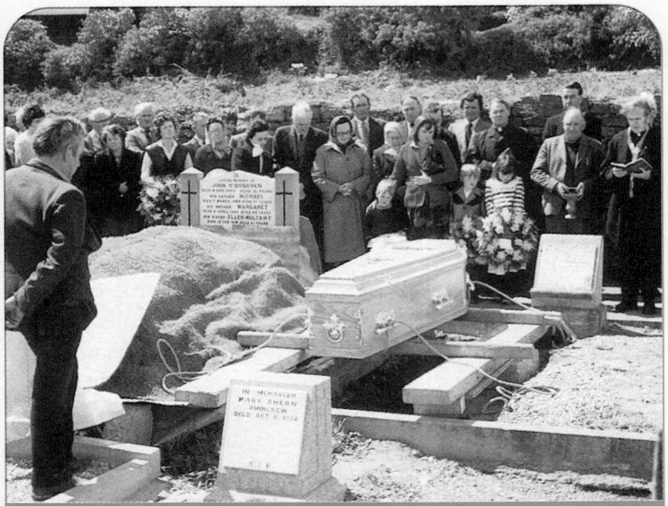

Death of a close friend, number 17 on the SRRS

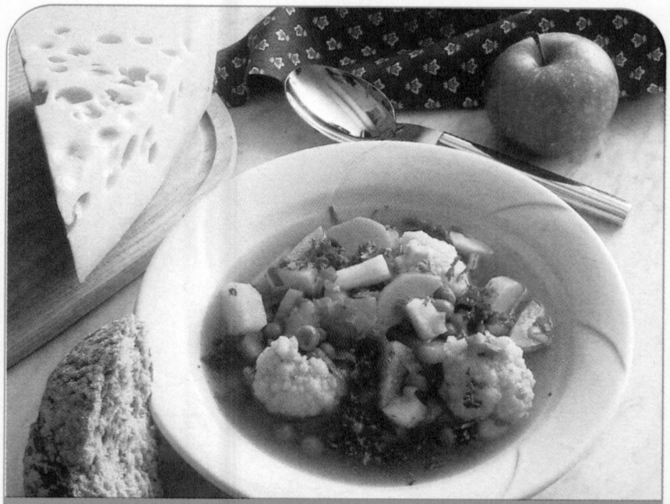
Change in eating habits to a vegetarian diet, number 40 on the SRRS

Christmas, number 42 on the SRRS

Questions

1 Briefly suggest how the life events pictured above might lead to stress.

2 Suggest reasons for their ranking on the Social Readjustment Rating Scale. For example, why is marriage rated as more stressful than Christmas?

Daily hassles and uplifts

Major life events don't occur every day. As their name suggests, *daily hassles* often do. Daily hassles are 'the irritating, frustrating, distressing demands that to some degree characterise everyday transactions with the environment' (Kanner et al., 1981). Table 2 lists the ten most common daily hassles experienced by 100 middle-aged adults.

A number of researchers argue that daily hassles lead to more stress and have a greater impact on physical and mental health than life events. In one study, using a hassles scale of 117 items, 100 middle-aged adults completed the scale each month for nine consecutive months. They also completed the SRRS life events scale. Hassles scores were a better predictor of psychological problems, such as depression and anxiety, than life events scores (Kanner et al., 1981).

The opposite of daily hassles – which get people down – are *daily uplifts* which, as their name suggests, give people a boost which makes them feel better. Table 3 lists the 10 most common daily uplifts experienced by 100 middle-aged adults.

Some studies combine the hassles and uplifts scales. For example, one study showed that people are likely to experience an increase in daily hassles and a decrease in daily uplifts a few days before the onset of a respiratory infection, eg a cold (Stone et al., 1987). The results of this study are shown in Figure 2.

Table 2 Daily hassles

1	Concerns about weight
2	Health of a family member
3	Rising prices of common goods
4	Home maintenance
5	Too many things to do
6	Misplacing or losing things
7	Outside home maintenance
8	Property, investment or taxes
9	Crime
10	Physical appearance

Kanner et al., 1981

Table 3 Daily uplifts

1	Relating well to spouse or lover
2	Relating well to friends
3	Completing a task
4	Feeling healthy
5	Getting enough sleep
6	Eating out
7	Meeting your responsibilities
8	Visiting, phoning or writing to someone
9	Spending time with the family
10	Finding your home a pleasant environment

Kanner et al., 1981

Figure 2 Hassles, uplifts and respiratory infection

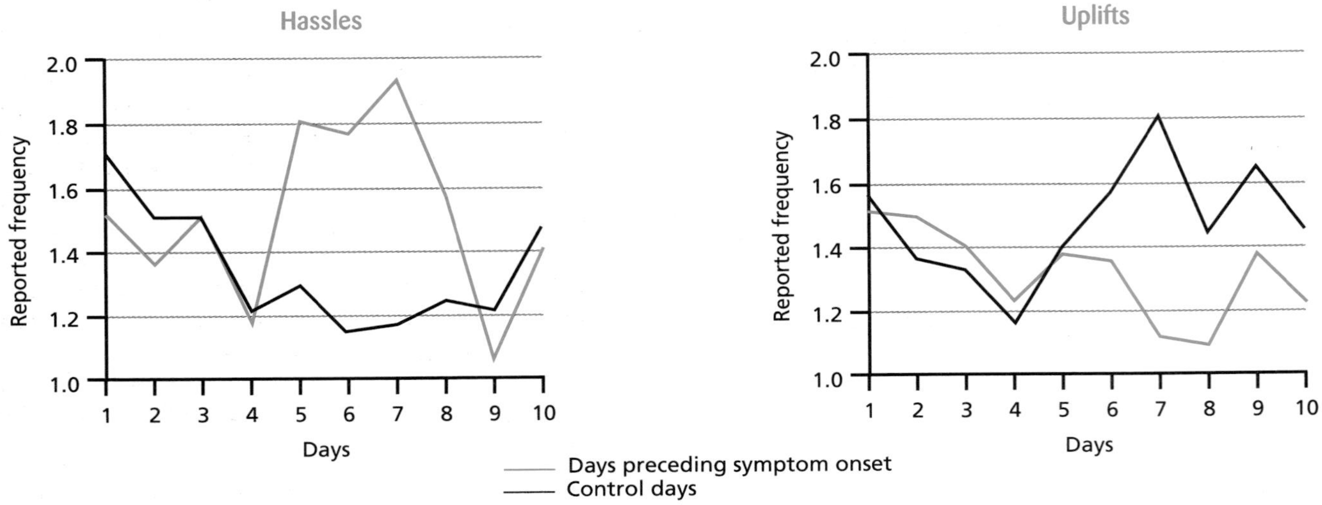

Number of undesirable events (hassles) in the 10 days before the onset of respiratory infection. Control days refer to a 10 day period which was not followed by a respiratory infection.

Number of desirable events (uplifts) in the 10 days before the onset of respiratory infection.

Adapted from Stone et al. 1987

How might daily hassles lead to stress and illness? First, their effect may be cumulative – the minor stresses produced by daily hassles may build up and wear people down, so making them more vulnerable to psychological and physical disorders. Second, the effects of daily hassles may combine with the effects of life events to produce higher levels of stress.

Evaluation The daily hassles scale has some of the same problems as the SRRS. The link between hassles and psychological and physical disorders is correlational. It is therefore difficult to separate cause from effect – to say what causes what. For example, the increase in hassles preceding a cold may be due to feeling rundown as a result of the early stages of the illness. Because of this, situations which people would normally take in their stride are interpreted and experienced as hassles. However, in the research outlined above (Stone et al., 1987), this criticism may not apply – two days before the onset of a cold the rates of hassles and uplifts had returned to average levels.

1.6 Workplace stressors

In recent years the workplace has been seen as the major source of stress. A Trades Union Congress survey claimed that two out of three workers experienced occupational stress. According to one report, stress has overtaken the common cold as the main cause of absence from work (Furedi, 1999). This section looks at some of the findings of research concerned with stress in the workplace.

Key terms

Daily hassles *Everyday events which people find annoying, irritating, frustrating and distressing.*

Daily uplifts *Everyday events which people find pleasurable and uplifting.*

Work overload One way of identifying work overload is in terms of the number of hours worked per week. This assumes that long hours result in work overload. A number of studies suggest a relationship between long hours, stress and ill-health. For example, a study of workers under the age of 45 in light industry found that those who worked over 48 hours a week were twice as likely to develop coronary heart disease than those who worked 40 hours or less (Breslow & Buell, 1960).

However, research indicates that it is the *perception* of work overload that is the important factor rather than the number of hours and the actual amount of work. In this sense, work overload is a perception held by a worker that they are required to work too long and/or too hard.

Repetitive work Jobs which require frequent repetition of a simple task have often been linked to indicators of stress. As noted earlier, a study of Swedish sawmill workers, who did little more than 'feed' machines with timber, indicated that they suffered from a high rate of stress-related illnesses – stomach and intestinal disorders, hypertension (high blood pressure) and frequent headaches. Urine analysis revealed high levels of adrenaline and noradrenaline which suggests they were experiencing stress (Frankenhaeuser, 1975; see also p 109).

Workers find repetitive jobs boring and monotonous. There is little opportunity to take pride in the job or feel a sense of achievement. Here's how one worker described the task he performed, day in and day out, at an engineering factory.

> 'I make these washers on this press. If I work fast I can take home good money. It's the same thing over and over again though. Put the blank on, drop the guard, that presses out the washer. I put it in that box and get the next blank. It's the same all day, over and over again. Sometimes it gets on top of you' (Cox, 1978).

Social isolation In some work situations, workers are isolated from each other. This often happens when machines control work operations, as in the case of the sawmill workers described above. Workers are tied to machines with little opportunity to move around the shop floor and talk to each other. Social isolation is related to various indicators of stress, for example high levels of adrenaline and noradrenaline (Cooper & Marshall, 1976).

Lack of control As noted earlier, people often experience stress when they believe they have little or no control over a situation. Lack of control is often associated with the sources of workplace stress outlined so far in this section. Many workers feel they have to accept work overload to keep their jobs, improve their chances of promotion or, in the case of overtime, to pay the bills. Lack of control is often a characteristic of repetitive work, especially when machines control the speed of work and the way the task is performed. And workers can do little about social isolation if they are tied to a machine.

Self-report studies indicate that workers experiencing stress often complain of a lack of control in the workplace. In particular, they feel excluded from decision-making processes. For example, a survey conducted by the Manufacturing, Science and Finance Union indicated that one of the main causes of stress according to their members was 'little or no involvement in decision making' (*Labour Research*, July, 1995).

Environmental factors A variety of environmental or physical aspects of the workplace have been linked with stress. These include temperature, humidity, noise, vibration, lighting and ventilation. For example, a number of studies have found that high noise levels in factories appear to be linked with hypertension, headaches and stomach and intestinal disorders (Bell et al., 1990).

Role ambiguity A role is a set of directives about how to behave when occupying a particular social position or status. Role ambiguity occurs when the guidelines for a role are unclear and ill-defined. It is regularly reported as one of the main factors contributing to stress in the workplace. For example, a survey in the USA based on a sample of 1500 respondents found that 35% were unclear about their job responsibilities and felt they had no clear guidelines for task performance. Role ambiguity appeared to be linked with low job satisfaction and low self-confidence (Kahn et al., 1964).

Role conflict As noted earlier, role conflict can be a source of stress. Role conflict occurs when the requirements of two or more roles conflict or when aspects of one particular role conflict. An example of the first instance is when a work role conflicts with a non-work role, such as the role of parent. A full-time job can conflict with the responsibilities of looking after young children. An example of the second instance – when aspects of a role conflict – is provided by middle management who have responsibilities to shop-floor workers and to higher management. Demands from higher management for greater output may conflict with demands from the shop floor for better working conditions (Arnold et al., 1991).

Evaluation Despite the large amount of research on stress in the workplace, it is difficult to pinpoint specific sources of stress and separate them from other factors which may contribute to stress. Take the example of noise in the workplace. It has been linked to stress and stress-related illness. But people who work in noisy environments often have low-income, low-skill, low-status jobs, they often work long hours and have little control over their work. Outside the workplace, low income and poor housing may add further pressures to their lives. It is difficult to separate the effect of noise at work from all the other factors which may affect stress levels and health (Banyard, 1996).

Many employers now take stress in the workplace very seriously. Stress is bad for business – it is seen to cause ill-health, absenteeism, high staff turnover and low job performance, all of which cost companies money. And in 1999, for the first time, workers in the UK successfully sued employers for stress and stress-related illness caused by work. Around a third of employers now offer stress counselling to their employees.

Some researchers believe that this emphasis on stress has got out of hand. They suggest that practically every emotional problem at work is now translated into the fashionable jargon of stress. According to the sociologist Frank Furedi (1999), 'After a while propaganda about stress will have the effect of convincing people that the everyday difficulties are indeed ruining their health. Worse still, we are in danger of creating a world where we lose confidence in people's ability to cope with the normal challenges associated with the world of work.' But this does not mean that stress is absent from the workplace. Nor does it remove responsibility from employers for reducing stress.

Key term

Role ambiguity *A situation in which the guidelines for a role are unclear and ill-defined.*

Summary

1 The transactional model of stress states that stress is a transaction between the individual and their environment. From this point of view, an event only becomes a stressor when the individual interprets and perceives it as such.

2 Research has indicated that situations with the following characteristics are likely to be perceived as stressors and experienced as stressful.

- Lack of control – when people feel they have little or no control over a situation.
- Unpredictability – when events cannot be predicted and, as a result, cannot be prepared for.
- Conflict and frustration which result from incompatible goals or courses of action.
- Life events – significant changes in a person's life which require a major readjustment to their normal routines.
- Daily hassles – everyday events which people find annoying, irritating, frustrating and distressing.

3 A number of workplace stressors have been identified. They include work overload, repetitive work, social isolation, lack of control, environmental factors, role ambiguity and role conflict.

Unit 2 Individual differences and stress

KEY ISSUES

1 What are individual differences?

2 How might they affect the perception of stressors and the experience of stress?

2.1 Individual differences

Unit 1 looked at the types of situations which are likely to be 1) perceived as stressors and 2) experienced as stressful. Some people are more likely than others to perceive situations as stressors and experience them as stressful. This unit asks why this is so. The short answer is because of individual differences.

Some of the more important factors which differentiate individuals are:

- **Culture** – the learned, shared behaviour of members of a society. To some extent people from different cultures see the world differently and behave in different ways.
- **Subculture** – the learned, shared behaviour of particular groups within a society, for example ethnic minority groups. While they share much of the mainstream culture, they may have distinctive norms, values and beliefs, for example, religious beliefs. In other words, they may have their own subculture.
- **Social class** – all modern industrial societies have a class system, a system of social inequality which divides people in terms of wealth and income, power and status.
- **Ethnicity** – to some extent members of ethnic minority groups have their own identity, lifestyle and subculture.
- **Gender** – there are important differences in identity and experience between men and women.
- **Age** – age differences can affect people's outlook, concerns and priorities, their interests and behaviour.
- **Individual experiences** – every individual has a unique life-history with experiences which are unique to themselves.
- **Personality** – people can be differentiated in terms of their personality characteristics.
- **Outlook on life** – the way individuals see the world. For example, some people see life in optimistic terms whilst others have a pessimistic view of the world.
- **Resources** – individuals differ in terms of the resources they have available for dealing with situations. Resources include time, energy, health, money and social support, (that is the amount of support available from others).
- **Biology** – to some extent every individual differs in terms of their biological makeup.

All the above factors contribute to individual differences. They can make a difference to the perception of possible stressors and the experience of stress. These factors are sometimes known as *stress moderators* because they modify the experience of stress.

Only some of the individual differences in the above list have been systematically researched in relation to stress. Those that have will form the basis of the rest of this unit.

2.2 Personality and behaviour patterns

Most of the research on individual differences and stress has focused on individual differences in *personality* and *behaviour patterns*. Personality is difficult to define and the term has been used in many different ways. A typical definition sees an individual's personality as their characteristic ways of behaving, thinking, feeling, reacting and perceiving the world. Behaviour patterns refer to a set of activities and reactions which are patterned in a certain way – they have certain common characteristics. At times, the terms personality and behaviour patterns are used interchangeably. For example, some researchers use the term Type A personality, others use Type A behaviour patterns. They are effectively referring to the same thing.

Activity 5 Individual differences

Item A Culture and divorce

In traditional Apache culture, divorce was simple, straightforward and frequent. To divorce his wife, a man simply took his few possessions and returned to his parents' wickiup (wicker hut). To divorce her husband, a woman removed his belongings and placed them outside his parents' wickiup.

Apache women

Item B Daily hassles

Daily hassles	Students (n=161)	Mothers (n=120)	Elderly (n=150)
Time pressure	1	2	4
Future security	2	4	3
Finances	3	1	4
Household	3	1	4
Neighbourhood	4	3	1
Health	4	3	1

Participants in this New Zealand survey were asked to rank the daily hassles on a scale of 1 to 4 with 1 being the most severe, 4 being the least severe. The mothers had one or more young children at home. (n = the number of participants in each group in the survey.)

Adapted from Zimbardo et al., 1995

Questions

1 Divorce is number 2 on the Social Readjustment Rating Scale. What does Item A suggest about cultural differences in the perception of stressors and the experience of stress?

2 Look at Item B.
a) What does it indicate about the importance of individual differences and stress?
b) Suggest reasons for the main differences in ranking by the three groups.

Type A personality and behaviour

During the 1950s, two heart specialists Friedman and Rosenman noticed that heart attack victims tended to have certain ways of behaving. They called these the Type A pattern (Friedman & Rosenman, 1974; see also p 106). Type A people are highly competitive, they are impatient, hostile, aggressive, impulsive, and they find it difficult to relax. Table 4 is a measure of Type A personality devised by Friedman and Rosenman. It gives a picture of how they see the Type A pattern.

The Type B pattern is the opposite of Type A. Type B individuals are not driven to succeed and impress, they can relax and do nothing without feeling guilty, they are not competitive and hostile, they are easy-going rather than impatient.

In a study entitled *Type A behaviour and your heart,* Friedman and Rosenman (1974) examined over 3500 healthy middle-aged men during an $8^1/2$ year period. They found that those with Type A patterns were twice as likely to have heart diseases than those with Type B patterns. Although some studies provided support for these findings, others did not. Later studies indicated that the crucial factor

Table 4 A measure of the Type A personality

Are you a Type A? Take this short test. If you check a majority of the items, you probably fit the Type A pattern.

----- 1 Do you find it difficult to restrain yourself from hurrying others' speech (finishing their sentences for them)?
----- 2 Do you often try to do more than one thing at a time (such as eat and read simultaneously)?
----- 3 Do you often feel guilty if you use extra time to relax?
----- 4 Do you tend to get involved in a great number of projects at once?
----- 5 Do you find yourself racing through yellow lights when you drive?
----- 6 Do you need to win in order to derive enjoyment from games and sport?
----- 7 Do you generally move, walk, and eat rapidly?
----- 8 Do you agree to take on too many responsibilities?
----- 9 Do you detest waiting in lines?
----- 10 Do you have an intense desire to better your position in life and impress others?

Friedman & Rosenman, 1974

which predicted heart disease, was hostility rather than the broad range of behaviour patterns included in Type A. For example, 118 male law students were given a personality test designed to measure hostility. Those with high scores were five times more likely than those with low scores to die before the age of 50 (Barefoot et al., 1989).

Cynical hostility A pattern of behaviour known as *cynical hostility* has recently been identified (Woodall & Matthews, 1993). It appears that people with this behaviour pattern are particularly prone to stress and stress-related illness. They are suspicious, resentful and distrustful of others, they frequently get angry and antagonistic and they rapidly become hostile when challenged.

Behaviour patterns, stress and illness What is the relationship between particular behaviour patterns, stress and illness? There are a number of possibilities. People with Type A and cynical hostility patterns may be more likely to perceive events as stressors and to react to them more strongly. The repetition of this response over a period of time may lead to stress-related illnesses and particularly to heart disease.

If an individual often reacts excessively to stressors, they are placing strain on several body systems: they experience raised blood pressure, increased heart rate and other symptoms produced by the arousal of the sympathetic nervous system. This may create wear and tear within the circulation system, perhaps damaging blood vessels and forcing the heart to pump blood at high pressure through narrowed blood vessels. In addition, the release of stress-related hormones, such as cortisol, from the adrenal glands tends to raise the fat content in the blood. The deposit of fats in arteries is an important factor leading to the narrowing of the arteries and heart disease.

On the other hand, these relationships are hard to prove. Certainly people who exhibit a great deal of hostility and aggression do appear to have higher levels of fats in their blood. But, they may just have a general tendency to overactivity within the autonomic nervous system (perhaps genetically inherited) so that both the hostility and the heart disease might be caused by this third factor. In other words, we cannot say that cynical hostility causes the heart illnesses (Bernstein et al., 1997).

Hardiness

Suzanne Kobasa (1979), claimed that people with a certain personality type – which she termed *hardiness* – are less likely to perceive events as stressors. And, if they do perceive them as stressors, they are likely to experience lower levels of stress.

Kobasa studied managers who worked for a public service company in a large American city. Using the Social Readjustment Rating Scale, she selected those who had experienced a relatively high number of life event stressors over the previous three years. She then compared those who were frequently ill with those who had few illnesses to see if she could discover any differences between the two groups. She found that those who were rarely ill had a personality type and outlook on life which she called hardiness.

Hardiness has three dimensions.

- **Challenge** – seeing change as a challenge rather than a threat.
- **Commitment** – getting directly involved in situations and focusing on solving problems.
- **Control** – believing that the individual has control over their own actions and can influence their environment.

Why were the hardy managers more healthy? First, they were less likely to perceive life events as stressors. Second, if they did see them as stressors, they tended to see them as a challenge rather than a threat. As a result, they were more likely to face the problem and take steps to solve it. They were therefore likely to experience the situation as less stressful.

Later evidence provides some support for the benefits of hardiness. For example, in one experiment, two groups of students were given a task, told they were being videotaped and that their performance would be evaluated. The first group had high scores on a measure of hardiness, the second group had low scores. The hardy group perceived the task as less threatening and showed fewer signs of frustration (Wiebe, 1991).

Evaluation Despite some support for Kobasa's findings, her concept of hardiness and her view of its relationship to stress and illness have been criticised. Some researchers have argued that hardiness, as such, makes little difference to the experience of stress and its relationship to illness. People who score highly on measures of hardiness may simply take better care of themselves and this accounts for their better health (Allred & Smith, 1989). Other researchers have argued that people who score low on measures of hardiness may simply interpret their experiences in a negative way. This, rather than low hardiness, may explain their experience of stress and their susceptibility to illness. And the tests designed to assess hardiness may be measuring *negative affectivity* (see below) rather than hardiness (Funk, 1992).

Negative affectivity

This term refers to a general tendency to experience dissatisfaction, distress and a range of negative emotions. People with high negative affectivity are more likely to perceive events as stressors and to experience a high level of stress. A review of research findings found a consistent, but fairly weak link between high negative affectivity and stress-related illnesses such as ulcers and heart disease (Friedman & Booth-Kewley, 1987).

Pessimistic explanatory style

Some people have a tendency to explain negative experiences in pessimistic terms. They tend to blame themselves for what's happened and see stressful events as outside their control. For example, a pessimistic explanatory style for divorce may state, 'It's my fault', 'I have problems with all my relationships', 'I can't see the situation changing'. They tend to see stressors in a very negative light and because of their pessimism about the past, present and future, often experience high levels of stress. They are likely to perceive stressors as long term and are pessimistic about their ability to deal with them. A study of 99 Harvard University graduates found that those with a pessimistic explanatory style at age 25 were more likely to be in poor health or dead at ages 45-50 (Peterson et al., 1988).

Dispositional optimism

This refers to people with an optimistic disposition and outlook on life. They tend to see things in a positive light and believe that everything will work out in the end. They are more likely to see stressors as short term and less likely to blame themselves for the situation. As a result they usually perceive fewer events as stressors and experience lower levels of stress. In one study, heart bypass patients with high scores on a questionnaire designed to measure dispositional optimism, recovered more rapidly in hospital and returned to normal life more quickly after their discharge (Scheier et al., 1989).

Conclusion Negative affectivity and pessimistic explanatory style appear to predispose people to stress and reduce their ability to deal effectively with stressful situations. On the other hand, dispositional optimism presents a picture of the stress-resistant individual who is much better able to cope with stressful situations.

Key terms

Personality *Characteristic ways of behaving, thinking, feeling, reacting and perceiving the world.*

Behaviour patterns *A set of activities and reactions which have certain common characteristics.*

Type A pattern *A type of personality and/or a set of behaviour patterns characterised by competitiveness, impatience, hostility and aggression.*

Cynical hostility *A type of personality and/or a set of behaviour patterns characterised by suspicion, resentment and hostility.*

Hardiness *A personality type which sees change as a challenge, which has a strong commitment to get involved and a belief that the individual can control their own actions and influence their environment.*

Negative affectivity *A general tendency to experience dissatisfaction, distress and a range of negative emotions.*

Pessimistic explanatory style *A tendency to explain negative events in pessimistic terms, often involving self-blame.*

Dispositional optimism *An optimistic disposition and outlook on life.*

2.3 Gender

There is some evidence of gender differences in the perception of stressors and the experience of stress. In one experiment, males and females were placed in a routine, non-stressful situation and then in a stressful situation – they were given an intelligence test. Females showed little increase in the secretion of adrenaline from one situation to the next. However, males showed a marked increase, which suggests that they perceived the test as a stressor and were experiencing stress (Johansson & Post, 1972). In general, research indicates that, compared to men, women show smaller increases in the standard physiological measures of stress – heart rate, blood pressure and secretion of 'stress-hormones' (Matthews et al., 1991).

A number of reasons have been suggested for these differences. First, biological differences between males and females may affect their physiological reaction to stress. Second, women are less likely to have Type A personalities and hostile behaviour patterns (Weidner & Collins, 1993). Third, the way women have traditionally been socialised for a female role, with an emphasis on caring, might make them less aggressive and competitive.

However, things might be changing. Type A behaviour patterns are linked to the male occupational role in Western society. The male work role often involves competition, aggression and striving for advancement. As women enter the labour force in increasing numbers and, in particular, increasingly enter traditional male occupations, their behaviour patterns may well become similar to those of men. There is evidence to support this view. One study found that in response to stressors, the levels of adrenaline in female engineering students and bus drivers were similar to those of men (Frankenhaeuser et al., 1983).

As noted in the previous unit, women often have the dual burden of paid employment and domestic tasks – housework and childcare. This not only involves more work, it can also result in role conflicts if the demands of being a wage earner and a mother conflict. This may increase the number of stressors in women's lives and their experience of stress. Evidence from a study of male and female white collar workers at the Volvo plant in Gothenburg, Sweden, suggests that this may be the case. At work, noradrenaline levels for both sexes were similar. But, after work, levels for men declined while those of women rose (Frankenhaeuser et al., 1989).

2.4 Class and ethnicity

Social class In general, research indicates that people in the lower levels of the class system live more stressful lives than people in higher levels. This appears particularly so for people living in poverty, at the bottom of the class system. One of the main reasons suggested for this, is the multitude of stressors in their environment – low income, substandard and overcrowded housing, high levels of unemployment, low social status and high levels of street crime and burglary (Pitts & Phillips, 1998).

Ethnicity Research into ethnicity and stress is limited. However, studies in the USA suggest there may be differences between African Americans and the white majority. The rate of hypertension – high blood pressure – is particularly high among lower class African Americans. Hypertension is generally regarded as a stress-related illness. Part of the explanation for this is to do with class rather than ethnicity. In general, lower-class African Americans have more severe stressors in their environment than lower-class whites. For example, their rate of unemployment is over twice that of their white counterparts and their income significantly lower.

However, this forms only part of the explanation. A study which carefully matched black and white women in terms of their income and class position found that black women were twice as likely to have hypertension (Adams-Campbell et al., 1993). One suggestion for this difference is the widespread racism in American society – in housing, occupation, leisure and day-to-day interaction. A major source of stress may be African-Americans' perception that, to some extent, their route to self-improvement is blocked by racism (Anderson, 1991).

Summary

1. Individual differences affect the perception of possible stressors and the experience of stress.
2. A number of personality types and behaviour patterns appear to predispose people to perceive events as stressors and to experience high levels of stress. These include:
   - Type A personality and behaviour patterns
   - Cynical hostility
   - Negative affectivity
   - Pessimistic explanatory styles.
3. Other individual differences appear to have the opposite effect. They include:
   - Type B personality and behaviour patterns
   - Hardiness
   - Dispositional optimism.
4. Differences in terms of gender, social class and ethnicity appear to affect the amount of stress people experience in their daily lives.

Unit 3 Measuring stress

KEY ISSUES

1 How is stress identified and measured?

2 How accurate are measurements of stress?

Research on stress stands and falls on the identification and measurement of stress. How do we know that stress is present? How can we measure the level of stress? This unit looks at these questions.

3.1 Physiological measures

The physiological stress response provides one way of identifying and measuring stress. Since stress involves physiological changes, measurements can be made from samples of blood, urine or saliva. The presence or level of certain hormones and neurotransmitter chemicals indicates the level of activity in particular nervous systems.

There are a number of problems with this approach. Simply measuring the level of a hormone does not tell us how stressed an individual is feeling. In addition, there are daily cycles in the production of hormones so levels will be affected by the time of day when samples are taken.

3.2 Laboratory experiments

Laboratory experiments provide an opportunity to control and measure certain stressors. For example, extremes of heat and cold are sometimes used as stressors in experiments. Temperature can be easily measured and controlled. Animal experiments provide examples of the control and measurement of stressors. Sleep deprivation experiments are conducted by placing the animal on an upturned flower pot in a pool of water. Every time it falls asleep, its nose drops into the water and it promptly wakes up. The length of sleep deprivation can be timed accurately. Animals are stressed by overcrowding and isolation. Again, these conditions can be timed and, in the case of overcrowding, the density of animals in a fixed area can be measured.

Laboratory experiments with humans have used all sorts of unpleasant experiences to induce stress. They include electric shocks, overcrowding and exposure to high and low temperatures. Again, there is ample opportunity for measurement. In the case of electric shocks, their number, duration and intensity can be measured accurately.

There are, however, a number of problems with laboratory experiments.

- Although they can measure certain aspects of a stressor, for example, temperature, this does not necessarily say anything about its impact on the individual. For example, a comfortable temperature for one person may be uncomfortably hot for another.
- An event or experience only becomes a stressor when it is perceived as such. Despite the accuracy of measurement in the laboratory, this does not tell us how the individual perceives the intended stressor.
- The laboratory is an artificial situation and participants tend to see it as such. For example, one experimental procedure involves participants submerging their arm in a bucket of ice cold water. This hardly reflects their experience of stress in life outside the laboratory.
- Laboratory experiments don't last long. At best they can only measure the strength of short-term stressors and the effect of short-term stress.
- Laboratory experiments raise ethical issues about the treatment of participants, both animal and human. For example, the British Psychological Society's guidelines for the use of animals in research state, 'If the animals are confined, constrained, harmed or stressed in any way the investigator must consider whether the knowledge to be gained justifies the procedure' (BPS, 1998).

3.3 Self-reports

Self-report studies ask people to report their perceptions of stressors and their experience of stress. These studies have the advantage of looking at stress from the point of view of those who experience it. Participants are often asked to keep diaries and, for example, report on daily hassles over a period of days, weeks or months. This overcomes one of the problems with many stress measures which provide only a one-off measure of stress, a snapshot of stress levels at a particular point in time. A diary report can note stress levels at various times during the day or week. The advantage of this can be seen from a study of stress in British drivers (Gulian et al., 1990). Drivers were asked to keep a diary of their feelings when driving, over a five day period. They reported feeling more stress in the evening and midweek. Their stress levels also appeared to be related to driving conditions, how well they'd slept, their age, health and driving experience, and whether or not they perceived driving as a stressful activity.

At best, however, self-report studies can only give a rough and ready guide to stress levels. Asking people to report on their feelings of stress cannot provide an objective and accurate measure of stress levels. Subjective feelings cannot be measured in the same way as temperature. In addition, people may exaggerate or minimise their experience of stress. For example, people with a pessimistic outlook may have a tendency to report higher stress levels than people with an optimistic outlook, even when their experience of stress is similar.

A variation on self-report studies asks participants to assess events which are then used as the basis for a questionnaire designed to measure stress. This method was used to construct the Social Readjustment Rating Scale (SRRS). A sample of 394 people were asked to rate life events in terms of the amount of social readjustment they required. There are a number of problems with this approach. First, many members of the sample may not have experienced some of the 43 life events they were asked to assess, for example death of a spouse and divorce, the top two items on the SRRS. Second, they were asked to make 'snap judgements' about social readjustment, something they had probably not considered before. Despite this, there was considerable agreement on the ranking from a sample composed of different age groups, men and women, Protestants and Catholics. However, the level of agreement was lower between African Americans and whites.

Triangulation

Often researchers combine various methods, a procedure known as *triangulation*. This can provide a means of checking on the accuracy of the data produced by different methods. For example, if physiological data contradicted

Key terms

Physiological measures *The measurement of physiological or bodily processes such as the levels of hormones and neurotransmitters, and heart rate.*

Self-report method *A method which asks people who are being studied to provide information about themselves.*

Triangulation *Using and comparing data produced from two or more research methods.*

Summary

1. There are various ways of measuring stress. Each has strengths and weaknesses.
2. Physiological measures provide evidence about the body's response to stress but this does not tell us how the individual is feeling – that is their experience of stress.
3. Laboratory studies can provide accurate measures of certain stressors. However, the laboratory situation is artificial, and limited to the study of short-term stress.
4. Self-report studies provide an opportunity to obtain people's perceptions of stressors and their experience of stress. However, they cannot provide objective and accurate measures of stress levels.
5. Triangulation provides a means of checking on the accuracy of data produced by different research methods.

data from self-report studies, then this leads the researcher to question the methods and the data they have produced.

Triangulation also produces a fuller picture as different methods produce different types of data. For example, a study of fire-fighters combined self-report and physiological measures. The heart rate of each fire-fighter was recorded when they were at work using a portable electrocardiogram. They also kept a diary recording events they perceived as stressful (Douglas et al., 1988).

References

Abbott, B.B., Schoen, L.S. & Badia, P. (1984). Predictable and unpredictable shock: Behavioural measures of aversion and physiological measures of stress. *Psychological Bulletin, 96*, 45-71.

Adams, P.R. & Adams, G.R. (1984). Mount Saint Helen's ashfall: Evidence for a disaster stress reaction. *American Psychologist, 39*, 252-260.

Adams-Campbell, L.L., Brambilla, D.J. & McKinley, S.M. (1993). Correlates of prevalence of self-reported hypertension among African-American and white women. *Ethnic Diseases, 3*, 119-125.

Allred, K.D. & Smith, T.W. (1989). The hardy personality: Cognitive and physiological responses to evaluative threat. *Journal of Personality and Social Psychology, 56*, 257-266.

Anderson, L.P. (1991). Acculturative stress: A theory of relevance to black Americans. *Clinical Psychology Review, 11*, 685-702.

Arnold, J., Robertson, I.T. & Cooper, C.L. (1991). *Work psychology.* London: Pitman.

Banyard, P. (1996). *Applying psychology to health.* London: Hodder & Stoughton.

Barefoot, J.C., Dodge, K.A., Peterson, B.L., Dahlstrom, W.G. & Williams, R.B., Jr. (1989). The Cook-Medley hostility scale: Item content and ability to predict survival. *Psychosomatic Medicine, 51*, 46-57.

Bell, P.A., Fisher, J.D., Baum, A. & Greene, T.C. (1990). *Environmental psychology*, (3rd ed.). Fort Worth: Holt, Rinehart and Winston.

Bernstein, D.A., Clarke-Stewart, A., Roy, E.J. & Wickens, C.D. (1997). *Psychology* (4th ed.). Boston: Houghton Mifflin.

Billings, A.G. & Moos, R.H. (1981). The role of coping responses and social resources in attenuating the stress of life events. *Journal of Behavioral Medicine, 4*, 139-157.

BPS (British Psychological Society). (1998). *Code of conduct, ethical principles and guidelines*, Leicester: BPA

Breslow, L. & Buell, P. (1960). Mortality from coronary heart disease and physical activity of work in California. *Journal of Chronic Disability,11.*

Brown, G.W. & Harris, T.O. (1978). *Social origins of depression: A study of psychiatric disorder in women.* London: Tavistock.

Brown, R. (1986). *Social psychology: The second edition.* New York: Free Press.

Canby, T.Y. (1990). Earthquake: prelude to the big one. *National Geographic, 177*, no 5, 76-105.

Cooper, C.J. & Marshall, J. (1976). Occupational sources of stress: A review of the literature relating to coronary heart disease and mental ill health. *Journal of Occupational Psychology, 49*, 11-28.

Cox, T. (1978). *Stress.* London: Macmillan.

Douglas, R.B., Blanks, R., Crowther, A. & Scott, G. (1988). A study of stress in West Midlands firemen, using ambulatory electrocardiograms. *Work and Stress, 2*, 309-318.

Frankenhaeuser, M. (1975). Sympathetic-adrenomedullary activity behaviour and the psychosocial environment. In P.H. Venables & M.J. Christie (Eds.), *Research in psychophysiology.* New York: Wiley.

Frankenhaeuser, M. (1983). The sympathetic-adrenal and pituitary-adrenal response to challenge; Comparison between the sexes. In T.M. Dembroski, T.H. Schmidt & G. Blumchen (Eds), *Biobehavioural bases of coronary heart disease.* Basel: Karger.

Frankenhaeuser, M., Lundberg, M., Fredriksson, B., Melin, M. & Thomisto, A., (1989). Stress on and off the job as related to sex and occupational status in whitecollar workers. *Journal of Organisational Behaviour, 10*, 321-346.

Friedman, H.S. & Booth-Kewley, S. (1987). The 'disease-prone' personality; A meta-analytic view of the construct. *American Psychologist, 42*, 539-555.

Friedman, M. & Rosenman, R.H. (1974). *Type A behaviour and your heart.* New York: Knopf.

Funk, S.C. (1992). Hardiness: A review of theory and research. *Health Psychology, 11*, 335-345.

Furedi, F. (1999). Time to put up or shut up. *Independent on Sunday*, 10th October.

Geer, J. & Maisel, E. (1973). Evaluating the effects of the prediction-control confound. *Journal of Personality and Social Psychology, 23*, 314-319.

Gulian, E., Glendon, A.I., Matthews, G. & Davies, D. (1990). The stress of driving: A diary study. *Work and Stress, 4*, 7-16.

Haralambos, M. (Ed.) (1996). *Sociology: A new approach* (3rd ed.). Ormskirk: Causeway.

Hazzard, A., Weston, J. & Gutterres, C. (1992). After a child's death: Factors related to parental bereavement. *Journal of Developmental & Behavioural Paediatrics, 13*, 24-30.

Holmes, T.H. & Rahe, R.H. (1967). The social readjustment rating scale. *Journal of Psychosomatic Research, 11*, 213-218.

Hunter, E.J. (1979, May). Combat casualities who remain at home. Paper presented at Western Regional Conference of the Interuniversity Seminar, 'Technology in Combat'. Navy Postgraduate School, Monterey, CA.

Johansson, G. and Post, B. (1972). Catecholamine output of males and females over a one-year period. *Rep. Psychol. Lab.*, University of Stockholm (379).

Kahn, R.L., Wolfe, D.M., Quinn, R.P., Snoek, J.D & Rosenthal, R.A. (1964). *Organisational stress: Studies in role conflict and ambiguity.* New York: John Wiley.

Kanner, A.D., Coyne, J.C., Schaeffer, C. & Lazarus, R.S. (1981). Comparison of two modes of stress measurement: Daily hassles and uplifts versus major life events. *Journal of Behavioural Medicine, 4*, 1-39.

Katz, R. & Wykes, T. (1985). The psychological difference between temporally predictable and unpredictable stressful events: evidence for information control theories. *Journal of Personality and Social Psychology, 48*, 781-790.

Kobasa, S.C. (1979). Stressful life events and health: An inquiry into hardiness. *Journal of Personality and Social Psychology, 37*, 1-11.

Lazarus, R.S. (1976). *Patterns of adjustment.* New York: McGraw-Hill.

Lundberg, U.(1976). Urban commuting: Crowdedness and catacholamine excretion. *Journal of Human Stress, 2*, 26-32.

Matthews, K.A., Davis, M.C., Stoney, C.M., Owens, J.F. & Caggiula, A.R. (1991). Does the gender relevance of the stressor influence sex differences in psychophysiological responses? *Health Psychology, 10*, 112-120.

Pennebaker, J.W. & Harber, K.D. (1991, April). *Coping after the Loma Prieta earthquake: A preliminary report.* Paper presented at the Western Psychological Association Convention, San Francisco, CA.

Peterson, C., Seligman, M.E.P. & Vaillant, G.E. (1988). Pessimistic explanatory style is a risk factor for physical illness: A thirty-five-year longitudinal study. *Journal of Personality and Social Psychology, 55*, 23-27.

Pitts, M. & Phillips, K. (Eds.) (1998). *The psychology of health: An introduction.* London: Routledge.

Sarafino, E.P. (1994). *Health psychology: Biopsychosocial interactions* (2nd ed.). New York: John Wiley.

Sarason, I.G., Johnson, J.H. & Siegel, J.M. (1978). Assessing the impact of life changes: Development of the Life Experiences Survey. *Journal of Consulting and Clinical Psychology, 46*, 932-946.

Scheier, M.F., Matthews, K.A., Owens, J., Magovern, G.J., Sr., Lefebvre, R.C., Abbott, R.A. & Carver, C.S. (1989). Dispositional optimism and recovery from coronary artery bypass surgery: The beneficial effects on physical and psychological well-being. *Journal of Personality and Social Psychology, 57*, 1024-1040.

Speisman, J., Lazarus, R.S., Mordkoff, A. & Davidson, L. (1964). Experimental reduction of stress based on ego defence theory. *Journal of Abnormal and Social Psychology, 68*, 367-380.

Stone, A.A., Reed, B.R. & Neale, J.M. (1987). Changes in daily event frequency precede episodes of physical symptoms. *Journal of Human Stress, 13*, 70-74.

Weidner, G. & Collins, R.L. (1993). Gender, coping, and health. In H.W. Krohne (Ed.), *Attention and avoidance.* New York: Springer-Verlag.

Weitz, R. (1989). Uncertainty and the lives of persons with AIDS. *Journal of Health and Social Behaviour, 30*, 270-81.

Wiebe, D.J. (1991). Hardiness and stress modification: A test of proposed mechanisms. *Journal of Personality and Social Psychology, 60*, 89-90.

Woodall, K.L. & Matthews, K.A. (1993). Changes in and stability of hostile characteristics: Results from a 4-year longitudinal study of children. *Journal of Personality and Social Psychology, 64*, 491-499.

Zimbardo, P., McDermott, M., Jansz. J. & Metaal, N. (1995). *Psychology: A European text.* London: Harper Collins.

9 Stress management

Introduction

Stress has become one of the major concerns of the new millennium. In the 'Popular Psychology' sections of American bookshops, book after book provides advice on coping with stress. The UK is following suit, with *The little book of calm* topping two million sales in 2000. Stress has become the focus of a cartoon series starring Stressed Eric, a harassed executive. And stress made British legal history in 1999 when Birmingham City Council was ordered by the courts to pay £67,000 to a former employee for personal injury caused by work-related stress. Unison, the trade union which backed her claim, has over 7000 more cases on its books.

Individuals and organisations are increasingly aware of the problems caused by stress. They are increasingly concerned about how to treat stress. This chapter looks at various methods of dealing with the negative effects of stress.

Chapter summary

- **Unit 1 looks at the use of drugs in stress management.**
- **Unit 2 examines biofeedback as a technique for reducing stress.**
- **Unit 3 considers cognitive-behavioural strategies which attempt to reduce stress by changing the way people think and behave.**
- **Unit 4 assesses the contribution of social support to stress reduction.**
- **Unit 5 presents a critical discussion of stress management.**

Unit 1 Drug treatment

KEY ISSUES

1. **Can drugs provide effective treatment for stress?**
2. **What are the disadvantages of drug treatment?**

Units 1 and 2 look at physiological approaches to stress management. These approaches are designed to reduce stress by altering bodily processes.

Stress is sometimes accompanied by anxiety and depression. Drugs can be used to treat these disorders.

Antianxiety drugs The most commonly prescribed antianxiety drugs, or anxiolytics, belong to a family of drugs known as *benzodiazepines*. These are also known as minor tranquillisers, and produced under trade names such as Librium and Valium.

Antianxiety drugs decrease arousal and relax the body by reducing tension in the muscles. Since the stress response involves high arousal, tranquillisers may, in some cases, reduce stress. But drugs have no direct effect on the stressor – for example, they do not mend a broken marriage or solve financial problems. However, they may put a person in a better frame of mind so they can cope more effectively with stressors.

There are a number of possible problems with benzodiazepines.

1 In many cases, when the medication is stopped, anxiety returns.

2 If taken in large doses over a long period of time, people can become psychologically and/or physically dependent on them.

3 There can be undesirable side effects such as drowsiness, impaired memory and depression.

4 They may reduce concentration which can be dangerous in situations such as driving (Comer, 1998).

Antidepressant drugs There are a number of antidepressant drugs which are manufactured under various trade names such as Prozac and Tofranil. Antidepressant drugs can reduce depression and so help the individual to cope more effectively with stressors. However, they can have many of the same problems as benzodiazepines. Antidepressants sometimes have undesirable side effects – in the case of Prozac, nausea, diarrhoea and dizziness. After the medication stops, depression can recur. Drugs may do little or nothing to solve the problem which led to stress in the first place. They may simply provide temporary relief rather than encouraging the individual to face up to and take steps to deal with the problem which led to their depression. In addition, these drugs may produce physical and/or psychological dependence where people feel they need drugs to cope with their problems. Again, this can be counterproductive.

Beta-blockers Long-term stress is often accompanied by high blood pressure which can lead to strokes and hypertension. Beta-blockers are drugs which slow the heart and reduce the strength of its contraction, so reducing blood pressure. They block receptors on the heart which are stimulated by noradrenaline. In this way, they decrease sympathetic nervous system activity. This probably has psychological as well as physiological effects. The individual may feel calm and relaxed as a result of suppression of the sympathetic nervous system.

As with all drug treatments, there is the possibility of side effects. Large doses of beta-blockers can lead to depression and impotence (Taylor, 1995).

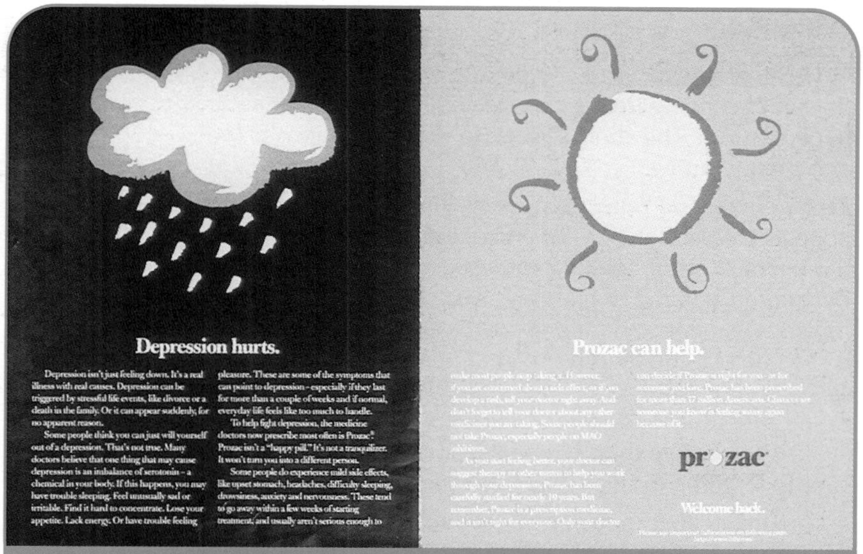

An advert for Prozac

Summary

1. Stress is often accompanied by anxiety and depression. Drugs are sometimes used to treat these disorders. They may reduce stress.
2. The stress response is often accompanied by high blood pressure. Beta-blockers can reduce blood pressure.
3. There are a number of problems with drug treatment.
   - The possibility of physical and psychological dependence
   - Undesirable side effects
   - After usage stops, the problem (eg depression) often returns
   - Drugs have no direct effect on the stressor.

Key terms

Antianxiety drugs or anxiolytics *Drugs prescribed to reduce anxiety.*

Benzodiazepines *Antianxiety drugs commonly known as minor tranquillisers. They decrease arousal and reduce tension in the muscles.*

Antidepressant drugs *Drugs prescribed to reduce depression.*

Beta-blockers *Drugs which slow the heart and reduce the strength of its contraction, so reducing blood pressure.*

Unit 2 Biofeedback

KEY ISSUES

1. **What is biofeedback?**
2. **What are the advantages and disadvantages of this technique?**

Biofeedback is a method which provides people with information about bodily processes such as their heart rate and blood pressure. Often people are unaware of these processes. Biofeedback allows them to 'see' or 'hear' them. For example, heart rate can be monitored and displayed visually on a computer screen. Alternatively, it can be converted into sound, with the tone increasing in pitch the higher the heart rate.

Biofeedback gives people both an awareness of their bodily processes and a means of measuring them. The aim is to help people to control them. Laboratory studies indicate that, with the help of biofeedback, participants can make significant short-term changes in their biological processes, for example raising their heart rate or lowering their blood pressure (Shapiro et al., 1970).

Biofeedback has been used to treat various stress-related illnesses such as migraine headache and hypertension. For example, migraine headache may result from the physiological stress response which involves a redistribution of blood from the skin and the gut to the brain. If a person is able to reverse this process, then the severity of their migraine might be reduced. An increase in body temperature indicates that they have achieved this. A thermometer on a finger provides temperature feedback and the aim is to increase the temperature.

Evaluation

Does biofeedback work? In particular, does it reduce stress, does it effectively treat stress-related illnesses such as hypertension? The short answer to these questions is we don't really know.

Biofeedback and relaxation Even when biofeedback appears to work, it may be relaxation, rather than biofeedback itself, which produces positive results. Relaxation training, which involves steadily relaxing the muscles, is often used alongside biofeedback. Some researchers argue that in the treatment of hypertension, relaxation techniques do more than biofeedback to reduce blood pressure. And, given that relaxation training is usually far less expensive than biofeedback, there is a case for simply learning to relax (Blanchard et al., 1979).

Biofeedback and control Biofeedback gives people a feeling of control. This sense of control, rather than biofeedback itself, may produce beneficial effects. Tension headaches are believed to result from tension in the muscles of the forehead. By attaching electrodes to a person's forehead, the amount of tension can be monitored and fed back as sound – a high pitch when the muscles contract, a low pitch when they are relaxed. Biofeedback has been effective in relaxing the muscles and reducing headaches. However, some studies have indicated that simply believing that muscle tension was being relaxed – even if it wasn't – can lead to a reduction in tension headaches (Holroyd et al., 1984).

This suggests that the key factor might be a sense of control. As noted in the previous chapter, a sense of control can play a major part in reducing stress.

Most of the time people can't be wired up to a heart monitor or walk round with a thermometer on the end of their finger. Can the supposed benefits of biofeedback be carried over into everyday situations to deal with the hassles of daily life? Some supporters of biofeedback believe that people can eventually learn to control their bodily processes without the use of monitoring devices (Turk et al., 1979). Other researchers disagree. However, in the case of tension headaches, there is evidence that people learn to recognise the beginning of tension and are able to reduce it without the help of monitoring devices (Tarler-Benlolo, 1978).

Biofeedback

Short-term benefits Biofeedback may well have short-term benefits, for example, short-term reductions in heartrate and blood pressure. But will this solve anything? In particular, does it deal with the real problems in people's lives? The answer is probably not. However, it may put people in a better frame of mind to deal with those problems.

Conclusion It is too early to celebrate the benefits of biofeedback. As one researcher said, 'Don't hold the party yet' (Melzack, 1975). From a survey of available evidence, Davison and Neale (1998) conclude, 'There is only limited evidence that biofeedback has any specific effects other than distraction, relaxation, and instilling a beneficial sense of control'.

Key terms

Biofeedback *A technique which allows people to monitor their bodily processes. This can give them some control over those processes.*

Summary

1. Laboratory studies indicate that people can exercise some control over their bodily processes with the help of biofeedback.
2. There is some evidence that biofeedback can bring improvements for hypertension and migraine sufferers. However, its effects are probably short term rather than long term.
3. Biofeedback is often used alongside relaxation techniques. Learning to relax may be more beneficial than biofeedback.
4. Biofeedback can give people a sense of control. It may be this, rather than biofeedback itself, which helps to reduce stress.

Unit 3 Psychological approaches

KEY ISSUES

1. **What are the main psychological approaches to stress management?**
2. **What are their strengths and weaknesses?**

Psychological approaches to stress reduction focus on changing the way people think and behave. They are usually known as cognitive-behavioural approaches because they involve cognitive changes – changes in the way people perceive stressors and think about stress – and behavioural changes – actual changes in their behaviour when they respond to and deal with stressful situations. Psychological approaches aim to provide the individual with control over their perception of stressors and their strategies for dealing with stress.

Type A behaviour

As outlined in Chapters 7 and 8, there is evidence which suggests that Type A behaviour patterns increase the risk of stress and coronary heart disease. If this is the case, then a change in these behaviour patterns should lead to a reduction in stress and heart disease. There is some evidence to support this. In one study, over 1000 men who had suffered a heart attack were divided into two groups. The first group were given standard cardiac counselling about reducing risk factors such as smoking and overactivity. In addition to this, the second group took part in a programme designed to reduce Type A behaviour. For example, they were discouraged from seeing stressors as direct personal challenges and from responding to them with aggression and hostility. After three years of counselling, the risk of a further heart attack for men on the Type A reduction programme was 7.2% annually compared to 13.2% for the men who received only standard cardiac counselling (Friedman et al., 1984).

Evaluation This research suggests three possibilities.

1 That a reduction in Type A behaviour reduces stress and, therefore, the risk of coronary heart disease.

2 The key factor was reducing the hostility component rather than the whole range of Type A behaviours (Haaga, 1987).

3 Since the group who took part in the Type A reduction programme received more attention, it was this, rather than a reduction in Type A behaviour, that accounted for their lower rate of heart attacks.

Stress management programmes

Stress management programmes are designed to reduce stress and improve coping skills. Many of these programmes have been developed by health psychologists. People who participate in such programmes either see psychologists on a one-to-one basis, or attend workshops where they are taught stress management techniques and given 'stress counselling'. In addition, there are numerous books and videos on stress management which allow you to 'do it yourself'.

Stress management is big business. Many large organisations employ 'stress consultants' to advise on work practices with the aim of reducing stress in the workplace. They are also employed to give stress management courses to workers.

Stress management programmes are also used to treat people with stress-related illnesses from migraine headaches to hypertension and coronary heart disease.

Stress as a transaction The transactional model of stress forms the basis of many stress management programmes. The transactional model argues that cognitive appraisal is the key to understanding stress. First, a possible stressor is appraised. It becomes a stressor if it is perceived as such. Second, coping abilities and resources for dealing with the situation are appraised. If, for example, abilities and resources are perceived as inadequate, then a high level of stress is likely (see pp 108-109 for a more detailed outline of the transactional model).

It follows from the transactional model that stress can be reduced by cognitive means – by changing the way stressors, coping abilities and resources are appraised. For example, many people worry about giving a speech to a large audience. A standard stress management technique for reducing this concern is to imagine those who might criticise you sitting naked in the audience. The key idea in many stress management programmes is *control* over the perception of stressors and coping strategies.

Increasing hardiness

The previous chapter outlined Kobasa's (1979) research on *hardiness* (see p 120). She claimed that people with a certain personality type, which she called hardiness, were more resistant to stress. People with this type of personality have the following characteristics.

- They see change as a challenge rather than a threat. As a result, they are less likely to perceive change as a stressor.
- They are more likely to face problems and take steps to solve them.
- They believe that people have control over their own actions and can influence their environment.

Hardiness training Kobasa's colleague, Salvator Maddi, founder of the Hardiness Institute in California, has designed a stress management programme based on the idea of hardiness (Maddi, 2000). The programme begins with a Hardi Survey Assessment which assesses people's level of hardiness. It then offers a series of programmes designed to increase hardiness – the HardiTraining Course, HardiWorkshops and HardiCoaching.

The HardiTraining Course is designed to build 'hardy attitudes'. It aims to help people to 'strengthen their beliefs about their effectiveness and coping strategies'. By doing this they will increase their ability to 'view disruptive changes in a more balanced, optimistic light, and to meet them head-on with constructive actions'. The following recipe is provided for increasing hardiness and reducing stress.

- Rather than focusing directly on 'stressful circumstances', they should be viewed in a broader perspective. By doing this, 'they won't seem so terrible after all'.
- Analysing stressful circumstances in order to understand and control them.

- Developing and carrying out an action plan in order to eliminate the stressful aspects of the situation.
- Accepting that some things cannot be changed, without becoming bitter or self-pitying about the situation.

The Hardiness Institute claims that by following these guidelines, individuals will become increasingly hardy and stress-resistant. They will gain 'stress mastery and personal power'.

Stress inoculation

This term was coined by the psychologist Donald Meichenbaum (1977). He argued that just as a person can be inoculated against a flu virus and become resistant to it, so they can be 'inoculated' against stress and become 'stress-resistant'. He developed a stress management programme which aimed to do just this.

Phase 1 First a person must identify the sources of stress in their life, examine how they cope with stressful situations, and consider alternative ways of coping. According to Meichenbaum, going through this process gives people a sense of control.

Phase 2 The next step is to learn a series of skills for dealing with stressful situations. This involves learning a list of coping self-statements, all of which are positive, reassuring and encouraging. At the same time negative self-statements which are self-critical and defeatist, must be identified and rejected. For example, before giving a speech, negative statements such as, 'I'll panic', 'I'll forget my lines', and 'I'll sound boring', must be replaced by positive statements such as 'I'm well prepared', 'I'm nervous but that means I'll give of my best'. Table 1 gives examples of coping self-statements to prepare, confront and cope with stressful situations.

Table 1 Coping self-statements

Preparation	I can develop a plan to deal with it.
	No negative self-statements, just think rationally.
Confrontation	One step at a time; I can handle this situation.
	Relax; I'm in control. Take a slow deep breath.
Coping	Don't try to eliminate fear totally; just keep it manageable.
	It's not the worst thing that can happen.
Self-reinforcement	I was able to do it because I was well prepared.
	I'm really pleased with the progress I'm making.

Adapted from Zimbardo et al., 1995

Phase 3 The final step is to appraise the performance. People must give themselves full credit for successful coping. Again the emphasis is on positive statements. If the speech referred to above went well, rather than saying 'I was lucky' or giving credit to 'a sympathetic audience', a statement like 'I put the work in so I deserved the applause' is far more appropriate. This can be self-reinforcing, increasing self-confidence and improving self-image. Examples of self-reinforcing statements are given in Table 1.

To become 'stress-resistant' a person must first practice with a therapist – the psychologist who is helping them to deal with stress. Then they must practice the approach in real life stress situations until it becomes 'second nature'. In addition, they must prepare their own list of coping self-statements – one that works best for them.

Stress management programmes offer a wide, and sometimes bewildering, range of cognitive-behavioural strategies. They often combine biofeedback and relaxation training with a variety of cognitive techniques designed to discourage negative and encourage positive thoughts and perceptions.

At times stress management programmes read like an instruction manual as the following examples indicate.

- Slow down – try to do things at a slower pace.
- Organise your life – disorganisation produces stress.
- Strike a balance – don't let one aspect of your life, for example work, get blown out of proportion.
- Write about your feelings – it will help you cope.
- Seek social support – support from family and friends can cushion the impact of stress.

(Above examples taken from Coon, 1998).

Many stress management programmes operate rather like a cafeteria. They offer a broad range of skills and techniques from which the individual chooses those that work best for them (Taylor, 1995).

Evaluation

How effective are stress management programmes? This is a difficult question to answer as there are many different programmes.

Aspects of stress management programmes have been built into treatment programmes for a variety of stress-related illnesses from migraine, to hypertension and coronary heart disease. They have met with some success. For example, stress management has been shown to reduce the risk of CHD (Carver & Humphries, 1982).

One advantage of stress management programmes is that they avoid the undesirable side effects of drug treatment. And, unlike drugs, some programmes deal directly with the stressor. They train people to identify stressors, to develop plans for dealing with them, and to take action to solve their problems.

Some of the benefits of stress management programmes may result from a perception of control rather than the detailed strategies they provide. Trained by an expert and armed with a list of instructions, the individual may feel in control of the situation. And this may lead to stress reduction.

Some stress management programmes have been criticised for failing to deal with the actual sources of stress. They may change perceptions and give a feeling of control but do they actually change the situation which gave rise to stress in the first place? In many cases the answer is no. For example, workplace stressors such as work overload, repetitive jobs and social isolation are not directly addressed by many stress management programmes. Such programmes may:

- Make it easier for people to live with stressors
- Give an illusion of control
- Cover up the real sources of stress so discouraging attempts to remove stressors
- Or, put people in a better frame of mind to deal with the actual causes of stress.

Stress management programmes can be seen as a smokescreen used by employers to exploit their workers. Rather than doing something about the actual causes of stress, for example work overload, apparently caring employers provide their workers with stress management programmes. This implies that the problem to be solved is stressed workers rather than stress-producing work situations.

Stress management programmes focus on the individual rather than the wider society. The individual follows their programme and practices their stress management techniques. But the real problem may be society as a whole. Rather than changing the individual, it might be society that needs changing. Western society emphasises achievement and competition. These emphases may be major stressors as people strive incessantly to achieve, and compete constantly for income and material possessions. As the market place becomes increasingly global, competition intensifies with calls to raise productivity, increase efficiency, reduce costs, meet deadlines and sell aggressively.

In this respect, stressors may be built into the very structure of society. It can be argued that by focusing on the individual, stress management programmes divert attention from the real problem – the wider society.

Unit 5 continues the evaluation of stress management programmes.

Key terms

Cognitive-behavioural approaches *Approaches to stress management based on cognitive and behavioural changes.*

Stress management programmes *A set of techniques and strategies designed to reduce stress and improve coping skills.*

Hardiness training *A training programme which aims to increase people's hardiness.*

Stress inoculation *A training programme which aims to make people resistant to stress.*

Coping self-statements *Positive statements about the self which aim to increase self-confidence, improve coping skills, and make the individual more resistant to stress.*

Summary

1. Cognitive-behavioural approaches argue that stress can be reduced by a) changing the way people perceive stressors and think about stress and b) changing the way they behave when responding to stressful situations.
2. There is some evidence that reducing Type A behaviour can reduce stress and stress-related illness.
3. Many stress management programmes are based on cognitive-behavioural approaches.
4. Stress management programmes have met with some success. They have the advantage of avoiding the undesirable side effects of drug treatment and of dealing directly with the stressor.
5. Stress management programmes have been criticised for failing to deal with the real causes of stress.
6. Stress management programmes deal with the individual rather than society. If major stressors are built into the structure of society, stress management programmes may divert attention from the real problem.

Unit 4 Social support

KEY ISSUES

1. **What is social support?**
2. **How might it reduce stress?**
3. **Are its effects always beneficial?**

Stress management programmes often advise people to seek social support. In general, research indicates that people with a wide network of family and friends experience less stress in response to a stressor and cope with it more successfully. Social support refers to the support available to the individual from others. Cohen and Wills (1985) identify four main aspects of social support.

Esteem support The experience of stress can lead to self-doubt and low self-esteem, especially when a person is having difficulty in coping. Love, care and attention from family and friends can reassure a person that they are valued and worthwhile. This can raise their sense of self-worth which, in turn, can help them to cope more effectively.

Informational support This refers to useful information provided by others. It can help a person to reappraise both a stressor and their coping strategy. It may involve advice from people who have experienced a similar situation, for example bereavement, divorce or unemployment. This advice may lead to more effective coping strategies.

Instrumental support This involves a range of activities which provide practical assistance. For example, it refers to a loan or gift of money to help a friend in financial difficulties. It includes services such as babysitting, gardening, home decorating, shopping, and caring for somebody when they are ill. Instrumental support, by making life easier, can help a person cope more effectively with a stressful situation.

Social companionship refers to spending time with other people – talking over a cup of coffee, going to the pub or cinema, going on holiday with friends. Social companionship can prevent people from dwelling on their problems, provide an opportunity for enjoyment, and put them in a better frame of mind to cope.

However, simply being surrounded by family and friends does not necessarily mean that a person experiences positive support. They may see the attention of others as an intrusion, and their attempts to help as interference. Many researchers argue that *perceived social support* – the amount of support a person feels they are receiving – is the key to understanding the relationship between social support and stress.

Benefits of social support

What evidence is there for the beneficial effects of social support? A large body of research indicates that people with a high level of social support are less prone to stress and more likely to cope with stress. For example, after an accident in 1979 at the Three Mile Island nuclear plant in the USA, people living nearby with high levels of social support experienced less stress than those with low levels of support (Fleming et al., 1982). A number of laboratory studies indicate the importance of social support. In one study women were placed in a stressful situation either alone or with a close friend. Blood pressure was used as a measure of stress. The women who were alone had significantly higher blood pressure than those accompanied by a friend (Kamarck et al., 1995).

Social support and health Research indicates that high levels of social support:

- Reduce the likelihood of illness
- Speed recovery from illness
- Reduce the risk of death from illness.

A large scale study in California looked at nearly 7000 people over a nine year period. It found that people with a large number of social contacts were less likely to die during this period than those with few social contacts (Berkman & Syme, 1979). A study of 133 women with breast cancer indicated that those who had more friendships and those who had jobs outside the home tended to live longer (Waxler-Morrison et al., 1991).

Evaluation

Social support can have a negative side. For example, people suffering from asthma may find their condition is made worse if they see their family as over-protective and over-concerned (Banyard, 1996).

The *matching hypothesis* suggests that social support is only effective when there is a match between an individual's needs and the type of support provided by those in their social network. For example, a person with financial difficulties may find it embarrassing to talk about their problem with family members, but may welcome a loan from a friend. A study of cancer patients indicated that different kinds of support are required from different members of the social network. Emotional support was required from family and close friends; informational support and advice from doctors and nurses. Receiving informational support from a family member can be seen as inappropriate and make matters worse. In general, being overly cheerful or trying to minimise the seriousness of the illness was seen as unhelpful, whether it came from family, friends, or doctors (Dakof & Taylor, 1990).

Overall, the evidence suggests that the effects of social support are beneficial – they usually reduce stress and help people to cope with stress. However, the relationship between stress and social support is not simple and

Summary

1. Research indicates that people with a wide social network experience less stress and cope with stress more effectively.

2. Research evidence indicates that high levels of social support:
   - Reduce the likelihood of illness
   - Speed recovery from illness
   - Reduce the risk of death from illness.

3. Social support can have negative effects. For example, it may be seen as an intrusion into a person's private life.

clear-cut. At times, people may feel overwhelmed by well-intentioned comfort, advice and offers of help. They may interpret 'support' as an intrusion into their private lives. In such cases, social support may add to the stress they are already experiencing.

Key terms

Social support *The support available to the individual from members of their social network. It includes esteem support, informational support, instrumental support and social companionship.*

Perceived social support *The amount of social support a person feels they are receiving.*

Matching hypothesis *Suggests that social support is only effective when there is a match between a person's needs and the type of support they receive.*

Activity 1 Social support

Item A A close-knit community

From early morning to late at night little groups formed and faded, trading with goodwill, candour or cattishness the detailed gossip of a closed society. Over a period the health, honesty, conduct, history and connections of everyone in the neighbourhood would be examined. Each would be criticised, praised, censured openly or by hint and finally allocated by tacit consent a position on the social scale.

Adapted from Roberts, 1973

Item B Pets

Research suggests that people live longer, and recover more quickly from an illness, if they have a pet. One study showed that pet owners were more likely to be alive one year after admission to hospital with a heart attack than similar people without pets. Another study found that when people stroked their own dog, their blood pressure fell. This did not happen when they stroked a strange dog.

Adapted from Baun et al., 1984

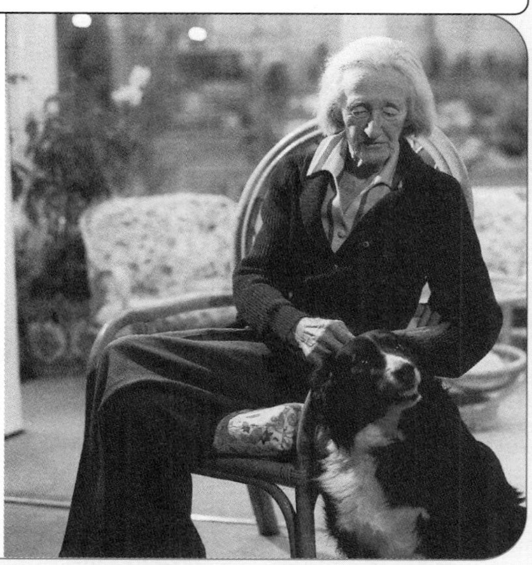

Questions

1 In a close-knit social network, social support can have both positive and negative effects. Discuss with some reference to Item A.

2 Read Item B. Suggest reasons for the apparent beneficial effects of pet ownership.

Unit 5 Stress management – a critical approach

KEY ISSUES

1. **Should the stress response be seen in a positive light?**
2. **How effective are stress management interventions in organisations?**

The 1990s could well be described as the decade of stress. The phrase 'I'm stressed' entered everyday conversation. The term stress was expanded to cover a multitude of negative emotions and experiences from anxiety and depression to feeling tired, worn out and fed up. Doctors are now diagnosing and treating stress and a rapidly growing stress management industry provides advice and treatment for individuals and organisations.

Stress is blamed for a whole range of physical illnesses and psychological disorders. It is said to be costing industry vast sums of money in absence from work and poor performance at work. Stress is now pictured almost exclusively in negative terms. It is sometimes seen as a new strain of disease, which, in the late 1990s, is reaching epidemic proportions.

5.1 Re-evaluating the stress response

In a paper entitled *Killing the messenger: The pathologising of the stress response*, Angela Patmore (1997) rejects the idea of stress as a disease which requires diagnosis and treatment. Stress itself is not the problem. The real problem is the causes of stress – the stressors. These are the things which require treatment. Patmore rejects many of the 'treatments' for stress proposed by the stress management industry. In her view, they do little or nothing to deal with the actual causes of stress. This section outlines some of her arguments.

The stress response should be seen as a positive response rather than a threat to individual wellbeing. It is a valuable survival mechanism which galvanises people 'into mental and physical activity, enhances awareness and prompts adaptation to change and challenge'. The stress response can be compared to a burglar alarm. It warns of a threat in the environment and galvanises the individual to take action and deal with the situation. But, many of the techniques of stress management are designed to calm people down and subdue the stress response. As a result, 'instead of looking for the burglar, we are taking the alarm down off the wall and throwing it in the dustbin'. In other words, the stress response – the alarm – should not be subdued. Instead, it should be used to identify the problem and to deal with it.

According to Patmore, many stress management techniques start from the assumption that the stress response is harmful. Since the stress response is activating and arousing, it follows that 'treatment' should be de-activating and de-arousing. This can be seen from a range of 'calming down' techniques such as biofeedback, muscle relaxation and deep breathing. Counselling and psychotherapy are often designed to reduce stress by damping down the stress response. And the same applies to drug treatments as the term tranquilliser suggests.

If the stress response is viewed as a valuable adaptive mechanism, then many stress management techniques are 'at best useless and at worst disabling'. By suppressing or closing down the stress response, they can prevent people from identifying the threat or challenge and prevent them from dealing with the threat or rising to the challenge. As a result, 'people are not being activated to help themselves'.

Patmore's ideas provide an important alternative to many of the arguments outlined in this chapter. She is one of the few researchers to challenge the accepted wisdom of stress management.

5.2 Stress management in organisations

Stress management is big business. Organisations are increasingly employing 'stress consultants' in an attempt to reduce or eliminate stress in the workplace. According to Rob Briner (1999), stress management intervention in organisations is based on the following assumptions. First, the way the organisation is structured and the way work is organised creates organisational stressors. These stressors cause undesirable states in employees such as psychological distress, ill-health and low job satisfaction. They also cause undesirable behaviours such as poor work performance, frequent absence from work and high turnover – a high level of resigning from work. Second, the way to deal with these problems is stress management intervention. This will reduce or remove organisational stressors which will lead to a reduction in undesirable employee states and behaviour.

Stress management intervention sometimes starts with a 'stress audit' or 'stress diagnosis' based on a questionnaire which asks employees to identify aspects of their jobs which they find 'stressful'. Partly on the basis of questionnaire results, the 'stress consultants' attempt to redesign jobs and working practices in order to eliminate stressors. For example, they may attempt to 'enrich' jobs by giving employees more responsibility and cutting out boring and tedious tasks with the aim of increasing job satisfaction. This, the argument goes, will reduce stress and improve both the wellbeing and performance of employees.

So far, so good, but Briner (1999) found little evidence to support either the assumptions or the practice of stress management intervention. He examined research evidence on the effects of stress on employee performance, absence and illness. He found the evidence was either weak – stress appears to explain only 2-3% of the variation in these factors – or non-existent. Briner then looked at a number of stress management interventions in organisations. At best, he found their effectiveness was limited and short term. Often the results were mixed. For example, one study found increases in job satisfaction and job commitment but also increases in absenteeism and job turnover (Cordery et al., 1991).

Briner concludes that at least part of the demand by organisations for stress management intervention is due to the current preoccupation in society with the idea of stress. As a result, the stress consultants, or 'stress busters' as they are sometimes called, are riding high on a wave of popular concerns and anxieties.

Summary

1. Many researchers and most people in the wider society see stress in a negative light.
2. Some researchers argue that the stress response should be seen as a valuable adaptive mechanism.
3. From this point of view, stress management techniques which aim to suppress the stress response may be harmful.
4. Despite their widespread use, stress management interventions in organisation may have, at best, limited benefits.

Activity 2 The culture of stress

Item A Stress and the media

One of the bestselling books of the new millennium.

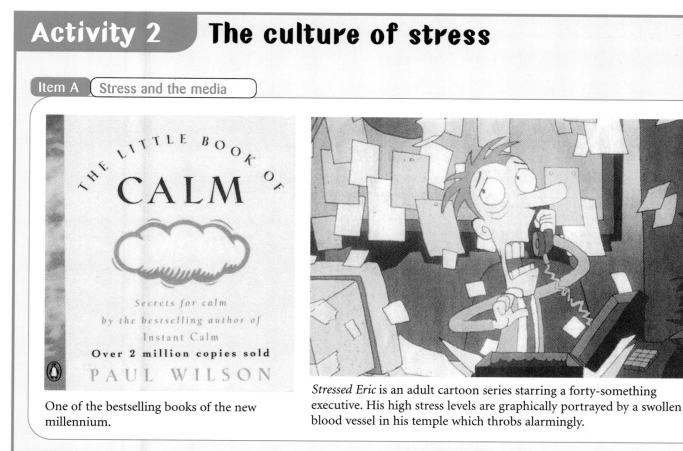

Stressed Eric is an adult cartoon series starring a forty-something executive. His high stress levels are graphically portrayed by a swollen blood vessel in his temple which throbs alarmingly.

Item B Stress management

The stress response is a signal that something is wrong in the environment, and that the real threat, whether at work or at home, should be urgently addressed. In so far as stress management prevents this from happening, it may be said to be harmful.

Adapted from Patmore, 1997

Questions

1. What does Item A indicate about current attitudes towards stress?
2. Which aspects of stress management might produce the 'harmful' effects referred to in Item B?

References

Banyard, P. (1996). *Applying psychology to health.* London: Hodder & Stoughton.

Baun, M.M., Bergstrum, N., Langston, M.F. & Thoma, L. (1984). Physiological effects of human animal bonding. *Nursing Research, 33*, 126-129.

Berkman, L.F. & Syme, S.L. (1979). Social networks, host resistance, and mortality: A nine-year followup study of Alameda County residents. *American Journal of Epidemiology, 109*, 186-204.

Blanchard, E.B., Miller, S.T., Abel, G.G., Haynes, M.R. & Wicker, R. (1979). Evaluation of biofeedback in the treatment of borderline essential hypertension. *Journal of Applied Behaviour Analysis, 12*, 99-109.

Briner, R. B. & Reynolds, S. (1999). The costs, benefits and limitations of organizational level stress interventions. *Journal of Organizational Behavior, 20*, 647-664.

Carver, C.S. & Humphries, C. (1982). Social psychology of the Type A coronary-prone behaviour pattern. In G.S. Saunders & J. Suls (Eds.), *Social psychology of health and illness.* Hillsdale, NJ: Erlbaum.

Cohen, S. & Wills, T.A. (1985). Stress, social support, and the buffering process. *Psychology Bulletin, 98*, 310-357.

Comer, R.J. (1998). *Abnormal psychology* (3rd ed.). New York: W.H. Freeman.

Coon, D. (1998). *Introduction to psychology: Exploration and application* (8th ed.). Pacific Grove, CA: Brooks/Cole.

Cordery, J.L., Mueller, W.S. & Smith, L.M. (1991). Attitudinal and behavioural effects of autonomous group working: A longitudinal field study. *Academy of Management Journal, 34*, 464-476.

Dakof, G.A. & Taylor, S.E. (1990). Victims' perceptions of social support: What is helpful from whom? *Journal of Personality and Social Psychology, 58*, 80-89.

Davison, G.C. & Neale, J.M. (1998). *Abnormal psychology* (7th ed.). New York: John Wiley & Sons.

Fleming, R., Baum, A., Gisriel, M.M. & Gatchel, R.J. (1982). Mediating influences of social support on stress at Three Mile Island. *Journal of Human Stress*, September, 14-23.

Friedman, M., Thoresen, C.E., Gill, J.J., Powell, L.H., Ulmer, D., Thompson, L., Price, V.A., Rabin, D.D., Breall, W.S., Dixon, T., Levy, R. & Bourg, E. (1984). Alteration of Type A behaviour and reduction in cardiac recurrences in post-myocardial infarction patients. *American Heart Journal, 108*, 237-248.

Haaga, D.A. (1987). Treatment of the Type A behaviour pattern. *Clinical Psychology Review, 7*, 557-574.

Holroyd, K., Penzien, D., Hursey, K., Tobin, D., Rogen, L., Holm, J., Marcille, P., Hall, J. & Chila, A. (1984). Change mechanisms in EMG biofeedback training: Cognitive changes underlying improvements in tension headache. *Journal of Consulting and Clinical Psychology, 52*, 1039-1053.

Kamarck, T.W., Annunziato, B. & Amateau, L.M. (1995). Affiliations moderate the effects of social threat on stress-related cardiovascular responses: Boundary conditions for a laboratory model of social support. *Psychosomatic Medicine, 57*, 183-194.

Kobasa, S.C. (1979). Stressful life events and health: An inquiry into hardiness. *Journal of Personality and Social Psychology, 37*, 1-11.

Maddi, S. (2000). www.hardinessinstitute.com

Meichenbaum, D.H. (1977). *Cognitive-behaviour modification.* New York: Plenum.

Melzack, R. (1975). The McGill Pain Questionnaire: Major properties and scoring methods. *Pain, 1*, 277-299.

Patmore, A. (1997). *Killing the messenger: The pathologising of the stress response.* Gosfield: Patmore.

Roberts, R. (1973). *The classic slum.* Harmondsworth: Penguin.

Shapiro, D., Tursky, B. & Schwartz, G.E. (1970). Control of blood pressure in man by operant conditioning. *Circulation Research, 26*, 127-132.

Tarler-Benlolo, L. (1978). The role of relaxation in biofeedback training. *Psychological Bulletin, 85*, 727-755.

Taylor, S.E. (1995). *Health psychology* (3rd ed.). New York: McGraw-Hill.

Turk, D.C., Meichenbaum, D.H. & Burman, W.H. (1979). Application of biofeedback for the regulation of pain: A critical review. *Psychological Bulletin, 86*, 1322-1338.

Waxler-Morrison, N., Hislop, T.G., Mears, B. & Can, L. (1991). The facts on social relationships on survival with women with breast cancer: A prospective study. *Social Science and Medicine, 3*, 177-183.

Zimbardo, P., McDermott, M., Jansz, J. & Metaal, N. (1995). *Psychology: A European text.* London: Harper Collins.

10 Defining psychological abnormality

Introduction

Darla Shaw refuses to throw anything away. In addition to what most people would regard as rubbish, she owns a large stock of theatrical costumes, a life-size Santa on skis, a papier-mâché mermaid and an assortment of stuffed alligators. Her collection grew to such an extent that she was forced to buy an abandoned opera house in order to store it. She finds time to play in a kazoo band and wears a fireman's coat in the winter (Weeks & James, 1995).

Does Darla's behaviour indicate some form of psychological abnormality? Or, is she merely eccentric? Before attempting to answer these questions, it is necessary to explore the idea of abnormality.

Abnormality is difficult to define. Views of abnormality change across cultures, they vary within cultures over time, and they vary from group to group within the same society. It is essential to examine views of abnormality since they form the basis for defining and identifying psychological disorders.

How do psychologists decide what is normal and what is abnormal? And once behaviour has been identified as abnormal, how do they then decide whether or not it constitutes a psychological disorder? The short answer is with great difficulty. Their attempts to answer these questions form the basis of this chapter.

Chapter summary

- **Unit 1 looks at abnormality in terms of deviation from statistical norms of behaviour and deviation from social norms.**
- **Unit 2 asks how failure to function adequately might provide indicators of psychological abnormality.**
- **Unit 3 looks at psychological abnormality as deviation from ideal mental health.**
- **Unit 4 examines the relationship between culture and ideas of abnormality.**
- **Unit 5 questions whether psychological disorders are really 'mental illnesses'.**

Unit 1 Statistical norms and social norms

KEY ISSUES

1. **Does behaviour which deviates from statistical norms indicate psychological abnormality?**
2. **Does behaviour which deviates from social norms indicate psychological abnormality?**

1.1 Deviation from statistical norms

In statistical terms, human behaviour is abnormal if it falls outside the range which is typical for most people. In other words, it is abnormal if it deviates from statistical norms.

This can be illustrated by the distribution of IQ (intelligence quotient) scores shown in Figure 1. The average score is 100 and most people fall around the middle. Those with very low or very high scores fall at the extremes. They are relatively few in number. In statistical terms they are abnormal – the word abnormal literally means away from the norm.

Figure 1 IQ distribution

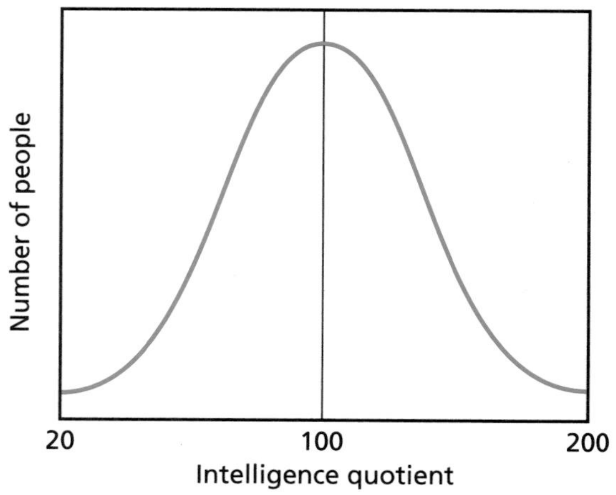

IQ distribution among adults. It forms a normal distribution curve.

Statistical infrequency forms the basis for diagnosing mental retardation which is classified as a psychological disorder. DSM-IV, the fourth edition of the American Psychiatric Association's *Diagnostic and statistical manual of mental disorders* (1994) defines mental retardation as an IQ of 70 and below. Around 2% to 3% of the population fall into this category (Barlow & Durand, 1999).

However, just because certain behaviours or characteristics are statistically infrequent does not necessarily mean they are *seen* as abnormal or as indicating a psychological disorder. They are more likely to be defined as such if they are considered undesirable. For example, being a genius is very rare, is usually regarded as highly desirable, and few, if any, would see it as a psychological disorder. On the other hand, being 'severely mentally retarded' is just as rare but is generally considered as undesirable, abnormal, and as requiring psychological treatment.

There are many examples of statistically infrequent behaviours which are not considered abnormal, either in general or in psychological terms. Olympic athletes, bestselling authors, famous painters, Oscar winning film stars, and singers with number one hits all deviate from statistical norms of human behaviour. Clearly, a definition of psychological abnormality cannot be based on statistical infrequency alone.

1.2 Deviation from social norms

Social norms are approved and expected ways of behaving in a particular society. For example, in all societies there are social norms governing dress. Members of society generally share norms that define acceptable male and female clothes and that specify appropriate dress for different age groups. For example, in British society a 70-year-old grandmother dressed as a male teenager would contravene the norms for both her gender and her age group. Norms of dress also specify appropriate and expected behaviour for particular occasions. A funeral, a day out on the beach, a working day in the office or on the building site – all these situations are governed by norms which specify appropriate dress.

In terms of social norms, abnormal behaviour can be seen as behaviour which deviates from or violates social norms. But does this type of 'abnormal behaviour' indicate psychological abnormality, does it indicate the presence of a psychological disorder? In certain cases, the answer may be yes.

The self-starvation of an anorexic is abnormal both in terms of social norms and psychological functioning. It deviates from social norms of eating behaviour and is classified by psychologists as a psychological disorder. The same applies to people with phobias – an extreme fear of something which leads them to avoid it at all costs. A phobia is classified as a psychological disorder. The behaviour that results from phobias often contravenes social norms. People with phobias for enclosed spaces, spiders, eating in public, or crossing a bridge sometimes behave in ways that are generally seen as strange, peculiar and bizarre. In other words, they deviate from accepted social norms.

But does *all* deviance from social norms indicate psychological abnormality. Quite clearly, the answer is no! Think about successive generations of young people from the 1950s to the present day. Their preferences in terms of music, hairstyles and clothes have often deviated from society's norms and been met with general disapproval. However, few would see their behaviour as an indication of psychological disorder. Think about those who violate not only social norms but also legal norms. Does the behaviour of burglars, bank robbers, joy riders, prostitutes and bigamists result from psychological disorders? Occasionally it might, but few psychologists would see this as the main reason for these activities.

Most people, most of the time, conform to social norms. In view of this, deviance from social norms can be seen as abnormal behaviour. In certain cases this may be due to psychological abnormality. In most instances, this is probably not the case. Because of this, deviance from social norms does not provide a sound basis for indicating psychological abnormality.

Key terms

Statistically infrequent behaviour *Behaviour which is uncommon. Statistically infrequent behaviour falls outside the range which is typical for most people.*

Social norms *Approved and expected ways of behaving in a particular society.*

Summary

1. Many behaviours which are statistically infrequent do not result from psychological abnormality. A definition of psychological abnormality cannot be based on statistical infrequency alone.
2. The behaviour of people with psychological disorders often deviates from social norms. However, in most instances, deviance from social norms does not indicate psychological abnormality.

Activity 1 Eccentricity

Item A John Slater

An eccentric is a person who deviates from established patterns of behaviour, in other words from social norms. Their behaviour strikes many people as odd. John Slater is an eccentric. He once walked from Land's End to John o'Groats in his bare feet, wearing only striped pyjamas and accompanied by his pet labrador, Guinness. Slater has been a Royal Marine bandsman, a truck driver, steward on a luxury yacht, social worker, salesman, insurance broker, waiter, driftwood artist, painter and decorator and fund-raiser. For most of the past ten years, he has lived in a cave, which is flooded with seawater at high tide. He says that he enjoys the 'cathedral-like silence in caves, which helps me to think and work things out'.

Adapted from Weeks & James, 1995

Item B Perfectly normal

John Slater's behaviour is very unusual, but does it indicate a psychological disorder? According to a study of 1000 eccentrics, the answer is quite definitely no. The study was based on in-depth interviews, personality questionnaires and a range of tests which reveal psychological disorders. The results showed that eccentrics had fewer disorders than the general population. Most eccentrics were happy and well-adjusted, they 'know they're different and glory in it'.

Adapted from Weeks & James, 1995

Item C Punks

Questions

1 What do Items A and B suggest about the problems of using deviance from social norms as an indicator of psychological disorders?

2 a) Judging from Item C, what social norms do punks break?

b) Is this a reason for seeing them as psychologically abnormal? Explain your answer.

Unit 2 Failure to function adequately

KEY ISSUES

1. **How might failure to function adequately provide indicators of psychological abnormality?**
2. **What are the strengths and limitations of these indicators?**

A failure to function adequately means that a person is unable to live a normal life, unable to experience the normal range of emotions, or engage in the normal range of behaviour. For example, they may be unable to hold down a job, they may be unable to take part in everyday activities like shopping, walking down the street or travelling by bus or train. They may see the world in ways which prevent them from normal participation in social life – for example, they may have 'visions' and hear 'voices' which others cannot see or hear. They may live in the depths of depression, unable to experience the normal range of emotions.

A failure to function adequately is sometimes seen as indicating both abnormal behaviour and psychological abnormality. This unit looks at various indicators of psychological abnormality which can be grouped under the heading of failure to function adequately. It has been argued that the more of these indicators that are present, and the more extreme they are, then the greater the likelihood of psychological disorder (Zimbardo et al., 1995).

2.1 Dysfunctional behaviour

In this case psychological abnormality is indicated by dysfunctional or maladaptive behaviour – behaviour which interferes with a person's ability to lead a normal, everyday life. For example, alcoholism is dysfunctional if it prevents a person from holding down a job; fear of crowds is dysfunctional if it prevents a person from shopping at the weekend.

Consider the case of Billy, a 13-year-old. He had no friends at school. Unlike most of the other children, he refused to attend any of the sports or social events connected with school. He dreaded being called on to speak in class, feeling physically sick at the prospect. Teachers were lucky to get a 'yes' or a 'no' out of him. Instead of eating at lunchtime, he locked himself in a cubicle in the boys' toilet. Billy was painfully shy. He was afraid of being embarrassed and humiliated in the presence of everybody except his parents. He was diagnosed as having a social phobia (Barlow & Durand, 1998). Billy's disorder is dysfunctional in the sense that it prevents him from leading a normal life.

Most people would probably agree that Billy's behaviour is dysfunctional. But there are plenty of examples which are not so clear-cut. What about the tramp who turns his back on conventional society, sleeps rough, doesn't eat properly and dies an early death as a result of his lifestyle? Who's to say that his behaviour is dysfunctional? He may be happy and fulfilled, he may see conventional lifestyles as dysfunctional and, psychologically, he may be perfectly normal.

In one sense behaviour that many people admire can be seen as dysfunctional in that it interferes with normal life, may harm physical health and even lead to death. For example, people have gone on hunger strike in support of causes such as animal rights and social justice. In 1924, Gandhi, one of the leaders of the movement for Indian independence, went on a 21 day fast to focus attention on and hopefully end the hostility between Hindus and Muslims in India. He had been ill for several months and knew the fast might be fatal. Although it could be seen as dysfunctional, few, if any, would see his behaviour as indicating psychological abnormality.

2.2 Personal distress

A failure to function adequately may be due to personal distress. And this distress may indicate psychological abnormality. Obviously personal distress is not limited to people with psychological disorders. For example, distress caused by the death of a close relative is seen as a normal and expected response. Sometimes, however, distress is a sign of psychological disorder. For example, distress is the main symptom of depression. People suffering from depression may experience disturbed sleep, constipation, headaches and constant tiredness. They are likely to feel intensely unhappy, to see themselves as undesirable and inadequate and their future as bleak and hopeless.

However, some psychological disorders do not involve personal distress. People with mania experience intense joy and elation – they are 'over the moon'. Psychopaths – people with antisocial personality disorder – show a complete disregard for the rights and feelings of others. They may lie, cheat and steal, verbally abuse and physically assault others, yet show no sign of shame, guilt or remorse. Their actions don't appear to cause them personal distress.

There is a further problem – how do we measure personal distress? Distress is a subjective experience – it refers to emotions and feelings which are very difficult to measure. And people's views about what counts as distress vary. One person may say they are very distressed whereas another person with similar feelings may say that they are a bit 'fed up'. This makes if difficult to measure and compare levels of distress.

Clearly there are problems with using personal distress as an indicator for psychological abnormality. However, combined with other indicators, it may help to identify certain psychological disorders.

2.3 Observer discomfort

People who frequently cause upset or discomfort to others are sometimes seen as unable to function adequately. Their behaviour can disrupt social interaction and damage social relationships. Others may find them embarrassing, threatening or upsetting. This is known as *observer discomfort*. It is sometimes seen as an indicator for psychological abnormality. From this point of view, alcoholics may be seen as abnormal if they bring distress to their friends and families. However, this indicator relies heavily on people's judgement and this will vary from person to person. For example, a streaker may cause acute embarrassment to some, but the reaction of others may range from annoyance, to amusement, to indifference. Indeed, observer discomfort may well say more about the observer than the observed.

2.4 Unpredictable behaviour

Unpredictable or unexpected behaviour is sometimes seen

as evidence of a failure to function adequately. And this type of behaviour may indicate psychological abnormality. Consider the following case of mania – an emotional state of extreme joy and elation, usually accompanied by hyperactivity and flights of fancy.

One morning, Mr W. told his wife he was quitting his job as a postman. He hardly slept that night, writing furiously at his desk. Next morning he withdrew the family savings and spent the lot on aquariums and a range of equipment for tropical fish. In a state of high excitement, he informed his wife that he had discovered a way to modify this equipment so that fish would live forever. 'We'll be millionaires,' he proclaimed (Davison & Neale, 1998). Mr W. was diagnosed as having mania. His behaviour was certainly unpredictable and unexpected – his wife got the shock of her life.

Behaviour is unpredictable and unexpected if it does not seem to fit the situation. For example, if people appear to over-react – if they appear over-enthusiastic, over-concerned, or over-anxious. But, who is to say whether someone is over-reacting, whether their response is out of proportion to the situation? Archimedes (287-212 BC), one of the greatest mathematicians of all time, is said to have jumped out the bath and run down the street shouting 'Eureka' ('I have found it') after coming up with the idea of displacement of volume in water. His behaviour was unpredictable and unexpected but hardly indicative of psychological disorder. And, if Mr W's fish *had* lived forever, maybe he would not have been diagnosed as manic.

2.5 Irrational behaviour

If a person's behaviour does not make sense to others, if others cannot communicate with them in a reasonable way, then the person's actions are often seen as irrational. This is sometimes taken as a indication of a failure to function adequately, and of psychological abnormality. Consider the following statement by a man hospitalised for schizophrenia.

'The inmates, here, hate me extremely because I am sane. They talk to me telepathically, continuously and daily almost without cessation, day and night. By the power of their imagination, they create extreme pain in my head, brain, eyes, heart, stomach and in every part of my body. By telepathy and imagination, they force me to say orally whatever they desire, whenever they desire and as long as they desire. I never said a word of my own. I never created a thought or image of my own' (Arieti, 1974). Most people would probably consider this statement to be irrational and, as a result, have difficulty communicating with the man. And they, like the psychiatrist who diagnosed his disorder, would probably see him as psychologically abnormal.

However, behaviour seen as irrational, may have nothing to do with psychological abnormality. The ideas of many of the world's greatest thinkers were often seen as irrational at the time – for example, Galileo who challenged the 17th century view that the earth was the centre of the universe and Darwin whose theory of natural selection challenged accepted views of the creation of humanity in the 19th century. From today's perspective, such thinkers were ahead of their time rather than irrational.

2.6 Conclusion

This unit has looked at five aspects of failure to function adequately. Each provides a possible indicator of psychological abnormality. Neither on their own nor together do these indicators provide a clear-cut and indisputable dividing line between psychological normality and abnormality. For example, personal distress *may* or *may not* indicate a psychological disorder. And a psychological disorder *may* or *may not* result in personal distress.

Where do we go from here? It has been argued that the more of these indicators that are present, and the more extreme they are, then the more likely they are to indicate psychological abnormality (Zimbardo et al., 1995). The problem is that this relies heavily on judgement. First, a judgement must be made on the presence or absence of these indicators – for example, is personal distress present? Second, a judgement must be made on the level of these indicators – for example, how extreme is the personal distress?

Judgements, by their very nature, are not hard and fast, they are interpretations and evaluations and to some degree will vary from person to person. And they will be influenced by the background of the person making the judgements. Most psychiatrists and psychologists are white, middle-class, university-educated males. To some extent, these factors will influence their judgements. Dougal Mackay puts it this way.

'In the final analysis, therefore, clinical intuition is used to determine whether the individual is to be regarded as normal or abnormal. The subjective nature of this criterion would suggest that there is a greater likelihood of the patient being described as "sick" if his experiences and behaviour do not closely resemble those of the psychiatrist who is assessing him' (1975).

All the indicators of psychological abnormality in this unit must be seen in the context of social norms. What counts as personal distress, observer discomfort, dysfunctional behaviour, unpredictable behaviour and irrational behaviour depend in large part on social norms. What would you make of the following behaviour? A man refused to speak to his mother-in-law and father-in-law. If he found himself alone in the house with his mother-in-law, he would cover himself with a blanket until she left. You may find this behaviour dysfunctional, unpredictable and irrational. However, in terms of traditional Cheyenne Indian norms, it is normal and expected (Stands In Timber & Liberty, 1967). As Robert Comer puts it, 'Efforts to define psychological abnormality typically raise as many questions as they do answers. The major difficulty is that the very concept of abnormality is relative: it depends on the norms and values of the society in question' (1998).

Despite all the problems of defining psychological abnormality, most researchers argue that it is real, it exists. People do have psychological disorders, in many cases these disorders cause them considerable pain and suffering, and they want an end to this pain and suffering. Activity 2 illustrates this point.

Key terms

Dysfunctional behaviour *Behaviour which interferes with a person's ability to lead a normal life.*

Personal distress *The distress and discomfort caused to a person by their own thoughts and actions.*

Observer discomfort *The unease and discomfort caused to a person by observing another's behaviour.*

Unpredictable behaviour *Behaviour which is unexpected, which cannot be predicted.*

Irrational behaviour *Behaviour which does not appear to be based on reason and logic – it does not seem to make sense.*

Summary

1. Failure to function adequately provides various indicators of psychological abnormality.
2. Indicators of psychological abnormality include dysfunctional behaviour, personal distress, observer discomfort, unpredictable behaviour and irrational behaviour.
3. It has been argued that the more of these indicators that are present, and the more extreme they are, then the more likely they are to indicate psychological abnormality.
4. Whether or not these indicators are present and how extreme they are relies heavily on the judgements of psychiatrists and psychologists.

Activity 2 Psychological disorders

Item A Depression

Katie was an attractive but very shy 16-year-old. She suffered from severe depression. This is how she described her situation in later years.

'The experience of depression is like falling into a deep, dark hole that you cannot climb out of. You scream as you fall, but it seems like no one hears you. Depression affects the way you interpret events. It influences the way you see yourself and the way you see other people. I remember looking in the mirror and thinking that I was the ugliest creature in the world.

Soon I found myself trying to sever the few interpersonal connections that I did have, with my closest friends, with my mother, and my oldest brother. I was almost impossible to talk to. I was angry and frustrated all the time. One day I went over the edge. My mother and I had a disagreement about some unimportant little thing. I went to my bedroom where I kept a bottle of whiskey or vodka or whatever I was drinking at the time. I drank as much as I could until I could pinch myself as hard as I could and feel nothing. Then I got out a very sharp knife that I had been saving and slashed my wrist deeply. I did not feel anything but the warmth of the blood running from my wrist.'

Adapted from Barlow & Durand, 1998

Item B Schizophrenia

Ann was bored with her marriage to Henry. She started to go dancing on her own and met Charles.

One evening she came home from dancing and told her mother that she was going to give Henry up, marry Charles, go to Brazil with him, and have twenty babies. She was talking very fast and part of her conversation was incomprehensible. She also told her mother that she was seeing the Virgin Mary in visions. She then went to her mother-in-law and told her to take Henry back because he was too immature. The following day Ann went to work and tried to get the entire office down on their knees to recite the rosary. A few days later, her mother took her to a priest, whom Ann told off in no uncertain terms. She finally spat at him. A psychiatrist was consulted. He diagnosed schizophrenia and recommended hospitalisation.

Adapted from Arieti, 1974

Item C Homeless and alone

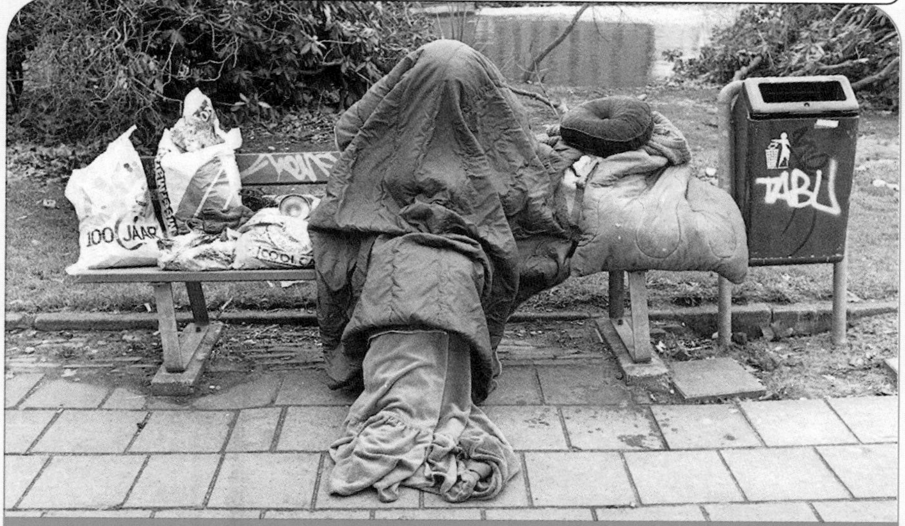

Homeless man – covering the head is often a sign of psychological disorder.

Question

To what extent do the following indicators of psychological abnormality fit Items A, B and C – dysfunctional behaviour, personal distress, observer discomfort, unpredictable behaviour, irrational behaviour?

Unit 3 Deviation from ideal mental health

KEY ISSUES

1. **What is psychological normality?**
2. **What are the problems with ideas of psychological normality?**

So far, this chapter has outlined ideas of abnormality. Why not reverse the procedure and start with normality? Then, once we have defined normality, the absence of it will indicate abnormality, just like the idea of good physical health gives us an idea of what ill health is.

Ideal psychological wellbeing

Normality is as difficult to define as abnormality. Marie Jahoda (1958) approached the problem by identifying various factors that were necessary for *optimal living* – living life to the full. Drawing on the work of a number of psychologists, she tried to identify the qualities a person needs in order to maximise their enjoyment of, and their satisfaction and fulfilment from life. The presence of these qualities indicates psychological health and wellbeing.

Jahoda's six 'elements for optimal living' are:

Positive view of self This involves self-awareness, self-acceptance and self-esteem. Self-acceptance means that people accept themselves as they are. Self-esteem means they have a fairly high regard for themselves.

Personal growth and development This refers to developing talents and abilities to the full. The more a person does this, the greater their psychological wellbeing.

Autonomy An autonomous person is able to act independently, make their own decisions, and find satisfaction from within themselves.

Accurate view of reality This means seeing the world as it really is, without distortion.

Positive relationships The ability to form close, warm and fulfilling relationships.

Environmental mastery This refers to effectively meeting the demands of situations and being sufficiently flexible to adapt to changing circumstances.

Evaluation

There are a number of problems with attempts to define psychological normality. First, like Jahoda's list of elements for optimal living, they tend to present a collection of ideal standards. This is likely to exclude the majority of people. Most people would fall short of these standards and therefore be considered 'abnormal' – as Mackay notes, the problem of using such standards as indicators of psychological wellbeing 'is that the majority of the population would have to be considered as maladjusted' (1975). As a result, the use of deviation from ideal mental health as an indicator of psychological abnormality produces a rather comical situation. The majority now become psychologically 'abnormal', even though in terms of statistical norms, they are the normal ones.

Second, Jahoda's view of mental health is culture-bound – largely based on and limited to a particular culture. It can be seen as a reflection of Western culture and, in particular, North American culture. Her emphasis on personal growth and development and individual autonomy reflects Western ideals of individualism. In many societies, this focus on the individual would be considered undesirable, unhealthy and abnormal. In such societies there is an emphasis on the group, on *collective* responsibilities, ties and obligations.

Third, Jahoda's ideals can be seen as value judgements – judgements based on beliefs about what is desirable and undesirable. Who is to say that close relationships with others are a sign of psychological wellbeing? Can't someone who keeps themselves to themselves live a happy and fulfilled life? Many of the elements for optimal living reflect not only Western culture but also Western *values*.

Key terms

Elements for optimal living *The qualities required in order to maximise satisfaction and fulfilment from life. These qualities have been seen as indicators of psychological wellbeing and normality.*

Value judgement *A judgement based on values which are beliefs about what is good and bad, desirable and undesirable.*

Summary

1. A number of attempts have been made to provide indicators for psychological wellbeing and normality. Jahoda's elements for optimal living is one example.
2. These indicators are usually presented as ideal standards. Most people therefore fall short of them. As a result, there are problems in using deviation from ideal mental health as an indicator of psychological abnormality
3. Jahoda's elements for optimal living tend to be culture-bound, in particular they tend to reflect Western culture.
4. They are based, at least in part, on value judgements, reflecting what is seen as good and desirable.

Unit 4 Culture and abnormality

KEY ISSUES

1. **How does culture affect views of psychological abnormality?**
2. **Are the same psychological disorders found in all cultures?**

Definitions of normality and abnormality are very important. They underlie what is seen as psychologically normal and abnormal. And, in particular, they underlie definitions of psychological disorders. As previous units have indicated, these definitions are based, in part, on value judgements, on beliefs about what is good and bad, desirable and undesirable. They are also based, in part, on social norms – on behaviour that is approved, expected and seen as appropriate. Values and social norms are part of culture. This suggests that, to some extent, definitions of psychological abnormality are culturally based. This view will now be examined.

4.1 Culture

Culture is the learned, shared behaviour of members of a society – their way of life. It includes social norms, values, attitudes and beliefs which are generally shared by people living in the same society. Culture varies from society to society. As a result, each society has its own ideas about what is normal and abnormal. Consider the following examples.

Two individuals, one from North America, the other from South America, are conversing in a hall 40 feet long. They begin at one end of the hall and finish at the other end, the North American steadily retreating, the South American relentlessly advancing. Each is trying to establish the 'accustomed conversation distance' defined by their culture. To the North American, his South American counterpart comes too close for comfort, whereas the South American feels uneasy conversing at the distance his partner demands (Hall, 1973). Among the Lakota Indians of South Dakota, it is regarded as improper to answer a question in the presence of others who do not know the answer. Such behaviour would be regarded as boastful and arrogant, and, since it reveals the ignorance of others, it would be interpreted as an attempt to undermine their confidence and shame them. Faced with a classroom of Lakota children, a white American teacher, who is unaware of their culture, might well regard their behaviour as abnormal (Klineberg, 1971).

What is considered normal in one culture may be seen as an indication of psychological disorder in another culture. Consider the following case which came to the author's attention during his stay at the University of Minnesota in Minneapolis, USA. Teachers at a Minneapolis school were convinced that one of their pupils had a psychological disorder. The pupil, a Chippewa boy, kept seeing thunderbirds – mythical birds. Unfortunately for him, nobody else at the school could see them. The boy's parents were called in and said they were delighted with their son's sightings. A psychiatrist was asked to examine the boy. He was concerned about the visions – they are often seen as a symptom of schizophrenia in Western psychiatry – but admitted that the boy seemed normal in every other respect. Luckily, a member of the anthropology department at the university who had studied the Chippewa was contacted. He explained that there was nothing wrong with the boy, in fact just the opposite. In traditional Chippewa culture, the thunderbird is a supernatural being and it is a great honour to have such visions. Far from seeing his behaviour as psychologically abnormal, the boy and his parents saw it as something to be proud of.

This example shows the danger of evaluating and interpreting other cultures in terms of one's own culture. This is known as *ethnocentrism*. In terms of American culture, the boy's behaviour is abnormal and may well indicate a psychological disorder. In terms of Chippewa culture, it indicates psychological wellbeing. Clearly, culture must be taken into account when making judgements about normality and abnormality.

Subculture The same argument applies to subculture. Some groups within society have certain social norms, beliefs and behaviour patterns which are different from those of the wider society. In other words, they have a distinctive *subculture*. While sharing may aspects of mainstream culture, they may have particular religious beliefs, family structures, dress codes, diets and speech patterns which set them apart from the wider society. For example, it has often been claimed that ethnic groups in the UK, such as African Caribbeans, Chinese, Cypriots, Pakistanis and Punjabi Sikhs, have their own subcultures.

To some extent, views of normality and abnormality vary from subculture to subculture. This has important implications. For example, Rack (1984) claims that African Caribbeans in Britain are sometimes diagnosed as 'mentally ill' on the basis of behaviour which is perfectly normal in terms of their subculture (see Item D, Activity 3). This is due to the ignorance of African-Caribbean subculture on the part of white psychiatrists. This may help to account for the fact that African Caribbeans in the UK are at least 3 times and up to 5 times more likely to be diagnosed as schizophrenic compared to the general population (Nazroo, 1997).

Conclusion The ideas of culture and subculture raise a number of fundamental questions. Is it possible to cut through culture and produce a culture-free definition of abnormality which is applicable to all societies? Is it possible to correctly identify psychological disorders in different cultures? There are no easy answers to these questions. It is difficult enough for psychologists to decide what counts as psychological abnormality in their own culture. This difficulty is magnified when they look at people from other cultures and subcultures.

The ideas of culture and subculture suggest that psychologists' views of abnormality and classifications of psychological disorders must be regarded with caution and continuously questioned.

Key terms

Culture *The learned, shared behaviour of members of a society. Culture includes social norms, attitudes, values and beliefs which are generally shared by people in a particular society.*

Subculture *Learned, shared behaviour which is distinctive to certain groups within a society. While sharing many aspects of the mainstream culture, these groups have certain social norms, values and beliefs which differ from the culture of society as a whole.*

Ethnocentrism *Judging, evaluating and interpreting other cultures in terms of the standards and beliefs of one's own culture.*

4.2 Culture change

Culture changes within the same society over time. Compare the culture of Victorian Britain with British culture today. There have been major changes in attitudes, values, norms and roles. This can be seen from the role of women. Not a single woman voted in national elections in the 19th century and many agreed with Queen Victoria's pronouncement, 'Let woman be what God intended, a helpmate for man, but with totally different duties and vocations'.

As culture changes, so do views of what counts as normal and abnormal behaviour. To take a simple example, the cover-all bathing costumes of Victorian times would be seen as laughable on today's beaches. And wearing today's swimwear on Victorian beaches would amount to a graphic display of abnormal behaviour.

If common-sense views about what is normal and abnormal change as culture changes, does the same apply to the views of psychiatrists and psychologists? Up to a point, the answer is yes. To some degree, their view of what counts as psychological abnormality reflects the culture of the day. The following example illustrates this.

In Britain, homosexuality was a criminal offence until 1967. It was classified as a psychological disorder from the 1920s until the 1970s. Homosexuality ran counter to practically every belief and norm of the time. It deviated from social norms and religious beliefs, it broke the law of the land and what were seen as the laws of nature. It was unacceptable, wrong, criminal and unnatural. Homophobia – hatred and fear of homosexuals – was widespread and gays were forced to keep their sexual orientation secret. And psychiatry made matters worse 'by inviting the harrassed and despised homosexual to see himself as sick' (Heather, 1976).

Activity 3 Culture and subculture

Item A The sun dance

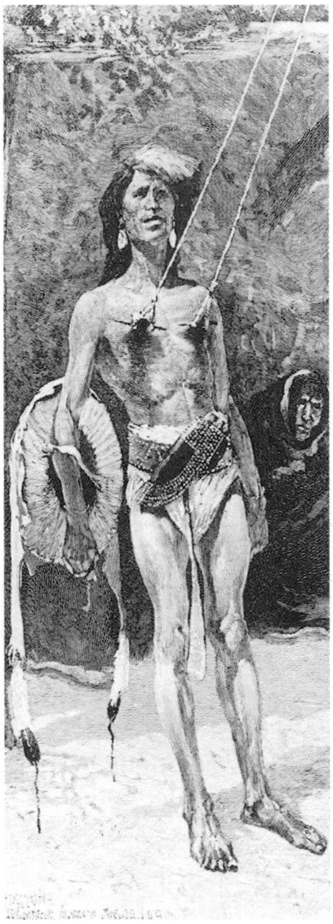
A sun dancer

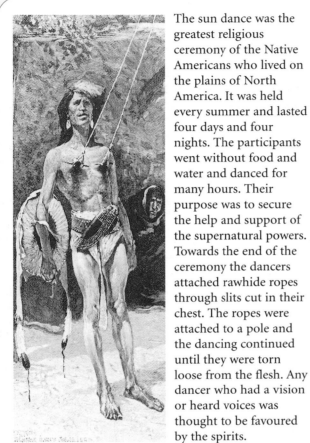

The sun dance was the greatest religious ceremony of the Native Americans who lived on the plains of North America. It was held every summer and lasted four days and four nights. The participants went without food and water and danced for many hours. Their purpose was to secure the help and support of the supernatural powers. Towards the end of the ceremony the dancers attached rawhide ropes through slits cut in their chest. The ropes were attached to a pole and the dancing continued until they were torn loose from the flesh. Any dancer who had a vision or heard voices was thought to be favoured by the spirits.

Adapted from Stands In Timber & Liberty, 1967

Item B Shamans

Sitting Bull, a shaman and chief of the Hunkpapa Lakota

Shamans obtain their power from the spirits. Shamans have the power to cure the sick, discover the whereabouts of an enemy and recover lost or stolen property. Often the cause of illness was diagnosed as a foreign object in the patient's body. Bull All The Time, a shaman of the Native American Cree people, cured several patients by sucking at the afflicted parts and pulling out respectively a bone, a black beetle and a morsel of meat.

Adapted from R.H. Lowie, 1954

Item C The Dobuans

Ruth Benedict's description of the culture of the Dobuan Islanders of Melanesia in the western Pacific provides a vivid illustration of cultural differences. Dobuan society was characterised by a distrust of others that verged on what we would call paranoia. For example, nobody ever left a cooking pot unattended for fear of poisoning. Benedict describes one man as pleasant and helpful, and he was considered crazy by other members of society.

Adapted from Benedict, 1934

Item D 'Hallucinations'

Nigel Copsey is a psychologist and an ordained minister. He spent two years studying the churches, temples and mosques of ethnic minority groups in London's East End. He found that many African Caribbean and Asian people refuse to talk about their religion to health workers for fear of being diagnosed as suffering from a psychological disorder. One pastor told him that many members of his congregation 'heard voices' and believed they were possessed by evil spirits. The pastor prayed alongside them to break the 'spell'. Only if the voices continued did he admit the possibility of psychological disorder.

Adapted from Copsey, 1997

Questions

1 Discuss the following statements with reference to Items A, B and C.

a) Views of abnormality vary from culture to culture.

b) What is normal in other cultures may be interpreted as psychological abnormality by Western psychiatrists.

2 'The line on the rainbow between normal and abnormal hallucinations is often very fuzzy indeed' (Bentall, 1990). Discuss with reference to Item D.

Many gay people accepted society's and psychiatrists' view of themselves and sought 'cures' for their 'illness'. Many of the attempts to 'cure' gays were based on *aversion therapy*. The idea was to associate unpleasant experiences with sexual attraction for men and so make men sexually undesirable. Often 'patients' were asked to bring photographs of people they found attractive – past or present lovers – to therapy sessions. They were then asked to look at the photographs during a course of electric shock treatment or nausea-inducing drugs which often made them violently sick.

In 1973, the American Psychiatric Association removed homosexuality from its *Diagnostic and statistical manual of mental disorders* (DSM). It was no longer classified as a 'sexual disorder'. As a result, large numbers of people were 'cured' in an instant. As Johnstone (1989) puts it, 'The most spectacular cure achieved by modern psychiatry was when homosexuality was dropped as a category of mental illness... and millions of people thus recovered overnight'.

Key terms

Aversion therapy *A technique which uses unpleasant or painful stimuli with the aim of changing behaviour patterns.*

This is a case of psychology reflecting changes in culture. From the 1970s onwards, homosexuality was increasingly seen as an acceptable alternative to heterosexuality. As social norms about sexual behaviour changed, so did psychology's view of what counted as a sexual disorder. Creating – some would say inventing – a psychological disorder on the basis of social norms can be extremely dangerous. Some of the consequences of this are outlined in Activity 4.

Activity 4 When gays needed 'treatment'

Item A 'Curing' homosexuality

The effects of aversion therapy could be devastating. In 1964 an 18 year old was admitted to a psychiatric ward in Chester. He recalls his interview with a psychiatrist. 'He asked me if I realised how revolting homosexuality was. He wanted to make me feel disgusted'. The 'patient' was locked in a room containing a bed, but no windows or furniture, and given a pile of erotic photographs of men. He was then pumped full of a drug which made him violently sick. This continued for 72 hours. The bed and room were eventually covered in his vomit, urine and faeces. Those three days of 'therapy', he says, have destroyed 30 years of his life.

Adapted from D'Silva, 1996

Item B Gay pride

Gay Pride march, London. Times change and so do psychological disorders.

Question

Items A and B show the dangers of creating a psychological disorder based on the social norms and attitudes of the day. What are those dangers?

4.3 Culture-bound syndromes

The case of homosexuality suggests that at least some so-called psychological disorders simply reflect cultural views of what is normal and abnormal. Homosexuality is found in every known society. In some societies it is seen as both abnormal and as a psychological disorder, in other societies it is seen as neither. For example, adolescent homosexuality was a common and accepted practice in ancient Athens and in the Mayan civilisation of Central America (Tannahill, 1989).

There are some behaviour patterns which are *not* found in every society. And some of these behaviour patterns are seen as psychological disorders. They are known as *culture-bound syndromes*. A syndrome is a collection of behaviours or characteristics. Culture-bound means they are limited to particular cultures. Table 1 provides examples of culture-bound syndromes.

The 1994 edition of DSM describes culture-bound syndromes as 'locality-specific patterns of aberrant behaviour and troubling experience that may or may not be linked to a particular DSM IV diagnostic category'. This means that culture-bound syndromes may be limited to particular cultures or they may be similar to Western psychological disorders but just expressed in a different way. Yap (1974) argues that it is possible to classify many, if not all, culture-bound syndromes in terms of Western categories. For example, he sees *amok* as a cultural expression of the Western disorder 'rage reaction'.

Table 1 Culture-bound syndromes

Disorder	Location	Description
Amok	Malaysia, Indonesia, Thailand	Wild, aggressive behaviour with attempts to kill or injure others. Begins with brooding and ends with exhaustion.
Koro	South East Asia	An intense fear that the penis will retract into the body and that once fully retracted will cause death. Attempts to stop the retraction of the penis often result in damage to the body.
Pibloqtoq	Greenland, Alaska, Canadian Arctic	An uncontrollable urge to tear off clothes, leave the warmth of the shelter and expose the body to cold, winter weather. Often involves running through the snow crying and screaming. Found amongst the Inuit (Eskimo).
Ghost sickness	North America	An extreme preoccupation with death and those who have died. Symptoms include nightmares, a sense of danger, hallucinations and feelings of suffocation. Found amongst certain Native American peoples.

Adapted from Berry et al., 1992

Other researchers believe that culture-bound syndromes are limited to certain cultures. Some researchers go further and suggest that many of the disorders listed in the DSM are culture-bound – they are limited to Western societies.

These views raise a number of important questions. They can be illustrated by looking at depression in different cultures. Depression is one of the most commonly diagnosed psychological disorders in the West. Does it exist in all societies, despite cultural differences?

First, people from different cultures describe what appears to be depression in different ways. For example, Chinese people often refer to 'exhaustion of their nerves' and their hearts being 'squeezed and weighed down'. Nigerians sometimes complain that 'ants keep creeping in parts of my brain' (Kleinman & Good, 1985). Do these examples merely illustrate different ways of describing the same disorder? Or, do they illustrate different disorders?

Second, the actual experience of what appears to be depression seems to vary from culture to culture. In the West people suffering from depression emphasise inner feeling states such as extreme sadness, helplessness and hopelessness. In may other cultures, depression is experienced in physical terms such as fatigue, loss of appetite, backache and headaches. Again, do these examples illustrate different ways of experiencing the same disorder? Or, do they illustrate different disorders?

There are no easy answers to these questions. Many researchers argue that a lot more research is needed before any firm conclusions can be reached (Berry et al., 1992).

Summary

1. Views of what counts as normal and abnormal behaviour vary from culture to culture.
2. Views of psychological abnormality vary from culture to culture.
3. As cultures change, so do ideas about normal and abnormal behaviour, and, in some cases, what counts as a psychological disorder.
4. So-called culture-bound syndromes may or may not be limited to particular cultures.
5. Psychological disorders identified and classified in the West may or may not be limited to Western cultures.

Conclusion The idea of culture shows how difficult it is to define abnormal behaviour in general and psychological abnormality in particular. Psychologists and psychiatrists are becoming increasingly aware of this difficulty. It is not just an academic debate. The difficulty of defining and identifying psychological abnormality can have serious consequences. It can result in perfectly healthy individuals being diagnosed as psychologically disordered and in people experiencing a psychological disorder going undiagnosed.

Key term

Culture-bound syndromes *Psychological disorders which appear to be limited to particular cultures.*

Unit 5 Psychological disorders and mental illness

KEY ISSUES

1. **What is the medical model and how does it view psychological abnormality?**
2. **Can mental illness be seen as a myth?**
3. **How can the idea of psychological abnormality be seen as a mechanism of social control?**
4. **Is psychological abnormality simply a 'cultural construct'?**

5.1 The medical model

This unit returns to the basic question: What is psychological abnormality? In terms of the *medical model*, psychological abnormality is an illness.

Around the middle of the 19th century the idea that abnormal behaviour resulted from 'mental illness' became increasingly popular. Many physicians believed that both physical illness and mental problems were caused by some organic or physical disorder. This view formed the basis for the development of psychiatry.

Psychiatrists are trained in medicine. They specialise in diagnosing and treating psychological disorders. Traditionally, psychiatrists have seen psychological problems as medical problems. From this point of view, people with psychological disorders are 'ill', they require 'treatment' which will hopefully 'cure' them of their 'mental illness'.

The medical model and the idea of mental illness have been strongly criticised. Part of this criticism is based on the idea that physical illness is distinct from psychological disorders.

Doctors can diagnose physical illness from physical symptoms such as raised blood pressure, high temperature or malignant growths and tumours. Many psychological disorders do not appear to have a physical or organic basis. As a result, psychiatrists have to base their diagnoses on people's thoughts, feelings and behaviours. This raises questions about the judgement of psychiatrists. In many cases doctors have clear-cut physical symptoms of illness. Psychiatrists usually have to rely on their interpretation of patients' reports about their feelings and behaviour.

Doctors can largely ignore questions of culture and subculture when diagnosing physical illness. As Mackay (1975) puts it, 'The clinical signs of tuberculosis are identical in Japan, England and Iceland'. However, as the previous unit has shown, the 'signs' of psychological disorders are not 'identical' in different cultures and subcultures.

Those who defend the medical model claim that advances in biopsychology are revealing that many psychological disorders do have a physical or organic basis. They point to recent research that indicates that disorders of the nervous system or genetic factors are associated with many psychological disorders. This point will be examined in more detail in the next two chapters.

5.2 The myth of mental illness

The psychiatrist Thomas Szasz rejects the whole idea of 'mental illness'. His views are summarised in the title of one of his books, *The myth of mental illness* (1961). Szasz argues that only a small minority of so-called mental illnesses can be seen as 'diseases of the brain'. These include Alzheimer's disease, which destroys neurons in the brain, and alcoholic poisoning. According to Szasz, the vast majority of 'mental illnesses' are 'problems in living'. The unhappiness, confusion, anxiety and fear that characterise many psychological disorders have nothing to do with 'mental diseases' or 'illnesses'. Instead, they are 'problems in living', for example problems in relationships with partners, families, friends and work colleagues. These are social, not medical problems. They should not be seen as 'diseases of the mind' which require 'treatment' to 'cure' them. This is why Szasz refers to mental illness as a myth. In his view it doesn't exist.

If mental illness doesn't exist, why was it invented? Szasz argues that throughout history human beings have concocted all sorts of ideas in an attempt to explain 'problems in living'. In the past, devils, witches, demons and evil spirits have all been blamed for 'problems in living'. And there has been a range of practitioners from priests, shamans and witchfinders to deal with these supernatural beings and solve the 'problems in living'. The latest in a long line of explanations is 'mental illness' and the latest in a long line of practitioners is the psychiatrist. In Szasz's words, 'Mental illness thus exists or is "real" in exactly the same sense in which witches existed or were "real" (1961).

Few psychiatrists or psychologists today would go as far as Szasz. However, there is a growing acceptance of the view that psychological disorders often result from social situations and social interaction.

5.2 Psychological abnormality and social control

According to Szasz the idea of mental illness does more than simply provide explanations for 'problems in living'. It also serves to control people whose behaviour breaks social norms and, in doing so, threatens the status quo – the way things are. Labelling someone as mentally ill means they can be controlled – they can be treated, hospitalised, removed from society and placed in secure accommodation. In this respect, the idea of mental illness can be seen as a mechanism of *social control*.

Those who have most to gain from preserving the status quo are those in power. Szasz (1989) takes the argument one step further by suggesting that the idea of mental illness has been used to control people who are seen to threaten the interests of the powerful. This view can be illustrated by the following examples.

Dr Samuel Cartwright was appointed by the Louisiana Medical Association to investigate the 'strange' behaviour of African-American slaves. His report, published in 1851, was entitled 'The diseases and physical peculiarities of the negro race'. He claimed to have discovered several 'diseases' unknown to the white race. One was a sensory disease which made African Americans insensitive 'to pain when being punished'. This discovery clearly justified the vicious treatment many slaves suffered. A second 'disease' was a 'mania to seek freedom' which Cartwright called 'drapetomania'. This 'mental disease' caused some slaves to escape from their masters. Clearly they needed to be caught and 'treated' so their 'illness' could be 'cured' (Zimbardo et al., 1995).

In the Soviet Union, from the late 1930s to the early 1970s, psychiatry was used as a weapon to silence those who opposed the communist system. Thousands of 'dissenters' were incarcerated in special psychiatric hospitals simply because they voiced their opposition to the state (Moynahan, 1994). Activity 5 provides further details of this practice.

The above examples illustrate how the idea of mental illness can be used as a means of social control. Labelling people as 'mentally ill' serves to punish them for breaking social norms and failing to conform to society's standards of morality. Like all punishments, it provides a warning and a deterrent to others. A *stigma* is often attached to mental illness. This is a mark of shame and disgrace. It implies that people are morally inferior and often leads to social rejection.

The idea of mental illness can be used by the powerful to discredit opinions and behaviours which challenge their position. Who would take someone seriously if they had been branded as mentally ill? In addition, the idea of mental illness can be used to justify the treatment of those who threaten the powerful. It is far easier to justify the removal of Soviet dissidents from society on the basis of their 'madness' than their political views.

Key terms

Medical model *An approach based on medicine which assumes there are basic similarities between physical illness and psychological disorders. Both are seen as illnesses which can be diagnosed and treated.*

Mental illness *A traditional term for psychological disorders which implies they are 'illnesses of the mind' which require treatment.*

Problems in living *The idea that psychological disorders are problems which result from social relationships. They are social rather than medical problems.*

Social control *Various mechanisms which encourage or enforce conformity to social norms. Also refers to the methods used by the powerful to control others in order to maintain their privileged position.*

Stigma *A mark of shame and disgrace. People stigmatised as 'mentally ill' sometimes experience social rejection.*

5.4 The problem of psychological abnormality

There is no clear-cut, objective way of defining and identifying psychological abnormality. What is seen as psychological abnormality rests heavily on the judgement of psychiatrists and psychologists. And their judgement depends in part on the culture of their society. Views of psychological abnormality vary from culture to culture and change as culture changes.

In addition, there are disagreements between psychologists, and between psychiatrists, about what counts as psychological abnormality. Many, particularly psychiatrists trained in medicine, see psychological abnormality as mental illness. Others reject the whole idea of mental illness and replace it with ideas such as 'problems in living'. All this suggests that psychological abnormality is

Activity 5 Mental illness and social control

Item A Slavery

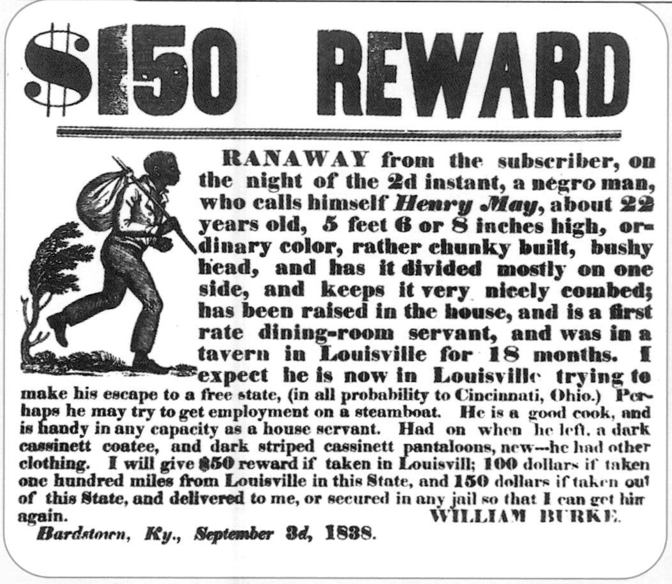
$150 REWARD

RANAWAY from the subscriber, on the night of the 2d instant, a negro man, who calls himself *Henry May*, about 22 years old, 5 feet 6 or 8 inches high, ordinary color, rather chunky built, bushy head, and has it divided mostly on one side, and keeps it very nicely combed; has been raised in the house, and is a first rate dining-room servant, and was in a tavern in Louisville for 18 months. I expect he is now in Louisville trying to make his escape to a free state, (in all probability to Cincinnati, Ohio.) Perhaps he may try to get employment on a steamboat. He is a good cook, and is handy in any capacity as a house servant. Had on when he left, a dark cassinett coatee, and dark striped cassinett pantaloons, new--he had other clothing. I will give $50 reward if taken in Louisvill; 100 dollars if taken one hundred miles from Louisville in this State, and 150 dollars if taken out of this State, and delivered to me, or secured in any jail so that I can get him again.

WILLIAM BURKE.

Bardstown, Ky., September 3d, 1838.

'Slave-drivers' whipping a slave. They will be whipped themselves if they refuse to do it.

Item B Soviet dissidents

President Khrushchev, leader of the Soviet Union from 1953 to 1964, regarded opposition to communism as so bizarre and irrational that it must be 'caused by mental disorder… clearly the state of such people is not normal'. As a result opponents of communism were confined in mental hospitals.

Professor Andrei Snezhnevsky, director of the Institute of Psychiatry at the Academy of Medical Sciences, provided an academic argument to support the labelling and confinement of dissidents. He stated that dissent was a symptom of schizophrenia.

Adapted from Moynahan, 1994

Item C Stigma

'For me, the stigma of mental illness was as devastating as the experience of hospitalisation itself. Prior to being hospitalised, I lived an enviable existence. Rewards, awards and invitations filled my scrapbook. The crisis of mental illness appeared as a nuclear explosion in my life. There was a binding, confining quality to my life, in part chosen, in part imposed. Repeated rejections, the awkwardness of others around me and my own discomfort and self-consciousness propelled me into solitary confinement.'

Adapted from Houghton, 1980

Question

1 How can Dr Cartwright's report (p 150) be used to explain and justify the behaviour illustrated in Item A?

2 Read Item B. How was the idea of mental illness used by the Soviet rulers to maintain their position?

3 Labelling people as mentally ill can be seen as a punishment and a deterrent. Discuss with reference to Item C.

a cultural construction – a meaning given to the behaviours of others which is shaped by the culture of society. In this sense, psychological abnormality doesn't have an objective reality, it doesn't really exist.

Most psychiatrists and psychologists would reject this view. They accept that there are all sorts of problems involved in defining and identifying psychological abnormality. But they stop short of saying that it doesn't really exist. This chapter closes with evidence to support this viewpoint. It is presented without criticism in order to illustrate the argument clearly.

Most psychological disorders are found and recognised in

all cultures. Schizophrenia provides an example. People with schizophrenia experience a sharp break with reality. They may have hallucinations and delusions, for example they may believe that thoughts are being inserted in their minds. According to the World Health Organisation (1979) schizophrenia is universal – it is found in every culture. This suggests that despite cultural differences, it is possible to identify the same disorder in all societies.

There is growing evidence that schizophrenia is an 'illness of the brain'. It may, at least in part, be caused by structural abnormalities in the brain, by brain damage resulting from viral infections, and by imbalances in the chemicals in the brain (Comer, 1998). In view of this, schizophrenia is not just a cultural construct, it is a real disorder with real physical causes.

Finally, most people with schizophrenia experience considerable suffering. Many feel an extreme sense of aloneness – they are completely isolated as no-one else shares their view of reality. Their suffering, like their disorder, is real (Westen, 1996).

Summary

1. The medical model sees psychological disorder as an illness which shares many similarities with physical illness.
2. Szasz rejects the whole idea of mental illness which he regards as a myth. He sees psychological disorders as problems in living, as social rather than medical problems.
3. The idea of psychological abnormality can be seen as a mechanism of social control which punishes people who deviate from social norms and who threaten the interests of the powerful.
4. Most psychologists and psychiatrists reject the view that psychological abnormality is simply a cultural construct. They argue that many psychological disorders are found and recognised in all cultures, that they often have 'real' organic causes and often cause 'real' suffering.

References

American Psychiatric Association (1994). *Diagnostic and statistical manual of mental disorders* (4th ed.). Washington, DC: Author.

Arieti, S. (1974). *Interpretation of schizophrenia.* New York: Basic Books.

Barlow, D.H. & Durand, V.M. (1999). *Abnormal psychology: An integrative approach* (2nd ed.). Pacific Grove, CA: Brooks/Cole.

Benedict, R. (1934). *Patterns of culture.* New York: Mentor.

Bentall, R.P. (1990). The illusion of reality: A review and integration of psychological research on hallucinations. *Psychological Bulletin, 107,* 82-95.

Berry, J.W., Poortinga, Y.H., Segall, M.H. & Dasen, P.R. (1992). *Cross-cultural psychology: Research and applications.* Cambridge: Cambridge University Press.

Comer, R.J. (1998). *Abnormal psychology* (3rd ed.). New York: W.H. Freeman.

Copsey, N. (1997). *Keeping faith: The provision of community health services within a multifaith context.* London: Sainsbury Centre for Mental Health.

D'Silva, B. (1996). *When gay meant mad. Independent on Sunday,* 4 August.

Davison, G.C. & Neale, J.M. (1998). *Abnormal psychology* (7th ed.). New York: John Wiley & Sons.

Hall, E.T. (1973). *The hidden dimension.* New York: Doubleday.

Heather, N. (1976). *Radical perspectives in psychology.* London: Methuen.

Houghton, J. (1980). One personal experience: Before and after mental illness. In I.G. Rabkin, L. Gelb & J.B. Lazar (Eds.), *Attitudes toward the mentally ill: Research perspectives.* Rockville, MD: National Institute of Mental Health.

Johnstone, L. (1989). *Users and abusers of psychology: A critical look at traditional psychiatric practice.* London: Routledge.

Jahoda, M. (1958). *Current concepts of positive mental health.* New York: Basic Books.

Kleinman, A. & Good, B. (1985). *Culture and depression: Studies in the anthropology and cross-cultural psychiatry of affective disorder.* Berkeley: University of California Press.

Klineberg, I. (1971). Race and IQ. *Courier,* November.

Lowie, R.H. (1954). *Indians of the plains.* New York: McGraw Hill.

Mackay, D. (1975). *Clinical psychology – theory and therapy.* London: Methuen.

Moynahan, B. (1994). *The Russian century.* London: BCA.

Nazroo, J.Y. (1997). *Ethnicity and mental health: Findings from a national community study.* London: Policy Studies Institute.

Rack, P. (1984). *Race, culture and mental disorder.* London: Tavistock.

Stands in Timber, J. & Liberty, M. (1967). *Cheyenne memories.* New Haven: Yale University Press.

Szasz, T. (1961). *The myth of mental illness: Foundations of a theory of personal conduct.* New York: Harper & Row.

Szasz, T. (1989). *Law, liberty, and psychiatry: An inquiry into the social uses of mental health practices.* Syracuse, NY: Syracuse University Press.

Tannahill, R. (1989). *Sex in history.* London: Sphere Books.

Weeks, D. & James, J. (1995). *Eccentrics: A study of sanity and strangeness.* New York: Villard.

Westen, D. (1996). *Psychology: Mind, brain and culture.* New York: John Wiley.

World Health Organisation. (1979). *Schizophrenia: An international follow-up study.* New York: John Wiley.

Yap, P.M. (1974). *Comparative psychiatry.* Toronto: University of Toronto Press.

Zimbardo, P., McDermott, M., Jansz, J. & Metall, N. (1995). *Psychology: A European text.* London: Harper Collins.

11 Models of abnormality

Introduction

The last chapter looked at definitions of abnormality. This chapter looks at models of abnormality. A model is a framework for understanding and explaining something. A model of abnormality provides an explanation for psychological disorders – an account of their origins and causes. It also provides suggestions for the treatment of those disorders.

Models of abnormality fall into two main groups. First, the biological or medical model which sees abnormality as the result of some underlying physical or organic problem, such as a dysfunction of the brain or the nervous system. Second, psychological models which see abnormality arising from psychological problems, caused by a person's thoughts, needs and experiences.

Chapter summary

- **Unit 1 traces the history of views of abnormality in the West to the early years of the 20th century.**
- **Unit 2 looks at the biological or medical model of abnormality.**
- **Units 3 to 6 look at psychological models of abnormality.**
- **Unit 7 outlines the sociocultural model of abnormality.**

Unit 1 A brief history of abnormality

KEY ISSUES

1. **How have views of psychological abnormality in the Western world changed over time?**
2. **To what degree have these views alternated between biological and psychological models?**

1.1 Before the 18th century

Both biological and psychological models of abnormality have been around for a long time.

Many ancient cultures held a kind of early psychological model. They believed that abnormality was due to possession by spirits. In these cultures, priests and shamans (religious curers) practised exorcism – chants, dances, prayers and laying on of hands – to expel the spirits. Some cultures practised trepanning – boring a hole in the skull to release the spirits – a treatment that a surprising number of patients seem to have survived.

The Greeks and Romans of classical times tended to favour a more biological model – the theory of humours, proposed by the 'father of medicine' Hippocrates (c.460-377 BC), and developed by Galen (c.130-200 AD). This theory suggested that both psychological abnormality and physical illness were caused by imbalances in four vital fluids, or humours, of the body. These fluids were blood, yellow bile, black bile, and phlegm. Galen believed that too much blood led to emotional instability; excess of yellow bile led to anger; excess of black bile led to melancholy or depression; and excess of phlegm led to lethargy. Under the influence of Galenic theory, exorcism was largely replaced by medical physicians prescribing diets, exercise and drugs.

In medieval times, the biological model declined and the idea of spirit possession was revived. The Christian church was suspicious of classical Greek and Roman ideas, including Galenic medicine, seeing them as 'pagan'. Wave after wave of plague and other contagious diseases hit Europe during this period. Galenic medicine failed to explain how people caught diseases from each other, or to cure the victims of these epidemics (Porter, 1997). Many people felt that disease was more likely to be the work of the Devil than the result of imbalances in bodily humours. Psychological disorders were often seen to result from possession by the Devil. By late medieval times, anyone deviating from the norms of society risked being accused of witchcraft and Devil-worship and of being tortured, hanged or burned at the stake.

Despite this, Galenic medicine did not entirely disappear. A few voices, like Paracelsus (1493-1541) and Johannes Weyer (1515-1588), insisted that abnormal people were sick rather than evil. 'Hospitals' were built, although many

Execution of witches in 1655

Two women visitors to Bedlam in the 18th century. They have bought tickets to view the antics of the patients.

of these were little better than zoos or prisons. St Mary's of Bethlehem in London (better known as Bedlam) was converted into a hospital for the 'insane' in 1547, and put its collection of chained up 'lunatics' on show to the paying public.

1.2 The 18th century

The first modern psychological model emerged in Paris in the 1790s. Philippe Pinel (1745-1826) suggested that psychological disorder was the result of stressful events in life, and that the abnormal needed sympathy and time to recuperate, not torture or chaining up. Under his guidance, Parisian hospitals like the Sâlpetrière became refuges (or asylums) for the psychologically disordered, designed to help the inmates recover – not to imprison them or put them on show. Pinel's humane treatment of his patients, involving such modern practices as occupational therapy and talking through problems, became known as 'moral treatment'. Similar developments took place in England (where Quakers opened the York Retreat in 1796) and later in America. Bedlam was finally closed and possession by the Devil, exorcism, and witchcraft were increasingly rejected as superstitious nonsense.

Pinel freeing patients from chains and shackles in Paris

The biological model of abnormality developed slowly during this period. Physicians continued to use bleeding (a leftover from Galen) for all manner of physical and mental disorders, and there was a flurry of interest in the healing powers of magnets, inspired by the claims of the notorious con-man Franz Anton Mesmer (1734-1815). In the meantime, governments were incarcerating every kind of 'deviant' (the sick, the 'mad', beggars, orphans, prostitutes, unmarried mothers and so on) in institutions – just in case crime, immorality or psychological disorder were as contagious as plague (Foucault, 1977).

1.3 The 19th century

In the 19th century, biology and medicine developed much more rapidly. Charles Darwin's theory of evolution (1859) drew attention to the importance of biological inheritance, and Louis Pasteur's discovery of germs in the 1860s at last explained how contagious diseases spread. Soon after, the idea that psychological disorders could have biological causes was strengthened by the discovery that 'general pariesis' (a form of insanity) was caused by syphilis – a sexually transmitted disease. From the 1840s, professional associations of 'mad-doctors' or 'alienists' (later called psychiatrists) were established in Europe and America, and by the 1860s, the German scientist Wilhelm Griesinger could confidently assert that all 'mental diseases are brain diseases'. Some of these diseases he thought were inherited, some due to infection.

Between 1883 and 1913, Griesinger's pupil Emil

Kraepelin (1855-1926) developed his classification system of psychological disorders. He distinguished between psychoses (true 'insanity' where the patient has lost touch with reality), neuroses (anxiety disorders), personality disorders, and retardation. All the classification systems used by psychiatry up to the present day are based on Kraepelin's original system (Stone, 1998). By the end of the 19th century, the biological or medical model of abnormality was dominant. Psychiatrists took control of the asylums and turned them into 'mental hospitals' housing large numbers of patients. 'Moral treatment' was seen as too time-consuming in terms of the attention it paid to the individual needs of patients. It was largely replaced by more economical treatments like physical restraint, cold baths, bleeding and purging – clearing out the stomach and the bowels.

Despite its triumph, however, 19th century psychiatry was not very optimistic about its chances of curing psychological disorders (Porter, 1997). The success rate of medical treatments was poor – psychiatrists claimed this was because many disorders were inherited and therefore incurable. The only solution many psychiatrists could see lay in eugenic programmes of selective breeding and sterilisation. In the first half of the 20th century, laws were passed in many Western countries, including the USA and Scandinavia, permitting the compulsory sterilisation of the mentally 'unfit' (Dowbiggin, 1998). In Nazi Germany in the 1930s, mental patients were gassed. Since then, eugenic programmes have been much less popular in psychiatric circles.

Summary

1. In ancient times, an early psychological model of spirit possession was widespread. This was treated by exorcism and trepanning.
2. In classical Greece and Rome, a biological model of imbalance of humours was favoured. This became known as the Galenic theory. Abnormality was treated with diets, exercise and drugs.
3. During the medieval period, spirit possession and exorcism revived, and the Galenic biological model declined.
4. In the 18th century, new psychological models emerged. Pinel's approach was influential, seeing abnormality as the result of stress, and treating it with 'moral treatment'.
5. Advances in biology and medicine led to the rise of psychiatry in the 19th century. By 1900, the biological model was dominant.

Unit 2 The biological (medical) model of abnormality

KEY ISSUES

1. **What are the main features of the biological model?**
2. **What are the implications for treatment of this model?**

2.1 Main features of the biological model

The biological model is favoured by medicine and psychiatry – the branch of medicine that specialises in mental disorders. The biological model was the dominant view of abnormality at the beginning of the 20th century. Despite serious challenges from various psychological models, it remains dominant today. The biological model uses the medical language of patient, symptoms, diagnosis, illness, disease, treatment and cure (Maher, 1966). Psychiatry tends to see abnormality as mental illness, although many psychiatrists now prefer the term disorder to illness.

The biological model classifies mental disorders. The main classification systems in use today are the ICD-10 (the World Health Organisation's *International Classification of Diseases*, 10th edition) published in 1993, and the American DSM-IV *(Diagnostic and Statistical Manual of Mental Disorders*, 4th edition*)* published in 1994.

Psychiatric systems classify disorders according to their symptoms. For example, both the ICD-10 and DSM-IV place depression in a category of mood disorders. The symptoms of depression include low mood, fatigue, loss of concentration, reduced sex drive, change in weight, disruption of normal patterns of sleep, slowed (or, in some cases, agitated) mental and physical activity, feelings of worthlessness or guilt, and preoccupation with death.

The biological model regards psychological disorders as a sign or symptom of an underlying physical or organic disorder – usually some dysfunction of the brain or nervous system. Different psychological disorders are believed to be caused by different organic disorders. Brain scanning techniques, such as PET or CAT scans, are often used to find evidence for the physical basis for psychological abnormality. In the case of depression, PET scans suggest that depressives have a lower uptake of glucose in the brain, which may explain the slower mental functioning and loss of concentration (Lingjaerde, 1983).

The brain dysfunctions and organic disorders that are believed to cause abnormality can arise in a number of ways. Some may be genetically inherited and run in families. Some may be caused by infection. Some may arise from damage to the nervous system, as a result of exposure to environmental pollution, alcohol or drug abuse, or the impact of life experiences like overwork or child abuse. Some people may be genetically more vulnerable to being harmed by certain experiences.

In the case of depression, the disorder has been linked to biological factors such as genetic inheritance and imbalances in neurotransmitter chemicals and hormones.

Genetic inheritance

According to the biological model, the presence of certain genes can predispose people to psychological disorders. In other words, certain genes can make people more vulnerable to disorders. Three types of studies – family studies, adoption studies and twin studies – have provided evidence to support this view.

Family studies In this type of study, the family tree of a person with a psychological disorder is traced to see if the disorder 'runs in the family'. Family study evidence suggests that a person is ten times more likely to suffer from a mood disorder such as depression if a parent or sibling (brother or sister) has a similar disorder (Weissman, 1987). The problem with these studies is that families tend to share home environments and this, rather than genetic inheritance, may cause disorders to run in the family.

Adoption studies These studies compare people who have been adopted with their biological and adoptive parents. Since they were raised apart from their biological relatives, similarities with their biological relatives would indicate genetic influences. In terms of depression, most studies show a higher rate of depression in their biological relatives – up to 20% of those relatives suffered from the disorder compared with 5-10% of their adoptive relatives, which is the rate for the general population (Harrington et al., 1993). The problem with evidence from adoptive studies is that unless the children have been adopted at or near birth, they have shared part of their life with their biological families. As a result, they may have learned abnormal behaviour from their biological parents. Again, it is difficult to separate genetic and environmental factors.

Twin studies These studies investigate how likely it is that pairs of twins share the same disorder. They compare identical (monozygotic) twins who have the same genes and fraternal (dizygotic twins) who share around 50% of their genes. If genes are a factor in psychological disorder, then we would expect a higher proportion of identical twins to share a disorder. A number of studies have confirmed this. For example, a study based on nearly 200 pairs of twins found that when an identical twin had depression, there was a 46% chance that the other twin would also have the disorder. The figure for fraternal twins was 20% (McGuffin et al., 1996).

However, twins not only share all or many of their genes, they also share much of their environment. Even when raised apart, they often live in the same neighbourhood, go to the same school, and spend time together. Again, it is difficult to separate genetic and environmental influences. In addition, samples of identical twins raised apart are small, so making it difficult to draw firm conclusions.

Biochemistry

The biological model suggests that psychological disorders may be due to an imbalance of chemicals in the nervous system and the endocrine system. In other words, there may be too much or too little of certain neurotransmitter chemicals and hormones. These biochemicals affect mood and behaviour. (See Chapter 7, pp 94-98, for a discussion of neurotransmitters and hormones.)

Neurotransmitters One theory links depression to low levels of the neurotransmitters serotonin and noradrenaline. However, the relationship between neurotransmitters and depression is complex – more research is needed to discover the exact biochemical mechanism of the disorder (Barlow & Durand, 1999).

Hormones People suffering from depression often have high levels of the hormone cortisol. Cortisol is sometimes referred to as a 'stress hormone' because it is produced in times of stress. The high levels of cortisol are not surprising as many depressive episodes are preceded by stressful events. Given this, the high levels of cortisol may be a result rather than a cause of depression – they may be produced as a response to stress rather than causing the disorder (Ladd et al., 1996).

2.2 Treatment and the biological model

The biological model states that psychological disorders are caused, at least in part, by biological factors. This suggests that treatment should address those factors. Many of the suggested treatments aim to change bodily functioning and alter biochemical levels.

Drug treatment A range of drug treatments have been developed which alter the body's biochemistry. For example, Prozac, an antidepressant drug, increases the level of the neurotransmitter serotonin. Antidepressants such as Prozac appear to be effective in 65-75% of cases. This suggests that depression is, at least in part, due to chemical imbalances.

However, drugs can have negative side effects. For example, Prozac, can cause insomnia, headaches and gastrointestinal disorders. And drugs can lead to physical addiction, especially if taken in high doses over long periods of time (Comer, 1998).

Gene therapy The Human Genome Project, which aims to map the complete genetic makeup of human beings, has been underway since 1990. However, gene therapy for genetically based disorders has hardly begun. One day, individually tailored genetic engineering may liberate those at risk from inherited disorders.

However, the evidence suggests that genes alone do not cause psychological disorders. They simply increase the probability that individuals will develop disorders. The *diathesis-stress model* states that psychological disorders result from an interaction between genes and the environment. Diathesis means a condition which makes an individual more susceptible to a disorder. When the diathesis – in this case a genetic predisposition – combines with certain life events such as stressors, the disorder is more likely to develop. The diathesis-stress model suggests that gene therapy, on its own, will not provide a 'magical cure' for psychological disorders.

Electroconvulsive therapy (ECT) ECT involves passing an electric current through the brain which causes a brain seizure or convulsions. It is sometimes used in cases of severe depression, though less so nowadays, partly because of side effects such as memory loss. Although it appears to reduce symptoms of depression in around 60-70% of cases, it is not clear how ECT works. However, it is known to release a variety of neurotransmitters in the brain (Comer, 1998).

Brain surgery This is the most extreme biological treatment for psychological disorders. It has a long history starting with trepanning in prehistoric times, though today it is only used as a last resort.

2.3 Evaluation of the biological model

Greater understanding In recent years, rapid advances in biochemistry and genetics have increased our understanding of the biological aspects of psychological disorders. However, this understanding is far from complete. The complexities of brain chemistry and human genetics have yet to be unravelled.

Inconclusive evidence The evidence is inconclusive. To what extent does neurotransmitter activity cause psychological disorders? What contribution do genes make to the onset of psychological disorders? The short answer is we don't really know. As yet, no specific genes have been identified that make major contributions to psychological disorders. Available evidence suggests that many genes may contribute to psychological disorders, each having a relatively small effect. However, the picture is far from clear (Barlow & Durand, 1999).

Reductionism This is the reduction of something to its most basic elements or parts. Can psychological disorders be reduced to biological factors, as extreme versions of the biological model suggest? The answer is probably no. Complex mental and emotional processes are unlikely to be caused solely by genes and neurotransmitters. At most, biological factors probably predispose people to psychological disorders as the diathesis-stress model suggests. In terms of this model, psychological disorders result from an interplay between biology and the environment.

Cause and effect As noted in the case of the role of hormones in depression, some biological changes may result from, rather than cause, psychological disorders. For example, if someone jumps out at you in the dark, it is fear that causes the adrenaline rush, not the adrenaline that causes the fear. In certain cases, biochemical imbalances may be caused by (rather than causing) psychological disorders.

The classification system Classification systems of psychological disorders are largely based on the biological or medical model. Critics question their claim to be objective and scientific for the following reasons. There are frequent and sudden changes in classifications including the appearance of new disorders, the re-classification of existing disorders, and the removal of other disorders – as in the case of homosexuality. At times these changes appear to reflect changes in attitudes in the wider society rather than the application of scientific knowledge.

Treatment Many of the treatments suggested by the biological model have been criticised as unethical and ineffective. Drug treatment can have negative side effects. It can lead to physical and psychological dependence. In addition, it may only treat the symptoms of a disorder rather than its cause. For example, drugs may simply readjust neurotransmitter levels and do nothing about the situation which caused the disorder in the first place. Many researchers would agree with Ronald Comer that 'drugs alone do not provide a long-term solution' to most cases of psychological disorders (Comer, 1998).

However, many psychiatrists and patients argue that drugs can relieve extremely distressing symptoms and place people in a better frame of mind to overcome their disorder (see Activity 1, Item B).

A humane approach? Supporters of the biological model claim that it is more humane than other models. It portrays psychological disorder as illness – something that just happens to a person. No blame is attached to the individual for suffering from the disorder. This is in contrast to some psychological models which imply that people cannot cope with life or have brought their disorders upon themselves. However, critics are doubtful that it really helps to see disorders as illness, since this encourages the 'patient' to depend on the 'doctor' and not to take any personal responsibility for their own recovery.

Key terms

Biological or medical model *A model which states that psychological disorders are caused, at least in part, by biological factors such as neurotransmitter imbalance and genetic inheritance.*

Diathesis-stress model *A model which states that psychological disorders are caused by an interaction between the environment and a condition – the diathesis – which makes people more susceptible to disorders.*

Summary

1. The biological model classifies psychological disorders in terms of their symptoms.
2. It assumes that psychological disorders have a biological basis.
3. It states that the presence of certain genes can predispose individuals to psychological disorders.
4. An imbalance of chemicals in the nervous system and endocrine system is seen as a major cause of psychological disorders.
5. Drug treatments which alter the body's biochemistry are seen as one of the main treatments for psychological disorders.
6. Evidence to support the biological model is inconclusive. The complexities of brain chemistry and human genetics are only partially understood.
7. Many researchers argue that biological factors are only part of the picture. They must be seen in a wider context, as the diathesis-stress model suggests.

Activity 1 The biological model

Item A Twins and psychological disorders

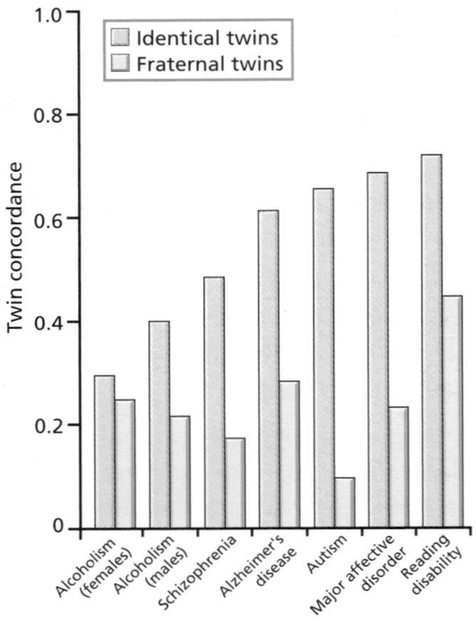

The bar chart shows the likelihood of twins having the same psychological disorder. Identical or monozygotic twins have the same genes. Fraternal or dizygotic twins share around 50% of their genes. The concordance level refers to the extent to which twins share a particular characteristic – in this case a psychological disorder. If the concordance level is 1, then each pair of twins in the study share a particular characteristic.

Adapted from Sarason & Sarason, 1996

Item B 'Magic bullets'

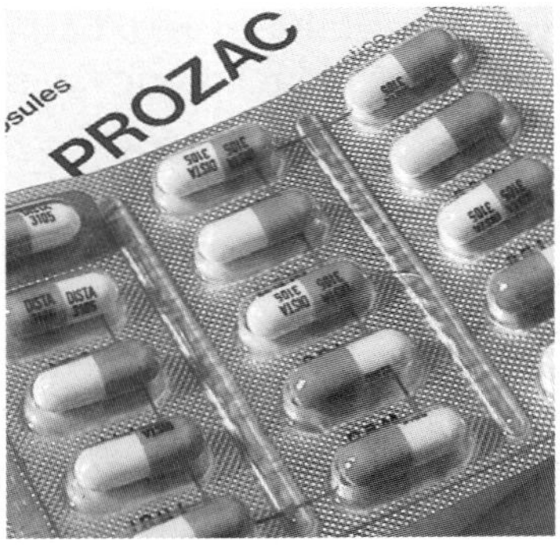

Sometimes known as 'magic bullets' because of their shape and the belief in their curative powers, Prozac has been prescribed to millions of people worldwide.

Prozac is extremely popular with many psychiatrists and people suffering from depression. In a book entitled *Listening to Prozac* (1993), Peter Kramer, an American psychiatrist, claims that Prozac not only reduced some of his patients' symptoms of depression, it also transformed their personalities and behaviour. He describes the case of Tess.

'Within weeks of starting Prozac, Tess settled into a satisfying dating routine. I'd never seen a patient's social life reshaped so rapidly and dramatically. Low self-worth and poor interpersonal skills – the usual causes of social awkwardness – are so deeply ingrained and difficult to influence that ordinarily change comes gradually, if ever. But Tess blossomed all at once.'

Despite this glowing report, there is evidence that Prozac may have harmful effects in certain cases. This evidence indicates possible links with violence and suicidal tendencies. For example, a 63-year-old man from Cornwall suffocated his wife and threw himself off a cliff in 1996. He had been taking Prozac for eleven days. His family blames the drug and has issued court proceedings against the manufacturers.

Adapted from Kramer, 1993 and Boseley, 1999

Questions

1. a) What support for the biological model is provided by Item A?
   b) Suggest an alternative explanation for the findings shown in Item A.
2. Not all psychiatrists are as optimistic about Prozac as Kramer in Item B. Briefly outline the case for and against drug treatment.

Unit 3 The psychodynamic model of abnormality

KEY ISSUES

1. **What are the main features of the psychodynamic model?**
2. **How does the psychodynamic model approach the treatment of psychological disorders?**

3.1 Main features of the psychodynamic model

The psychodynamic model of abnormality was the first major challenge to the dominance of the biological model since the days of Pinel and 'moral treatment'. Early contributions to the psychodynamic approach were made in France in the late 19th century by hypnotists like Jean Martin Charcot who worked at the Sâlpetrière in Paris, Pinel's old hospital.

In the 1880s, a Viennese doctor named Sigmund Freud (1856-1939) studied in Paris under Charcot. Drawing initially on the ideas of the French hypnotists, Freud went on to launch his own approach, *psychoanalysis,* in the 1890s.

Over the years, Freud attracted followers, many of whom eventually broke away and developed their own approaches. The term *psychodynamic* refers to psychoanalysis and its various offshoots. Despite their differences, the psychodynamic theories have certain things in common.

- They see the mind as active and complex, with some important mental processes operating unconsciously.
- They see psychological disorders as arising from some kind of mental conflict.
- The preferred form of treatment is the 'talking cure', encouraging the patient to talk through their problems, fantasies and fears to uncover the underlying mental conflicts.

3.2 Sigmund Freud and psychoanalysis

Freud's psychoanalysis is the most important of the psychodynamic theories. Freud's ideas developed and changed over time, becoming more complex as they progressed. The main ideas are as follows.

The psyche In Freudian psychoanalysis, the mind, or *psyche,* is seen as being governed by three main mental processes – innate drives, reason and morality. Freud (1923) divided the psyche into three parts.

- The unconscious mind or Id (Latin for 'it'). This is the largest part of the psyche. It is innate and is the source of our desires and impulses. It is entirely selfish and operates on the *pleasure principle,* concerned only with the gratification of its desires.
- The conscious mind or Ego (Latin for 'I'). This develops from the Id and is fully formed round about the age of 2 years. It works on the *reality principle* and is concerned with keeping our thoughts and actions in step with the real world and society.
- The Superego (Latin for 'above-I'), which contains our moral values – the ego ideal (what we would like to be) and the conscience (what we feel we ought to be). The Superego is formed around the age of 5 or 6 and regulates our thoughts and actions morally.

If the Id's cry is 'I want', the Superego says 'Thou shalt not', and the job of the Ego is to try to cope with their conflicting demands, as well as all the awkward restrictions imposed by reality and society.

Innate drives Freud saw human beings as motivated by innate or inborn drives. These drives take the form of impulses and desires and are rooted in the Id.

Much of their activity remains on an unconscious level. Freud (1920; 1923) identified two main drives. The first is Eros, the life drive (named after the Greek god of love), the active ingredient of which is the libido (Latin for 'lust'), the appetite for sensual and sexual pleasure. The second is Thanatos, the aggressive drive (named after the Greek god of death), which gives rise to our feelings of aggression towards others and towards the self.

Sigmund Freud (1856-1939)

Psychic conflict

In psychoanalytic theory, every individual experiences conflict between the different parts of the psyche. The root cause of this is that society can only exist if our unconscious sexual and aggressive impulses are kept in check. As a result, we are torn between our desires to gratify our impulses, and our wish to live in a peaceful, ordered society (Freud, 1930). This creates conflict between the pleasure principle and the reality principle within the individual psyche. The Id demands instant gratification for its erotic and aggressive desires, regardless of whether they are socially acceptable or even possible; the Ego tries to police these desires into acceptable and realistic channels; and the Superego seeks to impose moralistic rules to block many of the Id's desires altogether.

Ego defences In its struggle to referee the psychological civil war going on in our heads, the Ego uses a number of defence mechanisms. Among these defences are:

- **Displacement** Redirecting repressed desires and impulses on to a relatively safe target. For example, if we are angry with the boss, we take it out on the dog.
- **Sublimation** Transforming aggressive and sexual desires into some socially acceptable expression – for example, artists and musicians expressing these desires in their work.
- **Projection** Attributing your own unacceptable impulses to someone else. For example, a person who cannot acknowledge hating their brother accuses their brother of hating them.
- **Denial** An extreme form of self-protection which denies what has happened – for example, a terminal cancer patient refusing to accept they are dying.
- **Repression** This is the most important defence mechanism in Freud's theory. The Ego censors Id impulses and refuses to allow them access to conscious awareness. The Ego also uses repression to protect itself from threatening or traumatic experiences from the outside world. Traumas (from the Greek trauma meaning wound) may include experiences we all share, like the first realisation in childhood that we are not the centre of our mother's life. For some people, they may also include extremely painful experiences such as child abuse.

Without defences the Id would run amok, the Ego would be destroyed and society would be ripped apart. However, we pay a price for our defences.

Psychological disorder

It is repression in particular that leads to a range of psychological disorders which Freud called *neuroses* – anxiety disorders, panic attacks, hysteria, phobias and obsessive and compulsive behaviour. Repression pushes things out of conscious awareness – it does not make them go away. Repressed memories of traumatic experiences continue to haunt us, producing neurotic symptoms (Freud & Breuer, 1895). Repression of sexual and aggressive impulses can result in similar symptoms. These traumas and impulses often originate in childhood. Repression keeps them frozen in their childish state so we cannot grow out of them. We remain haunted and threatened by these childish anxieties and fears.

Struggles between the Ego and the Id cause neurosis, and struggles between the Ego and Superego cause moral anxiety. Psychoanalytic therapy can deal with these (see below). However, if Id impulses prove too strong for the Ego, the Id may invade the Ego and take control of it. This wrecks the reality principle, and insanity results (Freud, 1923). Freud did not think that insanity was treatable – certainly not by psychoanalytic techniques.

Depression Freud explained depression as arising from a sense of loss. Typically, when a person is bereaved, the process of mourning involves taking the character of the lost loved one into their own psyche, so 'keeping them alive'. If your feelings towards the lost loved one were positive, then the preserved loved one in your psyche will be loving and comforting.

However, if your feelings towards the loved one contained repressed hatred or resentment, then the preserved loved one in your psyche will turn malevolent and be punishing and hostile. Your hatred is directed back at your own Ego, leading to feelings of being unloved and worthless, and the Ego is destroyed by what it tried to preserve (Freud, 1917). Later losses reactivate this earlier bereavement, leading to depression. Depression can also arise if there is conflict between the Superego and Ego, where the Superego harasses the Ego as immoral and unworthy (Freud, 1923).

Later developments

Freud's followers developed psychodynamic thinking in a number of different ways. Some put more emphasis on the role of the Ego. Alfred Adler (1870-1937) focused on the Ego struggling for mastery over the self and seeking to adjust to society. Adler had a major influence on American psychodynamic theory and on the beginnings of humanistic psychology. In Britain, Freud's daughter Anna (1895-1982) did important work on the Ego and its defences. Others put more emphasis on the unconscious, like Carl Gustav Jung (1887-1961) whose interest in the religious and spiritual side of human nature has made him popular with more mystically inclined therapists and New Age groups.

British psychodynamic theory was greatly influenced by Melanie Klein (1882-1960) and *object relations theory*. This focuses on the importance of emotional bonds, especially with the mother, in the development of the child. Disruption of these bonds is seen as a source of psychological disorder.

John Bowlby's work on attachment (see Chapters 4 and 5) was influenced by object relations theory.

3.3 Treatment and the psychodynamic model

Psychoanalytic treatment is designed to uncover repressed impulses and traumatic memories and bring them to conscious awareness. Freud's favoured method was to focus on the patient's dreams. He believed that dreams contain repressed material in a disguised form (Freud, 1900).

Psychoanalysis invites patients to *free associate* on dreams, neurotic symptoms or childhood memories. Free association involves the patient letting their mind wander freely and saying whatever comes into their head. This in itself often uncovers repressed events and exposes uncomfortable desires. The psychoanalyst interprets the patient's words, dreams and behaviour, identifying and challenging their defence mechanisms.

Bringing repressed material to consciousness is a painful process and leads to the release of pent-up emotion. This process is known as *catharsis*. Neurotic symptoms should now disappear, leaving the patient with conscious awareness of what they had tried to repress. The patient is now able to grow out of their childish fears and anxieties, working through the repressed material, making sense of their experience, and coming to terms with it.

An important sign that therapy is actually taking place is when the patient engages in *transference*. This involves transferring repressed feeling towards others – for example, parents and siblings – in the patient's life, and 'taking them out' on the analyst. The patient loves, hates, fears or provokes the analyst, displacing pent-up feelings on to the analyst. When transference is over, psychoanalytic therapy is complete. The ultimate aim of psychoanalysis is to make the unconscious conscious, to cure neurotic symptoms, and to help the patient gain greater insight and self understanding.

3.4 Evaluation of the psychodynamic model

The psychodynamic model differs from the biological model in several important ways.

- It rejects the biological model's view that abnormality is sharply distinct from normality. Everybody suffers from mental conflicts, but some are more extreme than others.
- It does not try to explain psychological disorder in terms of brain dysfunction or inherited predispositions.
- It considers drug treatments, shocks and brain surgery as unhelpful in getting to grips with the underlying causes of psychological disorders.
- The psychodynamic model was more optimistic than early 20th century psychiatry, and held out the promise that some disorders at least could be cured.
- Although it accepted the broad outlines of psychiatric classification, the psychodynamic model has always focused on the individual case. Two people may be depressed, but their depression may have very different origins and meanings, and simply to label both as having 'mood disorder' does not get us very far.

In one important respect the psychodynamic model resembled the biological model. It retained a doctor-patient relationship, with the psychoanalyst taking the role of the professional and the patient seeking expert guidance.

The psychodynamic model is very controversial. It has been supported for producing powerful insights into the human mind and dismissed as little more than fantasy. First the criticisms.

It is unscientific Evidence supporting the psychodynamic model comes from clinical case studies of individual patients. These studies rely heavily on the therapist's interpretations and are open to bias. They are largely based on information acquired retrospectively – adults recalling their early years. The accuracy of childhood memories is open to question. In addition, concepts like Id, Ego and Superego and processes such as repression cannot be directly observed and measured. According to the philosopher Karl Popper (1959), psychodynamic theory fails to produce testable hypotheses and is simply not scientific.

Freud was quite prepared to go beyond empirical evidence – 'hard facts' and observable and measurable data – if his theories produced greater meaning and insight. If his findings could not be confirmed in the laboratory, then that was just too bad. For Freud, supporting evidence from Shakespeare's plays was of much greater significance than evidence from experimental psychology. Kline (1988; 1989) claims that there is strong evidence to support Freud's theory from real life, and that experimental psychology has yet to find a way of evaluating psychodynamic theory.

It does not work Eysenck (1952) published figures which suggested that psychodynamic therapy was worse than useless in the treatment of psychological disorders. However, this claim has been questioned. Psychoanalysis in the USA has been attacked as little more than a money spinner with some people spending their entire adult lives in analysis – which costs them a fortune. However, Freud's own cases usually lasted only a few weeks. And some recent studies suggest that short-term psychodynamic therapy can be beneficial to some patients (Messer et al., 1992).

It is deterministic and pessimistic Freud's theory has been criticised for suggesting that people's lives are dominated by unconscious drives and childhood experiences. Critics argue his theory is pessimistic because it offers little escape from these determining influences – people are pictured as prisoners of their drives and early experiences. However, Freud argued that this only happens if these factors are repressed. The whole point of psychoanalysis is to give people greater insight and the freedom to take control of their lives. Freud does claim that people have antisocial sexual and aggressive desires. But, in a more optimistic vein, he also claims that the Ego produces desires for social harmony (Freud, 1930).

It blames parents Critics argue that psychodynamic theory blames parents for all our ills. It does tend to see the individual as a product of their parenting. And there is evidence to support this view – for example the effects of child abuse on adult life. However, this evidence is controversial. The psychodynamic model has been accused of fuelling the recent panic over false memory syndrome and 'recovered memories' of child abuse which may not have actually occurred (see pp 31 and 42). But, by the late 1890s, Freud was convinced that many adult claims of sexual abuse during childhood were fantasies.

It is culture specific Critics have argued that psychodynamic theory only applies to the sexually repressed Victorian period and has little relevance to the relatively open and free sexual expression of more recent times. Others, for example feminists like Lynne Segal (2000), argue that it remains relevant and continues to provide important insights.

Positive views The psychodynamic model flourished between the 1920s and the 1960s, and is still influential today. Many psychiatrists were attracted by psychodynamic ideas and adopted them into their own practice.

Psychoanalysis has been the most influential psychological theory of the 20th century, having a significant effect on a whole range of disciplines from anthropology, women's studies and theology, to literary criticism and cinema studies.

By rejecting the sharp distinction between normality and abnormality, the psychodynamic model created greater sympathy for people with psychological disorders. In addition, psychoanalysis with its focus on talking as opposed to drugs, shocks and brain surgery, offered more humane treatment than the biological model. Finally, its supporters see the value of the model in its power to enhance our understanding of ourselves and from the number of people who testify how it has helped them in their own lives.

Key terms

Id *The unconscious mind which is the source of desires and impulses which spring from innate drives.*

Ego *The conscious part of the mind which keeps thoughts and actions in line with the demands of the wider society.*

Superego *The part of the mind which contains moral values – what people would like to be and think they ought to be.*

Ego defences *The various strategies used by the Ego to defend itself against Id impulses and traumatic experiences.*

Repression *The most important Ego defence. It prevents Id impulses and traumatic memories from entering conscious awareness.*

Free association *A technique used in psychoanalytic therapy in which the patient lets their mind wander freely.*

Catharsis *The release of pent-up emotion when the patient brings repressed material into conscious awareness.*

Transference *In therapy, where the patient directs their repressed feelings towards others on to the analyst.*

Summary

1. The psychodynamic model sees the mind as active and complex, with some mental processes operating unconsciously.
2. Psychological disorders arise from mental conflict – in particular conflict between the Id, Ego and Superego.
3. Repression is a major cause of psychological disorders. It pushes impulses and traumatic experiences out of conscious awareness, but they continue to threaten the individual.
4. Psychoanalytic treatment is designed to bring repressed material into conscious awareness. Once there, the patient can make sense of their experience and come to terms with it.
5. The psychodynamic model has been criticised as unscientific, deterministic, pessimistic, culture specific, and, in terms of the treatment it offers, as ineffective. However, its influence has been widespread and many individuals have nothing but praise for the way it has helped their lives.

Activity 2 The psychodynamic model

Item A The psyche

Item B Psychoanalysis

By the fourth therapy session, I realised that he had never mentioned his father. It seemed as if there wasn't and never had been a father. I asked myself: How could it be that this man who is so unhappy and has so many problems fails to even mention his father? I guessed that he was either so ashamed of his father that he couldn't talk about him or he harboured so much anger toward him that consciously or unconsciously he couldn't deal with it. I decided to wait and see what would happen rather than push the client in the direction of talking about something that was very sensitive for him.

During the ninth session he told me about a dream he had had the night before. A large dark man sat at a table and a small child watched from a corner as the man ate great quantities of food and ordered a small, frightened woman to bring him more and more. After he ate each helping, he would raise a gun and shoot down a few people who were standing in a row against the wall.

The client reported how frightened he had felt during the dream. As we discussed his associations to the dream, it became clear to me that the man in the dream represented his father. After several more sessions, he told me he felt very angry with me because I constantly told him what to do and verbally cut him down. After pointing out that in reality I had said almost nothing, I asked him if I seemed like the man in the dream. Finally the dike burst. For the rest of the session and the next one, all of his seething hatred toward his father came out. He blurted out that when he was a child he had seen his father strike his mother several times. When he saw this happen, he had wanted to kill his father.

Adapted from Sarason & Sarason, 1996

Questions

1 a) Identify the Id, Ego and Superego in Item A.
  b) Suggest how they may come into conflict.

2 Use the psychodynamic model to explain the client's behaviour in Item B.

Unit 4 The behavioural model of abnormality

KEY ISSUES

1. What are the main features of the behavioural model?
2. What is behavioural therapy?

4.1 Main features of the behavioural model

Learned behaviour

The behavioural model can be seen as a reaction to the psychodynamic model – it changes the focus from the mind to behaviour. *Behaviourism* was launched in the USA in 1913 by John Watson (1878-1958). Behaviourists insist that psychology should be the study of behaviour rather than the inner workings of the mind. Unlike mental processes, behaviour can be directly observed. This provides the foundation for a scientific psychology based on empirical evidence – 'hard facts' which can be observed and measured in the laboratory.

According to the behavioural model, all behaviour – both normal and abnormal – is learned. Many of these learned behaviours are useful – they help people to live normal and constructive lives. However, abnormal and maladaptive behaviours are also learned.

B.F. Skinner in the laboratory. Much of the evidence for operant conditioning was based on experiments with rats.

Behaviour is learned by a process known as *conditioning*. There are two main processes of conditioning – *classical conditioning* and *operant conditioning*.

Classical conditioning The idea of classical conditioning is illustrated by the following experiment conducted by John Watson and Rosalie Rayner (1920). A boy aged 11 months, known as Little Albert, was allowed to play with a white rat for several weeks. He showed no fear of the rat and appeared to enjoy playing with it. One day, when Albert reached for the rat, a steel bar was struck with a hammer behind his head. The loud noise frightened him. This was repeated five times, after which Albert became extremely frightened of the rat and did his best to avoid it. The experimenters had conditioned Albert to fear white rats (see p 223).

Classical conditioning involves learning an association between two stimuli – in the above example, the stimuli are the rat and the loud noise. The two are associated because the noise occurs in the presence of the rat. The learned response to one stimulus – in this case fright and avoidance – is extended to the other stimulus. Little Albert learned to fear and avoid white rats without the loud noise being present – he has learned a conditioned response.

Operant conditioning This view of learning was developed by the American psychologist B.F. Skinner (1904-1990). In operant conditioning, behaviour is learned by *reinforcement*. Positive reinforcement encourages certain behaviours by means of rewards – for example giving a child praise or sweets for 'good behaviour'. Negative reinforcement encourages behaviours by removing unpleasant events when those behaviours occur – for example, ceasing to scold children when they tidy their room. Behaviour which is ignored, that is given no reinforcement, becomes extinct or fades away. The use of punishment to suppress a behaviour is not always reliable.

Abnormal behaviour

According to the behavioural model, abnormal behaviour is learned in the same way as normal behaviour. The example of Little Albert showed how a phobia – an extreme and irrational fear – can be learned by a process of classical conditioning.

In terms of operant conditioning, abnormal behaviour can result from reinforcement. For example, the early stages of drug abuse can be encouraged by positive reinforcement – the pleasure or comfort associated with drug use (Carey & Carey, 1995). From a behavioural perspective, depression results from a lack of positive reinforcement (rewards) and/or an excess of unpleasant experiences (punishments).

This often involves a life change. For example, unemployment and retirement can lead to a loss of positive reinforcement – a loss of rewarding social relationships and reduced status and income. Life changes can also lead to unpleasant experiences such as the shame and stigma of unemployment or, in the case of retirement, being treated in terms of the negative stereotypes of old age.

Research by Lewinsohn et al. (1979) showed that depressed people received fewer positive reinforcements and are likely to have more unpleasant experiences than nondepressed people. The researchers found that a lack of positive social reinforcement – the approval and companionship of others – was particularly important.

4.2 Treatment and the behavioural model

According to the behavioural model, the problem is the behaviour and treatment – *behaviour therapy* – involves modifying or changing that behaviour. The idea of 'mental' or 'psychological disorder' is replaced by the idea of inappropriate or maladaptive behaviour. A behavioural therapist is more like a teacher than a doctor – their role is to teach new behaviours rather than to cure mental illnesses.

Classical conditioning Behaviour therapies based on classical conditioning include *systematic desensitisation* and *aversion therapy*. Systematic desensitisation (Wolpe, 1958) is used for deconditioning phobic fears. A phobia arises when something harmless has become associated with something frightening. In the Little Albert study, a white rat became associated with a frightening noise until the rat itself became an object of fear. In systematic desensitisation, the client is taught to relax and confront the feared object or situation in a calm and peaceful setting. The idea is that the object of fear will become associated with a pleasant feeling of relaxation and calm, and lose its frightening associations.

Aversion therapy is often used for treating addictions. It aims to change maladaptive behaviour by associating it with something unpleasant. For example, a client may be given an electric shock or a nausea (sickness) inducing drug whenever they reach for a cigarette. In this case, the idea is that they will associate unpleasant feelings with cigarettes and stop smoking.

Operant conditioning In behaviour modification programmes based on operant conditioning, the therapist rewards adaptive behaviour and withholds rewards from maladaptive behaviour. The idea is to change behaviour by applying reinforcement. An approach known as a *token economy* is based on this idea. It is sometimes used in schools, prisons and mental hospitals to change behaviour. Behaviour seen as appropriate is rewarded with tokens which can be exchanged for privileges such as longer breaks, sweets, or a movie. Tokens are withheld when behaviour is seen as inappropriate.

4.3 Evaluation of the behavioural model

Like the psychodynamic model, the behavioural approach is critical of the biological model. It rejects the view that normality and abnormality are sharply distinct. All behaviours are acquired in the same way. It rejects the idea that psychological disorders arise from underlying brain dysfunctions and biochemical imbalances. All disorders are maladaptive behaviours, arising from conditioning. It firmly rejects any role for inheritance in abnormality.

However, the behavioural approach is also very critical of the psychodynamic model, with its emphasis on concepts like the Id, Ego and Superego, and processes like repression. According to the behaviourists, all of these are unobservable and unmeasurable.

A scientific approach? Behaviourists claim that their approach is scientific – they focus exclusively on behaviour that can be directly observed and measured. Behaviourists claim support from a vast range of evidence from laboratory experiments.

Reductionist, determinist and demeaning? Behaviourists have been criticised for what many see as a simplistic and narrow view of human behaviour. Can all human behaviour be reduced to learning by association and reinforcement? Behaviourism is an entirely deterministic account of human behaviour. But are we really the prisoners of our conditioning? Much of the laboratory evidence for behaviourism comes from studies of non-human animals. How far can experiments on rats apply to human beings? Critics argue that a model which leaves out thoughts,

Key terms

Classical conditioning *A form of learning based on an association between two stimuli.*

Operant conditioning *A form of learning based on the use of reinforcement.*

Positive reinforcement *The encouragement of behaviours by means of rewards.*

Negative reinforcement *The encouragement of behaviours by removing unpleasant events when those behaviours occur.*

Systematic desensitisation *Confronting feared objects or situations in a calm and relaxed setting and associating these feelings with them.*

Aversion therapy *A technique which aims to change maladaptive behaviour by associating it with something unpleasant.*

Token economy *A technique which reinforces appropriate behaviour by giving or withholding tokens which can be exchanged for privileges.*

feelings and mental processes cannot capture the complexity of human nature and behaviour. Some see the behavioural model as reducing us to the status of rats (Heather, 1976).

Understanding causes Is abnormal behaviour caused by learning? Just because abnormal behaviour can be changed by behaviour therapy based on conditioning, this does not necessarily mean that the behaviour was learned this way in the first place. For example, if depression is lifted by positive reinforcement, this does not necessarily mean that it was caused by an absence of positive reinforcement. For behaviourism, changing maladaptive behaviour solves all psychological problems because the behaviour *is* the problem. Critics say that this is like treating measles by painting out the spots – it ignores the underlying causes. Many believe that the behavioural model fails to provide an adequate explanation for psychological disorders (Davison & Neale, 1998).

Treatment Behaviour therapy appears to be effective for certain disorders – for example, phobias – but not for others. Some forms of treatment have only limited, short-term benefits. For example, the effects of aversion therapy are often limited to the therapist's office and do not extend to the client's everyday life (Comer, 1998).

Ethical issues In some cases, treatment is imposed on people without their consent – for example, token economies in schools, prisons and mental hospitals. Aversion therapy can cause clients pain, or at least discomfort. By today's standards, some instances of aversion therapy are unethical – for example, the 'treatment' sometimes applied to homosexuals in the 1960s – see p 147. And some of the early experiments, for example Little Albert, would be completely out of bounds in terms of today's ethical guidelines.

Summary

1. The behavioural model argues that all behaviour – normal and abnormal – is learned in the same way.
2. There are two main processes of learning – classical conditioning and operant conditioning.
3. The behavioural model focuses on behaviour rather than the mind.
4. Behaviour therapy is concerned with changing abnormal behaviour. It uses techniques such as systematic desensitisation, aversion therapy and the token economy.
5. Behaviourists claim their approach is scientific – it is based on observable behaviour and supported by evidence from laboratory experiments. Critics claim it is too narrow and simplistic – in particular, it largely omits thoughts and feelings.

Activity 3 The behavioural model

Item A Obscene phone calls

A 32-year-old married man made up to twenty obscene phone calls a week to young women. His therapy involved making obscene calls to young women in a nearby office. They then met him in the presence of the therapist. The client found these meetings extremely unpleasant – he felt ashamed and embarrassed. He felt no strong urge to make further obscene calls, and over the next nine months no such calls were reported by people in the neighbourhood.

Adapted from Boudewyns et al., 1975

Item B Fear of criticism

A 35-year-old postman lived in fear of being criticised. The therapist created a list of anxiety-producing scenes. For example:

- Mrs Smith complains you are late delivering her mail.
- Your wife criticises you for forgetting to do the shopping on your way home.

The client was taught to relax deeply and imagine these scenes while remaining calm. Eventually, he learned to confront these imaginary situations without becoming anxious and agitated. Gradually, his fear of criticism in real life reduced.

Adapted from Davison & Neale, 1998

Questions

1 What types of behaviour therapy are being used in Items A and B?

2 With reference to Items A and B, suggest how they work.

Unit 5 The humanistic model of abnormality

KEY ISSUES

1. **What are the main features of the humanistic model?**
2. **What type of therapy does it recommend?**

5.1 The main features of the humanistic model

The humanistic model emerged during the 1950s and 1960s as a reaction against the psychodynamic and behavioural models. It accused both of being deterministic. It called itself 'the third force' in clinical psychology.

The humanistic model presents an optimistic picture of human beings. It emphasises the essential goodness and dignity of human nature. Every human being has the potential for *self-actualisation* – to find fulfilment, to achieve happiness, to discover meaning in life, and to develop self-understanding and a sense of self-worth. Problems arise when the road to self-actualisation is blocked.

Carl Rogers (1902-1987), one of the founders of humanistic psychology, argued that the potential for self-actualisation can be blocked in infancy (Rogers, 1951; 1959). Children need *positive regard*, particularly from their parents. They need to feel loved and accepted, needed and valued. From this, they develop a positive self-image and a feeling of self-worth. Positive regard needs to be unconditional and non-judgemental. If parents constantly place conditions on their love, for example, 'We'll only love you if you behave, if you do well at school ...', then children will tend to judge themselves and behave in terms of standards imposed by others, rather than becoming a person in their own right. If they are constantly criticised by their parents, then children will tend to develop a negative self-image and question their worth. This will tend to block the path to self-actualisation – they will be unlikely to develop self-acceptance and a positive view of self. Rogers does not suggest that parents should uncritically accept everything a child does. Instead, he states that the act rather than the child be criticised – for example, 'That was a bad thing to do' rather than, 'You are a bad girl'.

Unconditional positive regard during infancy and childhood opens the door to self-actualisation. It allows people to accept themselves, to recognise both their strengths and weaknesses; it encourages a sense of self-worth, and provides a route to self-fulfilment.

5.2 Humanistic therapy

Humanistic therapy aims to provide people with an opportunity to be honest with themselves. This is seen as a starting point for self-actualisation. Rogers' *client-centred therapy* focuses on people as individuals who can shape their own lives.

The therapist must not give advice, tell clients what to do, or interpret their behaviour. Instead, the therapist must create a warm, supporting and accepting environment which allows clients to discover themselves and search for their own, individual meanings. Therapists must show unconditional positive regard – they must be accepting and uncritical, sincere and genuine. This will encourage clients to be honest and accepting about themselves and to realise their potential for self-fulfilment and personal growth. This is the route by which they will recognise and become their true selves.

5.3 Evaluation of the humanistic model

The humanistic model rejects many aspects of the psychodynamic, behavioural and biological models. It rejects the psychodynamic view as too pessimistic and the behavioural view as demeaning. It refuses to accept the classification system of psychological disorders which is based on the biological model. It rejects the view that disorders have a biological basis. And it is opposed to treatments, such as drug therapy, recommended by the biological model.

The humanistic model was popular during the 1960s and early 70s, particularly in the USA. It reflected many of the ideas current at the time. The hippies' slogan 'love and peace', and their belief that if people could discover their true selves then the world would be a better place, mirrored aspects of the humanistic model. Today, the model has largely gone out of fashion with psychotherapists, but is extremely popular in the counselling industry.

In its favour, the humanistic model takes an optimistic view of human nature, seeing people as essentially good. It avoids the stigma – the shame – of mental illness with its reluctance to diagnose and label psychological disorders. Instead, its starting point is the road to psychological health and wellbeing. Critics often see this focus as counterproductive, arguing that many psychological disorders require specific types of treatment and, in some cases, medical treatment. They point to research which indicates that client-centred therapy is not particularly successful in providing 'cures' for disorders (Greenberg et al., 1994).

Some critics question the apparent optimism of the humanistic model. They suggest it implies that disorders result from personal failure – in particular, the failure to achieve self-actualisation.

Key terms

Self-actualisation *Realising the human potential for self-awareness, self-worth and self-fulfilment.*

Unconditional positive regard *Seeing others in a positive light and recognising their worth without any conditions.*

Client-centred therapy *A therapy which allows clients to discover and accept themselves without advice, judgement or criticism from the therapist.*

The humanistic model *A model which sees psychological well-being resulting from self-actualisation.*

Summary

1. The humanistic model sees human beings as essentially good.
2. Children need unconditional positive regard in order to develop self-acceptance and self-worth.
3. Problems arise when the route to self-actualisation is blocked.

Activity 4 Client-centred therapy

Item A Listening to the client

Client Yes, I know I shouldn't worry about it, but I do. Lots of things – money, people, clothes. I can't stand people laughing at me. I can't stand ridicule. That's why I'm afraid of kids. When I meet somebody I wonder what he's actually thinking of me. Then later on I wonder how I match up to what he's come to think of me.

Therapist You feel that you're pretty responsive to the opinions of other people.

Client Yes, but it's things that shouldn't worry me.

Therapist You feel that it's the sort of things that shouldn't be upsetting, but they do get you pretty much worried anyway.

Client Things just seem to be piling up, piling up inside of me. At home, I used to wear it off by socking the doors. It's a feeling that things were crowding up and they were going to burst.

Therapist You feel that it's a sort of oppression with some frustration and that things are just unmanageable.

Client In a way, but some things just seem illogical. I'm afraid I'm not very clear here but that's the way it comes.

Therapist That's all right. You say just what you think.

Adapted from Snyder, 1947

Question

What aspects of client-centred therapy are illustrated by Item A?

Unit 6 The cognitive model of abnormality

KEY ISSUES

1. **What are the main features of the cognitive model?**
2. **What is cognitive therapy?**

6.1 The main features of the cognitive model

The cognitive model developed in the 1960s and 70s and is very influential today. It draws ideas from all the psychological models discussed so far.

The cognitive model starts from the idea that to understand human behaviour, we must understand human thought. This involves understanding how people see themselves and the world around them, how they interpret and make sense of their own behaviour and the behaviour of others.

The cognitive model assumes that people's thoughts direct their emotions and behaviour. Psychological disorders are seen to result from 'errors in thinking', 'irrational assumptions' and 'negative perceptions' which are harmful to the individual.

Consider the following 'irrational beliefs'.

- I must always please others.
- I must always be perfect in what I do.

Anyone holding these beliefs is doomed to failure and disappointment. It is impossible to please all of the people all of the time. And no matter how hard a person strives, a life of perfection is beyond their reach.

Cognition and depression

Aaron Beck's (1967; 1997) theory of depression illustrates the cognitive approach to psychological disorders. According to Beck, negative thinking produces negative moods which can lead to depression. Beck uses the term *cognitive triad* to refer to the three main forms of negative thinking – negative views of 1) the self ('I am worthless'), 2) the world ('Everything is against me'), and 3) the future ('Nothing is ever going to change').

Negative thoughts can produce errors in thinking. These errors include:

- **Arbitrary inference** A conclusion based on insufficient evidence or no evidence at all. For example, my car broke down because I am a worthless person.
- **Selective abstraction** A conclusion based on one of many aspects of a situation. I forgot to put salt in the potatoes which ruined the entire dinner party and showed what a useless host I am.
- **Overgeneralisation** A generalisation based on a single, often trivial event. A teacher assumes that he is no good at his job because a student falls asleep in his class.

Beck argues that negative thoughts lead to negative emotions which can lead to depression.

There is plenty of evidence to support Beck's theory. Research indicates that compared to nondepressed people, depressed individuals are more negative in terms of themselves, the world, and the future. In addition, they are more likely to make the kind of errors in thinking that Beck identifies. The key question, however, is whether negative thinking precedes and contributes to the onset of depression or whether it results from depression and contributes to its maintenance. According to Davison and Neale (1998), 'the relationship in all likelihood works both ways; depression can make thinking more negative, and negative thinking can probably cause and certainly worsen depression'.

Longitudinal studies – studies of a group of people over time – are needed to investigate this question. The ongoing Temple-Wisconsin study of cognitive vulnerability to depression provides some preliminary answers. A sample of first year university students, none of whom was suffering from depression at the time, were assessed every few months. Results for the first 2½ years suggest that those students who were prone to negative thinking were more likely to become depressed. Seventeen per cent of high-risk participants (those with high scores for negative thinking) compared to 1% of low-risk participants (those with low scores) went on to experience a period of severe depression (discussed in Barlow and Durand, 1999).

6.2 Cognitive therapy

As the model implies, cognitive therapy for psychological disorders involves changing thoughts in order to change emotions and behaviour. Albert Ellis (1962), developed *rational-emotive therapy* which, as its name suggests, encourages rational thinking in order to change emotions. The therapist's job is to help their clients to recognise the irrational assumptions which govern their lives and to change them into rational and positive views of themselves and the world.

Beck's *cognitive therapy*, which is often used in cases of depression, encourages clients to challenge negative thoughts, and change them into more constructive ones. Clients are helped to recognise errors in thinking and encouraged to correct them. Beck claims that this will change their emotions and behaviour and, in many cases, lift their depression.

6.3 The cognitive model – evaluation

Successful treatment Research indicates that Beck's cognitive therapy is as successful as antidepressant drugs in treating depression (Hollon & Beck, 1994). This, in itself, provides support for the cognitive model.

Cause and effect The cognitive model has been criticised for seeing thoughts as the cause of psychological disorders. Critics argue that because people with depression tend to see the world in negative terms, then negative thinking is a consequence of their depression rather than its cause. However, as the provisional results of the Temple-Wisconsin study indicate, negative thinking, in and of itself, appears to make people more vulnerable to depression.

Origins of cognitive errors The cognitive model has been criticised for failing to explain where negative thoughts come from in the first place. However, Beck argues that experiences in childhood and adolescence, such as loss of a

Summary

1. The cognitive model assumes that people's thoughts direct their emotions and behaviour.
2. Cognitive errors and negative thoughts can affect mood and behaviour, and can lead to psychological disorders.
3. Therapy involves the correction of cognitive errors and the translation of negative thoughts into positive thoughts.

parent, rejection by friends or criticism from teachers, can produce a negative outlook. He believes that, in later life, negative beliefs and cognitive errors are triggered in situations which resemble the context in which they first develop. These situations may reflect, for example, a childhood loss or an adolescent failure.

Key terms

Cognitive model of abnormality *A model which states that psychological disorders are caused by errors in thinking, irrational assumptions and negative views of self, the world and the future.*

Cognitive therapy *A therapy which encourages people to identify, challenge and change cognitive errors and negative thoughts.*

Activity 5 Negative thoughts

Item A Thinking the worst

During an episode of depression

I remember an incident when I took the subway with my wife. She went through the turnstile before me and I was positive that she was going to desert me. She had probably had enough of me and was fed up with my behaviour.

After the depression had passed

Of course, nothing could have been further from the truth. Her kindness and devotion, compassion, concern and, more than anything else, her love, sustained me during my depression. She, more than anyone, helped me to get better.

Adapted from Endler, 1990

Item B Never satisfied!

Questions

1 a) Identify the cognitive error in Item A.
b) How might negative thoughts cause and reinforce depression?

2 How might a cognitive therapist encourage the people in Item B to challenge and change their negative thoughts?

Unit 7 The sociocultural model

KEY ISSUES

1. **What are the main features of the sociocultural model?**
2. **How does it differ from biological and psychological models of abnormality?**

7.1 The main features of the sociocultural model

The sociocultural model starts from the view that people are social and cultural beings. They are members of various social groups – families, communities and society as a whole – and they share a culture with other members of their society. From this perspective, their behaviour is shaped by their position in society, by their family relationships and occupational roles, and by the norms, values and beliefs of their culture. All these factors make them more or less vulnerable to psychological disorders.

Culture As the following chapter indicates, there is evidence of a rapid rise in eating disorders – anorexia and bulimia – in Western societies. One explanation for this is a change in the cultural ideal for the female figure. Reflected in models such as Kate Moss and Jodi Kidd, the 'ideal figure' is becoming thinner and thinner. Some researchers see this as one of the factors explaining the obsession to lose weight of young women with eating disorders.

The previous chapter outlined a number of culture-bound

syndromes – psychological disorders which are only found in particular cultures. The norms, values and beliefs of these cultures may be a factor in producing culture-bound disorders.

As Unit 1 indicates, ideas about what count as psychological disorders, what causes them and how they should be treated are partly shaped by culture. And, we don't have to go back hundreds of years to make this point. As noted in the previous chapter, homosexuality was classified as a psychological disorder until 1973. As culture changes, attitudes change, and in some cases, so do psychological disorders.

Family relationships A number of researchers argue that family relationships can make people more or less prone to psychological disorders. For example, conflict between parents may place a considerable strain on children which may make them more vulnerable to disorders. One explanation of eating disorders sees them as resulting from relationships within the family (see pp 180-181).

The class system This system of social division is found in all Western societies. In general, the lower a person's position in the class system, the lower their income, social status and power. And, the lower their position, the more likely they are to suffer from certain psychological disorders – for example, depression. One explanation of this finding states that the pressures and stress of life at the bottom of the class system makes people more vulnerable to a range of disorders (Zima et al., 1996).

Gender Women in Western societies are over twice as likely as men to be diagnosed as suffering from anxiety disorders and depression. One explanation for this is the cultural definition of women's roles and their position in society – in particular, their lack of power and control over their own lives. Compared to men, women are more likely to have low-status, low-skill and low-paid jobs. They are more likely to be dependent on state benefits and more likely to live in poverty (Haralambos & Holborn, 2000). And research suggests that marriage is no solution. Compared with unmarried women, wives are more likely to suffer from depression, other psychological disorders, and physical ill-health. In the words of the American sociologist Jessie Bernard (1976) 'In truth, being a housewife makes women sick'.

7.2 Evaluating the sociocultural model

The models of psychological abnormality outlined in this chapter have tended to focus on the individual. As a result, they have largely ignored the wider social and cultural influences on behaviour. There is growing evidence that part of the explanation for psychological disorders lies in culture and society.

Critics have argued that the sociocultural model fails to explain why particular *individuals* develop psychological disorders. However, this is not the point of the model. What it does explain is why certain *groups* of people are more vulnerable than others to certain psychological disorders.

The sociocultural model does not offer the kind of treatments or therapies suggested by the other models. In general, these models offer treatment on an individual level. The sociocultural model implies that changes in culture, society and social relationships are required to improve people's chances of recovering from psychological disorders. And just as, if not more importantly, these changes may actually reduce the extent of disorders.

However, changing culture and society is easier said than done. In most Western societies the gap between rich and poor has increased over the past thirty years. The rich and the powerful will not give up their privileges easily. Groups such as gays, women and ethnic minorities have had to organise, demonstrate and protest to improve their position in society and change the stereotypes and prejudices of the mainstream culture. The changes implied by the sociocultural model are far more difficult to put into practice than a course of treatment with a therapist.

The sociocultural model is an addition rather than an alternative to biological and psychological models of abnormality. It answers questions they cannot answer and provides a broader explanation of psychological disorders. Only in the last thirty years have psychologists recognised the importance of culture and society, a recognition that is long overdue (Comer, 1998).

Key term

Sociocultural model of abnormality *A model that sees certain groups of people as more or less vulnerable to psychological disorders as a result of their culture, their position in society, and their social relationships.*

Summary

1. To some extent, people's behaviour is shaped by their culture, their position in society and their social relationships. These factors can make them more or less prone to psychological disorders.
2. The sociocultural model implies that changes in culture and society are required to improve people's chances of recovering from psychological disorders, and to prevent those disorders from occurring in the first place.

Activity 6 Culture and society

Item A St Vitus dance

St Vitus dance

The engraving shows peasant women overcome by a psychological disorder known as St Vitus dance. This disorder is unique to medieval Europe. It began in Germany in the late 14th century and spread rapidly to Holland, Belgium, France and Italy. The dancers held hands and formed circles, dancing manically and deliriously for hours. They called out the names of spirits and seemed oblivious to bystanders, appearing neither to see nor hear them.

Adapted from Hayden, 1981

Item B The Jerusalem syndrome

Standing at the Wailing Wall, a 50-year-old Californian man, dressed in white robes made out of sheets, preaches the word of God. He claims he is the prophet Elijah and that God speaks to him on a daily basis. At any one time in Jerusalem there are several Jesus Christs and Virgin Marys, plus an assortment of prophets. All are convinced they are Biblical figures. They have what is known locally as 'Jerusalem syndrome'. They are foreign visitors who have been so enthralled with the Biblical sites, they have taken on new identities. Most get over Jerusalem syndrome in 4 or 5 days, when it's time to go home.

Adapted from *Today*, BBC Radio 4, 27.7.99

Item C Poor and powerless

Single mother in church crypt shelter for the homeless

Linda Jenkins is an unemployed single mother with three children living in Liverpool. She is 33, pale and careworn. She looks older. The only holiday she has had in years was a trip to a local seaside resort organised by Gingerbread, the single parent support group. Even then, she had to go collecting round the pubs to raise her contribution.

Life is a demeaning juggling act with the £103 a week she gets in benefit. Heating, hot water and electricity are turned on just before her children get back from school. Linda walks to the city centre markets to save a few pence on fruit and vegetables, and cuts off the ends of toothpaste tubes to squeeze out a little extra. Even her shoes are secondhand.

Linda describes her situation, 'It's horrible. I just don't see any future round here. I'm pushing my kids hard at school so they'll have a chance. I pray to God that they have itchy feet and just get out of here. I want to work. I want to go to college. But the kind of work someone unqualified like me can get won't cover the child-minding fees and I won't be a latchkey mother. There've been times when I've wanted to kill myself. I try to keep how hard it is from the kids. But Lawrence, the oldest, said to me when he was seven: "We're poor, aren't we?"'

Adapted from the *Observer*, 3.10.1993

Questions

1 How does the sociocultural model help to explain the behaviour in Items A and B?

2 Women's lack of power in society and control over their lives has been seen as a major reason for their higher rates of depression. Discuss with reference to Item C.

References

American Psychiatric Association (1994). *Diagnostic and statistical manual of mental disorders* (4th ed.). Washington, DC: Author.

Barlow, D.H. & Durand, V.M. (1999). *Abnormal psychology: An integrative approach* (2nd ed.). Pacific Grove, CA: Brooks/Cole.

Beck, A.T. (1967). *Depression: Clinical, experimental and theoretical aspects.* New York: Harper & Row.

Beck, A.T. (1997). Cognitive therapy: Reflections. In J.K. Zeig (Ed.), *The evolution of psychotherapy: The third conference.* New York: Brunner/Mazel.

Bernard, J. (1976). *The future of marriage.* Harmondsworth: Penguin.

Boseley, S. (1999). Revealed: The danger of taking Prozac. *The Guardian*, 4.9.1999.

Boudewyns, P.A., Tanna, V.L. & Fleischman, D.J.A. (1975). A modified shame aversion therapy for compulsive obscene telepone calling. *Behavior Therapy, 6*, 704-707.

Carey, K.B. & Carey, M.P. (1995). Reasons for drinking among psychiatric outpatients: Relationship to drinking patterns. *Psychology of Addictive Behavior, 9*, 251-257.

Comer, R.J. (1998). *Abnormal psychology* (3rd ed.). New York: W.H. Freeman.

Davison, G.C. & Neale, J.M. (1998). *Abnormal psychology* (7th ed.). New York: John Wiley & Sons.

Dowbiggin, I.R. (1998). *Keeping America sane: Psychiatry and eugenics in the United States and Canada* 1880-1940. Ithaca, NY: Cornell University Press.

Ellis, A. (1962). *Reason and emotion in psychotherapy.* Secaucus, NJ: Lyle Stuart.

Endler, N.S. (1990). *Holiday of darkness.* New York: Wiley-Interscience.

Eysenck, H. (1952). The effects of psychotherapy: An evaluation. *Journal of Consulting Psychology, 16*, 319-324.

Foucault, M. (1977). *Madness and civilisation.* London: Tavistock.

Freud, S. (1900). The interpretation of dreams. In A. Richards (Ed.) (1976). *The interpretation of dreams.* London: Pelican.

Freud, S. (1917). Mourning and melancholia. In A. Richards (Ed.) (1991). *On metapsychology.* London: Penguin.

Freud, S. (1920). Beyond the pleasure principle. In A. Richards (Ed.) (1991). *On metapsychology.* London: Penguin.

Freud, S. (1923). The ego and the id. In A. Richards (Ed.) (1991). *On metapsychology.* London: Penguin.

Freud, S. (1930). Civilisation and its discontents. In A. Dickson (Ed.) (1991). *Civilisation, society and religion.* London: Penguin.

Freud, S. & Breuer, J. (1895). Studies on hysteria. In A. Richards (Ed.) (1991). *Studies on hysteria.* London: Penguin.

Greenberg, L., Elliott, R. & Lietaer, G. (1994). Research on experiential psychotherapies. In A.E. Bergin & S.L. Garfield (Eds.), *Handbook of psychotherapy and behavior change.* New York: Wiley.

Haralambos, M. & Holborn, M. (2000). *Sociology: Themes and perspectives* (5th ed.). London: Harper Collins.

Harrington, R.C., Fudge, H., Rutter, M.L., Bredenkamp, D., Groothues, C. & Pridham, J. (1993). Child and adult depression: A test of continuities with data from a family study. *British Journal of Psychiatry, 162*, 627-633.

Hayden, M.R. (1981). *Huntington's corea.* New York: Springer-Verlag.

Heather, N. (1976). *Radical perspectives in psychology.* London: Methuen.

Hollon, S.D. & Beck, A.T. (1994). Cognitive and cognitive-behavioral therapies. In A.E. Bergin and S.L. Garfield (Eds.), *Handbook of psychotherapy and behavior change* (4th ed.). New York: John Wiley.

Kline, P. (1988). *Psychology exposed.* London: Routledge.

Kline, P. (1989). Objective tests of Freud's theories. In A.M. Colman & J.G. Beaumont (Eds.), *Psychology Survey No.7*, Leicester: British Psychological Society.

Kramer, P. (1993). *Listening to Prozac: A psychiatrist explores mood-altering drugs and the meaning of the self.* New York: Viking.

Ladd, C.O., Owens, M.J. & Nemeroff, C.B. (1996). Persistent changes in corticotropin-releasing factor neuronal systems induced by maternal deprivation. *Endocrinology, 137*, 1212-1218.

Lewinsohn, P.M., Youngren, M.A. & Grosscup, S.J. (1979). Reinforcement and depression. In R.A. Depue (Ed.), *The psychobiology of the depressive disorders.* New York: Academic Press.

Lingjaerde, O. (1983). The biochemistry of depression. A survey of monoaminergic, neuroendocrinological, and bio-rhythmic disturbances in endogenous depression. *Acta Psychiatrica Scandinavica Supplementum, 302*, 36-51.

Maher, B.A. (1966). *Principles of psychopathology: An experimental approach.* New York: McGraw-Hill.

McGuffin, P., Katz, R., Watkins, S. & Rutherford, J. (1996). A hospital-based twin register of the heritability of DSM-IV unipolar depression. *Archives of General Psychiatry, 53*, 129-136.

Messer, A.A. (1985). Narcissistic people. *Medical Aspects of Human Sexuality, 19*, 169-184.

Popper, K. (1959). *The logic of scientific discovery.* London: Hutchinson.

Porter, R. (1997). *The greatest benefit: A medical history of humanity from antiquity to the present.* London: Harper Collins.

Prochaska, J.O. & Norcross, J.C. (1994). *Systems of psychotherapy: A transtheoretical analysis* (3rd ed.). Pacific Grove, CA: Brooks/Cole.

Rogers, C.R. (1951). *Client-centered therapy.* Boston: Houghton-Mifflin.

Rogers, C.R. (1959). A theory of therapy, personality, and inter-personal relationships as developed in the client-centered framework. In S. Koch (Ed.), *Psychology: A study of a science Vol.3.* New York: McGraw-Hill.

Sarason, I.G. & Sarason, B.R. (1996). *Abnormal psychology* (8th ed.). Upper Saddle River, NJ: Prentice-Hall.

Segal, L. (2000). *Why feminism? Gender, psychology, politics.* Oxford: Polity.

Snyder, W.V. (1947). *Casebook of non-directive counseling.* Boston: Houghton Mifflin.

Stone, M. (1998). *Healing the mind.* London: Pimlico.

Watson, J.B. (1913). Psychology as the behaviourist sees it. *Psychology Review, 20*, 158-177.

Watson, J.B. & Rayner, R. (1920). Conditioned emotional reactions. *Journal of Experimental Psychology, 3*, 1-14.

Weissman, M. (1987). Advances in psychiatric epidemiology: Rates and risks for major depression. *American Journal of Public Health, 77*, 445-451.

Wolpe, J. (1958). *Psychotherapy by reciprocal inhibition.* Stanford, CA: Stanford University Press.

World Health Organization (1992). *The ICD-10 Classification of mental and behavioural disorders: Clinical descriptions and diagnostic guidelines.* Geneva: Author.

Zima, B.T., Wells, K.B., Benjamin, B. & Duan, N. (1996). Mental health problems among homeless mothers. *Archives of General Psychiatry, 53*, 332-338.

12 Eating disorders

Introduction

Food and thinness have been described as national obsessions. Judging by the sales of cookery books, the number of food and drink programmes on TV and the rapid growth of gourmet restaurants, the nation has never been so interested in food. And, judging from the number of slimming magazines, slimming products and slimming programmes, people have never been so preoccupied with thinness.

In recent years a new concern has entered the public consciousness – eating disorders. Hardly a week goes by without a tabloid newspaper accusing a pop star, actress or model of suffering from anorexia or bulimia. Recent victims of tabloid journalism include Victoria Beckham (Posh Spice), and Calista Flockhart who plays Ally McBeal.

Eating disorders first appeared in DSM, the American Psychiatric Association's *Diagnostic and statistical manual of mental disorders*, in the third edition published in 1980. This chapter examines the characteristics and explanations of the two main eating disorders – anorexia nervosa and bulimia nervosa.

Chapter summary

- **Unit 1 outlines the clinical characteristics of anorexia nervosa and bulimia nervosa.**
- **Unit 2 examines the main explanations of these disorders and the evidence on which these explanations are based.**

Unit 1 The characteristics and extent of eating disorders

KEY ISSUES

1. **What are the clinical characteristics of anorexia and bulimia?**
2. **How widespread are these eating disorders?**
3. **Are they modern disorders?**

1.1 Anorexia nervosa

Anorexia nervosa literally means 'loss of appetite for emotional reasons'. However, people with anorexia neither lose their appetite nor their interest in food – they usually have strong feelings of hunger and are preoccupied with food. Anorexics typically restrict their calorie intake to 600-800 calories a day. Their primary concern, often described as an obsession, is to lose weight. This drive for thinness is accompanied by an intense fear of being overweight. Failure to lose weight – or worse putting weight on – often leads to depression, anxiety and even panic. Anorexics usually take great pride in their ability to lose weight and to control their desire to eat. Many, however, are never satisfied with their weight loss, and this drives them deeper into the disorder.

Anorexics tend to have a distorted view of their body. They overestimate their body size and proportions. Where others see them as thin or even emaciated, they often see themselves as grossly overweight. Some accept they are thin but see certain parts of their body, for example their stomach, thighs or buttocks, as 'too fat'. This distorted image is maintained despite frequent measurements of body parts, weighing themselves and checking their body in a mirror.

Anorexia typically begins with a diet when a person is slightly overweight. It develops into a disorder when the pursuit of thinness is relentless, when food intake is severely restricted, when weight loss is rapid and the person becomes extremely thin. By the time anorexics are treated, they average 25% to 30% below normal weight for their height and age (Hsu, 1990).

For anorexics, their self-esteem and their estimation of themselves in the eyes of others depends on the appearance of their bodies. But they are in a no-win situation since, however much weight they lose, they remain dissatisfied and set themselves ever more stringent goals for weight loss. A possible consolation is the pride many take in their self-control, discipline and self-denial.

Food is never far from anorexics' thoughts. Some dream about it, some read cookbooks from cover to cover, others prepare gourmet meals for their families without taking a bite themselves. When they do eat, it is often in secret, sometimes accompanied by rituals such as cutting the food into tiny pieces.

Some anorexics are obsessed with exercise, often pushing

themselves to the point of exhaustion in order to lose even more weight.

DSM IV gives the following criteria for anorexia nervosa.

- Refusal to keep body weight at or above 85% of what is normal for height and age.
- Intense fear of gaining weight or becoming fat.
- Distorted body image.
- In females, absence of at least three consecutive menstrual periods.

DSM IV identifies two subtypes of anorexia – the restricting type which involves restricting food intake, and the binge-eating/purging type which involves bingeing on small amounts of food and then attempting to get rid of the food, usually by self-induced vomiting.

It is estimated that around 95% of anorexics are female, with more than 90% of the severe cases starting between the ages of 14 and 19 (Killian, 1994)

Anorexia can have very serious consequences. Estimates vary between 2% and 20% of anorexics dying from the disorder – as a result of medical problems brought about by starvation, or from suicide (Slade, 1995; Sullivan, 1995).

1.2 Bulimia nervosa

It was once thought the bulimia nervosa was merely a symptom of anorexia nervosa, but in 1978 the American Psychiatric Association recognised it as an eating disorder in its own right. The symptoms include:

- Recurrent episodes of binge eating.
- Recurrent inappropriate compensatory behaviour to prevent weight gain – eg vomiting, using laxatives (which cause emptying of the bowels), diuretics (which increase the output of urine), fasting, or excessive exercise.
- A minimum average of 2 binges per week for at least 3 months.
- An obsession with body shape and weight.

There are important similarities and differences between anorexia nervosa and bulimia nervosa. Bulimia nervosa means 'as hungry as an ox for emotional reasons'. The bulimic individual typically binges on a huge amount of calorie rich food, feels incredibly guilty, and then takes steps to remove the food from their body, either through vomiting, taking laxatives, or taking diuretics. For this reason it is often referred to as the 'binge-purge syndrome' even though there are some non-purging bulimics who rely on excessive exercise or fasting to remove the unwanted calories. Unlike the anorexic, however, the bulimic doesn't usually have an abnormally low weight because purging doesn't remove all the unwanted calories.

Like anorexia, bulimia usually starts with dieting. Once it gets underway, the bulimic consumes between 2000 and 5000 calories a day – up to twice as much as most people. The typical bulimic has one or two daily binges, gobbling high calorie food such as ice cream, sweets, cakes, crisps and biscuits until they feel uncomfortably full. A binge is preceded by a feeling of extreme tension which is relieved by eating. It is followed by guilt, disgust and self-reproach. To compensate for this, most bulimics follow a binge with a purge – they attempt to get rid of the unwanted food, usually by making themselves vomit, in an attempt to undo its effects.

Where the anorexic often feels in control of their food intake and takes pride in their self-discipline, the bulimic usually feels out of control and is ashamed of their lack of discipline. As the binge-purge cycle develops, bulimics are likely to feel useless and powerless and disgusted with their behaviour. As a result, they go to great lengths to conceal their activities from family and friends.

Like anorexics, bulimics are preoccupied with their body. Most feel that their self-esteem and popularity depend on their body shape and weight (Garfinkel, 1992). Despite their efforts, most have normal weight for their height and age. Purging is not particularly efficient. Even shortly after eating, vomiting removes only half the calories consumed and laxatives have little effect on calorie reduction.

It is estimated that 90% to 95% of bulimics are female. The disorder usually begins between the ages of 15 and 21. Over half recover within 5 years (Comer, 1998).

1.3 The extent of eating disorders

Anorexia and bulimia are usually presented in the media and by some researchers as modern disorders. If this is the case, then it suggests that eating disorders are related in some way to recent changes in society. However, as this section indicates, the evidence is not conclusive.

Statistics from Europe and the USA reveal a steady increase in reported cases of eating disorders from the 1950s onwards. Figures for the 1970s show a four-fold increase in cases of anorexia compared to the 1950s. This increase continued in the 1980s then appeared to level off in the 1990s (Barlow & Durand, 1999).

The increase in reported cases of bulimia has been even more dramatic. It has now overtaken anorexia as the main eating disorder. A joint five-year study conducted by the Institute of Psychiatry in London and Boston University in the USA reveals a rise from 15 out of 100,000 women suffering from bulimia in 1988 to just over 50 per 100,000 in 1993. The figure for anorexia remained steady at just over 20 per 100,000 (*Independent on Sunday, 1.12.1996*).

However, these figures must be treated with caution. Awareness of eating disorders, both by the public and professionals, has grown steadily. The American Psychiatric Association did not recognise bulimia as a separate disorder until 1978. Increasing awareness leads to increasing referral and diagnosis. Many of the statistics come from treatment centres and may not be representative of eating disorders in the wider society. As anorexia is a rare disorder, very large populations must be surveyed to reliably estimate its prevalence. Even if this was done, it is doubtful whether many anorexics would agree to participate in such a survey (Szmukler & Patton, 1995). One important study casts doubt on the reported rise in cases of anorexia. It was based on a detailed examination of clinical records from 1935 to 1979 for the town of Rochester in Minnesota (Lucas et al., 1991). It found no significant changes in the prevalence of anorexia during these years.

Available data indicates that bulimia was rare before the 1970s and has increased rapidly since then (Kendler et al., 1991). And despite the problems with measurement, most researchers believe that anorexia has increased in the last half of the 20th century, though they would be cautious about labelling it as a modern disorder (Szmukler & Patton, 1995). Evidence about the extent of eating disorders in earlier centuries is examined in Section 2.3.

Anorexia and bulimia are predominantly female disorders. However, there is some evidence from the 1990s that the proportion of young men suffering from eating disorders is increasing. The picture is not clear since this evidence is based on small samples, usually drawn from treatment centres. Some researchers now estimate that 10% of those suffering from eating disorders are male (Dobson, 1997).

Summary

1. Anorexia nervosa is an obsession with body weight and shape. It is an intense fear of gaining weight which results in a refusal to keep body weight at or above 85% of what is normal for height and age. Food intake is severely restricted.

2. Bulimia nervosa is also characterised by an extreme concern with body weight and shape. Bulimics typically have recurrent episodes of binge eating followed by purges aimed at removing food from their bodies.

3. Most anorexics and bulimics are female. The disorders usually begin between the ages of 14 and 21. Available evidence suggests that the extent of eating disorders grew rapidly during the last quarter of the 20th century.

Unit 2 Explanations of eating disorders

KEY ISSUES

1. **What are the main explanations of eating disorders?**
2. **What evidence are these explanations based on?**

2.1 Biological explanations

Biological explanations argue that the onset and/or development of eating disorders are, at least in part, due to genetic factors or to some biological abnormality or malfunction which may or may not be genetically based.

Genetic factors There is some evidence which suggests that eating disorders may have a genetic basis. Research indicates that female relatives of young women with eating disorders are between 5 and 10 times more likely than the general population to develop eating disorders themselves (Strober & Humphrey, 1987; Strober et al., 1990). However, this does not necessarily indicate genetic influence. Since relatives are likely to live together, the influence may be environmental rather than genetic.

Twin studies provide stronger evidence for the contribution of genetic factors to eating disorders. Holland et al. (1984) studied 30 pairs of female twins, with at least one twin in each pair having anorexia. They found that if an identical or monozygotic twin suffered from anorexia, there was a 55% chance that their twin would also suffer from the disorder. This compared to a 7% chance that fraternal or dizygotic twins would both suffer from anorexia. Since identical twins share the same genes and fraternal twins share about half of their genes, this suggests that genetic factors may contribute to anorexia. Similar studies for bulimia show less marked differences between identical and fraternal twins though they still indicate the possibility of some genetic influence.

Twin studies have two main problems – the samples are very small and they are not representative of twins in the wider society. Treasure and Holland (1995) estimate that a sample of 10,000-20,000 twin pairs would be needed to discover the importance of genetic factors for eating disorders.

Neurotransmitters and hormones There is considerable evidence of abnormalities in the regulation and levels of neurotransmitters and hormones in people suffering from eating disorders. In a series of studies Fichter and Pirke (1995) aimed to discover whether these abnormalities were a cause or a consequence of eating disorders. Their evidence provides 'overwhelming' support for the *starvation hypothesis*, that these abnormalities result from severely reduced food intake rather than cause it. Starvation experiments with healthy participants produced changes in hormone and neurotransmitter levels which were similar to those found in people suffering from eating disorders.

Once eating disorders are underway, what effects do the changes in neurotransmitters and hormones have? People with eating disorders often have high levels of anxiety. This may, in part, result from abnormally high levels of the neurotransmitter serotonin. Serotonin is made from tryptophan, an animo acid which comes from food. Reducing food intake reduces the amount of tryptophan, causing serotonin levels to drop, so reducing anxiety. This may make sense of the claim often made by people with eating disorders that if they don't eat, they feel better. If this argument is correct, neurotransmitter abnormality helps to maintain the disorder by discouraging the intake of food.

Gastric emptying Anorexics often complain that they are 'blocked' or excessively full after eating relatively small amounts of food. Research indicates that this may be related to their pattern of *gastric emptying* – the movement of food through the digestive system. Gastric emptying is delayed in anorexics. This produces a feeling of fullness which discourages eating. Caloric intake is reduced which results in weight loss. Delayed gastric emptying follows rather than precedes a severe reduction in food intake. It therefore serves to maintain or worsen the disorder rather than cause it. Quite why delayed gastric emptying results from extreme food reduction is an open question. It may be a mechanism that has evolved because of its survival value during periods of 'natural' starvation. It may, for example, increase the efficiency of nutrient absorption (Robinson & McHugh, 1995).

Biological explanations - evaluation Twin studies indicate a possible genetic basis which may predispose people – make them more vulnerable – to eating disorders. However, as noted earlier, these studies are based on very small and unrepresentative samples. Available evidence indicates that biological factors such as hormone and neurotransmitter levels and gastric emptying rates only become significant after the onset of eating disorders. In other words, they are a consequence rather than a cause of the disorders. To date, research into biological factors does not provide a convincing explanation for the cause of eating disorders, nor does it explain changes in their incidence over time – why their extent apparently increased rapidly over the past 25 years.

Key terms

Monozygotic twins *Twins who share the same genes – identical twins.*

Dizygotic twins *Twins who share approximately half their genes – fraternal twins.*

Neurotransmitter *A chemical used to communicate between neurons or nerve cells.*

Hormone *A chemical that circulates in the blood and activates particular cells or organs.*

Starvation hypothesis *The idea that abnormalities in the levels of neurotransmitters and hormones result from rather than cause severely reduced food intake.*

Gastric emptying *The movement of food through the digestive system.*

2.2 Psychodynamic explanations

Many of the early explanations for anorexia were based on psychodynamic theory. This suggests that some adolescents are frightened by the approach of adulthood because it involves moving towards sexual and social maturity and moving away from their parents. Anorexics are unable to face the growing separation from their parents and become fixated – excessively attached – to the oral stage of their development. This is the first stage of psychological development when infants are completely dependent on their caregivers, usually their mother. Anorexic behaviour is an unconscious attempt to return to the security of the oral stage of infancy. The disorder draws mother and adolescent closer together – the adolescent remains dependent and the mother retains her caring role.

Anorexia can be seen as a 'solution' to the daunting prospect of becoming a sexually mature adult. In Freudian theory, eating and sex are seen as related, and a refusal to eat can therefore be interpreted as a refusal of sexuality. Bruch (1978) argues that adolescent anorexics are unconsciously trying to prevent the onset of sexual maturity. A severe restriction of food can stop the development of secondary sex characteristics such as breasts, halt menstruation and give the body the appearance of a prepubescent girl. As a result, the girl appears sexually immature.

Pregnancy is associated with an adult role. Bruch suggests that pregnancy and 'fatness' are linked in the anorexic's mind. Restricting food intake can therefore be seen as an unconscious attempt to avoid pregnancy and the adult role that pregnancy implies.

Evaluation Psychodynamic theory has been criticised because it is based on ideas such as the unconscious which cannot be directly observed and measured. Despite this, there is evidence to support its views on anorexia. Anorexic adolescents look 'immature' and this could be one way to avoid the demands of 'maturity'.

Key term

Oral stage *In Freudian theory, the first stage of psychological development. During this stage the mouth is the focus of satisfaction.*

2.3 Cultural explanations

Anorexia and bulimia are often described as Western disorders. They are usually seen as developing from cultural ideals for the female form that are common in Western societies. If this is so, then the apparent rise of eating disorders over the past 50 years will be paralleled by a slimmer and slimmer ideal female figure. What evidence is there for these claims?

The past Evidence from the past is meagre. One of the earliest cases of self-starvation is Saint Catherine of Sienna in the 14th century. In Europe, from the Middle Ages to the 18th century there are reports of 'starving girls' denying themselves food for religious reasons. How widespread this behaviour was or whether it was actually anorexia nervosa, is difficult to determine. The term was first mentioned in the medical literature by Sir William Gull in 1874. Historical records provide little evidence of behaviour that could be described as bulimia. It appears to be a fairly recent development.

Although the evidence is sketchy, it suggests a number of conclusions. First, eating disorders were less common in past centuries in Europe. Second, self-starvation, which may indicate anorexia, had a somewhat different meaning – a concern with purity and spirituality. According to Szmukler and Patton (1995) it was not until the 1960s that fear of fatness became a major *identifying* characteristic of eating disorders and the main motive given by those who suffered from them. The evidence suggests that the meanings given to eating disorders and their prevalence (extent) are strongly influenced by culture.

Non-Western societies Available evidence indicates that eating disorders are extremely rare in non-Western societies. Reports from India, Africa, Malaysia, China and New Guinea indicate that when eating disorders are found, they occur in Westernised groups in the population – those most exposed to Western culture and, in particular, Western ideals of the female figure (DiNicola, 1990). Support for these findings is provided by a comparison of 50 Arab female undergraduates at universities in London and 60 similar undergraduates in Cairo, Egypt. There were 6 cases of bulimia in London, none in Cairo (Nasser, 1986).

For many researchers, the evidence suggests that eating disorders are strongly influenced by Western culture. However, one study questions this view. Dr Hans Hoek spent three years looking for cases of eating disorders in Curacao, a Caribbean island where being 'fat' is considered beautiful. None of the doctors he questioned had come across cases of eating disorders. However, after a painstaking search through 144,000 medical records, Hoek claimed to have found 8 cases of anorexia. This led Hoek to question the view that Western culture with its ideals of female slimness is a major influence on eating disorders (*Horizon*, 22.1. 1999).

Western culture Evidence from Western societies, particularly from the 1960s onwards, indicates the ideal female figure is slim and that this ideal is becoming increasingly slimmer. In the 1960s, fashion models such as Twiggy and Jean Shrimpton were often described as 'skinny'; by the 1990s, models such as Kate Moss and Jodie Kidd were sometimes described as 'emaciated'. A study by Garner et al. (1980) showed a 20 year trend to thinner ideals for young women. This trend was accompanied by the rise of the 'diet culture' – organisations such as Weight Watchers, books and magazines devoted to slimming diets, and supermarkets stacked with low-fat and no-fat food. In most cases, eating disorders in the West today appear to be motivated by a desire to be thin and are preceded by dieting.

Available evidence from the 1990s suggests that the proportion of young men with eating disorders is increasing. This may indicate a growing concern with slimness amongst young men. The 1990s have seen a rapid increase in the numbers and sales of magazines aimed at the teenage to thirty-something male market. Examples include *FHM*, *Loaded* and *Men's Health*. Judging by the often semi-naked images of young men portrayed in these magazines, particularly in the adverts, the ideal male figure is thin, sometimes 'super-thin'. Such images may reflect, reinforce and even create perceptions of the ideal male figure.

Evaluation The evidence suggests that the meanings, motivation and extent of eating disorders in the West are influenced by Western culture. However, evidence from the past and from non-Western societies is sparse and sketchy. Even evidence from the West on the extent of eating disorders over the past 50 years must be treated with caution as Section 1.3 indicated. However, even if we accept the influence of Western culture, it doesn't explain why some individuals succumb to eating disorders and others do not.

Activity 1 Culture and eating disorders

Item A Shape and culture

Researchers showed pictures of thin, normal and plump women to men of the Matsigenka, an isolated tribe in Peru. They preferred the plump 'apple-shaped' women, saying that the slender, 'wasp-shaped' women were skinny and probably recovering from diarrhoea. However, members of the tribe who had moved into towns and cities preferred the 'wasp-shaped' women.

Adapted from the Guardian, 26.11.1998

Item B Standards of beauty

'Seated Bather' by Renoir (1841-1919)

'Supermodel' Jodie Kidd

Item C Getting lighter

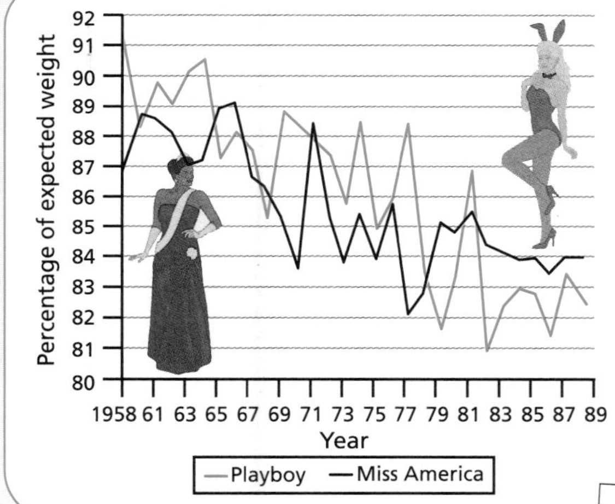

This graph shows the average body weight of Miss America contestants and *Playboy* centrefold models from 1959 to 1989 as a percentage of their expected weight in terms of age and height. Over 60% weighed 15% or more below expected weight which is one of the criteria for anorexia.

Adapted from Wiseman et al., 1992

Item D Slimming

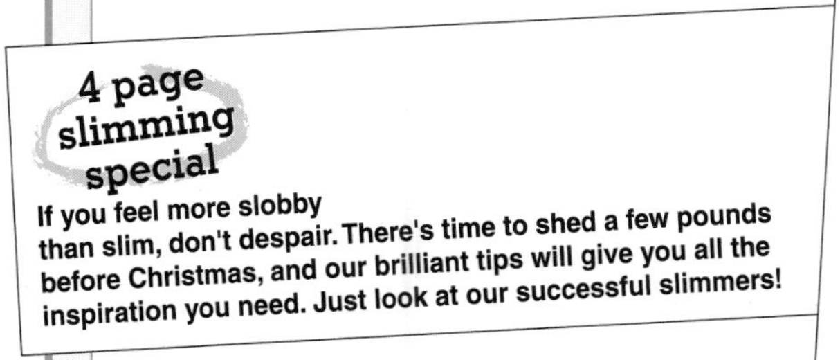

4 page slimming special

If you feel more slobby than slim, don't despair. There's time to shed a few pounds before Christmas, and our brilliant tips will give you all the inspiration you need. Just look at our successful slimmers!

6 SHOPPING TIPS TO HELP YOU STAY SLIM

* Always write a shopping list before going to the supermarket – and stick to it. And pay cash, too, so that you can't overspend.
* Never go shopping when you're feeling hungry.
* Try not to go to the supermarket on your own – if you're with someone else who knows you're on a diet, they won't let you sneak fattening things into your trolley
* Look out for low-calorie alternatives to your favourite treats.
* Remind yourself how much weight you've already lost when you walk past the cake counter.
* Make an effort with your appearance when you go shopping. If you look and feel good, you'll be positive about sticking to your diet.

Adapted from *Woman* magazine, 18.11.1996

Questions

1 The spread of Western culture is related to the rise in eating disorders. Briefly discuss with reference to Item A.

2 Use Item B to suggest why eating disorders may have become more widespread in the 20th century.

3 a) Outline the trends shown in Item C.

b) How might this help to explain the apparent increase in eating disorders?

4 a) What does the introduction to the 4 page slimming special in Item D imply about overweight people?

b) What do the slimming tips imply about 'successful' and 'unsuccessful' slimmers?

5 How might Item E help to explain the apparent rise in eating disorders among young men?

Item E Male models

Male models are getting thinner.

2.4 Behavioural explanations

From a behavioural view, eating disorders can be seen as learned behaviour which is maintained by positive reinforcement. Since slimness is so highly prized in Western culture, a young person who starts a diet, sticks to it and loses weight is likely to receive positive reinforcement or rewards – praise, approval, admiration – from others. At the same time, there is the pressure of punishment – being overweight can bring disapproval and even ridicule.

Giving positive reinforcement to a behaviour encourages repetition and even exaggeration of that behaviour. This may lead a person from extreme dieting to anorexia. A number of researchers have noted the pleasure and pride which many anorexics feel from not eating or eating very little (Gilbert, 1986). These feelings may develop into the main reinforcement for the disorder. Restricted eating may begin as a means to achieving a slim figure, but it may develop into an end in itself as the anorexic derives satisfaction from successfully controlling their intake of food (Wyrwicka, 1984).

Evaluation Behavioural views provide a fairly strong case for the maintenance or persistence of anorexia, but are weaker when attempting to explain its origin. Why, for example, doesn't every dieter travel the anorexic route from dieting to disorder given the positive reinforcements available along the way? The behavioural model is not particularly useful for explaining bulimia. It may help to explain purging – to reduce the anxiety produced by a binge. However, it fails to explain why bulimics binge in the first place (de Silva, 1995).

2.5 Cognitive explanations

Behavioural models tend to ignore cognitions – in particular they have little to say about what anorexics and bulimics think about their bodies. One of the main features of anorexia is distorted or faulty ideas about body weight and shape and about eating. For example, in the advanced stages of anorexia, many anorexics still see themselves as fat whereas others see them as pitifully emaciated – little more than skin and bone.

Garner and Bemis (1982) identify a number of *cognitive errors* or errors in thinking which underlie and influence the behaviour of anorexics. They include:

- **Selective abstraction** Selecting small parts of a situation and coming to conclusions on this basis, while ignoring other evidence. For example, 'I am very special if I am thin'.
- **Dichotomous reasoning** Thinking in terms of extremes. For example, 'If I am not in complete control, then I will lose all control'.
- **Magnification** Exaggerating the importance of events. For example, 'Gaining a pound will push me over the brink'.

The conclusions drawn from this type of thinking are never questioned or critically examined. As a result, they help to maintain the disorder. Wrapped up in faulty cognitions, the anorexic becomes increasingly isolated in their own little world, which from their point of view makes perfect sense.

Cognitive errors about body shape and weight are also found in bulimics. Many have normal weight for their age and height, yet regard themselves as grossly overweight. The key cognition in terms of bulimia appears to be, 'I have failed, so I might as well go on eating' (de Silva, 1995).

Evaluation Cognitive models help to explain the maintenance of eating disorders. They have the advantage of looking at the disorder from the point of view of the sufferer and showing how it makes sense in their eyes. However, as with behavioural models, cognitive perspectives largely fail to explain why some dieters develop an eating disorder and others do not. In other words, they are not very good at explaining the origins of eating disorders.

2.6 Family systems approaches

This is a general term used to describe approaches which explain behaviour in terms of interaction within the family unit. They see eating disorders as a response to things 'going wrong' within the family. Such families are sometimes described as *dysfunctional*. Family systems approaches draw on many of the approaches described so far. The following studies illustrate how these approaches may be combined to explain anorexia.

Hilde Bruch Bruch sees anorexia resulting from dysfunctional relationships between parents and their children. She claims that parents of anorexics tend to dominate their children, allowing them little control over their own lives. They decide when the child needs attention. They decide when the child is hungry, tired or upset and what to do about it. And often, they get it wrong. For example, they may feed the children when they are anxious rather than hungry. As a result, children may grow up confused, unable to rely on their own judgement. They fail to develop self-reliance, they look to others for guidance, are very sensitive to the wishes and opinions of others and vulnerable to criticism. In Bruch's words, such children 'experience themselves as not being in control of their behaviour, needs and impulses, as not knowing their own bodies' (Bruch, 1973).

Bruch (1973) interviewed the parents of 51 anorexic girls. They tended to be financially well-off and achievement oriented, placing considerable pressure on their daughter to succeed. However, this is not for their daughter's benefit. They saw her not as a person in her own right but as a person who can make *their* lives more satisfying and complete. Most of the girls were high achievers, but they excelled to please others and not to please themselves. This results in a lack of autonomy and a sense of who they are. Again the girls had little control over their own lives.

Adolescence brings increasing pressure for autonomy and independence. Added to this are the bodily changes resulting from the onset of puberty which are outside the young person's control. At this stage in their development, anorexics tend to feel particularly helpless and out of control. To overcome these feelings they seek extreme control over their own body. By controlling their diet, they can alter their body shape. As one anorexic told Bruch, 'You want to prove that you have control, that you can do it' (Bruch, 1978).

A number of studies have supported Bruch's findings. They indicate that anorexics feel they have little control over their lives, that they tend to seek approval and are extemely concerned about how others see them (Comer, 1998).

Salvador Minuchin According to Minuchin et al. (1978), anorexia is a response to relationships within dysfunctional families. Such families have the following characteristics.

- **Enmeshment** Family members are bound together in a tight and constricting network. This insistence on 'togetherness' swamps the young person who loses their sense of identity and self-control.
- **Overprotectiveness** Family members show extreme concern for each other's wellbeing.
- **Rigidity** There is pressure to keep things the way they are rather than changing to adapt to new situations such as adolescence.
- **Conflict** Family relationships tend to be in a state of constant conflict. This conflict is usually denied, covered up and unresolved.

Adolescence threatens the fragile stability of such families. It is a time when young people move towards independence and freedom from family ties. In the face of this threat, parents place pressure on the young person to adopt a 'sick role' in order to return them to the 'bosom of the family'. Anorexia provides a solution. The young person is drawn back into the family – parents protect her, worry about her, show concern for her. In this way the pattern of family relationships is maintained. In addition, the young person's illness deflects attention from the conflicts underlying family relationships.

There are two main criticisms of this study. First, some of the family characteristics identified by Minuchin et al. may, at least in part, be a result of anorexia rather than the cause. Parents of an anorexic child have good reason to be protective and concerned. Second, some studies have failed to confirm Minuchin et al's findings. For example, one study found wide variation in terms of enmeshment for families of anorexics (Dare et al., 1994).

Evaluation In their favour, family systems approaches do provide explanations for the origins of eating disorders. They do suggest why some people and not others develop eating disorders.

However, there are a number of problems with family studies. First, they are largely based on accounts by clinicians of their patients and their patients' families. This may produce biased samples – their patients may not be representative of those with eating disorders in the wider society. Many of the differences identified by clinicians between the families of those with eating disorders and 'normal' families disappear in community-based studies (Eisler, 1995). Second, many of the studies are retrospective – they look back on family interaction well after the disorder has started. As a result, much of the family behaviour reported may be a response to the disorder rather than a cause. Third, the evidence to support particular family studies is often sparse, based on very small samples and contradicted by evidence from other studies. From a survey of family studies, Eisler (1995) reaches the following conclusion: 'Families of both anorexics and bulimics vary considerably and do not conform to a single pattern'.

Key terms

Positive reinforcement *Rewards. Rewarding behaviour is likely to lead to that behaviour being learned and repeated.*

Cognitive errors *Faulty perceptions, mistaken ideas, errors in thinking.*

Dysfunctional families *Families in which relationships are harmful to their members.*

Summary

1. Genetic factors may predispose some people to eating disorders.
2. Biological factors such as abnormalities in neuro-transmitter and hormone levels are seen to result from and maintain eating disorders rather than cause them.
3. Psychodynamic explanations see eating disorders as an unconscious attempt to return to the oral stage of infancy.
4. Cultural explanations see them as a reflection of pressures to be slim.
5. Behavioural approaches see eating disorders as an extreme example of reinforcement for an ideal figure.
6. Cognitive explanations argue that faulty cognition contributes to the maintenance of eating disorders.
7. Family systems approaches see eating disorders as a response to dysfunctional family life.

Activity 2 Case studies

Item A Julie

At age 15, Julie was 5'1" and weighed 10 stone. Her mother, a well-meaning but overbearing and demanding woman, constantly criticised Julie about her weight. Her friends were kinder, but their comments were similar. Julie's confidence was not helped by the fact she'd never had a date. Her friends told her she was attractive and would have no trouble getting dates if she lost some weight.

Many unsuccessful diets followed, but this time Julie was determined to succeed. The pounds began dropping off. She experienced a new sense of control and mastery. Her new-found figure brought praise from her friends, even from her mother. At last, Julie began to feel good about herself. But, now she was in control, nothing could stop her dieting. By the time she received professional help, at age 17, Julie weighed 5 stone 5 pounds yet still thought she looked fine.

Adapted from Durand & Barlow, 1997

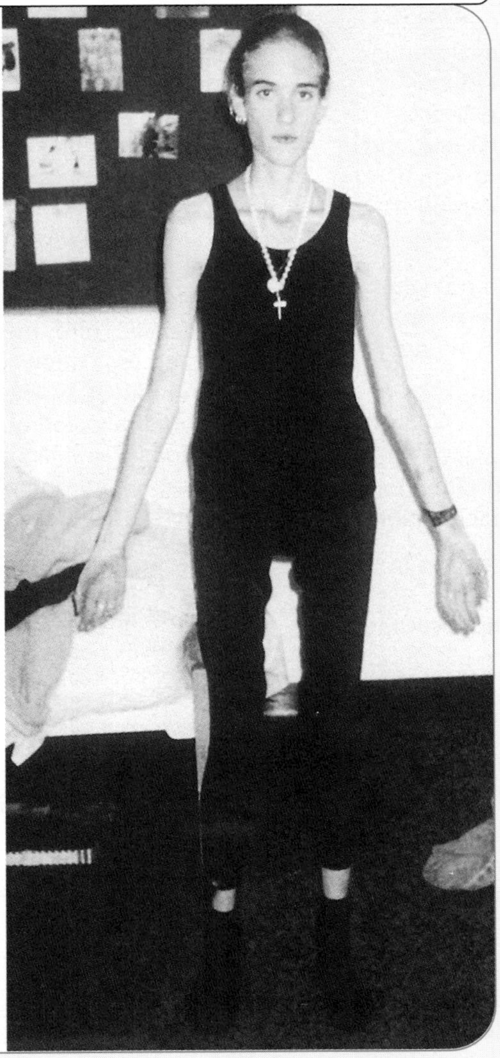

Item B Phoebe

Phoebe was a popular, attractive, intelligent all-American girl. She excelled at everything she did. At high school she achieved top grades and was considered a model student. She was elected home-coming queen and prom queen and appeared to have the world at her feet. She played for several of the school teams and was a poised and confident ballet dancer. She was headed for a leading university.

Yet Phoebe was haunted by a secret thought. She was convinced she was fat and ugly and saw this as a threat to her popularity and success. She began to restrict her eating at age 11. Later she began the occasional binge. One day, sat alone in front of the TV, she ate two big boxes of candy. Depressed, guilty and desperate, she forced herself to vomit. It was the perfect solution – she felt an overwhelming sense of relief. From then on her life became a secretive binge-purge cycle. This continued until her second year at university when, realising things had got totally out of control, Phoebe sought professional help.

Adapted from Durand & Barlow, 1997

Question

Using some of the preceding theories of eating disorders, explain the behaviour of Julie and Phoebe.

References

Barlow, D.H. & Durand, V.M. (1999). *Abnormal psychology: An integrative approach* (2nd ed.). Pacific Grove, CA: Brooks/Cole.

Bruch, H. (1973). *Eating disorders: Obesity, anorexia nervosa, and the person within.* New York: Basic Books.

Bruch, H. (1978). *The golden cage: The enigma of anorexia nervosa.* Cambridge, MA: Harvard University Press.

Comer, R.J. (1998). *Abnormal psychology* (3rd ed.). New York: W.H. Freeman.

Dare, C., LeGrange, D., Eisler, I. & Rutherford, J. (1994). Redefining the psychosomatic family: Family process of 26 eating disordered families. *International Journal of Eating Disorders, 16,* 211-226.

de Silva, P. (1995). Cognitive-behavioural models of eating disorders. In G. Szmukler, C. Dare & J. Treasure (Eds.), *Handbook of eating disorders: Theory, treatment and research.* Chichester: Wiley.

DiNicola, V.F. (1990). Anorexia multiforme: Self-starvation in historical and cultural context. II: Anorexia nervosa as a culture reactive syndrome. *Transcultural Psychiatric Research Review, 27,* 245-286.

Dobson, R. (1997). Anorexia – now it's Nineties man who suffers. *Independent on Sunday*, 8.6.1997.

Durand, V.M. & Barlow, D.H. (1997). *Abnormal psychology: An introduction.* Pacific Grove, CA: Brooks/Cole.

Eisler, I. (1995). Family models of eating disorders. In G. Szmukler, C. Dare & J. Treasure (Eds.), *Handbook of eating disorders: Theory, treatment and research.* Chichester: Wiley.

Fichter, M.M. & Pirke, K.M. (1995). Starvation models and eating disorders. In G. Szmukler, C. Dare & J. Treasure (Eds.), *Handbook of eating disorders: Theory, treatment and research.* Chichester: Wiley.

Garfinkel, P.E. (1992). Evidence in support of attitudes to shape and weight as a diagnostic criterion of bulimia nervosa. Special section: Eating disorders in DSM-IV. *International Journal of Eating Disorders, 11*, 321-325.

Garner, D.M. & Bemis, K.M. (1982). A cognitive-behavioural approach to anorexia nervosa. *CognitiveTherapy and Research, 6*, 123-150.

Gilbert, S. (1986). *Pathology of Eating.* London: Routledge & Kegan Paul.

Hoek, H.W. (1999). Interview in *Horizon.* BBC TV, 22.1.1999.

Holland, A.J., Murray, R., Russell, G.F.M. & Crisp, A.H. (1984). Anorexia nervosa: A study of 34 pairs of twins and one set of triplets. *British Journal of Psychiatry, 145*, 414-419.

Hsu, L.K.G. (1990). *Eating disorders.* New York: Guilford Press.

Kendler, K.S., Maclean, C., Neale, M., Kessler, R., Heath, A. & Eaves, L. (1991). The genetic epidemiology of bulimia nervosa. *American Journal of Psychiatry, 148*, 1627-1637.

Killian, K.D. (1994). Fearing fat: A literature review of family systems understandings and treatments of anorexia and bulimia. *Family Relations, 43*, 311-318.

Lucas, A.R., Beard, C.M., O'Fallon, W.M. & Kurlan, L.T. (1991). 50-year trends in the incidence of anorexia nervosa in Rochester, Minn.: A population-based study. *American Journal of Psychiatry, 148*, 917-922.

Minuchin, S., Rosman, B.L. & Baker, L. (1978). *Psychosomatic families.* Cambridge, MA: Harvard University Press.

Nassar, M. (1986). Comparative study of the prevalence of abnormal eating attitudes among Arab female students of both London and Cairo universities. *Psychological Medicine, 16*, 621-625.

Robinson, P.H. & McHugh, P.R. (1995). A physiology of starvation that sustains eating disorders. In G. Szmukler, C. Dare & J. Treasure (Eds.), *Handbook of eating disorders: Theory, treatment and research.* Chichester: Wiley.

Slade, P. (1995). Prospects for prevention. In G. Szmukler, C. Dare & J. Treasure (Eds.), *Handbook of eating disorders: Theory, treatment and research.* Chichester: Wiley.

Strober, M. & Humphrey, L.L. (1987). Familial contributions to the etiology and course of anorexia nervosa and bulimia. Special Issue: Eating disorders. *Journal of Consulting and Clinical Psychology, 55*, 654-659.

Strober, M., Lampert, C., Morrell, W., Burroughs, J. & Jacobs, C. (1990). A controlled family study of anorexia nervosa: Evidence of familial aggregation and lack of shared transmission with affective disorders. *International Journal of Eating Disorders, 9*, 239-253.

Sullivan, P.F. (1995). Mortality in anorexia nervosa. *American Journal of Psychiatry, 152*, 1073-1075.

Szmukler, G.I. & Patton, G. (1995). Sociocultural models of eating disorders. In G. Szmukler, C. Dare & J. Treasure (Eds.), *Handbook of eating disorders: Theory, treatment and research.* Chichester: Wiley.

Treasure, J. & Holland, A. (1995). Genetic factors in eating disorders. In G. Szmukler, C. Dare & J. Treasure (Eds.), *Handbook of eating disorders: Theory, treatment and research.* Chichester: Wiley.

Wiseman, C.V., Gray, J.J., Mosimann, J.E. & Ahrens, A.H. (1992). Cultural expectations of thinness in women: An update. *International Journal of Eating Disorders, 11*, 85-89.

Wyrwicka, W. (1984). Anorexia nervosa as a case of complex instrumental conditioning. *Experimental Neurology, 84*, 579-589.

13 Conformity and minority influence

Introduction

Very few people live in isolation from other human beings. Apart from the occasional hermit who chooses to live alone, or unfortunates such as Robinson Crusoe forced by circumstances to live a solitary existence, human beings live in social groups. As members of society, they interact on a regular basis with other human beings. Their behaviour is influenced by others and they, in turn, influence the behaviour of others. As such, people are social beings. These fairly obvious observations form the basis of social psychology. Put simply, social psychology is the study of people as members of social groups – it is the study of the social side of human behaviour.

This is the first of three chapters on social psychology. It looks at conformity. It examines why most people, most of the time, conform to the accepted standards of behaviour of the groups to which they belong. In this respect, it looks at how the majority influence the behaviour of the minority. The chapter also looks at the other side of the coin – how minorities can sometimes influence the behaviour of the majority of people in a social group.

Chapter summary

- **Unit 1 looks at conformity or majority influence. It outlines some of the experiments conducted to investigate conformity and examines various explanations for conformity.**
- **Unit 2 looks at minority influence. It examines ways in which a minority can influence the behaviour of a majority.**

Unit 1 Conformity – majority influence

KEY ISSUES

1. **What are social norms?**
2. **Why do most people conform to social norms?**
3. **What are social roles?**
4. **What encourages conformity to social roles?**

Social influence is the influence of social factors on behaviour. It refers to the effect that the presence of others has on the way people think, feel and behave. *Conformity* is a major aspect of social influence. The term conformity is used in two main ways. First, it refers generally to following the accepted ways of behaving of particular groups within society, or of society as a whole. Second, it refers to a change in the behaviour of a minority which results from the influence of the majority. The minority changes its behaviour so that it matches the behaviour of the majority. In this sense, conformity is also known as *majority influence*.

1.1 Social norms

The idea of social norms provides a key to understanding social influence in general and conformity in particular. Social norms are the accepted standards of behaviour of social groups. These groups range from friendship and work groups to nation states. Thus in British society norms of acceptable behaviour include queuing for public transport, waiting in line at a post office counter or a fastfood takeout and taking your turn in a doctor's waiting room.

There are norms defining appropriate behaviour for every social group. For example, students, workers, partygoers, friends, neighbours, patients in a hospital and drinkers in a pub are all usually aware of the norms governing their

Bedouin eating, Syria 1923

behaviour. And, as the individual moves from group to group, their behaviour changes accordingly.

Social norms vary from society to society. This can be seen clearly from norms concerning food. In traditional Bedouin society of North Africa, sheep's eyes are regarded as a delicacy whereas in the West they are not even considered fit to eat. The Bedouin eat with their fingers and a loud and prolonged burp at the end of a meal is a compliment to the host. In the West such behaviour would be considered the height of bad manners. Or, as a social psychologist might say, it would not conform to Western norms of eating behaviour.

Norms provide order in society. Imagine a situation in which 'anything goes'. The result is likely to be confusion and disorder. This can sometimes be seen in the classroom if teacher and students fail to establish a set of norms for conducting a lesson. Norms help to make social life predictable and comprehensible. If there were no norms stating how people should express pleasure or irritation, warmth or hostility, it would be difficult to understand how others felt, to predict their behaviour and respond to them in appropriate ways.

It is difficult to see how human society could operate without social norms. Human beings need social norms to guide and direct their behaviour, to provide order and predictability in social relationships and to make sense of and understand each others' actions. These are some of the reasons why most people, most of the time, conform to social norms.

Key terms

Social influence *The influence of others on the attitudes, beliefs and behaviour of the individual.*

Conformity *1) Acting in terms of the accepted behaviour of a social group. 2) A change in the behaviour of a minority to fit the behaviour of the majority.*

Social norms *The accepted and expected ways of behaving of a social group.*

Activity 1 Social norms

Item A Kikuyu women, Kenya

Item B Tibetan nuns in 1904

Item C Russian women in 1890

Questions

Use the pictures to discuss the following statements.

1 Most people conform to social norms.
2 Social norms vary from society to society.
3 Social norms are learned rather than innate or inborn.

1.2 Why do people conform?

Social psychologists have identified two main factors which encourage conformity. First, people conform when they are unsure about what to do in a particular situation. They seek guidance from others, whom, they see as better informed than themselves, and conform to their behaviour and opinions. This is called *informational social influence*. Second, people conform because they want to be liked. They conform to the behaviour of others in order to gain their approval. This is called *normative social influence* (Deutsch & Gerard, 1955).

Informational social influence When people are uncertain about what to do, they often look to others for guidance. This can happen when they find themselves in a novel situation – their first day at work, college or university, their first dinner party or visit to the opera. They want to do the right thing but may lack the appropriate information. Observing others can provide this information. For example, at your first formal dinner party you may be presented with a bewildering array of cutlery. Watching more experienced guests will guide your selection – they know the norms which fit the situation. This is known as informational social influence – people conform because the behaviour of others provides information and guidance for appropriate action.

Sometimes situations are ambiguous and ill-defined. Consider the following example. A fire alarm goes off. Has it gone off accidentally, is it an unannounced fire drill, or is there a fire? Again, people look to others for guidance. They may ask what others think and observe what they do. And, if they appear to know the answer, people may well conform to their behaviour.

Informational social influence is based on the need to be right. When people are unsure of their own judgement, they often accept the judgement of others. When they are uncertain about what to do, they often accept the actions of others as a guide.

Normative social influence All social groups have norms which define appropriate behaviour for their members. In general, conforming to group norms brings acceptance and approval, while nonconformity can bring disapproval and even rejection. People are social beings, they have a need to belong, to feel part of a social group. Because of this, social groups can place considerable pressure on individuals to conform to group norms. Conformity is rewarded with approval and praise. Nonconformity is punished with disapproval, ridicule and even ostracism – the individual is shunned by group members.

Normative social influence involves altering behaviour to fit the expectations of others. People yield to group pressure and behave in a way that others consider appropriate, reasonable and desirable in order to gain social acceptance and approval.

So far, this section has examined the two main forms of social influence which encourage conformity. It now considers two types of conformity – *public compliance* and *private acceptance*.

Public compliance How many times have you agreed with what your friends say, while privately rejecting their opinions? How often have you 'gone along' with the behaviour of others and acted in a similar manner despite disapproving of this course of action? These are examples of public compliance. People often conform in public to the norms of others even though these norms contradict their privately held beliefs.

Public compliance often occurs in response to normative social influence. In the presence of others people often act in terms of social norms and give the impression they approve of those norms in order to gain acceptance and approval.

Private acceptance In this case people conform to the norms of others because they believe those norms are right. This can result in a change to their private beliefs and attitudes. They *internalise* the norms of others – make them their own and act in terms of them. Private acceptance is a more powerful and longlasting influence than public compliance. It can result in a genuine change in beliefs and attitudes. For this reason, private acceptance is also known as *conversion* – the individual is 'converted' to the beliefs of others.

Key terms

Informational social influence *Being influenced by others to conform to their behaviour because of uncertainty about how to behave.*

Normative social influence *Being influenced by others to conform to their behaviour because of a desire to gain their approval.*

Public compliance *Conforming to the behaviour of others despite privately disagreeing with their behaviour.*

Private acceptance *Conforming to the behaviour of others because their behaviour is seen to be right.*

Activity 2 Normative and informational influence

Item A At the golf club

Elaine, Ingrid, Pauline and Mary-Anne were enjoying a drink in the clubhouse after a round of golf. Elaine was telling the others a story. She had been asked by a neighbour if she could arrange a game of golf for a 15-year-old boy from Finland who was in England on holiday. She asked John, the young assistant professional, to play with him. 'Do you know,' Elaine said, 'I got the shock of my life. The boy from Finland was black and my neighbour hadn't even told me. So I went to John and apologised. Not that I've got anything against blacks,' she added. The other women nodded and murmured agreement.

However, Mary-Anne, who recounted this story later, was taken aback. 'I was disgusted with Elaine's attitude,' she said. 'But I was even more disgusted with myself. I had given Elaine every indication that I was in complete agreement with her.'

Story told to author 15.2.1998

Item B The Martians are coming

New York Times

Radio Listeners in Panic, Taking War Drama as Fact

Many Flee Homes to Escape 'Gas Raid From Mars'—Phone Calls Swamp Police at Broadcast of Wells Fantasy

A wave of mass hysteria seized thousands of radio listeners throughout the nation between 8:15 and 9:30 o'clock last night when a broadcast of a dramatization of H. G. Wells's fantasy, "The War of the Worlds," led thousands to believe that an interplanetary conflict had started with invading Martians spreading wide death and destruction ... Jersey ... York ... and radio stations here and in other cities of the United States and Canada seeking advice on protective measures against the raids.

The program was produced by Mr. Welles and the Mercury Theatre on the Air over station WABC and the Columbia Broadcasting System's coast-to-coast network, from 8 to 9 o'clock.

The radio ... as prese...

'The girls huddled around their radios trembling and weeping in each other's arms. They separated themselves from their friends only to take their turn at the telephone to make long distance calls to their parents, saying goodbye for what they thought might be the last time. Terror-stricken girls, hoping to escape from the Mars invaders, rushed to the basement of the dormitory.'

Orson Welles broadcasting War of the Worlds

With these words, an American college student recalls the reaction of herself and her friends to a radio broadcast in 1938. The broadcast was a radio play by Orson Welles based on H.G. Wells' *War of the Worlds*, a novel about an invasion from Mars. It was so realistic that hundreds of thousands of people, who missed the announcement that it was only a play, were convinced the Martians had invaded. There was widespread panic at the news that millions had been killed by Martian death rays.

Many people just didn't know how to respond. They turned to family and friends to see whether they should believe what they'd heard. They interpreted what they saw in terms of the radio programme. One person looked out of his window and saw that Wyoming Avenue was 'black with cars. People were rushing away, I figured'. Another recounted, 'No cars came down my street. Traffic is jammed on account of the roads being destroyed, I thought.'

Thousands fled towns and cities and took to the hills.

Adapted from Cantril, 1940

Questions

1 Read Item A.
   a) Is Mary-Anne's behaviour an example of normative social influence or informational social influence?
   b) Is it an example of public compliance or private acceptance?
   Give reasons for your answers to both questions.

2 How can the idea of informational social influence help to explain the behaviour described in Item B?

1.3 Experimental studies of conformity

This section examines a number of experiments designed to investigate conformity. They were conducted in laboratory situations.

Sherif – the autokinetic effect

Muzafer Sherif (1935) devised an experiment to investigate the development of group norms and conformity to those norms. He used the *autokinetic effect* – an optical illusion in which a stationary spot of light in a darkened environment appears to move around. Sherif divided his participants into two groups. The first group was tested individually. Each participant sat alone in a darkened room, looking at a stationary point of light. They were told the light was actually moving and asked to estimate how far it moved. Each participant made one hundred estimates. At first the estimates varied widely before settling down to a fairly standard pattern – a *personal norm*. However, there were considerable differences between the estimates which each participant produced. For example, some thought the light was moving an inch or so, others believed it moved as far as ten inches.

The participants were then placed in small groups of two or three. At first, the estimates of group members varied widely – each member based their estimate on their personal norm. Then their estimates steadily converged, becoming more and more similar. Finally, the group reached a consensus – an agreement. A group norm had developed to which the participants conformed. This can be seen from Figure 1 which shows the results of one group's estimates.

Figure 1 Formation of a group norm

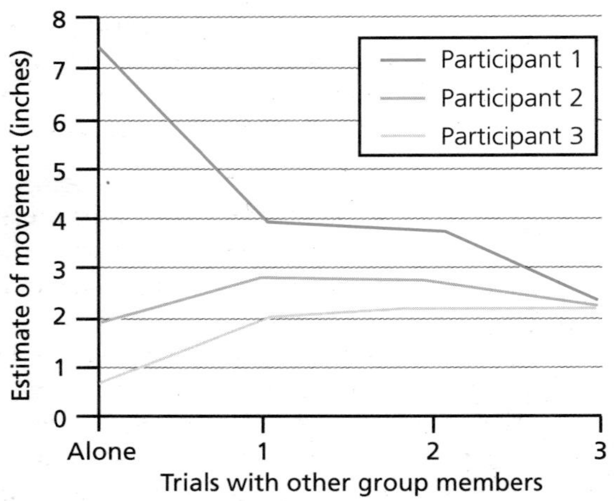

Sherif reversed the procedure with the second set of participants. They began in small groups and each group rapidly developed a group estimate to which each member conformed. Finally, these participants were tested individually. Each was placed alone in the darkened room and asked again to estimate the movement of light. Their answers, as individuals, mirrored those of their group. In other words, they continued to follow the group norm despite the fact that nobody else was there.

Sherif's experiment demonstrates a number of things. First, it shows how group norms develop. Second, it shows how individuals conform to group norms. Third, it shows the effect of informational social influence. The situation was ambiguous. In fact there was no correct answer (other than the answer 'no movement') since the light was not moving. In this situation, participants were happy to adjust their own judgements to fit those of others. Finally, the experiment provides an example of private acceptance. Participants internalised the group norm and made it their own. Even when they sat alone in the darkened room, they continued to base their individual estimates on the group norm.

Majority influence Strictly speaking, Sherif's experiment is not an example of conformity in terms of majority influence. Majority influence means a majority influences a minority who then conform to the majority view. There was no majority or minority in Sherif's experiment, simply a number of people who had different views. They then came together and formed a collective view (van Avermaet, 1996).

Jacobs and Campbell (1961) conducted a variation of Sherif's experiment to assess the importance of majority influence. They used groups of four, made up of three confederates or stooges (accomplices who worked with the researchers) and one 'real' participant. The three confederates gave either very large or very small estimates of how far the light had moved. In almost every case the participant conformed to their estimate. One by one the confederates were replaced by participants. As each new participant entered the group, they accepted the group norm. Finally, all the confederates were removed and the four participants continued to agree on the group norm. This study shows that a majority can have a significant influence on the judgements of a minority.

Solomon Asch

The task given to the participants in Sherif's study was ambiguous since there was no correct answer other than 'no movement'. In this situation conformity is to be expected as people look to others for guidance. But what about a situation where people are sure that the judgements of the majority are wrong? Will they conform then? This was the question asked by Solomon Asch (1951, 1956) in a series of experiments conducted in the early 1950s.

Asch designed a simple, straightforward and unambiguous task. Participants were presented with two cards. On one card was a single 'standard' line, on the other were three 'comparison' lines. Participants were asked to judge which of the comparison lines was equal in length to the standard line. Various pairs of cards were used. Figure 2 shows one example.

Figure 2 Line judgement task

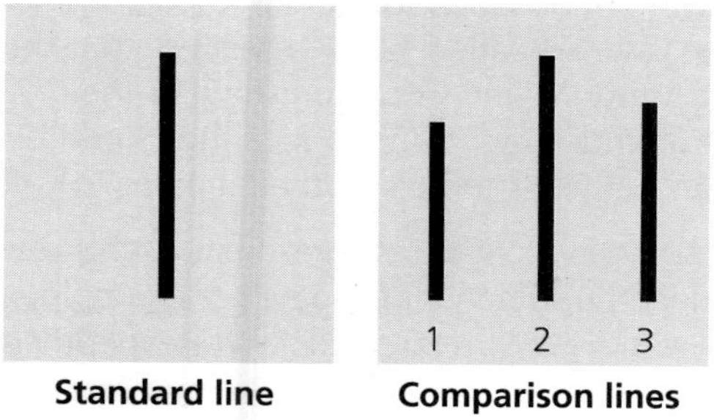

First, a control group of 37 participants were given the task. A control group is used for comparison with the experimental group. The factors expected to influence the experimental group's behaviour – in this case pressure to conform – are removed. The participants were simply asked to judge the comparison lines without any social pressure to conform to the judgements made by other people. Thirty-five members of the control group made no errors, one made a single error and one made two errors. This indicates that the task was straightforward and unambiguous.

In the experimental situation, there was only one participant, the rest were confederates working with Asch. The participant was seated at a table along with 6 to 8 confederates. He thought they were participants like himself and did not realise that the entire experiment was about his behaviour. The comparison lines were presented and each person was asked to state their judgements aloud. The participant was seated near the end of the table and was next to last to state his judgements. To begin with, the confederates gave accurate judgements and the participant readily agreed – after all, the answers were obvious. Then, on one comparison task, *all* the confederates gave the same wrong answer. They continued to do this on 12 of the 18 trials, that is for 12 out of the 18 pairs of cards. Asch repeated the experiment with a number of different participants. The question is, would the participants fall into line and conform to judgements which were obviously wrong?

There was a surprising amount of conformity. In the control group only 0.7% of the judgements were incorrect. In the experimental groups, 37% of the judgements made by the participants were incorrect. Of the 125 participants in the experimental groups, only 25% gave the correct answer in every case compared with 95% in the control group.

Why did so many participants conform to what was clearly an incorrect judgement? A small minority stated that they actually saw the lines in the same way as the rest of the group. Some participants recognised that they saw things differently from the group but concluded that their own perceptions must be inaccurate. They thought they must be suffering from eye strain or they had been seated in an awkward position from which it was difficult to see the cards. Other participants remained convinced that they were right yet, despite this, they still conformed. According to one such participant, 'Here was a group; they had a definite idea; my idea disagreed; this might arouse anger. I was standing out as a sore thumb. I didn't want particularly to make a fool of myself. I felt I was definitely right but they might think I was peculiar' (Asch, 1955). This quotation is typical of the reasons given by participants who were convinced they were right yet still conformed. It is clearly a case of normative social influence. These participants didn't want to 'rock the boat', 'stand out like a sore thumb' and risk the disapproval of other group members. It was a case of public compliance rather than private acceptance. They knew they were right but went along with the majority and gave the wrong answer. The power of majority influence can be seen from their behaviour. They were tense, they sweated, squirmed, mumbled and giggled – sure signs of the pressure they were under to conform to the majority view.

'Faceless' conformity

The participants in Asch's experiment were presented with a group of people who all gave answers that were clearly incorrect. In a face-to-face situation, the pressure to conform was considerable. Was it the actual presence of others which generated this pressure?

Asch's conformity experiment. The participant is seated second from the right at the table.

Crutchfield (1955) devised a version of the Asch experiment which did not involve face-to-face communication. Each participant was placed in a separate booth, facing a screen which displayed questions and what they believed were the answers of the other participants. The questions were simple and the correct answers obvious. In around half the cases, the answers displayed on the screen were incorrect. Each participant believed they were the last to answer, after having seen everybody else's answers. In fact, the answers on the screen were placed there by the experimenter – they were not those of the other participants.

Crutchfield's results were similar to those of Asch. For example, on an Asch-type perceptual task the conformity level was 30% – in other words, 30% of the responses conformed to the wrong answer. These participants had clearly been influenced by what they believed to be the answers of their fellow participants. This experiment indicates that pressure to conform can operate without face-to-face communication. Even an awareness of the presence of unknown and unseen others is sufficient to generate this pressure.

Evaluation

Laboratory experiments The findings of Sherif, Asch and Crutchfield are drawn from experiments in laboratories. Laboratory settings and the tasks involved in experiments are a long way from normal, everyday life. After all, how many people sit in a darkened room staring at a light or match lines on cards when the answer is obvious? If participants define the situation as artificial and the tasks as unreal, can the results of experiments be generalised to life outside the laboratory? These are standard criticisms of laboratory experiments in psychology. They refer to the issue of ecological validity – the extent to which research findings can be generalised to other settings. Some researchers argue that if the experiment bears little relationship to the outside world, if the tasks are artificial and 'unreal', then the experiment has low ecological validity. As a result, its findings may be limited to the laboratory; it may not be possible to generalise the results to other settings.

However, the experimental method can be defended. In fact, it can be argued it has certain advantages over normal, everyday social settings. Asch's line-matching experiments illustrate this. Why create an artificial situation in which people – the confederates – behave in such an unreal manner? Why confront participants with complete strangers? The answer is that if participants conform in this setting it will show the power of *pure* group pressure. The confederates' judgements are clearly wrong. They are complete strangers – the participants will never see them again so in this respect their disapproval won't mean that much. The experiment has therefore created a situation to indicate the power of group pressure. Everything else that might encourage conformity has been stripped away. We would be unlikely to find a similar situation to study outside the laboratory.

Time Asch's experiments were conducted in the early 1950s in the USA. Can the results be generalised to other times and other places? The relatively high level of conformity in Asch's research was seen by some as a reflection of American society in the 1950s. This was a time when non-conformity was discouraged. The McCarthy 'witch hunts' – investigations into so-called unAmerican activities – hounded anybody suspected of communist sympathies, accusing them of treason. Thousands lost their jobs and hundreds were imprisoned for failing to conform to the 'American Way'. So-called 'subversives', such as the playwright Arthur Miller, were punished for their non-conformist attitudes by having to face the House of unAmerican Activities to defend their actions.

There is some evidence to suggest that Asch's results may, in part, reflect the society of his day. For example, Nicholson et al. (1985) replicated Asch's experiment (repeated it under the same conditions) and found lower conformity levels. This may be due to changes in American society, but it could also be due to other factors such as differences in the samples. Despite these differences, most social psychologists agree with Elliot Aronson that, 'decades of research indicate that conformity for normative reasons can occur simply because we do not want to risk social disapproval even from complete strangers we will never see again' (Aronson et al., 1997).

Culture Can Asch's findings be generalised to other places, in particular other cultures? Different societies have different cultures. Culture is the learned, shared behaviour of members of a society. It includes norms, values, attitudes and beliefs. To some extent, people from different cultures see the world in different ways. Culture can affect the results of experiments in two main ways. First, people from different cultures may see experiments in different ways. They may give different meanings to the tasks they are asked to perform. They may, therefore, respond differently to the same stimulus. If so, the results of experiments may reflect cultural differences. Second, the importance placed on conformity may differ from culture to culture. If so, we need to understand the culture in order to understand the results of experiments.

Asch's experiments have been replicated in 13 countries outside the USA. In the original experiments 37% of the judgements were incorrect. However, in the experiments conducted in other societies the percentage of errors varied considerably – from 14% in Belgium to 51% in Zimbabwe (Smith & Bond, 1993). As with the Asch experiments, the participants in Belgium and Zimbabwe were students, in the case of Zimbabwe, Bantu students. Many reasons have been suggested for these variations, including minor changes in experimental design. However, the main reason put forward to explain these variations is cultural differences.

Social psychologists have made a distinction between *individualist* and *collectivist* cultures. In individualist cultures, a high value is placed on individual freedom, self-help, self-reliance and individual responsibility. By comparison, collectivist cultures place more emphasis on collective responsibility, group cooperation, collective effort and dependence on social groups. As a result, group pressure to conform – majority influence – is greater in collectivist cultures. Results from the Asch experiments conducted in different societies show that the percentage of errors is higher in collectivist cultures. This suggests that the pressure to conform is higher in collectivist cultures (such as the Bantu of Zimbabwe) than in individualist cultures (such as the USA). This indicates that culture is an important variable affecting human behaviour. It must, therefore, be taken into account in order to understand and assess the results of psychological research (Moghaddam et al., 1993; Smith & Bond, 1993).

Key terms

Autokinetic effect *An optical illusion in which a stationary spot of light in a darkened environment appears to move.*

Personal norm *A standardised belief or behaviour of a particular person.*

Individualist cultures *Cultures which emphasise the individual – individual freedom and personal responsibility.*

Collectivist cultures *Cultures which emphasise the group – group responsibility and collective effort.*

1.4 Factors affecting conformity

The previous section has indicated a number of factors which affect levels of conformity. These include the ambiguity of the situation as in the Sherif experiments, the unanimity of the group as in the Asch experiments, and the cultural background of the participants. This section briefly reviews some of the other factors that can affect levels of conformity.

Group identification Research has indicated that normative social influence is stronger in groups to which people feel they belong. Within such groups the costs of non-conformity are higher than in groups of strangers. People have more to lose if they offend or upset their family, friends and workmates. To what extent do feelings of belonging to and identifying with groups influence conformity?

Abrams et al. (1990) attempted to answer this question using experiments based on those of Sherif and Asch. The participants were psychology students. They were placed in two groups, one containing people they believed were fellow psychology students, the other containing people they were told were students of ancient history. In Abrams' version of Sherif's autokinetic experiment, the convergence of estimates, which Sherif found in all groups, only occurred in the 'psychology group'. In Abrams' version of Asch's line judgement experiment, the level of conformity in the 'psychology group' was even higher than in the original Asch experiment. However, the level of conformity in the 'ancient history' group was considerably lower.

These experiments added a new dimension to studies of conformity. It appears that social influence to conform is stronger when people identify with a group. In this case the participants saw the 'psychology group' as people like themselves, as peers. As a result, they expected to share their attitudes and beliefs, they expected to agree with them and wanted to fit in with them. Approval from those they saw as their peers meant more to them than approval from the 'ancient history' group. There is less pressure to conform when people are seen as different from ourselves.

Group size Experiments have indicated that group size has an important effect on conformity. Asch (1951) found that in a one-to-one situation – one participant and one confederate – the confederate's incorrect answers make little difference. After all, it is only one person's judgement against another. However, if there are two confederates, the participant's error rate, and therefore conformity, rises to 13%. With three confederates, conformity rises still further to 33%. Asch found that conformity does not rise much beyond this level, no matter how big the group gets. The results from one of his experiments are shown in Figure 3.

Figure 3 Group size and conformity

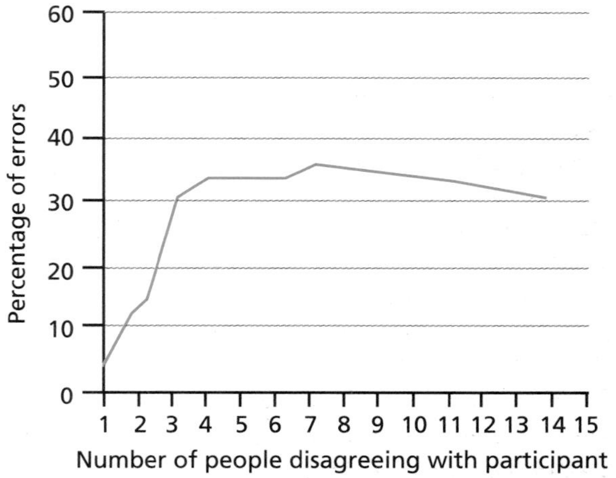

Social support In another version of his conformity experiment, Asch (1955) gave the participants a 'supporter' or 'ally'. This confederate gave the correct answer in every case, while other confederates continued to give wrong answers. No longer was the participant alone; social support had been provided. In this situation, the conformity rate reduced dramatically to an average of 5.5%. A number of other studies have produced similar results. It appears that having someone to 'back us up' gives people the confidence to resist normative social influence.

Personality Research has indicated that there are wide differences in conformity between individuals. This has led some researchers to argue that this reflects differences in personality. They claim that some people have personality characteristics which predispose them to conform. For example, Asch (1956) suggested that people with low self-esteem – a low opinion of themselves – tend to conform because they are more likely to fear disapproval and rejection from the group. Research has indicated that the following characteristics are associated with conformity: low self-esteem, a high need for social approval, feelings of inferiority and insecurity, high levels of anxiety and low IQ (Hogg & Vaughan, 1995).

However, the relationship between personality and conformity is not as clear-cut as this research suggests. Some studies have found little or no relationship between them. One of the main findings is that there is little consistency in people's behaviour. In one situation they conform, in another situation they don't. If their personality was the main factor affecting their behaviour, then this inconsistency would be unlikely. It appears that the social situation is more important in accounting for conformity than differences in personality (Aronson et al., 1997).

Gender For many years it was assumed that women were more conforming than men. Research indicated that though gender differences in conformity were small, they did exist. The methodology of these studies, and therefore their findings, have been criticised. Eagly and Carli (1981) found that male researchers were more likely to find higher levels of conformity in women than female researchers. This may, in part, be due to male researchers using tasks in their experiments which were more familiar to male participants.

Support for this view comes from a conformity experiment conducted by Sistrunk and McDavid (1971). Male and female participants were asked to identify various things while being subjected to group pressure to give the wrong answer – and so conform. Some participants were given traditionally male items (eg, a wrench), others were given traditionally female items (eg, different types of needlework), while others were given 'neutral' items (eg, identifying rock stars). Conformity for women was highest on male items, conformity for men was highest on female items, and for 'neutral' items, conformity levels were similar for both sexes – see Figure 4.

This study indicates that there are no significant differences in conformity behaviour between women and men. It also suggests that gender differences revealed by other studies may be due to the nature of the experiments rather than any real differences between men and women.

Figure 4 Gender and conformity

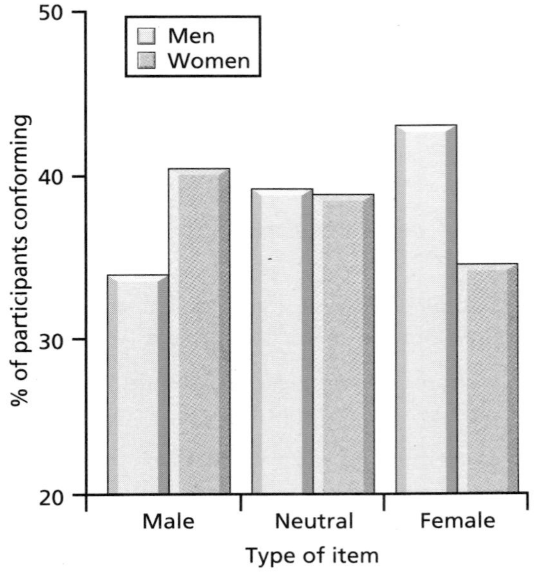

Adapted from Hogg and Vaughan, 1995

Key term

Group identification *The degree to which people feel they belong to a social group.*

Activity 3 Factors affecting conformity

Item A Culture and conformity

According to J.W. Berry (1967) societies whose economy is based on hunting and fishing will have different values than those based on agriculture. The successful hunter needs to be adventurous, assertive and independent. By comparison, the successful farmer needs to cooperate with others and recognise his or her dependence on the social group. This can be seen during planting and harvest seasons. In view of these differences, we should expect farming societies to place a higher value on conformity than hunting societies.

Berry tested this proposition by comparing a hunting and fishing society, the Inuit (Eskimos) of Baffin Island in Canada, with a farming society, the Temne of Sierra Leone in West Africa. Participants from each society were given an Asch-type conformity task. As predicted, the Temne had a significantly higher conformity rate than the Inuit. In the words of one Temne, 'When the Temne people choose a thing, we must all agree with the decision – this is what we call cooperation'. By comparison, the Inuit usually disregarded the incorrect answers of the group. When they did conform, and agreed to the incorrect answer, they did so with 'a quiet, knowing smile'.

Adapted from Berry, 1967

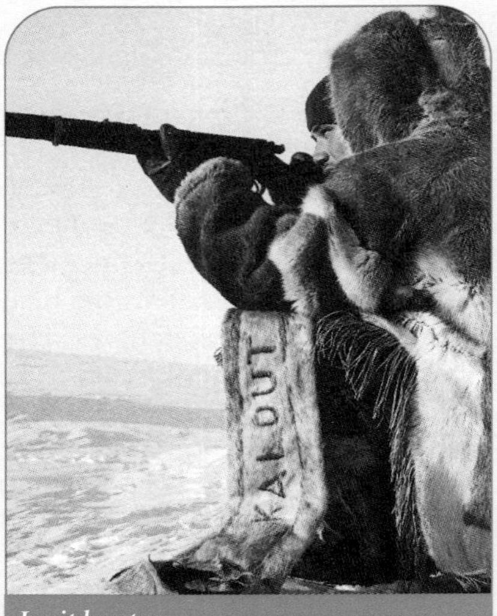

Inuit hunter

Item B Where do I belong?

I was born and raised in England. I was a student at the University of Minnesota in the USA for four years. During that time, I got to know about twenty students from England at the university. Around half of them decided to stay in America. It was noticeable that these students developed American accents. Those students, like myself, who returned home retained their English accents.

Story told to author, 15.10.1997

Questions

1 Read Item A. Why do we need to take culture into account when interpreting the results of conformity experiments?

2 Use the idea of group identification to explain the behaviour of the two groups of students in Item B.

3 Read Item C. Suggest reasons for the high level of conformity in Latino gangs.

Item C Latino gangs

Los Angeles has 570 Latino gangs. They are split into two groups. The Chicanos, Mexican-Americans born in the US, who often don't speak any Spanish. Their rivals are those Latino gangs whose members are recent immigrants from Mexico and other Spanish speaking countries and who have evolved a language of their own called *calo*. Older members (*veteranos*) are held in great respect by their 'home boys', having defended the honour of the *barrio* (territory) for over a decade or more of fierce urban warfare.

Each gang has its own initiation ceremony. For example, to become a Playboy, a prospective member has to get 'jumped in' – beaten up – by a minimum of three gang members and has only limited means to defend him or herself. While the beating takes place, others look on and count up to 13 slowly. Once initiated, members take on nicknames and adopt the dress codes of their comrades.

Hand signals and tattoos are important signifiers of gang loyalties. Tattoos are usually done by *carnals* (fellow gang members) often using home-made instruments. They cannot be removed by the authorities and are thus a symbol of defiance.

Adapted from *The Observer*, 6.2.1994

1.5 Conformity and social roles

This unit began with an introduction to social norms, one of the major organising principles of human society. It closes with an introduction to social roles. Like norms, roles guide and direct human behaviour.

In the words of William Shakespeare:

All the world's a stage,
And all the men and women merely players:
They have their exits, and their entrances;
And one man in his time plays many parts.
(*As You Like It*, Act 2, Scene 7)

These lines capture the essence of social roles. They are parts people play as members of social groups. Think of the roles you play in a single day. Before leaving home you may perform the role of son or daughter, brother or sister, husband or wife. At school or college you are a student in class, a friend at breaktime, and maybe a team member if you play a sport. On the way home you may be a customer in a shop and in the evening you probably return to your roles as a family member or a friend.

Attached to each role is a 'script' which states how the role should be played. For example, solicitors are expected to have a detailed knowledge of certain aspects of the law, to support their clients' interests and respect the confidentiality of their business. Solicitors' attire is expected to be sober, their manner restrained and their standing in the community beyond reproach.

Roles are social. They involve social relationships in the sense that an individual plays a role in relation to other roles. Thus the role of doctor is played in relation to the role of patient, the role of husband in relation to the role of wife.

Roles organise and regulate social life. They provide guidelines for action and give social life order and predictability. Interacting in terms of their respective roles, teacher and student, for example, know what to expect, what to do and how to do it.

With each social role you adopt, your behaviour changes to fit the expectations both you and others have of that role. If these expectations are not met, you may fail in your role. Imagine your teacher arriving in a bathing costume, playing a guitar and singing the psychology lecture to the class. This may well disrupt the lesson and students may have difficulty knowing how to respond.

There is considerable pressure to conform to social roles. Consider the so-called 'breaching experiments' conducted by the American sociologist Harold Garfinkel (1967). He asked his students to go into familiar situations and behave in unexpected ways, in other words, to dispense with normal role play. Some went into department stores and haggled over the price of goods, others went home to their families and behaved as if they were lodgers. The students had stepped out of their roles. They were not playing the parts of customers, sons, or daughters, as they should. The response to their actions was confusion, incomprehension, and even anger and hostility.

Social roles provide an example of social influence in general and conformity in particular. Most of us, most of the time, conform to the guidelines provided by the roles we perform. We conform to the expectations of others, we respond to their approval when we play our roles well, and to their disapproval when we play our roles badly. But how far will this conformity go? Would you follow your role to the letter even if this conflicted with deeply held beliefs? Could you lose yourself so completely in your role that your behaviour was totally out of character? These are some of the questions examined in the following section.

The Stanford Prison experiment

Philip Zimbardo and his colleagues (Haney, Banks & Zimbardo, 1973) recruited students from Stanford University in California, to play the roles of prisoners and guards in a mock prison. On the basis of interviews, psychological tests and physical examinations, those chosen to participate were judged to be mentally and physically healthy.

With the cooperation of the local police department, the 'prisoners' were arrested and handcuffed at their homes, taken to a police station and placed in a detention cell. They were then blindfolded and taken to the 'prison' in the basement of the psychology department at the university. There, they were locked in their cells 24 hours a day, while the 'guards' were rotated on 8 hour shifts.

On arrival, the prisoners were stripped, sprayed with a delousing solution (a deodorant spray) and forced to stand naked in the prison yard. They were then dressed in a loose-fitting smock stamped with an ID number, rubber sandals, a cap made from a nylon stocking and a lock chain attached to one ankle. From then on they were referred to only by number, not by name, and in reply to the guards, they had to say 'Mr Correctional Officer, Sir'. The guards were supplied with khaki shirts and trousers, reflecting sunglasses, whistles, police nightsticks and handcuffs.

The guards appeared to relish their new roles, performing them with vigour and authority. Any misbehaviour from the prisoners resulted in loss of privileges such as reading books or writing letters. But, as time went on, the guards became increasingly brutal and ground the prisoners down. At the first hint of protest or rebellion, loss of privileges now became loss of food, sleep, blankets and washing facilities. The guards kept inventing new forms of punishment such as solitary confinement (in a cupboard) and cleaning toilets with bare hands. Prisoners were routinely woken in the middle of the night and marched out to the cell yard to be counted. The guards verbally abused the prisoners, taunting and humiliating them.

For most of the time, the prisoners obeyed. Most shuffled round their cells, helpless and apathetic. Although one began a hunger strike, the rest did exactly as they were told. But the strain was telling. On the third day, one prisoner was released from the experiment because of 'acute emotional disturbance'. Another was released after developing a psychosomatic rash over most of his body. The

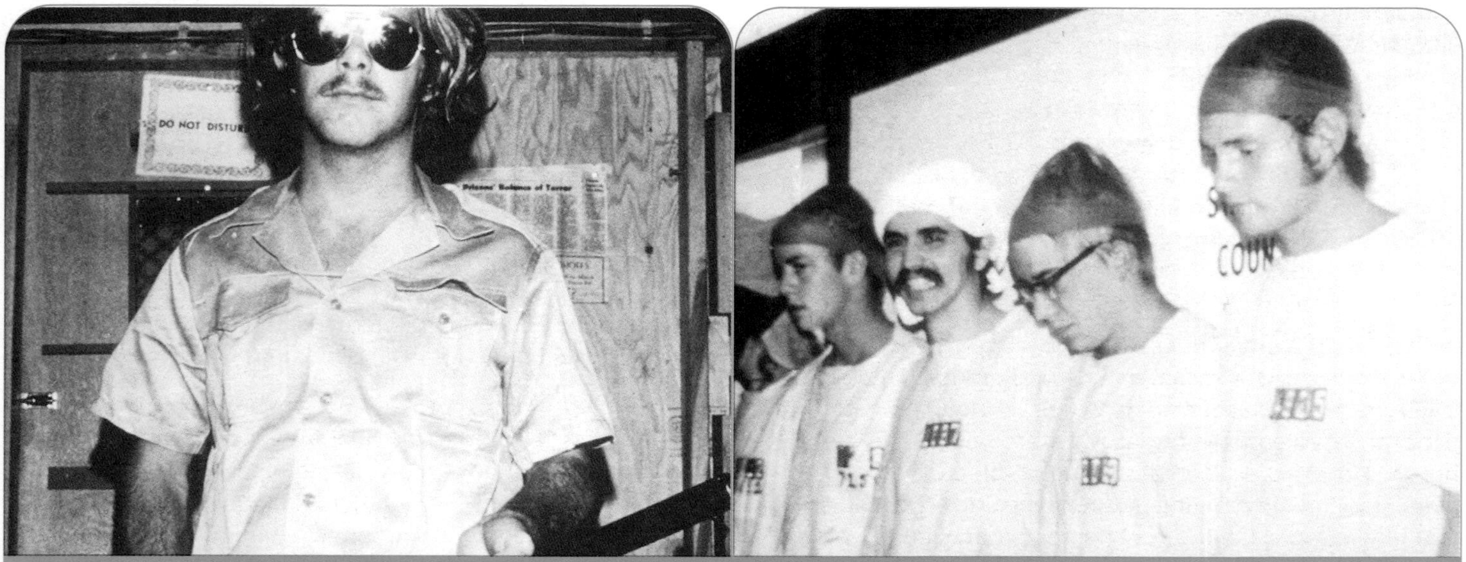

A guard and prisoners in the Stanford prison

experiment had been designed to last for two weeks; the researchers decided to end it after six days.

The participants had assumed their roles rapidly. As the days went by, they developed their roles. A 'good' guard was tough, aggressive and arrogant. Even the less aggressive guards publicly conformed to this role model.

As for the prisoners, their role was soon established. They stuck to the rules so that the guards would have no reason to punish them. They even sided with the guards against the prisoner on hunger strike. Rather than becoming a hero, he was simply a nuisance who drew attention to the prisoners and caused trouble. The other prisoners rejected him.

Evaluation According to the researchers, the Stanford Prison experiment shows the power and potency of social influence. In many respects the participants became the roles they were playing. Normal, well-adjusted university students became either brutal overseers or pathetic subordinates. Clearly their roles had a powerful influence on their behaviour. Or did they?

For a start, the prison, built in the basement of the psychology department of Stanford University, was hardly realistic. The participants were given little indication of how to behave. For example, the guards were told simply to 'maintain the reasonable degree of order within the prison necessary for its effective functioning'. In a real prison, new guards and prisoners are subject to detailed rules, and are trained and guided by more experienced officers and 'old lags'. Critics have argued that without such rules and guidance, Zimbardo's experiment is unlikely to tell us much about how people really behave in prisons.

Moreover, the experiment was just that, an experiment. The prison was a mock prison, the participants were in 'fancy dress' acting out parts they had been told to play. They had probably seen movies like *Cool Hand Luke* (1967), which portrays stereotypes of brutal prison guards, with the most vicious guards wearing reflecting sunglasses. This suggests that when Zimbardo issued the guards with similar sunglasses (which are very impractical indoors!), he was providing them with a cue to 'play' the guards in films like *Cool Hand Luke*. Were the participants then simply behaving like actors in a movie? Most of the guards in the experiment later claimed this was exactly what they were doing. Critics have argued that the Stanford Prison experiment shows little more than play-acting on a film set, and tells us virtually nothing about the effect of roles on people's behaviour in real life.

The following points can be made to counter this criticism. First, if the prisoners were simply play-acting, why did they show symptoms of stress, symptoms that were so severe that the experiment had to be stopped after only six days. Second, why did the guards' aggression towards the prisoners steadily intensify? Doesn't this indicate that the guards became increasingly involved in their roles, that they were identifying with their roles?

From this point of view, the experiment shows how readily people adopt social roles and conform to them. It shows the power of social influence.

The Stanford Prison experiment has also been criticised on ethical grounds. This criticism is examined on pages 228-229.

Key term

Social roles *The parts people play as members of a society, for example mother, son, teacher, student. Each role has a 'script' which states how the role should be performed.*

Summary

1. Informational social influence encourages conformity when people are unsure of the correct response. It is based on the desire to be right. It can lead to private acceptance – conforming to the norms of others because they are seen to be right.

2. Normative social influence encourages conformity because people seek the approval of others. It is based on the desire to be liked and accepted. It can lead to public compliance – conforming to group norms in public – but it does not necessarily lead to private acceptance.

3. Sherif's experiment, based on the autokinetic effect, indicates that the presence of others leads to the formation of group norms and conformity to those norms. It is an example of informational social influence.

4. Asch's line-matching experiments show that people are sometimes prepared to deny what they know to be true in order to gain the approval of the group. This is an example of normative social influence.

5. A number of factors influence levels of conformity. They include culture, whether or not people identify with the group, the size of the group and the level of social support for nonconformity.

6. According to Zimbardo et al., the Stanford Prison experiment shows how readily people conform to social roles.

Unit 2 Minority influence

KEY ISSUES

1. **What is minority influence?**
2. **What factors affect minority influence?**
3. **How have psychologists seen conformity – as a 'good' or a 'bad' thing?**

Unit 1 has been primarily concerned with majority influence – the pressures on the minority to conform to the views and behaviour of the majority. This unit looks at the possibility of reversing the direction of social influence – the minority influencing the majority. This is known as *minority influence* or *innovation*. Minority influence occurs when a minority 'rejects the established norm of the majority of group members and induces the majority to move to the position of the minority' (Turner, 1991).

2.1 Consistency

The French social psychologist Serge Moscovici argued that minorities are most likely to influence majorities if they are consistent in their views. They must be consistent over time, in other words, they must not change their views. And, they must be consistent among themselves, that is they must all hold the same views.

Moscovici designed a series of experiments to examine minority influence. One of these experiments will now be described (Moscovici et al., 1969).

The participants were first given eye tests to ensure they were not colour-blind. They were then placed in a group consisting of four participants and two confederates. They were shown 36 slides which were clearly different shades of blue and asked to state the colour of each slide out loud. In the first part of the experiment the two confederates answered green for each of the slides. They were totally consistent in their responses. In the second part of the experiment they answered green 24 times and blue 12 times. In this case they were inconsistent in their answers. Would the responses of the two confederates influence those of the four participants? In other words, would there be minority influence?

Here are the results. First, those of a control group. A control group is used for comparison with an experimental group. The factors expected to influence the experimental group's behaviour are removed. So, in this case, the control group did not include confederates. Only 0.25% of the control group's answers were green, the rest were blue. For the experimental group, 1.25% of the participants' answers were green when the confederates gave inconsistent answers (ie, 24 green, 12 blue). This rose to 8.42% green when the confederates answers were consistent (ie, 36 green). These results are shown in Figure 5.

Figure 5 Percentage of green responses given by participants

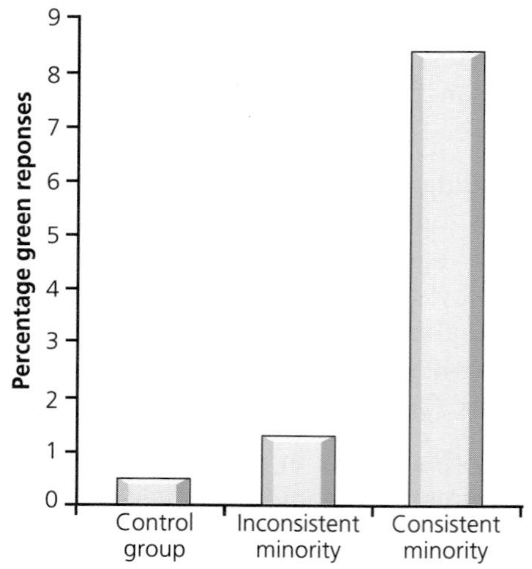

Moscovici's experiment suggests that minorities can influence majorities. However, it indicates that this influence is much more effective when the minority are consistent in their responses. When the minority gave inconsistent answers, they were largely ignored by the majority. Later research has largely confirmed these findings.

Moscovici (1985) sees consistency as the key to minority influence for the following reasons.

- The minority speaks with a single voice. There are no ifs, buts and maybes; no contradictions. Consistency leaves the majority in no doubt about the alternative views being expressed.
- This gives the impression that the minority are convinced they are right and are committed to their viewpoint.
- As a result, the minority appear confident and assured. This can lead to the majority taking the minority view seriously. The majority will therefore be more likely to question their own views.
- A consistent minority disrupts established norms and creates uncertainty, doubt and conflict.
- One way to resolve this conflict and to remove the uncertainty is for the majority to accept the minority view.

Moscovici argues that majority influence tends to be based on public compliance. It is likely to be a case of normative social influence. In this respect, power of numbers is important – the majority have the power to reward and punish with approval and disapproval. And because of this, there is pressure on minorities to conform. Since majorities are often unconcerned about what minorities think about them, minority influence is rarely based on normative social influence. Instead, it is usually based on informational social influence – providing the majority with new ideas, new information which leads them to re-examine their views. In this respect, minority influence involves private acceptance – converting the majority by convincing them that the minority's views are right.

Flexibility and compromise A number of researchers have questioned whether consistency alone is sufficient for a minority to influence a majority. They argue that the key is how consistency is interpreted by the majority. If the consistent minority are seen as inflexible, rigid, uncompromising and dogmatic, they will be unlikely to change the views of the majority. However, if they appear flexible and compromising, they are likely to be seen as less extreme, as more moderate, cooperative and reasonable. As a result, they will have a better chance of changing majority views (Mugny & Papastamou, 1980).

Some researchers have gone further and suggested that it is not just the *appearance* of flexibility and compromise which is important but *actual* flexibility and compromise. This possibility was investigated by Nemeth and Brilmayer (1987). Their experiment was based on a mock jury in which groups of three participants and one confederate had to decide on the amount of compensation to be given to the victim of a ski-lift accident. When the consistent minority (the confederate) argued for a very low amount and refused to change his position, he had no effect on the majority. However, when he compromised and moved some way towards the majority position, the majority also compromised and changed their view. This experiment questions the importance of consistency. The minority position changed, it was not consistent, and it was this change that apparently resulted in minority influence.

Key term

Minority influence *When a minority changes the beliefs and/or behaviour of a majority.*

2.2 Other factors affecting minority influence

Group identification

People tend to identify with people they see as similar to themselves. For example, men tend to identify with men, African Caribbeans with African Caribbeans, psychology students with psychology students, and so on. Research indicates that if the majority identify with the minority, then they are more likely to take the views of the minority seriously and change their own views in line with those of the minority. For example, one study showed that a gay minority arguing for gay rights had less influence on a straight majority than a straight minority arguing for gay rights (Maass et al., 1982). The non-gay majority identified with the non-gay minority. They tended to see the gay minority as different from themselves, as self-interested and concerned with promoting their own particular cause.

Zeitgeist

Zeitgeist is a German word meaning 'spirit of the times' or 'mood of the times'. Zeitgeist refers to the prevailing attitudes and values in society at a particular time. Research indicates that if the minority viewpoint is in line with the prevailing zeitgeist, then the majority will be more likely to accept it. For example, in Western societies today, the zeitgeist is more likely to support equality for women than it was fifty years ago. One study conducted in the 1970s indicated that minorities were more likely to influence majorities if they argued in favour of women's rights rather than against them (Paicheler, 1976).

The problem with this argument is that, in one sense, the minority is not really a minority because their views are in line with the current zeitgeist, with the attitudes and values of the majority in society. The argument doesn't tell us how the zeitgeist changed in the first place. For example, how did views supporting equality for women – once a minority view – become accepted by the majority in society?

Social cryptoamnesia One answer to this question is provided by the idea of *social cryptoamnesia* – a kind of social forgetting (Perez et al., 1995). Minority ideas are often rejected because people find it difficult to identify with those who put them forward. Women's rights provides an example. Many men *and* women found it difficult to identify with the suffragettes in the early 20th century and the feminists of the mid-20th century. Social cryptoamnesia states that people tend to forget those who put forward the new ideas but remember the ideas themselves. This allows them to take on minority ideas without identifying with the minority. For example, equal rights for women ceases to be associated with 'crazy' suffragettes or 'pushy', 'strident' feminists. Equality for women now makes sense and appears reasonable. Minority influence is therefore indirect and delayed. It becomes detached and removed from the minority who first promoted it and takes effect some time after it first appeared. In this way the idea of social cryptoamnesia provides an explanation for how the zeitgeist changes (Perez et al., 1995).

Argument refutation and desertion

An interesting experiment conducted by Russell D. Clark III (1990) indicates two possible factors that can increase minority influence. First, if the minority can refute the majority's arguments, that is, show them to be incorrect. Second, if one or more members of the majority desert the majority and support the minority position.

Clark based his experiment on the play *Twelve Angry Men* in which a son is accused of murdering his father and a jury discusses the trial and reaches a verdict. Clark's findings indicated that the more of the majority's arguments that the minority could refute, the more influence they had. It also showed that desertion by majority members to the minority increased minority influence. The minority was most effective when these factors were combined – refuting majority arguments and desertion by majority members.

2.3 Evaluation

Most of the research on minority influence is based on experiments conducted in laboratories. This raises the question of ecological validity. Is it possible to generalise from the findings of laboratory research to other settings? Edward Sampson (1991) is particularly critical of laboratory research on minority influence. He makes the following points.

Real groups The participants in laboratory experiments are rarely 'real groups'. More often than not they are a collection of students who do not know each other and will probably never meet again. As such they are very different from minority groups in the wider society who seek to change majority opinion. For example, members of women's rights, gay rights and animal rights organisations, people in black power and black consciousness groups, and members of pressure groups such as Greenpeace and Friends of the Earth are very different from participants in laboratory experiments. They operate in different settings with different constraints. They often face much more determined opposition. They are committed to a cause, they often know each other, provide each other with considerable social support and sometimes devote their lives to changing the views of the majority.

Power and status Laboratory experiments are largely unable to represent and simulate the wide differences in power and status that often separate minorities and majorities. As Sampson (1991) notes, history is littered with examples of how majorities can crush minorities who attempt to express divergent views. Student pro-democracy demonstrators in Tiananmen Square in Beijing were powerless in the face of government forces. In 1989 they were brutally swept aside by troops and tanks and many were later executed (see p 216).

A lack of power is often linked to a lack of social status. Ethnic minorities, women, gays, the poor and the underprivileged tend to have low status in society. As a result, their views are often ignored.

Protest Minorities do influence majorities. Western societies now have laws protecting the rights of groups such as ethnic minorities, gays, women and the disabled. But minority influence does not triumph simply because of the consistency of their arguments or their willingness to be flexible or to compromise. Often it results from massive protests such as the civil rights demonstrations by African Americans in the 1950s and 60s and the uprisings in Eastern Europe which overthrew the communist regimes in 1989.

Conclusion Edward Sampson does not suggest we ignore the laboratory findings on minority influence – they provide important insights. But neither should we ignore 'the harsh realities of life'. In his words, 'we need to see the broader social contexts in which minorities are able to wield influence and the conditions under which they are ruthlessly put down or even benignly pacified' (Sampson, 1991).

Key terms

Zeitgeist *The spirit of the times. The prevailing attitudes and values in society at a particular time.*

Social cryptoamnesia *A tendency to forget the people who put forward new ideas but to remember the ideas themselves. Minority ideas become part of the ideas of the majority, but the majority forget where they came from.*

2.4 Conformity – the case for and against

Most of the research on conformity has been North American and has focused on the way majority pressure can control and distort the judgement of the individual. American researchers have tended to see conformity in a negative light, as a threat to individual liberty. This view has been seen as a reflection of American culture which emphasises (at least after the McCarthy era of the early 1950s) individual freedom and self-reliance (Moghaddam et al., 1993; Smith & Bond, 1993). Starting from the assumption that independence is good and conformity is bad can influence both research design and the way that the results of research are interpreted.

It can be argued that conformity studies are often designed to highlight the dangers of conformity. The Stanford Prison experiment can be seen in this light. Looking back on the experiment, Zimbardo et al. (1995) see it as a valuable warning to us all. However, it would have been equally possible to set up an experiment to show the positive effects of conformity, eg to ask participants to play caring roles in a hospital situation. Asch's line-matching experiment is presented in hundreds of psychology textbooks as an example of majority influence. Yet only 37% of the judgements made by the participants were incorrect. In other words, in 63% of their judgements they were not swayed by the influence of the majority. This emphasis can be interpreted as a reflection of the values Americans place on individuality and independence. By focusing on the minority of incorrect judgements, they portray the Asch experiment as a warning of the threat of majority influence to individual freedom.

This preoccupation with majority influence may help to explain why it was European psychologists, particularly the Frenchman Moscovici, who developed the study of minority influence. It has been argued that conformity is viewed in a more positive light in Europe where it is more likely to be seen as the outcome of negotiation rather than the imposition of majority views.

Whether conformity is seen as a good or a bad thing depends in part on culture. Different cultures view conformity in different ways. In non-Western societies, particularly traditional, small-scale societies, researchers have noted a greater emphasis on group solidarity and a more positive view of conformity. For example, the traditional culture of Australian aborigines states that problems should be solved by groups rather than individuals and decisions should be unanimous. When approached by psychologists to take IQ tests, aborigines were reluctant to take the tests as individuals and found it difficult to understand the request to do so (Haralambos & Holborn, 2000).

The above paragraphs raise a number of important points. First, we should guard against ethnocentrism, ie seeing things solely from the point of view of our own culture and assuming that view is correct. There are different ways of seeing conformity and we should not assume that our view is the only one and that everybody shares it. Second, everybody – psychologists included – sees the world through the lens of their own culture. Thus, to some degree, psychologists' views of conformity will reflect their cultural backgrounds. This will influence the research they conduct and their interpretation of the results.

In general, it makes little sense to talk about conformity as 'good' or 'bad'. Such judgements depend in a large part on the circumstances. All societies require a certain level of conformity in order to function. Imagine a situation where social norms were constantly violated – people refusing to pay for groceries at the supermarket or to stop at a red light, or ignoring greetings from friends. The result would be confusion, disorder, even chaos. As Zimbardo and Leippe (1991) put it, conformity 'lubricates the wheels of social interaction'. On the other hand, conformity can be seen as harmful, producing 'blind' obedience and herd-like behaviour.

Similarly, non conformity can be seen as 'good ' or 'bad' depending on the situation. A certain level of nonconformity can be seen as beneficial to society. If conformity were total, society would stagnate – there would be no change, no improvement, no new ideas, no creativity. There would be no inventions which 'break the rules', there would be no advances in science or in society. In the words of Moghaddam et al., 'Almost all great intellectual and social movements began as minority movements. Think, for example, of the opposition faced by Galileo and other scientists who argued that the earth is not the centre of the universe, and of the ridicule and resentment confronting the suffragettes in their struggle for women's rights'. Nonconformity has also been seen as positive in order to resist behaviour which is cruel or evil, as, for example, opposing dictatorships such as Hitler's in Germany. But nonconformity can also have its downside. Breaking social norms can be obstructive and even dangerous. For example, disobeying the Highway Code can endanger life and limb. Nonconformity is not necessarily a sign of independent-mindedness or creative thinking. It can be a result of personal inadequacy, obstinacy or sheer bloody-mindedness.

Summary

1. Minority influence occurs when a minority rejects the norms of the majority and the majority accepts the position of the minority.

2. According to Moscovici, consistency is the key to minority influence – consistency of views within the minority and over time. Minority influence is usually based on informational social influence and on private acceptance.

3. Later research indicates that minority influence will be more effective if the minority appear flexible and ready to compromise.

4. Majorities are more ready to accept the minority view if they can identify with the minority.

5. Minority views are more likely to be accepted if they are in line with the prevailing zeitgeist in society.

6. The zeitgeist may be changed by social cryptoamnesia – the majority accepts minority views but forgets where they came from.

7. Minority influence is more likely to be effective if majority ideas can be refuted and if majority members desert to the minority.

8. Much of the research on conformity has been based on the assumption that conformity is a bad thing. This can influence both research design and how the results of the research are interpreted.

9. Without a certain degree of conformity, it is difficult to see how social life could operate. However, without minority influence, there would be no social change and society would stagnate.

Activity 4 Minority influence

Item A Trial by jury

In October 1997, a jury in Boston, Massachusetts found 19-year-old English nanny Louise Woodward guilty of the murder of the baby she was caring for. The nine women and three men considered the evidence for three days. Immediately after the trial, when asked for their first impressions, the jury were split evenly down the middle. Next morning, four members thought Louise was guilty, four thought she was innocent and the others were unsure. By day three, it was ten guilty, two innocent until finally all agreed to a guilty verdict.

According to Tracey Mannix, aged 24, the youngest member of the jury, four jurors were convinced of Louise's guilt from the start. They didn't waver in their conviction and refused to give an inch. They wore down the other members and forced a guilty verdict through. Tracey said 'I held out as long as I could. It was the toughest decision of my life. I just believed, given the evidence, she did not kill that baby.'

Adapted from *The Mirror*, 3.11.1997

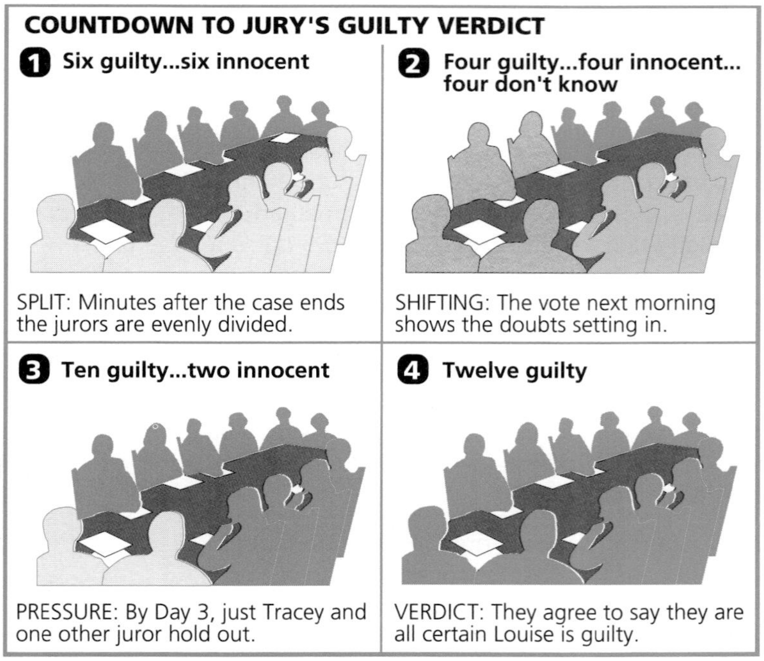

COUNTDOWN TO JURY'S GUILTY VERDICT
1 Six guilty...six innocent
SPLIT: Minutes after the case ends the jurors are evenly divided.
2 Four guilty...four innocent... four don't know
SHIFTING: The vote next morning shows the doubts setting in.
3 Ten guilty...two innocent
PRESSURE: By Day 3, just Tracey and one other juror hold out.
4 Twelve guilty
VERDICT: They agree to say they are all certain Louise is guilty.

Item B The White House cat

US President Calvin Coolidge shocked the fashionable guests at the White House breakfast by pouring his heavily creamed coffee into a saucer. Taken aback but unfailingly polite, Coolidge's guests did the same. They waited wide-eyed for the President to take the first sip. At which point Coolidge picked up the saucer, leaned over, and presented it to the White House cat.

Item C Protest and demonstration

Protest and demonstrations by African Americans in the 1950s and 60s led to civil rights legislation giving minority groups equal rights under the law.

Questions

1. Explain the behaviour of the jury in Item A.
2 Explain the behaviour of the guests in Item B.
3 What support does Item C provide for Sampson's (1991) statement that 'we need to see the broader social contexts in which minorities are able to wield influence'?

References

Abrams, D., Wetherell, M., Cochrane, S., Hogg, M.A. & Turner, J.C. (1990). Knowing what to think by knowing who you are: Self-categorisation and the nature of norm formation, conformity and group polarisation. *British Journal of Social Psychology, 29* (part 2), 97-119.

Aronson, E., Wilson, T.D. & Akert, R.M. (1997). *Social psychology* (2nd ed.). New York: Addison Wesley Longman.

Asch, S.E. (1951). Effects of group pressure on the modification and distortion of judgements. In H. Guetzkow (Ed.), *Groups, leadership and men.* Pittsburgh: Carnegie

Asch, S.E. (1955). Opinions and social pressure. *Scientific American, 193,* 31-35.

Asch, S.E. (1956). Studies of independence and conformity: A minority of one against a unanimous majority. *Psychological Monographs, 70* (9, Whole No. 416).

Berry, J.W. (1967). Independence and conformity in subsistence-level societies. *Journal of Personality and Social Psychology, 7,* 415-418.

Cantril, H. (1940). *The invasion from Mars: A study in the psychology of panic.* New York: Harper & Row.

Clark, R.D., III. (1990). Minority influence: The role of argument refutation of the majority position and social support for the minority position. *European Journal of Social Psychology, 20,* 487-497.

Crutchfield, R.A. (1955). Conformity and character. *American Psychologist, 10,* 191-198.

Deutsch, M. & Gerard, H.B. (1955). A study of normative and informational social influences upon individual judgement. *Journal of Abnormal and Social Psychology, 51,* 629-636.

Eagly, A.H. & Carli, L.L. (1981). Sex of researchers and sex-typed communications as determinants of sex differences in influenceability: A meta-analysis of social influence studies. *Psychological Bulletin, 90,* 1-20.

Garfinkil, H. (1967). *Studies in ethnomethodology.* Englewood Cliffs, NJ: Prentice Hall.

Haney, C., Banks, C. & Zimbardo, P.G. (1973). Interpersonal dynamics in a simulated prison. *International Journal of Criminology and Penology, 1,* 69-97.

Haralambos, M. & Holborn, M. (2000). *Sociology: Themes and perspectives* (5th ed.). London: Collins Educational.

Hogg, M.A. & Vaughan, G.M. (1995). *Social psychology: An introduction.* Hemel Hempstead: Prentice Hall/Harvester Wheatsheaf.

Jacobs, K.C. & Campbell, D.T. (1961). The perpetuation of an arbitrary tradition through several generations of a laboratory microculture. *Journal of Abnormal and Social Psychology, 62,* 649-658.

Maass, A., Clark, R.D., III & Haberkorn, G. (1982). The effects of differential ascribed category membership and norms on minority influence. *European Journal of Social Psychology, 12,* 89-104.

Moghaddam, F.M., Taylor, D.M. & Wright, S.C. (1993). *Social psychology in cross-cultural perspective.* New York: W.H. Freeman.

Moscovici, S. (1985). Social influence and conformity. In G. Lindzey & E. Aronson (Eds.), *Handbook of social psychology* (3rd ed., vol. 2). New York: Random House.

Moscovici, S., Lage, E. & Naffrechoux, M. (1969). Influence of a consistent minority on the responses of a majority in a colour perception task. *Sociometry, 32,* 365-380.

Mugny, G. & Papastamou, S. (1980). When rigidity does not fail: Individualisation and psychologisation as resistances to the diffusion of minority innovations. *European Journal of Social Psychology, 10,* 43-62.

Nemeth, G.J. & Brilmayer, A.G. (1987). Negotiation versus influence. *European Journal of Social Psychology, 17,* 45-56.

Nicholson, M., Cole, S.G. & Rocklin, T. (1985). Conformity in the Asch situation: A comparison between contemporary British and US university students. *British Journal of Social Psychology, 24,* 59-63.

Paicheler, G. (1976). Norms and attitude change: 1. Polarisation and styles of behaviour. *European Journal of Social Psychology, 6,* 405-427.

Perez, J.A., Papastamou, S. & Mugny, G. (1995). 'Zeitgeist' and minority influence – where is the causality: A comment on Clark (1990). *European Journal of Social Psychology, 25,* 703-710.

Sampson, E.E. (1991). *Social worlds, personal lives: An introduction to social psychology.* New York: Harcourt Brace Jovanovich.

Sherif, M. (1935). A study of some social factors in perception. *Archives of Psychology, 27,* no. 187.

Sistrunk, F. & McDavid, J.W. (1971). Sex variable in conforming behaviour. *Journal of Personality and Social Psychology, 17,* 200-207.

Smith, P.B. & Bond, M.H. (1993). *Social psychology across cultures: Analysis and perspectives.* Hemel Hempstead: Harvester Wheatsheaf.

Turner, J.C. (1991). *Social influence.* Buckingham: Open University Press.

van Avermaet, E. (1996). Social influence in small groups. In M. Hewstone, W. Stroebe & G.M. Stephenson (Eds.), *Introduction to social psychology* (2nd ed.). Oxford: Blackwell.

Zimbardo, P.G. & Leippe, M. (1991). *The psychology of attitude change and social influence.* New York: McGraw-Hill.

Zimbardo, P.G., McDermott, M., Jansz, J. & Metaal, M. (1995). *Psychology: A European text.* London: Harper Collins.

14 Obedience to authority

Introduction

It's your first day at university, you're excited, apprehensive and not sure what to do. You go to your first psychology lecture. The lecturer begins by telling you the rules. He assigns seats in the lecture theatre and you go where you're told. You must not talk in lectures, you require permission to leave early and you must bring your textbook to every lecture. So far, so good, apart from the weight of the textbook.

Then the lecturer's demands become less reasonable. 'You must use a pencil to take notes. Take your watch off. Keep both hands on the desktop at all times.' Finally, you are told, 'Stick two fingers up your nose and quack like a duck'.

This is a demonstration sometimes used by psychology lecturers in the USA (Halonen, 1986). Would you obey the lecturer and end up quacking with two fingers up your nose? You'd probably be surprised how many students do just that.

This is a rather silly example but it illustrates one of the main issues examined in this chapter. How far would people go if ordered to do something by those in authority? Would they obey orders which they thought immoral? For example, would they torture and kill defenceless men, women and children? Would they take their own lives if ordered to do so? Under certain circumstances people have done all these things.

This chapter looks at obedience, a major form of social influence.

Chapter summary

- **Unit 1 considers the view that certain people are prone to obedience because of their personality type.**
- **Unit 2 outlines and assesses experimental studies of obedience.**
- **Unit 3 examines resistance to authority – why some people refuse to obey those who have the right to give orders.**

Unit 1 Obeying others

KEY ISSUES

1. **What is obedience?**
2. **Can obedience be seen as a problem?**
3. **Is there an 'obedient personality'?**

Stanley Milgram, one of the leading researchers into the psychology of obedience, notes that conformity and obedience have an important factor in common. Both involve changes in a person's behaviour due to social pressure. Both are forms of social influence. However, they differ from one another in important ways.

- Obedience involves a direct requirement to change behaviour in response to authority whereas conformity is a change in behaviour in response to group norms.
- Obedience involves people of different social status – those in authority and those subject to authority. Conformity usually occurs in groups whose members have a similar social status, for example peer groups.
- Obedience results from the direct exercise of power – those in charge usually have the power to ensure that their directives are followed. Conformity occurs primarily from a desire for acceptance within the group.

Milgram illustrates the difference between obedience and conformity with the experience of a new recruit in the army. 'He scrupulously carries out the orders of his superiors. At the same time he adopts the habits, routines and language of his peers. The former represents obedience and the latter conformity.' Thus a person *obeys* when they 'comply with authority', they *conform* when they 'go along with their peers who have no special right to direct their behaviour' (Milgram, 1974).

1.1 Obedience – is it a problem?

People usually obey others for one of two main reasons. First, because they see the authority of others as right and lawful – as *legitimate authority*. In this case, they are likely to obey willingly. Second, they may obey others because they are forced to, or because they fear the consequences of not obeying. In this case, they are likely to see the authority of others as illegitimate, and attempts to enforce obedience as *coercion*.

The question of whether obedience can be a problem is to some extent a political one. Right-wing political philosophies see obedience as essential to the wellbeing of society. Conservatives often blame society's ills, such as crime and delinquency, on a decline of obedience resulting from a 'breakdown of authority'. Fascists prized obedience as a great virtue, admiring strong government and emphasising the importance of order in society. Hitler, in a speech in 1928, stated, 'We must teach the people to recognise authority and leadership', and in 1933 he exhorted his storm-troopers to 'submit to this overwhelming need to obey'. Fascist rulers were commonly referred to simply as 'the Leader': Mussolini was 'Il Duce', Hitler was the 'Führer' – both terms meant leader.

By contrast, more liberal political perspectives see obedience as potentially dangerous, especially when, in their view, obedience to so-called legitimate authority results in evil and inhumane actions. Liberals prefer to stress the importance of each person making their own individual decisions. They are more likely to question the requests and demands of authority figures.

Milgram accepts the necessity for some kind of legitimate authority. He points out that we happily and reasonably accept the authority of others in their specific domains. As he put it, 'We expose our throats to a man with a razor blade in the barber's shop, but would not do so in a shoe store' (Milgram, 1974). In all societies, from the smallest hunting and gathering bands to the largest nation states, there is some system of authority. It ranges from the authority of parents, teachers and employers, to the authority of the state represented in institutions such as parliament and the police. It is difficult to see how human society could operate without some degree of obedience to some system of authority.

While accepting this view, social psychologists recognise that obedience can lead to actions which they regard as unreasonable, morally wrong and even dangerous. American psychologists often refer to this type of obedience as 'destructive obedience'. Much of the early research was concerned with obedience to Nazi policies of genocide during the Second World War. It asked why people obeyed orders which violated the most basic moral codes of humane behaviour.

Key terms

Obedience *Obeying the requests and demands of others.*

Legitimate authority *Authority which is considered right. It is often supported by the law.*

Coercion *Forced obedience. The authority of those who enforce coercion is considered illegitimate and wrong.*

1.2 Personality or situation?

This section contrasts two views of obedience. The first states that some people are more prone than others to obey because of the nature of their personalities. The second states that those who obey do so because of the situation in which they find themselves.

The authoritarian personality

Theodore Adorno (1950) and his colleagues started their research shortly after World War II. They began by investigating anti-Semitism (prejudice against Jews) in order to understand the treatment of Jews in Nazi Germany. They claimed that people with a certain personality type – which they called the *authoritarian personality* – were more prone to obedience than others. On a personality questionnaire, people with this personality type emphatically agreed with statements such as 'Obedience and respect for authority are the most important virtues children should learn'. They were submissive to those in authority and inclined towards unquestioning obedience. They looked up to their 'superiors' and often treated those beneath them with contempt. They believed in a rigid social structure with everybody in their place, and tended to be prejudiced against minority groups.

Adorno claimed that people with authoritarian personalities had childhoods which were dominated by a strict and punitive father who demanded absolute obedience. They developed a defence mechanism of *displacement*, targeting the anger they felt for their father at safer targets such as minority groups. They were conditioned to value strength and perceive the world to be full of people who need to be defeated, as they were defeated in childhood. They learned to fear and obey authority from an early age.

Evaluation Adorno used the idea of the authoritarian personality to explain obedience to authority in fascist societies. He argued that fascism encouraged the development of this type of personality. This led to hostility towards minority groups, particularly Jews, and to the obeying of orders to oppress and murder Jewish people.

Despite later research which supports the existence of authoritarian personalities, critics have argued that Adorno's theory is hardly sufficient to explain the slaughter of millions of Jews in Nazi Germany. First, fascism developed in

Germany some ten years before the persecution of the Jews began. This is hardly enough time for German families to adopt the child-rearing practices needed to produce authoritarian personalities, or for their children to reach adulthood and obey the orders of the Nazi leadership. Second, Adorno's theories cannot explain why whole communities share the same prejudices and obey the same orders, or why attitudes and behaviour change rapidly over short periods of time (Zimbardo et al., 1995). Third, evidence suggests that Nazi officials were not so much authoritarian as merely bureaucratic. Hannah Arendt (1963) studied the trial of Adolf Eichmann who was judged to be responsible for the murder of millions of Jews in Nazi Germany. She found his obedience to authority differed little from that of officials in any bureaucratic organisation. He was simply a cog, albeit a major one, in a massive bureaucratic machine, obeying the orders of his superiors just like any good bureaucrat. He appeared ordinary, even dull and boring, fitting neatly into the stereotype of the bureaucrat. Arendt referred to his behaviour, and similar actions, as the 'banality of evil'. In this sense, evil can be seen as a commonplace response to the demands of authority. In Arendt's words, it is 'terrifyingly normal'.

In situations such as Hitler's Germany, the demand for obedience was overpowering. There was tremendous pressure for people to obey, whatever their personality type. Even without such pressure, there is evidence that obedience to authority is a normal part of social situations and has nothing necessarily to do with personality type.

Key terms

Authoritarian personality *A personality type which results in people being more likely to respect authority figures and to obey them without question.*

Displacement *Directing the anger and frustration from the source which caused them on to another, usually less threatening, target such as minority groups.*

Summary

1. Obedience and conformity are both forms of social influence. However, whereas obedience results from pressure to comply with authority, conformity results from pressure to behave in terms of group norms.
2. According to Adorno, people with authoritarian personalities are more prone to obedience.
3. Situational explanations see obedience as a product of the situation rather than a reflection of personality.

Activity 1 Obeying orders

Item A The final solution

In 1941, Rudolf Hoess was placed in charge of the extermination camp at Auschwitz. He received his orders from the head of the SS in Berlin who, in turn, received his orders directly from the Fuhrer, Adolf Hitler. Hoess was told:

'The Fuhrer has ordered the final solution of the Jewish question and we – the SS – have to carry out this order. It will be onerous and difficult and will require your full personal commitment without regard for any difficulties that may arise.'

Hoess took his orders very seriously. He wrote, 'On receiving this grave order, I returned at once to Auschwitz'.

Five years later, Hoess made the following statement during his trial for war crimes in 1946.

'The final solution of the Jewish question meant the complete extermination of all Jews in Europe. I was ordered to establish extermination facilities at Auschwitz in June 1941.

I visited Treblinka to find out how they carried out their extermination. The camp commandant at Treblinka told me he had liquidated 80,000 in the course of half a year.

He used monoxide gas and I did not think his methods were very efficient. So when I set up the extermination building at Auschwitz, I used Zyklon B, which was crystallised prussic acid which we dropped into the death chamber from a small opening. It took from three to fifteen minutes to kill all the people in the death chamber, depending on climatic conditions. We knew when the people were dead because their screaming stopped. We usually waited about half an hour before we opened the doors and removed the bodies. After the bodies were removed our special commandos took off the rings and extracted the gold from the teeth of the corpses.

Another improvement we made over Treblinka was that we built our gas chambers to accommodate 2,000 people at one time, whereas at Treblinka their ten gas chambers only accommodated 200 people each.'

Quotations from Noakes & Pridham, 1988 and Brooman, 1985.

Auschwitz, 1945

Item B My Lai

The My Lai massacre took place on 16 March 1968 during the Vietnam War. Under the command of Lieutenant William Calley, US Army Charlie Company 'swept through' the small South Vietnamese village of My Lai. Calley ordered his men to shoot the villagers, whom he suspected of being enemy sympathisers. The official body count was 128 but unofficial estimates put the figure at 500. They were unarmed civilians and included women, children and old people.

One American soldier was asked to explain why he personally killed over 50 Vietnamese during the massacre. 'Why did I do it? Because I felt like I was ordered to do it, and it seemed like I was doing the right thing.'

Adapted from *The New York Times*, 25.11.1969

Item C What would you have done?

Many Americans were outraged when Lieutenant William Calley was tried and convicted for his part in the killing of Vietnamese civilians at My Lai. These Americans believed he was simply carrying out the policy set forth by his superiors. In a national sample, 51% said that if they had been soldiers in Vietnam and were ordered to kill innocent civilians, they would have done so. Given their view that one must obey orders, these people saw the Army's legal case against Calley as a betrayal. But other people in the sample took a different view, holding that we must each accept ultimate responsibility for our own actions.

Lieutenant William Calley

Adapted from Rubin & McNeil, 1987

Questions

1 Read Item A. Hoess was concerned about 'efficiency' and 'improvement' in his 'extermination facility'. What does this suggest about the way he saw his work?

2 On the basis of Items A, B and C, which best explains the behaviour of those who murdered innocent civilians – personality or situation?

3 People often say one thing and do another. Why is this important to bear in mind when interpreting the data from the national sample in Item C?

Unit 2 Experimental studies of obedience

KEY ISSUES

1 **What do experimental studies reveal about obedience?**

2 **What are the problems of studying obedience in laboratory situations?**

A number of experimental studies have investigated the degree to which obedience arises from the situation people find themselves in. It is easy to see how people are likely to obey commands they dislike or feel are morally wrong if the penalty for disobedience is imprisonment or death. But what if they are not forced? Will people still obey, even if obedience goes against their ethical values?

The answer appears to be yes. Contrary to popular belief, the high level of obedience Hitler's regime commanded in Germany and Austria (as well as in many occupied territories) was not in the main due to direct force. Evidence suggests that there was a mass willingness on behalf of tens of thousands of people to cooperate with the Nazi regime and obey Hitler's edicts, even to the extent of shopping neighbours to the Gestapo (the Nazi secret police) and helping to round up Jews to be sent to Auschwitz and other extermination camps (Goldhagen, 1996). This was commonly interpreted on the Allied side as being due to the German 'national character', which was depicted as authoritarian, militaristic and obedient. The American psychologist Stanley Milgram was sceptical of this idea, and thought it likely that obedience owed more to the situation than to culture or national character. He suspected that Americans, despite their perception of themselves as rugged individualists, would be just as likely to obey orders to harm others given the 'right' situation. It was this idea that Milgram set out to investigate in a series of experiments conducted in the early 1960s.

2.1 Stanley Milgram

The participants in Milgram's first experiment were forty men, aged between twenty and fifty, whose jobs ranged from unskilled labourers to school teachers and engineers (Milgram, 1963). They were recruited by a deceptive newspaper advertisement which asked for volunteers for a 'study of memory' rather than for the obedience experiment that Milgram conducted (see p 224). They were paid $4 plus travelling expenses for taking part in the experiment.

When the participants arrived they were told that the experiment was designed to investigate whether punishment improves learning. Each participant was told they would either play the role of 'teacher', or the role of 'learner'. The teacher would give the learner tests and deliver an electric shock – the punishment – for each incorrect answer. Each participant was introduced to another person – a mild-mannered, middle-aged man they thought was a fellow participant but who was in fact a 'stooge', a confederate working with Milgram. Then the participants and the confederate drew lots for their roles as teacher and learner but the draw was rigged – the genuine participants were always allocated the role of teacher while the confederate always played the role of learner. Several versions of the experiment were used. The following describes the first experiment.

The participants watched as the confederate was strapped into a chair – 'to prevent excessive movement' – and attached to electrodes – to deliver the electric shock. In practice no shock was delivered. The confederate was asked whether he had any medical conditions and announced he had a heart ailment.

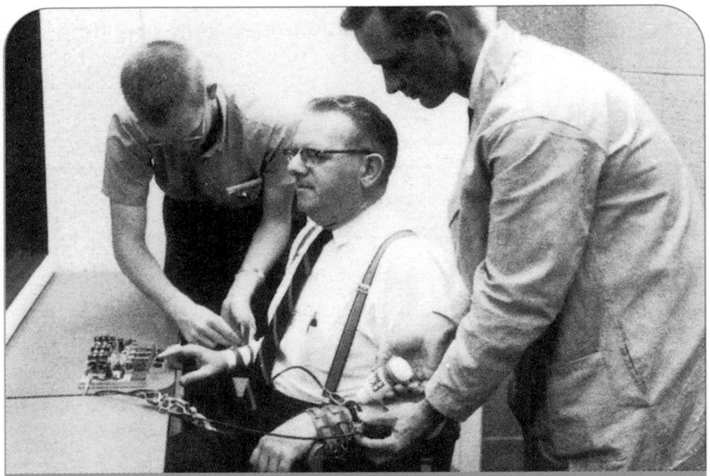

The experimenter (right) and a participant (left) attach electrodes to the confederate's wrists.

The participant was then led into another room and seated in front of a large generator. He was told that this generator could administer shocks to the confederate via the electrodes which had been attached to him. The confederate was out of sight in the next room but communication was made possible via an intercom. The participant was instructed to ask the confederate questions about word pairs. Each time the confederate made a mistake, the participant was told to administer an electric shock, increasing the voltage by 15 volts for each incorrect answer. The generator had a row of switches which indicated shocks from 15 volts up to 450 volts. The switches were labelled 'Slight Shock' to 'Danger – Severe Shock', with the final two switches being labelled XXX. The participant was given a sample electric shock of 45 volts to demonstrate that the generator was indeed capable of delivering a dose of electricity. This shock came from a hidden battery – the generator was a mock-up and incapable of generating electricity.

During the experiment the confederate kept making mistakes. He protested about the shocks, crying out in pain and saying that his heart was bothering him. Many of the participants were visibly upset. Some were laughing nervously – an indication of emotional disturbance. Signs of tension included trembling, stuttering, biting lips and digging fingernails into palms of hands. Three participants had uncontrollable seizures, one of which was severe enough to halt the experiment. They frequently asked the experimenter whether they should continue to administer shocks, many pleading to be allowed to stop.

The experimenter remained calm and responded with a standardised set of verbal prods.

1. Please continue.
2. The experiment requires you to continue.
3. It is absolutely essential that you continue.
4. You have no other choice, you *must* go on.

Only if the participant refused to continue after the fourth and final prod was the experiment terminated.

The results of the experiment were as follows. All the participants gave shocks up to and including the level of 'Intense Shock' as labelled on the generator. 65% of the participants continued to the maximum of 450 volts – they obeyed the instructions to the letter.

Follow-up experiments

In a series of follow-up experiments, Milgram (1974) investigated factors which may vary the level of obedience. They included the following.

Proximity of the victim The presence of the confederate in another room resulted in a psychological as well as a physical distance between him and the participant. The common phrase is 'out of sight, out of mind'. Participants could not see the suffering of their victim. They were less willing to follow orders when they could see the confederate and least willing when they were required to force his hand onto the electrode – then obedience fell from 65% to 30%.

Milgram (1974) draws a comparison with a bomber pilot to illustrate the importance of proximity. The pilot 'can reasonably suppose that his weapons will inflict suffering and death, yet this knowledge is divested of affect (emotion) and does not arouse in him an emotional response to the suffering he causes'. Distance prevents him from seeing the death and destruction his bombs produce.

Proximity of experimenter When the experimenter was in the same room as the participant, 'breathing down his neck' as it were, the level of obedience was high. If the experimenter was in another room, giving instructions over the telephone, obedience fell to 20.5%. In this situation, participants often said they were administering shocks when in fact they weren't doing so.

Perceived authority Because the experiment was conducted at Yale, a prestigious Ivy League university, the participants perceived it as very important. Because of the status of the university, they were convinced of the integrity of the experimenter. These factors encouraged them to obey the experimenter and continue with the experiment. When the experiment was conducted in a run-down office building and the experimenter did not wear a scientist's lab coat, obedience fell to 47.5%. Some of the participants questioned the legitimacy of the experimenter. This did not happen at Yale.

Whether or not people obey depends on how they perceive the person giving the orders. In one experiment, the experimenter and the confederate changed places. The experimenter told the participant to stop the shocks while the confederate told him to continue. In this situation all the participants refused to give further shocks. The demands of the experimenter – the authority figure – were clearly more influential.

Social support If a participant wanted to disobey the experimenter, he was more likely to do so if he was with other participants who supported his views. In one experiment Milgram introduced two confederates who refused to continue. The participants' obedience fell to 10%.

Individual differences Obedience depends in part on individual differences – differences in people's personalities, experiences, backgrounds and so on. Milgram found that participants who had gone on to higher education were less obedient, possibly because they had been taught to think for themselves and were more likely to be in occupations where they gave rather than received orders. He also found that participants with a military background tended to be more obedient, possibly because they had been trained to obey orders. Gender appeared to make no difference to levels of obedience. Milgram repeated his experiment using 40 female participants – 65% continued to the highest voltage level.

2.2 Methods

Milgram claimed that his experiments indicate that in the 'right' situation ordinary people will obey orders from those in authority, even if obedience goes against deeply held moral beliefs. A number of Milgram's critics reject this claim. They argue that his findings reflect flaws in the design of his experiment. They believe that the methods Milgram used in his research produced the behaviour he observed. In other words, the behaviour of his participants does not reflect how people would normally behave in response to orders from an authority figure.

Milgram's methodology has been criticised on two main grounds – *internal validity* and *external validity*.

Internal validity

An experiment has internal validity if it measures what it is intended to measure. Milgram's experiments were designed to measure obedience to authority. If they actually measured obedience, then they are internally valid. But did they measure what they were intended to measure?

Did Milgram's participants really believe that they were inflicting painful electric shocks on a middle-aged man with a heart condition? As with all laboratory experiments, participants may define the situation as 'artificial', 'unreal' and 'false'. As a result, they may see through Milgram's deception and realise they are not really inflicting painful shocks. They may 'play along' to please the experimenter and to earn their fees. They may pretend to show signs of distress – trembling, stuttering and groaning – in order to add realism to their performance (Orne & Holland, 1968). If this is the case, then Milgram's experiments are not measuring obedience to authority – they are not internally valid.

Milgram rejects these criticisms claiming that, 'with few exceptions subjects (participants) were convinced of the reality of the experimental situation' (Milgram, 1963). A questionnaire given to participants a year after the experiment asked if they believed they were really inflicting painful shocks. 56.1% 'fully believed', 24% 'had some doubts' but on balance believed, 11.4% had doubts but thought probably not, 6.1% 'just weren't sure' and only 2.4% were 'certain' the shocks were not real.

Were the signs of distress shown by the participants genuine? The answer is probably yes judging from the observations of those who watched the experiments. This is how one observer described a participant.

> 'I observed a mature and initially poised businessman enter the laboratory smiling and confident. Within 20 minutes he was reduced to a twitching, stuttering wreck, who was rapidly approaching a point of nervous collapse' (Milgram, 1963).

Participants interviewed after the experiment gave every indication that their distress was real. During the experiment, several had expressed their tension in terms of nervous laughter. They were at pains to point out that this did *not* mean they enjoyed inflicting shocks.

Milgram claims that his experiments were internally valid. But, even if this claim is accepted, can his findings be applied beyond the four walls of the laboratory? In other words, can his findings be generalised?

External validity

External validity refers to the extent to which the findings of a research study can be generalised to other settings, other people and other times. Can Milgram's findings be generalised to other settings outside the laboratory and outside the USA? Can they be generalised to other people? For example, do the findings of Milgram's first experiment apply to people other than American males between the ages of 20 and 50? And, do the findings apply to other time periods apart from the 1960s when Milgram conducted his experiments?

The laboratory setting Both the setting and the relationships involved in experiments are very different from the world outside the laboratory. In particular, the experimenter/participant relationship is distinct from all other relationships. Participants agree to do what the experimenter asks them within a limited time in a laboratory situation. They assume that the experimenter will not harm them and will take full responsibility for whatever happens in the experiment. Given this unique relationship and setting, it is not surprising that most of the participants in Milgram's experiments did what they were told and obeyed the experimenter. As a result, it is not possible to generalise from Milgram's findings since they simply reflect the experimenter/participant relationship (Orne & Holland, 1968).

Milgram (1992) makes the following response to this argument. He states that the relationship between experimenter and participant is little different from the relationship between any authority figure and those subject to their authority. Since the relationships are essentially the same, it is possible to generalise from the laboratory to the wider society. In view of this, Milgram claims that his experiments have high external validity.

People, settings and times As noted earlier, Milgram repeated his first experiment with 40 female participants. Sixty-five per cent continued to the highest voltage level, the same percentage as his male participants. This suggests that in terms of gender his findings can be generalised. Do they apply to people in other societies with different cultures? This question is examined in detail in Section 2.6. Various versions of Milgram's experiments have been conducted in a number of countries. Complete obedience – continuing to the highest voltage level – ranges from 16% to 90%, compared to 65% for Milgram's studies of US males and females. These differences may reflect differences in the experimental design and procedures and/or differences in culture between the participants. In view of this, it is not possible to say with any degree of certainty whether Milgram's findings can be generalised to other societies.

Nor is it possible to say whether Milgram's findings can be generalised to other time periods. Milgram's experiments were conducted in the 1960s. In the USA, the last version of his experiments was published in 1976. Because of changing ethical standards, researchers are no longer able to conduct this type of research. (The ethical issues raised by Milgram's research are examined in the following chapter.)

No firm conclusions can be reached about the external validity of Milgram's experiments. However, a number of studies using different methods and approaches have provided some support for his findings. Two of these studies will now be examined.

Key terms

Internal validity *The extent to which an experiment measures what it is intended to measure.*

External validity *The extent to which the findings of an experiment can be generalised; the extent to which they apply outside the laboratory.*

2.3 Obedience in a job interview

There is a further question about the external validity of Milgram's research. The participants had been told they were taking part in a memory and learning experiment. Then, with no warning, they were sat down in front of a shock generator and told to give shocks to an apparently unwilling victim. They had very little time to think about the situation and to consider what they should do. If they had the time – as they probably would in everyday life – would they have behaved in the same way? A possible answer to this question is given by the second experiment described below.

Two Dutch psychologists, Meeus and Raaijmakers (1987), designed a series of experiments which help to answer these questions. The experiments were a variation on Milgram's research. However, rather than inflicting physical harm, the participants were required to inflict psychological harm. They were asked to interview applicants for a job. Unknown to the participants, the applicants were confederates of the experimenter. At the time, unemployment in Holland was high – failing the interview would be a serious blow to the applicants who were all presented to the participants as unemployed. At various points in the interview, participants were told to make 'stress remarks' to put the applicant under pressure, for example, 'If you continue like this you'll fail the test' and 'This job is too difficult for you. You are more suited to lower functions'. Participants were told the job required people who could handle stress, and that it was therefore necessary to put the applicants under stress to ensure they would be able to cope with the demands of the job.

There were 15 'stress remarks' which increased steadily in severity, just as the shock levels in Milgram's experiments. Participants were instructed to make *all* the remarks – they must continue no matter how much the applicant complained or appeared to suffer. They were prodded by the experimenter, as in the Milgram experiments, and told it was necessary to see how the applicant performed under stress.

At the start of the interview, applicants appeared confident, assured and at ease. As the interview developed they became increasingly distressed. They complained that the remarks were ruining their chances of getting a job they desperately needed. They pleaded with the interviewer to stop making abusive remarks, they became angry and refused to answer further questions and finally fell into a state of despair. As a result, they failed to get the job.

Despite finding the interview distasteful, unfair and humiliating for the applicant, 22 out of the 24 participants continued to the end. They obeyed the experimenter – the authority figure. In a control group without a prodding experimenter, *none* of the participants continued to the end.

As noted earlier, one of the criticisms of Milgram's experiments was that the participants had little opportunity to consider their actions. As such, the experiments lacked external validity – in real life people usually have time to think about what they should do. To counter this criticism, Meeus and Raaijmakers conducted a further experiment. They sent participants a letter detailing the interview procedure a week before the experiment. This gave them plenty of time outside the laboratory in their normal surroundings to decide whether they would go ahead and behave in this way. Despite this time to consider, the same proportion of participants continued to the end of the experiment as those in the 'no-warning' experiment. This suggests that, at least in this respect, the experiment was externally valid – in other words the findings could be generalised to situations outside the laboratory (Meeus & Raaijmakers, 1987).

2.4 Obedience in a hospital

So far, this unit has examined studies of obedience conducted in laboratories. Because laboratories are to some extent artificial and unreal settings, these studies are open to the criticism of lacking both internal and external validity. The following study of obedience is a field experiment – an experiment conducted in a normal, everyday social setting.

The experiment was conducted by Hofling and his colleagues (Hofling et al., 1966). The setting was a number of psychiatric hospitals in the USA. The participants were 22 staff nurses on night duty. An unknown 'doctor' (actually a confederate of Hofling) telephoned each staff nurse with instructions to give medication to a patient. The medication was a drug with a maximum daily dosage of 10mg. This was clearly stated on the label. The doctor asked the nurses to administer 20mg, twice the recommended maximum. The doctor said that he would sign the necessary authorisation papers when he arrived at the hospital in about 10 minutes time.

Twenty-one out of the twenty-two nurses obeyed the telephoned instruction and prepared the medication before they were stopped and the situation explained to them. In doing so, they broke a number of important hospital rules. First, they accepted instructions over the telephone, something which is forbidden as they cannot be certain that the caller is a genuine doctor. Second, they accepted instructions from a doctor they had never heard of, which is forbidden for the same reason. Third, the medication was an unauthorised drug for the wards in question. Fourth, doubling the maximum dosage might seriously endanger the patients.

Why were the nurses prepared to obey the doctor? In their role as nurses, it is the norm to accept orders from the higher authority of a doctor. In addition, the doctor who telephoned promised to take responsibility by signing the authorisation papers. When questioned later, the nurses said that doctors often telephoned instructions and got very annoyed if nurses attempted to stick to hospital regulations.

Hofling interviewed 12 experienced nurses asking them what they would have done in this situation. Ten said they would refuse to follow the doctor's instructions. He also interviewed 21 student nurses, asking the same question. All of them stated that they would disobey the doctor. This is important as it suggests that what people say in an interview may be very different from what they do in everyday life.

Hofling's research is important because it studied obedience in a real-life setting. As such, it is more realistic than the relatively artificial context of the laboratory.

2.5 Explaining obedience

This section examines theories which have been put forward to explain obedience.

Seeing authority as legitimate

People tend to obey others if they recognise their authority as morally right and/or legally based. This response to legitimate authority is learned in a variety of situations, for example in the family, school and workplace. It is particularly obvious in organisations with a clearly marked hierarchy of authority such as the army and the civil service. Although the pressures to obey are not as severe as in totalitarian societies such as Nazi Germany, they are still powerful. Disobedience may result in a reprimand, demotion or loss of employment.

Obedience to legitimate authority can become 'second nature' – unthinking and taken for granted. It can also lead to the removal of individual responsibility – since people are only following orders they cannot be held personally responsible for the consequences. Their job is simply to translate the order into action as efficiently as possible. In this respect, obedience has nothing necessarily to do with personality. Instead, it is the result of a social situation – learning to obey and being subject to legitimate authority.

Milgram saw obedience as an essential part of all social life. In his words, 'Obedience is as basic an element in the structure of social life as one can point to. Some system of authority is a requirement of all communal living, and it is only the man living in isolation who is not forced to respond, through defiance or submission, to the commands of others' (Milgram, 1974).

Obedience to authority is learned from an early age, it is reinforced in schools and required in the workplace. Its importance can be seen clearly from both Milgram's and Hofling's experiments.

Milgram's experimenter was in charge, he was an authority figure who directed the participants. His integrity and status were indicated by the prestige of the institution – Yale University; by the significance of the experiment – an important scientific investigation; and by the uniform he wore – a lab coat. When these factors were removed and the experiment was conducted in a rundown office building, the participants who administered the maximum shock dropped from 65% to 47.5%.

The nurses in Hofling's experiment were used to the hierarchy of authority in the hospital. Under normal circumstances there was no question that doctors gave orders and nurses obeyed. Nor was there much question that doctors could bend the rules, judging from what the nurses said after the experiment.

The perception of authority as legitimate provides a major explanation for obedience.

Allocation of responsibility

During Milgram's experiments, a number of participants pestered the experimenter to take responsibility for the situation. They typically asked, 'Who is going to take the responsibility if anything happens to that gentleman?' They were determined to absolve themselves of any personal responsibility and to see themselves as simply carrying out orders from a higher authority. Milgram called this 'being another person's agent', a situation known as the *agentic state*. During the debrief one participant who had administered the maximum shock indicated that he wouldn't have been overconcerned if the victim died – he was just doing a job he was told to do.

In Hofling's hospital experiment, personal responsibility was partly removed from the nurses. The doctor promised to sign the authorisation papers when he arrived at the hospital ten minutes after his phone call.

There is considerable evidence both from experiments and real life that the removal of personal responsibility encourages obedience. Time and time again, in war crimes trials from World War II in the 1940s to the civil wars in the former Yugoslavia in the 1990s, those on trial stated they were simply following orders, doing their job, and therefore not personally responsible for their actions.

The just world hypothesis

If people are ordered to inflict harm on others, they may justify their actions with the *just world hypothesis.* Lerner (1980) argues that people have a need to believe that the world is fair and just, and that everybody gets what they deserve. Victims are often said to deserve their fate. For example, some people see AIDS as God's punishment of gays for their 'deviant' sexual behaviour. Nazi propaganda stated in no uncertain terms that the Jews deserved everything they got. They were portrayed as responsible for practically every ill of German society, from inflation, to unemployment, to crime, to disease. This is known as *victim derogation.*

Inflicting pain on others can result in *cognitive dissonance* – a clash between two contradictory attitudes held by the same person. Festinger (1957) suggested that if a person holds two conflicting views, or if their actions contradict their beliefs, then a state of tension results which must be reduced. People need consistency, they strive to match their attitudes and behaviour.

Many of Milgram's participants experienced cognitive dissonance. They saw themselves as kind and decent people, yet found themselves inflicting pain on another human being. This produced a contradiction between their self-perception and their behaviour. The resulting tension led to cognitive dissonance. Rather than changing their self-perception and seeing themselves as cruel and inhumane, they were more likely to derogate the victim and see his suffering as deserved.

The just world hypothesis can resolve the contradictions which produce cognitive dissonance. It can state that bad things happen to those who deserve them. In this respect, it can encourage following orders to inflict pain on others.

Dehumanisation

Dehumanisation means denying people their humanity. They may be seen as less than human, or as an impersonal object, or as something that doesn't really exist. Dehumanisation can encourage people to obey orders which involve harming others.

There are many techniques for dehumanising the victim. One of the simplest is to forget about them. For example, one of Milgram's participants stated, 'You really begin to forget that there's a guy out there, even though you can hear him ... I just concentrated on pressing the switches and reading the words' (Milgram, 1974). Another method is to remove a person's individuality. Victims of torture sometimes have their heads covered with bags, so that the torturers cannot see their victims' faces and are not moved by their humanity. Defining people as less than human can provide justification for inhuman treatment. For example, slaves have often been seen as a lower form of human life.

Language is an important part of this process. Veterans of the Vietnam war speak of 'search and destroy' missions and 'sweeping through' enemy villages. Often this involved the murder of innocent civilians. When confronted with this reality, the veterans were uncomfortable and preferred their own sanitised terms. Similarly, the Nazis spoke of 'the final solution' which really meant the genocide of the Jewish people. In the civil war in the former Yugoslavia, the slaughter of thousands of men, women and children was glossed with the phrase 'ethnic cleansing'. And Nato officials often referred to the deaths of civilians as a result of their air strikes in Serbia as 'collateral damage'. In Milgram's words, 'Euphemisms come to dominate language as a means of guarding the person against the full moral implications of his acts' (Milgram, 1974).

Dehumanisation means that normal standards for treating human beings can be ignored, morality can be suspended, and orders which result in harm to others can be accepted and carried out and justified.

Gradual commitment

Milgram's participants were encouraged to obey the experimenter by the gradual steps they were asked to take. They started with a practice session, then went on to the real thing, beginning with the 15 volt switch and gradually moving up the voltage scale. The initial act of obedience – administering 15 volts – was not too difficult. The increases were gradual – in 15 volt increments – each step only slightly worse than the one before. What difference would an extra 15 volts make? Not a lot. However, a jump from 15 to 450 volts is something else. It is unlikely that the participants would have taken this step.

The first step in this gradual commitment is known as the *foot-in-the-door effect* (Freedman & Fraser, 1966). Agreeing to a small, seemingly harmless effect can pave the way to obeying larger, more harmful orders.

Key terms

Agentic state *Being another person's agent and, as a result, not being personally responsible for the consequences of following orders given by that person.*

Just world hypothesis *The idea that people need to believe that the world is just and fair and that everybody gets what they deserve.*

Victim derogation *Reducing the dignity and worth of a victim, so making them appear more deserving of their suffering.*

Cognitive dissonance *A clash between two conflicting beliefs held by a person, or a contradiction between their beliefs and behaviour. It results in a state of tension.*

Dehumanisation *Denying people their humanity – seeing them as less than human or as impersonal objects. It means that normal standards for treating human beings can be ignored.*

Foot-in-the-door effect *The first step in a commitment to a path of action.*

Activity 2 Why obedience?

Item A Learning to obey

Children are taught to obey from an early age. They are told what to wear, how to eat and drink, how to go to the toilet and so on. Lessons learned during childhood often last a lifetime. As the following quotation suggests, this may well be essential for the wellbeing of human society. 'Every day society is submitted to a terrible invasion: within it a multitude of small barbarians is born. They would quickly overthrow the whole social order and all the institutions of society if they were not well-disciplined and educated.'

R. Pinot quoted in Goodman, 1967

Item B Mass suicide

In 1978, 913 members of an American religious cult, the People's Temple, were found dead, deep in the jungle in Guyana. They had moved there four years earlier from San Francisco and set up an agricultural commune called Jonestown. The cult leader, the Reverend Jim Jones, had ordered his followers to take their own lives as a sign of their religious dedication. They drank a mixture of Kool-Aid (a soft drink) and cyanide. According to the few survivors, most people took their lives willingly, with mothers giving the cyanide to their children, then drinking it themselves.

Adapted from *Chronicle of America*, 1989

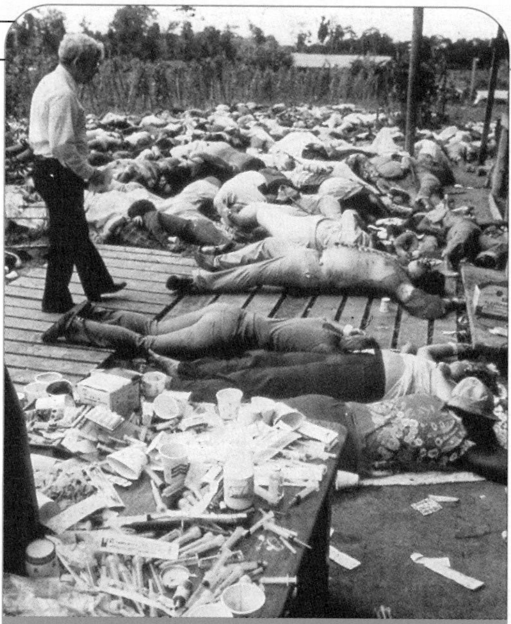

Dead cult members in Jonestown

Item C Authority, obedience and blame

After Germany's defeat in 1945, 21 leading Nazis were put on trial for war crimes at Nuremberg. All pleaded their innocence, none accepted personal blame. When presented with incriminating evidence, most claimed they were simply following orders issued by a higher authority. Former Nazi SS officer Adolf Eichmann admitted at his trial in 1960 that he had played a part in 'liquidating' the Jews. In his defence he claimed he was simply doing his job, following orders, and was 'only a little sausage' in the Nazi war machine. The historian Klaus Fischer described him as a 'normal' human being 'who followed orders without question and served his employer loyally and efficiently'. Looking back on his time as Commandant of Auschwitz concentration camp, Rudolph Hoess wrote, 'Unknowingly, I was a cog in the chain of the great extermination machine of the Third Reich'. Apart from their 'work', most of these men appeared to live normal lives, with families and friends, and saw themselves as decent, law-abiding citizens.

Adapted from Lee 1989 and Fischer 1995

Item D 'My Struggle'

Mein Kampf ('My Struggle') was written by Adolf Hitler. Published in 1925, it became a bestseller in Germany. Hitler wrote: 'Was there any form of filth or crime without at least one Jew involved in it? If you cut such a sore, you find – like a maggot in a rotting body – a Jew. By defending myself against the Jew, I am fighting for the work of the Lord.'

This cartoon appeared in the German magazine Der Sturmer ('The Stormer') in 1934. It shows Jews draining the blood of innocent German children.

Item E 'Gooks'

Vietnamese prisoners led by US marines during the Vietnam war. The Americans referred to the Vietnamese as 'gooks'.

Item F Gradual commitment

The 1967-1974 Greek military regime had great success in taking ordinary civilians and making them into official torturers. The military rulers selected stable, well-adjusted fishermen, farmers, carpenters, civil servants, shoemakers, cooks, lorry drivers, and small businessmen for 'special training.' During their training, the men were gradually introduced to brutality. They were often kept from eating, urinating, and defecating for days at a time. They were ordered to eat lighted cigarettes. They were 'forced to run while beaten until there were drops of sweat hanging from the ceiling' (Haritos-Fatouros, 1988).

At the end of the training, the apprentice torturers had to swear on their knees their undying allegiance and obedience to the military rulers. After enduring torture themselves, they first watched more experienced torturers and then gradually joined in unbelievably sadistic torture of citizens who were suspected of being disloyal to the military rulers. Through these carefully orchestrated indoctrination procedures, ordinary citizens were turned into obedient and efficient torturers.

Adapted from Lord, 1997

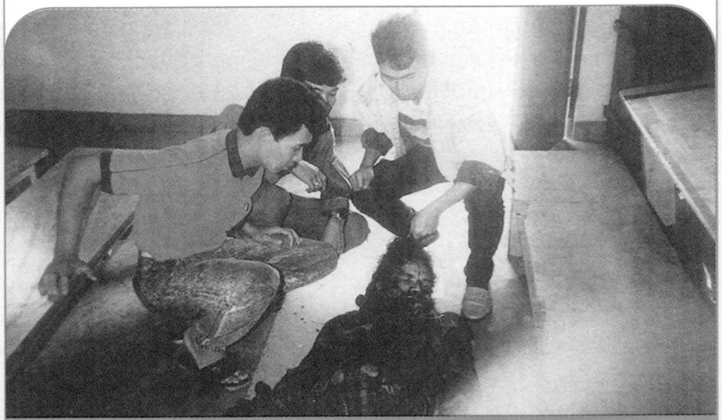

Indonesian secret police torturing an East Timorese man

Questions

1 With reference to Item A, briefly discuss the view that,
a) Obedience is learned from an early age.
b) Obedience is necessary for human society.

2 Use the idea of legitimate authority to explain the mass suicide described in Item B.

3 Read Item C. Explain the relationship between responsibility, obedience and authority.

4 Read Item D. Use the ideas of the just world hypothesis and cognitive dissonance to explain obedience to orders to commit atrocities against Jewish people.

5 Look at Item E.
a) How might the term 'gook' help to dehumanise the Vietnamese?
b) How might this make it easier for American soldiers to obey orders during the Vietnam war?

6 Explain the part played by gradual commitment in ensuring that the torturers in Item F obeyed orders.

2.6 Culture and obedience

Most of the studies of obedience have been conducted in the USA. Many have been conducted in laboratory settings where the participants have tended to be white American middle-class males. Can the results of these studies be generalised to other groups within the same society or to other societies? For example, can they be generalised to ethnic groups within the USA, such as African Americans and Hispanics, or to countries outside the USA, particularly non-Western societies?

This leads to the question of *culture*. Culture is the learned, shared behaviour of members of society and includes social norms, values and beliefs. Culture varies from society to society. To some extent, each society has its own distinctive norms, values and beliefs which provide guidelines and directives for the behaviour of its members.

Within each society, particular groups have their own *subculture*. They share some of the norms and values of the wider society but also have their own norms and values. For example, many Hispanics in the USA speak Spanish and have distinctive tastes in food and music.

To what extent will cultures and subcultures affect behaviour in terms of obedience, and, in particular, laboratory experiments on obedience? The short answer is we don't really know. However, it is very unlikely they will have no effect.

Milgram's experiments have been conducted in a number of countries. Complete obedience – where participants continued to the maximum shock level – ranged from over 90% in Spain, to over 80% in Italy, Germany and Austria, to 73% in Jordan, 50% in the UK, and 40% for Australian males and only 16% for Australian females. To some researchers, these results generally support Milgram's findings. They indicate that his findings are not limited to the USA, that they are not simply a product of American culture. Other researchers disagree. They see the findings from various countries as very different. Complete obedience ranges from 90% to 16% compared to 65% for Milgram's studies of US males and females.

Not all the experiments conducted outside the USA are exact replications of Milgram's research – the samples and the procedures are not exactly the same. For example, the Jordanian research, where complete obedience was 73%, was conducted by a female experimenter and the participants were children, aged 6 to 16 of both sexes (Shanab & Yahya, 1977). In the USA, Milgram found the same level of complete obedience for males and females – 65%. In Australia, the figure for male participants was 40%, for female participants, 16%. Part of this gender difference may be due to the fact that Australian women were asked to give shocks to a female 'victim', whereas the 'victims' for Australian men and Milgram's participants were male (Kilham & Mann, 1974).

It is not possible to say whether the variation in findings between countries is due to differences in experimental design or to differences in culture. The answer may well be both (Smith & Bond, 1993).

Levels of obedience in laboratory settings depend in part on the meanings given to laboratories, science and scientists. And these meanings might differ from culture to culture. In the West, science and scientists usually have high status. As a result, a scientist in a laboratory situation may well command a high level of obedience, as Milgram's experiments indicate. This may not apply to other societies. For example, after the 1979 revolution in Iran, universities were closed and scientists who were trained in the West were at best regarded with suspicion. Fathali Moghaddam, who was there at the time, writes, 'In this context, the scientist in the white lab coat would have made a pathetic authority figure, but the mullah (religious leader) would have made a very powerful one' (Moghaddam et al., 1993).

Moving outside the laboratory, there is plenty of evidence to indicate that culture has an important influence on obedience. Studies of obedience training of children in different cultures shows considerable variation in the types and levels of obedience required (Berry et al., 1992). And as cultures change, so do expected levels of obedience. This can be seen by comparing family relationships in the West in the 19th century with those of today. The authoritarian

Victorian husband and father is, for most women and children, a thing of the past.

The psychology of obedience has been largely based on studies conducted in American society by American social psychologists. A considerable amount of research is needed before we know whether or not these findings apply to different societies with different cultures.

Summary

1. Milgram's experiments indicate that most people will obey authority figures when placed in the 'right' situation. Obedience in such situations is likely even if it results in harm to others.
2. Critics of Milgram argue that his experiments lacked both internal validity and external validity.
3. Support for Milgram's findings comes from experiments in Holland where participants had time to consider whether or not to obey orders and from a field experiment in American hospitals – a real life situation – where nurses obeyed orders with potentially harmful consequences.
4. Obedience is often a response to legitimate authority – authority regarded as morally right and/or legal.
5. People are more likely to obey if they can absolve themselves of responsibility for their actions.
6. Where obedience results in harm to others, people are more likely to obey if a) their actions can be justified by the just world hypothesis – the world is fair and people get what they deserve; b) their 'victims' can be dehumanised – deprived of their human characteristics; c) their commitment is gradual.
7. Studies of obedience have been largely based on American culture. Because of this, we cannot be sure whether or not the results can be applied to other cultures.

Unit 3 Resistance to authority

KEY ISSUES

1. **How important is the example and support of others for resisting authority?**
2. **Do individual differences play a part in resistance?**
3. **What part can conformity to group norms play in resistance?**

Units 1 and 2 may have given the impression that resistance to authority is a rare occurrence. It isn't. For example, many individuals conscripted into the armed forces, such as conscientious objectors, refuse to join. During the Vietnam War, thousands of American 'draft dodgers' avoided conscription, either through opposition to the war or simply for self-preservation. During the Nazi regime, many German citizens sheltered Jews and helped to smuggle them out of the country. Millions of people have joined together to overthrow established authority as in the French revolution of 1789 and the Russian revolution of 1917. And it is important to remember that 35% of Milgram's participants refused to go further than the 'intense shock' level, despite being told they '*must* go on'.

3.1 Social support

There is evidence to indicate that when a person is provided with social support and/or role models for resisting authority, they are more likely to disobey directives from above. In other words, if an individual joins with others to resist, or is presented with the example of others resisting, then disobedience is more likely. Often both kinds of social support – joining with others and the presence of role models for resistance – occur in the same social situation.

Milgram's experiments In one experiment, Milgram assigned two confederates to join the participants in the role of teacher. The first confederate refused to continue beyond the 150 volt shock, the second beyond the 210 volt shock. In this situation, only 10% of the participants obeyed the experimenter and continued to the highest voltage level. Those who refused to go further were supported by the role models provided by the confederates.

The MHRC experiment The importance of social support can be seen from an experiment designed to encourage resistance to authority (Gamson et al.,1982). Participants were contacted by a non-existent company, MHRC – Manufacturers' Human Relations Consultants – and asked to take part in discussions about how legal cases are affected by the views of the local community. They were placed in groups of nine and asked to discuss the following case. They gave MHRC permission to videotape their discussions.

Mr C was manager of a petrol station. The oil company which owned the station hired a private detective to investigate his lifestyle. Mr C was living with a woman but they were not married. The company cancelled his franchise on the station, claiming that his behaviour offended the moral standards of the local community and would result in loss of business. Mr C sued the oil company for breach of contract and invasion of privacy.

After a general discussion, the experimenter – who called himself the coordinator – asked three members of each group to argue that Mr C's domestic arrangements had caused them offence. A further three participants from each group were then asked to do the same. Finally, each group member was asked to speak individually. They were told to say that Mr C's behaviour was offensive, that he should lose his franchise and that they intended to boycott the service station. The coordinator then asked them to sign affidavits – written statements taken under oath – allowing MHRC to edit the videotapes as they saw fit and to use them as evidence in court.

Most of the participants objected strongly to this procedure. They realised that their 'evidence' was being distorted and insisted on an assurance that the court would be told that these weren't their real views. There were 33 groups in the experiment. In 16 groups, every member refused to sign the affidavit, in 9 a majority refused and in the remaining 8 a minority refused. Most participants therefore resisted authority.

Why did so many participants disobey the coordinator? First, the experiment was designed to encourage resistance. Mr C's treatment by MHRC was clearly unacceptable to most fair-minded people. Judging from the results of a questionnaire given before the discussions, most participants saw nothing wrong with his behaviour. In addition, asking the participants to argue against their own views then directing them to sign affidavits allowing MHRC to use their statements as evidence in court clearly violated normal standards of behaviour. Second, the participants had the example and support of other group members for resistance. During the discussions they were given breaks which provided ample opportunity to share their views with others and question the morality of the coordinator's directives. During these breaks, the decision to disobey was formulated and often became a group norm.

Moving from small-scale experiments to the wider society, there is considerable evidence that resistance to authority is often a collective act involving role models for resistance and support from like-minded others. This can be seen in strikes, protests, demonstrations, riots and revolutions.

3.2 Attitudes and individual differences

As discussed earlier, Milgram found that individual differences – differences in attitudes, experiences and backgrounds – influenced whether or not people resisted authority. One of his participants, Gretchen Brandt, refused to go beyond the 210 volt level. She was raised in Nazi Germany and told the experimenter, 'Perhaps we have seen too much pain'. Another participant, who had lived in Holland during the Nazi occupation, also refused to continue to the maximum voltage. These participants had been sickened by the suffering they had seen during the Nazi regime and regarded the pain apparently inflicted in Milgram's experiments as morally unacceptable. Compared to the participants who obeyed, they were calm and self-assured – they were in no doubt that their refusal was right.

In the MHRC experiment, most of the groups who disobeyed contained members with previous experience of dissent – they had participated in strikes, protests and demonstrations against authority. They often provided role models for other group members.

Participants' attitudes towards authority were assessed by a questionnaire given at the start of the MHRC experiment. There was a close link between anti-authority attitudes and disobedience on the one hand, and pro-authority attitudes and obedience on the other. Thus members of groups with a high level of pro-authority attitudes were most likely to obey and sign the affidavit.

Attitudes on their own, however, do not provide a sufficient explanation for obedience and resistance. Almost all of Milgram's participants were disturbed about the pain they thought they had inflicted – after the experiment many expressed dismay about their behaviour. But the pressure of the situation led them to shelve their attitudes and beliefs and do as they were told. Situational forces and constraints often outweigh attitudes and beliefs.

3.3 The role of conformity in disobedience

The previous chapter indicated the power of the group to enforce conformity to group norms and group standards. How far was the disobedience of participants in the MHRC experiment due to conformity to group norms rather than resistance to authority? There is evidence which suggests that for some participants, their refusal to obey the coordinator was due mainly to social pressures to conform to group norms. When faced with the choice of obedience or conformity, many participants 'were uncertain at this point, waiting to see what others would do, delaying decision as long as possible. Ultimately, they were faced with an unavoidable choice – to sign or not to sign – and loyalty to the group became one major factor in their decision.' One participant stood up to the coordinator, making it clear where the strongest pressure lay. 'I didn't personally say anything I didn't believe, but I'm not going to sign this either, if the rest of the group isn't signing' (Gamson et al., 1982).

Evaluation

Studies of resistance to authority indicate there are many factors involved. It is difficult to tease out these factors and weigh their influence. For example, just how important were social support, individual differences and conformity to the results of the MHRC experiment?

Much of the research on resistance to authority is based on laboratory experiments. To what extent can conclusions based on such artificial social situations be generalised to the real world? As the following activity indicates, this world is a lot messier than controlled experiments which have been set up to assess the importance of specific variables.

Key terms

Social support *Support provided by others for an individual.*

Individual differences *Differences in personality, attitudes, experiences and social factors (eg, gender, ethnicity, social class and culture) between people.*

Summary

1. It appears easier for groups rather than individuals to resist authority. This is probably due to the influence of social support.
2. Individual differences help to explain why some rather than others resist authority.
3. In a group context, conformity to group norms can increase resistance.

Activity 3 Resisting authority

Item A Tiananmen Square

In April 1989, hundreds of thousands of students, supported by people from all walks of life, gathered in Tiananmen Square in Beijing. They were demanding democratic reforms and protesting against the autocratic leadership of the People's Republic of China. The demonstration developed into an occupation of the Square and the demonstrators ignored government orders to disperse and return to their homes.

On May 20th the government ordered the army to clear the Square. For nearly two weeks the troops, many of them young, inexperienced conscripts, could not – or chose not to – obey those orders. Late in the night of June 23rd, seasoned troops, backed by tanks and armoured cars were sent in. They fired indiscriminately, killing many hundreds, perhaps thousands.

Adapted from Spence & Chin, 1996

A student blocks the path of a column of tanks in Tiananmen Square

Item B Conscientious objection

On August 18 1916, at an army barracks at Warley in Essex, 26-year-old Clifford Allen, a pacifist, was court-martialled for refusing to agree to any form of military or non-combatant service. He told the officers trying him, 'I believe in the inherent worth and sanctity of every human personality, irrespective of the nation to which a man belongs'.

Adapted from Gilbert, 1994

Item C Resistance groups

Hans and Sophie were brother and sister. They were members of the White Rose, a resistance group which opposed Hitler's rule in Nazi Germany. They distributed leaflets which were highly critical of the Nazi regime. In 1943 they were arrested by the Gestapo, Hitler's secret police. Their sister Inge wrote the following account of Hans and Sophie's last days.

'Everyone who came into contact with Hans and Sophie – the other prisoners, the pastors at the prison, the guards, and even the Gestapo officers – were deeply moved by their courage and their noble bearing. Their calm and composure made for a strange contrast to the hectic tension of that place. Their activities worried party and government officials right up to the top levels.

Two days after their arrest, it became clear to them that they could expect the death sentence. There was only one thing to do: remain prudent and rational, involve as few people as possible, and embody, in all clarity, the freedom of the human spirit.

When the last morning came, Hans asked his cellmate to bid goodbye to our parents. Then he gave him his hand, kindly, almost ceremoniously, and said, 'We want to say goodbye while we're still alone'. With that, he turned around without a word and wrote something on the white prison wall. There was silence. He had barely put the pencil down when the guard came to handcuff him and lead him into court. The words on the wall were Goethe's words, words which his father had often murmured when pacing back and forth, the pathos of which had sometimes made Hans smile: *Allen Gewalten zum Trutz sich erhalten* (To stand defiant before overwhelming power).

When Sophie left her cell for the last time, a piece of paper remained behind – an indictment, in one word, Freedom.'

Adapted from Steinhoff, Pechel & Showalter, 1991.

Questions

1 Read Item A.
   a) Assess the importance of social support in resisting authority.
   b) Why did the army send in 'seasoned' troops?

2 How do Clifford Allen's words in Item B help to explain his resistance to authority?

3 Read Item C. Explain Hans and Sophie's behaviour while in prison.

References

Adorno, T.W., Frenkel-Brunswik, E., Levinson, D.J. & Stanford, R.M. (1950). *The authoritarian personality.* New York: Harper.

Arendt, H. (1963). *Eichmann in Jerusalem: A report on the banality of evil.* New York: Viking.

Berry, J.W., Poortinga, Y.H., Segall, M.H. & Dasen, P.R. (Eds.) (1992). *Cross-cultural psychology: Research and applications.* Cambridge: Cambridge University Press.

Brooman, J. (1985). *Hitler's Germany.* Harlow: Longman.

Chronicle of America. (1989). Farnborough: J L International Publishing.

Festinger, L. (1957). *A theory of cognitive dissonance.* Stanford, CA: Stanford Univerity Press.

Fischer, K.P. (1995). *Nazi Germany: A new history.* London: Constable.

Freedman, J.L. & Fraser, S.C. (1966). Compliance without pressure: The foot-in-the-door technique. *Journal of Personality and Social Psychology, 4,* 195-202.

Gamson, W.B., Fireman, B. & Rytina, S. (1982). *Encounters with unjust authority.* Homewood, ILL: Dorsey Press.

Gilbert, M. (1994). *First World War.* London: BCA.

Goldhagen, D.J. (1996). *Hitler's willing executioners: Ordinary Germans and the Holocaust.* Boston: Little Brown.

Goodman, M.E. (1967). *The individual and culture.* Homewood: Dorsey.

Halonen, J.S. (1986). *Teaching critical thinking in psychology.* Milwaukee, WI: Alverno Productions.

Haritos-Fatouros, M. (1988). The official torturer: A learning model for obedience to the authority of violence. *Journal of Applied Social Psychology, 18,* 1107-1120.

Hofling, K.C., Brotzman, E., Dalrymple, S., Graves, N. & Pierce, C.M. (1966). An experimental study in the nurse-physician relationship. *Journal of Nervous and Mental Disorders, 143,* 171-180.

Kilham, W. & Mann, L. (1974). Level of destructive obedience as a function of transmitter and executant roles in the Milgram obedience paradigm. *Journal of Personality and Social Psychology, 29,* 696-702.

Lee, S. (1989). *Nazi Germany.* Oxford: Heinemann.

Lerner, M.J. (1980). *The belief in a just world: A fundamental delusion.* New York: Plenum.

Lord, C.G. (1997). *Social psychology.* Fort Worth: Harcourt Brace.

Meeus, W.H.J. & Raaijmakers, Q.A.W. (1987). Administrative obedience as a social phenomenon. In W. Doise & S. Moscovici (Eds.), *Current issues in European social psychology* (Vol.2). Cambridge: Cambridge University Press.

Milgram, S. (1963). Behavioral study of obedience. *Journal of Abnormal and Social Psychology, 67,* 371-378.

Milgram, S. (1965). Some conditions of obedience and disobedience to authority. *Human Relations, 18,* 57-76.

Milgram, S. (1974). *Obedience to authority.* London: Tavistock.

Milgram, S. (1992). *The individual in a social world* (2nd ed.). New York: McGraw-Hill.

Moghaddam, F.M., Taylor, D.M. & Wright, S.C. (1993). *Social psychology in cross-cultural perspective.* New York: W. H. Freeman.

Noakes, J. & Pridham, G. (Eds.) (1988). *Nazism 1919-1945.* Exeter: University of Exeter Press.

Orne, M.T. & Holland, C.C. (1968). On the ecological validity of laboratory experiments. *International Journal of Psychology, 6,* 282-293.

Rubin, Z. & McNeil, E.B. (1987). *Psychology: Being human* (4th ed.). New York: Harper & Row.

Shanab, M.E. & Yahya, K.A. (1977). A behavioural study of obedience in children. *Journal of Personality and Social Psychology, 35,* 530-536.

Smith, P.B. & Bond, M.H. (1993). *Social psychology across cultures: Analysis and perspectives.* Hemel Hempstead: Harvester Wheatsheaf.

Spence, J. & Chin, A. (1996). *The Chinese century.* London: Harper Collins.

Steinhoff, J., Pechel, D. & Showalter, D. (1991). *Voices from the Third Reich: An oral history.* London: Grafton Books.

Zimbardo, P.G., McDermott, M., Jansz, J. & Metaal, N. (1995). *Psychology: A European text.* London: Harper Collins.

15 Ethics and research

Introduction

Ethics are a set of moral principles, a set of beliefs about what is right and wrong. In terms of research, ethics are the moral principles which guide research. Psychological associations in many countries now have a set of ethical guidelines for conducting research. Psychology departments in universities usually have an ethics committee to ensure that research conducted by members of the department is in line with these guidelines.

There is a growing awareness that those who participate in research have rights and that researchers have responsibilities and obligations. For example, should participants be informed about the purpose of the research and what exactly their participation involves? Should researchers make every effort to ensure that participants come to no physical or psychological harm? Is it ever justifiable to deceive participants about the purpose of the research and the true nature of the tasks they may be asked to perform? These are some of the questions this chapter examines.

Chapter summary

- **Unit 1 looks at the development of ethical guidelines for research. It outlines recent guidelines, focusing on those of the British Psychological Society.**
- **Unit 2 examines the ethics of Milgram's obedience research.**
- **Unit 3 considers the ethical issues raised by Zimbardo's prison simulation experiment.**

Unit 1 Ethical guidelines for research

KEY ISSUES

1. **How have ethical guidelines for research developed?**
2. **What are the main ethical issues in research with human participants?**

1.1 The development of ethical guidelines

The Nuremberg Code

After World War II (1939-1945) Nazi doctors stood trial at Nuremberg for experiments they conducted on prisoners in German concentration camps. The world was horrified by the revelations of their 'research'. Jews, Gypsies, Poles and Russians were subjected to appalling treatment in the name of science. They were thrown into icy water to see how they would react to extreme cold. Every detail of their behaviour was clinically and carefully recorded – how they writhed in pain, foamed at the mouth and went into death rattles. Other experiments included infecting prisoners with malaria, typhoid and jaundice, dosing or injecting them with a variety of poisons, and placing them in decompression chambers which sometimes resulted in ruptured lungs and death (Fischer, 1995). On August 19th, 1947, seven of the Nazi doctors received death sentences and the remaining sixteen were imprisoned.

One positive outcome of these horrific experiments was the Nuremberg Code, a code of ethics which forms the basis for research in medicine and psychology and the social sciences in general. The Code outlined the responsibilities and obligations of researchers and the rights of participants. These include:

- Participation in research should be voluntary.
- Participants should be informed of any risks involved.
- They should be free to withdraw from an experiment at any point *and* made aware of this right from the start.
- Participants should be told about the purpose of the research and given details about their involvement.
- Researchers should make sure participants come to no physical or psychological harm.
- Experiments should be stopped immediately if such harm is occurring (Homan, 1991).

Human rights

The Nazis used Jews, Gypsies, Poles and Russians in their experiments because they regarded them as a lower form of humanity. They also used them because, in the words of one doctor, they were the cheapest experimental animals, cheaper even than rats (Fischer, 1995). Clearly, this is an extreme example of a disregard for human rights. A further positive outcome of the atrocities of the Second World War was the United Nations' Universal Declaration of Human Rights in 1948. Article 1 states that, 'All human beings are born free and equal in dignity and rights'. Article 5 states that, 'No one shall be subjected to torture or to cruel, inhuman or degrading treatment or punishment'.

The UN Declaration reflected an increasing concern with human rights which has continued to the present day. This concern is mirrored in the codes of ethics for medical and social science research, including psychology. For example, the British Psychological Society's code states that participants 'should be able to expect to be treated with the highest standards of consideration and respect' (BPS, 1998).

From 'subjects' to 'participants'

The growing concern with the dignity and rights of all human beings is reflected in the change from 'subjects' to 'participants'. Those who took part in research used to be known as 'subjects'; today they are increasingly referred to as 'participants'. 'Subjects' implies that people are subordinate to others, that they are under the control and authority of others. As the British Psychological Society (BPS) notes, the term 'subject' can seem impersonal, disrespectful and even derogatory (BPS, 1998).

The term 'subject' can also imply that people can be seen and treated as 'objects' in experimental research. This reflected psychology's concern with science and the scientific method. The natural sciences, such as physics and chemistry, study the behaviour of matter. Matter is manipulated in controlled experiments in order to discover the laws which underlie its behaviour. Psychology has often applied the same approach to human beings. In the past, though to a lesser extent today, 'subjects' were manipulated in experiments in order to discover the principles underlying human behaviour.

Psychologists are increasingly realising that people who participate in experiments are very different from the passive objects which are manipulated in natural science experiments. For example, interviews with people who have taken part in psychology experiments have shown that they often work out what is expected from them and do their best to give experimenters what they want (Silverman, 1977). Now the 'passive subject' of the psychology experiment is more likely to be seen as the 'active participant'.

This view places participants in a new light. Increasingly, they are seen not as objects to be manipulated but as people who are actively involved and cooperating with the experimenter. In the words of the British Psychological Society, 'Good psychological research is possible only if there is mutual respect and confidence between investigators and participants' (BPS, 1998). This focus on respect leads to an increasing concern with the rights of participants and the responsibilities of researchers.

Codes of conduct for research

During the 1960s and 1970s, there were growing demands for explicit and detailed ethical guidelines for psychological research. These demands were triggered by a number of controversial experiments, in particular, Milgram's (1963) obedience experiments (see pp 205-208) and Zimbardo's prison simulation study (Haney, Banks & Zimbardo, 1973; see pp 194-195). Participants in both studies experienced considerable stress. They were instructed to do things which, under normal circumstances, they would probably see as unacceptable. And, in the case of Milgram's research, participants were deceived about the purpose of the research and the nature of the tasks they were instructed to perform.

Ethical issues were now on the agenda. Milgram and Zimbardo were stongly criticised by some of their colleagues and strongly supported by others. Partly as a result of this debate, professional associations of psychologists in a number of countries produced codes of conduct for research with human participants. In 1978, the British Psychological Society published its *Ethical principles for research on human subjects*. This was revised in 1990, further amended in 1992, and republished in 1993 and 1998 with the title *Ethical principles for conducting research with human participants*. It is noticeable that 'on' has changed to 'with' and 'subjects' to 'participants'.

Ethical considerations are now a major concern in research. The BPS (1998) states that, 'In all circumstances, investigators must consider the ethical implications and psychological consequences for the participants in their research. The essential principle is that the investigation should be considered from the standpoint of all participants; foreseeable threats to their psychological wellbeing, health, values or dignity should be eliminated.'

Psychological associations such as the BPS now have committees which are responsible for ethical issues and for reviewing and updating codes of conduct. In addition, psychology departments in universities usually have ethics committees which examine research proposals to ensure they are in line with codes of conduct.

1.2 The BPS ethical principles

This section looks at codes of conduct for research, focusing on the British Psychological Society's *Ethical principles for conducting research with human participants* (1998).

Informed consent

Participants must give their consent to take part in research and this consent must be 'informed'. This means that information must be made available on which to base a decision to participate or not. According to the BPS, 'The investigator should inform the participants of all aspects of the research ... that might reasonably be expected to influence willingness to participate' (BPS, 1998).

In practice, this means participants should be told:

- They are volunteers – they have a free choice whether or not to participate in the research and are free to withdraw whenever they wish, even if they have been paid to take part.
- The objectives of the research – in general terms, what the investigator is looking at.
- The experiences they will undergo during the actual research.
- The expectation that there is no risk – participation is not expected to lead to psychological or physical harm.

In a nutshell, participants should be told what they are letting themselves in for. Only then are they in a position to give informed consent.

Special safeguards are needed for certain participants. In the case of young people under 16, consent should also be obtained from their parents. In the case of people who have difficulties with communication and understanding, every attempt must be made to obtain 'real consent'. Where this is not possible, approval must be obtained from those 'well-placed to appreciate the participant's reaction, such as the person's family' and from an independent advisor (BPS, 1998). When people are detained in institutions such as prisons or psychiatric hospitals, care must be taken to ensure their consent is freely given. The same applies to participants over whom the researcher has authority and influence – his or her students, clients or employees. These relationships must not be used to place pressure on them to participate in the research.

Finally, if there is any possibility of 'harm, unusual discomfort, or other negative consequences' resulting from participation, the investigator must inform not only participants but also independent advisors. All must give their consent (BPS, 1998).

A major problem with informed consent is the possibility that the researcher will 'give the game away' – reveal what they expect to find. Participants may then act in terms of these expectations and so invalidate the experiment – they will not be responding to the factors which the experiment is designed to examine. As a result, a case can be made for withholding information. This case will be examined in the following section.

Deception

Deception means that information is withheld from participants, they are misled about the purpose of the study and the events that will take place during an experiment. According to the BPS, 'Intentional deception of the participants over the purpose and general nature of the investigation should be avoided whenever possible'. In particular, deception is unacceptable if it leads to 'discomfort, anger or objections from the participants' when the deception is revealed after the research has been completed (BPS, 1998).

However, both the BPS and the American Psychological Association agree that in certain cases deception is unavoidable. For example, the BPS states that, 'It may be impossible to study some psychological processes without withholding information about the true object of the study or deliberately misleading the participants' (BPS, 1998). In such cases the researcher must 1) make sure that alternative procedures which avoid deception are not available; 2) consult with colleagues about how participants might be affected by the deception; 3) reveal the deception to participants immediately after the research has been completed.

Opinion on the use of deception in research is divided. Some feel that it is wrong and, no matter how useful, should be avoided (Baumrind, 1979). However well-intentioned, deception involves lies and manipulation. Some researchers argue that it shows a disrespect for participants and views them as objects to be manipulated at will (Kelman, 1967). And informed consent is not possible if deception is involved – participants will have no idea what they are letting themselves in for.

Others argue that deception is often essential. Many experiments just would not work without it. For example, participants in Asch's experiments on conformity were told they were taking part in a study of perception – the way people judge line lengths – rather than study of social influence. They were led to believe that the other members of the experimental group were participants like themselves rather than confederates. It is difficult to see how this experiment could have been conducted successfully without deception (see pp 188-189). A similar case can be made for Sherif's use of deception in his autokinetic experiment. If the participants had been told that the light was actually stationary, the experiment would not have worked (see p 188).

Those who support the use of deception do so on the assumption that it is harmless, trivial and short-lived. It is short-lived, as in most cases participants are told about the deception immediately after the experiment. It is trivial in the sense that most participants see it as unimportant. It is harmless as there is no evidence of any long-term harm to participants (Elms, 1982). In fact, the vast majority of participants enjoy taking part in experiments which involve deception and often express admiration for the researcher for staging a skilful deception (Christensen, 1988).

Activity 1 Deception

Item A Acceptable deception?

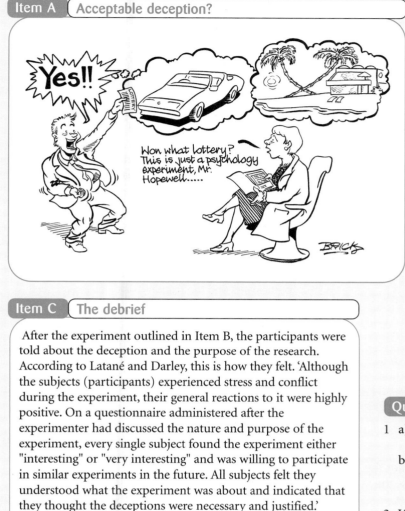

Yes!!
LOTTERY
Won what lottery?
This is just a psychology experiment, Mr. Hopewell.....
BRICK

Item B The bystander effect

Darley and Latané designed an experiment to investigate the 'bystander effect'. Their hypothesis was the greater the number of bystanders who witness an emergency, the less likely any one of them is to help. The participants were students. Each sat in a separate room discussing university life over an intercom with one or more students in other rooms. Then one of the participants appeared to have a seizure and cried out, 'I'm gonna die er er I'm gonna die, er help'. In fact, there was only one real participant, all the others were pre-recorded voices. When participants believed they were the only ones listening to the student having a seizure, 85% left the experimental room and offered help within a minute and 100% offered help within 2½ minutes. When participants believed there was another student listening, fewer offered help and took longer to do so. When participants believed there were four other students listening, even fewer offered help and took even longer – 31% helped in the first minute and after 6 minutes (when the experiment ended) only 62% had offered help.

Adapted from Darley & Latané, 1968

Item C The debrief

After the experiment outlined in Item B, the participants were told about the deception and the purpose of the research. According to Latané and Darley, this is how they felt. 'Although the subjects (participants) experienced stress and conflict during the experiment, their general reactions to it were highly positive. On a questionnaire administered after the experimenter had discussed the nature and purpose of the experiment, every single subject found the experiment either "interesting" or "very interesting" and was willing to participate in similar experiments in the future. All subjects felt they understood what the experiment was about and indicated that they thought the deceptions were necessary and justified.'

From Latané & Darley, 1970

Questions

1 a) How would you feel if you were the participant in Item A?
  b) Assuming that the experiment was to investigate reactions to a big lottery win, do you feel the deception is justified?

2 With reference to Item C, provide brief arguments to a) support and b) reject the experimenters' claim that the deception in Item B was necessary and justified.

Protection from harm

The BPS ethical guidelines state that, 'Investigators have a primary responsibility to protect participants from physical and mental harm during the investigation' (BPS, 1998). However, no investigation is entirely free from risk. The guiding principle is that risk should be no greater than the risks participants are exposed to in their normal lifestyles.

Participants should be encouraged to contact the investigator after the research if they have any worries or concerns. As Latané and Darley (1970) note in Activity 1, Item C, participants 'experienced stress and conflict' during the seizure experiment. This stress and conflict may continue after the experiment along with self-doubt and low self-esteem for those participants who did not offer help to an apparently dying student. If the research results 'in undesirable consequences for participants, the investigator has the responsibility to detect and remove these consequences' (BPS, 1998). However, this is easier said than done, especially if participants are ashamed of their behaviour during an experiment and wish to conceal their shame.

As noted in the previous section, there is no evidence of any long-term harm to participants in psychological research (Elms, 1982). However, people's responses to questionnaires and comments in interviews about their experience of participating in research cannot be taken at face value. They may disguise their true feelings for a variety of reasons.

Confidentiality Protection from harm also involves confidentiality. Participants may be asked personal and private questions. They must be told that there is no compulsion to answer these questions, and, if they do answer, their replies will be treated in confidence. If the research is published, they should remain anonymous. If this cannot be guaranteed, they should be told in advance and have the right to withdraw.

During experiments, participants may behave in ways they don't wish to be made public. The same safeguards apply – there should be no way they can be identified. Without such safeguards, participants may experience worry and stress.

Research outside the laboratory where the investigator observes behaviour 'must respect the privacy and psychological wellbeing of the individuals studied'. Invasion of privacy can result in unease or distress. According to the BPS, unless people have given their consent, they should only be observed in situations where they would expect to be observed by strangers (BPS, 1998). This largely limits observational research to public places.

Withdrawal from investigations Participants should have the right to withdraw from an investigation at any time. This applies even if they have been paid to take part. They should be told this at the start of the investigation. No attempt should be made to encourage or persuade them to remain should they wish to withdraw. This is an important right since staying against their will may result in considerable stress.

Debriefing

Debriefing involves a full disclosure – telling it all – after the investigation is complete. Typically, researchers discuss the aims of the research with participants, making sure they understand how they have contributed to meeting those aims. Any deception is disclosed, explained and justified. Attempts are made to undo any negative effects of the research experience. For example, if participants experience guilt, anxiety or lowered self-esteem as a result of their behaviour during an experiment, they are given reassurance and support. Researchers attempt to remove any feelings of discomfort and distress and ask participants to get back in touch should such feelings continue.

Codes of conduct for research state that all participants have a right to a debriefing session after the investigation has been completed. But does debriefing work? A review of the research on debriefing indicates that if it is done with 'care, effort and vigilance', then it does work (Holmes, 1976). However, others are not so sure. Participants may be reluctant to express negative feelings during debriefing. They may feel embarrassed, they may not wish to upset the researcher, and as a result their negative feelings may continue (Fisher & Fyrberg, 1994).

Key terms

Informed consent *A voluntary decision to participate in research based on information about the aims of the research and the tasks the participants will be asked to perform.*

Deception *Purposely misleading participants about the aims of the research and/or the nature of the tasks they are asked to perform. This is done by withholding information and/or providing false information.*

Debriefing *The procedure at the end of the research which involves a full disclosure of the aims of the research and the reasons for the tasks which participants have performed. Any deception is explained and justified. Attempts are made to undo any negative effects of the research experience.*

Summary

1. In terms of research, ethics are the moral principles which guide research. They involve the rights of participants and the responsibilities of researchers.
2. Ethical guidelines for research in psychology were influenced by the concern for human rights following World War II. This concern was reflected in the Nuremburg Code and the Universal Declaration of Human Rights.
3. Increasingly, participants are seen not as objects to be manipulated but as people who cooperate with researchers. This is reflected in the change in terminology from 'subjects' to 'participants'. It indicates increased respect for those who take part in research.
4. Demands for ethical guidelines for psychological research were triggered by controversial experiments in the 1960s and 1970s, in particular Milgram's obedience experiments and Zimbardo's prison simulation study.
5. The main ethical principles for conducting research with human participants are:
   - Informed consent
   - Avoidance of deception if at all possible
   - Protection of participants from physical and psychological harm
   - Confidentiality and respect for privacy
   - The right to withdraw from investigations at any time
   - Debriefing.

Activity 2 Ethics and research

Item A Little Albert

Little Albert was a healthy, well-balanced baby. John Watson and Rosalie Rayner felt they would 'do him relatively little harm' by carrying out the following experiment in 1919 when Albert was 11 months old. They wanted to see if emotional responses could be learned, in particular, could fear be learned.

Albert was presented with a white rat – he showed no fear of the rat. Could he be conditioned to fear it? A four foot steel bar was suspended near Albert's head and struck with a hammer. On the third strike he 'broke into a sudden crying fit'. The rat was then presented to Albert and as he reached out to touch it, the bar was struck. This was done several times. Then the rat was presented to Albert without the bar being struck. The result was dramatic. 'The instant the rat was shown, the baby began to cry. Almost instantly he turned sharply to the left, fell over on left side, raised himself on all fours and began to crawl away so rapidly that he was caught with difficulty before reaching the edge of the table'. Watson and Rayner were extremely pleased with this result. In their words, 'This was as convincing a case of a completely conditioned fear response as could have been theoretically pictured'. However, no attempt was made to decondition Little Albert, ie to remove his fear of rats.

Adapted from Watson & Rayner, 1920

Item B Invasion of privacy?

Evidence for a study of the relationship between stress and the invasion of 'personal space' was obtained by observation in a men's public toilet. The observer hid in a cubicle and used a periscope to watch the urinals. As expected, men took longer to urinate when a confederate occupied an adjoining urinal.

Adapted from Middlemist et al., 1976

Questions

1 Read Item A. What aspects of this experiment would be considered unethical in terms of today's standards?

2 Are the research methods in Item B justifiable? Give reasons for your answer.

Unit 2 The ethics of Milgram's obedience research

KEY ISSUES

1 **What ethical issues were raised by Milgram's experiments?**

2 **How did Milgram defend himself against his critics?**

This unit examines the ethical issues involved in Milgram's experiments designed to study obedience to authority. These experiments are outlined on pages 205-208. Some commentators have described them as amongst the most unethical in psychological research.

2.1 Deception

Milgram's experiments were masterpieces of deception. They were elaborate, stage-managed hoaxes. The props were excellent, the performances of the experimenter and the confederate were accomplished.

The deception began even before the participants were selected. Figure 1 is a copy of a newspaper advertisement placed by Milgram. It asked for 'men to help us complete a scientific study of memory and learning'. In fact, the research was a study of obedience.

The stage was set at the beginning of the experiment. The participants were falsely informed that:

> 'We want to find out just what effect different people have on each other as teachers and learners, and also what effect *punishment* will have on learning in this situation. Therefore, I'm going to ask one of you to be the teacher here tonight and the other one to be the learner' (Milgram, 1963).

Participants then drew slips of paper from a hat to see who would be a teacher and a learner. The draw was fixed so the participant was always a teacher and a confederate the learner.

The 'punishment' was a series of electric shocks of increasing severity given by the teacher (the participant) to the learner (the confederate). Unknown to the participant, the shocks were not real.

At the start of the experiment the confederate was strapped into an 'electric chair'. Electrodes were attached to his wrist and electrode paste applied to 'avoid blisters and burns'. The performance was convincing.

The apparatus used in Milgram's experiments was

realistic. This is how Milgram (1963) described the 'shock generator'.

> 'The instrument panel consists of 30 lever switches set in a horizontal line. Each switch is clearly labelled with a voltage designation that ranges from 15 to 450 volts.
>
> Upon depressing a switch: a pilot light corresponding to each switch is illuminated in bright red; an electric buzzing is heard; an electric blue light, labelled "voltage energizer", flashes; the dial on the voltage meter swings to the right; various relay clicks are sounded.
>
> The upper left-hand corner of the generator is labelled Shock Generator, Type ZLB, Dyson Instrument Company, Waltham, Mass. Output 15 Volts – 450 Volts.
>
> Details of the instrument were carefully handled to insure an appearance of authenticity. The panel was engraved by precision industrial engravers, and all components were of high quality. No subject in the experiment suspected that the instrument was merely a simulated shock generator.'

Just to make sure the deception worked, participants were given a 'sample shock' from a battery wired into the 'generator'.

In one experiment, the participants heard what they assumed to be the learner's cries of protest and pain as the voltage level increased. Exclamations of 'Ugh!' were followed by shouted protests and later by agonised screams. This deception was accomplished by an audio-tape which had been carefully prepared before the experiment (see Table 1 for a transcript of this tape).

Milgram's experiments were based on deception

Figure 1 Milgram's newspaper advertisement

WE WILL PAY YOU $4.00 FOR ONE HOUR OF YOUR TIME

Persons Needed for a Study of Memory

* We will pay five hundred New Haven men to help us complete a scientific study of memory and learning. The study is being done at Yale University.
* Each person who participates will be paid $4.00 (plus 50c carfare) for approximately 1 hour's time. We need you for only one hour: there are no further obligations. You may choose the time you would like to come (evenings, weekdays, or weekends).
* No special training, education, or experience is needed. We want:

Factory workers	Businessmen	Construction workers
City employees	Clerks	Salespeople
Laborers	Professional people	White-collar workers
Barbers	Telephone workers	Others

All persons must be between the ages of 20 and 50. High school and college students cannot be used.

* If you meet these qualifications, fill out the coupon below and mail it now to Professor Stanley Milgram, Department of Psychology, Yale University, New Haven. You will be notified later of the specific time and place of study. We reserve the right to decline any application.
* You will be paid $4.00 (plus 50c carfare) as soon as you arrive at the laboratory.

TO: PROF. STANLEY MILGRAM, DEPARTMENT OF PSYCHOLOGY, YALE UNIVERSITY, NEW HAVEN, CONN. I want to take part in this study of memory and learning. I am between the ages of 20 and 50. I will be paid $4.00 (plus 50c carfare) if I participate.

NAME (Please print)..

ADDRESS..

TELEPHONE NO .... Best time to call you ....

AGE .... OCCUPATION .... SEX ....

CAN YOU COME:

WEEKDAYS .... EVENINGS .... WEEKENDS ....

The 'shock generator'

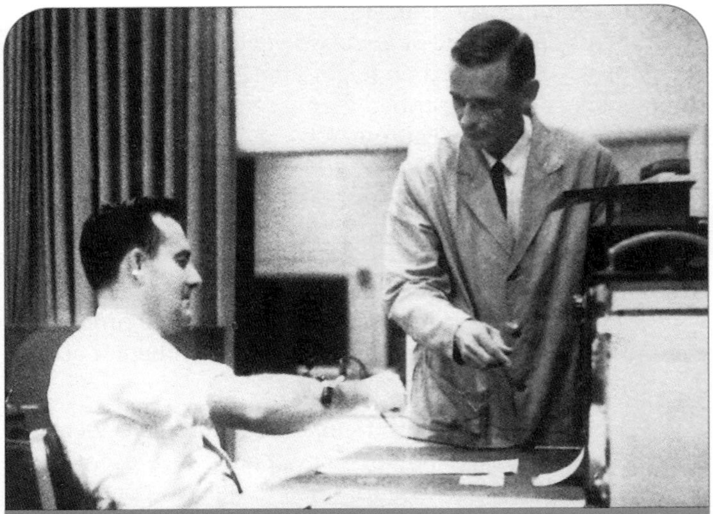

Participant receives 'sample shock'

from beginning to end. Everything was false – the initial advert, the briefing before the experiments began, the equipment and the behaviour of the confederate. And, according to Milgram (1963) 'with a few exceptions', the deception worked. Nearly all the participants 'were convinced of the reality of the experimental situation' and that 'they were administering shocks to another person'.

Criticism and defence Milgram has been criticised for deceiving the participants in his experiments. He makes two main points in his defence. First, without deceptions – or 'technical illusions' as he prefers to call them – the experiments would not have worked. In Milgram's words, 'illusion is used when necessary in order to set the stage for the revelation of certain difficult-to-get-at truths'. Thus, for example, if participants were aware that the shocks weren't real and that the learner was really a confederate, then these 'truths' could not have been revealed.

Second, Milgram claimed that if participants later accept that deception has been necessary and worthwhile, then it is justified. In Milgram's words, 'The central moral justification for allowing a procedure of the sort used in my experiment is that it is judged acceptable by those who have taken part in it' (Milgram, 1974). Judging from the debriefing sessions which followed Milgram's experiments, most participants found the deception acceptable – 83.7% said they were 'glad to have been in the experiment', only 1.3% said they wished they had not been involved.

2.2 Informed consent

Deception means that informed consent is not possible. This is particularly so in Milgram's experiments where the deception was widespread and carefully planned. Informed consent needs information, not misinformation.

Milgram admits that his participants were 'misinformed', a term he prefers to 'deceived'. However, he argues that since misinformation is essential for experiments such as his, there are two ways of dealing with the problem of consent. First, *prior general consent,* that is obtaining the consent of participants to take part in an experiment and telling them that they may be misinformed about its purpose. Second, *presumptive consent* which means asking 'reasonable people', who are not taking part, whether the experiment is acceptable and how they think the participants would react. If they think everything is OK, then they have given presumptive consent.

2.3 Protection of participants

The ethical guidelines of the British Psychological Society state that, 'Investigators have a primary responsibility to protect participants from physical and mental harm during the investigation' (BPS, 1998). How do Milgam's experiments measure up to this?

Table 1 shows the learner's (confederate's) responses to various shock levels. Above 330 volts there was an ominous silence – the learner ceased to respond. This could suggest he had either passed out or was dead.

Table 1 Learner's responses

75 volts	Ugh!
90 volts	Ugh!
105 volts	Ugh! *(louder)*
120 volts	Ugh! Hey this really hurts.
135 volts	Ugh!!
150 volts	Ugh!!! Experimenter! That's all. Get me out of here. My heart's bothering me. Let me out of here! You have no right to keep me here! Let me out! Let me out of here! Let me out! Let me out of here! My heart's bothering me. Let me out! Let me out!
210 volts	Ugh!! Experimenter! Get me out of here. I've had enough. I won't be in the experiment any more.
225 volts	Ugh!
240 volts	Ugh!
255 volts	Ugh! Get me out of here.
270 volts	*(Agonised scream)* Let me out of here. Let me out of here. Let me out of here. Let me out. Do you hear? Let me out of here.
285 volts	*(Agonised scream)*
300 volts	*(Agonised scream)* I absolutely refuse to answer any more. Get me out of here. You can't hold me here. Get me out. Get me out of here.
315 volts	*(Intensely agonised scream)* I told you I refuse to answer. I'm no longer part of this experiment.
330 volts	*(Intense and prolonged agonised scream)* Let me out of here. Let me out of here. My heart's bothering me. Let me out, I tell you. *(Hysterically)* Let me out of here. Let me out of here. You have no right to hold me here. Let me out! Let me out! Let me out of here! Let me out!

Adapted from Milgram, 1974

Many of the participants were visibly shaken by their experiences. This is how an observer, watching through one-way glass, describes one of them. 'I observed a mature and initially poised businessman enter the laboratory smiling and confident. Within 20 minutes he was reduced to a twitching, stuttering wreck, who was rapidly approaching a point of nervous collapse. He constantly pulled on his earlobe, and twisted his hands. At one point he pushed his fist into his forehead and muttered: "Oh God, let's stop it". And yet he continued to respond to every word of the experimenter, and obeyed to the end' (Milgram, 1963).

Milgram describes what he calls 'signs of extreme tension' in the participants. 'Many subjects (participants) showed signs of nervousness in the experimental situation, and especially upon administering the more powerful shocks. In a large number of cases the degree of tension reached extremes that are rarely seen in sociopsychological laboratory studies. Subjects were observed to sweat, tremble, stutter, bite their lips, groan, and dig their fingernails into their flesh. These were characteristic rather than exceptional responses to the experiment'.

'One sign of tension was the regular occurrence of nervous laughing fits. Fourteen of the 40 subjects showed definite signs of nervous laughter and smiling. The laughter seemed entirely out of place, even bizarre. Full-blown, uncontrollable seizures were observed for 3 subjects. On one occasion we observed a seizure so violently convulsive that it was necessary to call a halt to the experiment. The subject, a 46-year-old encyclopaedia salesman, was seriously embarrassed by his untoward and uncontrollable behaviour' (Milgram, 1963).

Short-term and long-term effects Clearly, in the short term, many participants were extremely distressed. But does this amount to 'psychological harm'? And what about the long term – did participants experience any lasting harm?

Milgram has been severely criticised for putting participants through this experience (Baumrind, 1964). In his defence he says 1) he didn't expect it to happen and 2) there was no long-term harm.

Milgram had discussed his experiments at length with colleagues beforehand. None had expected the participants to reach the shock level where the learner protested and showed pain. The 'extreme tension' that resulted was neither anticipated nor intended.

While admitting the obvious short-term distress, Milgram argued there was no evidence of any long-term harm. He hired a psychiatrist to interview 40 participants one year after the experiments. There was no indication of any harmful effects – most felt their participation had been rewarding and informative. However, what people say in an interview does not always reveal their true feelings. What about the small minority who said they wished they had never taken part? And could all the participants live happily with the knowledge that they were capable of inflicting pain – in some cases extreme pain – on a fellow human being? These questions will be examined further in the section on debriefing.

2.4 The right to withdraw

The British Psychological Society states that at the start of an investigation, researchers 'should make plain to participants their right to withdraw from the research at any time', whether they are being paid for participating or not (BPS, 1998). What opportunities did Milgram's participants have to withdraw from his experiments?

First, Milgram refers to his participants as 'volunteers'. This is perhaps stretching the meaning of the word since they had little idea what they were 'volunteering' for. There was no informed consent on which to base a free choice.

Second, Milgram does admit that once participants have agreed to take part, there is an obligation not to withdraw. However, even though they accepted payment, the participants were told, 'Of course, as in all experiments, the money is yours simply for coming to the laboratory. From this point on, no matter what happens, the money is yours' (Milgram, 1963). However, they were not explicitly told they were free to withdraw at any time. In fact, the whole point of the research was to encourage them to stay until the end. This can clearly be seen by the following procedures.

The experimenter made it very difficult for the participants to withdraw. Participants who appeared unwilling to continue with the experiment were encouraged, cajoled or bullied (depending on your point of view) to carry on. Here's how Milgram (1963) described the procedures.

'At various points in the experiment the subject may turn to the experimenter for advice on whether he should continue to administer shocks. Or he may indicate that he does not wish to go on. It was important to standardise the experimenter's responses to these inquiries and reactions.'

'If the subject indicated his unwillingness to go on, the experimenter responded with a sequence of "prods", using as many as necessary to bring the subject into line.

Prod 1: Please continue. *Or* Please go on.

Prod 2: The experiment requires that you continue.

Prod 3: It is absolutely essential that you continue.

Prod 4: You have no other choice, you *must* go on.

The prods were always made in sequence: Only if Prod 1 had been unsuccessful, could Prod 2 be used. If the subject refused to obey the experimenters after Prod 4, the experiment was terminated. The experimenter's tone of voice was at all times firm, but not impolite. The sequence was begun anew on each occasion that the subject balked or showed reluctance to follow orders.'

Given that the whole point of the experiments was to see how far participants would go in response to orders, there is justification for the prods. But, at the same time, the prods made it difficult for them to withdraw. Prod 4, in fact, forbids withdrawal – 'You have no other choice, you *must* go on'.

2.5 Debriefing

The British Psychological Society states that participants should be debriefed after an investigation. They should be given sufficient information to understand the purpose of the research. Any deception should be revealed. They should have the opportunity to discuss their experiences with the researcher in order to clear up any misunderstandings. This also allows the researcher to pick up on any 'negative effects' of the research experience and, hopefully, remove them (BPS, 1998).

In terms of this aspect of ethical conduct, Milgram comes out well. After each experiment, the participants were interviewed and given a battery of psychological tests to make sure they hadn't experienced any negative effects. The aim was to ensure that they left the laboratory 'in a state of wellbeing'. Participants were told that their behaviour during the experiment was perfectly normal and that they shouldn't feel ashamed or blame themselves. They were told the shocks were not real, and it was smiles all round as they met, shook hands with and chatted to their 'victim' (the confederate). Every effort was made 'to reduce any tension that arose as a result of the experiment' (Milgram, 1963). The debrief, or 'dehoax' as Milgram called it, was careful and thorough. As mentioned earlier, 40 participants were interviewed by a psychiatrist one year after the experiment. No long-lasting harmful effects were discovered.

At the debriefing, the experimenter explained the purpose of the research to the participants. He said their contribution provided important insights into the dangers of 'blind obedience'. Later the participants were sent a summary of the results and a questionnaire asking them what they felt about their participation. 83.7% said they were 'very glad' or 'glad' to have taken part and only 1.3% said they were 'sorry' or 'very sorry'. 74% indicated that they had learned something of real personal significance from their experience.

2.6 Conclusion

Milgram's research has been branded as unethical for what others see as deliberate deception, a lack of informed consent, a disregard of the right to withdraw, and a failure to protect participants from psychological harm. As the previous sections indicate, Milgram has defended himself on all these counts. His final defence rests on the importance of the research.

Milgram argues that the significance of his findings justifies the methods he used. He therefore suggests that, up to a point, the end justifies the means. In his words, 'If this experiment serves to jar people out of their complacency, it will have served its end' (Milgram, 1974). Milgram points to the wider significance of his findings. 'If an anonymous experimenter can successfully command adults to subdue a 50-year-old man and force on him painful electric shocks against his protests, one can only wonder what government, with its vastly greater authority and prestige, can command of its subjects' (Milgram, 1965).

Some researchers agree with Milgram. For example, Erikson (1968) believes that Milgram made 'a momentous and meaningful contribution to our knowledge of human behaviour'. However, the psychiatrist Bruno Bettelheim states, 'These experiments are so vile, the intention with which they were engaged in is so vile, that nothing these experiments show has any value' (quoted in Miller, 1986). Ironically, Bettelheim experienced the very thing that inspired Milgram's research – he had been interned in a German concentration camp.

Milgram's experiments led to a long and heated debate about ethical issues in research. Shortly after the publication of his first paper in 1963, he was suspended from the American Psychological Association. After an investigation, the Association decided his research was ethically acceptable. Throughout the 1960s and early 1970s there were many replications (repetitions) of Milgram's experiments. However, times were changing. The last replication in the USA was published in 1976. Given the present ethical guidelines, it is very unlikely that Milgram's experiments could be conducted today.

Summary

1. Milgram's experiments have been seen as unethical because:
    - Participants were not in a position to give informed consent
    - The experiments involved widespread deception
    - Participants experienced psychological harm, at least in the short term
    - They were discouraged from withdrawing, and in some cases ordered not to withdraw, from the experiments.
2. In his defence, Milgram argued that:
    - Informed consent was not possible as participants had to be misled for the experiments to work
    - Deception was essential in order to reveal 'difficult-to-get-at truths'
    - There was no evidence that participants suffered any long-term harm
    - Ordering participants not to withdraw was an essential part of the experiments – after all, the whole point of the research was to study obedience
    - Most of the participants saw the experiments as worthwhile and were pleased to have taken part
    - The importance of the findings justifies the methods used.

Unit 3 The ethics of Zimbardo's prison experiment

KEY ISSUES

1. **What ethical issues were raised by Zimbardo's prison simulation experiment?**
2. **What arguments did Zimbardo make in defence of his research procedures?**

Informed consent

Like Milgram, Zimbardo placed a newspaper advertisement asking for 'volunteers' to take part in an experiment (see pp 194-195 for an outline of Zimbardo's study). Participants were offered $15 a day and told the experiment was to last for two weeks. Unlike Milgram, Zimbardo openly stated the aim of his research – 'a psychological study of prison life' (Haney, Banks & Zimbardo, 1973).

The participants were told they would be randomly assigned to the roles of prisoner or guard. They signed a contract which stated that those playing the role of prisoner agreed to a suspension of their 'basic civil rights', except for the right to freedom from physical abuse. They were informed that they had no right to privacy and, as prisoners, they would be harassed. No instructions were given about how to play the role of prisoner or what to expect during the experiment.

Those assigned to the role of guards were told they must 'maintain the reasonable degree of order within the prison necessary for effective functioning'. Apart from being told they must not use physical force, no details of how to play their role were given.

According to Zimbardo, the only breach of the principle of informed consent was the arrest of the prisoners in their homes at the start of the experiment. There were two reasons for this breach. First, the local police only gave their approval for the mock arrests a few minutes before the experiment took place. As a result, there was not time to inform the participants that they were going to be 'arrested' at home. Second, the researchers wanted the arrests to come as a surprise in order to add realism to the experiment.

Official approval Zimbardo made every effort to gain official approval for his research. Before the experiment was carried out, it was approved by the Psychology Department at Stanford University, by the University Committee of Human Experimentation and the Office of Naval Research which sponsored the research.

Deception

As noted above, the researchers failed to inform the prisoners about their arrest. As Zimbardo admitted, this can be seen as deception.

Participant arrested outside his home by local police

Zimbardo was just as interested in the behaviour of the guards as he was in the behaviour of the prisoners. However, the participants who played the role of guards believed he was primarily interested in the behaviour of the prisoners. Zimbardo made no attempt to correct this false impression.

Apart from the information in the contract, participants were given little or no indication of what to expect. In other words, they were kept in the dark. As it turned out, the researchers themselves failed to predict how the experiment would develop. However, it can be reasonably argued that telling the participants what to expect would lead to *expectancy bias*. Participants may behave in terms of the researchers' expectations which would lead to invalid results.

Protection from harm

Zimbardo made every effort to ensure the participants were psychologically and physically fit to take part in the experiment. Seventy-five people replied to his advertisement. Each person was interviewed and completed a lengthy questionnaire about their 'physical and mental history'. Twenty-one were selected to take part in the experiment. They were judged to be the 'most stable (physically and mentally)' and the 'most mature'.

The aim of the experiment was to create and maintain 'a psychological state of imprisonment'. For ethical reasons, many aspects of prison life which might harm the prisoners were forbidden – physical punishment, racism and rape. However, the experiment was designed to simulate the social relationships and psychology of prison life – power, control, oppression, humiliation and powerlessness. And this is how things got out of hand.

The guards behaviour became increasingly 'negative, hostile, insulting and dehumanising'. Five of the prisoners

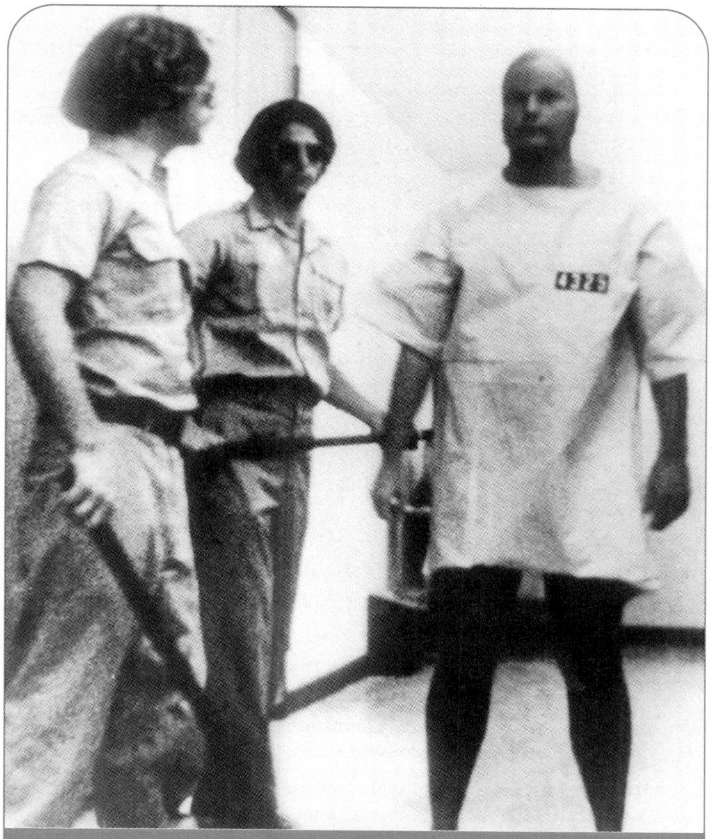
Guards and prisoner

had to be 'released' because of 'extreme emotional depression, crying, rage and acute anxiety'. One of them developed a 'psychosomatic rash' which covered large parts of his body. The experiment was planned to last for two weeks. After six days the researchers decided to end it. In Zimbardo's words, 'we had to close down our mock prison because what we saw was frightening'.

There is no doubt that the prisoners were suffering during the experiment. They were deteriorating rapidly, both psychologically and physically. In addition, the proceedings may have caused harm to the guards. Zimbardo recognised this. In his words, 'Volunteer prisoners suffered physical and psychological abuse hour after hour for days, while volunteer guards were exposed to the new self-knowledge that they enjoyed being powerful and had abused this power to make other human beings suffer' (Zimbardo, 1973).

It was the failure to protect the prisoners from harm which resulted in considerable criticism of the prison simulation experiment. Some critics argued that the researchers should have anticipated what happened and should not have conducted the research in the first place (Savin, 1973).

Key term

Expectancy bias *Invalid findings resulting from participants acting in terms of researchers' expectations of how they will behave.*

Zimbardo argued that there was no way of predicting such extreme behaviour. In addition, the 'release' of five prisoners, then the abandonment of the experiment after six days, indicates that steps were taken to protect the participants from harm.

Debriefing

Thorough debriefing sessions were held with participants on a one-to-one basis and in groups. They completed questionnaires on their experience of the research, then further questionnaires after several weeks, several months and then every year. Zimbardo (1973) concluded, 'We are sufficiently convinced that the suffering we observed, and were responsible for ... did not extend beyond the confines of that basement prison'. In other words, the participants did not experience any long-term harm – the debriefing revealed 'no lasting negative effects'. The participants were 'basically healthy and they readily bounced back from that highly charged situation' (Zimbardo et al., 1995).

Conclusion

Do the benefits of the prison simulation experiment outweigh the costs? Can the suffering of the prisoners be justified? Some critics answer these questions with a resounding no (Savin, 1973). However, the researchers disagree. None of the participants showed any ill-effects *after* the experiment. They were fully debriefed by professional counsellors who explained the aims of the experiment and what had been learned from it. And the participants appreciated what they had learned. In Zimbardo's words, 'The participants had all learned an important lesson: to never underestimate the power of socially negotiated situations and interpersonal influences to overwhelm the personalities and intentions of even the brightest, most emotionally resilient and moral among us' (Zimbardo et al., 1995).

Summary

1. Zimbardo argued that he and his colleagues made every attempt to ensure that the prison simulation experiment was ethically sound.
   - Informed consent was obtained
   - Deception was minimised
   - Every effort was made to protect the participants
   - What happened could not be predicted
   - There was no indication of lasting harm to the participants
   - The findings were valuable and provided a lesson in what can happen in the wider society.
2. Critics argued that what happened during the experiment should have been anticipated and, however valuable the findings, the end does not justify the means.

References

Baumrind, D. (1964). Some thoughts on ethics of research: After reading Milgram's 'Behavioral Study of Obedience'. *American Psychologist, 19,* 421-423.

Baumrind, D. (1979). The costs of deception. *IRB: A Review of Human Subjects Research, 6,* 1-4.

BPS (British Psychological Society). (1998). *Code of conduct, ethical principles and guidelines.* Leicester: BPS.

Christensen, L. (1988). Deception in psychological research: When is its use justified? *Personality and Social Psychology Bulletin, 14,* 664-675.

Darley, J.M. & Latané, B. (1968). Bystander intervention in emergencies: Diffusion of responsibility. *Journal of Personality and Social Psychology, 8,* 377-383.

Elms, A.C. (1982). Keeping deception honest: justifying conditions for social scientific research strategies. In T.L. Beauchamp & R. Faden (Eds.), *Ethical issues in social science research.* Baltimore, MD: Johns Hopkins University Press.

Erikson, M. (1968). The inhumanity of ordinary people. *International Journal of Psychiatry, 6,* 278-9.

Fischer, K.P. (1995). *Nazi Germany: A new history.* London: Constable.

Fisher, C.B. & Fyrberg, D. (1994). Participant partners: College students weigh the costs and benefits of deceptive research. *American Psychologist, 49,* 417-427.

Gross, R.D. (1994). *Key studies in psychology* (2nd ed.). London: Hodder & Stoughton.

Haney, C., Banks, C. & Zimbardo, P. (1973). Interpersonal dynamics in a simulated prison. *International Journal of Criminology and Penology, 1,* 69-97.

Holmes, D.S. (1976a). Debriefing after psychological experiments 1. Effectiveness of postdeception dehoaxing. *American Psychologist, 31,* 858-867.

Holmes, D.S. (1976b). Debriefing after psychological experiments II. Effectiveness of postexperimental desensitising. *American Psychologist, 31,* 868-875.

Homan, R. (1991). *The ethics of social research.* Harlow: Longman.

Kelman, H.C. (1967). Human use of human subjects: The problem of deception in social psychological experiments. *Psychological Bulletin, 67,* 1-11.

Latané, B. & Darley, J.M. (1970). *The unresponsive bystander: Why doesn't he help?* Englewood Cliffs, NJ: Prentice Hall.

Middlemist, R.D., Knowles, E.S. & Matter, C.F. (1976). Personal space invasions in the lavatory: Suggestive evidence for arousal. *Journal of Personality and Social Psychology, 33,* 541-546.

Milgram, S. (1963). Behavioral study of obedience. *Journal of Abnormal and Social Psychology, 67,* 371-378.

Milgram, S. (1965). Some conditions of obedience and disobedience to authority. *Human Relations, 18,* 57-76.

Milgram, S. (1974). *Obedience to authority: An experimental view.* New York: Harper & Row.

Miller. A.G. (1986). *The obedience experiments: A case study of controversy in social science.* New York: Praeger.

Savin, H.B. (1973). Professors and psychological researchers: Conflicting values in conflicting roles. *Cognition, 2,* 147-149.

Silverman, I. (1977). *The human subject in the psychological laboratory.* New York: Pergamon.

Watson, J.B. & Rayner, R. (1920). Conditioned emotional reactions. *Journal of Experimental Psychology, 3,* 1-14.

Zimbardo, P.G. (1973). On the ethics of intervention in human psychological research: With special reference to the Stanford prison experiment. *Cognition, 2,* 243-256.

Zimbardo, P.G., McDermott, M., Jansz, J. & Metaal, M. (1995). *Psychology: A European text.* London: Harper Collins.

16 Quantitative and qualitative research methods

Introduction

In their research, psychologists use a range of different methods which produce a variety of different types of data. This chapter looks at a number of these methods and assesses their advantages and disadvantages.

Chapter summary

- **Unit 1 distinguishes between quantitative and qualitative data.**
- **Unit 2 looks at the three main types of experiments – laboratory, field and natural experiments.**
- **Unit 3 examines investigations using correlational analysis.**
- **Units 4, 5 and 6 look at non-experimental research methods – observation, questionnaire surveys and interviews.**

Unit 1 Quantitative and qualitative data

KEY ISSUES

1. **What is the difference between quantitative and qualitative research methods?**
2. **What kinds of data does each produce?**

Psychologists use research methods to gather data. Data can be *quantitative* – in the form of numbers, or *qualitative* – in the form of a description.

Research methods such as laboratory experiments and questionnaire surveys are more likely to produce quantitative data. Methods such as unstructured, in-depth interviews and participant observation (where the researcher joins the group they are observing) are more likely to produce qualitative data – a detailed description of behaviour.

The distinction between quantitative and qualitative data is illustrated in Activity 1. To appreciate the difference, it is a good idea to read Items A and B now, then answer the questions when you have read this unit.

Some researchers argue that unless human behaviour is expressed in the form of numbers, it cannot be accurately measured. Without accurate measurement, conclusions will be based on impressions and will be little more than opinions. Accurate measurement is essential if cause and effect relationships are to be established. Some researchers argue that the establishment of cause and effect relationships is the basis of science. They believe that for psychology to be a science, quantitative data is essential.

Other researchers tend to favour qualitative research methods. They argue that qualitative data has greater depth, it is more meaningful, it produces a richer and more detailed picture of behaviour. In particular, they believe it is more likely to give a picture of life from the point of view of the people they are studying. It is more likely to capture subtleties, nuances and shades of meaning than the numerical data provided by quantitative methods.

In practice, many researchers use both quantitative and qualitative methods. They recognise the strengths and weaknesses of each and see the different types of data as suitable for different purposes. For example, the findings produced by a participant observation study might form the basis for a laboratory experiment. And quantitative and qualitative data can be used together as 1) a means of checking the other and 2) building up a more complete picture of human behaviour.

Key terms

Quantitative data *Data in the form of numbers.*

Qualitative data *Descriptive data.*

Unit 2 Experiments

KEY ISSUES

1. **What are the main types of experiment?**
2. **What are the advantages and disadvantages of each?**

2.1 Laboratory experiments

The following experiment, which was briefly outlined in Chapter 1 (see p 20), illustrates the main features of a laboratory experiment.

Activity 1 Quantitative and qualitative data

The following items are taken from *Violence against wives* (Dobash & Dobash, 1980). The study was based on in-depth interviews with 109 women who had experienced battering. During each interview a number of specific questions were asked which provided data which could be quantified.

Item A Qualitative data

He punched me, he kicked me, he pulled me by the hair. My face hit a step. He had his bare feet, you know, with being in bed, and he just jumped up and he pulled on his trousers and he was kicking me. If he had his shoes oh, God knows what kind of face I would have had. As it was, I had a cracked cheek-bone, two teeth knocked out, cracked ribs, broken nose, two beautiful black eyes – it wasn't even a black eye, my whole cheek was just purple from one eye to the other. And he had got me by the neck and, you know, he was trying, in fact, practically succeeded in strangling me. I was choking, I was actually at the blacking-out stage. I was trying to pull his fingers away, with me trying to pull his fingers away, I scratched myself, you know, trying to get his fingers off. He hit me and I felt my head, you know, hitting the back of the lock of the door. I started to scream and I felt as if I'd been screaming for ages. When I came to, he was pulling me up the stairs by the hair, I mean, I think it was the pain of him pulling me up the stairs by the hair that brought me round again.

Item B Quantitative data

Types of injuries resulting from the first, worst, and last violent episode*

Injuries	Violent episode: First		Worst		Last	
	Number	%	Number	%	Number	%
Bruises to face and/or body	101	74	182	64	148	70
Abrasions	0	0	2	1	3	1
Burns	0	0	4	1	5	3
Cuts	18	13	48	17	27	13
Hair torn out	5	3	13	5	10	5
Fractured bones or broken teeth	6	5	11	4	9	4
Internal injuries, miscarriages	4	3	8	3	2	1
Knocked unconscious	2	1	14	5	7	3
Total	136	100	282	100	211	100

* We recorded up to five *different* types of physical injuries in any single violent episode. These figures reflect only the *different* types of injuries, and not the number of times a particular type of injury was received.

Question

What are the advantages and disadvantages of the types of data in Items A and B?

A researcher wishes to find out the effect of light on plant growth. In order to do this, it is necessary to identify and control all the variables or factors which affect plant growth. This is difficult to do outside a laboratory since variables such as temperature and humidity cannot be controlled. Within a laboratory, there is a greater chance of controlling such variables.

The researcher conducts the following experiment. Every variable except light is held constant – kept the same. For example, plants of the same species and size are kept at the same temperature and humidity; they are grown in the same type of soil and given the same amount of water. Only the light is varied. For example, one group of plants is exposed to the same type and intensity of light for a longer period of time than another group. Since nothing else varies, any difference in growth between the two groups of plants is due to differences in the amount of light they receive.

From this simple example, some of the main features of a laboratory experiment can be identified.

- **Control** The researcher has a greater chance of controlling the variables. One variable is manipulated and changed (the duration of exposure to light), the other variables are held constant (the same temperature, humidity etc).
- **The independent variable** This is the variable that is manipulated by the researcher. In the above example, the independent variable is the duration of exposure to light.
- **The dependent variable** This is the variable that is measured by the researcher. In the above example, the dependent variable is growth. The purpose of the experiment is to see if the dependent variable is affected by the independent variable. In psychology experiments, the dependent variable is usually the performance of the participants.

- **Cause and effect** In an experiment it is possible to establish a cause and effect relationship between the independent variable and the dependent variable. In terms of the above example, variations in exposure to light cause variations in growth.
- **Quantification** Experiments usually produce quantitative data – data in the form of numbers, for example, 4 hours and 30 minutes, 5 millimetres, and so on.
- **Objective measurement** Ideally, measurement in experiments should be objective. This means it is not affected by personal judgements. For instance, the duration of exposure to light can be measured quantitatively in hours, minutes and seconds, plant growth in millimetres, and so on. These quantitative measurements are unlikely to be affected by personal judgements.
- **Replication** This means repeating the experiment under exactly the same conditions by the same or other researchers. If the variables have been controlled and if the measurements are objective and the data quantified, then replication is possible. If the same results are then obtained, then there is a greater likelihood that the findings of the experiment are reliable.

The laboratory experiment in psychology

The laboratory experiment has dominated large areas of research in psychology. For instance, it has been particularly important in memory research, as the first three chapters indicate. The following example provides an illustration of a laboratory experiment in memory research.

A researcher wishes to investigate the effect of noise on memory. Noise is the independent variable which is manipulated. The dependent variable is the performance of participants on a memory test. One group of participants takes the test in a quiet room, another group in a room with loud music playing. There are two *conditions* – a quiet condition and a noisy condition. Quietness and noisiness are two values or levels of the independent variable.

Apart from the independent variable – level of noise – the researcher attempts to keep all other variables constant. For example, lighting, temperature and the size of rooms are the same. Participants are given the same instructions, the same test, and the same amount of time in which to do it.

The performance of the participants in the two conditions is measured. If participants in the quiet condition perform differently on the memory test that those in the noisy condition, then this suggests that noise affects memory.

It is important to ensure that the only difference between the two conditions is the difference in the value of the independent variable – in this case the level of the noise. If any other variables intrude – for example, if one room was hotter than the other, or if one group of participants had been partying all night and had hangovers – then the researcher would not know if the results were due to the independent variable or one of these other variables. As a result the experiment has been confounded or ruined. Uncontrolled variables which affect the results are known as *confounding variables*.

Key terms

Variables *Factors which affect behaviour. Variables can vary or change. For example, temperature can increase or decrease.*

Control of variables *The ability to control the value of variables. The researcher can keep them constant (the same) or change their value.*

Cause and effect relationship *When one variable is shown to cause a change in another variable.*

Independent variable *The variable that is manipulated by the researcher to see if it has an effect on the dependent variable.*

Dependent variable *The variable that is measured by the researcher – in psychology this is usually the performance of the participants.*

Replication *Repeating an experiment in exactly the same way to see if its results are reliable.*

Confounding variables *Uncontrolled variables which interfere with the experiment and affect the dependent variable.*

Summary The experiment is an investigation into the effect of an independent variable on a dependent variable. In its simplest form, there are two conditions, in which participants are presented with one value of the independent variable in one condition, and the other value of the independent variable in the other condition. The performance of the participants – the dependent variable – in condition 1 is measured and compared with the performance of the participants in condition 2. The only way to know whether the independent variable has had an effect on the dependent variable is by making sure that all variables which might confound the experiment have been controlled or eliminated.

Advantages of laboratory experiments

Control The laboratory experiment gives the researcher a greater opportunity to control variables than any other research method.

Cause and effect By controlling variables and reducing or even eliminating the effect of confounding variables, the researcher can be more confident about establishing cause and effect relationships between the independent variable and the dependent variable.

Replication Because laboratory experiments are conducted under controlled conditions, they are easier to replicate than studies conducted using other research methods.

Quantification It is easier to quantify the results of an experiment in the controlled conditions of a laboratory. It is then possible to use statistical tests to indicate how likely it is that the results are due to the action of the independent variable.

Time and money Laboratory experiments are often less expensive and time-consuming than other research methods. This is particularly true for the study of events that rarely occur in everyday life such as an eyewitness observing a robbery. Showing participants a film of a robbery in the laboratory is far less expensive and time-consuming than waiting for a similar event to occur in real life.

Specialised equipment Laboratories provide the opportunity to use specialised equipment which may be unavailable or difficult to use in other research settings – for example, instruments for measuring brain activity.

Disadvantages of laboratory experiments

Psychology and science Laboratory experiments were developed by the natural sciences – physics, chemistry and biology. They enable the scientist to show that, under controlled conditions, matter always reacts in the same way to an external stimulus. For example, water always boils at the same temperature. Matter is compelled to react in this way because it has no consciousness. It has no awareness, meanings or motives which direct its behaviour.

Although most psychologists see psychology as a science, they differ over how far the methods of the natural sciences are appropriate for the study of human beings. Some are in favour of laboratory experiments. Others are less sure. They argue that there is a fundamental difference between the subject matter of psychology and the natural sciences. In particular, human beings have consciousness, matter does not. As a result, human beings can give different meanings to situations and act in terms of those meanings rather than simply reacting to the situation itself. Assume the loud music played in the memory experiment described earlier was classical music. Participants will give meaning to the music – some may like classical music, others may not; some may have particular associations with the music. As a result, they are not simply reacting to the noise level. And the meaning they give to the music may affect their performance on the memory test. Considerations such as these do not affect water boiling at a particular temperature.

Some psychologists argue that the laboratory experiment is not appropriate for the study of human beings. Since every aspect of the experiment will be given meanings by the participants, it is not possible to say with any certainty what is directing the participants' actions. This argument lies behind some of the following objections to the use of laboratory experiments in psychology.

Demand characteristics These are cues or clues in an experiment that convey the researcher's hypothesis to the participant. For example, participants try to make sense of experiments and give meaning to the tasks they perform. They may try to guess what the experiment is about and how the researcher expects them to behave. They may act in terms of these expectations and try to please the researcher (Orne, 1962). If they do this, they are responding to demand characteristics rather than to the independent variable.

The researcher/participant relationship In a laboratory experiment, the relationship between the researcher and the participant is distinct from all other relationships outside the laboratory. Participants assume that the researcher will take full responsibility for whatever happens in the experiment. As a result of this unique relationship, participants may behave in ways they would never dream of outside the laboratory (Orne & Holland, 1968). This is one of the criticisms of the Milgram obedience experiments (see pp 205-208). The willingness of some of the participants to deliver supposedly high-voltage shocks to an apparently helpless 'victim', may well reflect the researcher/participant relationship. This relationship may be unique to experimental situations.

Evaluation apprehension Some participants may experience *evaluation apprehension* – they may be worried about how they appear to the researcher and what the researcher might think about them. For example, they may try to look good and behave in ways which are socially acceptable. This is known as the *social desirability effect*.

Laboratory experiments are designed to measure response to independent variables. If participants are concerned about how they appear to the researcher, then this might affect their response to the independent variable.

Investigator or experimenter effects This refers to the ways in which researchers influence the behaviour of participants. For example, a smile, a frown, or a questioning look from the experimenter might encourage participants to behave in particular ways. The same applies to the characteristics of the experimenter – whether they are male or female, black or white, attractive or unattractive, cheerful or solemn, and so on. All these factors may affect the participants' behaviour.

Researchers sometimes expect and hope that experiments will produce certain results. These hopes and expectations may influence participants. For example, a smile when their behaviour matches the expected findings may encourage participants to continue to behave in that way (Rosenthal, 1966).

Artificiality Both the laboratory setting and the tasks participants are asked to perform can appear artificial and unrealistic.

In a laboratory experiment, participants are removed from their everyday settings. They are directed by an experimenter, often in the company of complete strangers. For many people, this is a brand new experience far removed from their everyday lives. It can appear artificial and 'unreal'.

Sometimes the tasks participants are asked to perform

appear meaningless. For example, learning nonsense syllables in memory experiments may make little sense to participants. However, not all experimental tasks are as artificial as this. Some experiments attempt to simulate life outside the laboratory – for example, experiments on eyewitness testimony which show participants a film of an accident or a robbery. But even this is a long way from the real thing.

Ecological validity This refers to the extent to which the findings of an experiment can be generalised to settings outside the laboratory. Critics argue that participants are unlikely to behave normally and naturally in a laboratory because of the artificiality of the setting and the tasks. As a result, it is unlikely that their behaviour in the laboratory will reflect their behaviour in other settings. If this is the case, then laboratory experiments will tend to have low ecological validity – it is unlikely that their findings will apply to other settings.

Samples Who are the participants who take part in laboratory experiments? Particularly in the USA, they tend to be white, middle-class, male undergraduate students in their late teens and early twenties. Can the results of experiments based on this type of sample be generalised to other cultures, other places and other times? According to some researchers, the answer is no (Sears, 1986).

There is considerable evidence that a wide range of social factors such as gender, social class, ethnicity, age and culture affect the way people behave and see the world. It can be argued that unless these factors are represented in samples, then generalisations from laboratory experiments are unjustified.

Culture Human beings live in different societies with different cultures – different norms, values, beliefs and attitudes. As a result, they may respond to the same experiment in different ways. For example, a number of researchers have argued that the Strange Situation, a procedure developed in the USA, is not appropriate for classifying and measuring infant attachment across cultures (see pp 58-59). Similar criticisms can be made of many laboratory experiments which have been designed in

Key terms

Demand characteristics *The cues in an experiment which convey the researcher's hypothesis to the participants.*

Evaluation apprehension *A concern by participants that they are being judged and evaluated by the researcher.*

Social desirability effect *The tendency for participants to behave in ways which are socially acceptable and desirable.*

Investigator or experimenter effects *Ways in which the expectations, behaviour, appearance and social characteristics of the researcher affect the behaviour of participants.*

Ecological validity *The extent to which the findings of an experiment can be generalised to settings outside the laboratory.*

Western societies. They may be inappropriate for use in other societies with different cultures.

Limitations There are many types of behaviour which are difficult, if not impossible to study in laboratory experiments. For example, complex social behaviours like falling in love; frightening or dangerous situations such as stalking or physical assault; and mental or cognitive events such as dreaming or imagining are difficult to reproduce in a laboratory setting. And in some cases, such as physical assault, it would be unethical to do so.

Ethical issues Laboratory experiments raise a number of ethical issues. As outlined in Chapter 15, the British Psychological Society states that researchers should obtain the informed consent of participants and, wherever possible, avoid deceiving them. This raises a problem. If participants are told everything about the experiment before taking part, this may invalidate the whole experiment. For example, if participants are aware of how they are expected to behave, they may well act accordingly. Some researchers argue that deception is sometimes necessary to avoid the effect of demand characteristics. Others reject this view, seeing deception as unethical.

Activity 2 Eyewitness testimony

Participants watched a film about a car accident. They described what happened, as if they were eyewitnesses giving evidence. They were divided into three groups and each group was asked a slightly different question. The questions and answers are shown below.

Question	Verb	Estimated MPH
About how fast were the cars going when they_____ each other?	smashed	40.8
	bumped	34.0
	contacted	30.8

Adapted from Loftus & Palmer, 1974

Questions

1 What is the independent variable in this experiment?

2 What is the dependent variable in this experiment?

3 What data is quantified?

4 How many conditions are there? What are they?

5 What cause and effect relationship is suggested by the results?

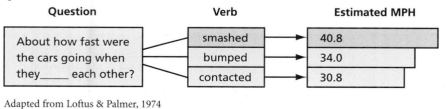

2.2 Field experiments

Field experiments are conducted outside the laboratory in normal social situations such as the classroom, the workplace, the hospital or the street. The researcher still manipulates the independent variable and measures the dependent variable. However, compared to the laboratory experiment, the researcher has far less control over variables which might affect the participants' behaviour. For example, if the field experiment was conducted on the street, the researcher cannot control the weather or the number of people present.

Hofling et al's (1966) study of obedience in the hospital outlined in Chapter 14 (p 209) is an example of a field experiment. The participants were 22 staff nurses on night duty in psychiatric hospitals in the USA. They were telephoned by an unknown 'doctor' (a confederate of Hofling) and instructed to give medication to a patient. All but one of the nurses obeyed this instruction and prepared the medication before they were stopped and the situation explained to them. In doing so, they broke a number of hospital rules. For example, they were forbidden to accept instructions over the telephone and from an unknown doctor.

Field experiments may have certain advantages over other research methods such as interviews. After completing his experiment, Hofling interviewed 12 experienced nurses and asked them what they would have done in this situation. Ten said they would refuse to follow the doctor's instructions. Hofling also interviewed 21 student nurses. All of them said they would disobey the doctor. This suggests that what people say in an interview may be very different from what they do in everyday life.

Activity 3 indicates a further advantage of the field experiment. It suggests that the way people behave in their natural settings may be different from the way they perform in a laboratory experiment.

Activity 3 Field experiments

Item A Helping on the New York subway

The following field experiment was designed to examine 'helping behaviour'. It was conducted on subway trains in New York City during a $7^1/2$ minute journey between Harlem and the Bronx. Students played the role of 'victims' who were either drunk or ill, black or white. The students were male, between 26-35 years of age, three were white and one was black. In the drunk condition, the victim smelled of alcohol and carried a bottle in a brown paper bag. In the ill condition, the victim carried a black cane. In both conditions, the victims were dressed identically and collapsed – apparently drunk or ill – in a train compartment. There were between 40 and 45 passengers in the compartment and 8 or 9 close to the victim. Around 45% of the passengers were black, 55% white.

Adapted from Piliavin et al., 1969

Item B The results

The New York subway

Help for the victim was provided by one or more passengers in 81 of the 103 trials. This is high compared with previous laboratory experiments which indicated a much lower rate of assistance. Evidence from laboratory experiments also suggested that as the number of bystanders increases, the likelihood that any individual would help decreases (Darley & Latané, 1968 – see p 221). There was no evidence to support this from the subway experiment. If anything, the opposite occurred.

The 'ill' victim was more likely to be helped than the 'drunk' victim. In the ill condition, ethnicity appeared to make no difference to helping. In the drunk condition, the victim was more likely to be helped by a member of his own ethnic group.

Adapted from Piliavin et al., 1969

Questions

1. Why is this a field study?
2. How is the independent variable manipulated in this study?
3. What variables cannot be controlled in this study?
4. Judging by Item B, why is it important to conduct field experiments as well as laboratory experiments?

Advantages of field experiments

Realism Since they are conducted in normal social settings, field experiments are often more realistic and true to life than laboratory experiments. As a result, participants are more likely to behave normally and naturally. Because of this, some researchers believe that field experiments have higher ecological validity than laboratory experiments – that there is a greater likelihood of generalising their findings to other settings.

Validity Compared to other research methods, evidence suggests that the data from field experiments may have higher validity. As the hospital experiment indicates, interview data may not give a true picture of how people actually behave in real life. And, as the subway experiment suggests, the way people behave in the laboratory does not necessarily reflect their behaviour in more natural settings.

Demand characteristics Compared to laboratory experiments, it is less likely that demand characteristics will affect participants' behaviour. The participants don't know they are taking part in an experiment. As a result, they will not be aware of the purpose of the experiment. In addition, they will be unlikely to respond in terms of the researcher/participant relationship; they will be less likely to be influenced by investigator effects.

Disadvantages of field experiments

Control of variables Field experiments do not provide the control available in the laboratory. For example, in the subway experiment, the researchers had no control over the number or ethnicity of the commuters in the train compartment. As a result, there is a greater chance of uncontrolled variables affecting participants' behaviour.

Replication Because many variables cannot be controlled, it is difficult to replicate field experiments precisely. For example, it is not possible to exactly reproduce the 103 trials in the subway experiment.

Time and money Field experiments are often more time-consuming and expensive than laboratory experiments. However, compared to observational research (discussed in Unit 4), they usually cost less and take less time.

Sampling The researcher often has little control of the sample of participants who take part in a field experiment. For example, in the subway experiment, apart from selecting the route, the researcher had no control over who was present in the compartment.

Specialised equipment Often, it is not possible to use technical equipment in field experiments – for example equipment to measure physiological changes.

Ethical issues Participants in field experiments are unable to give informed consent – they don't even know they are taking part in an experiment. As a result, they are deceived. In many cases, participants in field experiments are not debriefed after the experiment. Sometimes, a debrief can do more harm than good. Ethical guidelines for research in psychology state that participants should be protected from psychological harm. In the hospital experiment, the researchers later explained the situation to the nurses. However, the nurses still had to live with the realisation that they had been prepared to give their patients an overdose of a drug which might have caused serious injury.

2.3 Natural experiments

A natural experiment is the study of the effects of a naturally occurring event. It is not set up and controlled by the researcher. The difference in the situation before and after the event is taken to be the independent variable and its effect on behaviour, the dependent variable. The eruption of Mount St Helens in the USA in 1980 provides an example (see p 112). Although there were warnings, the exact time of the eruption could not be predicted, nor was the scale and power of the blast anticipated. Sixty people were killed and the blast of hot gas, ash and rock destroyed an area of 150 square miles.

Psychologists studied the behaviour of people in the small agricultural town of Othello near the disaster area. After the eruption they found a 198% increase in stress-related illness, a 235% increase in the diagnosis of mental health problems and an 18.6% increase in the death rate. Crisis calls to the emergency services increased dramatically, as did appointments at the local mental health clinic (Adams & Adams, 1984).

Natural experiments usually look at behaviour before and after a naturally occurring event. In the case of the Mount St Helens experiment, researchers noted differences in behaviour before and after the eruption. They assumed that changes in behaviour resulted from the eruption.

The researcher has no control over the variables in a natural experiment. As a result, it is difficult to establish cause and effect relationships with any degree of certainty. This can be seen clearly from Activity 4 which looks at the possible effects of zero tolerance policing on crime rates.

Advantages of natural experiments

Realism Natural experiments are realistic – they are based on real-life events. They avoid the artificiality of laboratory experiments.

Demand characteristics and investigator effects Natural experiments minimise demand characteristics and investigator effects. In many cases, the researcher is not present when the event occurs. And, in many cases, participants have no idea their behaviour is being studied.

Research opportunities Often natural experiments give researchers the opportunity to study events that could not be simulated in a laboratory experiment or created in a field

Activity 4 Zero tolerance policing

In 1994, William J Bratton was appointed police commissioner for New York City. He introduced the policy of zero tolerance policing. This meant that the police clamped down on all types of crime, however petty and insignificant. No longer did they turn a blind eye to people riding bikes on the sidewalk, urinating in public, petty drug dealers, graffiti, beggars and street prostitution. In Brattons' words, 'If you don't stop the small offenders, it emboldens the really bad guys. It creates an atmosphere of lawlessness.' Within two years of the introduction of zero tolerance, homicides in New York City were halved and robberies dropped by a third. Everybody was impressed, but was this due to zero tolerance policing?

Stop-and-search in Harlem, New York City

The USA experienced a crime wave from 1990 to 1993. This coincided with an economic recession and high unemployment. Since then, 10.5 million new jobs have been created in the USA. In addition, there has been a decline in the crack-cocaine epidemic and longer prison sentences have kept many criminals locked up and off the streets for much longer periods.

Zero tolerance policing was later introduced in Washington DC. There was little change in the crime rate. In some American cities which did not introduce zero tolerance policing, the reduction in the crime rate was similar to that of New York City.

Adapted from Chaudhary & Walker, 1996

Questions

1 Some researchers assume that zero tolerance policing resulted in a reduction in the crime rate. What are the possible uncontrolled variables which suggest that this might not be the case?

2 Why is it difficult to establish cause and effect relationships from natural experiments?

experiment. The Mount St Helens eruption is an obvious example.

Ethical issues It can be argued that natural experiments are ethically sound for the following reasons. The events on which they are based would happen anyway and researchers are unlikely to have much effect on the behaviour of those they are studying.

Disadvantages of natural experiments

Lack of control Researchers have no control over the variables in a natural experiment. They simply study what naturally happens.

Cause and effect Because of this lack of control, the researcher is unlikely to establish cause and effect relationships with any degree of certainty. As the example of zero tolerance policing indicates, there are many possible causes for the drop in the crime rate.

Replication and generalisation It is not possible to replicate natural experiments. The events on which they are based are one-off situations which will not occur again with exactly the same characteristics. As a result, it is difficult to make generalisations from natural experiments.

Ethical issues There may be ethical problems in certain situations. For example, people's experience of natural disasters can be traumatic. They don't want an intrusive researcher asking questions if they are still in shock after an earthquake; and after they have got over the initial shock, they might not want to be reminded of the situation as they attempt to rebuild their lives.

2.4 Quasi-experiments

Natural experiments are an example of *quasi-experiments*.

Quasi means almost. In a quasi-experiment, the researcher lacks the degree of control found in true experiments.

Quasi-experiments usually take place in natural settings outside the laboratory. In such settings, the researcher may be unable to control important variables. First, the researcher may be unable to control the independent variable. This can be seen clearly from natural experiments. In terms of the examples given in this section, the researcher is unable to control a natural disaster or a policy of zero tolerance policing. In a true experiment, the researcher would be able to systematically manipulate the independent variable and control a range of other variables which might affect the participants' behaviour. As the activity on zero tolerance policing shows, this is not possible in a natural experiment. A number of uncontrolled factors, other than zero tolerance policing, may have affected the reduction in the crime rate. Because of this, the researcher cannot be confident about establishing cause and effect relationships.

Second, in a natural setting, the researcher is often unable to select participants and assign them to one condition or another. For example, in the New York subway experiment, the researchers simply relied on participants who happened to be in the train compartment. In a true experiment, participants are randomly assigned to the different conditions. It is assumed that random assignment will cancel out differences between the participants. As a result, differences in their behaviour in the various conditions are seen to reflect different levels of the independent variable. In a quasi-experiment, differences in behaviour may be due to differences between the groups of participants. Again, this makes it difficult to establish cause and effect relationships.

In summary, quasi-experiments lack the controls of a true experiment – in particular, they lack control of the independent variable and/or participants are not randomly assigned to different conditions. Despite this, quasi-experiments can produce valuable data. Their findings can suggest cause and effect relationships. And these findings are often supported by evidence from other studies. In addition, because they often take place in natural settings, quasi-experiments avoid the criticism of artificiality and lack of realism which is sometimes levelled at laboratory experiments.

Summary

1. Supporters of laboratory experiments argue that their value lies in:
   - Control of variables
   - Establishing cause and effect relationships
   - Objective measurement
   - Ease of replication.
2. There are a number of possible disadvantages to laboratory experiments. They include:
   - Demand characteristics
   - Investigator effects
   - Low ecological validity
   - Inappropriateness for different cultures
   - Limited to certain types of behaviour.
3. Compared to laboratory experiments, field experiments are likely to have the following advantages:
   - Greater realism
   - Less likely to be affected by demand characteristics and investigator effects

   and the following disadvantages:
   - Less control of variables
   - More difficult to replicate
   - More costly and time-consuming
   - Less control of samples
   - Often not possible to use technical equipment.
4. Natural experiments have the following advantages:
   - Realism
   - Minimal demand characteristics and investigator effects
   - Unique research opportunities

   and the following disadvantages:
   - No control over variables
   - Cannot establish cause and effect relationships
   - Cannot be replicated
   - Difficult to generalise.
5. Quasi-experiments lack the controls of true experiments. The researcher is sometimes unable to control the independent variable and may be unable to randomly assign participants to different conditions.

Unit 3 Investigations using correlational analysis

KEY ISSUES

1. **What is correlational analysis?**
2. **What are its advantages and disadvantages?**

Correlational analysis is a technique for analysing data rather than a research method as such. Thus, correlational analysis can be used for analysing data produced by different research methods – by laboratory and field experiments, questionnaire surveys, interviews and so on.

Correlational analysis is a statistical technique which measures the strength of relationships between two or more variables. As such, it requires quantitative data – data in the form of numbers. For example, correlational analysis can be used to measure the relationship between the amount of revision – measured in hours and minutes – and examination performance – measured in the number of marks.

It is possible to obtain a numerical measure of the strength of the relationship between variables. This measure is known as the correlational coefficient. Correlational coefficients vary between –1 (perfect negative correlation) to +1 (perfect positive correlation) with 0 showing no correlation at all between the variables.

A positive correlation refers to a relationship where an increase in one variable is accompanied by an increase in another variable. For example, an increase in revision is accompanied by an increase in examination marks. A negative correlation refers to a relationship in which an increase in one variable is accompanied by a decrease in another variable. For example, an increase in visits to the pub is accompanied by a decrease in examination marks. A correlation of zero indicates no relationship between the variables. For example, there may be a zero correlation between hair colour and examination marks. (Correlational analysis is examined in more detail in Chapter 18).

Correlation and causation If there is a high positive or negative correlation between two variables, this does not necessarily mean that one causes the other. For example, there is often a high positive correlation between the sales of cold drinks and the yellowness of grass, yet neither of these factors is causing the other. The explanation for this correlation lies with a 'hidden third factor', namely the temperature. On hot summer days the grass tends to turn to yellow and everyone wants cold drinks.

Correlational analysis in psychological research

Correlational analysis is widely used in psychology. The following example indicates some of the advantages and disadvantages of this technique.

Life events, stress and illness Life events are significant changes in a person's life which disrupt their normal routines. Examples include marriage, the death of a close relative and moving house. As outlined in Chapter 8 (pp 113-114), Holmes and Rahe (1967) argued that life events produce high levels of stress. They devised the Social Readjustment Rating Scale (SRRS) in which 43 life events were ranked in terms of the degree of 'social readjustment' they required. Each life event was assigned a number of 'life change units' from 100 (death of husband or wife) to 11 (minor violations of the law such as a speeding ticket). A person's 'stress score' is the sum of the life change units of events they have experienced during a period of 12 months.

Correlational analysis was then used to discover whether there was a relationship between stress scores and incidence of future illness. A survey of studies using the SRRS indicates a correlation coefficient of 0.3 (Sarafino, 1994). This suggests a relationship, but not a particularly strong one.

Does a high 'stress score' produce a greater chance of illness? Not necessarily. Some illnesses can develop undetected over long periods of time. Some of the life events included in the SRRS may result from the early stages of an illness rather than causing that illness. Possible examples are changes in eating and sleeping habits, trouble with in-laws or the boss, and sex difficulties, all of which may be a response to a developing illness (Brown, 1986).

This example shows why correlational analysis cannot establish cause and effect relationships. It indicates three possibilities. First, high stress scores might lead to illness. Second, illness might lead to high stress scores. Third, both high stress scores and illness might result from some other unknown factor.

Advantages of correlational analysis

Strength of relationships Correlational analysis measures the strength of relationships between variables. It can be applied to numerical data produced by a range of research methods.

Further research Correlational analysis can identify relationships between variables. This may open up new lines of research. Further experimental research may indicate the probability of the relationship being causal or not.

Disadvantages of correlational analysis

Causation A high correlation between two variables cannot, on its own, show that one variable is causing the other. The correlation may be caused by a third factor. Even if a causal relationship exists, correlation does not show the direction of causation – for example A might cause B or B might cause A.

Key term

Correlational coefficient *A numerical measure of the strength of the relationship between two or more variables.*

Summary

1. Correlational analysis provides a numerical measure of the strength of the relationship between variables. It is widely used in psychological research.
2. A high correlation between two variables does not necessarily indicate a cause and effect relationship.

Unit 4 Observational research

KEY ISSUES

1. **What are the main types of observational research?**
2. **What are their advantages and disadvantages?**

4.1 Naturalistic observation

Naturalistic observation refers to the observation of behaviour in its natural setting. The researcher makes no attempt to influence the behaviour of those being observed. In fact, researchers do their best not to intervene and manipulate variables. The aim is to observe naturally occurring behaviour.

Naturalistic observation is widely used in zoology and ethology where non-human animals are observed in their natural habitat. It is also used to study human behaviour.

Naturalistic observation may be *disclosed* – where the observer informs the people he or she is studying that they are being observed. Or, it may be *undisclosed* – where the observer remains hidden and/or attempts to disguise the real reason for their presence.

Naturalistic observation is sometimes defined as *non-participant observation*. This means that researchers do not participate in the behaviour they are observing and, most of the time, those they are observing are unaware of the researcher's presence. It is possible to observe human behaviour in this way – for example the researcher may find an inconspicuous place on a street, in a shopping centre or a museum from which to observe undetected. Alternatively, behaviour can be filmed using hidden video cameras.

Naturalistic observation tends to be limited to public places and specific aspects of behaviour. For example, it might be used to study behaviour at a pelican crossing. The researcher might note who waits for the 'green man' before crossing the road. At first sight, this seems a rather trivial study. However, if the findings showed that males and young people were more likely to cross on red than females and older people, this may indicate gender and age differences in risk taking. And if this finding was reflected in risk taking in a range of other situations, then it ceases to be trivial and may indicate general tendencies in human behaviour.

Systematic observation Naturalistic observations are often conducted systematically. The researcher may use a *behaviour schedule* – a checklist of precisely defined behaviours which are recorded as and when they occur. For example, a behaviour schedule for aggressive behaviours in a primary school playground included the following categories: bite, chase, hit, push-pull and wrestle (Strayer & Strayer, 1976). These behaviours were ticked off systematically as they occurred. This provides quantitative data which can be directly compared with the results of similar studies using the same behaviour schedule. However, there are a number of problems with this approach. First, only behaviours which fit the categories on the schedule are recorded. Second, the researcher has no information about the meaning of these behaviours to those concerned. For example, is a 'hit' in the playground study an aggressive or a playful act?

Advantages of naturalistic observation

Realism and natural behaviour The researcher is able to observe behaviour which occurs naturally in a real-life setting. No attempt is made to change that behaviour. As a result, it is likely that people will behave normally.

Low demand characteristics and investigator effects When people are unaware they are being observed, their behaviour will not be influenced by demand characteristics or investigator effects.

New ideas Naturalistic observation can provide new ideas for research which can be examined systematically in later studies.

Testing existing findings Naturalistic observation can be used to discover whether the findings of laboratory experiments are reflected in real-life situations.

Disadvantages of naturalistic observation

Lack of control The researcher has no control over the variables – for example, the number and social characteristics of the participants. As a result, cause and effect relationships cannot be established. Observations can describe behaviour but are unlikely to tell us why it took place.

Observer bias As Chapter 3 on eyewitness testimony has shown, observers interpret what they see, they are selective in what they notice, and they tend to see what they expect to see. Observer bias can be reduced by using a behaviour schedule. However, this places limits on the behaviour recorded and discourages observation of behaviour not listed on the schedule.

Meanings Naturalistic observation provides little information about the meanings which direct the behaviour of those observed. This raises problems for the analysis and interpretation of observational findings.

Limitations Naturalistic observation tends to be limited to public places and specific aspects of behaviour. It is unlikely to provide a picture of the way of life of a group of people.

Ethical issues In many cases, people have no idea they are being observed. As a result, they have no opportunity to give informed consent. According to the British Psychological Society's ethical guidelines for research, unless people give their consent, observational research is only acceptable in places where they would expect to be observed by strangers (BPS, 1998). However, a glance from a stranger is very different from the close scrutiny of naturalistic observation. People may well object to this scrutiny as an invasion of their privacy. They may also object to being filmed by hidden video cameras.

4.2 Controlled observation

Controlled observation takes place in a natural setting, but the researcher intervenes and manipulates certain aspects of the situation. An illustration of controlled observation is provided in Activity 5, which looks at the behaviour of macaque monkeys.

Certain features of their natural environment were changed in order to study the extent to which the monkeys could learn new behaviour patterns. It is important that the environment remains unaltered apart from the changes introduced by the researcher. This means that any changes in behaviour are probably due to the changes introduced by the observer. And, because they remain in their normal environment, the monkeys can respond to these changes as naturally as possible.

Activity 5 Controlled observation

Japanese macaques washing potatoes

Paddling in the sea

For a number of years Japanese researchers have been studying the behaviour of macaque monkeys on islands in northern Japan. On one island, the macaques lived in the forest in the interior. The researchers tried to discover whether they could change the behaviour of the monkeys. They began by dumping potatoes in a clearing in the forest. The macaques picked them up, sniffed them inquisitively and tasted them. Gradually they changed their eating habits, and potatoes, a food previously unknown to them, became their main diet. The researchers then began moving the potatoes towards the shoreline, and the macaques followed. The potatoes were regularly dumped on the beach and the troupe took up residence there rather than in the forest. Then, without any encouragement from the researchers, a number of brand new behaviour patterns developed.

Some of the macaques began washing potatoes in the sea before eating them, a practice which was soon adopted by the whole group. Some of the younger monkeys began paddling in the sea then took the plunge and learned how to swim. Their elders followed suit and swimming became normal behaviour for the whole troupe. Finally, some of the more adventurous youngsters began diving into the sea from rocks on the shoreline. Other members of the troupe imitated them but some of the older macaques decided that this time they would not follow the lead of the youngsters.

Adapted from Kawamura, 1963

Questions

1 Why is this a controlled observation?

2 Why is it important that it be conducted in the macaques' natural environment?

Advantages of controlled observation

Natural setting Controlled observation allows researchers to study behaviour in natural settings.

Focus Controlled observation enables researchers to focus on what they want to study. In the case of the macaques, intervention meant the researchers were able to observe the extent to which new behaviour patterns could be learned. Without intervention, they might observe the macaques for years without seeing any significant change in behaviour.

Disadvantages of controlled observation

Disturbing natural settings Intervention means that the natural setting has been disturbed – in this respect it is no longer natural. For example, the macaques were provided with a new supply of food. And, for the first time in their existence, they no longer had to forage for food.

4.3 Participant observation

How do we really know how people behave in their normal, everyday settings? One way is to join them – to participate in their daily activities and observe what they say and do. This research method is known as *participant observation*. It was used by Erving Goffman (1968) when he took on the role of a member of staff in order to study the experience of patients in a psychiatric hospital in Washington DC. It was also used by the white journalist John Howard Griffin (1960), who dyed his skin black in order to discover what it was like to live as an African American in the southern states of the USA.

Supporters of participant observation see it as an important means of obtaining rich qualitative data. It provides an opportunity to observe people in their natural settings as opposed to the artificial surroundings of the laboratory. It enables researchers to see what people actually do, as opposed to what they say they do when interviewed. It provides an opportunity to capture the meanings which direct behaviour in everyday life.

Gaining entry Participant observation only works if the researcher can gain entry into the group and obtain some degree of acceptance and trust. Researchers sometimes inform those they are studying about their research. For example, William Whyte (1955), told the Italian-American gang he observed in Boston, Massachusetts, that he was studying the area – they assumed he was gathering material for a book. Sometimes researchers disguise their real purpose for joining the group. This is known as covert (hidden) research. For example, Festinger et al. (1956) found that the only way to observe a small religious sect was to pretend to be a 'true believer' and become a member of the group.

Conducting research As far as possible, researchers try not to influence the behaviour of those they observe. Most researchers simply watch and listen and attempt to blend into the background.

Participant observation is often informal, unplanned and unstructured – it consists of 'hanging around'. In his study of pilfering from the docks in St Johns, Newfoundland, Mars (1982) wandered round the wharves and sheds chatting to the dockers, and hung round the bars with them in the evening.

Recording data can be difficult. Researchers usually write up the day's findings each evening, when events are still fresh in their mind. However, this relies on the researcher's memory which is inevitably partial and selective.

Participant observation can be a long and difficult process. Some researchers spend over a year 'in the field', often cut off from the normal social supports of family and friends.

Some of the advantages and disadvantages of participant observation can be seen from Activity 6.

Advantages of participant observation

Normal behaviour Since those observed are in their normal, everyday environment, they are likely to behave naturally. The presence of an observer may affect their behaviour. However, most participant observers believe that once they have gained acceptance and trust, people revert to their normal behaviour.

Insight and new directions Observation can provide fresh insights and new directions for research as the quote from Whyte (1955) indicates (see Activity 6, Item A).

Insider's view By watching and listening, the participant observer has the chance to discover how people see the world in which they live – their meanings, concerns and priorities.

Qualitative data Participant observation can provide a rich source of qualitative data – from detailed accounts of conversations in bars and on streetcorners to vivid descriptions of people's feelings as they experience the ups and downs of everyday life.

Practicality Sometimes the only way to study a group is to join it. The Italian-American gang studied by Whyte were suspicious of outsiders. Only when he gained their trust and acceptance did he obtain any worthwhile data.

Disadvantages of participant observation

Observer bias Researchers interpret the behaviour of those they observe. They watch and listen and try to make sense of the behaviour of others. To some extent, these observations will be affected by the researcher's own beliefs, values and sympathies.

Observer effects The presence of the researcher will, to some degree, affect the behaviour of those observed. As Hargreaves' (1967) study indicates, some teachers changed their behaviour in his presence (see Activity 6, Item B).

Sample size Sample sizes are small. The researcher can only be at one place at one time and can only obtain an in-depth picture of a small group of people.

Quantitative data The type of data obtained by participant observation does not lend itself to quantification. Descriptions of everyday life are difficult to translate into numbers.

Replication Because participant observation relies so heavily on the interpretive skills and personal qualities of the observer, it is difficult to replicate. Participant observation is often unsystematic – there are no fixed procedures. Again, this makes replication difficult, if not impossible.

Generalisation Small samples make if difficult to generalise. Also, because participant observation studies look at people at particular times and in particular settings, it is difficult to

Activity 6 Participant observation

Item A Cornerville

The following extract is taken from William Whyte's study of an Italian-American gang in Boston in an area he called 'Cornerville'.

'As I sat and listened, I learned the answers to questions that I would not even have had the sense to ask if I had been getting my information solely on an interviewing basis. When I had established my position on the street corner, the data simply came to me without very active efforts on my part.'

Adapted from Whyte, 1955

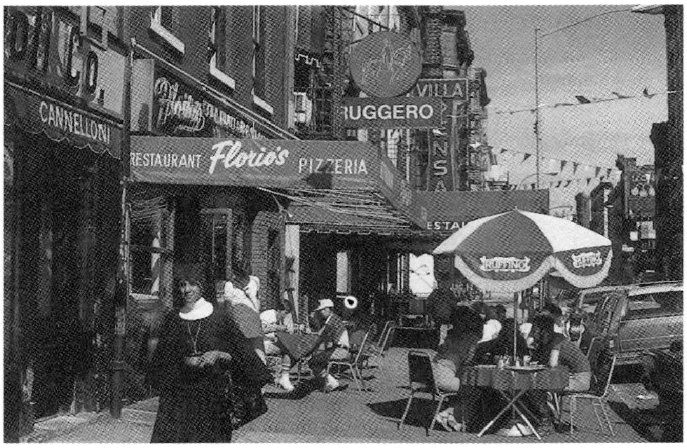

Whyte's research was carried out in the Italian-American community of South Boston. Many east coast American cities have large Italian communities. This picture shows 'Little Italy' in New York.

Item B In the classroom

The following extract is taken from David Hargreaves' study of an all-boys secondary school in England. He sat at the back of the classroom to observe lessons. Later, he talked to some of the boys about the behaviour of the teachers. This is what they said.

'When you're in he tries to act calmly as though he's a little angel and all that.'

'They put on a show for you. They put the good act on, smiles and all that, and when you've gone out …'

'Like if Mr O's getting mad 'cos someone's ripped a book or something, but if you're in he seems to drop it. If you weren't there, he'd get real mad.'

Adapted from Hargreaves, 1967

Item C On the street

Elliot Liebow studied African-American 'streetcorner men' – unemployed men who hung round on street corners – in Washington DC. He chose participant observation because he wanted 'an inside view, a clear first-hand picture of the life of ordinary people, on their grounds and on their terms'. Liebow claims that, 'Taking this inside view makes it easier to avoid structuring the material in ways that might be alien to the material itself'.

Adapted from Liebow, 1967

Question

What are the advantages and disadvantages of participant observation indicated by Items A, B and C?

generalise to other times and settings.

Time, money and personal cost Participant observation is often costly and time-consuming. Researchers can spend over a year 'in the field'. There are also personal costs – time away from friends and family and sometimes high levels of stress and even danger. For example, Haralambos (1994) was threatened with guns on more than one occasion during his research on the south side of Chicago.

Ethical issues Covert (hidden) observation involves deception – people don't know they are being observed. Even when researchers reveal the reasons for their presence, they rarely tell the whole truth. Often those observed have insufficient information to give fully informed consent.

Key terms

Naturalistic observation *Observation of behaviour in its normal social setting. Usually, the researcher does not participate in this behaviour and those observed are unaware of the researcher's presence.*

Behaviour schedule *A checklist of precisely defined behaviours which are recorded as and when they occur.*

Controlled observation *The researcher controls one or more of the factors in a natural setting and observes the behaviour that results.*

Participant observation *Observation of behaviour in its normal social setting. The researcher participates in the activities of those observed.*

Summary

1. Naturalistic observation has the following advantages:
   - Realism and natural behaviour
   - Low demand characteristics and investigator effects
   - It can generate new ideas
   - It can be used to test existing findings

   and the following disadvantages:
   - Lack of control of variables
   - Observer bias
   - Little information about meanings
   - Tends to be limited to public places and specific aspects of behaviour
   - Ethical problems.
2. Controlled observation allows researchers to observe behaviour in natural settings and to focus on what they want to study. However, intervention by the researcher disturbs the setting.
3. Participant observation has the following advantages:
   - Realism and natural behaviour
   - Insight and new directions for research
   - Provides a rich source of qualitative data
   - Can be the only practical way of studying certain groups

   and the following disadvantages:
   - Observer bias
   - Observer effects
   - Small samples
   - Lack of quantitative data
   - Difficult to replicate
   - Difficult to generalise from findings
   - Often time-consuming, with high financial and personal costs
   - Ethical problems.

Unit 5 Questionnaire surveys

KEY ISSUES

1. **What are questionnaire surveys?**
2. **What are they used for?**

5.1 Surveys

A *survey* is the systematic collection of the same type of data from a large number of people. This data is usually collected by means of a *questionnaire* – a printed list of questions. In most cases, everybody in the survey is asked the same questions. The type of data collected by surveys is illustrated by the following examples. Twenty-six per cent of all households in 1997 had a home computer. In 1997, *Sugar* was the most popular magazine for 11-14 year old girls – it was read by 47% of the age group. In 1998, 61% of households participated in the Saturday draw of the National Lottery. (All figures are for the UK and taken from *Social Trends*, 1999).

Nearly all surveys are based on a sample of the population to be investigated – the Census is an exception, it requires information on all members of a society. 'Population' refers to everybody in the group to be studied. The population might be 16-19 year old students, manual workers, divorced men, single women and so on. A sample is a selection of part of the population. Samples are necessary because researchers rarely have the time and money to study everybody in the population.

Most researchers try to select a sample which is representative of the population. This means that the sample should have the same characteristics as the population as a whole. For example, if a sample of 16-19 year old students contained only females who were taking A level psychology, it would not be representative. With a representative sample, the researcher can be more confident of generalising from the survey findings, that is applying them to the population as a whole. (Sampling techniques are examined in the following chapter.)

Surveys are sometimes divided into two types – the *descriptive* and the *analytic survey* (Oppenheim, 1992).

Descriptive surveys, as their name suggests, simply describe aspects of the population under study. The information they provide is often based on the question 'How many?' For example, 'How many people attend church on Sundays?' or 'How many people intend to vote Liberal Democrat in the next general election?'

Analytic surveys are designed to discover relationships between variables – for example, the relationship between age, gender and church attendance. Correlational analysis is often used to calculate the strength of these relationships, but as noted earlier, this type of analysis cannot establish cause and effect relationships.

5.2 Questionnaires

The questionnaire is the main method of collecting data for surveys. It consists of a list of pre-set questions.

Types of questions There are two main types of questions used in questionnaires – *closed* and *open questions*. In closed questions, the various responses are fixed by the researcher. Respondents – those who answer the questions – are required to give 'yes' or 'no' answers or to choose between a fixed number of alternatives. The following example is taken from the annual British Social Attitudes Survey. It shows the percentage of respondents who selected each alternative.

How often do you ...

Make a special effort to sort glass or tins or plastic or newspapers and so on for recycling?	%
Always	19
Often	23
Sometimes	30
Never	21
Not available where I live	6

From Jowell et al., 1994

Closed questions are easy to quantify and therefore appropriate for correlational analysis. However, they limit the respondent's choice and freedom of expression.

Open questions allow respondents to answer in their own words. They are particularly appropriate for finding out respondents' opinions and their views of their own behaviour. For example, the question 'Why did you vote Liberal Democrat?' allows respondents to give their own views in their own way.

Open questions are more difficult to quantify. Researchers have to *code* the answers – interpret and classify them – in order to state, for example, that 40% of respondents voted Liberal Democrat because of the party's policy on education. (The design of questionnaires and the analysis of questionnaire data is discussed in more detail in the following two chapters).

Administering questionnaires Questionnaires can be administered – given to respondents – in a number of ways. They can be sent through the post or printed in newspapers and magazines. They can be handed to the respondent and collected later. They can be read out and filled in by the researcher as the respondent answers verbally. In this case, they take the form of structured interviews. This involves the problem of interviewer effects which is discussed in the following unit.

Advantages of questionnaire surveys

Time and money Questionnaires are a fast, efficient and relatively inexpensive method of collecting data.

Large samples Because questionnaires are fast and cheap, questionnaire surveys can be based on far larger samples than are available to other research methods.

Quantitative data Particularly in the case of closed questions, questionnaire data is easy to quantify. As a result, it is suitable for statistical analysis.

Generalisation If the sample is representative, it is possible to generalise from the findings of a questionnaire survey.

Replication Since the questions are standardised and selection procedures for the sample are usually explicit, questionnaire surveys are easy to replicate.

Disadvantages of questionnaire surveys

Response rate The response rate – the percentage of people in the sample who actually complete the questionnaire – is sometimes low – often well below 50% for postal questionnaires and well below 5% for questionnaires in newspapers and magazines. This may destroy the representativeness of the sample. Those who do not complete the questionnaire may differ in important respects from those who do.

Limitations on response Questionnaires often place limits on what respondents wish to say, particularly in the case of closed questions.

Demand characteristics Respondents may give answers

which they think the researcher expects or wants. There may also be social desirability effects – respondents may try to present themselves in the best possible light.

Sensitive areas Respondents may refuse to reveal information which they find embarrassing, eg sexual behaviour, or which may cause them problems if reported to the authorities, eg criminal behaviour.

Ambiguity of questions Questions may be open to different interpretations. If respondents interpret questions differently, then their answers are not directly comparable.

Summary

Questionnaire surveys have the following advantages:

- Fast, efficient, relatively inexpensive
- Large samples
- Provide quantitative data
- Easy to replicate

and the following disadvantages:

- Sometimes low response rate
- Limited possible responses
- Demand characteristics
- Refusal to reveal sensitive information
- Possible ambiguity of questions.

Key terms

Questionnaire *A list of pre-set questions.*

Questionnaire survey *The collection of the same type of data from a large number of people by means of a questionnaire.*

Descriptive survey *The collection of data which can be used to describe a population.*

Analytic survey *A survey designed to discover relationships between variables.*

Closed questions *Questions where the various responses are fixed by the researcher.*

Open questions *Questions where the responses are not fixed – respondents can answer them in their own way.*

Coding questionnaires *Classifying answers into different types.*

Unit 6 Interviews

KEY ISSUES

1. **What are the main types of interview?**
2. **What are their advantages and disadvantages?**

Interviews involve the researcher asking the respondent questions. However, some interviews are more like a discussion or a conversation than a question and answer session. Interviews fall between two extremes – *structured interviews* and *unstructured interviews*. In the middle are *semi-structured interviews* which are a mixture of the two types.

6.1 Structured interviews

A structured interview is simply a questionnaire which is read out to the respondent. The interviewer writes down the answers. All respondents are given the same questions in the same order. Structured interviews are sometimes known as *formal interviews* because there is little opportunity for informal conversation. They are also known as *directive interviews* because the interviewer directs the proceedings. Structured interviews have many of the same advantages and disadvantages as questionnaires.

Advantages of structured interviews

Focus They allow researchers to focus on exactly what they want to find out.

Time and money Most are relatively short and inexpensive.

Quantifiable data Much of the data is easily quantified.

Replication Since respondents are asked the same questions in the same order, they are easy to replicate.

Comparable data Assuming the questions mean the same thing to all respondents, the data can be directly compared since all respondents are answering the same questions.

Interviewer assistance The interviewer is on hand to clear up any ambiguity or misunderstanding with the questions.

Disadvantages of structured interviews

Lack of flexibility The questions are predetermined which leaves little room for respondents to develop their answers or move into areas which interest them. As a result, there is less chance of the richer qualitative data that unstructured interviews often produce.

Investigator or interviewer effects Because they are answered in the presence of an interviewer, there is a greater chance of investigator effects than in a questionnaire survey. For example, with certain questions respondents might give different answers to male and female interviewers. However, investigator effects are probably less likely than in unstructured interviews.

6.2 Unstructured interviews

Unstructured interviews are more like a conversation. They are sometimes called *informal interviews* because the atmosphere is relatively relaxed and friendly. They are sometimes known as *non-directive interviews* because the interviewer is usually less directive and, at times, the respondent decides which direction the interview will take. And, they are sometimes called *in-depth interviews* because they tend to 'dig more deeply' into the respondent's beliefs, attitudes and feelings.

As part of their training, interviewers are encouraged to develop *rapport* – a friendly and understanding relationship with the respondent. However, they must maintain a certain distance or the respondent may be unduly influenced if they become too friendly. When conducting an unstructured interview, interviewers are taught to be non-directive – they must avoid asking leading questions and allow respondents to express themselves in their own way. This does not mean they have a chat about something and nothing. Interviewers have certain topics they wish to cover and, at times, they must steer respondents towards these topics.

Advantages of unstructured interviews

Respondent's viewpoint Opportunities are provided for respondents to give their own point of view in their own way. They are able to talk about things which interest them, rather than simply responding to pre-set questions. This can produce new and important insights.

Qualitative data Unstructured interviews can produce rich and detailed qualitative data, especially when the respondent feels the interviewer is sympathetic and understanding.

Developing answers The interviewer has the opportunity to develop the respondent's answers by asking further questions. Interviewers can 'dig deeper'.

Sensitive areas Unstructured interviews are particularly suitable for covering sensitive areas because they provide an opportunity for trust to develop between interviewer and respondent. For example, postal questionnaire surveys were used in London to find out why people did not apply for welfare benefits to which they were entitled. The response rate was very low, partly due to fear and suspicion of authority. Research indicated that the best way to obtain answers was to use unstructured interviews, with skilled interviewers who could develop rapport (Fielding, 1993).

Disadvantages of unstructured interviews

Investigator or interviewer effects Unstructured interviews involve a face-to-face relationship between interviewer and respondent, and often the discussion of intimate personal details. Because of this they are 'wide open' to interviewer effects. For example, the interviewer's beliefs and values can affect the respondent's answers (see Item B, Activity 7).

Key terms

Structured interview *A pre-set list of questions which is read out to the respondent by the interviewer.*

Unstructured interview *Questions and discussion about particular topics. The questions are not pre-set, the direction of the interview is not pre-determined.*

So can the personal qualities of the interviewer – for example, whether they have a sense of humour or a concern for others. And so can the social characteristics of the interviewer – their gender, ethnicity, age, social class and so on (see Item C, Activity 7). And, in a face-to-face situation, social desirability effects may also influence the respondent's answers.

Lack of comparable data Because of a lack of structure and the fact that interviews can take very different directions, it is difficult to directly compare the data from unstructured interviews.

Lack of quantitative data It is difficult to code and quantify much of the qualitative data produced by unstructured interviews.

Replication and generalisation Because each interview is different, and because each involves a unique social relationship, it is not possible to exactly replicate an unstructured interview. And, for the same reasons, it is difficult to generalise from unstructured interviews.

Summary

1. Structured interviews have the following advantages:
   - Directly focused
   - Relatively short and inexpensive
   - Quantitative data
   - Comparable data
   - Easy to replicate
   - Interviewer assistance

   and the following disadvantages:
   - Lack of flexibility
   - Interviewer effects (though less than unstructured interviews).
2. Unstructured interviews have the following advantages:
   - Provide respondent's viewpoint
   - Rich, detailed qualitative data
   - Allow the interviewer to develop respondent's answers
   - Suitable for sensitive areas

   and the following disadvantages:
   - Interviewer effects and social desirability effects
   - Lack of quantitative data
   - Lack of comparable data
   - Difficult to replicate and generalise from.

Activity 7 Interviews

Item A Three interviews

Interview 1 An eight-year-old black boy from Harlem in New York is interviewed by a 'friendly' white interviewer who presents him with a toy jet plane and asks him to describe it. The setting is formal. There are long silences followed by short two or three word answers, which hardly provide an adequate description of the plane.

Interview 2 Another black boy from Harlem is interviewed. Again the setting is formal but this time the interviewer is black and raised in Harlem. The boy responds in much the same way as the boy in the first interview.

Interview 3 The boy and the interviewer are the same as in the second interview. This time the interviewer sits on the floor, the boy is provided with a supply of crisps and his best friend is invited along. The change is dramatic. The boy is enthusiastic, talkative, and gives a detailed description of the toy plane.

Adapted from Labov, 1973

Harlem, New York

Item B Interviewer effects (1)

In 1914, 2000 destitute men ('down-and-outs' with no means of support) were questioned by two interviewers in the USA. They were asked, among other things, to explain their situation. One of the interviewers was a strong supporter of prohibition – forbidding by law the manufacture and sale of alcoholic drinks. There was a strong tendency for the men he interviewed to blame their situation on alcohol. The second interviewer was a strong supporter of socialist political views. He believed that private industry should be brought into public ownership and that making a profit should take second place to the welfare of the workers. The men that he interviewed were much more likely to explain their misfortune in terms of the industrial situation.

Adapted from Deming, 1971

Item C Interviewer effects (2)

Eight hundred and forty African Americans were interviewed in North Carolina during the 1960s. All the interviewers were female, 13 were African American, 9 were white. Important differences were revealed between the responses obtained by black and white interviewers. For example, a significantly higher proportion of those interviewed by blacks said they approved of civil rights demonstrations and school desegregation. In addition, more respondents refused to give answers to these questions when faced by a white interviewer.

Adapted from Williams, 1971

Questions

1 Suggest reasons for the similarities and differences between the three interviews in Item A.

2 a) Explain the responses to the two interviewers in Item B.

b) What problem does this raise for researchers?

3 Suggest reasons for the different responses obtained by black and white interviewers in Item C.

6.3 Conclusion

Over a century ago, the German philosopher Wilhelm Dilthey distinguished between what he called 'scientific psychology' and 'humanistic psychology'. The prime objective of scientific psychology is to be scientific at all costs. It adopted the methods of the natural sciences – particularly the laboratory experiment – and applied them to human behaviour. The prime objective of humanistic psychology is to be as true as possible to the complexities and subtleties of human nature. And if this means losing the scientific status of psychology, then so be it.

Even today, we see 'scientifically-minded' psychologists preferring experimental methods, believing that only by controlling variables, objective measurement and replication can cause and effect relationships be established. On the other hand, 'humanistically-minded' psychologists tend to prefer non-experimental methods such as unstructured interviews and participant observation where the sheer richness and diversity of human experience can be explored. Each group remains highly critical of the other.

However, things are not locked into a stalemate. Many psychologists fall between these extremes. They recognise that no one method is entirely satisfactory – all have their strengths and weaknesses. Some argue that if a variety of methods are applied to the same question, and broadly similar results are obtained, then researchers can be more confident about their findings. This use of different methods is known as *triangulation*. It enables researchers to overcome the limitations imposed by any one method and can result in a deeper understanding of human behaviour.

References

Adams, P.R. & Adams, G.R. (1984). Mount Saint Helen's ashfall: Evidence for a disaster stress reaction. *American Psychologist, 39*, 252-260.

BPS (British Psychological Society). (1998). *Code of conduct, ethical principles and guidelines.* Leicester: BPS.

Brown, R. (1986). *Social psychology: The second edition.* New York: Free Press.

Chaundhary, V. & Walker, M. (1996). The petty crime war. *The Guardian*, 21.11.96.

Deming, W.E. (1971). On errors in surveys. In B.J. Franklin & H.W. Osborne (Eds.), *Research methods.* Belmont: Wadsworth.

Dobash, R.E. & Dobash, R. (1980). *Violence against wives.* Wells: Open Books.

Festinger, L., Riecken, H.W. & Schachter, S. (1956). *When prophecy fails.* Minneapolis: University of Minnesota Press.

Fielding, M. (1993). Qualitative interviewing. In N. Gilbert (Ed.), *Researching social life.* London: Sage.

Goffman, E. (1968). *Asylums.* Harmondsworth: Penguin.

Griffin, J.H. (1960). *Black like me.* New York: Signet.

Haralambos, M. (1994). *Right on: From blues to soul in black America.* Ormskirk: Causeway Press.

Hargreaves, D.H. *Social relations in a secondary school.* London: Routledge & Kegan Paul.

Hofling, K.C., Brotzman, E., Balrymple, S., Graves, N. & Pierce, C.M. (1966). An experimental study in the nurse-physician relationship. *Journal of Nervous and Mental Disorders, 143*, 171-180.

Holmes, T.H. & Rahe, R.H. (1967). The social readjustment rating scale. *Journal of Psychosomatic Research, 11*, 213-218.

Jowell, R., Curtice, J., Brook, L. & Ahrendt, D. (Eds.) (1994). *British social attitudes: The 11th report.* Aldershot: Dartmouth.

Kawamura, S. (1963). The process of sub-culture propagation among Japanese macaques. In C.H. Southwick (Ed.), *Primate social behaviour.* New York: Van Nostrand.

Labov, W. (1973). The logic of nonstandard English. In N. Keddie (Ed.), *Tinker, tailor … the myth of cultural deprivation.* Harmondsworth: Penguin.

Liebow, E. (1967). *Tally's corner.* Boston: Little Brown.

Loftus, E.F. & Palmer, J.C. (1974). Reconstruction of automobile destruction: An example of the interaction between language and memory. *Journal of Verbal Learning and Verbal Behavior, 13*, 585-589.

Mars, G. (1982). *Cheats at work: An anthropology of workplace crime.* London: Allen & Unwin.

Oppenheim, A.N. (1992). *Questionnaire design, interviewing and attitude measurement.* London: Pinter.

Orne, M.T. (1962). On the social psychology of the psychology experiment: With particular reference to demand characteristics and their implications. *American Psychologist, 17*, 776-783.

Orne, M.T. & Holland, C.C. (1968). On the ecological validity of laboratory deceptions. *International Journal of Psychiatry, 6*, 282-293.

Piliavin, I.M., Rodin, J. & Piliavin, J. (1969). Good Samaritanism: An underground phenomenon? *Journal of Personality and Social Psychology, 13*, 289-299.

Rosenthal, R. (1966). Covert communication in the psychological experiment. *Psychological Bulletin, 67*, 356-367.

Sarafino, E.P. (1994). *Health psychology: Biopsychological interactions* (2nd ed.). New York: John Wiley.

Sears, D.O. (1986). College sophomores in the laboratory: Influences of a narrow data base on psychology's view of human nature. *Journal of Personality and Social Psychology, 51*, 515-530.

Social Trends. (1999). London: the Stationery Office.

Strayer, F.F. & Strayer, J. (1976). An ethological analysis of social antagonism and dominance relations among preschool children. *Child Development, 47*, 980-989.

Whyte, W.F. (1955). *Street corner society* (2nd ed.). Chicago: University of Chicago Press.

Williams, J.A. Jr. (1971). Interviewer-respondent interaction. In B.J. Franklin, & H.W. Osborne (Eds.), *Research methods.* Belmont: Wadsworth.

17 Research design and implementation

Introduction

Research studies require careful planning and organisation. The organisation of a study is called the research design. This chapter looks at research design and how studies may be carried out or implemented.

Chapter summary

- **Unit 1 looks at aims and hypotheses in research studies.**
- **Unit 2 examines some of the main features of research design, focusing on experiments.**
- **Unit 3 outlines the main sampling procedures used to select participants for research.**
- **Unit 4 examines ways in which the relationship between researchers and participants can affect research.**
- **Unit 5 looks at the design of naturalistic observations, questionnaire surveys and interviews.**

Unit 1 Aims and hypotheses

KEY ISSUES

1. **How can aims be formulated?**
2. **What are the different types of hypotheses and why are they used?**

1.1 Formulation of aims

No research study takes place without an aim in mind. Where does the aim for a research project come from? Sometimes it reflects the researcher's personal interests, observations and concerns. For example, Stanley Milgram was horrified by the slaughter of the Holocaust. He wanted to know why apparently normal people followed orders which resulted in the deaths of millions of innocent people.

Often the aims of research derive from other researchers' theories and studies. For example, Bowlby's theory of maternal deprivation and Freud's idea of repressed memories have formed the basis for a large number of studies. Later research builds on the findings of earlier research and develops existing knowledge. For example, Milgram's obedience experiments have been repeated in various societies in order to see how culture affected their findings.

Sometimes research seeks to discover a solution to a practical problem. For example, the aim of some childcare studies is to improve day care facilities. And many studies of stress aim to provide methods for managing and reducing stress.

Once researchers have decided on an area to investigate, for example obedience or memory, they need to state the purpose of their research in a clear and precise way. For example, it is not sufficient to say, 'I'm going to study memory'. This is only a first step. In practice, most worthwhile studies have a much more specific aim, for example, 'This study aims to investigate the effects of noise on memory'.

It is important to ensure that the aim is realistic in terms of available resources, and that it is ethically acceptable. For example, if research funds were low, a study of attachment behaviour in six different cultures would probably be unrealistic. And, in terms of today's ethical guidelines, a replication of Milgram's obedience experiments would be considered unacceptable.

1.2 Hypotheses

Many research studies focus the aim more narrowly by translating it into a hypothesis. This turns the aim into a testable statement. For example, Darley and Latané (1968) designed an experiment to test the hypothesis that the greater the number of bystanders who witness an emergency, the less likely any one of them is to help (see p 221). The hypothesis is usually a prediction of what the researcher expects to happen. The research study is therefore a means of testing whether or not the hypothesis is supported by the findings.

Alternative and null hypotheses

In an experiment where the researcher is manipulating an independent variable (eg noise) and measuring a dependent variable (eg participants' performance on a memory test), it is customary to state two contradictory hypotheses – the *alternative hypothesis* and the *null hypothesis*. (In an experiment, the alternative hypothesis is also known as the *experimental hypothesis*.)

These two hypotheses cover the two possible outcomes of the experiment. Either the independent variable will have an effect on the dependent variable, or it will not. The alternative (or experimental) hypothesis states that it will. The null hypothesis states that it will not.

In terms of the effect of noise on memory experiment outlined in the previous chapter (see p 233), the two hypotheses could be presented like this:

- The alternative hypothesis states that noise will have an effect on performance of the memory task.
- The null hypothesis states that noise will not have an effect on performance of the memory task.

By stating both hypotheses, the researcher is spelling out the options. One of these options must be true. One of the hypotheses has to be correct.

Statistical tests are generally used to decide between the hypotheses. The researcher can reject the null hypothesis and accept the alternative hypothesis only if they can be more than 95% sure that the results are due to the action of the independent variable. If they are not this sure, they must reject the alternative hypothesis and accept the null hypothesis.

Most experiments have an alternative and null hypothesis. Correlational studies usually have both an alternative hypothesis and a null hypothesis (which predicts no correlation). Qualitative studies always have an aim but may not have an actual hypothesis.

Directional and non-directional hypotheses

In formulating the alternative hypothesis there is an additional decision that must be made – whether the hypothesis is directional or non-directional.

A *directional hypothesis* not only predicts that the independent variable will have an effect, it predicts what that effect will be. In the effect of noise on memory experiment, for example, a directional hypothesis will not just state that loud noise will have an effect on performance of the memory task, it will predict that loud noise will have the effect of impairing performance on the task.

A *non-directional hypothesis* simply states that the independent variable will have an effect and does not predict the direction of the effect. In the above example, it simply says that noise will have an effect on performance of the memory task.

The researcher must decide which form of the alternative hypothesis to use in each particular experiment. They cannot cheat and use both! The directional form has the advantage of being more precise, but the researcher must give good reasons why a directional hypothesis is being used. By and large, researchers can only use a directional hypothesis if they are confident of the direction of the effect of the independent variable. If they are not confident, they *must* use a non-directional hypothesis.

Some researchers do not think psychologists can ever be sufficiently confident to use a directional hypothesis. This might be a bit extreme. In the effect of noise on memory experiment, a directional hypothesis may well be justified since it is reasonable to assume that if loud noise has any effect, it will act as a distraction. However, in a study into whether people do better in exams in the morning or the afternoon, a non-directional hypothesis would probably be more appropriate.

It is important to note that this choice of two forms of hypothesis only applies to the alternative hypothesis. The null hypothesis is always a straight statement that the independent variable will not have an effect (or, in the case of a correlational study, that there will be no relationship between the variables).

Key terms

Null hypothesis *A hypothesis which states that the independent variable will have no effect on the dependent variable.*

Alternative hypothesis *In an experiment, a hypothesis which states that the independent variable will have an effect on the dependent variable.*

Directional hypothesis *A form of alternative hypothesis which states the direction of the effect of the independent variable.*

Non-directional hypothesis *A form of alternative hypothesis which does not state the direction of the effect of the independent variable.*

Summary

1. Research studies begin with a general aim which is increasingly focused.
2. In many studies, the aim is translated into a hypothesis which turns the aim into a testable statement.
3. If the researcher is more than 95% sure that the independent variable has had an effect, the alternative hypothesis can be accepted. If not, the null hypothesis must be accepted.

Unit 2 Research design

KEY ISSUES

1. **How are variables operationalised?**
2. **How might pilot studies improve research design?**
3. **What are the main features of experimental design?**
4. **How are reliability and validity assessed and improved?**
5. **How do ethical issues affect research design?**

2.1 Operationalisation

In an experiment, the researcher manipulates the independent variable to discover its effect on the dependent variable. In order to do this, it is necessary to *operationalise* these variables. This means defining the variables in such a way that they can be manipulated and precisely measured. For example, in the effect of noise on memory experiment, noise can be operationalised as so many decibels, and memory can be operationalised as performance on a memory test. Each operational definition provides quantitative data – numbers of decibels and scores on the memory test. Without operational definitions, it is not possible to measure the results of an experiment with any degree of precision. Nor is it possible to replicate the experiment since this requires the use of the same measuring instruments.

Sometimes it is more difficult to operationalise variables. Consider the following hypothesis: the more favouritism an adult shows to a child, the more the child will like the adult. Operationalising variables such as 'favouritism' and 'liking' requires considerable ingenuity. And when such variables are operationalised, are they actually measuring what they are intended to measure? For example, psychologists have operationalised aggression as delivering electric shocks, honking car horns, and pressing a button to make it difficult for others to complete a task. Are all these behaviours measuring the same thing? Despite these problems, it is often necessary to operationalise variables in order to do research.

2.2 Pilot studies

Pilot studies are sometimes carried out before the full-scale research project begins. They are a small-scale version of the real thing. Based on a small sample, they are usually quick, easy to conduct and inexpensive.

Pilot studies are used to make sure the research design works. For example, a questionnaire can be piloted with a small sample to make sure that the instructions are clear and that the questions make sense and mean the same thing to all the participants. Any errors in the design of the questionnaire can hopefully be corrected before the main research begins.

Pilot studies can also be helpful in operationalising variables. The previous chapter looked at a naturalistic observation of aggressive behaviour in a primary school playground (see p 241). Aggressive behaviour was operationalised by using a behaviour schedule which included the following items: bit, chase, hit, push-pull and wrestle (Strayer & Strayer, 1976). Preliminary observation of children in the playground may result in a more comprehensive schedule – for example, the addition of further items such as pinching. It may also indicate the importance of verbal aggression and lead the researcher to add examples of this to the schedule. And, as a final check, the improved schedule can be piloted before the actual research begins.

Pilot studies can reveal demand characteristics and provide an opportunity for the researcher to reduce them. For example, participants may guess the hypothesis under investigation and behave accordingly. A debrief after the pilot study may reveal this and lead to design changes which reduce demand characteristics. If changes are made, then it is advisable to pilot the new design.

Finally, a pilot study may show that the research design is completely impractical and send the researcher back to the drawing board.

2.3 Participant design

One of the most important features of experimental design is the way participants are allocated to groups when they take part in an experiment. This is called the *participant design*. The main purpose of participant design is to ensure that individual differences between the participants do not confound the results of the experiment. Suppose that in the effect of noise on memory experiment, participants in the quiet condition have normal hearing, while those in the noisy condition have impaired hearing. Clearly, this difference in hearing ability will affect the results. It becomes a confounding variable. The researcher cannot be sure whether a difference in performance between the two groups is due to the independent variable (noise level), or to the difference in hearing ability, or to both.

Individuals differ in many ways – personality, intelligence, physical skills, experience, sexual orientation, age, gender, social class, ethnicity, nationality and culture. Any, some, or all of these factors can affect their performance in an experiment. The researcher must find some way of eliminating, or at least minimising, the effects of individual differences in order to make sure that it is the effect of the independent variable that is being measured.

The three main types of participant design will now be examined.

Repeated measures design

The repeated measures design uses the same participants in each condition. For example, in the effect of noise on memory experiment, the *same* participants would be used in the quiet and noisy conditions. This eliminates the effect of individual differences since the same people are tested in each condition. As a result, a participant's performance in condition 1 can be directly compared with their performance in condition 2.

The repeated measures design has the added advantage of reducing the number of participants required. More participants would be needed if different participants were used in each of the two conditions. However, there are disadvantages to the repeated measures design.

There may be practical difficulties. For example, in the effect of noise on memory experiment, the researcher would need two memory tests of equivalent difficulty. And, if there was a period of time between the conditions, it is not always possible to get all the participants back!

Demand characteristics can be high as participants may realise what the experiment is about once they begin the second condition and see how it differs from the first. This is particularly true of experiments involving deception.

Similar problems arise if the experiment is studying the effectiveness of two training techniques – it is not easy for participants to unlearn what they have learned in the first condition. In these circumstances, two groups of participants are needed, one to do each condition.

Order effects This refers to the effects created by the order of the conditions. Because each participant does each condition, their performance in the second condition may be influenced by their performance in the first condition. They may learn a skill in the first condition which improves their performance in the second condition. This is called a *practice* or *transfer* effect. On the other hand, participants may get tired or bored by the time they do the second condition and this might impair their performance. Unless order effects are eliminated, they will become confounding variables.

Counterbalancing This technique aims to eliminate order effects. The order in which the participants do the conditions is counterbalanced. Some do condition 1 first, others start with condition 2. Counterbalancing only works if the effect of doing condition 1 then condition 2 is the same as doing them in the reverse order. It is difficult to be sure that this is the case.

Matched participants design

This participant design uses a different group of participants for each condition. Each participant in condition 1 is matched with a participant in condition 2 in terms of one or more variables. For example, they may be matched in terms of intelligence. The two participants with the highest IQ are randomly assigned, one to condition 1, the other to condition 2. The same applies to the two participants with the next highest IQ, and so on. This ensures that the groups are directly comparable in terms of IQ.

Sometimes participants are matched in terms of their performance on the experimental task. For example, in the effect of noise on memory experiment, the researcher may decide to match the participants in terms of memory skills. They are given a preliminary memory test and then assigned to groups on the basis of their scores. This means that their scores in the actual experiment should reflect noise level rather than memory ability.

The matched participants design has several advantages. It eliminates order and practice effects, and ensures that participants do not become fatigued by doing both conditions. It also saves the researcher from finding two sets of different but equivalent materials. For example, if a matched participants design was used in the effect of noise on memory experiment, only one memory test, not two, would be needed.

The main disadvantage is knowing what to match the participants for. It is all very well matching them for memory ability in a memory experiment, but what if hearing sensitivity, age, gender, ethnicity, IQ and so on affect performance? It would be extremely difficult and time-consuming to find participants who could be matched on a range of individual differences. And, even if this were possible, the researcher cannot be sure they have been matched on the right things. In addition, if matching involved a test before the experiment, this can be a source of demand characteristics.

Independent groups design

In this participant design, there are different participants in each condition but no attempt is made to match them. Instead, participants are randomly assigned to each condition, for example by tossing a coin or using a random number table. This means that each participant has an equal chance of being assigned to each of the conditions. The assumption is that reasonably comparable groups will emerge entirely by chance, provided the sample is fairly large. As a result, individual differences should cancel each other out and therefore have little effect on the results.

The independent groups design has a number of advantages. It avoids order effects. It is less costly and time-consuming than the matched participants design. However, control over individual differences is left to chance. This may have the desired effect of producing comparable groups of participants by cancelling out differences between them. But it may not. Using large samples and randomly allocating participants to conditions increases the likelihood of producing comparable groups, but it does not guarantee it.

Key terms

Repeated measures design *The same participants are used in all the conditions. Also known as related samples, related measures and within-group design.*

Matched participants design *Different participants are used in each condition but they are matched in terms of one or more variables, for example intelligence and memory ability. Also known as matched pairs and matched groups design.*

Independent groups design *Different participants are used in each condition. They are randomly allocated to the conditions. Also known as independent measures, independent participant and between-groups design.*

Order effects *The effect of the order of the conditions on the performance of the participants in the repeated measures design.*

Practice or transfer effect *An example of an order effect in which a skill learned in the first condition can affect performance in later conditions.*

Counterbalancing *A technique which aims to eliminate order effects.*

Random assignment *The random allocation of participants to each condition. Each participant has an equal chance of being assigned to each condition.*

2.4 Controlling variables

The previous section looked at three types of participant design which aim to control the effects of individual differences on the results of experiments. This section takes a wider view of the problem of controlling variables.

Extraneous variables

In an experiment an independent variable is manipulated to see if it has an effect on a dependent variable – the performance of the participants. However, there are many other variables which might have an effect on the dependent variable. These are known as *extraneous variables*. In order to measure the effect of the independent variable, it is essential that the extraneous variables are controlled. If this isn't done, then extraneous variables may spoil or confound the experiment. In other words, they may become *confounding variables*.

Systematic variation Some extraneous variables operate systematically, that is they vary from one condition to the next and so affect condition 1 differently from the way they affect condition 2. As a result, they may become confounding variables. For example, in the effect of noise on memory experiment, suppose participants in the noisy condition were in a hot room, while those in the quiet condition were in a cool room. Any difference in performance between the two sets of participants could be due to noise *or* temperature. Temperature may have become a confounding variable.

Similarly, suppose the participants in the noisy condition were 6th form students, and those in the quiet condition were pensioners. The researcher would not know whether the performance of the two groups was due to the action of the independent variable (noise level) or to their age. Age may have become a confounding variable.

Extraneous variables which operate systematically must be controlled in order to prevent the experiment from being spoiled or confounded. Ways of controlling extraneous variables are discussed on page 256.

Random errors Other extraneous variables do not operate systematically – they do not affect all the participants in a particular condition. Some participants in condition 1 might be affected by them and some participants in condition 2. These unsystematic effects are sometimes known as *random errors*. For example, a participant in one condition may have stomach ache. The researcher may sneeze in front of another participant. A wasp may buzz round the head of a third participant. Random errors do not confound the experiment because they do not make condition 1 consistently different from condition 2. However, they may still have some effect.

The effect of random errors can be indicated by having a control condition in the experiment to which the independent variable is not applied. The performance of the participants in the control group can be regarded as due to random errors, and their performance can then be compared to that of the experimental group. Many experiments in psychology compare an experimental group with a control group in this way.

The purpose of statistical testing is to estimate how likely it is that random errors have affected the dependent variable. If the test indicates that their effect was small, ie there is less than a 5% chance that they caused the change in the dependent variable, then the researcher can conclude that the results were due to the action of the independent variable, and accept the experimental hypothesis. Although it is not possible to get rid of random errors, statistical testing is a way of dealing with them.

Types of extraneous variables

There are three main types of extraneous variables which can affect the results of an experiment. They are *participant variables, situational variables* and *investigator variables*.

Participant variables refer to differences between the participants which might affect their performance. They include individual differences such as personality, intelligence, age and a range of social characteristics such as ethnicity and social class. They also include factors such as how participants feel on the day of the experiment and how much attention they give to the tasks they are performing.

Situational variables refer to the setting and circumstances of the research which may affect the performance of the participants. They include things like heat, light, noise, time of day and size of room. They also include the instructions given to participants and the procedures they follow.

Investigator variables refer to the personal and social characteristics and the behaviour of the researcher which may affect the performance of the participants. For example, the personality and appearance of the researcher and their age, gender, ethnicity and social class.

Controlling participant variables

Section 2.3 looked at the control of participant variables. Participant variables are controlled by participant design. There are three main types of participant design used in experiments – repeated measures design, matched participants design and independent groups design. Each type of participant design attempts to ensure that there are no consistent differences between the participants in the various conditions. The idea is to minimise the effects of individual differences on the performance of the participants. However, as noted earlier, there are problems with all three types of experimental design.

Controlling situational variables

Situational variables can be controlled in three main ways: standardisation, randomisation and counterbalancing.

Standardisation This refers to keeping variables constant, that is the same. For example, in a laboratory experiment, factors such as light, temperature and the time of day can be kept constant for all participants in all conditions. It is assumed that if everybody experiences constant situational variables, then these variables won't change their performance in the various conditions.

The procedures which participants follow and the tasks they perform must be the same in each condition. Participants must be given the same instructions and the same length of time to complete the tasks. Any variations in these factors can affect the performance of the participants and confound the experiment.

However, too much standardisation can be a problem. For example, if the researcher attempted to control every aspect of the environment, then the situation might become so artificial that there would be little chance of generalising the findings beyond the laboratory walls.

Randomisation Even in the highly controlled setting of a laboratory, it is not always possible to standardise situational variables. For example, it may not be possible to test all participants at the same time of day. In this case, randomisation offers an alternative to standardisation. Participants are randomly allocated to different times of the day. Here, the researcher assumes that random allocation will cancel out the effect of testing at different time periods.

Sometimes experiments are conducted outside the laboratory. For example, they may be conducted in participants' homes. This prevents standardisation of a number of situational variables, for example lighting and temperature. Rather than trying to control these variables, the researcher assumes that if participants in each condition experience a similar *range* of lighting and temperature, then these situational variables will cancel each other out. In order to be fairly sure that this happens, large samples are needed. This adds time and expense, but it can result in a more realistic experiment.

Counterbalancing can be used to deliberately cancel out situational variables. For example, if participants are being tested at different times of day, half the participants in condition 1 perform the experiment in the morning and half in the afternoon. The same applies to the participants in condition 2. The assumption is that this will cancel out the effect of testing at different times of day.

All three techniques of controlling situational variables may be used in one experiment. Instructions and procedures are usually standardised. In a repeated measures design, order effects can be eliminated by counterbalancing. Other situational variables may be dealt with by a mixture of standardisation and randomising according to the circumstances and the researcher's judgement. Designing experiments is quite an art.

Controlling investigator variables

Counterbalancing can also be used to control investigator variables. For example, if there were two researchers, a cheerful young woman for condition 1 and a solemn older

Key terms

Extraneous variables *Variables other than the independent variables which may affect the dependent variable.*

Confounding variables *Extraneous variables which affect the dependent variable in a systematic way and confound the experiment.*

Random errors *Extraneous variables which do not affect the dependent variable in a systematic way, but may still have some effect.*

Participant variables *Differences between participants which may affect their performance.*

Situational variables *The setting or circumstances of the research which may affect the performance of the participants.*

Investigator variables *The personal and social characteristics and the behaviour of the researcher which may affect the performance of the participants.*

man for condition 2, then participants may respond differently to each. However, if half the participants in each condition were dealt with by each researcher, then this may cancel out any effects of the different researchers' characteristics.

Investigator variables and their control are examined in more detail in Unit 4.

2.5 Reliability and validity

Reliability

Researchers aim to produce results which are both reliable and valid. Results are reliable if they are consistent. For example, if researchers replicate an experiment, using the same methods of observation and measurement, and obtain the same results, then both the methods and the data they produce are seen as reliable. Reliability matters – researchers can only trust results if they are reliable. However, reliability does not mean that the results are accurate. Nor does it mean that the methods are measuring what they are intended to measure. Take the following example.

A milometer in a car produces consistent readings between two towns. Every time the journey is made, it measures the same distance – 25 miles. This measurement is reliable because it is consistent. However, it is not accurate – the actual distance is 30 miles. The milometer is faulty.

And, the milometer may not be measuring what it is intended to measure, ie distance. It may be measuring something completely different. For example, due to incorrect wiring, it might be measuring fuel consumption.

In terms of this example, the measuring instrument is reliable – it produces consistent measurements – but it is not valid. A valid measuring instrument produces accurate measurements and measures what it is supposed to measure.

Assessing reliability

There are various methods of checking reliability.

Replication This refers to repeating a research study under exactly the same conditions. For example, in a laboratory experiment, it means using the same procedures in the same setting. Participants are given the same instructions and required to perform the same tasks. The sample is the same – for example in both experiments participants are 18-20 year old, middle-class British females. If the same results are obtained, then those results are seen as reliable.

Exact replication is practically impossible. Participants will not be exactly the same as those in the first experiment. The same usually applies to the researcher and the setting. However, if a later experiment is basically similar to an earlier experiment and produces similar results, then many researchers accept the results as reliable (Shaughnessy & Zechmeister, 1997).

In practice, few researchers attempt exact replications, mainly because it does little to advance their careers. For example, psychology journals rarely publish replications. To make a name for themselves, researchers need to publish new and exciting research, rather than simply repeating what went before (Graziano & Raulin, 1997).

A number of techniques have been developed for assessing the reliability of particular research methods. Some of these will be examined in Unit 5.

Validity

The results of a research study may be reliable but this does not necessarily mean they are valid. Valid results are accurate. A valid measuring instrument produces accurate measurements of what it is intended to measure. Returning to the example of the use of a behaviour schedule for measuring aggression in a school playground (see p 253), the schedule may produce results which are reliable but not valid. All the observers may obtain the same results – a reliable measure – but what they record as aggression may simply be non-aggressive play. If so, they are not measuring aggression. Their measurements are not valid because their measuring instrument – the behaviour schedule – is not measuring what it is designed to measure.

Research studies can be assessed in terms of *internal validity* and *external validity*.

Internal validity

Internal validity is the extent to which the findings of an experiment can be attributed to the effect of the independent variable. An experiment is internally valid when the findings have not been affected by confounding variables. In other words, the findings are due to the action of the independent variable. For example, in the effect of noise on memory experiment, if participants' performance on the memory test (the dependent variable) was due to variation in the noise level (the independent variable), then the experiment is internally valid. However, if their performance was affected by extraneous variables, such as differences in room temperature between the conditions, then the experiment does not have internal validity.

Establishing internal validity In order to establish internal validity, the researcher must control extraneous variables which might affect the dependent variable. In other words, the researcher must prevent extraneous variables from becoming confounding variables. Many of the techniques which aim to do this have already been examined. They include participant designs, such as the repeated measures design, which aim to prevent individual differences between participants from confounding the results. They include controlling situational variables and investigator variables. And they include attempts to reduce demand characteristics, investigator effects and social desirability effects (examined in Unit 4). The greater the control of extraneous variables, the more confident the researcher can be that the experiment is internally valid.

External validity

External validity refers to the extent to which research findings can be generalised. Simply because a research study has internal validity does not mean its results can be generalised. For example, an experiment may have internal validity but its findings may not apply to people beyond the laboratory walls.

A research study has high external validity if its findings can be generalised to other populations, other settings and other times.

Populations Can the findings be generalised to similar populations to those used in the research study? For example, if the study was based on a sample of female undergraduates, can the findings be applied to all female undergraduates? Can the findings be generalised further – for example, to male undergraduates, or more widely to people of different age, ethnic and social class groups? The term *population validity* refers to the extent to which findings can be generalised to other populations.

Settings Can the findings be generalised to other settings and situations? For example, can the findings of the New York subway experiment on helping behaviour be generalised to other settings such as the street, the school playground and the workplace? The term *ecological validity* refers to the extent to which findings can be generalised to other settings. (Ecological validity is sometimes used to mean external validity though, strictly speaking, it refers to settings.)

Times Can the findings be generalised to other times? For example, are the findings of studies conducted in the 1950s, such as Asch's conformity experiments in the USA, still valid today? As noted in Chapter 13, nonconformity was widely discouraged in 1950s' America (see p 190). The term *temporal validity* may be used to refer to the extent to which findings can be generalised to other times.

The highest level of external validity is when findings can be generalised to all populations, all settings, and all times.

Establishing external validity

How can researchers increase the external validity of their studies? How do they know the extent of the external validity of their research?

Sampling In general, researchers assume that the more representative the sample, the more likely the results can be generalised to a wider population. For example, if the sample reflects the general population in terms of a range of factors such as age, gender, ethnicity and social class, then the results of the study are more likely to have high population validity – they are more likely to apply to the population as a whole. (Sampling methods are examined in Unit 3.)

Partial replication This refers to repeating a study with a change in one or more of the variables, for example a change in the sample, setting or time (Shaughnessy & Zechmeister, 1997). Milgram partially replicated his original obedience experiment using female rather than male participants. The results were similar, indicating that, in terms of gender, the experiment had high population validity. Partial replications of Milgram's experiment were conducted using samples from different countries. The results varied indicating that, in these cases, population validity was lower (see p 213). Milgram also used a partial replication by changing the setting from a laboratory in Yale University to a rundown office building. Here the results indicated fairly low ecological validity – obedience was much lower in the office building (see p 210).

Realism Some researchers assume that the more realistic a research study, the higher its external validity. From this viewpoint, laboratory experiments are often seen as artificial and unrealistic. Because of this, it is unlikely that participants' behaviour in the laboratory will reflect their behaviour in the world outside. As a result, laboratory experiments are seen to have low external validity.

However, greater realism does not necessarily mean higher external validity. For example, field experiments are usually more realistic than laboratory experiments since

Key terms

Reliability *Measurements and findings are reliable if they are consistent.*

Replication *Repeating a research study under exactly the same conditions.*

Partial replication *Repeating a research study with a change in one or more of the variables, eg a different type of sample or setting.*

Validity *Measurements and findings are valid if they are accurate.*

Internal validity *The extent to which the findings of an experiment can be attributed to the effect of the independent variable.*

External validity *The extent to which research findings can be generalised to other populations, settings and times.*

Population validity *The extent to which research findings can be generalised to other populations.*

Ecological validity *The extent to which research findings can be generalised to other settings.*

Temporal validity *The extent to which research findings can be generalised to other times.*

Triangulation *Comparing the results of research studies which use different researchers and different methods.*

they are conducted in 'natural' settings. But this does not automatically mean that their results have higher ecological validity. As noted earlier, the findings of the New York subway experiment may not generalise to other settings.

Triangulation This is a term used to compare the results of research studies using different investigators and different methods (O'Connell Davidson & Layder, 1994). Triangulation can be used to assess the external validity of research results. For example, if laboratory experiments, field experiments, observational research, questionnaire surveys and interviews on the same topic produce similar results, then the researcher can be more confident about generalising from those results. In other words, triangulation of methods which produce similar results may indicate high external validity.

2.6 Ethical issues

When designing their research, investigators must make sure it complies with ethical guidelines. Ethical issues in psychological research are discussed in detail in Chapter 15. This section summarises and develops some of the points made earlier. It is based on the British Psychological Society's ethical guidelines for research with human participants (BPS, 1998).

Protection from harm Researchers must protect participants from physical and psychological harm. They must not offend participants' values or undermine their dignity. No risk, stress or harm greater than that normally encountered in everyday life should be permitted. If researchers are in any doubt about this, they must consult with independent judges, drawn from the same population as the participants, and ask them how they would feel about taking part in the study. This is especially important if the participants are of different age, gender, social class, ethnicity or culture to the researcher.

Informed consent Participants must be given sufficient information on which to base a decision whether or not to take part in the research. In particular, they must be informed about any aspects of the study which might influence their willingness to participate. In the case of young people under 16, researchers must obtain both their consent and that of their parents or guardians. In the case of adults with 'impairments in understanding or communication', the researcher should consult a member of the person's family, their doctor or obtain approval from independent advisors.

Care must be taken to make sure consent is freely given. This is particularly important when participants are in institutions such as prisons or psychiatric hospitals and in the case of students who are asked to participate in experiments as part of their course requirements. There is a danger of coercion when participants are not volunteers – they may be pressured to take part.

Deception Whenever possible, deception should be avoided. Some researchers insist that deception is never justified, as it demeans the participant and turns psychological research into a con trick (eg Baumrind, 1979; Korn, 1987). Others argue that deception is sometimes justified – without it certain experiments simply would not work. When deception is used, the researcher should check with independent judges, for example members of an ethics committee, to make sure it won't cause the participants distress.

Debriefing Participants must be fully debriefed after the research. Any deception must be revealed. Participants who have experienced guilt, anxiety or stress as a result of the research should be reassured and supported immediately after completion of the study. Immediate debriefing is especially important when deception has been used.

Withdrawal from investigation Participants have the right to withdraw from an investigation at any time, whether or not they have been paid to take part. They should be informed of this right at the start of the investigation. Participants also have the right to withdraw their results, even after the research has been completed.

Confidentiality Participants' identity must not be revealed. Often research deals with personal and sensitive areas. Researchers must make it clear that participants cannot be identified when research results are published.

Privacy In studies based on observation, the researcher must respect the privacy of those observed. Unless they give their consent, observational research should be limited to settings where people normally expect to be observed by strangers.

Giving advice If researchers believe that participants have physical or psychological problems which might threaten their future wellbeing, they have a responsibility to inform them. However, researchers should not lay claim to competence they do not possess or pose as experts.

Psychological research and society What use should be made of psychological research? This is an ethical question which the British Psychological Society does not address in its ethical guidelines. For Hans Eysenck (1969) in his *Technology of consent*, psychology should make its expertise available to the powers that be to engineer a more ordered and obedient society. For George Miller, in his *Psychology as a means of promoting human welfare* (1969), psychology should never become a tool in the hands of the powerful. Instead, it should 'give itself away' to citizens for use in their own lives, and to defend themselves against attempts by government, business and advertisers to manipulate them. The ethics of 'What is psychology for?' and 'Who are psychologists working for?' are perhaps even more important than the ethics of research procedures.

Summary

1. Variables in a research study need to be operationalised in order to measure changes in the independent variable and the dependent variable.
2. Pilot studies can be used to improve research designs.
3. Wherever possible, researchers must control extraneous variables and prevent them from becoming confounding variables.
4. Participant design aims to control the effects of extraneous variables arising from differences between participants.
5. Replication can be used to assess the reliability of the findings of a research study.
6. The results of research may be reliable, but this does not necessarily mean they are valid.
7. Internal validity is threatened by extraneous variables.
8. External validity can be improved by effective sampling techniques and assessed by partial replication and triangulation.
9. Research design and implementation should comply with ethical guidelines for research.

Unit 3 Sampling procedures

KEY ISSUES

1. **What are the main methods of sampling?**
2. **What are their advantages and disadvantages?**

Sampling refers to the way participants are selected for research studies. Sampling is important if the researcher wishes to generalise the findings of a particular study to a larger population. In order to do this, the sample must be representative of the wider population.

The term population refers to the total number of people in the group to be studied. The population might be teenage boys, middle-class housewives, bus drivers, divorced men, African Caribbeans living in Britain, and so on. The term *target population* is used to refer to the population to be investigated.

Ideally, the researcher should study the entire target population. In practice, this is usually impracticable – it would cost too much and take too long. Researchers therefore select a sample from the target population. If they are going to generalise from their findings to the population as a whole, then the sample must represent that population. For example, if the study was based on teenage boys in Britain, the sample should be drawn from different social classes, different ethnic groups and different parts of the country. A sample of boys drawn solely from middle-class households would produce a biased sample – it would not represent the target population.

There are various ways of selecting samples. The main ways are outlined below.

Opportunity samples

Also known as convenience samples, *opportunity samples* are the most common sampling technique used in psychological research. Opportunity samples are made up of anyone who is available to take part in the research – anyone who is handy and convenient. Since most researchers are based in university psychology departments, opportunity samples are usually composed of undergraduate students, and, more often than not, students taking psychology courses. According to one estimate, around 75% of the participants in British and American studies are students (Valentine, 1992).

Students may be convenient but they are hardly representative of the population as a whole. They tend to be young, middle-class, male (though in recent years this is changing), white, and more intelligent and literate than the general population. And, because of the popularity of psychology in the USA, the students in research studies tend to be American. Studies using opportunity samples have been criticised for lacking external validity. Students are a narrow and distinctive band of the population as a whole. As a result, generalisations from studies based on opportunity samples of students must be treated with considerable caution.

The use of students in research also raises ethical issues. Students taking psychology courses are often asked to participate in research as part of the course requirements. They are usually offered alternatives, such as writing papers, but these are often hard work compared to taking part in research. As a result, there is pressure for students to participate. Some researchers regard this as unethical (Korn, 1988).

Random samples

A *random sample* gives every member of the target population an equal chance of being selected for the sample. Every name is given a number and a list of random numbers is then used to select the sample. Ideally, this will result in a representative sample, assuming the sample is large enough. However, this cannot be guaranteed. Because the sample is random, a disproportionate number of, for example, men or young people might be selected. If the target population is the general population, researchers often select a random sample from the electoral register. This automatically excludes those not old enough to vote. And certain groups, such as the poor, are under-represented on the electoral register because many have not registered to vote.

In many cases, it is difficult to obtain a list of members of the target population from which to select a random sample. For example, lists of people with criminal records or psychological disorders are not readily available.

In practice, researchers do not randomly sample entire target populations. If this were possible, they'd end up with people from all over the country which would make their research too costly and time-consuming. Instead, they often choose a particular place – a university, a town, or a district – and draw a random sample from the local telephone directory or electoral register. However, care is needed. For example, if the sample is intended to represent the population as a whole, then choosing a retirement resort like Bournemouth can result in an over-representation of wealthy, elderly and white people.

Despite all these difficulties, a random sample does avoid the possibility of researchers selecting a sample which supports their hypothesis. And random samples are more likely to represent the target population than the opportunity samples so often used in psychological research.

Stratified samples

A random sample does not necessarily produce a representative sample. A *stratified sample* offers a partial solution to this problem. It allows researchers to make sure that certain aspects of the target population which are relevant to their research are reflected in the sample. The population is divided into separate 'strata' in terms of one or more characteristics, for example age, gender, ethnicity and social class. A random sample which reflects the proportion of those characteristics in the target population is then drawn from the strata. For example, if the aim is to reflect gender divisions in the UK, then 51% of the sample will be randomly selected from the female stratum and 49% from the male stratum. In terms of gender, the sample will be representative of the population as a whole.

Quota samples

Quota samples are similar to stratified samples. They are often used by market researchers. For example, the researcher may require 20 women between the ages of 30 and 45 to fill her quota. If she was using a questionnaire in a town centre, she would probably select the first available people who met her requirements that passed by. This is the main difference between quota and stratified samples – in a quota sample, participants are not selected randomly.

Quota sampling has certain advantages. It is quicker, cheaper and easier than stratified sampling. However, it can lead to a more biased sample. For example, stopping people on the street during working hours would exclude many people in paid employment.

Snowball sampling

Sometimes researchers have great difficulty in obtaining a sample. First, lists of members of the target population may not be available. Second, members of the target population might not wish to be identified – for example, burglars, heroin users, prostitutes or members of a Masonic Lodge. One possibility is to use an existing network of members of the target population. This is the basis of *snowball sampling*, so-called because it is like rolling a snowball.

Snowballing works like this. The researcher finds a member of the target population. They are asked to find another person who fits the sample, and so on until the sample is complete.

Snowballing has the obvious advantage of providing a sample where other methods might fail. However, it is unlikely to provide a representative sample since it relies on personal networks and personal recommendations.

Volunteer sampling

Snowballing is an example of *volunteer sampling* which involves people volunteering to participate in research. Researchers sometimes advertise for volunteers on university notice boards or in newspapers – see Milgram's advertisement on p 224. Sometimes questionnaires are included in newspapers or magazines.

Volunteer sampling is a quick, cheap and easy way of obtaining participants but it is not without its problems. The participants are self-selected – they choose themselves – and, as a result, they may differ in important respects from those who did not volunteer. As a result, they may not be representative of the population being investigated. According to Rosenthal (1965), volunteers tend to be more intelligent, younger, less conventional, less authoritarian, more sociable, and more in need of social approval than the general population. Because of this, generalisations from volunteer samples should be treated with caution.

Cross-cultural samples

In recent years, psychologists have become increasingly aware of the dangers of generalising their findings across cultures. Findings from a study based on a sample of white, male, middle-class, American undergraduate students cannot be automatically generalised to other cultures whose members have different norms, values, attitudes and beliefs.

Samples based on members of different cultures show this clearly. They indicate the limits to the external validity of much of the research conducted in Western societies. This has been shown when Ainsworth's Strange Situation and Milgram's obedience experiments have been used in different societies (see pp 58-59;213). Culture can make a significant difference to people's responses to laboratory and field experiments. Because of this, increasing numbers of psychologists are calling for *cross-cultural samples* – samples drawn from members of different cultures (Moghaddam et al., 1993; Smith & Bond, 1993).

Critics have made similar points about the under-representation of a range of social groups in samples. Such groups include women, the working class, ethnic minorities, the disabled and gays. As a result, psychologists have been accused of bias in selecting and generalising from their samples. Some researchers see the under-representation of women as an example of *androcentrism* (seeing the world through male eyes), and the under-representation of other cultures as an example of *ethnocentrism* (seeing the world through the eyes of your own culture).

Conclusion

Without a representative sample of the target population, researchers cannot generalise their findings with any degree of confidence. As a result, the external validity of their research is likely to be low.

Psychologists have tended to rely on opportunity samples of undergraduate students. This is a serious drawback. These samples may only represent the people who make them up – that is undergraduate students. This suggests that many of the findings about human behaviour which psychologists claim to have discovered may have limited application. Fortunately, psychologists are increasingly aware of this possibility as can be seen with the growing calls for more cross-cultural research.

Summary

1. Samples are necessary because researchers are rarely able to study the whole target population.
2. Researchers can only be confident in generalising from their findings if the sample is representative.
2. Most psychological research is based on opportunity samples which are unlikely to be representative of wider populations.

Key terms

Sample *The selection of part of a larger population in order to indicate what the larger population is like.*

Target population *The population under investigation from which the sample is drawn.*

Representative sample *A sample that represents the larger population.*

Biased sample *A sample that does not represent the target population.*

Opportunity sample *A sample made up of anybody who is available.*

Random sample *A sample which is randomly selected from the target population.*

Stratified sample *A sample which reflects the proportion of certain characteristics in the target population. Members of the sample are randomly selected.*

Quota sample *Similar to a stratified sample except that participants are not randomly selected.*

Snowball sample *A sample drawn from introductions provided by members of the target population.*

Volunteer sample *A sample drawn from people who volunteer to take part in the research.*

Cross-cultural sample *A sample drawn from members of different cultures.*

Activity 1 Problems with samples

Item A A self-selected sample

Shere Hite's *The Hite report on the family* (1994), based on a questionnaire survey, presented some dramatic figures about the 'dark side' of family life. According to the survey, more than one in four women 'have no memory of affection by their father'. Four out of ten fathers frighten their sons with their violent tempers. 31% of girls and young women 'report sexual harassment or abuse by a male family member'. Hite distributed 100,000 questionnaires in magazines such as *Penthouse* in America, *Women against fundamentalism* in Britain and *Nouvelles questions feminists* in France. Her statistics come from the 3% who responded.

Adapted from Kellner, 1994

Will the readership of 'Penthouse' provide a representative sample?

Item B A student sample

In a study of eyewitness testimony, Loftus and Burns (1982) showed participants two filmed versions of a crime. In one version, the robbers made a clean getaway without any violence. In the other version, a small boy was shot in the face as the robbers escaped. Loftus and Burns found that the inclusion of violence in the film impaired participants' memory for other details occurring up to two minutes before the shooting happened.

This experiment was conducted at the University of Washington. The sample consisted of 226 students who volunteered to take part in order to fulfil a course requirement.

Adapted from Loftus and Burns, 1982

Questions

1 Why should we question Hite's findings in Item A?

2 Critically assess the sample in Item B.

Unit 4 The relationship between researcher and participants

KEY ISSUES

1. **How might the relationship between researcher and participants affect the results of research?**
2. **What can be done to control this possibility?**

Most research studies involve a social relationship between researchers and participants. In any social relationship, those involved will influence each other's behaviour. Social relationships in a research study are unusual, particularly from the participants' viewpoint. Many have never been the focus of research. How will this affect their behaviour? This unit looks at how the relationship between researchers and participants might affect the findings of research studies.

A special relationship

According to Orne (1962), in a laboratory experiment, the relationship between the researcher and the participant is distinct from all other relationships outside the laboratory. Participants agree to do what the researcher asks them within a limited period of time in a strange place. Some might withdraw from the experiment, but most continue to the end. They assume that the researcher will not harm them and will take full responsibility for what happens during the experiment. In view of this special relationship and unusual setting, it is not surprising that participants sometimes behave in ways that are very different from their behaviour outside the laboratory.

This raises serious questions about the internal validity of laboratory experiments. Are participants responding to the independent variable or to the special relationship with the researcher? In other words, is the experiment measuring what it is supposed to measure? For example, are Milgram's experiments measuring obedience or do their findings simply reflect the researcher/participant relationship? (Orne & Holland, 1968)

Consider the following experiments. In one experiment, participants picked up snakes which they had been told were poisonous. In another experiment, they picked coins out of an acid solution which they were told would burn their hands (Orne, 1969). They were willing to do this because they believed the researcher would protect them from harm – and they were right! These experiments contained cues which informed the participants that there was no real danger. And they behaved accordingly. These cues are known as *demand characteristics*.

Demand characteristics

Demand characteristics are the cues or clues in an investigation that convey the researcher's hypothesis to the participant (Orne, 1962). In doing so, they influence the participants' behaviour. When entering a laboratory, participants try to make sense of the situation. Often this involves asking themselves what the experiment is all about. In answering this question, they may well try to guess the researcher's hypothesis. (Sometimes the term demand characteristic is used more generally to refer to any aspect of the researcher's behaviour or the research design which indicates to participants how they are expected to behave.)

The following experiment conducted by Orne and Scheibe (1964) shows how demand characteristics can operate. Two groups of participants were asked to sit for four hours in a small but comfortable room. The first group were told they were taking part in a sensory deprivation experiment. They signed a form which released the researcher from any liability for what might happen. They were provided with a 'panic button' which they could press if the experience became too much for them. At the end of four hours, the participants reported finding the experiment extremely stressful. The second group were simply asked to sit in the room for four hours. They were told nothing about sensory deprivation, and given no panic button to press or release form to sign. Although a little bored, they experienced no stress.

The first group experienced stress simply because they expected to – there was nothing essentially stressful about sitting in a comfortable room for four hours. However, the way the experiment was set up gave participants clues about how they ought to feel. They believed they knew what the researcher's hypothesis was and behaved accordingly. This experiment shows how cues in the research setting can become demand characteristics.

This can have serious consequences for research. In an experiment, participants may be responding to demand characteristics rather than the independent variable. If so, demand characteristics become confounding variables and reduce the internal validity of the experiment.

Investigator effects

Researchers are human beings with their own hopes and expectations. In terms of their research, they hope and expect that the results will turn out as predicted and support their hypothesis. They are often emotionally involved in their work – they have put considerable time and energy into their research and their career may depend on the expected outcome. As a result, they might influence participants' behaviour to support their hypothesis. However, they usually have little or no awareness of doing this.

The various ways in which researchers influence the behaviour of participants are known as *investigator effects*. In the context of experiments, they are sometimes known as *experimenter effects*.

Consider the following experiment conducted by Rosenthal and Fode (1963a). Two groups of participants were given identical sets of photographs of people. They were asked to judge how successful the people were on a scale of -10 (total failure) to +10 (extremely successful). Researchers who conducted the experiment with the first group were told that the participants would rate the pictures positively. Researchers with the second group were told the participants would rate the pictures negatively. And this is exactly what happened! It appears that the researchers' expectations were communicated to the participants who then made judgements in line with these expectations. This is known as the *expectancy effect*. It is an example of a *self-fulfilling prophecy* – an expectation that is conveyed to others who then act to make it come true.

Expectancy effects are another example of demand characteristics. They are particularly likely to occur in the enclosed setting of a laboratory where the researcher is in direct communication with participants. In this context, the researcher's manner and tone of voice, a nod, a smile, or a frown, can influence participants' behaviour. This type of influence can also operate in the face-to-face situation of an unstructured, in-depth interview.

Individual differences No two researchers are the same. They may differ in terms of personality, age, gender, ethnicity, social class, and so on. To some extent, their personal and social characteristics will have some effect on the behaviour of participants.

As the previous chapter indicated, African American respondents may give different answers to black and white interviewers (see Activity 7, Item C, p 249). Self-conscious researchers are often anxious, fidgety and less courteous. Female researchers tend to be more friendly to male participants. The same applies to male researchers with female participants – they are likely to use a different tone of voice and lean closer towards them (Rosenthal, 1967). All these differences between researchers can have some effect on the behaviour of participants.

Participant effects

Just as researchers can affect the outcome of a research study, so can participants.

Evaluation apprehension This refers to the concern felt by participants that they are being judged or evaluated by the researcher (Rosenberg, 1969). Many participants want to make a good impression and present themselves in the best possible light. As a result, they may hide certain aspects of their normal behaviour which they think might be interpreted in a negative way. This can have serious consequences for research. For example, respondents in an interview may give answers they think are socially desirable. This is known as the *social desirability effect*. It can be clearly seen from the following example.

Interviews were conducted in New York to investigate the relationship between psychological disorders and ethnicity. People were asked whether or not they had experienced a list of symptoms associated with psychological disorders. Compared with Jewish people, Irish Americans and African Americans, Puerto Ricans reported experiencing more of the symptoms and therefore appeared to have a higher rate of psychological disorders. However, it was then found that the symptoms were regarded as less undesirable by Puerto Ricans than by members of other ethnic groups. As a result, they were more likely to admit to them (Phillips, 1971).

The Hawthorne effect The following research was conducted at the Hawthorne plant of the Western Electricity Company in Cicero, Illinois (Roethlisberger & Dickson, 1939). Factors affecting the productivity of five female workers were investigated. Variables such as lighting and heating, the length of rest periods and the value of bonus payments were systematically manipulated. But, no matter what changes were made, productivity remained consistently high – even when working conditions and bonus payments worsened.

One interpretation of these results is known as the *Hawthorne effect* (named after the plant). It states that participants' behaviour is affected by their awareness that others are interested in them. The workers knew they were taking part in an experiment, they were flattered by the interest shown in them and did their best to please the researchers. As a result, they were not responding to changes in the various independent variables – lighting, bonus payments and so on. Instead they were responding to the attention being paid to them.

Individual differences Like researchers, participants vary in terms of their personal and social characteristics. These factors can affect their behaviour in a research situation. For example, some participants are cooperative and do their best to help the researcher; others do just the opposite – the 'screw you effect' (Masling, 1966). Some might be suspicious or even fearful of the researcher. All these factors can affect participants' behaviour in the presence of a researcher.

Controlling demand characteristics, investigator and participant effects

Clearly researchers wish to reduce and ideally eliminate these effects. A number of techniques have been developed for this purpose. Some are examined below, others are outlined in the following unit which looks at the design of various research methods.

Blind procedures In some studies, participants know the general aim of the research. However, demand characteristics can be reduced by concealing from them which condition they are in. This is known as the *single-blind procedure*. However, it does not stop participants from guessing the condition and acting accordingly. It doesn't really matter whether their guess is right or wrong. It will still affect their behaviour.

With a *double-blind procedure* research assistants are used to direct the experiment. Neither they, nor the participants, know which condition the participants are in. This technique is often used in drug studies. Participants in the experimental group are given the drug, those in the control group are given a pill which looks identical but does not contain the drug. Neither the research assistant nor the participants know which pill is being taken.

Deception One of the most common techniques for reducing demand characteristics is to deceive participants. For example, Milgram deliberately misled his participants by telling them they were taking part in 'a study of memory and learning' when, in fact, they were taking part in an obedience experiment (see p 223). Today, most researchers would regard such blatant deception as unethical. However, in some circumstances, researchers see it as acceptable to withhold the aim of the research from participants. Again, however, this does not prevent participants from guessing the aim and acting accordingly.

Automation One of the most effective ways of reducing investigator effects is to remove the researcher from the scene of the experiment. For example, instructions to participants can be tape recorded or presented on a computer screen. In this respect, the experiment is 'automated'.

Alternative research methods Many of the effects discussed in this unit apply particularly to laboratory studies. Here participants are aware they are the focus of research and they usually communicate directly with the researcher. Field experiments and naturalistic observations often avoid these problems.

Conclusion

Despite various techniques to control demand characteristics, investigator effects and participant effects, it is generally agreed that they cannot be eliminated. They threaten both the internal and external validity of research studies. They threaten internal validity because participants may be responding to demand characteristics rather than the independent variable. As a result, the findings of the experiment cannot be generalised – they are limited to the experimental situation. Some researchers have even suggested that laboratory experiments should be removed from the repertoire of research methods in psychology. For example, Orne (1962) is sceptical about the possibility of laboratory experiments producing anything approaching real-life behaviour.

However, many researchers reject this view. While accepting that experiments have their problems, they still see them as an important research method. Experimental research has provided valuable insights which are often supported by triangulation – by the use of data produced by other research methods.

Key terms

Demand characteristics *The cues in a research study which convey the hypothesis to the participants.*

Investigator or experimenter effects *Ways in which researchers influence the behaviour of participants.*

Expectancy effects *The tendency for participants to behave in ways the researcher expects them to behave.*

Evaluation apprehension *A concern felt by participants that they are being judged by the researcher.*

Hawthorne effect *The effect on participants' behaviour of their awareness that others are interested in them.*

Single-blind procedure *Concealing from participants the condition they are in.*

Double-blind procedure *Concealing from both participants and research assistants which condition the participants are in.*

Summary

1. Social relationships between researchers and participants will affect the behaviour of participants in a research study.
2. This is particularly so in the enclosed situation of a laboratory experiment where researchers and participants communicate directly.
3. Various aspects of this communication can become confounding variables which threaten both the internal and external validity of research studies.
4. While it is possible to reduce demand characteristics and investigator and participant effects, there is general agreement that they cannot be eliminated.

Activity 2 Influencing responses

Item A Clever Hans

Clever Hans was a performing horse who amazed his audiences in Berlin during the early years of the 20th century. Spectators would ask him to solve mathematical problems and he gave the answer by tapping his hoof. And, practically every time, he got the answer right. How did he do it? When asking a question, spectators would lean forward very slightly or move their eyes up and down without being aware of it. When Hans reached the correct answer by tapping his hoof, the spectator would straighten up or glance up. This signalled to Hans that it was time to stop.

Adapted from Goodwin, 1998

Clever Hans and his owner

Item B Social desirability

Survey after survey has revealed a high level of church attendance in the USA, far higher than the UK. Yet figures produced by the churches in America sometimes tell a rather different story. For example, a survey conducted by Gallup indicates that 35% of Episcopalians in the USA had been to church in the last 7 days. Yet figures from the churches showed that only 16% actually did so.

Adapted from Bruce, 1995

Item C Bright rats and dull rats

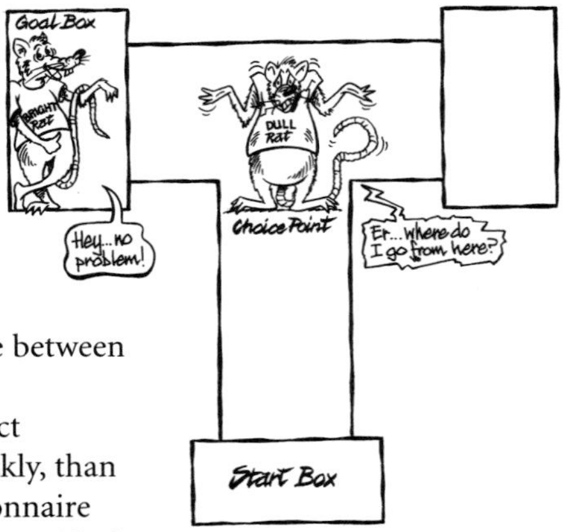

Members of two groups of students were each given five rats and asked to train them on a T-maze task. Students in the first condition were told that their rats were bred to be 'maze-bright'; those in the second condition were told that their rats were 'maze-dull'. In fact, the two groups of rats were randomly selected from the same stock – they only difference between them was in the minds of the students.

The 'maze-bright' rats made more correct responses, and they made them more quickly, than the 'maze-dull' rats. Results from a questionnaire after the experiment indicated that students with the 'maze-bright' rats rated their rats as cleaner, tamer, more pleasant and more intelligent than did students with 'maze-dull' rats. They also estimated that they handled their rats more gently and more often.

Adapted from Rosenthal & Fode, 1963 (b)

Questions

1 What parallels can be drawn between Clever Hans's performance and investigator effects?

2 Use the idea of social desirability effects to explain the difference between the two sets of figures in Item B.

3 Use the idea of investigator effects to explain the behaviour of the two groups of rats in Item C.

Unit 5 Designing naturalistic observations, questionnaire surveys and interviews

KEY ISSUES

1. **How might research studies using these methods be designed?**
2. **What problems are involved and how might they be overcome?**

5.1 Designing naturalistic observations

Naturalistic observation is the observation of behaviour in a natural setting, that is a setting in which the behaviour normally occurs. Examples include the street, the school playground, the workplace or a shopping centre. Events are allowed to occur naturally – they are not manipulated or controlled by the observer. The researcher tries to remain unobtrusive – usually those observed are not aware of the researcher. As a result, the researcher's presence does not affect the behaviour of those observed.

Aim and hypothesis

As with all research studies, the researcher begins with an aim – for example:

> 'The aim of the study is to observe gender differences in the behaviour of primary school children in the school playground.'

Sometimes this aim can be refined further and expressed as a hypothesis:

> 'It is predicted that girls will be more cooperative in their play, and boys more competitive.'

Because naturalistic observation does not involve the manipulation of variables or permit cause-and-effect relationships to be established, it is not usually necessary to state a null hypothesis.

Sampling procedures

Having decided on the aim of the study, the researcher must now select a sample of people to observe. The size of the sample will depend in part on the resources – time and money – available. Ideally the sample will be representative of the wider population. How typical of primary school children will a sample drawn from the school round the corner be? Probably not very typical – most primary schools are neighbourhood schools often drawing children from particular social class and ethnic groups. In order to reflect such social differences, the researcher might select samples from a number of schools in different areas.

Time sampling This refers to the intervals at which observations are made. For example, the researcher may decide to observe children in the playground for ten minutes during morning, lunchtime and afternoon breaks. Systematic time sampling allows the observations of different researchers to be directly compared and means the study can be replicated using the same procedures.

The importance of time sampling can be seen from the following example. A researcher wishes to observe the behaviour of people using a pelican crossing. It is important to observe behaviour at different times of the day and night. First, there are different volumes of traffic at different time periods. Second, there are different types of people using the crossing at different times. At mid-morning during a weekday, those observed will be unrepresentative since most employed people will be at work. Those in the street at midnight will be even more unrepresentative.

Event sampling Here the researcher decides which events or behaviours are going to be sampled. In any situation, a wide range of behaviours can occur. The researcher decides which of these are relevant to the study and records them on a checklist or behaviour schedule each time they occur.

Situation sampling This refers to sampling the behaviour to be observed in different circumstances and locations. As noted earlier, samples for an observation of primary school children's play might be drawn from different schools with children of different ethnic and social class backgrounds. In addition, children from this age group might be observed playing in different settings – in the street, the park or at home. Situation sampling can increase the external validity of a study. If the same behaviour is observed in different settings with children of different backgrounds, then the researcher can be more confident of generalising from the study's findings.

The behaviour schedule

The researcher needs to decide which behaviours are relevant to the study and how to identify and measure them. Returning to the study of children playing, the researcher will need to clearly identify which behaviours indicate cooperative play and which indicate competitive play. A pilot study – an initial observation of children playing – will be useful in this respect. The researcher may identify behaviours such as:

- Shares toy with another child
- Gives toy to another child
- Explains to another child how to use toy

as examples of *cooperative* play, and behaviours like:

- Refuses to share toy
- Takes toy from another child
- Warns another child not to touch.

as examples of *competitive* play.

Once these behaviours have been identified and precisely defined, they are entered on a behaviour schedule or checklist. The observer can then simply tick them off as and when they occur. Usually, researchers devise a behaviour schedule which suits their particular study. However, some 'off the shelf' schedules are available – for example the Bales' Interaction Process Analysis (Bales, 1950) for verbal behaviour in small group interactions.

Rather than simply measuring the frequency of behaviours, the researcher might also want to measure their intensity. For example, if aggressive behaviour is being observed, the researcher might want to measure the level of aggression. This may involve rating how loudly one person shouted at another or how hard they pushed them. This type of rating is open to the observer's interpretation. For example, one observer might think a shove is a normal part of everyday life and give it a rating of 3 out of 10. Another observer might interpret it as a sign of real aggression and give it a rating of 8 out of 10.

Reliability How reliable are the results of naturalistic observations? One way to answer this question is to use the same behaviour schedule with two or more observers and test for *inter-observer reliability*, ie the degree of consistency between the observers' results. As a general rule, if there is 85% or above agreement, then inter-observer reliability is seen as high (Shaughnessy & Zechmeister, 1997). However, this does not necessarily mean the results are valid. For example, two observers might make the same errors because behaviours have been inadequately defined on the schedule.

Some form of mechanical recording – video, audio or photographic – can serve as a means of checking the reliability of observations. However, recording behaviour without consent raises ethical issues.

Observing others

In naturalistic observations, the researcher usually tries to be unobtrusive, but this is not always easy. Ticking boxes on a behaviour schedule is fairly straightforward if the researcher sits in a café watching people using a pelican crossing. But how can the researcher remain inconspicuous observing children in a playground? The problem is magnified if the researcher wants to get close enough to hear what people are saying.

A possible solution is for the researcher to openly observe people. This is known as *disclosed observation* (as opposed to *undisclosed observation*). However, disclosed observation may influence people's behaviour. They may become self-conscious. This may result in demand characteristics if they ask questions such as, 'What am I supposed to be doing?' and 'How am I expected to behave?' This may result in unnatural behaviour – quite different from the kind of behaviour naturalistic observations are designed to record. However, many researchers believe that people revert to their normal behaviour once they get used to the presence of an observer.

Key terms

Time sampling *Sampling behaviour at specific times and for specific lengths of time.*

Event sampling *Sampling specific behaviours from a range of behaviours.*

Situation sampling *Sampling the same behaviour in different situations and locations.*

Inter-observer reliability *The degree of consistency between the observations of different researchers.*

Ethical issues Observing people without their consent can be seen as an invasion of privacy. The British Psychological Society's ethical guidelines state that naturalistic observation without consent is only acceptable in public places where people expect to be seen by strangers (BPS, 1998). The street is an obvious public place, but what about a pub or a club? The definition of a public place is not clear-cut.

5.2 Designing questionnaire surveys

A questionnaire is a list of questions. A questionnaire survey involves collecting information from a sample of people by means of a questionnaire. Those who answer the questionnaire are known as respondents.

Aim and hypothesis

As with all research studies, the researcher begins with an aim. The choice of aim will affect the design of the questionnaire – in particular the choice of questions. Oppenheim (1992) identifies two main types of survey in terms of the data they produce. Descriptive surveys record attitudes and behaviours and simply collect information on 'how many' – for example 40% of respondents prefer westerns to thrillers. Analytic surveys are designed to test hypotheses. For example, the hypothesis might state that film preference is related to social characteristics. In this case, respondents might be asked a series of questions which identify their social class, ethnicity, gender, age group, sexual orientation, religion and so on. This will allow the researcher to discover possible relationships between social factors and film preferences.

Sampling procedures

Having decided on the aim of the survey, the researcher must now decide on who will take part and how to select them. Ideally, the sample should be representative of the target population in order to generalise from the findings of the survey. If the aim of the study is a descriptive survey of the adult population, then a random sample drawn from the electoral register will probably be adequate. However, if the study is an analytic survey designed to test a hypothesis, then a stratified sample may well be more appropriate. For example, if the researcher is examining the relationship between film preference, gender and age, then a stratified sample, which includes gender and age groups in proportion to their numbers in the general population, will probably be selected.

Opportunity samples – samples drawn from whoever is convenient – are unlikely to be representative. However, they may be useful as a basis for a pilot study. For example, an opportunity sample may indicate a strong relationship between social class and film preference. This may lead the researcher to use a stratified sample in which one of the strata is social class. (Sampling procedures are examined in more detail in Unit 3.)

Administering the survey

Concerns about sampling may influence how the questionnaire is administered. Postal questionnaires have a low response rate. As a result, they are unlikely to provide a representative sample. The same applies to questionnaires reproduced in newspapers and magazines. First, the readership is unlikely to be representative. Second, those who answer the questionnaire are unlikely to be representative of the readership – they are likely to differ in important respects from those who do not respond.

Questionnaires administered by an interviewer – structured interviews – have a much higher response rate. However, they are more expensive and more likely to produce investigator effects (see Unit 4). But, they have the advantage of allowing the interviewer to correct any misunderstandings respondents might have with the questions.

Designing questions

Designing questions is quite an art. In general, they should be clear, simple and mean the same thing to all respondents. And, obviously, they should provide the information which the researcher requires. Here are some things to avoid.

- **Leading questions** These questions encourage respondents to give particular answers. For example, 'Any sensible person would want to ban fox hunting. Do you agree?' Some respondents might agree simply to appear sensible.
- **Ambiguity** Questions which can be interpreted in various ways should be avoided. For example, 'Do you drink coffee often?' can mean different things to different respondents. How often is often? Questions should be clear and precise. For example, 'How many cups of coffee do you drink a day?'
- **Loaded questions** These are questions which contain emotive language. For example, 'Do you think right-wing extremists should be allowed to stand for Parliament?' Emotive language can encourage respondents to give particular answers.
- **Jargon** Technical jargon should be avoided, simply because most respondents will not know what it means. For example, phrases like 'role conflict' and 'role ambiguity' are likely to confuse many people.
- **Double-barrelled questions** These contain two options within a single question. For example, 'Do you think crime is due to bad housing and poor education?' A respondent who blames bad housing but not poor education would have difficulty answering this question. It should be rewritten as two separate questions.
- **Negatives** The use of negatives can often confuse respondents. For example, 'Would you not trust a secondhand car salesman?'
- **Complex questions** Respondents can get lost with long, complex questions. For example, 'While equal opportunity legislation may reduce discrimination against minority groups, it may have the reverse effect by antagonising those who are responsible for discrimination, so reinforcing the very behaviour it was designed to eradicate. Do you agree?'
- **Impossible questions** Some questions are just impossible to answer accurately. For example, 'How many Mars bars have you eaten in the last five years?' Probably, the only respondents who are able to provide an accurate answer are those who can't stand Mars bars – and never eat them!

Even apparently straightforward questions may be misunderstood. A man who had an extremely busy sex life answered 'no' to the question 'Are you sexually active?' In his words, 'I just lie there' (Zimbardo et al., 1995). There is always a danger of misunderstanding, but care in framing questions can reduce this.

It is always advisable to pilot a questionnaire, using people drawn from the same target population as the respondents. This can highlight any problems with the questions – whether they can be answered, whether they will be answered (some respondents may refuse to answer sensitive questions) and whether they will mean the same thing to all respondents. In addition, the pilot study may indicate whether respondents will answer truthfully. If this leads to a revision of the questionnaire, it is advisable to pilot the new version.

The format of questions

Questions can be *closed* or *open*.

Closed questions Closed or fixed-response questions provide the respondent with a set of possible responses which are fixed by the researcher. For example, the respondent may be asked to select from the following alternatives.

☐ Married
☐ Cohabiting
☐ Single
☐ Separated
☐ Divorced
☐ Widowed

Respondents may be asked to give their opinion by selecting an answer from alternatives provided. For example, 'What do you think of the service provided by state-run hospitals?'

- ☐ Very good
- ☐ Fairly good
- ☐ Neither good nor bad
- ☐ Not very good
- ☐ Not good at all

Another variation is to ask respondents to rank the alternatives provided. An example of this type of question is given below.

> Which do you feel are the most important factors in choosing a university? Please rank the following in order of importance to you. Number them from 1= most important, to 7= least important.
>
> Closeness to a town or city.
> Good academic reputation.
> Good chance of getting a job after graduation.
> Attractive campus.
> Good social facilities.
> Good accommodation.
> Availability of real ale.
>
> From Newell, 1993

This type of question limits the respondent's range of choice. One way round this is to add a further alternative: 'Other factors, please specify'.

Closed questions have a number of advantages. The responses are easily quantified – put into a numerical form. For example, 55% of respondents chose their university because it had a good academic reputation. Closed questions are easy to code – to classify the answers into particular types. In fact, they are pre-coded – the categories are pre-set and the respondent simply has to choose one or rank some. Ease of quantification and coding means that a questionnaire consisting of closed questions is relatively quick and easy to process and analyse. However, closed questions can limit respondents' choices. Although the researcher can add, 'Other factors, please specify', the respondent does not have the freedom to express their answers in their own way.

Open questions This freedom is provided by open or free-response questions. Here the researcher simply asks a question, for example, 'What are your views on abortion?' and leaves space on the questionnaire for respondents to write in their answer. Often people do not have a clear-cut view. For example, they might favour abortion in cases of rape and where the child might be born with severe disabilities, but they may reject abortion as an option for all parents. Open questions allow respondents to qualify their answers, to give shades of opinion, and to express themselves in their own way. However, open questions are often difficult to code. The kind of answers they produce do not fit easily into a particular category.

Reliability and validity

Reliability Reliability of coding can be assessed by giving two or more researchers the same questions to code. If there is a high level of agreement, then the coding is seen as reliable.

Validity Is the data obtained from questionnaire surveys valid? In other words, are respondents giving accurate answers, are they telling the truth? To what degree does social desirability affect their responses? Are their answers influenced by how they think they ought to behave and what they think they ought to believe? Where evidence from other sources about respondents' behaviour is available, it is possible to check on the validity of their answers. One study found that 40% of respondents gave inaccurate answers about their contributions to a charity, 25% provided inaccurate information about whether they had registered to vote and had voted in a recent election, and 17% lied about their age (Parry & Crossley, 1950).

Respondents may be unwilling to give honest answers about sensitive issues, as indicated by the 17% who lied about their age in the above example. Respondents often shy away from answering questions about sexual behaviour. Guaranteeing anonymity may help the sensitive to overcome their inhibitions, but may not prevent the boastful from bragging about their supposed 'exploits'.

Respondents are sometimes influenced by social desirability – their answers may reflect how they think they ought to behave rather than how they actually behave. In the above example, those who gave inaccurate answers about their contributions to charity may have deviated from the truth and given a socially desirable answer in order to 'look good'.

When respondents are asked what they would do in particular situations, do their answers reflect what they'd actually do? In Milgram's first obedience experiment, 65% of men aged 20-50 applied shocks to the highest level. Before conducting the experiment, Milgram asked a similar group of men what they would do. Most said they would not continue to the highest level (Milgram, 1974).

The evidence presented in this section raises serious questions about the validity of questionnaire data.

Ethical issues

Confidentiality should be guaranteed and this should be made clear to all respondents. When the results are coded and published, there should be no way of identifying the respondents. Both the aims of the research and the uses to which the data will be put should be made clear. Questionnaire surveys are often used by big businesses to promote their products. For example, a Burger King survey indicated that 75% of respondents preferred their Whoppers to Big Macs. However, a McDonald's survey reported that 85% of respondents preferred Big Macs (see Activity 3, Item B). Clever phrasing of the questions by both companies produced the desired results (Goodwin, 1998).

5.3 Designing interviews

Interviews range from structured interviews, which consist of a questionnaire read out by an interviewer, to unstructured interviews which are more like a conversation. The semi-structured interview is mid-way between these two extremes.

Structured interviews

The design of structured interviews is similar to the design of questionnaires. The various do's and don'ts of question design apply to both. The key difference is the presence of an interviewer.

As with questionnaires, each respondent in a structured interview is presented with the same questions in the same order. Ideally, each respondent should experience an identical interview. In this way, they are responding to the actual questions rather than differences between the questions, their order, and the interviewer.

Interviews are face-to-face encounters. Different interviewers may produce different responses from respondents. In order to minimise investigator effects, the following approach is often recommended. Interviewers should be pleasant, friendly and businesslike. They should not become emotionally involved. Questions should be phrased in a neutral way. Interviewers should not communicate their feelings about respondents' answers – for example, they should not express approval or disapproval. The interviewer should always be in control. For example, if the respondent is allowed to direct the interview, then the result will be different interviews for each respondent. As a result, the data will not be directly comparable. In the words of one researcher, 'losing control of the interview is almost always a methodological disaster' (Hessler, 1992). The goal of a standardised interview for each respondent is lost.

The above outline of how to conduct an interview is found in many 'traditional', 'orthodox' textbooks on research methods. Although it applies particularly to structured interviews, some of its guidelines are also recommended for unstructured interviews. However, not all researchers agree with the use of this approach for unstructured interviews.

Unstructured interviews

Unstructured interviews are not standardised. The interviewer has a number of topics to cover, but the questions are usually not pre-set. Unstructured interviews are less formal, more open-ended, flexible and free-flowing than structured interviews. They are sometimes called in-depth interviews because the aim is to 'dig deeper', to find out exactly what the respondent means, and to give respondents the opportunity to develop their answers and to express themselves freely. Some researchers argue that this means that an unstructured interview must be conducted very differently from a structured interview.

Conducting unstructured interviews One of the keys to a successful unstructured interview is the relationship between interviewer and respondent. According to many researchers, trust is essential for honest, sincere answers, especially on sensitive topics. The respondent needs to feel that the interviewer is sympathetic and understanding and is interested in what they have to say (Glesne & Peshkin, 1992).

This approach is not always possible. Diane Scully's *Understanding sexual violence* (1990) was based on interviews with convicted rapists. She found some of the men 'personally repulsive' and some of the stories they told 'horrible'. Unable to take a warm and caring approach, she adopted a neutral, non-judgemental position. In her words, 'no one tells his or her secrets to a visibly hostile and disapproving person'. To some extent, she gained the trust of the respondents by hiding her true feelings. Some might see this as unethical, but without it there was little chance of obtaining valid data.

Unstructured interviews are often spontaneous and unpredictable. Although the interviewer guides them to some extent – for example covering topics relevant to the research – the type of control used in structured interviews is absent. Respondents must be allowed to express their answers in their own way. However, interviewers are allowed to probe – to ask respondents to clarify, qualify and develop their answers.

Unstructured interviews are largely non-directive. This means that the interviewer is not constantly directing the course of the interview. At times, as in a normal conversation, respondents must be allowed to direct the interview into areas which interest them.

Investigator effects

As noted in the previous chapter, the personal and social characteristics of the interviewer can affect the respondent's answers (see pp 248-249). For example, middle-aged female interviewers may obtain far more information from retired women than young male interviewers. In fact, the young man may not even get past the door (van Kammen & Stouthamer-Loeber, 1998). Some researchers have suggested matching interviewers and respondents in terms of age, gender, ethnicity and social class on the assumption that respondents are more likely to 'open up' to people like themselves.

Unstructured interviews are wide open to demand characteristics, investigator effects and social desirability effects. They are face-to-face relationships in which respondents are often asked to divulge very personal information. In this kind of relationship, demand characteristics can flourish – some respondents can be easily led into saying what the researcher wants to hear (see Activity 3, Item C). And, faced with an interviewer, social desirability effects are likely. However, these effects may well be reduced if the interviewer appears sympathetic, understanding and non-judgemental – respondents may feel more able to admit their faults and weaknesses and the less desirable aspects of their behaviour.

Validity and reliability

Because of the free-ranging, conversational and unpredictable nature of unstructured interviews, their reliability is low. Two different interviewers may well obtain very different data from the same respondent. By comparison, structured interviews are generally seen as having greater reliability.

However, some researchers argue that what unstructured interviews lose in reliability, they gain in validity. Compared to structured interviews, they are more likely to produce richer data, to capture shades of opinion and reveal the meanings which direct behaviour. In these respects, unstructured interviews are more likely to produce valid data.

Summary

1. Naturalistic observation is the observation of behaviour in its natural setting. Usually, those observed are unaware of the observer's presence.
2. Various sampling procedures can be used – time sampling, event sampling and situation sampling.
3. A behaviour schedule is often used to record behaviours.
4. Questionnaire surveys are designed to survey relatively large numbers of people. Representative samples are normally used in order to generalise the findings to the target population.
5. Questions in the survey require careful construction.
6. There are doubts about the validity of some questionnaire data.
7. Interviews are particularly susceptible to demand characteristics, investigator effects and social desirability effects.
8. Although the reliability of unstructured interviews is low, some researchers see their potential for producing valid data as high.

Activity 3 Conducting research

Item A Naturalistic observation

A researcher observed the behaviour of car drivers at a stop sign. He stood at the intersection next to the stop sign, holding a clipboard. He soon noticed that all the cars came to a complete halt. He then concealed himself and found that although many of the drivers slowed down, they went across the intersection without stopping.

Adapted from Underwood & Shaughnessy, 1975

Item B Whopper or Big Mac?

Burger King conducted a questionnaire survey comparing their Whoppers to McDonald's Big Macs. The key question asked, 'Do you prefer your hamburgers flame-broiled or fried?' Seventy-five per cent of the respondents said they preferred flame-broiled – the process used for Whoppers. On the basis of this response, Burger King claimed that most people preferred Whoppers to Big Macs.

Another survey asked, 'Do you prefer a hamburger that is grilled on a hot, stainless-steel grill or by passing the raw meat through an open gas flame'. Over half the respondents selected the first option – the McDonald's method. When the question contained the information that flame-broiled burgers – the Whoppers – were reheated in a microwave oven before being served, 85% said they preferred Big Macs.

Adapted from Goodwin, 1998

Item C Demand characteristics

During the late 1960s many African Americans rejected the idea that 'white is right' and stopped trying to copy white Americans. Being black became something to be proud of rather than ashamed. The researcher believed that this outlook was reflected in African-American 'soul' music. The following extract quotes a small part of an interview with Jay Butler, a black disc jockey from Detroit.

Interviewer The song *Take me as I am* by Solomon Burke. What's it about?

Jay Butler It's just about a guy and his woman and he's telling her not to try and change him, to take him as he is.

Interviewer But don't you think it could have a deeper meaning, that it's saying accept me as a black man, not as a poor substitute for a white man?

Jay Butler Yeah. You got a point there. The black community wants to be accepted as black American. I don't wanna be a white American, I wanna be a black American. It's like the Detroit Emeralds' song *I'm an ordinary man, take me the way I am.* There's a two-fold meaning in all these soul songs. Take Solomon Burke's *Take me as I am.* This song might be about a guy and his girl, but it means more at this period of time. Back in the 1950s we were trying to be accepted by white Americans on their terms. Now accept me as I am, accept my nappy (tightly curled) hair, accept me period.

Adapted from Haralambos, 1994

The interviewer (left)

Questions

1 What does Item A indicate about investigator effects?

2 a) Briefly explain why different results were obtained by the two surveys in Item B.

b) What lessons does this contain for constructing questions?

3 How might demand characteristics have influenced the respondent's answers in Item C?

References

Bales, R.F. (1950). *Interaction process analysis: A method for the study of small groups.* Reading, Mass: Addison-Wesley.

Baumrind, D. (1979). The costs of deception. *IRB: A Review of Human Subjects Research, 6,* 1-4.

BPS (British Psychological Society). (1998). *Code of conduct, ethical principles and guidelines.* Leicester: BPS.

Bruce, S. (1995). Religion and the Sociology of Religion in M. Haralambos (Ed.). *Developments in Sociology, Vol 11.* Ormskirk: Causeway.

Darley, J.M. & Latané, B. (1968). Bystander intervention in emergencies: Diffusion of responsibility. *Journal of Personality and Social Psychology, 8,* 377-383.

Eysenck, H. (1969). The technology of consent. *New Scientist, 42,* 688-690.

Glesne, C. & Peshkin, A. (1992). *Becoming qualitative researchers: An introduction.* New York: Longman.

Goodwin, C.J. (1998). *Research in psychology: Methods and design* (2nd ed.). New York: John Wiley & Sons.

Graziano, A.M. & Raulin, M.L. (1997). *Research methods: A process of inquiry* (3rd ed.). New York: Longman.

Haralambos, M. (1994). *Right on: From blues to soul in black America.* Ormskirk: Causeway.

Hessler, R. (1992). *Social research methods.* St. Paul: West Publishing.

Kellner, P. (1994). The figures are Shere nonsense. *Sunday Times,* 27.2.94.

Korn, J.H. (1987). Judgements of acceptability of deception in psychological research. *Journal of General Psychology, 14,* 205-216.

Korn, J.H. (1988). Students' roles, rights, and responsibilities as research participants. *Teaching of Psychology, 15,* 74-78.

Loftus, E.F. & Burns, T.E. (1982). Mental shock can produce retrograde amnesia. *Memory and Cognition, 10,* 318-323.

Masling, J. (1966). Role-related behaviour of the subject and psychologist and its effect upon psychological data. In D. Levine (Ed.), *Nebraska Symposium on Motivation.* Lincoln: University of Nebraska Press.

Milgram, S. (1974). *Obedience to authority: An experimental view.* New York: Harper & Row.

Miller, G. (1969). Psychology as a means of promoting human welfare. *American Psychologist, 24,* 1063-1075.

Moghaddam, F.M., Taylor, D.M. & Wright, S.C. (1993). *Social psychology in cross-cultural perspective.* New York: W.H. Freeman.

Newell, R. (1993). Questionnaires. In N. Gilbert (Ed.), *Researching social life.* London: Sage.

O'Connell Davidson, J. & Layder, D. (1994). *Methods, sex and madness.* London: Routledge.

Oppenheim, A.N. (1992). *Questionnaire design, interviewing and attitude measurement.* London: Pinter.

Orne, M.T. (1962). On the social psychology of the psychology experiment: With particular reference to demand characteristics and their implications. *American Psychologist, 17,* 776-783.

Orne, M.T. (1969). Demand characteristics and the concept of quasi-controls. In R. Rosenthal & R.L. Rosnow (Eds.), *Artifact in behavioral research.* New York: Academic Press.

Orne, M.T. & Holland, C.C. (1968). On the ecological validity of laboratory deceptions. *International Journal of Psychiatry, 6,* 282-293.

Orne, M.T. & Scheibe, K.E. (1964). The contribution of nondeprivation factors in the production of sensory deprivation effects. *Journal of Abnormal and Social Psychology, 68,* 3-12.

Parry, H.J. & Crossley, H.M. (1950). Validity of responses to survey questions. *Public Opinion Quarterly, 14,* 61-80.

Phillips, D.L. (1971). *Knowledge from what?* Chicago: Rand McNally.

Roethlisberger, F.J. & Dickson, W.J. (1939). *Management and the worker.* Cambridge, Mass: Harvard University Press.

Rosenberg, M.J. (1969). The conditions and consequences of evaluation apprehension. In R. Rosenthal & R.L. Rosnow (Eds.), *Artifact in behavioral research.* New York: Academic Press.

Rosenthal, R. (1965). The volunteer subject. *Human Relations, 18,* 389-406.

Rosenthal, R. (1967). Covert communication in the psychological experiment. *Psychological Bulletin, 67,* 356-367.

Rosenthal, R. & Fode, K.L. (1963a). Three experiments in experimenter bias. *Psychological Reports, 12,* 491-511.

Rosenthal, R. & Fode, K.L. (1963b). The effect of experimenter bias on the performance of the albino rat. *Behavioral Science, 8,* 183-189.

Scully, D. (1990). *Understanding sexual violence.* London: Harper Collins.

Shaughnessy, J.J. & Zechmeister, E.B. (1997). *Research methods in psychology* (4th ed.). New York: McGraw-Hill.

Smith, P.B. & Bond, M.H. (1993). *Social psychology across cultures: Analysis and perspectives.* Hemel Hempstead: Harvester Wheatsheaf.

Strayer, F.F. & Strayer, J. (1976). An ethological analysis of social antagonism and dominance relations among preschool children. *Child Development, 47,* 980-989.

Underwood, B.J. & Shaughnessy, J.J. (1975). *Experimentation in psychology.* New York: Wiley.

Valentine, E.R. (1992). *Conceptual issues in psychology* (2nd ed.). London: Routledge.

van Kammen, W.B. & Stouthamer-Loeber, M. (1998). Practice aspects of interview data collection and data management. In L. Bickman & D.J. Rog (Eds.). *Handbook of applied social research methods.* Thousand Oaks, CA: Sage.

Zimbardo, P., McDermott, M., Jansz, J. & Metall, N. (1995). *Psychology: A European text.* London: Harper Collins.

18 Data analysis

Introduction

The previous two chapters looked at methods of data collection. This chapter looks at ways of analysing data once it has been collected. Analysis involves categorising and classifying the data, looking for relationships or links between the data, identifying themes running through the data, and discovering meanings underlying the data. In general, analysis involves making sense of data.

This chapter looks at ways of analysing qualitative and quantitative data.

Chapter summary

- **Unit 1 examines various methods of analysing qualitative data.**
- **Units 2, 3 and 4 outline statistical methods of analysing quantitative data.**

Unit 1 The analysis of qualitative data

KEY ISSUES

1. **What is qualitative data?**
2. **What are the main methods of analysing qualitative data?**

Qualitative data refers to information collected by researchers which is not in the form of numbers. It includes information from interviews, questionnaires and observational research which has not been collected in, or translated into, a numerical form. Examples of qualitative data include a passage from an interview in which a respondent describes their work experience, a written answer to a questionnaire in which a respondent outlines their views on child rearing practices, and data from participant observation of students in a classroom.

Content analysis

Content analysis has been widely used in media research. It has been used for analysing the content of television and radio programmes, books, newspapers, magazines and comics, and popular songs and nursery rhymes. Many of the techniques used in content analysis have been applied to the analysis of qualitative data from interviews, questionnaires and observations.

The following example illustrates typical features of content analysis. It is based on an analysis of gender roles in six reading schemes, including the *Janet and John* and *Ladybird* series, which were widely used in primary schools during the 1960s (Lobban, 1974).

First, a sample of the materials to be analysed is examined. In terms of the above example, three books from each of the series might be selected.

Second, categories are created in terms of which the data can be classified and organised. The categories reflect the purpose of the research – in this case an analysis of gender roles. Categories developed from the reading schemes included objects, activities and roles that are linked to girls, those that are linked to boys, and those that are linked to both.

Third, a larger sample is selected and the researcher classifies data from the books in terms of the various categories. Table 1 presents the results of this analysis for the six reading schemes.

Themes The classification of data into categories is usually only a first step. Once this has been done, further analysis can take place. For example, the researcher might look for themes which are common to many of the categories in Table 1. The following themes might be identified from the way boys and girls are presented in the reading schemes.

- Boys are presented as more adventurous than girls
- As physically stronger
- As having more choices
- Girls are presented as more caring than boys
- As more interested in domestic matters
- As followers rather than leaders.

The researcher may then widen the focus and, for example, relate these themes to adult roles such as the mother-housewife role and gender divisions in the labour market. For instance, women are concentrated in the caring professions – nursing, social work and primary school teaching. Men outnumber women in leadership roles such

Table 1 Gender roles that occurred in three or more of the six schemes

Gender for which role was allocated	Toys and Pets	Activities	Taking the lead in activities that both boys and girls take part in	Learning a new skill	Adult roles presented
Girls only	1 Doll 2 Skipping rope 3 Doll's pram	1 Preparing the tea 2 Playing with dolls 3 Taking care of younger siblings	1 Hopping 2 Shopping with parents 3 Skipping	1 Taking care of younger siblings	1 Mother 2 Aunt 3 Grandmother
Boys only	1 Car 2 Train 3 Aeroplane 4 Boat 5 Football	1 Playing with cars 2 Playing with trains 3 Playing football 4 Lifting or pulling heavy objects 5 Playing cricket 6 Watching adult males in occupational roles 7 Heavy gardening	1 Going exploring alone 2 Climbing trees 3 Building things 4 Taking care of pets 5 Sailing boats 6 Flying kites 7 Washing and polishing Dad's car	1 Taking care of pets 2 Making/building 3 Saving/rescuing people or pets 4 Playing sports	1 Father 2 Uncle 3 Grandfather 4 Postman 5 Farmer 6 Fisherman 7 Business owner 8 Policeman 9 Builder 10 Bus driver 11 Bus conductor 12 Train driver 13 Railway porter
Girls and boys	1 Book 2 Ball 3 Paints 4 Bucket and spade 5 Dog 6 Cat 7 Shop	1 Playing with pets 2 Writing 3 Reading 4 Going to the seaside 5 Going on a family outing			1 Teacher 2 Shop assistant

Adapted from Lobban, 1974

as managers. The researcher may then ask how the themes identified in the reading schemes form a part of gender socialisation – the way boys learn to be men and girls learn to be women. For example, how do these themes steer men and women into 'men's jobs' and 'women's jobs'?

Observational research

In many ways the analysis of data from naturalistic observation uses the same methods as content analysis. The example of observation of aggression in the school playground was outlined earlier – see page 241. Based on preliminary observations, a behaviour schedule was drawn up with categories such as 'pushing' and 'hitting', and these behaviours were recorded as and when they occurred. This is a fairly straightforward procedure that usually produces quantitative data. However, it is fairly limited in scope. It is suitable for the behaviour of pedestrians at pelican crossings and drivers at traffic lights which can be readily observed, classified and counted. But it is not particularly suitable for more complex behaviour patterns. It can be argued that behaviour schedules fail to capture the richness of life as it is lived, that they are unable to discover the meanings which direct behaviour. How is it possible to analyse more complex behaviour patterns observed in natural contexts?

Behaviour in a mental hospital Erving Goffman's classic study, *Asylums* (1968), is an investigation of the behaviour of inmates in a mental hospital in Washington DC. Goffman spent a year in the hospital in the role of a member of staff. As a participant observer, he watched and listened, and amassed a vast quantity of data. How could he make sense of it all?

Goffman did not decide in advance what was relevant. He did not start with pre-set categories in which to classify the data. Instead, he simply watched and listened. Categories, themes and patterns gradually emerged from his observations. Here is an example of how he organised and made sense of his data.

Goffman identified a pattern of behaviour which he called the *mortification process*. He recognised this process time and time again during his stay at the mental hospital. It consisted of 'a series of abasements, degradations, humiliations, and profanities of self' in terms of which inmates were stripped of their former identities and treated as 'mental cases' who had little social significance and 'were hardly capable of acting like a fully-fledged person at all'. The idea of a mortification process connected a range of apparently unconnected behaviours, it identified a common theme underlying those behaviours, and made sense of them.

On entry to mental hospitals, inmates are often stripped of various supports which help them to maintain their former self-concepts. Their clothes, an important symbol of identity, are sometimes removed. Their possessions, a further symbol of identity, may be taken away and stored for the duration of their stay. They may be washed, disinfected and have their hair cut. They may be issued with a new 'identity kit' such as regulation clothes and toilet articles. Such standardised articles tend to remove individuality.

Once the entry phase is over, the inmate settles down to a range of 'mortifying experiences'. Each day is strictly timetabled into a set of compulsory activities controlled by the staff. Inmates are allowed little freedom of movement, few opportunities for self-expression, and little chance to show initiative or take decisions. Their actions are scrutinised and assessed by the staff in terms of the rules and regulations of the institution. A demeaning system of rewards and privileges is administered to encourage obedience and 'appropriate behaviour'. Watching TV, an extra cup of coffee or a cigarette are awarded for 'good behaviour', or withheld from those who don't 'toe the line'. Many of the behaviours demanded from inmates are degrading – for example, in some mental hospitals, a spoon is the only utensil provided for them to eat with.

Goffman found that his idea of a mortification process identified a theme running through a large number of apparently differing behaviours. It connected those behaviours and made sense of them. Time and time again the mortification process told inmates they were less than human.

Goffman's study is generally regarded as a classic. However, it relies heavily on his interpretation of the behaviour he observed. Did he get it right? Here are Goffman's thoughts about this question.

'I want to warn that my view is probably too much that of a middle-class male; perhaps I suffered vicariously about conditions that lower-class patients handled with little pain. Also, unlike some patients, I came to the hospital with no great respect for the discipline of psychiatry' (Goffman, 1968).

Discovering meanings

The analysis of qualitative data often aims to discover the meanings which underlie what people say and do. There is no simple recipe for doing this. It relies heavily on the interpretive skills of the researcher, and is best illustrated by example.

Look at the newspaper headlines in Figure 1. They refer to men and women infected with AIDS through blood transfusions and mother to child transmission of AIDS in the womb.

What meanings lie behind these headlines? One interpretation runs as follows. The word 'innocent' crops up again and again. This suggests that the people concerned do not deserve to be infected – it is not their fault. As one headline states, they come from 'ordinary families', and this kind of thing does not, and should not, happen to 'ordinary people'. This implies that unlike 'ordinary people', 'typical' AIDS victims are not so 'innocent' – in some way they deserve their fate, in some way they are guilty for what happens to them.

Here is another example of interpreting meanings, from the Glasgow University Media Group's (1976) analysis of the reporting of industrial disputes on television news. Trade unionists were typically asked, 'What are you doing to end the strike?' whereas the typical question put to managers was, 'How much production or exports have you lost?' The assumption appears to be that unions cause strikes. Shop

Figure 1 Newspaper headlines

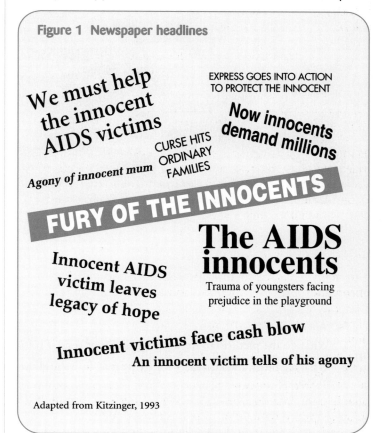

We must help the innocent AIDS victims
EXPRESS GOES INTO ACTION TO PROTECT THE INNOCENT
Now innocents demand millions
CURSE HITS ORDINARY FAMILIES
Agony of innocent mum
FURY OF THE INNOCENTS
The AIDS innocents
Trauma of youngsters facing prejudice in the playground
Innocent AIDS victim leaves legacy of hope
Innocent victims face cash blow
An innocent victim tells of his agony

Adapted from Kitzinger, 1993

stewards were often accused by TV interviewers of 'acting irresponsibly', 'destroying the company' and 'cutting their own throats'. The implication is that the blame for strikes lies with workers and trade unions. Other factors which may have caused the strike, such as bad management, low wages despite high profits, or high inflation, were largely ignored. This type of analysis looks closely at the words and phrases people use and the assumptions that lie behind them. In this case, the researchers concluded that the view that unions cause industrial problems underpinned television news coverage.

The interpretation of meanings is a long way from the 'hard' empirical data and number crunching of many laboratory experiments. Researchers may provide evidence to support the meanings they claim to have discovered. But, in many cases, they are a long way from demonstrating that their interpretations are correct. Despite this, the search for meanings is important. Meanings guide and direct human behaviour. And the analysis of meanings that underlie qualitative data is often convincing, plausible and insightful.

Summary

1. The analysis of qualitative data often starts with categorising and classifying the data.
2. The researcher may then look for themes and patterns which run through and link the data.
3. There is no simple way of discovering and interpreting the meanings which underlie behaviour. This type of analysis relies on the interpretive skills of the researcher.

Activity 1 Analysing qualitative data

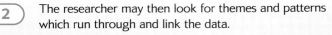

Item A Gender roles in reading schemes

Item B African-American blues songs

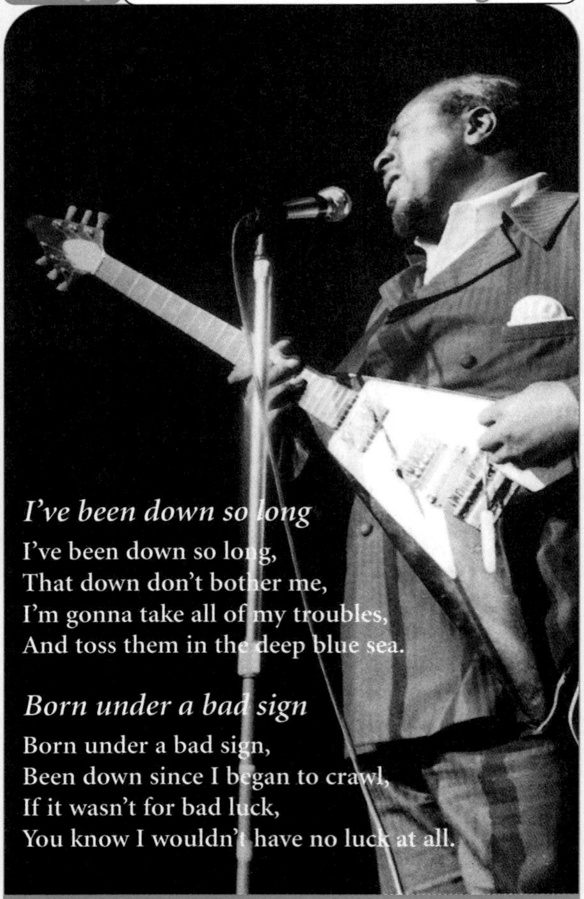

I've been down so long
I've been down so long,
That down don't bother me,
I'm gonna take all of my troubles,
And toss them in the deep blue sea.
Born under a bad sign
Born under a bad sign,
Been down since I began to crawl,
If it wasn't for bad luck,
You know I wouldn't have no luck at all.

Blues singer Albert King who recorded these songs.

Questions

1. What do the pictures in Item A suggest about gender roles?
2. What attitudes and strategies for living may lie behind the lyrics in Item B?

Unit 2 Quantitative data

KEY ISSUES

1. What is quantitative data?
2. How can quantitative data be presented?

Many research methods, particularly experiments and questionnaires, are designed to provide *quantitative data*. Quantitative data takes the form of measurements or scores in the form of numbers. There are four main types or *levels* of measurement.

2.1 Levels of measurement

Nominal level of measurement This is the simplest *level of measurement*. The data it provides is known as nominal data. The researcher identifies categories of objects or behaviours, and simply counts how many instances there are in each category.

For example, an investigation of a fruit bowl reveals 6 apples, 3 oranges, 15 grapes and 2 bananas. The types of fruit are the categories, and the researcher counts how many there are of each type of fruit.

People's behaviour can be recorded as nominal data. In the observation of children's aggressive behaviour in the playground (see p 241), a behaviour schedule was drawn up and a tally made of how many times each type of behaviour occurred – see Table 2. Collecting nominal data simply involves counting the number of instances in each category.

Table 2 Behaviour schedule for 10 minute observation of children at play

Behaviour	Number of occurrences
Bit	1
Chased	3
Hit	2
Pushed/pulled	5
Wrestled	2

Ordinal level of measurement Ordinal data is ordered or ranked according to its position on a scale.

Positions in a race provide an example of ordinal scale measures. The runners are ordered in terms of their finishing positions – 1st, 2nd, 3rd, and so on.

Ordinal data is also provided by attitude scales, where a respondent rates items, for example types of soft drink, in order of preference.

Ordinal scales simply provide a rank order. They do not measure how far apart the items on the scale are. For example, they do not state the time between the runners or how much more a respondent liked drink A compared with drink B.

Interval level of measurement Interval measurements go one step further than ordinal scales. They place items on a scale with fixed intervals, for example temperature in degrees Celsius. It is now possible not only to rank items but also to show how far apart they are.

Temperature provides a good example. If town A has a temperature of 40°C, town B has a temperature of 30°C, and town C of 20°C, this tells us not only the order of the three towns in terms of temperature, but also the difference in temperature between them.

However, it is not possible to say that town A is twice as hot as town C. This is because the zero point on the Celsius scale is not a true or absolute zero. In other words, a temperature of 0°C does not mean no temperature at all since lower temperatures, eg minus 5°C, are possible.

Ratio level of measurement A ratio scale is simply an interval scale with a true or absolute zero point below which no values can occur. This provides a baseline for comparing scores. Time is a good example of this. Suppose participant A takes 25 seconds to complete a task, participant B takes 50 seconds, and participant C takes 75 seconds. It is possible to say that B took twice as long as A to complete the task, and C took three times as long as A. This is possible because the scale starts at zero seconds.

In psychological research, ratio scales are simply regarded as a form of interval scale.

Key terms

Quantitative data *Measurements or scores in the form of numbers.*

Nominal level of measurement *A count of the number of instances in each category.*

Ordinal level of measurement *Placing data into a rank order.*

Interval level of measurement *Placing data on a scale with fixed intervals.*

Ratio level of measurement *Placing data on an interval scale with an absolute zero point.*

Activity 2 Levels of measurement

Item A Girl bands

Female and male teenagers were asked whether or not they liked girl bands.

	Likes girl bands	Dislikes girl bands
Female	42	12
Male	37	18

(Taken from a student research project.)

The Corrs

Item B Soaps

A respondent is asked to rank a list of 5 television soaps in order of preference (the favourite earning a score of 5, the least favourite a score of 1). The following result was obtained.

Emmerdale	5
Coronation Street	4
Brookside	3
Neighbours	2
EastEnders	1

(Taken from a student research project.)

Item C War of the ghosts

A replication of the *War of the ghosts* experiment (see p 37) produced the following results. Condition 1 shows the number of correctly recorded details from the story recalled by each participant immediately after hearing the story. Condition 2 shows the number of correctly recorded details a week later.

Participant Number	Condition 1 (immediate recall)	Condition 2 (recall 1 week later)
1	33	25
2	18	4
3	27	15
4	11	14
5	19	8
6	22	15
7	7	3
8	31	22
9	22	12
10	9	8
11	26	18
12	15	6

Questions

1 Why is the data in Item A a nominal level of measurement?

2 Why is the data in Item B an ordinal level of measurement?

3 What kind of data is shown in Item C?

2.2 Frequency distributions

Measurements of participants' behaviour obtained directly from a research study are called *raw scores*. They have not yet been organised or processed. Raw nominal scores are often quite easy to interpret. Look at Item A in Activity 2. It is quite clear from this data that girl groups are popular with both teenage boys and teenage girls, and are especially popular with girls. Raw ordinal scores are often fairly straightforward too. It is fairly clear what the scores in Item B show.

Raw interval and ratio scores are often less clear. Look at the data in Activity 2 Item C. It is not very easy to see any pattern in these raw scores, or to get much impression of what effect (if any) time has on recall of details from the *War of the ghosts* story.

In order to get a clearer picture of raw results, they can be rearranged into a *frequency distribution*. The total number of times each score occurs is called its *frequency*. A frequency distribution is a table showing the frequencies of all the scores.

Suppose a study was conducted into the number of hours a sample of 10 male and 10 female psychology students spent revising the day before an AS level exam – see Table 3. For convenience, all figures are rounded up or down to the nearest hour.

Table 3 Revision time (in hours)

Males	Females
5	4
4	5
3	3
6	4
1	2
2	3
3	4
5	3
8	4
1	5

A frequency distribution of this data would look like this:

Table 4 Frequency distribution of revision time

Revision time (hours)	Males	Females
1	2	0
2	1	1
3	2	3
4	1	4
5	2	2
6	1	0
7	0	0
8	1	0

Table 4 shows that two males did approximately 1 hours revision; one male and one female did approximately 2 hours, and so on. The frequency distribution provides a clearer picture of the layout of the scores. It shows that male students varied more widely in their revision times than female students.

Grouped frequency distributions

A frequency distribution does not have to show each individual score. If, for example, there are over 100 scores, the table would be too large and confusing. A clearer picture is produced by grouping scores into *class intervals* – in Table 5 the class intervals used are 1-2, 3-4, and so on.

Grouped frequency distribution of the data in Table 3 would look like this:

Table 5 Grouped frequency distribution of revision time

Revision time (hours)	Males	Females
1-2	3	1
3-4	3	7
5-6	3	2
7-8	1	0

Grouped frequency distributions often provide a simpler and clearer picture. For example, the data from the *War of the ghosts* experiment in Activity 2, Item C would be a lot clearer presented in the form of a grouped frequency distribution table.

2.3 Pictorial presentation of frequency distributions

Many people find numerical data easier to understand if it is presented in a pictorial form. This section looks at ways of presenting frequency distributions in the form of charts, graphs and diagrams.

Bar charts

Bar charts provide a simple and effective way of presenting and comparing data, particularly nominal data. The bar chart in Figure 2 illustrates data from the behaviour schedule shown in Table 2 on p 279. The height of each bar gives the frequency of each type of behaviour.

Figure 2 Aggressive behaviour in the school playground

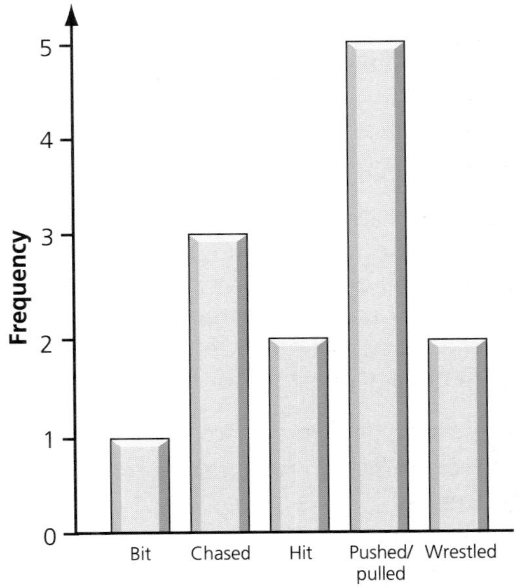

The bar chart in Figure 2 illustrates, at a glance, the frequency distribution of the five types of aggressive behaviour. Because each bar represents a different category of data, the bars are presented separately with spaces between them. Different categories of data are known as *discrete data*. The bars can be drawn in any order.

Histograms

Histograms are mainly used to present frequency distributions of interval and ratio data. They can also be used for grouped frequency distributions. The horizontal axis is a *continuous* scale, for example of time as shown in

Figure 3. On a histogram there are no spaces between the bars. A histogram showing the frequencies of revision times for female students, taken from Table 4, would look like this:

Figure 3 Frequencies of revision times for females

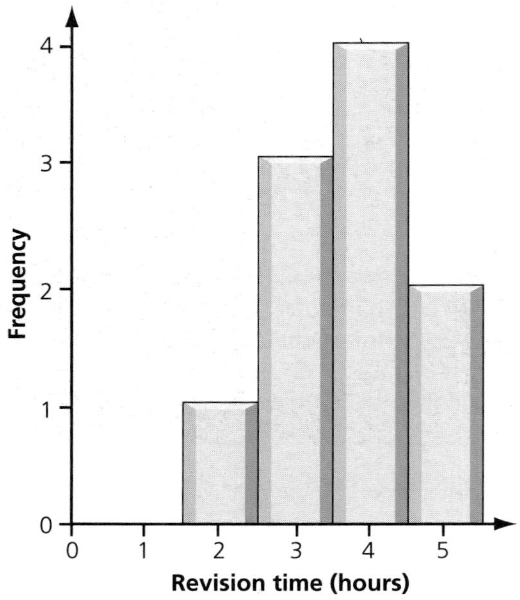

Frequency polygons

Frequency polygons are an alternative way of presenting the same information shown on a histogram. They are often used to compare two or more sets of data. A frequency polygon is drawn by plotting the frequencies of each score, then joining the successive points with straight lines. Figure 4 shows the frequency polygons for the revision times of male and female students, taken from Table 4.

Figure 4 Frequencies of revision times for males and females

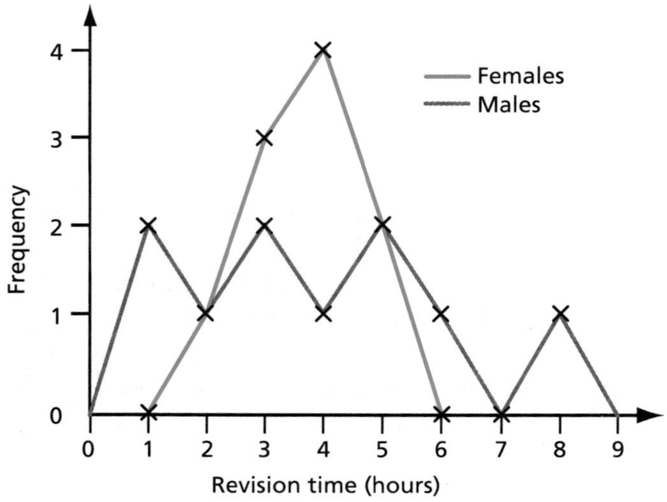

It allows a direct comparison of the frequency distributions of male and female revision times to be made.

Stem and leaf diagrams

A *stem and leaf diagram* is a quick and efficient way of displaying *actual* data in the form of a frequency distribution. Table 6 shows the raw scores from condition 1 of the replication of the *War of ghosts* experiment (see Activity 2, Item C, p 280).

Table 6 Raw scores

33
18
27
11
19
22
7
31
22
9
26
15

To create a stem and leaf diagram, all the scores between 0 and 9 are laid out in a horizontal line from the smallest to the largest. Scores from 10 to 19 are placed on a second line; those from 20 to 29 on a third line, and so on. This is shown below.

7	9		
11	15	18	19
22	22	26	27
31	33		

To convert Table 6 into a stem and leaf diagram, the scores 7 and 9 must be thought of as 07 and 09. For each line of the diagram, the stem is the first digit of the score and the numbers on the leaves are the second digits of each score. The frequency of scores for each line can be noted, as shown in Table 7.

Table 7 Stem and leaf diagram

Stem	Leaves				Frequency
0	7	9			2
1	1	5	8	9	4
2	2	2	6	7	4
3	1	3			2

The stem and leaf diagram groups scores together as in a grouped frequency distribution, while retaining information on individual scores. When laid on its side, a stem and leaf diagram looks like a histogram for a grouped frequency distribution.

Activity 3 Eyewitness testimony

The following experiment was designed to investigate eyewitness testimony.

Two groups of nine participants were asked to watch a video of an event staged in a bank. The first group saw a man paying in money to a bank clerk. The second group saw a man with a gun threatening a customer. Both events lasted exactly 8 seconds. The participants' estimates (in seconds) of the length of these events is shown below.

Condition 1 (man paying in money)	Condition 2 (man with gun)
10	20
12	24
11	23
10	22
11	20
11	23
12	25
13	19
9	23

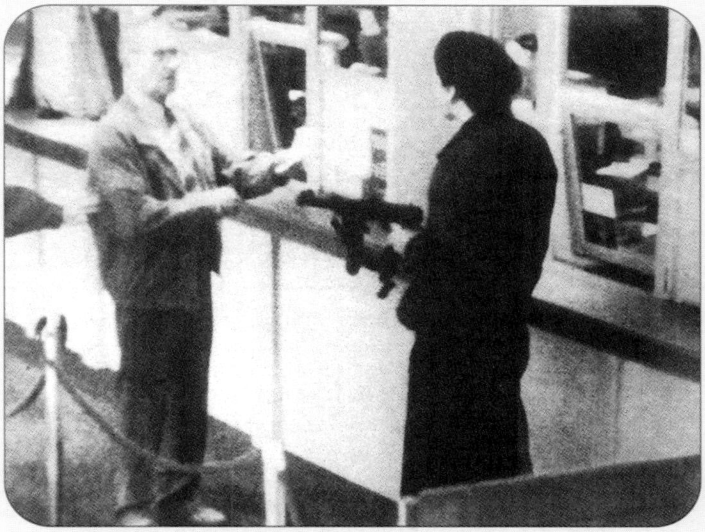

Questions

1 a) Draw up a frequency distribution (see Table 4) of the data in conditions 1 and 2.

b) Draw up a grouped frequency distribution (see Table 5) of the data in conditions 1 and 2, using suitable class intervals.

c) What does each frequency distribution tell you?

2 a) Draw a histogram for each condition (see Figure 3).

b) Draw frequency polygons of the two frequency distributions (see Figure 4).

c) What does each graph tell you about the results obtained in the experiment?

3 a) Draw up a stem and leaf diagram of the data in the two conditions, noting the frequency (see Table 7).

b) Describe the advantages of a stem and leaf diagram.

Key terms

Raw scores *Unprocessed scores taken directly from a study.*

Frequency *The total number of times a score occurs.*

Frequency distribution *The distribution of the frequencies of all scores.*

Grouped frequency distribution *A frequency distribution in which scores are grouped into class intervals.*

Bar chart *A chart in which the height of each bar shows the frequency of each score.*

Histogram *A type of bar chart showing a grouped frequency distribution or continuous data.*

Frequency polygon *A graph which shows a frequency distribution as frequencies joined by straight lines.*

Stem and leaf diagram *A diagram which shows grouped frequency distribution. It also shows individual scores.*

Summary

1. Quantitative data takes the form of scores or measurements.
2. There are four main levels of measurement – nominal, ordinal, interval and ratio.
3. Raw interval and ratio scores are easier to interpret when arranged into a frequency distribution.
4. There are various ways of presenting frequency distributions. They can be presented as individual scores or grouped scores, and in tables or in graphical form.

Unit 3 Analysing quantitative data

KEY ISSUES

1. **What is central tendency? What are the advantages and disadvantages of each measure of central tendency?**
2. **How is the spread (dispersion) of scores measured? What are the advantages and disadvantages of each measure?**

In an experiment, an independent variable is manipulated to see if it has an effect on the performance of the participants – the dependent variable. Two sets of scores are obtained – one from each condition. These two sets of scores need to be compared to see if there is any noticeable difference between them. In order to compare two sets of scores, it is necessary to summarise them. A set of scores can be summarised by:

1) a measure of *central tendency*, that is, a single score that represents the whole set;
2) a measure of the *spread* or *dispersion* of the scores.

With this information it is possible to compare two or more sets of scores.

3.1 Measures of central tendency

There are three measures of central tendency – the *mode*, the *median* and the *mean*.

- The mode is the most common score.
- The median is found by arranging the scores from lowest to highest, and taking the middle score. If there is an even number of scores, the median is given by the average of the two middle scores.
- The mean is found by adding up the total of all the scores and dividing by the number of scores.

The following formula is used to work out the mean.

$$\text{Mean} = \frac{\text{total of all scores}}{\text{number of scores}}$$

This formula can be written using the following symbols.

$$\bar{x} = \frac{\Sigma x}{n}$$

where $\bar{x}$ (pronounced 'x bar') is the mean,
Σ (the Greek letter sigma) stands for 'the sum of',
x represents each score,
n is the number of scores.

Data from Table 8 can be used to show how the mode, median and mean are worked out. The table shows the number of minutes taken to solve a puzzle by participants working in normal and very hot temperatures.

Table 8 Time taken to solve a puzzle

Participant number	Condition 1 normal (minutes)	Participant number	Condition 2 hot (minutes)
P1	7	P6	11
P2	5	P7	7
P3	4	P8	8
P4	5	P9	12
P5	2	P10	9

Table 9 shows the mode, median and mean for the data in conditions 1 and 2.

Mode, median and mean – advantages and disadvantages

Mode The mode is the most frequently occurring score or item of data. It is the only measure that can be used for nominal data. For example, the mode for the types of behaviour shown in Table 2 is 'pushed/pulled' which occurs 5 times. (The mean cannot be used for nominal data – it would make no sense to average the behaviours in Table 2 because they are different kinds of behaviour. Nor could the median be used because there is no order to the data.)

Sometimes, the mode does not provide an overall summary of a set of scores. For example, the most

Table 9 Mode, median and mean

Condition 1	Condition 2
Mode Scores: 7, 5, 4, 5, 2 The mode is the most common score. Mode = 5 minutes	**Mode** scores: 11, 7, 8, 12, 9 There is no mode.
Median Arrange the scores in order: 2, 4, 5, 5, 7 The median is the middle score. Median = 5 minutes	**Median** Scores in order: 7, 8, 9, 11, 12 Median = 9 minutes
Mean $\bar{x} = \frac{\Sigma x}{n}$ $= \frac{7+5+4+5+2}{5}$ $= \frac{23}{5}$ = 4.6 minutes	**Mean** $\bar{x} = \frac{\Sigma x}{n}$ $= \frac{11+7+8+12+9}{5}$ $= \frac{47}{5}$ = 9.4 minutes

Both the mean and the median show that participants in the hot condition take roughly twice as long to solve the puzzles.

frequently occurring score may be the highest or the lowest score, and is located away from the centre of the distribution.

Median The median is the middle score or measurement. It can be used for ordinal, interval and ratio data. It is more likely to provide a measure of central tendency than the mode. However, it can give a misleading impression when scores are clustered in low and high groups. For example, the median for the following scores is six.

1 2 3 6 27 48 63

Mean The mean provides a typical score for interval and ratio data. However, a single extreme score – known as a *rogue score* or *outlier* – results in the mean giving a misleading impression of central tendency. Suppose that in the example in Table 8, participant 1 took 67 minutes to complete the puzzle. The mean for condition 1 now shoots up to 16.6. This gives the impression that people solve puzzles faster in a hot room, when in fact most do not. When rogue scores affect the mean, the median can often give a better measure of central tendency.

Key terms

Mode *The most common score.*

Median *The middle score when the scores are arranged from lowest to highest.*

Mean *The total of all scores divided by the number of scores.*

Central tendency *A typical or representative score which tends to be found near the centre of the distribution of scores.*

Rogue score *An extreme score which can result in the mean giving a misleading impression. Also called an outlier.*

3.2 Dispersion

In order to summarise a set of scores, a measure of central tendency is important, but on its own it is not enough. Consider the following sets of scores.

Table 10 Sets of scores

Set A	35	48	49	50	50	54	57
Set B	2	25	47	50	50	79	90

The mean of each set it 49, the mode 50, and the median 50, yet these are clearly very different sets of data. The main difference between them is the spread of the scores. Set A spreads from 35 to 57, while set B has a much larger spread from 2 to 90.

The spread of scores is also known as *dispersion* or *variability*. In order to clearly summarise a set of scores, it is as important to measure spread or dispersion as it is to measure central tendency.

This can be done a number of ways.

The range

This is the simplest and most obvious way to measure the dispersion of a set of scores. It is obtained by subtracting the lowest score from the highest. The range of a Set A is 57–35=22. The range of Set B is 90-2=88. This shows how much greater the spread of scores in Set B is. There are problems with the range, however.

First, although with a small range we can see that the scores are tightly clustered, with a large range, we do not know how the scores are dispersed. Set B, for example, has one very low score, three near the mean, and two high scores. The range gives us no information about this.

Second, the range is vulnerable to rogue scores or outliers. Suppose the last score in Set A was not 57 but 136, this would bump up the range of Set A to 101, giving a misleading impression of the real dispersion of scores in Set A.

Interquartile range

The *interquartile range* avoids the problem of rogue scores by ignoring the highest 25% and the lowest 25% of the scores. It is a measure of the range of the middle 50% of the scores. This is shown in Figure 5 using scores from Set A.

Figure 5 The interquartile range

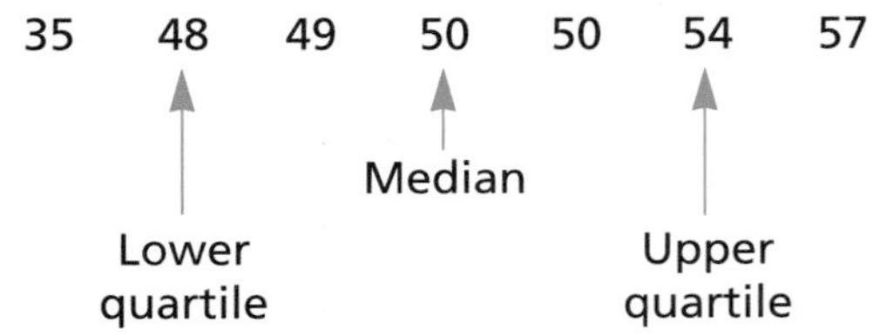

The interquartile range = upper quartile minus lower quartile.

The interquartile range is the difference between the upper and lower quartiles. To find the lower quartile, use the formula 1/4 $(n+1)$ where n= the number of scores. For the scores in Set A, this is 1/4 (7+1) = 2. The lower quartile is the second score which is 48. To find the upper quartile, use the formula 3/4 $(n+1)$. For the scores in Set A, this is 3/4 (7+1) = 6. The upper quartile is the sixth score which is 54.

The interquartile range for the scores is Set A is 54−48 = 6.

The interquartile range is especially valuable with ordinal data, and has the advantage of not being distorted by rogue scores. However, it does lose a lot of information, since 50% of the scores are discarded.

Box plots

Box plots are used to show the range and interquartile range of a set of scores. Box plots are also known as *box and whisker plots*. Figure 6 shows a box plot for the scores in Set A and Set B.

Figure 6 Box plots for Set A and Set B

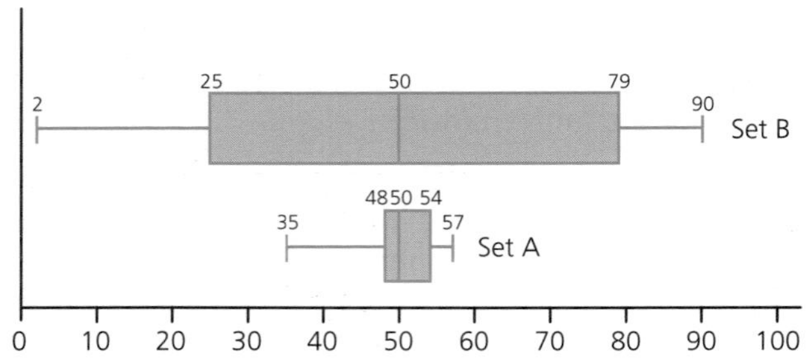

The 'boxes' show the interquartile range of the scores. The 'whiskers' show the range of the data from the lowest score on the left to the highest score on the right. The vertical line in the boxes shows the median.

Box plots provide a clear image of the dispersion of different sets of scores, enabling direct comparisons to be made. They lose less information than the interquartile range, since highest and lowest scores are indicated by the whiskers.

Key terms

Range *A measure of spread or dispersion of scores given by taking the lowest score from the highest.*

Interquartile range *The range of the middle 50% of the scores.*

Box plot *A way of showing both the range and the interquartile range on the same diagram. Also known as a box and whisker plot.*

Standard deviation

We have already looked at two measures of spread – the range and the interquartile range. The range measures the spread of all scores. It can be affected by rogue scores, or outliers, and can be misleading. The interquartile range only measures the spread of the middle 50% of the scores.

A third measure, called *standard deviation*, is more precise. It gets round the problems of range and interquartile range. Standard deviation measures the average deviation (difference) of each score or item of data from the mean. Every score is involved in the calculation. Standard deviation involves the mean of a set of scores. Because of this, it can only be used with interval and ratio data. Nominal and ordinal data do not have means.

Standard deviation (sd) is given by the formulae:

$$\text{sd} = \sqrt{\frac{\Sigma(x - \bar{x})^2}{n}} \quad \text{or} \quad \text{sd} = \sqrt{\frac{\Sigma x^2}{n} - \bar{x}^2}$$

where n is the number of items of data and

$(x - \bar{x})$ is the difference between each score or item of data and the mean.

Look at the sets of scores in Table 11. They show the number of seconds taken by participants to complete a task without alcohol (condition 1) and with alcohol (condition 2).

Standard deviation can be calculated using the formulae shown above, or by using a statistical calculator. Tables 13 and 14 show two methods for calculating standard deviation using the scores from Table 11.

Use whichever method you find easiest to perform calculations.

Table 11 Times (in seconds) to complete a task

Condition 1 (without alcohol)	Condition 2 (with alcohol)
3	3
4	6
4	6
5	9
5	9
5	9
6	11
6	13
7	15

The results of the numerical analysis from Tables 13 and 14 can be summarised as:

Table 12 Summary

	Mean	Standard deviation
Condition 1	5 seconds	1.15 seconds
Condition 2	9 seconds	3.50 seconds

Table 14 provides the following information. The means tell us that the participants in condition 2 (with alcohol) took nearly twice as long to complete the task as the participants in condition 1 (without alcohol).

The standard deviations tell us that the spread of scores in condition 2 was much greater than the spread in condition 1. Scores in condition 1 are clustered around the mean; those in condition 2 are more widely spread out.

These findings indicate that alcohol has two effects.

- First, it increases the average time taken to perform a task.
- Second, it exaggerates differences in task performance – slowing some people down a lot, and others hardly at all.

Standard deviation is the most commonly used measure of dispersion for interval and ratio data. It gives an indication of how far the average participant deviates from the mean. As Table 12 indicates, it provides a precise and useful summary of the spread of data.

Table 13 Standard deviation – method 1

Using $\text{sd} = \sqrt{\frac{\sum(x-\bar{x})^2}{n}}$

Condition 1

First calculate the mean.

$$\bar{x} = \frac{\sum x}{n} = \frac{45}{9} = 5$$

The mean is 5 seconds.

x	$x-\bar{x}$	$(x-\bar{x})^2$
3	-2	4
4	-1	1
4	-1	1
5	0	0
5	0	0
5	0	0
6	1	1
6	1	1
7	2	4
$\sum x = 45$		$\sum(x-\bar{x})^2 = 12$

$$\text{sd} = \sqrt{\frac{\sum(x-\bar{x})^2}{n}}$$

$$= \sqrt{\frac{12}{9}}$$

$=1.15$ seconds, to 2 decimal places

Condition 1 has a mean of 5 seconds and a standard deviation of 1.15 seconds.

Condition 2

First calculate the mean.

$$\bar{x} = \frac{\sum x}{n} = \frac{81}{9} = 9$$

The mean is 9 seconds.

x	$x-\bar{x}$	$(x-\bar{x})^2$
3	-6	36
6	-3	9
6	-3	9
9	0	0
9	0	0
9	0	0
11	2	4
13	4	16
15	6	36
$\sum x = 81$		$\sum(x-\bar{x})^2 = 110$

$$\text{sd} = \sqrt{\frac{\sum(x-\bar{x})^2}{n}}$$

$$= \sqrt{\frac{110}{9}}$$

$=3.50$ seconds, to 2 decimal places

Condition 2 has a mean of 9 seconds and a standard deviation of 3.50 seconds

Table 14 Standard deviation – method 2

Using $\text{sd} = \sqrt{\frac{\sum x^2}{n} - \bar{x}^2}$

Condition 1

First calculate the mean.

$$\bar{x} = \frac{\sum x}{n} = \frac{45}{9} = 5$$

The mean is 5 seconds.

x	x^2
3	9
4	16
4	16
5	25
5	25
5	25
6	36
6	36
7	49
$\sum x = 45$	$\sum x^2 = 237$

$$\text{sd} = \sqrt{\frac{\sum x^2}{n} - \bar{x}^2}$$

$$= \sqrt{\frac{237}{9} - 5^2}$$

$$= \sqrt{1.33...}$$

$= 1.15$ seconds, to 2 decimal places

Condition 1 has a mean of 5 seconds and a standard deviation of 1.15 seconds.

Condition 2

First calculate the mean.

$$\bar{x} = \frac{\sum x}{n} = \frac{81}{9} = 9$$

The mean is 9 seconds.

x	x^2
3	9
6	36
6	36
9	81
9	81
9	81
11	121
13	169
15	225
$\sum x = 81$	$\sum x^2 = 839$

$$\text{sd} = \sqrt{\frac{\sum x^2}{n} - \bar{x}^2}$$

$$= \sqrt{\frac{839}{9} - 9^2}$$

$$= \sqrt{12.22...}$$

$=3.50$ seconds, to 2 decimal places

Condition 2 has a mean of 9 seconds and a standard deviation of 3.50 seconds

Activity 4 Caffeine and concentration

The data below is taken from an investigation into the effect of caffeine on concentration.

The participants in condition 1 were given no caffeine. Those in condition 2 drank five cups of strong coffee. The scores show the number of maths problems each participant solved correctly in 10 minutes.

Participant number	Condition 1 (no coffee)	Condition 2 (coffee)
1	5	9
2	4	3
3	3	1
4	2	1
5	7	7
6	3	5
7	4	1
8	5	9
9	4	2
10	6	7

(Taken from a student research project.)

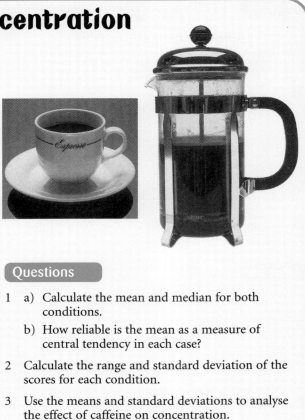

Questions

1 a) Calculate the mean and median for both conditions.

b) How reliable is the mean as a measure of central tendency in each case?

2 Calculate the range and standard deviation of the scores for each condition.

3 Use the means and standard deviations to analyse the effect of caffeine on concentration.

The normal distribution

Look at Figure 7 which shows the distributions of marks obtained by the same group of students in three different psychology exams. The distributions are shown as *frequency curves*. Frequency curves are often used instead of frequency polygons in order to represent a large number of scores.

The first diagram shows a *positive skew*. This is caused by many students getting low scores – the exam may have been too hard.

The third diagram shows a *negative skew*. This is caused by many students getting high scores – the exam may have been too easy.

The second diagram shows a *normal distribution* of marks. The exam is well matched to the ability of the students.

The mode is always at the highest point in the curve. The median always divides the area into two equal parts. If the data in a distribution is skewed, it is better to use the median as a measure of central tendency, and the interquartile range as a measure of spread (dispersion). The reasons for this can be seen by looking at the skewed distribution diagrams in Figure 7.

For the normal distribution the mode = median = mean.

When interval or ratio scores are clustered symmetrically around the mean, a special frequency distribution is produced. This is called the *normal distribution*. The normal distribution is important in nature. Many naturally occurring phenomena are normally distributed – for example, the heights of women in the UK, the number of branches on yew trees, and so on. Some would say that psychological features like IQ are normally distributed too (see p137).

An interesting feature of a set of data that is normally distributed is the relationship between the area below the curve (which represents the number of scores or items of data), the mean, and the standard deviation.

This relationship is shown in Figure 8.

Since the data is symmetrically distributed about the mean, 50% of the area lies on either side of the mean.

Roughly 68% of the area, 34% being either side of the mean, lies within a standard deviation of the mean, that is from $\bar{x}$ – sd to $\bar{x}$ + sd.

Roughly 95% of the area, 47.5% being either side of the mean, lies within 2 standard deviations of the mean, that is from $\bar{x}$ – 2sd to $\bar{x}$ + 2sd.

Roughly 99.8% of the area, 49.9% being either side of the

Figure 7 Frequency curves

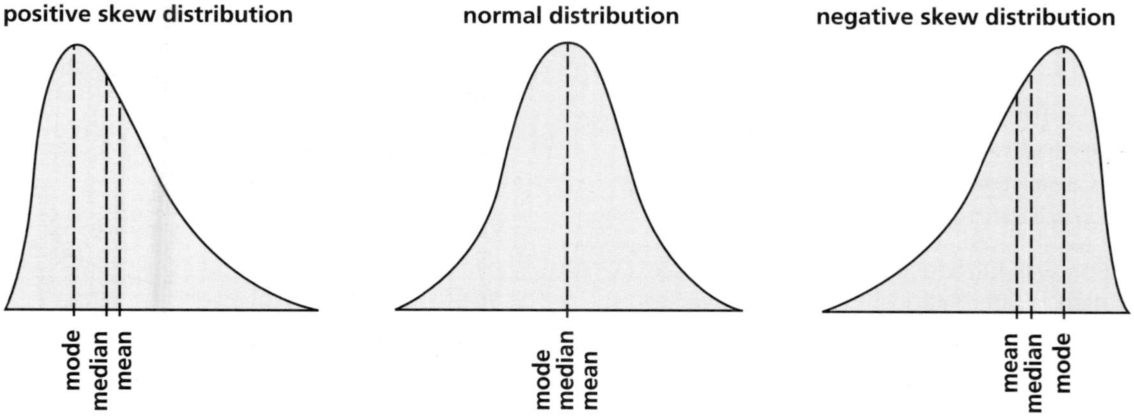

Figure 8 Normal distribution, mean and standard deviation

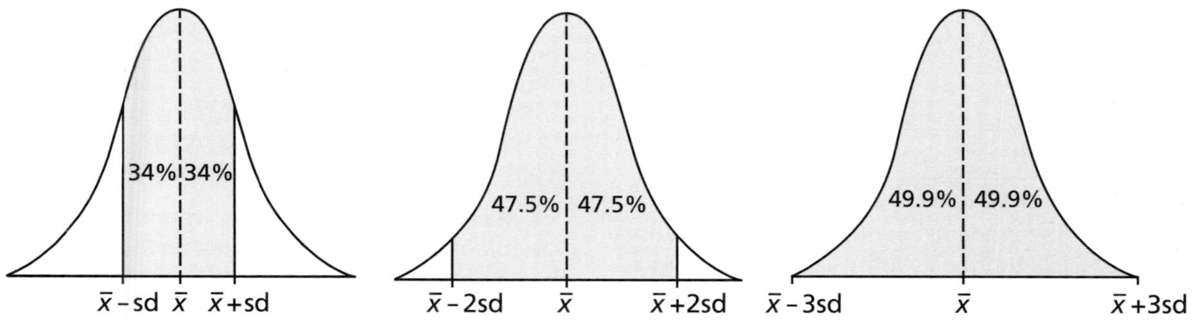

mean, lies within 3 standard deviations of the mean, that is from $\bar{x}$ – 3sd to $\bar{x}$ + 3sd.

The above information can be used for analysing any normal distribution. For example, suppose the heights of men in Manchester are normally distributed, about a mean height of 70 inches, with a standard deviation of 2 inches. This information allows us to build up an accurate picture of the heights of men in Manchester. For example, Figure 8 shows that:

68% of men are between 68 and 72 inches tall.

50 – 47.5 = 2.5% of men are shorter than 66 inches.

0.1%, 1 in 1000, are taller than 76 inches.

Summary

1. There are two main measures for summarising quantitative data.
   - A measure of central tendency – a single score that represents the whole set of scores.
   - A measure of the spread or dispersion of the scores.
2. The range provides a simple measure of dispersion. It is the difference between the lowest and highest scores. However, when the range is used, rogue scores can give a misleading impression of the overall spread of the data.
3. The interquartile range overcomes this problem by measuring the range of the middle 50% of a set of scores. However, in doing so, it loses 50% of the scores.
4. Standard deviation is a more precise measure of dispersion. Every score is involved in the calculation.

Key terms

Standard deviation *A measure of the average deviation of each score from the mean.*

Normal distribution *A frequency distribution in which the scores are symmetrically arranged around the mean.*

Skewed distribution *A frequency distribution in which the scores are asymmetrical (not symmetrically arranged around the mean).*

Unit 4 Correlation

KEY ISSUES

1. **What is correlation?**
2. **What is a scattergraph?**
3. **How may a correlation coefficient be calculated?**

The idea of correlation was introduced in Chapter 16 – see pp239-240. Correlation is the relationship between two sets of data. A correlation exists when two different measures vary together. For example, there is a correlation between intelligence, measured by scores on an IQ test, and examination results, measured by GCSE grades, if the two measures vary together.

Investigations into the relationship between the crime rate and the unemployment rate, between smoking and the incidence of cancer, and between age and income, may all reveal correlations.

4.1 The scattergraph

A study is conducted into students' performance in a maths test (maximum score 10) and their performance in a physics exam (maximum score 100%). The results are shown in Table 15.

Table 15 Maths and physics scores

Participant	Maths score	Physics score
1	10	77
2	8	63
3	9	68
4	2	37
5	9	42
6	7	56

These results can be drawn on a *scattergraph*, as shown in Figure 9.

Each cross on the graph represents the maths *and* physics scores of one participant. It is not necessary to identify the participants by numbering the crosses. It is the overall *trend* which matters. A *line of best fit* can be drawn, by eye, to show the trend. It does not have to go through the origin of the graph, ie the zero. The line of best fit shows the relationship between the two sets of data. It can be seen immediately that students who did well on the maths test tended to do well on the physics exam.

This suggests that the maths test is a good predictor of performance in physics, and could be used by the school or college to estimate how well applicants for the physics course are likely to get on.

Figure 9 Scattergraph of maths and physics scores

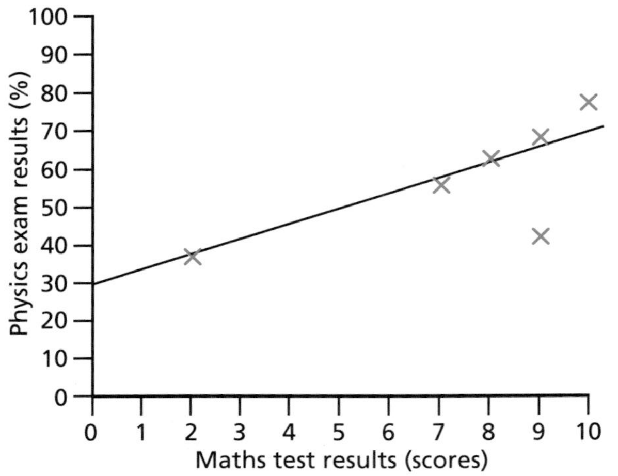

The scattergraph in Figure 9 shows a *positive correlation*. As scores on one variable (the maths test) increase, so do scores on the other variable (the physics exam).

A *negative correlation* exists when the scores on one variable increase and the scores on the other variable decrease. For example, the more pints students drink the night before the physics exam, the lower their marks.

A *zero correlation* exists when there is no relationship between the variables. For example, there is a zero correlation between marks in the physics exam and the heights of students.

4.2 Correlation coefficients

The strengths of the relationship between two sets of data can be measured with a *correlation coefficient.* A *perfect positive correlation* has a coefficient of +1. As the scores on one variable increase, so do the scores on the other variable, in exactly the same proportion – for example, the number of litres of petrol bought and the price paid.

A *perfect negative correlation* has a coefficient of –1, for example the amount of money spent on petrol and the amount of money left in your pocket. When there is no correlation, the coefficient is 0.

Correlation coefficients are illustrated in Figure 10.

With a strong correlation, it is possible to use the scores on one variable to predict the scores on the other variable. The stronger the correlation, the more reliable the prediction. In Figure 9, the scattergraph suggests that the relationship between the scores on the maths test and the physics exam is sufficiently strong to use the maths test to predict performance in physics.

Figure 10 Scattergraphs and correlation coefficients

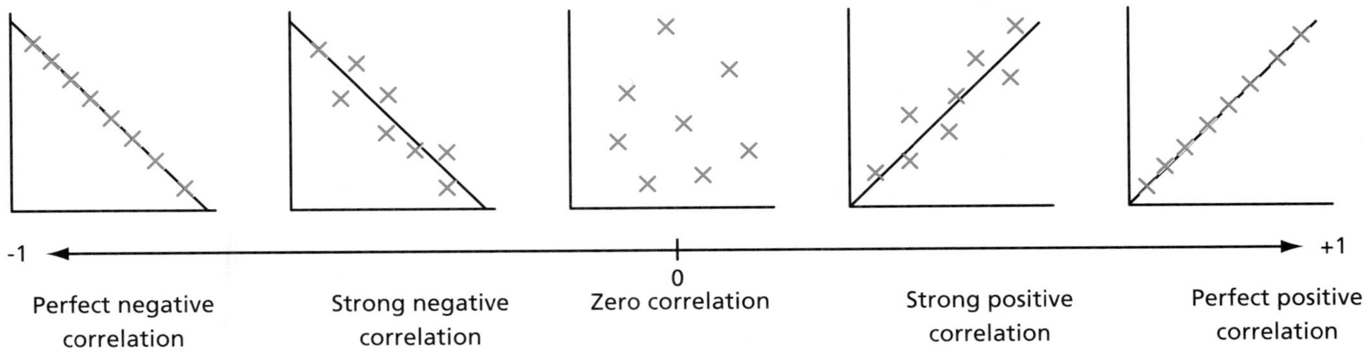

Calculating a correlation coefficient

Spearman's coefficient of rank correlation is a useful way of quantifying the strength of the correlation between variables.

Spearman's coefficient of rank correlation, r_s, is calculated using the following formula

$$r_s = 1 - \frac{6 \sum d^2}{n(n^2 - 1)}$$

where d is the difference in the rank of the score in each set of data (that is, d = rank in set 1 – rank in set 2) and n is the number of items of data. Table 16 shows the rank orders for the maths and physics scores.

Table 16 Rank order of scores

Participant	Maths score	Physics score	Rank order (maths)	Rank order (physics)	d	d^2
1	10	77	6	6	0	0
2	8	63	3	4	-1	1
3	9	68	4.5	5	-0.5	0.25
4	2	37	1	1	0	0
5	9	42	4.5	2	2.5	6.25
6	7	56	2	3	-1	1
						$\sum d^2 = 8.5$

To rank the scores, the lowest score is given the rank of 1 (eg the score of 2 in maths), the next lowest is given the rank of 2 (eg the score of 7 in maths), and so on. When there are equal scores (eg two scores of 9 in maths) the scores are given the next two available ranks (in this example, ranks 4 and 5). The ranks are then divided between the equal scores – in this example both scores are given the rank of 4.5. Since ranks 4 and 5 have now been occupied, the next score gets the rank of 6.

As Table 16 shows, the difference (d) between each pair of ranks is calculated. Each value of d is then squared (d^2). This makes all the values positive.

Using this example, Spearman's coefficient of correlation (r_s) is calculated as follows.

$$r_s = 1 - \frac{6 \sum d^2}{n(n^2-1)}$$

$$= 1 - \left(\frac{6 \times 8.5}{6(6^2-1)} \right)$$

$$= 1 - \left(\frac{6 \times 8.5}{6(36-1)} \right)$$

$$= 1 - \left(\frac{6 \times 8.5}{6 \times 35} \right)$$

$$= 1 - \frac{51}{210}$$

$$= 1 - 0.242...$$

$$= 0.76 \text{ to 2 decimal places}$$

Spearman's coefficient of rank correlation for the relationship between maths and physics scores is 0.76. This is a strong positive correlation.

Correlation coefficients of:

0.5 to 1 for positive correlation and

– 0.5 to –1 for negative correlation

are considered to provide reliable predicted values. They indicate reasonably strong correlations. The closer the values of r_s to 1 and –1 respectively, the stronger the correlations, and the higher the reliability of prediction.

One weakness of Spearman's coefficient of rank correlation is that it only indicates linear correlation – that is, relationships which go in one direction only. Some correlations are non-linear – they may begin as positive and then become negative (or vice versa). This is illustrated in Figure 11 which shows the relationship between how enjoyable people found a party and the number of guests present.

Figure 11 Relationship between enjoyment and number of guests

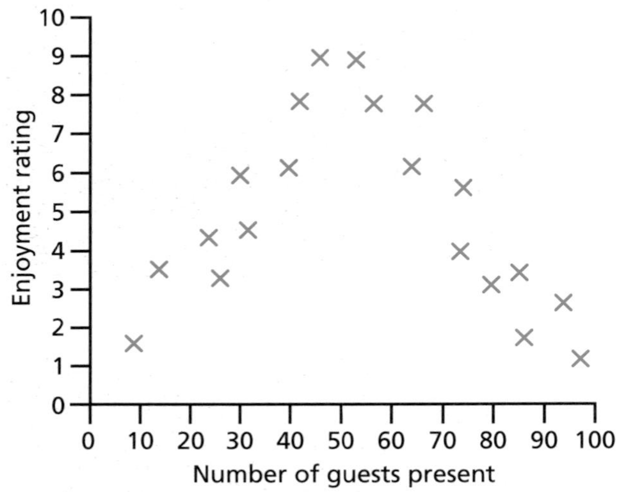

As more people arrive, the party becomes more lively and enjoyable. However, the party then becomes increasingly crowded and less and less enjoyable. The Spearman coefficient of rank correlation gives a zero correlation for these two sets of data. This gives the mistaken impression that there is no correlation when, in fact, there is quite a striking one – it is just that it is non-linear. It is important to draw a scattergraph in order to see what the correlation coefficient is telling us.

Correlation and causation

Correlations, no matter how strong, do not necessarily indicate cause and effect relationships (see p240). For example, people's enjoyment of the party may have nothing to do with the number of guests, despite the correlation shown in Figure 11. The enjoyment rating might have declined because of the host's choice of music. She might have replaced dance music with her favourite Cliff Richard CDs after half the guests had arrived.

Even if there is a cause and effect relationship, correlation does not indicate the direction of causation – it does not show what causes what. For example, there may be a correlation between schizophrenia and imbalances of dopamine. However, this does not tell us whether the dopamine imbalance causes schizophrenia, or whether schizophrenia causes the dopamine imbalance. And, returning to the point made in the previous paragraph, there may be an unknown third factor which causes both.

Even a very strong correlation coefficient does not necessarily show any real relationship between the variables. Snedecor (1946) provides a delightful example of a near perfect negative correlation of –0.98 between the birth rate in the UK and the production of pig iron in the USA between 1875 and 1920. Despite this impressive correlation coefficient, it is highly unlikely that these factors are related.

Key terms

Correlation *The relationship between two or more variables or sets of data.*

Positive correlation *As scores on one variable increase, so do scores on the other variable.*

Negative correlation *As scores on one variable increase, scores on the other variable decrease.*

Correlation coefficient *A measure of the strength of the correlation.*

Scattergraph *A graph which illustrates the relationship between two or more variables. Also known as scattergram and scatter plot.*

Summary

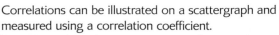

1. Correlations can be illustrated on a scattergraph and measured using a correlation coefficient.
2. Spearman's coefficient of rank correlation is a simple and useful method of producing correlation coefficients. However, it cannot measure non-linear correlations.
3. Correlations do not necessarily indicate cause and effect relationships.

Activity 5 Oasis and Blur

Item A Student ratings

Students were asked to rate two bands on a scale of 1 to 10, with ten being the highest rating. The results are shown below.

Ratings for two bands

Participant	Oasis rating	Blur rating
1	4	9
2	5	7
3	10	2
4	8	3
5	9	5
6	1	9
7	5	5
8	3	6
9	8	2
10	7	7

(Taken from a student research project.)

Oasis

Blur

Questions

1 a) Draw a scattergraph of the data.
  b) What does the graph show?

2 a) Calculate Spearman's coefficient of rank correlation for the data.
  b) What does the correlation show?

References

Glasgow University Media Group (1980). *Bad news.* London: Routledge.

Goffman, E. (1968). *Asylums.* Harmondsworth: Penguin.

Kitzinger, J. (1993). Understanding AIDS. In J. Eldridge (Ed.), *Getting the message: News, truth and power.* London: Routledge.

Lobban, G. (1974). Data report on British reading schemes. *Times Educational Supplement,* 1.3.1974.

Snedecor, G.W. (1946). *Statistical methods* (4th ed.). Ames: Iowa State College Press.

Author index